Make the Gra
Your Atomic Dog Online Edition.

The Atomic Dog Online Edition includes proven study tools that expand and enhance key concepts in your text. Reinforce and review the information you absolutely 'need to know' with features like:

- **Review Quizzes**
- Key term Assessments
- Interactive Animations and Simulations
- Notes and Information from Your Instructor
- Pop-up Glossary Terms
- A Full Text Search Engine

Ensure that you *'make the grade'*. Follow your lectures, complete assignments, and take advantage of all your available study resources like the **Atomic Dog Online Edition.**

How to Access Your Online Edition

If you purchased this text directly from Atomic Dog ....
Visit atomicdog.com and enter your email address and password in the login box at the top-right corner of the page.

If you purchased this text NEW from another source....
Visit our Students' Page on atomicdog.com and enter the **activation key located below** to register and access your Online Edition.

If you purchased this text USED from another source....
Using the Book Activation key below you can access the Online Edition at a discounted rate. Visit our Students' Page on atomicdog.com and enter the **Book Activation Key in** the field provided to register and gain access to the Online Edition.

Be sure to download our *How to Use Your Online Edition* guide located on atomicdog.com to learn about additional features!

This key activates your online edition. Visit atomicdog.com to enter your Book Activation Key and start accessing your online resources.

1515HDTNJ

For more information, give us a call at (800) 310-5661 or send us an email at support@atomicdog.com.

*Some online Editions do not contain all features.

Criminal
Justice

Criminal Justice

Seventh Edition

Sue Titus Reid, J.D., Ph.D.
Florida State University

Australia • Canada • Mexico • Singapore • Spain • United Kingdom • United States

Criminal Justice
Sue Titus Reid

Printed in the
United States of America
2 3 4 5 6 7 8 09 08 07 06

For more information, please contact Thomson Custom Solutions, 5191 Natorp Boulevard, Mason, OH 45040. Or you can visit our Internet site at
http://www.thomsoncustom.com

For permission to use material from this text or product, contact us by:
Tel (800) 730-2214
Fax (800) 730 2215
http://www.thomsonrights.com

The Adaptable Courseware Program consists of products and additions to existing Thomson products that are produced from camera-ready copy. Peer review, class testing, and accuracy are primarily the responsibility of the author(s).

Criminal Justice
Sue Titus Reid—Seventh Edition

BOOK ISBN 1-592-60223-1
PACKAGE ISBN 1-592-60225-8

Library of Congress Control Number:
2005930792

International Division List

Asia (Including India):
Thomson Learning
(a division of Thomson Asia Pte Ltd)
5 Shenton Way #01-01
UIC Building
Singapore 068808
Tel: (65) 6410-1200
Fax: (65) 6410-1208

Australia/New Zealand:
Thomson Learning Australia
102 Dodds Street
Southbank, Victoria 3006
Australia

Latin America:
Thomson Learning
Seneca 53
Colonia Polano
11560 Mexico, D.F., Mexico
Tel (525) 281-2906
Fax (525) 281-2656

Canada:
Thomson Nelson
1120 Birchmount Road
Toronto, Ontario
Canada M1K 5G4
Tel (416) 752-9100
Fax (416) 752-8102

UK/Europe/Middle East/Africa:
Thomson Learning
High Holborn House
50-51 Bedford Row
London, WC1R 4L$
United Kingdom
Tel 44 (020) 7067-2500
Fax 44 (020) 7067-2600

Spain (Includes Portugal):
Thomson Paraninfo
Calle Magallanes 25
28015 Madrid
España
Tel 34 (0)91 446-3350
Fax 34 (0)91 445-621

To: H.H.A. Cooper
President, Nuevevidas International, Inc., a security consulting firm
Adjunct professor, University of Texas, Dallas

Brief Contents

Contents

Preface

One of the most serious domestic problems in the United States is crime. U.S. crime and incarceration rates are among the highest in the world, and the country faces immense problems associated with criminal activity. The concern for crime extends beyond the nature and frequency of occurrence to include official and unofficial reactions to crimes. Criminal justice systems appear inadequate to prevent crime and are questionable systems for coping with crimes that do occur.

Some react with bitter criticism of U.S. criminal justice systems but with no meaningful suggestions for improvement. Others take the law into their own hands and fight back, wounding and, in some cases, killing those who attempt to victimize them. Still others take a close look at the systems with the hope of retaining the best parts and changing those that need improvement. The last view is taken in this text, which also considers the interrelationships of the various parts of the system, for it is important to understand that a change in one area of a criminal justice system may and usually does have a significant impact on other areas of that system.

Significant changes have been made in previous editions of this text, with the number of chapters being reduced from 18 to 14 and then to 12. These changes were made after the author used an edition with 18 chapters and discussed with adopters the difficulties she experienced in covering that much material in a traditional semester. The cost of texts was another consideration.

With the increase in textbooks' size and production costs (resulting from more color and greater photography), the student's cost for purchasing criminal justice texts has escalated. Second-hand copies are expensive, too, with students receiving only a small portion of the original price for resale. In addition to the cost of the text, the student has the additional costs of a study guide, should he or she choose to utilize one.

The publishers and author of this text decided that it is possible to write and produce a book that contains sufficient and up-to-date coverage of criminal justice issues, along with an inclusion of charts, graphs, and other study aids, while keeping the price within a more reasonable range for the average student budget. We believe the format and coverage of this text provides an excellent alternative to the more expensive, four-color, hardbound texts.

The text retains the author's reputation of including the most recent information on topics discussed. All topics have been checked for the latest information available at the time of publication. All legal citations, including cases and statutes, have been checked to determine whether they have been altered or overruled by subsequent legislation or court decisions. Where possible, issues are illustrated with recent cases, although some older cases are used because they represent "classic" statements on the law and are still in effect or because they represent the latest U.S. Supreme Court decisions on these issues.

Along with recent scholarly research in the social sciences, this seventh edition retains the practice of using recent current events from popular sources to illustrate what is happening in criminal justice. These events are updated to the latest point in the book's publication.

Chapter Format

Each chapter contains an overview, an outline of the chapter's content, and a list of learning objectives, which are designed to suggest to students what they should be learning during their progression through the chapter. Combined with the study questions and the summary, these objectives provide an excellent study guide for each chapter. Key terms are bold faced within the chapter and defined in the margin as well as in the Glossary at the end of the text. The material within the chapters is illustrated and emphasized further by tables, figures, and Spotlights. Most chapters include a Professions feature, which will enlighten those students who are seeking a career in the criminal justice field. Each chapter closes with a detailed summary, followed by essay questions that are designed to help students analyze the subjects covered in that chapter.

Organization of the Text and Important Content Changes

The text is divided into five parts. Part 1, "Introduction to Criminal Justice Systems," contains two chapters. The first, "Criminal Justice: An Overview," covers issues regarding punishment, criminal law, the concept of crime, and the purposes of the criminal law. The chapter's topics are illustrated with references to such crimes as the terrorist acts of 11 September 2001; the 2005 murders of a judge and others in Atlanta and of a judge's family in Chicago; the Washington, D.C., area snipers of 2002; the serial killing of Kansas's defendant Dennis L. Rader; and recent U.S. Supreme Court cases, such as the following: *Lawrence* v. *Texas* (concerning sodomy), *Ashcroft* v. *Free Speech Coalition* (concerning virtual child pornography), and *U.S.* v. *Oakland Cannabis Buyers' Cooperative* and *Ashcroft* v. *Raich* (concerning the use of marijuana for medicinal purposes).

The recent approach of treating rather than punishing first and second nonviolent drug offenders is discussed in light of the Idaho and California statutes. Another new addition to the substance abuse discussion is that of date rape, including mention of the club drugs Ecstasy and GHB and legislation concerning these drugs, as well as the conclusion of the trial and capture of Andrew Luster, convicted of multiple date rapes after giving his victims club drugs. A new section on fetal abuse includes information on criminalizing the use of controlled substances during pregnancy and changing the definition of murder to include the purposeful death of a fetus. This topic is illustrated by the case involving the deaths of Laci Peterson and her unborn son and the trial, conviction, and sentencing of Scott Peterson, Laci's husband, for those murders.

Chapter 2 contains the latest official data on crime and victimization, emphasizing crimes, offenders, and victims, along with the interrelationships between the last two. The accuracy of crime data is questioned in light of a 2003 report on a study of data collection in New York City. The chapter contains more information on the eight serious crimes, as well as offenders and victims, by the categories of age, race, and gender. It also informs the reader of the recent changes in the use of the term *index crimes* by the FBI. New figures graph trends in serious violent and property crimes, as well as crime victimization rates by the victims' gender. The USA Patriot Act, which was enacted shortly after 9/11/01, is introduced; it is discussed in greater detail in a subsequent chapter. The discussion on hate crimes is updated with mention of the recent U.S. Supreme Court case on cross burning, *Virginia* v. *Black*.

Part 2, "Entry into Criminal Justice Systems: Policing," contains three chapters. Chapter 3, "The Emergence and Structure of Police Systems," covers the history of policing, noting some of the problems of policing at the local, state, and federal levels. It includes updates on a spotlight from the previous edition, which featured police problems within the Los Angeles Police Department (LAPD). The new version of Spotlight 3-1 contains the latest information on the investigation into the Rampart scandal and the taped beating of a teen by LAPD officers in the summer of 2002. New Spotlight 3-2 explains vigilantism in light of airline passengers who take action during flight to subdue suspected terrorists, such as Richard Reid, the would-be shoe bomber, who was subsequently convicted and incarcerated.

Chapter 3's discussion of Scotland Yard is updated with recent information on allegations of racism, while the analysis of rural policing contains a report on drugs in small towns. The latest problems and evaluations of the Federal Bureau of Investigation (FBI) are noted, along with a detailing of the new Department of Homeland Security (DHS) and the changes that resulted in other federal departments as a result of the establishment of the DHS. New legislation, such as the Public Health Security and Bioterrorism Response Act of 2002 and the Enhanced Border Security and Visa Entry Reform Act of 2002, are noted. The discussion of the national Community-Oriented Policing (COPS) program is updated, including the 2006 Bush budget proposal, which virtually eliminates the program.

Chapter 4, "Policing in a Modern Society," explores the structure and function of policing, featuring additional information on the recruitment, training, and education of police, including problems that occur when "overqualified" people apply. The case of *City of Canton, Ohio* v. *Harris,* concerning negligent hiring and previously discussed in Chapter 5, was moved to Chapter 4 and is the focus of Spotlight 4-1. New efforts to train persons to assist police (such as training truck drivers to look out for terrorists) are noted, along with a discussion of the USA Patriot Act and some of the constitutional issues raised by that legislation.

Chapter 4 also contains several recent U.S. Supreme Court cases, such as *People* v. *Illinois* (concerning stopping all motorists in an area in which a crime has occurred); *Illinois* v. *Lidster* (concerning stopping all motorists at the same intersection at the same late hour and handing them a flier describing a fatal hit-and-run accident; *United States* v. *Arvizu, Florida* v. *J.L.,* and *Bond* v. *United States* (all involving searches and seizures); *Maryland* v. *Pringle* (concerning whether police may arrest everyone in a car when they have probable cause to arrest a speeding driver and find illegal drugs and a "wad" of cash); *United States* v. *Banks* (considering the reasonable time for police to wait, after knocking and announcing, before they break into a house); *United States* v. *Drayton* (analyzing whether police may enter a bus and ask questions without telling passengers that they are free to leave); and *Illinois* v. *McArthur* (considering whether police may restrict a person from entering his or her home if they have probable cause to believe that illegal drugs are contained therein and may be disposed of). A 2003 Texas case permitting a body cavity search without a warrant is mentioned, along with a 2003 case involving a strip search of an African American woman at the Miami International Airport. A section on racial profiling is also included.

New to Chapter 4 is a discussion of crime scene investigations (CSI) and the establishment of the CSI Institute at the University of New Haven in Connecticut. The chapter includes a discussion of interrogation in the case of police who went to the home of a 17-year-old, told him they needed to go to the police station, and got a confession. The defendant was convicted. Finally, recent U.S. Supreme Court cases concerning the *Miranda* warning issue are included: *Missouri* v. *Seibert, United States* v. *Fellers,* and *United States* v. *Petane. Illinois* v. *Caballes* (upholding the use of drug-sniffing dogs during a routine traffic stop) was decided in January 2005.

Chapter 5, "Problems and Issues in Policing," is devoted to a close look at the major problems and issues of policing. A new spotlight on intimate partner violence provides data for the chapter's discussion of this important topic, which includes police response to domestic violence, as well as domestic violence among police. The Spotlight on police suicides was expanded and updated with 2003 examples. The blue code of silence is illustrated by the example of a female officer who won a case on this issue. The discussion of the Mollen Commission was updated, and the topic of police brutality was enhanced by new examples and the LAPD policy on the topic. A discussion on early detection systems enhances the topic of police department control of conduct. New topics in Chapter 5 include drugs and policing, the impact of terrorism on policing, and federal regulation of policing. The section on affirmative action features the recent U.S. Supreme Court decisions of *Grutter* v. *Bollinger* and *Gratz* v. *Bollinger.*

The three chapters in Part 3, "Processing a Criminal Case: Criminal Court Systems," explore the procedures and issues that arise from arrest through sentencing and appeals. Chapter 6, "Criminal Court Systems," sets the stage for this discussion with an overview of court systems. It contains numerous updates on topics such as the following: the au pair case involving Louise Woodward; the Michael Skakel trial, conviction, and appeal; judicial salaries; and the U.S. Supreme Court.

Chapter 7, "Prosecution, Defense, and Pretrial Procedures," begins with an analysis of the role of lawyers in criminal court systems and proceeds through the pretrial procedures.

It examines the roles of prosecutors and defense attorneys historically and currently, paying close attention to the modern problems of providing an adequate defense for indigent defendants. Professions 7-1 contains an open letter from the president of the American Bar Association (ABA) to all ABA members one year after the 9/11/01 terrorist attacks. The letter emphasizes the importance of the legal profession. New data on the economics of practicing law are introduced. A recent Florida case involving two young teens accused of murdering their father is included to illustrate the issue of prosecutorial discretion, along with other information on prosecutorial abuse. Former U.S. Attorney General John Ashcroft's controversial rules concerning filing federal charges are discussed, along with his ruling that limited plea bargaining in federal cases. The chapter includes significant updates on the right to counsel, especially the right to the effective assistance of counsel. The Texas "sleeping counsel" case (*Burdine* v. *Texas*) was updated; the issue of whether a defendant, who was convicted of murder and sentenced to death, had received ineffective assistance of counsel because his attorney had previously represented the alleged victim in the defendant's case (*Mickens* v. *Taylor*) is presented. Other cases involving the issue of effective assistance of counsel are also cited.

New to Chapter 7 is the case of the Green River (Seattle, Washington) serial killer, Gary L. Ridgway, along with an update on the case of Lionel Tate, Florida's 12-year-old who was convicted of murder and sentenced to life without parole. His conviction was reversed in December 2003 by a Florida appellate court, and Tate was released from prison in 2004, although subsequent legal problems may send him back to prison. Also new to Chapter 7 is a discussion of the recent U.S. Supreme Court decisions concerning the detention of "enemy combatants" without permitting them to see counsel: *Rasul* v. *Bush* and *Hamdi* v. *Rumsfeld*.

Chapter 8, "Trial, Sentencing, and Appeal," describes the basic procedures of the trial, sentencing, and appeal phases of criminal cases. The recentness of the discussions is illustrated by the following: *Miller-El* v. *Cockrell*, a 2005 U.S. Supreme Court case that involved a prosecutorial decision to eliminate 10 of 11 African Americans from the jury pool in a case involving an African American defendant; recent pardons issued in Texas after the only witness in a case was indicted on three perjury charges; the U.S. Supreme Court's refusal to review the case of a lawyer who was pardoned by President Bill Clinton and argued that the pardon should remove his disbarment; and *Atkins* v. *Virginia*, a U.S. Supreme Court decision holding that it is unconstitutional to execute a mentally retarded person.

Chapter 8 also updates the discussion on capital punishment with the inclusion of recent cases such as *Ring* v. *Arizona, Blakely* v. *Washington*, and *Summerlin* v. *Stewart*. The three strikes and you're out sentencing issue was expanded by the inclusion of the U.S. Supreme Court's decisions in *Ewing* v. *California* and *Lockyer* v. *Andrade*. Also included are two cases decided by the U.S. Supreme Court in 2004, *United States* v. *Booker* and *United States* v. *Fanfan*, both involving questions left unanswered by *Blakely*.

Data on capital punishment are updated through early 2005, and additional information is provided on the topic of truth in sentencing.

Part 4, "Confinement and Corrections," focuses on corrections, with three chapters examining the methods of confining offenders in total institutions or of placing them in the community under supervision. The discussion begins in Chapter 9, "The History and Structure of Confinement," with a look at the history of prisons and jails and a discussion of the federal and state prison systems. Attention is given to the problems of local jails and boot camps. The discussion of privatization of prisons and jails was updated. The chapter contains new information on maxi-maxi prisons (see Spotlight 9-2), women's prisons; boot camp closings; prison and jail populations; and the cost of prison and jail expansion and operations. The chapter also provides updated information on the federal Bureau of Prisons (BOP), which is now the largest prison system in the United States, with a population that is growing at a faster rate than state prison populations. New Figure 9-1 graphs the U.S. incarceration rates between 1980 and 2003.

Chapter 10, "Life in Prison," discusses inmates and correctional officers and the interaction between them. Particular attention is given to the methods of social control that involve inmates and officers. How inmates cope with the pains of imprisonment, along with a distinction between the adjustment of women and men is noted. Special attention is given to AIDS and other medical issues in prisons, along with the growing problems of dealing with inmates who are physically challenged, elderly, or mentally ill. The chapter also notes the special problems of female inmates, as well as of female correctional officers.

New to this edition's Chapter 10 are the following: an update on the 2000 settlement of Attica civil actions; recent information on sexual relations between correctional officers and inmates, along with information concerning female correctional officers who have been apprehended for having sex with male inmates; recent information on prison litigation; a new Spotlight (10-3) on the growth of the female as compared with the male inmate population; more information on the special needs of female inmates; a new Spotlight (10-4) on the Prison Rape Elimination Act of 2003; information on TB and hepatitis C among inmates; a brief discussion of *Sell* v. *United States,* involving the forced medication of defendants to make them competent to stand trial, along with the implications of the case for prison inmates; a case involving a hostile working environment for female correctional officers; updates on jail and prison suicides; and inclusion of the murder of defrocked priest John J. Geoghan in a Massachusetts prison.

Part 4 closes with Chapter 11, "Community Corrections, Probation, and Parole," which examines the preparation of inmates for release, the problems they face upon release, and the supervision of offenders in the community. The chapter contains a section on the diversion of nonviolent drug offenders, which discusses drug courts and statutory provisions for treatments, topics mentioned earlier in the text and expanded here as they relate to offenders in the community. Spotlight 11-1 features portions of the California statute providing for treatment, rather than punishment, of nonviolent first- and second-time drug offenders. Spotlight 11-2 includes highlights about probation and parole in 2003. Chapter 11 also includes information on family drug courts designed to help addicted mothers recover and regain custody of their children. A new section on diversion of mentally challenged persons focuses on mental health courts. Extensive new information is included on electronic monitoring as well as parole, with both topics including mention of noted persons involved, such as Andrew Luster and Kathy Boudin. A new section on constitutional issues includes three topics: search and seizure (including the 2001 case of *United States* v. *Knights,* permitting a probation officer to search and seize within a probationer's home); the Americans with Disabilities Act (ADA); and updated information on probation and parole revocation. Significant new material on probation—especially probation conditions—is included. Finally, the discussion of Megan's Laws includes the two cases decided by the U.S. Supreme Court in 2003, upholding the statutes in Alaska and Connecticut, against challenges of *ex post facto* and due process violations, respectively.

The final part of the text, Part 5, "Juvenile Justice: A Special Case," contains Chapter 12, on juvenile justice systems, a special approach that was developed for the processing of juveniles who get into trouble with the law or who are in need of supervision or care because of neglectful parents or other guardians. This chapter, entitled "Juvenile Justice Systems," explains juvenile justice systems, contrasts those systems with adult criminal court systems, and considers the changes in juvenile justice systems that have resulted from decisions of the U.S. Supreme Court, as well as those of lower courts. The legal implications of racial and gender issues were updated. The issue of substance abuse among juveniles is highlighted in Spotlight 12-3, which discusses the 2004 report of the National Center on Substance Abuse at Columbia University (CASA). The chapter also includes a 2003 report by the ABA concluding that some juveniles are not getting effective legal representation. It updates the discussion on juvenile curfews; all data (including data on juveniles in adult jails and prisons); and the discussion of juveniles and capital punishment, including a case decided by the U.S. Supreme Court in March 2005, concerning whether it is constitutional to execute a person for a murder committed at the age of 17. That case, *Roper* v. *Simmons,* is the topic of Spotlight 12-4.

Chapter 12 contains new information on the following topics: Megan's Laws and juveniles; drug courts and juveniles; constitutional violations of juvenile rights within correctional institutions; and the Louisiana system and its problems, along with an update on the Georgia juvenile system. The chapter also includes recent information on facilities for female juvenile offenders, with a special look at Florida, which has one of the few maximum-security institutions for youthful women; a discussion of respite care, which gives families and troubled youths a break from living with each other and, through counseling, aims at reuniting the family as soon as possible; and a new case on a juvenile's right to counsel. *Yarborough* v. *Alvarado* concerns the issue of whether police must give juveniles the *Miranda* warning before they interrogate them at a police station.

Two appendices assist the reader with legal issues. Appendix A reprints selected amendments to the U.S. Constitution. Those amendments are cited throughout the text. Appendix B explains the abbreviations and references that are used in legal case citations. Individual indexes assist the reader who desires quick access to names, subjects, and legal cases cited in the text.

Print Edition and Online Edition

Criminal Justice, 7e, is available online as well as in print. The Online Edition chapters demonstrate how the interactive media components of the text enhance presentation and understanding. For example,

- Animated illustrations help to clarify concepts.
- Clickable glossary terms provide immediate definitions of key concepts.
- Highlighting capabilities allow you to emphasize main ideas. You can also add personal notes in the margin.
- The search function allows you to quickly locate discussions of specific topics throughout the text.

You may choose to use just the Online Edition, or both the online and print versions together. This gives you the flexibility to choose which combination of resources works best for you. To assist those who use the online and print versions together, the primary heads and subheads in each chapter are numbered the same. For example, the first primary head in Chapter 1 is labeled 1-1, the second primary head in this chapter is labeled 1-2, and so on. The subheads build from the designation of their corresponding primary head: 1-1a, 1-1b, etc. This numbering system is designed to make moving between the Online Edition and the print book as seamless as possible.

Finally, next to a number of figures in the print version of the text, you will see an icon similar to the one in the margin on the left. This icon indicates that this figure in the Online Edition is interactive in a way that applies, illustrates, or reinforces the concept.

Supplements

Atomic Dog is pleased to offer a robust suite of supplemental materials for instructors using its textbooks. These ancillaries include a Test Bank, PowerPoint® slides, and an Instructor's Manual.

The Test Bank for this book includes approximately 70 items per chapter, including 20 true/false, 40 multiple choice, 5 completion, and 5 short answer questions. The Test Bank offers not only the correct answer for each question, but also a reference—the location in the chapter where materials addressing the question content can be found.

A full set of over 200 PowerPoint® Slides is available for this text. This is designed to provide instructors with comprehensive visual aids for each chapter in the book.

The Instructor's Manual for this book includes key terms, chapter outlines, learning objectives, and additional web resources for each chapter.

Acknowledgments

Throughout my writing career, special colleagues and friends have been supportive and encouraging, and to them I give my unconditional thanks. In particular, I would like to thank David Fabianic, Professor, University of Central Florida, for his friendship for over 30 years and his consistent use of this text. Another friend, as well as former colleague, who has been supportive of my writing from the beginning is Marilyn Mather, now retired, who taught with me at Cornell College in Mt. Vernon, Iowa, in the 1960s. A third friend of over 30 years is H.H.A. "Tony" Cooper , a prolific writer and internationally recognized authority on security and terrorism. Cooper, who is president of Nuevevidas International, Inc., a security and terrorism consulting firm based in Dallas, Texas, is also an adjunct professor at the University of Texas–Dallas. Thanks, Tony, for your encouragement, your humor, your advice, your concern; to you this book is dedicated.

As always, my family has supported my writing and the long hours that it involves. To my sister, Jill Pickett, and her family, husband Roger, son Clint (along with his wife Stephanie), and daughter Rhonda Sue, thanks for all the memories. Clint and Stephanie have enlarged our family with a beautiful daughter Cherith, who promises to keep us all at a high energy level.

Although the writing of this revision took place in my New Hampshire home, most of the editing and proofing occurred during my weekly travels to and from my teaching position at Florida State University in Tallahassee, Florida. During those long hours on the road, in airports, and in the friendly skies, I encountered what seemed like more than my share of airplane delays due to scheduling, mechanical, or weather issues. My rescheduling and my delays were eased by the Delta managers and agents in Portland, Maine, Tallahassee, Florida, and especially Atlanta, Georgia. Many of the Atlanta Delta Crown Room agents were helpful, but to the following I owe special thanks: Alex Espinosa, John Grogan, Laura H. Hambley, Libby T. Hunt, Thomas H. Hunt, Jan Kimbrough, Jeffrey Penzkowski, and Bobbi J. Russell. In particular, I am grateful to Jeff Penzkowski, who met one of my rescheduled flights, and quickly escorted me to my connecting flight. Jeff, the agents in Boston did not think I could make my flight, which was scheduled to leave four minutes after I was to arrive in Atlanta. Even with the 10 extra minutes provided by an early arrival, had you not met the flight, boarding pass in hand, I would never have made the connection. You gave new meaning to the phrase, "A Delta agent will be meeting this flight."

My weekly travels left my twin Persians in need of care, which was lovingly supplied by their cat nanny, Sandy Louis, who also checked on the house during those cold winter days and nights. Sandy was assisted by another cat person and dear friend, Paulette Chambers.

Almost daily e-mails from my college roommate, Heide Trept van Hulst, and my friend Chris Morales, both of whom supplied humor just when I needed it, gave me energy and determination even on the most difficult days.

A new computer was installed and many computer issues were resolved by Robin Reid, who also supplied frequent e-mail encouragements. I am also indebted to my local police chief, Karl F. Myers, who rescued me from my car stuck in the first New Hampshire snowstorm and lent me his copy of the *Uniform Crime Reports 2003*, available before I could get my own copy. Without the efforts of these two men, this edition would not have been completed on time.

The author would like to thank the following individuals for reviewing the text:

Liqun Cao, *Eastern Michigan University*
Ofc. Steve Cohen, *Florida Fish and Wildlife Conservation Commission*
Douglas Davenport, *Truman State University*
Richard Dewey, *Indian River Community College*
Michelle Jones, *Community College of Baltimore County*
Alexis J. Miller, *Middle Tennessee State University*
Michael Eric Siegel, *University of Maryland University College*
Charles M. ViVona, *Felician College*

Finally, the production of this book was facilitated by my colleagues and friends at Atomic Dog Publishing. To Christine Abshire, developmental editor; Lori Bradshaw, production coordinator; Victoria Putman, vice president of production; and Deb DeBord, copy editor, thanks for your professional assistance, your understanding, and your encouragement.

About the Author

Sue Titus Reid, professor and Director of the Undergraduate Program in the Reubin O'Donovan Askew School of Public Administration and Policy at Florida State University, Tallahassee, has taught law students, graduate students, and undergraduate students in many states. In 2000 she received a university teaching award at Florida State University. She has served on the board of the Midwest Sociological Society and the executive staff of the American Sociological Association. She has served as chairperson, associate dean, and dean. In 1985 she held the prestigious George Beto Chair in criminal justice at the Criminal Justice Center, Sam Houston State University, Huntsville, Texas.

Dr. Reid was influenced in her choice of career by her family background and early experiences in a small East Texas community. She graduated with honors from Texas Woman's University in 1960 and received graduate degrees in sociology (M.A. in 1962 and Ph.D. in 1965) from the University of Missouri–Columbia. In 1972 she graduated with distinction from the University of Iowa College of Law. She was admitted to the Iowa Bar that year and later to the District of Columbia Court of Appeals. She has been admitted to practice before the U.S. Supreme Court as well.

Dr. Reid is unique among authors in the criminal justice field because of her distinguished qualifications in both law and the social sciences. Her first major publication, *Crime and Criminology,* 1976, now in its eleventh edition, has been widely adopted throughout the United States and in foreign countries. Dr. Reid's other titles include *The Correctional System: An Introduction,* and *Criminal Law,* sixth edition. She has contributed a chapter to the *Encyclopedia of Crime and Justice,* as well as to other books, in addition to publishing scholarly articles in both law and sociology. Dr. Reid's contributions to her profession have been widely recognized nationally and abroad. In 1982 the American Society of Criminology elected her a fellow "for outstanding contributions to the field of Criminology." Other national honors include the following: Who's Who among Women; Who's Who in Criminal Law; 2,000 Notable Women (Hall of Fame for Outstanding Contributions to Criminal Law, 1990); Personalities of America; and Most Admired Woman of the Decade, 1992. Her international honors include International Woman of the Year, 1991–1992; International Who's Who of Intellectuals; International Order of Merit, 1993; Distinguished Alumna Award, 1979, Texas Women's University; Who's Who in American Law; The World's Who's Who of Women; Who's Who of American Women; Who's Who in American Education; and Research Board of Advisors, American Bio. Institute, Inc.

Dr. Reid has traveled extensively to widen her knowledge of criminal justice systems in the United States and in other countries. In 1982 she was a member of the People-to-People Crime Prevention delegation to the People's Republic of China. Her several trips to Europe included a three-month study and lecture tour of ten countries in 1985.

Sue Titus Reid, J.D., Ph.D.
Professor and Director of the Undergraduate Program
Reubin O'D. Askew School of Public Administration and Policy
Florida State University

1 Criminal Justice: An Overview

2 Crime, Offenders, and Victims

Introduction to Criminal Justice Systems

Criminal justice systems throughout the world vary considerably; even within the United States there are differences among the various state systems. The federal system has unique features, too. All criminal justice systems, however, face common issues, such as a punishment philosophy; definitions of the conduct to be included in the criminal law; definitions of the elements of crimes; and crime data collection. Criminal justice professionals must decide how to respond to crime victims and how to process the accused and sanction the convicted.

Part 1 of this text features U.S. criminal justice systems. The first chapter presents an overview of the punishment philosophies on which these systems are based and explores the reality of how they work. Chapter 1 also contains an overview of criminal law, beginning with the nature and philosophical bases of punishment. It mentions the components of criminal justice systems and discusses the meaning of criminal law as compared with civil law, the sources of criminal law within the context of the adversary system, and the constitutional limits of criminal law. The concept of crime is explored in greater detail, with consideration given to the elements of crimes. The final section analyzes the reach of criminal law, looking in particular at crimes against public morality, such as sexual behavior, child pornography, and substance abuse, considering the legal use of marijuana for medical purposes and, finally, looking at the changing nature of criminal law that today, in some jurisdictions, characterizes as murder the killing of a fetus.

Chapter 2 discusses the methods for securing and analyzing crime and victimization data. It includes an analysis of the characteristics of offenders and of victims.

The chapters in Part 1 set the stage for the subsequent and more extensive analyses of the basic parts of criminal justice systems—police, prosecution and defense, courts, and corrections—that constitute the remainder of the text.

Criminal Justice: An Overview

The peace and tranquility of Oklahoma City and the nation were shattered on 19 April 1995, when a bomb ripped through the federal building, resulting in the deaths of 168 people, including children and infants. Timothy McVeigh was found guilty of those crimes and executed in June 2001. In a federal trial Terry L. Nichols was found guilty of conspiracy and of manslaughter, but not of murder, and was sentenced to life in prison. Subsequently he was tried in Oklahoma for *state* crimes of murder, which carry the death penalty. He was convicted but not sentenced to death. Michael Fortier, who knew about the plans to bomb the building but did not report them to authorities, was convicted and sentenced to 12 years in prison, a reduction from the maximum sentence because of his cooperation with federal prosecutors.

At the time, the Oklahoma City bombing was the most atrocious terrorist act on American soil in history, but the number of deaths and property damage were exceeded on 11 September 2001 in a series of terrorist acts known commonly as the *Attack on America.* On that day terrorists overpowered the crew of four U.S. commercial aircraft, flying two of them into the Twin Towers of the World Trade Center in New York City; another into the Pentagon in Washington, D.C.; and a fourth into a field in Shankesville, Pennsylvania. This plane was perhaps flying toward another target in Washington, D.C., perhaps the U.S. Capitol or the White House, but crashed after passengers apparently attempted to stop the hijackers. Approximately 3,000 people lost their lives in these terrorist attacks; the World Trade Center was demolished; the Pentagon was damaged; and untold numbers of persons lost money or jobs as a result of the economic effects of these unbelievable terrorist acts.

Numerous other shocking crimes have been committed in the United States in recent years. In late March 2005, a shooting rampage on an Indian reservation in Red Lake, Minnesota, left 10 people dead and others injured. This was the deadliest school rampage since 15 were killed at Columbine High School in Littleton, Colorado, in April 1999, and was attributed to a loner, Jeff Weise, who killed himself in the rampage. Among the victims was Weise's grandfather and his companion.

Also in March 2005 the nation's judicial system was the focus of two violent attacks. Inside an Atlanta, Georgia, courtroom, Superior Court Judge Rowland W. Barnes and his court reporter, Julie Ann Brandau, were fatally shot.

L E A R N I N G
OBJECTIVES

After reading this chapter, you should be able to do the following:

- **List, define, and illustrate the major punishment philosophies**
- **Discuss the importance and impact of discretion in criminal justice systems**
- **List and describe briefly the major components of criminal justice systems**
- **Explain the difference between *civil law* and *criminal law***
- **Contrast the *inquisitory* and the *adversary* systems**
- **Explain what is meant by constitutional limits on criminal law**
- **List and analyze the sources of law**
- **Define *crime*, explain how crimes are classified, and discuss the meaning of the general elements of a crime**
- **Explain criminal *defenses***
- **Explain the pros and cons of including sexual behavior, child pornography, and substance abuse within the reach of criminal law**
- **Evaluate the impact of one state's decision to allow gay and lesbian marriages**
- **Analyze the issues involved in the legal use of marijuana for medical purposes**
- **Consider the legal issues involved in legislation encompassing a fetus as a person**

Outside the courtroom Sgt. Hoyt Teasley was shot and killed; Cynthia Hall, a guard, was overpowered, shot, and wounded. After the alleged offender, Brian Nichols, 33, escaped the courthouse, he allegedly shot and killed David Wilhelm, an off-duty federal customs agent, and committed other crimes, including his final one: the kidnapping of Ashley Smith, who became a heroine by talking Nichols into turning himself in to authorities.

Prior to the Atlanta shootings, Judge Joan Humphrey Lefkow of the United States District Court in Chicago, found her mother, Donna Humphrey, 89, and her husband, Michael F. Lefkow, 64, dead in the Lefkow home. Both were victims of gunshot wounds. Bart A. Ross, 57, who killed himself after police stopped his car, stated in a suicide note that he was responsible for these killings.

In February 2005 law enforcement authorities arrested Dennis L. Rader, 59, in Wichita, Kansas. Rader was charged with multiple counts of first-degree murder, as evidence was said to link him with the serial killings that terrorized that city off and on for three decades. Rader, who selected for himself the initials B.T.K. (bind, torture, and kill), was an unlikely suspect. The husband, father of two, active church member, and long-time member of the community, aroused no suspicion with regard to his criminal life. He was finally linked to the killings through information on a computer disk that he sent to a local television station. According to the pastor of a local church, that disk was traced to a computer in his church. The pastor recalled showing Rader, the president of the church, how to use the computer in order to print information concerning a church meeting over which Rader presided.

The randomness of such crimes causes fear. For example, many were frightened by the sniper attacks in the Washington, D.C./Maryland/Virginia area in 2002. Ten people were killed and three were injured. John Allen Muhammad, 41, and Lee Malvo, 17, were arrested in October 2002 and tried for those crimes. Both men were convicted of some of these murders. Muhammad was sentenced to death. Malvo was sentenced to life in prison without parole.

All crimes are of concern, and this text will focus on many of them. The lasting impact of the 9/11/01 events, however, will be noted where applicable, as the terrorist acts of that day affected U.S. criminal justice systems in particular and American life in general in significant ways.

Professions 1-1

Criminal Justice Careers

Most of the chapters of this text include a focus on careers. Although it is not possible to discuss most of the careers available in criminal justice or to prepare students for applying for specific jobs, it is thought that some exposure to job possibilities is beneficial. This career focus constitutes a brief overview.

Careers in criminal justice encompass a wide range of activities, from custodial services to high levels of administrative and professional positions, such as that of a U.S. Supreme Court justice. They include professions in law, psychology, criminology, sociology and other social sciences, architecture, accounting, physical sciences, and many other fields. Persons in criminal justice may be investigating criminal activities on the streets or in the labs, engaging in administrative activities in a wide variety of settings, counseling adult or juvenile offenders,

designing prisons or jails, supervising persons on parole or probation, training correctional officers or other personnel, supervising shop or other job assignments or training in correctional facilities, teaching college students in criminal justice, and engaging in many more kinds of activities. These and other positions require training and education ranging from a high school education and on-the-job training to a Ph.D. or a law degree, perhaps with experience.

The purpose of this text is to introduce you to criminal justice systems and their functions. Not all of you will become employed in the field, but even for those who do not, the information should be of general usefulness in related professions.

Enjoy your excursion through one of the most important and challenging areas of employment.

▶ Criminal justice system
The entire system of criminal prevention, detection, apprehension, trial, and punishment.

The purpose of this chapter is to analyze some of the issues in a **criminal justice system** regarding the imposition of punishment in criminal courts before looking briefly at the systems that impose that punishment and the criminal law on which punishment is based. Emphasis on careers is included, too, as noted in Professions 1-1.

The chapter begins with a look at the nature and meaning of punishment, along with the historical and current acceptable philosophies underlying punishment. But in reality societies punish for other reasons, some of which are illegal. It is important to understand the reality of any criminal justice system, and attention is given in this chapter to the wide discretion of decision making in criminal justice systems.

The basic components of criminal justice systems—police, prosecution, courts, and corrections—are noted. An overview of criminal law follows, with an examination of the distinction between criminal and civil law, an exploration of the adversary system, and a brief explanation of the constitutional limitations on criminal law. The sources of criminal law are mentioned briefly. The concept of crime is analyzed in terms of the ways in which crimes are classified and the basic elements of a crime. Brief attention is given to defenses to criminal allegations. The chapter continues with a discussion of how far the criminal law should reach in its efforts to control behavior, looking closely at the areas of sexual behavior, child pornography, and substance abuse, which some would argue constitute crimes against morality. Two relatively new areas of legal concern conclude the chapter. First is a discussion of legalizing the use of marijuana for medicinal purposes. Second is the topic of fetal abuse, which focuses on criminalizing the use of illegal drugs by pregnant women, as well as defining a fetus as a *person* for purposes of murder statutes.

1-1   The Nature and Philosophical Bases of Punishment

▶ Sanction A penalty or punishment that is imposed on a person in order to enforce the law.

A criminal justice system is designed to prevent people from violating its rules and to **sanction**, or impose legal punishments on, those who do. The issues arise, however, regarding the behavior that should be covered by **criminal** punishments, who should be sanctioned, and which sanctions should be applied. These issues are discussed in various chapters throughout the text, but at this point we look at the philosophical bases for punishment.

▶ Criminal A person found guilty of an act that violates the criminal law.

Consider the two cases described in Spotlight 1-1. Most people have no difficulty contrasting the cases of Henry Brisbon Jr. and Hans Florian, in view of the number and nature

Spotlight 1-1 Two Cases of Murder?

In all U.S. criminal justice systems the crime of murder requires intent, but the presence of that element does not ensure a conviction for murder. Consider the following cases, both of which apparently involved an intent to kill. Do you think the crimes should be treated alike? Would the death penalty be an appropriate punishment for either or both cases?

In the first case, a young woman driving a Chevrolet Caprice along Interstate 57 in southern Cook County, Illinois, on the night of 3 June 1973 was forced off the highway by a car occupied by four men. With one of the men pointing a gun at her, she was ordered to remove her clothing and climb through a barbed wire fence at the side of the road. Henry Brisbon Jr. responded to her pleas for life by thrusting a shotgun into her vagina and firing. She was in agony for several minutes before her assailant fired the fatal shot at her throat.

In less than an hour, Brisbon had committed two more murders. Brisbon's next victims, also riding in their car along I-57, were planning to be married in six months. When they pleaded that their lives be spared, Brisbon told them to lie on the ground and "kiss your last kiss," after which he shot each in the back. Brisbon took $54 in cash, two watches, an engagement ring, and a wedding band from his victims. He was arrested and convicted of these crimes, but, because the death penalty in Illinois had been invalidated, he was given a term of 1,000 to 3,000 years. While serving that term he killed an inmate and was sentenced to death under the state's new death penalty statute.

During an earlier incarceration, Brisbon was involved in 15 attacks on guards and inmates and was responsible for beginning at least one prison riot. He hit a warden with a broom handle and crashed a courtroom during a trial. Despite these acts of violence, Brisbon said, "I'm no bad dude . . . just an antisocial individual." He blamed his problems on the strict upbringing by his Muslim father, who taught him to dislike white people—the result: "I didn't like nobody." How did he feel about his victims? "All this talk about victims' rights and restitution gets me. What about my family? I'm a victim of a crooked criminal system. Isn't my family entitled to something?"[1]

How should Illinois have reacted to the crimes of Henry Brisbon? At the trial that resulted in his death sentence, the prosecutor described Brisbon as "a very, very terrible human being, a walking testimonial for the death penalty." The attorney who prosecuted him for the I-57 murders said, "On the day he dies . . . I plan to be there to see that it's done. Nobody I've heard of deserves the death penalty more than Henry Brisbon."[2]

Brisbon remains on death row in Illinois. In February 2003, noted lawyer and best-selling novelist Scott Turow was interviewed on National Public Radio (NPR) about the death penalty and specifically about Brisbon. Turow had just published *Reversible Errors,* his novel about a lawyer who was trying to free a man facing imminent execution. Turow had visited Brisbon in the supermax prison in Thames, Illinois. According to Turow,

> Henry Brisbon tends to be the poster child for capital punishment in Illinois . . . in addition to having been convicted twice of murder, . . . he's got an atrocious disciplinary record, over 250 disciplinary incidents, many of them involving . . . serious acts of alleged violence.[3]

Turow went on to point out that such dangerous persons as Brisbon evoke little if any sympathy but that it is the most atrocious cases that are most likely to produce mistakes in prosecution, leading to the conviction of the innocent. This is because of the enormous public pressure on law enforcement officials to obtain convictions in these cases. In Turow's judgment, the supermax prisons, such as the one in which Brisbon is incarcerated, are sufficiently secure to mitigate the possibility that he will kill again.[4]

In contrast to the case of Brisbon is that of Hans Florian. In March 1983, Florian, age 79, went to the hospital to visit his 62-year-old wife of 51 years, who was suffering from a disease that eventually would make her senile and helpless. Florian had placed his wife in a nursing home because he was unable to care for her, but, when she became too ill for that facility, she was hospitalized. Florian visited his ailing wife daily. On each visit he placed her in a wheelchair and pushed her around the floor of the hospital to give her a change of scenery. On the day in question, he wheeled her into a stairwell and shot her in the head, ending her life quickly. Friends claimed that Florian was not a murderer. He killed his wife because he loved her so much that he wanted her to be rid of her suffering.[5]

Florian was charged with first-degree murder. Should he have been convicted of that charge? Apparently his act was premeditated and without legal justification. If convicted, should he have been sentenced to death?

1. "An Eye for an Eye," *Time* (24 January 1983), p. 30.
2. Ibid.
3. "Scott Turow Discusses the Death Penalty," Show: *Fresh Air* (National Public Radio 18 February 2003), 12:00 noon.
4. Ibid.
5. "When Is Killing Not a Crime?" *Washington Post* (14 April 1983), p. 23.

of the killings Brisbon committed. But a case can be made that the legal elements of first-degree murder were present in both cases. Brisbon remains on death row in Illinois and may never be executed due to the moratorium on executions announced by Illinois Governor George Ryan in 2000 and continued in 2003 by his successor.

In the second case mentioned in Spotlight 1-1, that of Hans Florian, the grand jury refused to indict. Similar cases have, however, resulted in indictments, trials, convictions, and incarcerations. For example, consider another case that received national media attention. In 1990, Florida officials approved the release from prison of Roswell Gilbert, age 81, who was incarcerated for murdering his ailing wife in what he called a mercy killing. Gilbert was convicted of first-degree murder and sentenced to 25 years-to-life in prison. He served several years before his release for health reasons. Should Gilbert have been convicted of first-degree murder on facts similar to those of Florian and others? All these persons claimed they acted out of love when they killed their terminally ill spouses, who begged to be relieved of their sufferings. If Gilbert deserved to serve time in prison, why should he have been released for medical reasons?[1] Gilbert died in 1994.

These cases may be analyzed in terms of four objectives recognized historically as bases for punishment: **incapacitation, retribution, rehabilitation,** and **deterrence.** These objectives are defined and analyzed in historical perspective in Spotlight 1-2, which also mentions other factors that might be considered in punishment. The debate over which of these objectives ought to be the basis for punishment continues. The main punishment philosophies in vogue in the past century were rehabilitation and deterrence, with the former dominating the scene until recently and the latter the dominant philosophy today. Both continue to influence legislation and court decisions.

Rehabilitation has been described as the rehabilitative ideal, which is based on the premise that human behavior is the result of antecedent causes that may be known by objective analysis and permit scientific control. The assumption is that the offender should be treated, not punished. In the mid-1900s, social scientists endorsed the rehabilitative ideal and began developing treatment programs for institutionalized inmates. The ideal was incorporated into some statutes, proclaimed by courts, and supported by presidential crime commissions.

The demise of the rehabilitative ideal was emphasized in a 1982 magazine headline: "What Are Prisons For? No Longer Rehabilitation, but to Punish and to Lock the Worst Away." The article referred briefly to the original purpose of U.S. prisons: not only to punish but also to transform criminals "from idlers and hooligans into good, industrious citizens." It concluded, however, that

> no other country was so seduced for so long by that ambitious charter. The language, ever malleable, conformed to the ideal: when a monkish salvation was expected of inmates, prisons became penitentiaries, then reformatories, correctional centers and rehabilitation facilities.[2]

The simple fact is that prisons did not work as intended. The result was a movement toward more severe and definite sentences. California, a state that used the rehabilitation philosophy, led the way in returning to a punitive philosophy by declaring in its statutory changes in 1976 (to become effective the following year) that "the purpose of imprisonment for crime is punishment."[3] Likewise, the U.S. Congress eliminated rehabilitation as a goal in the federal system.[4]

There has been recent evidence, however, of a movement back to rehabilitation. Since 2001, California law has provided for treatment rather than incarceration for nonviolent drug offenders convicted of first or second offenses, and Idaho provides for treatment rather than criminal prosecution for some cases of substance abuse in order that those persons "may lead normal lives as productive members of society."[5]

The second and more recognized punishment philosophy in vogue today is *deterrence*. Deterrence is based on the assumption that, if punishments are unpleasant or severe enough, people will not engage in criminal behavior. This philosophy is one of the main justifications for punishment in U.S. criminal justice systems. There are two types of deterrence: individual (or specific) and general. *Individual deterrence* refers to the effect of punishment in preventing a particular individual from committing additional crimes. In the past this form of deterrence often involved incapacitation, or taking actions to make it impossible for a particular offender to repeat the crime for which he or she had been convicted. Today incapacitation usually takes the form of incarceration (or milder forms of restraint, such as house arrest) or capital punishment. In recent years, however, attempts

▶ **Incapacitation**
A punishment theory usually implemented by imprisoning an offender to prevent the commission of any other crimes by that person. In some countries (and in earlier days in the United States), incapacitation involved mutilation, such as removing the hands of thieves and castrating sex offenders.

▶ **Retribution** *See* **just deserts.**

▶ **Rehabilitation** A punishment philosophy based on a belief that the offender can and will change to a law-abiding citizen through treatment programs and facilities. Rehabilitation may be most likely to occur in community-based programs rather than during incarceration in penal institutions. The "rehabilitative ideal" was embodied in probation, parole, the indeterminate sentence, and the juvenile court.

▶ **Deterrence** A punishment philosophy based on the assumption that the acts of potential offenders can be prevented. *Individual deterrence* refers to the prevention of additional criminal acts by the specific individual being punished; *general deterrence* refers to the presumed effect that punishing one offender will have on other potential offenders.

Spotlight 1-2   Punishment Philosophies

1. *Incapacitation of the offender.* In the past, corporal punishment involved incapacitating the offender by making it impossible for him or her to commit further offenses of a like nature. The hands of a thief were cut off; the eyes of a spy were gouged; rapists were castrated; prostitutes were disfigured to make them unattractive. Another form of incapacitation in earlier days was to brand the offender with a letter symbolizing the crime; thus, an adulteress was branded with the letter *A*. The assumption was that, if people knew the nature of this person's criminal activity, they would avoid him or her. In modern times incapacitation has been accomplished primarily through incarceration.

2. *Retribution.* Historically, revenge has been one of the most important justifications for punishment. The philosophy of revenge, or retribution, is the eye-for-an-eye doctrine, which can be traced back for centuries.

   Not only was revenge acceptable, but it was expected. The victim (or the victim's family) was expected to avenge the offender. Private revenge was replaced by official government punishment, and today the philosophy of revenge has been replaced by that of retribution, which is widely recognized as an appropriate reason for punishment. The earlier "eye-for-an-eye, tooth-for-a-tooth" approach is not recognized legally today, but the U.S. Supreme Court has approved retribution as a basis for punishment.[1]

3. *Rehabilitation.* For years the rehabilitation philosophy dominated U.S. criminal justice policies. It is based on the belief that offenders can be changed through proper treatment and care. Some can be rehabilitated outside institutions; others may require confinement for this goal to be accomplished. Rehabilitation through treatment is

seeing a comeback in some jurisdictions today, as subsequent discussions of drug abuse show.

4. *Protection of society: deterrence theory.* Deterrence implies that punishment is imposed to keep people from victimizing others. **Individual deterrence** refers to preventing the apprehended offender from committing criminal acts, whereas **general deterrence** assumes that punishing that offender will keep others from engaging in criminal acts. Potential offenders will refrain from criminal behavior after seeing the punishment imposed on actual offenders.

5. *Preservation of social solidarity.* It has been suggested that the only justification for punishment is that it upholds society's norms and prevents private revenge. According to sociologist Emilé Durkheim, the true function of punishment "is to maintain social cohesion intact."[2] Thus, punishment may reinforce the morals of society and bind its members closer together in their fight against offenders.

6. *Reparation or restitution.* The reparation or restitution approach to punishment assumes that the victim should be returned to his or her former position. This approach has been used mainly in civil cases but recently has become more acceptable in criminal cases. Although injured persons (or the family of a deceased individual) may not be restored to their former positions by money, a financial contribution from offenders (or from society) eases the burdens caused by the crime. This type of punishment is more workable when victims have suffered crimes against property.

1. See Gregg v. Georgia, 428 U.S. 153 (1976).
2. Emilé Durkheim, *The Division of Labor in Society* (New York: Free Press, 1984), p. 108.

have been made to use more traditional methods of incapacitation, such as the castration of sex offenders.

In Texas, for example, there has been a movement to castrate inmate Larry Don McQuay, a convicted pedophile, but legal and other problems have prevented that, even though McQuay has asked to be castrated. In California, however, a statute enacted in 1996 that took effect in 1997, was the first to provide for chemical castration for repeat child sexual offenders. Under this statute persons who are convicted of a second offense against a child under the age of 13 must undergo weekly injections of Depo-Provera, a drug that reduces sexual desire. It is doubtful that a statute providing for involuntary surgical castration of sex offenders would survive constitutional challenges, although the California statute provides that those offenders for whom the law prescribes mandatory chemical castration may *choose* surgical castration instead.[6]

The second type of deterrence, *general deterrence,* is based on the assumption that punishing individuals convicted of crimes will set an example for potential violators, who, being rational people and wishing to avoid such pain, will not violate the law. Pro and con opinions as to whether this is the case may be based on conjecture, faith, or emotion, with

▶ **Individual deterrence**
See **deterrence.**

▶ **General deterrence**
See **deterrence.**

▶ **Just deserts** The belief that those who commit crimes should suffer for those crimes; also the amount or type of punishment a particular offender deserves to receive.

little significant empirical data. This approach leads to dogmatic statements, which cloud the issues and should be examined carefully.

A third punishment philosophy in vogue today is the justice approach, or the **just deserts** model. It is based on two philosophies, deterrence and retribution, and constitutes a reaction against the perceived ineffectiveness of rehabilitation.[7] The retribution basis assumes that offenders will be assessed the punishment they deserve in light of the crimes they have committed. It presumes that appropriate punishments will deter those criminals from engaging in further criminal acts and deter others from committing crimes.

Under the justice model an incarcerated person should be allowed to choose whether to participate in rehabilitation programs. The only purpose of incarceration is to confine for a specified period of time, not to rehabilitate the criminal. The offender receives only the sentence he or she deserves, and that sentence is implemented according to fair principles.

The justice model sounds good. People should be punished in accordance with what they deserve. But try applying it to the cases discussed in Spotlight 1-1 and the accompanying text. Which, if any, of the offenders *deserve* to be executed? If Brisbon is not executed, will more people commit atrocious murders such as those he committed? If he is executed, will people who contemplate such murders refrain from them? How about mercy killing? Did incarcerating a Florida mercy killer deter others from such acts? Would incarceration have deterred Florian from committing that offense again, or was imprisonment unnecessary for specific deterrence in his case? Or is it possible that, regardless of the stated underlying punishment philosophies accepted by a society, the reality is that particular decisions are sometimes made for other reasons? Is it also possible that reactions to crime are due to other reasons, such as politics?

1-2   The Role of Discretion in Punishment

It is characteristic of criminal justice systems throughout the world that decisions may be made for political reasons that have little if anything to do with the issues. A large body of scholarship has developed in an attempt to explain criminal justice systems as an area where critical decisions are made by those in power for the purpose of maintaining control over those not in power. It is alleged, for example, that in the United States women, minorities, and the poor can expect the blunt end of justice, whereas white men make all the important decisions legislatively, administratively, and judicially.

Others disagree with this position, and the conflict may be expected to continue. But as long as **discretion** is possible, decisions may be made for political reasons. *Discretion* means that individuals may use their own judgment to make decisions. The text discussion of Spotlight 1-1 contains examples of the exercise of discretion. Hans Florian was not tried for the murder of his wife, but Roswell Gilbert, who took his wife's life under similar circumstances, was convicted and served prison time. The jury could have chosen not to convict him, as has been the case in other so-called mercy killings. Thus, the jury had considerable discretion. In Gilbert's case, the governor exercised his discretion in releasing Gilbert before the completion of his sentence.

▶ **Discretion** In the criminal justice system, authority to make decisions based on one's own judgment rather than on specified rules. The result may be inconsistent handling of offenders, as well as positive actions tailored to individual circumstances.

Discretion may be exercised by various persons within criminal justice systems, including police, prosecutors, judges or justices, correctional officials, and paroling authorities. In addition, defense attorneys exercise discretion in determining which defenses to advance at trial. Defense and prosecutors exercise discretion in plea bargaining.

Discretion is inevitable within criminal justice systems, although the degree to which it is permitted varies. Discretion may be abused, but it is not necessarily a negative aspect of the system. It is possible to establish guidelines for the exercise of discretion, but it is not possible to eliminate all discretion. In addition, attempts to abolish discretion in one area of the system may increase it in others. Thus, for example, if longer sentences are instituted to control crime but juries perceive these sentences as being too harsh, they might acquit rather than convict persons whom they believe are guilty. In such cases, the system would have no alternative but to free the accused. On the other hand, conviction of more offenders with longer sentences has clogged courts and prisons, creating serious problems of overcrowding in both areas.

1-3   Components of Criminal Justice Systems

Criminal justice systems are composed of several components and processes, and they differ throughout the world. Figure 1-1 diagrams the most common model in the United States, although states organize and operate their systems in different ways. The federal system has some unique features as well. The various criminal justice systems have many common features, which are emphasized throughout this text.

In the United States, the most common organization of criminal justice systems is one consisting of four institutions: police, prosecution, courts, and corrections (noted at the top of Figure 1-1). The different stages are discussed in more detail where appropriate throughout the text.

A case may enter the system when a crime is reported to the police or when police observe behavior that appears to be criminal. After a crime has been reported, police may conduct a preliminary investigation to determine whether there is sufficient evidence that a crime was committed. If so and the suspect is a juvenile, he or she may be processed through the juvenile rather than the adult division of the system.

Not all arrested suspects proceed to the end of the criminal justice system. In fact, most cases do not go that far for a number of reasons. Police may decide that no crime has been committed or that a crime has been committed but there is not enough evidence on which to arrest a suspect. A suspect may be arrested but released quickly for lack of evidence. Persons who remain suspects through booking, the initial appearance, and the preliminary hearing may be dismissed, or the charges may be dropped at any of those stages. These decisions may be made for lack of evidence or other reasons, some of them highly controversial, such as political pressures. Even after formal charges have been made against the accused, they may be dropped or reduced.

Suspects who proceed to trial may not be convicted. Despite strong evidence against them, they may be acquitted. They may be convicted but placed on probation, fined, or sentenced to work in the community in place of being sent to prison. Those sent to prison may not serve their full terms.

Criminal justice systems are a process as well as a set of stages, and many factors affect how a suspect experiences the system. Throughout the text those factors are considered, but first, attention must be given to the basis of criminal justice systems, criminal law.

1-4   Criminal Law: An Overview

This overview of criminal law begins with the differences between civil and criminal law. Criminal and civil law, however, are not always distinguishable; in some instances they overlap.

1-4a   Criminal and Civil Law Distinguished

Criminal law may be defined by contrasting it with **civil law,** which pertains to private rights. Criminal laws provide the basis for the actions that take place in criminal justice systems. They define acts that are so threatening to society (not just to the individual victim) that they require that offenders be prosecuted by the government. They define punishments that may be imposed on offenders.

Civil laws provide a vehicle for legal redress for those who are harmed by others. They are used to uphold certain institutions, such as the family. Civil laws regulate marriage and divorce or dissolution, the handling of dependent and neglected children, and the inheritance of property. They protect legal and political systems, organize power relationships, and establish who is superordinate and who is subordinate in given situations.

Civil and criminal cases are governed by different procedural rules; there are differences in the evidence that may be presented and in the extent of proof needed to win the case. Whether the action is civil or criminal may determine the type of court in which the trial is held. In some cases, the act may not be considered a crime the first time it occurs. For example, a first offense of driving while intoxicated is considered a traffic violation and

Criminal law Statutes defining acts so offensive that they threaten the well-being of the society and require that the accused be prosecuted by the government. Criminal laws prescribe punishments that may be imposed on offenders.

Civil law Distinguished from criminal law as that law pertaining to private rights.

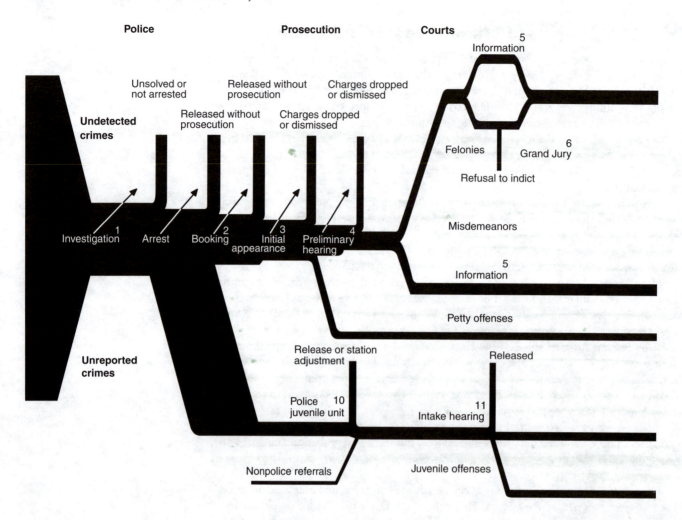

1. May continue until trial.
2. Administrative record of arrest. First step at which temporary release on bail may be available.
3. Before magistrate, commissioner, and justice of the peace. Formal notice of charge, advice of rights. Bail set. Summary trials for petty offenses usually conducted here without further processing.
4. Preliminary testing of evidence against defendant. Charge may be reduced. No separate preliminary hearing for misdemeanors in some systems.
5. Charge filed by prosecutor on basis of information submitted by police or citizens. Alternative to grand jury indictment; often used in felonies, almost always in misdemeanors.
6. Review whether government evidence sufficient to justify trial. Some states have no grand jury system; others seldom use it.

Figure 1-1
Institutions and Stages in American Criminal Justice Systems
Source: President's Commission on Law Enforcement and Administration of Justice, *The Challenge of Crime in a Free Society* (Washington, D.C.: U.S. Government Printing Office, 1967), pp. 8–9.

not a crime in some jurisdictions, but a second or third offense may be a crime. And the first offense might be considered a crime if a person is killed as a result.

The distinction between a civil and a criminal violation is important. The repercussions of being accused of violating a criminal law are more serious than those of violating a civil law. In addition to the possibility of a prison sentence, persons accused of a crime may expect social repercussions even if they are acquitted. Some people lose their jobs as soon as they are charged with a crime, particularly when it involves sexual offenses. It is important that the criminal law not be taken lightly and that the term *criminal* be used only in referring to people who have been convicted of a *criminal* offense.

Because of the serious impact of a criminal conviction, the law provides greater safeguards for those accused of crimes than for those facing civil suits. The most important safeguards are embodied in the concept of the adversary system.

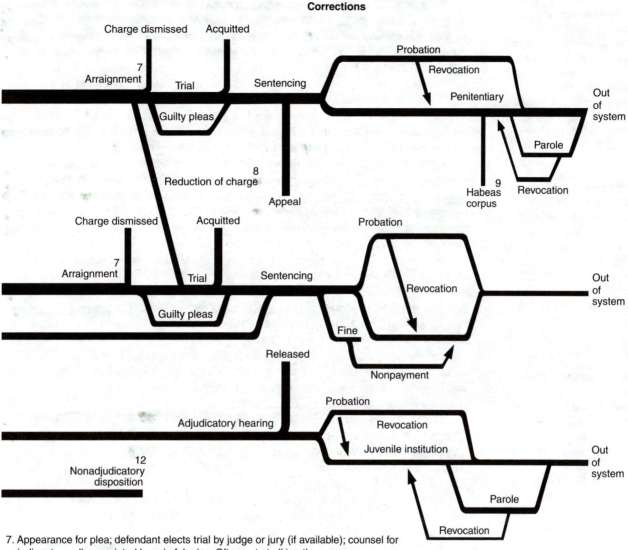

7. Appearance for plea; defendant elects trial by judge or jury (if available); counsel for indigent usually appointed here in felonies. Often not at all in other cases.
8. Charge may be reduced at any time prior to trial in return for plea of guilty or for other reasons.
9. Challenge on constitutional grounds to legality of detention. May be sought at any point in process.
10. Police often hold informal hearings, dismiss or adjust many cases without further processing.
11. Probation officer decides desirability of further court action.
12. Welfare agency, social services, counseling, medical care, etc. for cases where adjudicatory handling not needed.

1-4b The Adversary System

U.S. criminal justice systems are **adversary systems,** in contrast to the **inquisitory system** characteristic of some other countries. The two approaches may be distinguished in several ways. The adversary approach presumes that the accused are innocent. They do not have to prove their innocence; that burden lies with the state (or the federal government if it is a federal trial). In contrast, the inquisitory system presumes guilt, and the accused must prove that they are innocent. This difference between the two approaches is related to another basic contrast: the inquisitory approach places a greater emphasis on conviction than on the *process* by which that conviction is secured.

Adversary system   One of two primary systems for settling disputes in court. The accused is presumed to be innocent. A defense attorney and a prosecuting attorney attempt to convince a judge or a jury of their versions of the case. *See also* **inquisitory system.**

▶ **Inquisitory system**   (page 11)
A system in which the defendant must prove his or her innocence, in contrast to the adversary system, which has a presumption of innocence, requiring the state (or federal prosecutors in federal cases) to prove the defendant's guilt.

▶ **Due process**   The constitutional principle that a person should not be deprived of life, liberty, or property without reasonable and lawful procedures that must be made available in any criminal action, including postconviction procedures such as prison disciplinary hearings or parole revocations.

▶ **Equal protection**   All persons under like circumstances must receive essentially the same treatment in criminal justice systems; they may not be discriminated against because of race, gender, minority status, ethnicity, disability, or religion.

The adversary approach requires following proper procedures designed to protect the rights of the accused. Those procedures are guided by two important principles: **due process** and **equal protection,** concepts considered necessary to create a system in which the accused has a fair chance against the tremendous powers of the prosecutor and the resources of the state. Theoretically, the protections prevent the prosecutor from obtaining a guilty verdict for an innocent defendant. In reality, justice does not always prevail.

The impossibility of explaining exactly what is meant by the concept of due process is illustrated by the comment of a former U.S. Supreme Court justice, who said that due process "cannot be imprisoned within the treacherous limits of any formula. 'Due process' is not a mechanical instrument. It is not a yardstick. It is a process."[8]

The basis for the right to due process and equal protection comes from the Fourteenth Amendment to the Constitution (see Appendix A), which guarantees that we shall not be deprived "of life, liberty, or property, without due process of law." Nor may we be denied "the equal protection of the laws." The U.S. Supreme Court has decided numerous cases in which it has been argued that the due process or equal protection rights of individuals have been violated. It would take an extensive course in constitutional law to explore these concepts adequately, but we can look at them briefly. They are explained in more detail where relevant in subsequent chapters.

The concept of due process means that those who are accused of crimes and who are processed through a criminal justice system must be given the basic rights guaranteed by the U.S. Constitution. For example, defendants may not be subjected to unreasonable searches and seizures. When questioned by police about acts that, upon conviction, may involve a jail or prison term, they do not have to answer until they have an attorney. If they do not wish to talk then, they may remain silent. If they cannot afford an attorney, the state must provide one for them. They do not have to testify against themselves at trial. Certain rules of evidence must be followed during the trial.

Defendants may not be tried twice for the same offense; once a judge or jury has decided that the defendant is not guilty, the state (or federal government) may not bring these same charges again in an effort to wear down the accused. In short, the state must conduct the criminal trial and the processes preceding and following that trial by the rules embodied in the U.S. Constitution, as interpreted by the U.S. Supreme Court, and according to the established procedural statutes of the relevant jurisdiction. State trials must also follow the procedural safeguards established by their respective state constitutions and legislatures, as interpreted by their state courts.

The equal protection clause of the Fourteenth Amendment is also the focus of frequent lawsuits. That clause means that in general the government may not infringe on the rights of persons solely because of characteristics such as race, age, national origin, ethnicity, religion, or gender. Some jurisdictions have added disability and sexual orientation by statute, constitutional amendment, or judicial decision.

1-4c Constitutional Limitations on Criminal Law

The adversary model comes under attack frequently. Critics assert that it hinders law enforcement and, consequently, crime prevention and control. There is no question that observation of defendants' due process and equal protection rights creates obstacles for law enforcement. If authorities could accuse anyone of a crime regardless of available evidence, search and seize at will, interrogate suspects for unlimited periods of time when those suspects do not have an attorney, coerce confessions physically and psychologically, and so on, there could be more convictions, but the resulting loss of individual freedom and liberty is not tolerable in U.S. criminal justice systems.

In addition to the constitutional limits of due process and equal protection, state legislatures and Congress are limited by the federal Constitution (and interpretations of that document by lower federal courts and the U.S. Supreme Court) in how they may define criminal law. They are limited in criminal procedure as well. Throughout the text these limitations are discussed wherever relevant, but a few that are of importance to a general understanding of criminal law are noted here.

Criminal laws cannot be vague or too broad. Laws may not specify everything that is prohibited; they must be flexible. However, to avoid being held unconstitutional due to vagueness, laws must meet three criteria: (1) they must give notice or warning to all who are subject to them; (2) they must protect against arbitrary and discriminatory enforcement; and (3) they must not unreasonably deny other rights, such as the First Amendment rights to free speech, religion, and so on (see Appendix A). With regard to breadth, a statute should not "sweep within its ambit other activities that constitute an exercise" of other constitutional rights.[9]

Another constitutional limitation of particular importance in criminal justice is that of the Eighth Amendment's prohibition against **cruel and unusual punishment** (see Appendix A). The issue arises frequently in capital punishment cases, and, although the U.S. Supreme Court has ruled that capital punishment per se is not unconstitutional, it may be so if applied arbitrarily and capriciously.

The conflict between the legitimate concern of governments to maintain peace and control and the rights of citizens to be free of unreasonable governmental interference may be expected to continue.

1-5　Sources of Criminal Law

Although many people think of law as those provisions written in the statute books after passage by legislatures, laws come from three sources: constitutions, statutes, and court decisions. State legislatures enact statutes that apply to actions in their respective states. Congress enacts statutes that apply to the federal government as well as to the District of Columbia. These statutes are called **statutory law.** They apply only to the **jurisdiction** in which they are passed, with the exception that no state may enforce statutes conflicting with the rights guaranteed by the U.S. Constitution. That document and state constitutions are also sources of law.

Some statutes define the procedures that are appropriate for law enforcement. These are called *procedural laws.* Others define the elements that are necessary for an act to constitute a violation of the civil or criminal law. They are called *substantive laws.* For example, the crime of murder may be defined as the killing by one human being of another with malice aforethought. Convicting a person of murder under that statute requires proof of these elements: that a person was killed, that the person was killed by the accused, and that the killing involved malice aforethought.

What does *malice aforethought* mean? It refers to the requirement of an intent to kill and the absence of any legal justification for that killing. But, if the statute does not define that element, then court decisions, another source of law, may be used for a definition. Law that comes from court decisions is called **case law.** Much U.S. case law is derived from or influenced by **common law,** which consists of those customs, traditions, judicial decisions, and other materials that guide courts in decision making but that have not been enacted by legislatures into statutes or embodied in the U.S. Constitution.

The common law developed in England after the Norman Conquest in 1066. Previously there was no distinction among law, custom, religion, and morality. Decisions might vary in different communities. The Normans wanted to establish some unity, so the king employed representatives to travel to the various jurisdictions. These representatives kept the king informed about the various decisions and carried news to each jurisdiction of what was happening in the others. "The result of all this was that the legal principles being applied began to be similar, or common, in all parts of England. Thus, the terms 'Common Law of England,' and 'Common Law.'"[10] English common law has had a significant impact in the United States.

Another source that is important to an understanding of criminal law is **administrative law.** State legislatures and Congress delegate rule-making power to state and federal agencies. For example, prison officials are given authority to make rules that regulate the daily operations of their institutions; the Federal Bureau of Investigation (FBI) is granted power to make rules governing the enforcement of laws under its jurisdiction. Such rules must be made according to specific procedures and guidelines. These rules are very important, but normally the violation of administrative rules is not viewed as criminal.

Cruel and unusual punishment The punishments prohibited by the Eighth Amendment to the U.S. Constitution, as interpreted by the courts. Some examples are torture, prison conditions that "shock the conscience," excessively long sentences, and the death penalty for rape but not murder of an adult woman.

Statutory law Law that the legislature has originated and passed by a written enactment.

Jurisdiction The lawful exercise of authority; the area within which authority may be exercised, such as the geographical area within which a particular police force has authority. Courts may have *original* jurisdiction to hear the case; if more than one court has authority to hear the same case, those courts have *concurrent* jurisdiction. *Appellate* jurisdiction is the power of a court to hear a particular case on appeal. *Exclusive* jurisdiction means that only one court may hear the case.

Case law Legally binding court interpretations of written laws or rules made by the courts. *See also* common law.

Common law Broadly defined, the legal theory and law that originated in England and are common in the United States as well. More specifically, common law consists of the guidelines, customs, traditions, and judicial decisions that courts use in decision making. It is contrasted with constitutions and written laws.

Administrative law (page 13) Rules and regulations made by agencies to which power has been delegated by a state legislature or by the U.S. Congress. Administrative agencies investigate and decide cases concerning potential violations of these rules.

Violation of administrative rules may become criminal under some circumstances. Suppose that an administrative agency with the power to enforce rules concerning pure food discovers that a restaurant is serving spoiled food. Although this is not a criminal action (assuming it is not intentional), the agency may issue an order to the restaurant to stop the practice. If the practice is not stopped, the administrative agency may get a court order for enforcement; if that order is violated, the restaurant officials may be cited for a criminal offense. Even in those cases, however, persons who do not comply with the court order are not viewed in the same way as those who violate the criminal law, and data on violations of administrative rules and regulations are not a part of official crime data.

1-6   The Concept of Crime

Crime An illegal act of omission or commission that is punishable by the criminal law.

A **crime** may be defined as an "act or omission prohibited by law for the protection of the public, the violation of which is prosecuted by the state in its own name and punishable by incarceration."[11] Some jurisdictions define certain acts as violations or infractions. Those acts may be subject to fines or other minor penalties in the criminal law or to civil penalties, but the commission of those acts is not considered criminal. When an act is not defined or processed as a crime, it should not be labeled as a crime.

1-6a   Classification of Crimes

Crimes may be classified according to the seriousness of the offense; two main categories are used for this purpose. The term **misdemeanor** refers to the less serious offenses, whereas **felony** is used to classify the more serious ones. Generally misdemeanors are punishable by a short jail term, fine, probation, or some other penalty that does not involve incarceration in a prison. Felonies are normally punishable by more than a year in jail, incarceration in a prison, or capital punishment, although in some cases they, too, involve alternative punishments, such as community service or even a fine or probation.

Misdemeanor A less serious offense, punishable by a fine, probation, or a short jail term, in contrast to a felony, a more serious crime.

Crimes may be classified as *mala in se* and *mala prohibita*. *Mala in se* refers to acts that are considered criminal in nature, such as murder and rape. *Mala prohibita* refers to acts that are not universally regarded as criminal; they are criminal because the legislature has designated them as crimes. Examples of *mala prohibita* crimes are laws regulating the private, consensual sexual conduct of adults, the use of some drugs, and the use of alcohol by certain age groups.

Felony A serious offense, such as murder, armed robbery, or rape. Punishment ranges from execution to imprisonment in a state or federal institution but also includes probation, community work service, fines, and other less punitive sanctions, as well as a combination of these measures.

1-6b   Elements of a Crime

Certain elements must be proved before a person can be convicted of a crime. These vary from crime to crime and from jurisdiction to jurisdiction, but some common elements distinguish crime from noncrime.

An Act

Mala in se Actions that are intrinsically immoral, such as murder, forcible rape, and robbery.

In U.S. criminal justice systems, a person may not be punished for his or her thoughts; an act, or the omission of an act, must be committed, although some crimes do not require an act in the traditional definition of the term. For example, in the crime of conspiracy, which involves an agreement between two or more people to commit an illegal act, the agreement constitutes the act. Two parties may be convicted of conspiracy to commit a crime even though only one (or neither) is convicted of that crime. In addition, a crime may be committed when a person is an accomplice to another who commits the criminal act.

Mala prohibita Actions that are wrong because legislation prohibits them, although there may not be general agreement that they are wrong in themselves.

A crime may be committed when a person has made an attempt to commit—but has not committed—an act defined as a crime. The person must have made a substantial attempt to commit the crime. A very early English case established the crime of attempt. The defendant was accused of putting a lighted candle and some combustible materials in the house he was renting. The house was not burned, but the defendant was convicted. The court said, "The intent may make an act, innocent in itself, criminal; nor is the completion of an act, criminal in itself, necessary to constitute criminality."[12]

Failure to act may also constitute a crime but only when a person has a legal duty to act. If a child is drowning and two people watch without making any effort to rescue the child, the lack of action of one may be a crime, whereas that of the other might not meet the requirements of a criminal act of omission. In the first instance, the observer is a parent with a legal duty to aid the drowning child. Conversely, if the other person is not a close relative, has no contractual obligation to the child, and has not placed the child in that position of peril, he or she may not have a legal duty to come to the aid of the child. Failure to do so does not constitute a crime, no matter how reprehensible the lack of action may be from a moral point of view.

In order for an act to be criminal, it must be voluntary. A driver who has a sudden epileptic seizure, loses control of the car, strikes another car, and injures or kills another human being has not necessarily committed a crime. But a driver who has had prior attacks of a similar nature might be found guilty of a crime for recklessly creating a situation of danger to others by driving a car when he or she knows such attacks may occur.

An Unlawful Act

A crime is an act prohibited by the criminal law. A person cannot be punished for acts that may be considered socially harmful but that are not prohibited by the criminal law. As noted earlier, the law must be reasonably clear about the conduct that is prohibited. A statute will be declared void when "men of common intelligence must necessarily guess at its meaning and differ as to its application."[13]

An Intent

For an act to be a crime, the law requires the element of intent, or *mens rea*, a guilty mind. This is to distinguish those acts that may be harmful to others but for which the actor had no immoral or wrongful purpose. Negligent actions may cause harm to others, who may recover damages in a civil suit, but the law requires a guilty or an immoral mind for those acts to be considered criminal. Former U.S. Supreme Court Justice Oliver Wendell Holmes Jr. described the meaning of this distinction when he said, "Even a dog distinguishes between being stumbled over and being kicked."[14]

The intent requirement is complex. Neither court decisions nor scholarly legal writings provide an easily understood meaning. The intent requirement may vary from crime to crime, but it is clear that some kind of intent must be present in order for an act to constitute a crime. In simple terms, an intent to do something means that the actor intends to bring about the consequences of his or her actions or engages in acts that are reasonably certain to bring about the negative effects. The actor does not have to intend the *specific* result that occurs. A person who fires a gun into a crowd, intending to kill a specific person; misses that person; and kills another could be convicted of murder. In this example, the intent comes from the evidence that the individual purposely and knowingly took the action that resulted in the death of another. Usually this is the easiest kind of case in which to prove intent, but the required intent need not be that obvious. Criminal intent may be found in cases in which the action is extremely reckless or grossly negligent.

The definition of criminal intent in cases of reckless and negligent behavior is not easy. Part of the Texas Penal Code, reproduced in Spotlight 1-3, illustrates one way to define those kinds of culpability, as well as the two more common kinds of intent: purposely and knowingly.

Intent may not be required in some cases, such as those in which people are held responsible for the criminal acts of others. For example, the owner of a bar might be charged with a crime after one of his employees serves liquor to an underage person who drives negligently and kills another. Nor is knowledge that a crime is being committed required in all circumstances. To illustrate, sexual intercourse with a person under the legal age of consent may be defined as the crime of *statutory rape* even though the alleged victim consented to the act. Historically the law has presumed that young women must be protected and thus could not legally consent to sex. In recent years some of these laws have been revised or eliminated.

> **Mens rea** The criminal intent of the accused at the time the criminal act is committed.

Spotlight 1-3   **General Requirements of Culpability**

Texas Penal Code, Chapter 6 (2004)
Section 6.02. Requirement of Culpability.

(a) Except as provided in Subsection (b), a person does not commit an offense unless he intentionally, knowingly, recklessly, or with criminal negligence engages in conduct as the definition of the offense requires.

(b) If the definition of an offense does not prescribe a culpable mental state, a culpable mental state is nevertheless required unless the definition plainly dispenses with any mental element....

Section 6.03. Definitions of Culpable Mental States.

(a) A person acts intentionally, or with intent, with respect to the nature of his conduct or to a result of his conduct when it is his conscious objective or desire to engage in the conduct or cause the result.

(b) A person acts knowingly, or with knowledge, with respect to the nature of his conduct or to circumstances surrounding his conduct when he is aware of the nature of his conduct or that the circumstances exist. A person acts know-

ingly, or with knowledge, with respect to a result of his conduct when he is aware that his conduct is reasonably certain to cause the result.

(c) A person acts recklessly, or is reckless, with respect to circumstances surrounding his conduct or the result of his conduct when he is aware of but consciously disregards a substantial and unjustifiable risk that the circumstances exist or the result will occur. The risk must be of such a nature and degree that its disregard constitutes a gross deviation from the standard of care that an ordinary person would exercise under all the circumstances as viewed from the actor's standpoint.

(d) A person acts with criminal negligence, or is criminally negligent, with respect to circumstances surrounding his conduct or the result of his conduct when he ought to be aware of a substantial and unjustifiable risk that the circumstances exist or the result will occur. The risk must be of such a nature and degree that the failure to perceive it constitutes a gross deviation from the standard of care that an ordinary person would exercise under all the circumstances as viewed from the actor's standpoint.

The Concurrence of Act and Intent

For an act to be a crime, the act and the intent must occur together. It is not sufficient to have a criminal intent today but not commit the act until later. *A* might intend to kill *B* today but not do so. One week later, after *A* and *B* have resolved their differences, they go hunting. *A* accidentally falls while preparing to shoot a deer; the gun fires; *B* is killed. *A* should not be charged with murder because, at the time he fired, he did not have the criminal intent required for the crime of murder.

The importance of the concurrence of act and intent, along with the issue of causation (discussed in the "Causation" section), has been raised recently in the cases of persons who know they have **AIDS (acquired immune deficiency syndrome)** or are HIV positive and have sexual relations without disclosing to their partners that they have the virus or the disease. Some recent cases illustrate the legal issues.

Nushawn J. Williams, 22, pleaded guilty to two counts of reckless endangerment after he became the first person to be charged under the recently enacted New York statute that criminalizes knowingly having sexual relations without informing a partner of one's HIV status. Williams also pleaded guilty to other sex-related offenses, including statutory rape. Prosecutors alleged that Williams had had unprotected sex with as many as 48 women during one year (four of them were known to have had children by Williams), but most of the identified women refused to cooperate with the prosecution; thus, charges were not filed in those cases. In an interview Williams boasted that he had had unprotected sex with more than 300 women. He said, "Yeah, I gave them a death sentence, but it wasn't knowingly." Williams was denied parole in August 2001 and again in July 2003.[15]

HIV- or AIDS-infected persons who are convicted of a crime for having unprotected sex may argue that they did not have an intent to harm the alleged victim. A 1998 Michigan case, however, held that the intent requirement is implicit in the irresponsible conduct. The court made the analogy of driving a car while under the influence of a controlled substance. The person may not intend to harm anyone, but the general intent to do so is implicit in that reckless and irresponsible act.[16]

In contrast to the state statutes involved in these two examples, some states have chosen to use existing statutes to prosecute the act of having unprotected sex when you know you are HIVpositive or have AIDS. In 1993, for example, Texas repealed its statute that

> **AIDS (acquired immune deficiency syndrome)**   A deadly disease that attacks the immune system; it is communicated through exchange of body fluids, especially during sexual activity and blood transfusions, but it can also be transmitted in other ways.

criminalized *exposing to AIDS/HIV*. Legislators noted that the statute had not been used frequently and had some problems; they argued that existing statutes, such as attempted murder, would cover the crime.[17]

In fact, Texas did convict an inmate who, knowing he was HIV positive, spat at a correctional officer and yelled words to the effect that, if he were going down, he would take everyone with him. Despite the defendant's offer of evidence that neither the HIV virus nor AIDS can be transmitted by saliva, under the facts of this case, the jury was permitted to find Curtis Weeks guilty of attempted murder.[18]

In a similar case, the state of New Jersey upheld an inmate's conviction for biting a correctional officer.[19] In a Florida case, however, the trial court dismissed attempted murder charges against HIV-positive Pamela Super, who had bitten her daughter repeatedly. The judge ruled that there is insufficient evidence to substantiate transmittal of the virus through saliva. Super entered a guilty plea to child endangerment.[20]

One final example demonstrates the need to read cases carefully. A Maryland appellate court held that, in the case of Dwight Ralph Smallwood, who was told to use condoms before having sex (because of his HIV status), the state could not assume from his act alone that he had had the requisite intent for attempted second-degree murder and assault with attempt to murder when he raped three women without using condoms. The court held that in each case the state must prove specific intent. The court distinguished the New Jersey and Texas cases by the announced intentions of the defendants in each.[21]

Causation

The final element of all crimes is that there must be proof that the result is caused by the act. If *A* shoots and hits *B*, wounding *B* slightly, *A* may be charged with attempted murder (if the elements of that crime can be proved). But *A* should not be charged with murder if *B* dies of causes unrelated to the act of shooting. **Causation** in criminal law is very intricate and complex. It is important to know, however, that legal cause is a crucial element that must be proved before a person is convicted of a crime.

In addition to proving an act, an intent, concurrence of the act and the intent, and causation, for some crimes the prosecution must prove the existence of **attendant circumstances,** which are facts surrounding an act. For example, a statute may provide for a higher penalty if the crime is committed against a police officer, in which case the prosecution would have to prove that the victim was an officer.

1-6c Defenses to Crimes

In the 1800s, the classical school of criminologists advocated that punishment should fit the crime. All who committed a particular crime should have the same penalty. Members of the positive school, in contrast, advocated that some exceptions should be made. For example, because of their infancy, children should not have the same criminal responsibility as adults; indeed, children below a certain age should not be charged with crimes. Those who have serious mental problems to the extent that either they do not know what they are doing or they cannot control their actions should not be criminally responsible. Exceptions, or **defenses,** thus crept into the law.

Defenses to criminal culpability have varied over the years, and, like all areas of law, this one is in transition, with new attempts at criminal defenses occurring often, although some defenses have been traditional in many societies.[22]

1-7 The Reach of Criminal Law

The acts covered within criminal law vary from time to time and from jurisdiction to jurisdiction. Some of these acts result from reactions to technology. For example, one of the fastest growing crimes in the world today is **identity theft,** which is relatively new as a crime. On 18 June 2003, CBS aired a special report on identity theft, reporting on a recent crackdown in California in an effort to combat this widespread crime that can victimize anyone and cause years of turmoil. In the examples cited by CBS, thieves were stealing mail

> **Causation** In criminal law, the requirement that the act must be the cause of the harmful consequence.

> **Attendant circumstances** Facts surrounding a crime, which are considered to be a part of that crime and which must be proved along with the elements of the crime.

> **Defenses** Responses by the defendant in a criminal or civil case. They may consist only of a denial of the factual allegations of the prosecution (in a criminal case) or of the plaintiff (in a civil case). If the defense offers new factual allegations in an effort to negate the charges, there is an affirmative defense.

> **Identity theft** The stealing of an individual's social security number or other important information about his or her identity and using that information to commit crimes, such as removing funds from the victim's bank account.

from boxes in apartment buildings. From the mail, they secured important identifiers, which permitted them to secure the identities of numerous people and use that information to steal their money. According to CBS, for some victims, "straightening out their financial life can become a full-time job."[23]

Most people would not have an issue with extending the criminal law to cover such new crimes as identity theft. Some do, however, contend that expanding the law to cover some acts is unreasonable. The following sections discuss some of those acts.

1-7a   Crimes against Public Morality

Historically the purpose of criminal law has been the subject of extensive debate. Some people argue that only clearly *criminal* acts should be included and that the criminal law should not be used to try to control behavior that many people do not consider wrong. Others take the position that the criminal law is the most effective method of social control and therefore should embrace even those acts that some consider to be *mala prohibita* rather than *mala in se*. The issues arise most frequently when the criminal law embraces areas of private morality, such as consensual adult sexual behavior and substance abuse, or goes beyond the historical coverage of a crime, such as murder, by including a fetus. We begin with consensual sexual behavior.

Sexual Behavior

In a 1969 publication two scholars referred to U.S. criminal laws as the most moralistic in history—characterized by sex offense statutes designed "to provide an enormous legislative chastity belt encompassing the whole population and proscribing everything but solitary and joyless masturbation and 'normal coitus' inside wedlock."[24] In recent years many states have repealed criminal statutes that proscribe sexual behavior between consenting adults. They have limited criminal statutes to sexual behavior that is the result of force against any person, that is committed consensually but with an underage or a mentally or physically incompetent person, or that is committed in public. Some states retain the common law approach, however, and provide criminal penalties for adult consensual sexual behavior that is considered deviant by some members of the population. In a controversial decision in 1986, *Bowers* v. *Hardwick*, the U.S. Supreme Court upheld the right of states to do so. This case involved consensual sexual behavior between two men in the privacy of their Georgia home, where police had gone for legal reasons. Although this case had not been reversed by the U.S. Supreme Court, in 1998 the Georgia Supreme Court held that the state's statute on which the case was based violates the Georgia constitution.[25] As Spotlight 1-4 indicates, in June 2003 the U.S. Supreme Court decided another case, *Lawrence* v. *Texas*, involving the issue of private and consenting sexual behavior between same-gender persons; in that case, the Supreme Court overruled *Bowers* v. *Hardwick*.

This discussion of prohibitions against oral and anal sex is the kind of information used by those who oppose recognizing most civil rights for gays and lesbians. Many changes have been made not only in the laws regarding sexual behavior but also in the recognition of civil rights such as health and other benefits of employment (now extended by some companies to same-gender partners). Although these changes do not involve *criminal* acts, they are important in understanding changes that have been or may be made in criminal laws concerning sexual behavior. In that sense, it is relevant that the subject of marriage is the area of same-gender rights that has been fought over most bitterly. Vermont became the first state to move toward that recognition. In December 1999, the Vermont Supreme Court unanimously ruled that gays and lesbians who are committed to each other should receive benefits similar to those provided for heterosexual couples. The court did not recognize marriage per se but did hold that the state constitution's "common benefits clause" means that same-gender couples should be afforded the benefits and protections provided by the state for opposite-gender couples. This would include health and life insurance, provisions for inheritance, medical visitation rights, and medical and other proxy decisions. The court left it to the state legislature to determine the specifics of making such

| Spotlight 1-4 | **The U.S. Supreme Court Rules on Same-Gender Sex** |

Lawrence v. *Texas*[1]

Liberty protects the person from unwarranted government intrusions into a dwelling or other private places. In our tradition the state is not omnipresent in the home. And there are other spheres of our lives and existence, outside the home, where the state should not be a dominant presence. Freedom extends beyond spatial bounds. Liberty presumes an autonomy of self that includes freedom of thought, belief, expression, and certain intimate conduct....

The question before the Court is the validity of a Texas statute making it a crime for two persons of the same sex to engage in certain intimate sexual conduct.

In Houston, Texas, officers of the Harris County Police Department were dispatched to a private residence in response to a reported weapons disturbance. They entered an apartment where one of the petitioners, John Geddes Lawrence, resided. The right of the police to enter does not seem to have been questioned. The officers observed Lawrence and another man, Tyron Garner, engaging in a sexual act. The two petitioners were arrested, held in custody over night, and charged and convicted before a Justice of the Peace.

The complainants described their crime as deviate sexual intercourse, namely anal sex, with a member of the same sex (man) ... The petitioners exercised their right to a trial *de novo* [a new trial] in Harris County Criminal Court. They challenged the statute as a violation of the Equal Protection Clause of the Fourteenth Amendment and of a like provision of the Texas Constitution. Those contentions were rejected. The petitioners, having entered a plea of nolo contendere [meaning the defendant will not contest the charges], were each fined $200 and assessed court costs of $141.25....

[The constitutional challenges were rejected and the convictions were affirmed by the Court of Appeals for the Texas Fourteenth District.]

We granted *certiorari* to consider three questions:

1. Whether petitioners' criminal convictions under the Texas Homosexual Conduct law that criminalizes sexual intimacy by same-sex couples, but not identical behavior by different-sex couples—violate the Fourteenth Amendment guarantee of equal protection of laws?
2. Whether petitioners' criminal convictions for adult consensual sexual intimacy in the home violate their vital interests in liberty and privacy protected by the Due Process Clause of the Fourteenth Amendment?
3. Whether *Bowers* v. *Hardwick* should be overruled?

The petitioners were adults at the time of the alleged offense. Their conduct was in private and consensual. ...

[The U.S. Supreme Court ruled in the affirmative on all issues and, among other statements, made the following:]

The central holding of *Bowers* has been brought into question by this case, and it should be addressed. Its continuance as precedent demeans the lives of homosexual persons....

Bowers was not correct when it was decided, and it is not correct today. It ought not to remain binding precedent. *Bowers* v. *Hardwick* should be and now is overruled....

The Texas statute furthers no legitimate state interest which can justify its intrusion into the personal and private life of the individual.

Had those who drew and ratified the Due Process Clauses of the Fifth Amendment or the Fourteenth Amendment known the components of liberty in its manifold possibilities, they might have been more specific. They did not presume to have this insight. They knew times can blind us to certain truths and later generations can see that laws once thought necessary and proper in fact serve only to oppress. As the Constitution endures, persons in every generation can invoke its principles in their own search for greater freedom.

1. Lawrence v. Texas, 41 S.W.3d 349 (Tex.App. 2001), *rev'd*, 539 U.S. 558 (2003).

provisions available. The term *marriage* (recognized by the court as an institution involving a man and a woman) was not used, but the point is clear: gender can no longer determine the availability of "common benefits."[26]

In November 2003, however, the highest court in Massachusetts, by a 4-to-3 vote, became the first state court to hold that the state constitution precludes denying marriage to same-gender couples. According to the Massachusetts Supreme Judicial Court, "The question before us is whether, consistent with the Massachusetts Constitution, the commonwealth may deny the protections, benefits and obligations conferred by civil marriage to two individuals of the same sex who wish to marry." The court held that it may not do so. "The Massachusetts Constitution affirms the dignity and equality of all individuals. It forbids the creation of second-class citizens."[27] The U.S. Supreme Court refused to review the case. The decision by the Massachusetts court concerning that state's constitution would normally affect only that state. But the U.S. Constitution has a "full faith and credit clause," through which states recognize actions in other states. Although most states have enacted statutes prohibiting same-gender marriages, it is possible that those statutes will be declared unconstitutional under the U.S. Constitution now that the U.S. Supreme Court has held that it is unconstitutional to prohibit sexual behavior between same-gender consenting adults in private when the behavior is not illegal among heterosexuals.

Child Pornography

The attempts of Congress to prohibit the use of children in pornography serves as another example of the use of the criminal law to ban sexual behavior. It is not illegal for adults to view pornography, but it is illegal to produce or possess pornography involving children, as this is seen as sexual exploitation of children. Congress has enacted various statutes aimed at such prohibitions. In a recent case, the U.S. Supreme Court held that the production or possession of *virtual child pornography,* which is created by computer simulations rather than through the use of children, does not violate federal statutes. By a 6-to-3 vote the Court, emphasizing the First Amendment right to free speech (see Appendix A), ruled that the provisions of the Child Pornography Prevention Act of 1996 (CPPA) that criminalize virtual child pornography are unconstitutional. Although the justices acknowledged the need (and the right) to prohibit children from viewing pornography or being involved in its production, they nevertheless took the position that "speech within the rights of adults to hear may not be silenced completely in an attempt to shield children from it."[28] A big issue in the continued fight against using real children in pornography will be for the prosecution to prove beyond a reasonable doubt that, in any given example of pornography involving children, *actual* children were used.

A 2003 statute enacted by Congress and signed by President Bush was designed to protect children from pornography as well as other forms of sexual abuse, kidnapping, and other crimes. The lengthy statute is entitled the Prosecutorial Remedies and Other Tools to End the Exploitation of Children Today Act of 2003 (the Protect Act).[29]

There are many other areas involving public morality in which some people take the position that the criminal law should not be used to attempt to regulate behavior. Some of those areas are prostitution, sexual behavior between heterosexuals who are not married to each other, and public nudity under some circumstances (such as on beaches designated for that purpose).

Substance Abuse

The second
Another major area of acts in which the use of the criminal law to regulate behavior is questioned is that of substance abuse. Although many people would agree that the criminal law is an appropriate mechanism for controlling the sale of drugs, there is no general agreement with regard to its use to control the *use* of some drugs, such as marijuana.

Considerable debate has occurred concerning the role of the criminal law in attempting to regulate substance abuse. Several reasons are given for including acts related to substance abuse within the criminal law. First is the symbolic value of the legislation: by criminalizing the acts, society makes it clear that they are unacceptable. Second, it is assumed that criminalization has a deterrent effect; if the act is a crime, most people will decline to commit it. This reason requires more careful consideration. There is no significant evidence that the threat of criminal punishment is a deterrent to public drunkenness. In fact, in 1986, a California court concluded that jailing public drunks might even be counterproductive.[30]

Some people take the position that alcoholism is a disease, not a condition over which the alcoholic has control. It is not clear which position the U.S. Supreme Court would take on the issue. In 1988 in *Traynor* v. *Turnage,* a case involving veterans' benefits, the U.S. Supreme Court upheld the statutory categorization of alcoholism as "willful misconduct" when the alcoholism is unrelated to mental illness, but the Court noted that it did not have to decide whether alcoholism is a disease. According to the justices, "It is not our role to resolve this medical issue on which the authorities remain sharply divided."[31]

Since *Traynor* v. *Turnage,* some medical scientists have reported evidence of a hereditary basis for alcoholism. If sufficient evidence suggests that the tendency toward substance abuse is inherited, we have to face the question of whether the use of alcohol and other drugs should be decriminalized and, if so, in what way. For example, should the criminal law retain jurisdiction over the selling of alcohol and other drugs to minors? Should driving under the influence (DUI) of a controlled substance result in *criminal* liability if the driver cannot control his or her drinking? Given the high percentage of highway deaths caused by drunk drivers, one could argue that this criminalization should continue. But does it have a deterrent effect?

It is also maintained that, because the use of alcohol (and other drugs) is related to criminal behavior, substance abuse should come under the jurisdiction of the criminal law, but the relationship between substance abuse and crime must be analyzed carefully. An earlier study of inmates disclosed that many of them had been *using* alcohol or other drugs at the time of their criminal acts. Even if some of the inmates exaggerated their reports of alcohol use, the researchers concluded, "It is clear that alcohol has played a major role in the lives of many prison inmates." Furthermore, almost half the inmates said they had been drinking just before the commission of the criminal acts for which they were incarcerated at the time of the study. More than three-fifths reported that they had been drinking heavily.[32]

Later studies confirm that a large number of inmates as well as arrestees test positive for alcohol or other drugs.[33] Substance abuse violations also account for a large percentage of the increase in crime and, consequently, jail and prison populations.[34]

Although it is unreasonable to ignore the possible effect of substance abuse present in so many instances when crimes are committed, the concurrence of alcohol or other drug abuse with criminal activity does not necessarily mean that there is a direct cause-and-effect relationship. It is possible that the use of alcohol and other drugs represents a lifestyle adopted by some offenders and has nothing to do with the commission of crimes. In those cases, attempts to enforce laws regulating the abuse of alcohol and other drugs will not have a significant long-term effect on criminal activity. Nevertheless, many scholars who have studied the impact of substance abuse on crime have concluded that the relationship is significant. An example is the work of James A. Inciardi and Anne E. Pottieger, who, although acknowledging that the evidence does not *prove* that substance abuse *causes* crime, concluded the following:

> It is clear to us that drugs are driving crime. That is, although drug use does not necessarily initiate criminal careers among users, it freezes users into patterns of criminality that are more intensive and unremitting than they would have been without drugs.[35]

Another area in which substance abuse and crime are related is that of **date rape.** So-called club drugs, such as gamma hydroxybutyrate (GHB), may be dropped into the drinks of unsuspecting dates, who are then victimized by forced sexual acts. GHB causes unconsciousness quickly and it cannot be smelled or tasted. Victims may have no memory of an alleged sexual attack. Another drug used in date rapes is Ecstasy, which highlighted a famous trial in 2003. In February, Andrew Luster, 39-year-old grandson of the founder of the Max Factor (cosmetics) company, was convicted in absentia (he fled to Mexico during his February trial but was captured in June and returned to the United States to serve his term) of numerous counts of rape and sodomy of unconscious victims, as well as possession of Ecstasy, poisoning, and sexual battery. Luster was sentenced to 124 years in prison.

The seriousness of club drugs has led to numerous legislative attempts to curb their use. A law passed in 2000 increased the penalties for possessing and distributing GHB and moved that drug into the category of drugs that receives the highest regulations under the federal Controlled Substances Act, the Schedule I drugs.[36] Bills introduced into the U.S. Congress in 2002 and 2003 were designed to crack down on Ecstasy and other club drugs. The Reducing Americans' Vulnerability to Ecstasy (RAVE) Act amended existing federal laws to increase the civil and criminal penalties for persons responsible for putting teenagers at risk of using Ecstasy and other club drugs by preventing the leasing of, renting of, or profiting from any place in which the drugs are used. The bill became a law when it was signed by President George W. Bush in April 2003. The RAVE act amends the controlled substance provision of the Comprehensive Drug Abuse and Prevention Act of 1970.[37]

▶ Date rape Forced sexual acts that occur during a social occasion. The alleged victim may have agreed to some intimacy but not to the activities defined in that jurisdiction as constituting the elements of rape.

1-7b   The Use of Marijuana for Medicinal Purposes

Another use of the criminal law to control substance abuse is that of laws prohibiting growing, distributing, and prescribing marijuana for any purpose. The sale and possession of marijuana is a serious offense, with long penalties in many states. In the federal system, marijuana is a Schedule I drug, meaning it is one of the drugs that cannot be prescribed by doctors for any reason. However, in California and a few other states, it is legal under state law to use marijuana for medical reasons with a prescription from a physician. The drug relieves pain and other symptoms in some diseases and is tolerated by some patients who do not respond well to other drugs.

Federal authorities have taken the position that the prescription of marijuana for medical reasons violates federal law and have focused on prosecuting those in California who violate these laws. They have had some success, with the U.S. Supreme Court reversing a lower federal court in California and ruling that the necessity defense is not available to a defendant who grows marijuana for medicinal reasons. That means that the defendant charged with violating the federal Controlled Substance Act by growing marijuana cannot defend that this was done because the drug is necessary for medical treatment. The U.S. Supreme Court reasoned that, when Congress included marijuana as a Schedule I drug, meaning it cannot be prescribed by physicians for any reason, and provided no exceptions, that is exactly what Congress meant. However, federal prosecutors wanted to avoid the harsh penalties of the federal statute and thus petitioned the California court to issue an injunction prohibiting anyone from providing marijuana for medical reasons. The Supreme Court did so, and that permits federal prosecutors to process through the civil rather than the criminal court anyone who grows, sells, or uses marijuana for medicinal purposes.[38]

Some defendants, however, have been charged with violation of the federal criminal controlled substances statute. For example, Ed Rosenthal was convicted in February 2003 by a California jury that was not given evidence during the trial that Rosenthal had permission from Oakland, California, officials to grow marijuana for medicinal purposes. After they found this out, some jurors demanded that Rosenthal be retried. The judge refused but, at the sentencing hearing, Rosenthal, who had faced up to 100 years in prison and a fine of $4.5 million, was sentenced to only one day in prison and three years of court supervision.

On the issue of using marijuana for medicinal purposes, a panel of the Ninth Circuit Court of Appeals in California ruled that the government may not revoke the medical licenses of physicians who prescribe marijuana for medicinal reasons. A hearing by the full court was denied, and the U.S. Supreme Court refused to review the case.[39]

Finally, in June 2005, the U.S. Supreme Court ruled in a case involving the use of marijuana for medical reasons. The two plaintiffs in *Ashcroft* v. *Raich* were using marijuana to ease the pain from their respective diseases; no other medications had given them relief. The Supreme Court held that the federal Controlled Substances Act is within the proper exercise of federal power "even as applied to the troubling facts of this case." Advocates of the medical use of marijuana must now convince Congress to change the federal statute.[40]

1-7c   Fetal Abuse

Fetal abuse   The abusing of a fetus, which may or may not lead to its death. In some jurisdictions any resulting injury may lead to legal culpability; in a few states, killing a fetus may result in murder charges.

Another area in which there is controversy concerning the use of the criminal law is **fetal abuse.** Two areas of focus are included here: the abuse of a fetus by a pregnant woman who abuses drugs and the killing of a fetus.

There is sufficient evidence that consumption of alcohol and other drugs by pregnant women may cause harm to their fetuses that warnings are given and criminal sanctions are imposed. The toughest drug laws regarding harm to a fetus are found in South Carolina, which provides that a pregnant woman who uses drugs and her fetus dies may be charged with murder. One woman who used crack cocaine during her pregnancy and gave birth to a stillborn fetus was charged and convicted of murder. Her conviction was upheld in 2003 by the South Carolina Supreme Court.[41] Although the U.S. Supreme Court has not ruled on this issue, it has held that a state may not force pregnant women suspected of drug abuse to be drug tested involuntarily if the primary purpose of the test is to report their actions to the police.[42]

Another expansion of the criminal law in the area of fetal abuse is illustrated by the definition of murder in the California criminal statutes. The state previously defined murder as "the unlawful killing of a human being with malice aforethought." The current statute adds "or a fetus" after the words *human being*.[43] (Exclusions are made for legal abortions.) This change in the common law definition of murder, which has been followed in other states as well, has led to murder convictions for defendants accused of killing a woman and her fetus. The California position gained national and worldwide focus in the criminal trial of Scott Peterson for the murders of his wife, Laci, who disappeared from their home on Christmas Eve, 2002, and their unborn son, already named Conner. The double murder charge provided the special circumstances required by California law to try a defendant for capital murder. Peterson was convicted of first-degree murder for his wife's death and second degree murder for Conner's death. He was sentenced to death. As a result of this case, Congress passed a federal statute entitled the Unborn Victims of Violence Act of 2004 (also known as Laci and Conner's Law) to change the federal criminal code and that of the military code to protect unborn children fom assault and murder.[44]

1-7d   Conclusion on the Reach of the Criminal Law

Even if we decide that all of the acts discussed in this section of the chapter should be included within the criminal law, we should consider carefully what penalties to assess. What is accomplished by jailing a pregnant woman who uses drugs, other than to prevent her from harming her fetus further? Given that perhaps worthy goal, is it necessary to incarcerate her? What if she has other children to care for? And is that jail term worth the cost to society when new facilities must be constructed to handle the large populations of incarcerated people?

This discussion of criminalizing acts some consider against public morality, legalizing the use of marijuana for medicinal purposes, and fetal abuse raises the issue of whether the criminal law is used too extensively and therefore goes beyond the purpose of protecting the public's safety and welfare and interferes with the behavior of private persons. Those who take this position argue that the criminal law is being used to encompass acts without victims. They assert that the results are harmful in the long run: police may invade personal rights of privacy in order to enforce the law; minorities and other unpopular groups may be harassed; courts, jails, and prisons may be overcrowded as a result of processing these people through criminal justice systems; black markets may develop to supply prohibited products, such as alcohol and other drugs; and attempts to enforce unpopular and unsupported criminal statutes may create disrespect for the law. Critical police resources may be diverted from more important functions.

Supporters argue that the criminal law is a necessary symbol of morality and that removal of *mala prohibita* acts from the criminal law would place society's stamp of approval on the behaviors in question. Resolution of these two positions regarding the use of the criminal law to control morality involves religious, moral, and ethical considerations, as well as legal and empirical issues. In the final analysis, the answer may be a personal one. But it is clear that, whatever position is taken, it will have important repercussions on criminal justice systems.

Chapter Wrap-Up

This chapter begins the text with an overview of criminal justice systems and criminal law. Although the systems differ, all may be analyzed first in terms of punishment philosophies: retribution, incapacitation, social solidarity, revenge, rehabilitation, deterrence, and just deserts. In present-day United States the philosophies of deterrence and retribution, often combined in the just deserts approach, are dominant. Just a short time ago U.S. systems were dominated by the philosophy of rehabilitation, and today some efforts are being made to bring back that emphasis.

The role of discretion was discussed because it is crucial to criminal justice systems. It exists at all levels, and it cannot be eliminated. But it can be controlled by some measures, and, if left unchecked, it can result in unfairness to defendants. After an overview of discretion the chapter turned to a brief look at the components of criminal justice systems, using a diagram of general U.S. approaches for illustrative purposes. All of the elements of the systems are discussed in more detail throughout the text.

Crucial to all criminal justice systems is the basis for those systems, criminal law. A criminal justice system is based on a society's willingness to grant legal authority to some individuals to impose punishment. Criminal law provides that basis in modern societies, and this chapter began its overview of criminal law with a distinction between criminal and civil law. Criminal law has existed for centuries, predating and forming the basis for much of our civil law.

Criminal justice systems may be based on either the adversary or the inquisitory model. U.S. systems follow the adversary model, in which all accused are presumed innocent and the state must prove guilt. In contrast is the inquisitory system, in which the accused are presumed guilty and must prove their innocence. The adversary system is characterized by due process and equal protection. Other constitutional limitations include the prohibition of statutes that are vague or too broad and the imposition of cruel and unusual punishment.

Criminal law emerges from statutes enacted by the legislative branches of government, administrative rules and regulations, constitutions, and court decisions. All of these are important sources of law.

Criminal law is based on the concept of crime, which must be defined legally to fall within criminal justice systems. Crimes are classified as serious (felonies) or less serious (misdemeanors). Crimes may be classified as *mala prohibita*, criminal because they are so designated by society, or *mala in se*, criminal per se. Crimes have elements that must be proved before a person is convicted. Those include an illegal act that concurs with a guilty mind, attendant circumstances, and causation. Some acts that fit these elements may not be considered criminal because the accused has an acceptable defense.

Scholars, politicians, and the general public continue to debate what the reach of the criminal law should be. This chapter considered whether consensual sexual behavior between consenting adults in private, the use of children in pornography, and substance abuse should be included within the criminal law's reach. It also discussed whether we should legalize the use of marijuana for medicinal purposes. Finally, it analyzed recent developments in the law regarding the status of a fetus.

This overview chapter on criminal justice systems and criminal law set the stage for more detailed analyses of the components of the systems. The next chapter focuses on another foundation important to the understanding of criminal justice systems—the collection and analysis of data on crime, offenders, and crime victims.

Key Terms

administrative law (p. 14)
adversary system (p. 11)
AIDS (p. 16)
attendant circumstances (p. 17)
case law (p. 13)
causation (p. 17)
civil law (p. 9)
common law (p. 13)
crime (p. 14)
criminal (p. 4)
criminal justice system (p. 4)
criminal law (p. 9)

cruel and unusual punishment (p. 13)
date rape (p. 21)
defenses (p. 17)
deterrence (p. 6)
discretion (p. 8)
due process (p. 12)
equal protection (p. 12)
felony (p. 14)
fetal abuse (p. 22)
general deterrence (p. 7)
identity theft (p. 17)
incapacitation (p. 6)

individual deterrence (p. 7)
inquisitory system (p. 12)
jurisdiction (p. 13)
just deserts (p. 8)
mala in se (p. 14)
mala prohibita (p. 14)
mens rea (p. 15)
misdemeanor (p. 14)
rehabilitation (p. 6)
retribution (p. 6)
sanction (p. 4)
statutory law (p. 13)

Apply It

1. Briefly summarize the recent terrorist and other violent crimes that have occurred on U.S. soil.
2. Explain and distinguish among deterrence, rehabilitation, incapacitation, and retribution. Explain how these punishment and sentencing philosophies relate to the justice model of punishment.
3. Discuss the punishment implications of the cases discussed in Spotlight 1-1.
4. How do you think discretion should be regulated in criminal justice systems? Be specific in discussing the process in terms of specific personnel, such as police, prosecutors, judges, and juries. Consider your answer at the end of the course to determine whether your personal views have changed.
5. Contrast civil and criminal law.
6. Distinguish between the adversary and the inquisitory systems of criminal justice.
7. Explain the meaning of due process and equal protection. What other constitutional limitations are placed on criminal law?
8. Do you think capital punishment is cruel and unusual punishment? A life sentence without parole for drug

possession? For drug sales? Would your answer to the last two questions depend on the amount of drugs?
9. List and discuss the sources of criminal law.
10. How are crimes classified?
11. Discuss the basic elements of a crime.
12. What are criminal defenses?
13. Should the criminal law be used to control any or all of the following: premarital sex, extramarital sex, same-gender sex, driving while intoxicated, use of drugs, use of seat belts?
14. Analyze the U.S. Supreme Court decision concerning the sexual behavior of gay men.
15. What do you think will be the impact of the decision of the Massachusetts Supreme Judicial Court concerning gay and lesbian marriages?
16. What position should the criminal law take on the use of marijuana for medicinal purposes?
17. Under what theory should a fetus be considered a person for purposes of homicide statutes?
18. Should pregnant women who use illegal drugs be prosecuted for the *criminal* abuse of a fetus?

Endnotes

1. See "Clemency Granted to a Mercy Killer," *New York Times* (2 August 1990), p. 9.
2. "What Are Prisons For? No Longer Rehabilitation, but to Punish—and to Lock the Worst Away," *Time* (13 September 1982), p. 38.
3. Cal. Penal Code, Article 1, Section 1170 (2005).
4. U.S. Code, Article 28, Section 994(k) (2005).
5. See Cal. Penal Code, Section 1210.1 (2005); Idaho Code, Section 39-301 (2004).
6. Cal. Penal Code, Section 645 (2005).
7. See, for example, Ernest van den Haag, *Punishing Criminals: Concerning a Very Old and Painful Question* (New York: Basic Books, 1975); and David Fogel, *We Are the Living Proof: The Justice Model for Corrections* (Cincinnati, Ohio: Anderson, 1975).
8. Joint Anti-Fascist Refugee Committee v. McGrath, 341 U.S. 123, 162–163 (1951), Justice Frankfurter, concurring.
9. Thornhill v. Alabama, 310 U.S. 88, 97 (1940).
10. Hazel B. Kerper, *Introduction to the Criminal Justice System* (St. Paul, Minn.: West, 1972), p. 27.
11. Model Penal Code, Section 1.104(1).
12. Rex v. Scofield, Cald. 397, 400 (1784).
13. Connally v. General Construction Company, 269 U.S. 385, 391 (1926).
14. Oliver Wendell Holmes Jr., *The Common Law*, as cited in Morissette v. United States, 342 U.S. 246, 252 (1952).
15. "Drifter Gets Four to Twelve Years in H.I.V. Case," *New York Times* (6 April 1999), p. 1B; "Man Guilty of Spreading AIDS Virus Says He Had Hundreds of Sex Partners," *New York Times* (29 July 1999), p. 19; "Niagra Street Fire Damage Is Estimated at $90,000," *Buffalo News* (New York) (1 August 2003), p. 2C.
16. People v. Jensen, 586 N.W.2d 748 (Mich.App. 1998).
17. "Texas AIDS Law Off Books in '94: No Convictions Obtained in Statute's Brief History," *Houston Chronicle* (5 September 1993), p. 1C.
18. Weeks v. State, 834 S.W.2d 559, 561 (Tex.Ct.App. 1992), *sum. judgment granted sub nom.*, 867 F.Supp. 544 (S.D.Tex. 1994), *subsequent appeal sub nom.*, 55 F.3d 1059 (5th Cir. 1995).
19. Smith v. State, 621 A.2d 493 (N.J.Sup. 1993), *certification denied*, 634 A.2d 523 (N.J. 1993).
20. "Mom with AIDS Sentenced for Biting Her Child," *Orlando Sentinel* (23 April 1993), p. 1B.
21. Smallwood v. State, 680 A.2d 512 (Md. 1996).
22. For more details on defenses, see Sue Titus Reid, *Criminal Law*, 6th ed. (New York: McGraw-Hill, 2004), pp. 116–203.
23. "Crackdown in California against Identity Theft," CBS Morning News (18 June 2003).
24. Norval Morris and Gordon Hawkins, *The Honest Politician's Guide to Crime Control* (Chicago: University of Chicago Press, 1969), p. 15.
25. Bowers v. Hardwick, 478 U.S. 186 (1986), *overruled by* Lawrence v. Texas, 539 U.S. 558 (2003). See also Powell v. State, 510 S.E.2d 18 (Ga. 1998).
26. Baker v. State, 744 A.2d 864 (Vt. 1999).
27. Goodridge v. Department of Public Health, 798 N.E.2d 941 (Mass. 2003), *cert. denied sub nom.*, 125 S. Ct. 618 (2004).
28. Ashcroft v. Free Speech Coalition, 535 U.S. 234 (2002).
29. The Prosecutorial Remedies and Other Tools to End the Exploitation of Children Today Act of 2003 (the Protect Act), Public Law 108-21 (30 April 2003).
30. Sundance v. Municipal Court, 729 P.2d 80 (Cal. 1986).
31. Traynor v. Turnage, 485 U.S. 535 (1988), *superseded by statute as stated in* Larrabee v. Derwinski, 968 F.2d 1497 (3d Cir. 1992).
32. Bureau of Justice Statistics, *Prisoners and Alcohol* (Washington, D.C.: U.S. Department of Justice, January 1983).
33. See, for example, Executive Office of the President, Office of National Drug Control Policy, *Drug Data Summary* (Washington, D.C.: The White House, April 1999), p. 2.
34. See National Institute of Justice, *Drug Use Forecasting, Annual Report on Adult and Juvenile Arrestees* 1995, referred to in *The National Drug Control Strategy, 1997* (Washington, D.C.: The White House, February 1977), pp. 19–20.
35. James A. Inciardi and Anne E. Pottieger, "Drug Use and Street Crime in Miami: An (Almost) Twenty-Year Retrospective," in *The American Drug Scene*, 3d ed., ed. Inciardi and Karen McElrath (Los Angeles, Calif. Roxbury, 2001), pp. 319–342; quotation is on pp. 337–338.
36. The Controlled Substances Act is codified at U.S. Code, Title 18, Section 812(b) (2005).
37. The Reducing Americans' Vulnerability to Ecstasy (RAVE) Act of 2003 amended the Comprehensive Drug Abuse and Prevention Act of 1970, U.S. Code, Title 21, Sections 801-966 (2005).
38. U.S. v. Oakland Cannabis Buyers' Cooperative, 532 U.S. 483 (2001), *injunction granted sub nom.*, 2002 U.S. Dist. LEXIS 10660 (N.D.Cal. 10 June 2002).
39. Conant v. Walters, 309 F.3d 629 (9th Cir. 2002), *reh'g. denied, reh'g. en banc, denied sub nom.*, 2003 U.S. App. LEXIS 3932 (9th Cir. 2003), *cert. denied*, 540 U.S. 946 (2003).
40. Raich v. Ashcroft, 352 F.3d 1222 (9th Cir. 2003), *cert. granted*, Ashcroft v. Raich, 124 S.Ct. 2909 (2004), *and vacated, remanded subnom*, 125 S.Ct 2195 (2005).
41. State v. McKnight, 576 S.E.2d 168 (S.C. 2003), *cert. denied sub nom.*, 540 U.S. 819 (2003).
42. Ferguson v. Charleston, 532 U.S. 67 (2001).
43. Cal. Penal Code, Section 187(a)(b)(2005).
44. Unborn Victims of Violence Act of 2004, U.S. Code, Title 18, Section 1841 (2005).

Crime, Offenders, and Victims

In October 2000, the Federal Bureau of Investigation (FBI) released crime data for 1999, and for the eighth consecutive year serious crimes reported to police declined, this time by 7 percent. This was the longest consecutive period of decreases during the period the FBI had kept records. Murder (including nonnegligent manslaughter) was down 8.5 percent; robberies were down 4 percent; forcible rape fell 4 percent; and aggravated assault declined by 10 percent. Burglaries declined by 10 percent, auto thefts decreased by 7.7 percent, and larceny-thefts dropped by 5.7.[1]

These figures for 1999 were encouraging, and even more so was the fact that a year later the FBI announced that there had been virtually no change in serious crimes in 2000, compared with 1999, and in 2000 overall serious crimes were down 14 percent over 1996 and 22 percent over 1991.[2] In 2001, crime data showed the first increase in serious crime in a decade, rising by 2.1 percent, but the October 2003 release of the 2002 crime data showed little change over the previous year, with serious crime dropping only 1.1 percent. That overall figure included a 2 percent drop in serious violent crimes and a .9 percent drop in serious property crimes. Murders increased by 1 percent between 2001 and 2002, but the 2002 figure was 34 percent lower than a decade earlier.[3] In 2003, violent crimes decreased by 3 percent, whereas property crimes decreased by only 0.2 percent.[4] Later discussions in this chapter contain more details about the 2003 changes in crime data.

It is important that these (and other) crime data be analyzed carefully. It is possible, for example, that crimes will increase again, especially with the weak economy, the increase in the teenage population, a decrease in courts and law enforcement personnel due to budget cuts, and the rise in the number of inmates returning to communities from prison. It is thus important to analyze crime data in light of changing demographics and other variables.

It must also be understood that the collection of crime data is not as precise as some would have us believe. Not all crimes are reported to the police, although as Figure 2-1 notes (see Section 2-1), crime reporting has improved in recent years. Not all reported crimes are cleared by arrest; fewer still are cleared by conviction. This means that no data source is complete in its measure of criminal activity. Additional problems exist when comparisons are made among jurisdictions.

L E A R N I N G
OBJECTIVES

After reading this chapter, you should be able to do the following:

- **List and evaluate the major sources of crime and victimization data**
- **Recognize the importance of misdemeanors in criminal justice systems**
- **List and explain four reasons that crime data may not be accurate**
- **Discuss reasons for the nonreporting of crime by victims**
- **List and define the eight serious crimes as categorized by the Federal Bureau of Investigation**
- **Analyze and summarize recent crime data, noting changes in the rates of violent and property crimes**
- **Explain the meaning of *hate crime* and analyze the recent U.S. Supreme Court decision relating to this crime**
- **Discuss the demographic characteristics of offenders**
- **Define victimology and describe and criticize the sources of victimization data**
- **List the major variables used to analyze victimization data and explain the meaning of each**
- **Explain the relationship between victims and offenders according to crime data and predict your chances of becoming a crime victim, given your current lifestyle**
- **Consider the effects of the 9/11/01 terrorist attacks on U.S. citizens**
- **Discuss ways in which criminal justice systems have attempted to respond to the needs of victims and evaluate each**

Despite the impossibility of detecting all criminal activity or prosecuting and convicting all guilty parties who are detected, crime data serve an important function. They are needed by official agencies to determine policies and budgets. They are utilized by police officials, who must decide the best use of their officers and their resources.

Crime data may be used by official agencies and by private citizens who are determined to make their communities safer for all who live there. Social scientists who study criminal behavior use crime data, both official and unofficial, in their analyses of why and under what circumstances people commit criminal acts. Crime data might also be used for political reasons in an effort to convince voters of the success or failure of crime prevention efforts.

The point is not to dismiss crime data because of problems of inaccuracy but, rather, to analyze carefully the various sources of data and to determine which are best for a particular purpose. This chapter examines and analyzes the most common methods for collecting crime data: official reports of reported crimes, data secured from victims, and data from self-report studies. Following the description of data sources, the discussion compares those sources and analyzes the problems of collecting data by each method. The chapter contains an overview of the amount and types of crime and offenders as determined by official data as well as by data collected from victimization studies. Finally, the chapter looks at crime victims as well as the relationship between victims and offenders, the fear of crime, and how criminal justice systems treat victims.

2-1   Sources of Crime Data

There are two major sources of official crime data in the United States: the *Uniform Crime Reports (UCR)* and the National Crime Victimization Survey (NCVS). Table 2-1 explains the purposes of these two sources and their differences. The *UCR* reports crime data that come to the attention of police through their own observations or through reports from others. The *UCR* includes two crimes not included by the NCVS—murder and arson.

Reporting to the police of violent crime increased from an annual average of 43%, 1992–99, to 49% in 2000

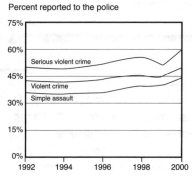

Percent reported to the police

Note: Serious violent crime includes rape, sexual assault, robbery, and aggravated assault and excludes simple assault.

- In 2000, 39% of the 25.4 million violent and property crimes were reported to the police according to the National Crime Victimization Survey. Violent crimes were reported at a higher percent than property crimes.

- Violence against females was more likely to be reported than violence against males. Higher percentages of violence against older persons than younger persons were reported to law enforcement.

- Overall violent crime was more likely to be reported to the police if the victim perceived that the offender was under the influence of drugs/alcohol.

- When violent crime was committed by an armed offender, it was more likely to be reported to the police.

- A higher percentage of violence in which the victim was injured was reported to the police. Ninety Percent of violence in which the victim was shot was reported to the police.

- Overall violent crime committed by strangers was reported to police at a higher percentage than was violent crime committed by nonstrangers.

- Robbery was less likely to have been reported to the police when the victim thought the offender was a gang member (46% for gang members and 59% for nongang members).

- Violent crime was most often reported in an effort to "prevent future violence," "stop the offender," or to "protect others."

- Violent crime was most often not reported to police because it was deemed a "private/personal matter," was considered "not important enough," or because it was "reported to another official."

Figure 2-1
Reporting Crime to the Police, 1992–2000

Source: Timothy C. Hart and Callie Rennison, Bureau of Justice Statistics, *Reporting Crime to the Police, 1992–2000* (Washington, D.C.: U.S. Department of Justice, March 2003), p. 1.

T A B L E **2-1**	Comparison of the *Uniform Crime Reports* and the National Crime Victimization Survey	
	Uniform Crime Reports	**National Crime Victimization Survey**
Offenses measured	Homicide Rape Robbery (personal and commercial) Assault (aggravated) Burglary (commercial and household) Motor vehicle theft Arson	Rape Robbery (personal) Assault (aggravated and simple) Household burglary Larceny (personal and household) Motor vehicle theft
Scope	Crimes reported to the police in most jurisdictions: considerable flexibility in developing small-area data	Crimes both reported and not reported to police: all data are available for a few large geographic areas
Collection method	Police department reports to FBI or to centralized State agencies that then report to FBI	Survey interviews: periodically measures the total number of crimes committed by asking a national sample of 49,000 households emcompassing 101,000 persons age 12 and over about their experiences as victims of crime during a specific period
Kinds of information	In addition to offense counts, provides information on crime clearances, persons arrested, persons charged, law enforcement officers killed and assaulted, and characteristics of homicide victims	Provides details about victims (such as age, race, sex, education, income, and whether the victim and offender were related to each other) and about crimes (such as time and place of occurrence, whether or not reported to police, use of weapons, occurrence of injury, and economic consequences)
Sponsor	Department of Justice Federal Bureau of Investigation	Department of Justice Bureau of Justice Statistics

Source: Bureau of Justice Statistics, *Report to the Nation on Crime and Justice: The Data,* 2d ed. (Washington, D.C.: U.S. Government Printing Office, 1988), p. 1.

Murder is not included in NCVS data because those data are based on interviews with crime victims. Arson is not included because it is too difficult to measure with the techniques used in the NCVS.

Of the two sources, the *UCR* is used more frequently. Despite their differences, the two sources may complement each other, but a comparison should be based on this realization. The *UCR* and the NCVS are based on different time periods, definitions of the included crimes, and methods of counting crime.

Each source has limitations, as noted in the respective discussions. But neither can estimate the extent to which a few offenders are responsible for large numbers of crimes. These reports disclose only how many crimes were reported (not how many of those crimes were traced to the same offenders) and how many arrests were made (not how many times a particular person was arrested). More specialized studies disclose that a large percentage of those who enter prison to serve time were convicted previously of other criminal offenses. Although these repeat offenders are relatively few, many authorities suspect that they account for a large amount of crime.

2-1a   *Uniform Crime Reports (UCR)*

The *Uniform Crime Reports (UCR)* consists of crime data collected by the FBI. The FBI publishes the official report yearly, usually in the fall. Originally, seven crimes were selected, because of their seriousness and frequency, to constitute the *UCR* Crime Index. Known as Part I, or **index offenses,** they included murder and nonnegligent manslaughter, forcible rape, robbery, aggravated assault, burglary, larceny-theft, and motor vehicle theft. Congress added arson to the crime index in 1979.

In June 2004, the FBI ceased using the concept of *index offenses* for reporting data because of its concern that this category was misleading. For example, overall most serious crimes are property crimes, with larceny-theft constituting almost 60 percent of serious crimes. Thus, if one jurisdiction had a large increase in larceny-theft, that could raise its overall crime index offense data significantly even though it had an insignificant increase in serious violent crimes. But we have all become accustomed to seeing these data, so the crime index offense data for 2002, the last use of the measure, are included in Figure 2-2.

Each month law enforcement agencies report the number of **crimes known to the police**—that is, the number of Part I offenses verified by police investigation of the complaint. A crime known to the police is counted even if no suspect is arrested and no prosecution occurs. If a criminal activity involves several different crimes, only the most serious one is reported as a Part I, or serious, offense. If a victim is raped, robbed, and murdered, only the murder is counted in the *UCR*. Offenses known to police do not show how many persons were involved in a particular reported crime. The data are used to calculate a **crime rate.** The national crime rate is calculated by dividing the number of Part I reported crimes by the number of people in the country (data obtained from census reports). The result is expressed as a rate of crimes per 100,000 people.

In addition, the *UCR* reports the number of Part I offenses that are cleared. Offenses are cleared in two ways: (1) when a suspect is arrested, charged, and turned over to the judicial system for prosecution and (2) by circumstances beyond the control of the police. For example, a suspect's death or a victim's refusal to press charges may signal the end of police involvement in a reported crime. Crimes are considered cleared whether or not the suspect is convicted.

Several persons may be arrested and one crime cleared, or one person may be arrested and many crimes cleared. The clearance rate is the number of crimes solved, expressed as a percentage of the total number of crimes reported to the police. The clearance rate is critical in policy decisions because it is one measure used to evaluate police departments. The higher the number of crimes solved by arrest, the better the police force looks in the eyes of the public.

Violent crimes are more likely than property crimes to be cleared by arrest. This is because victims (or families, in the case of murder) are more likely to report violent than property crimes and to act more quickly. Victims of personal violence, as compared with victims of property crimes, are more likely to be able to give police pertinent information

---

► Uniform Crime Reports (UCR)
Official crime data, collected and published by the Federal Bureau of Investigation (FBI) and based on "crimes known to the police"—crimes that are reported to or observed by the police and that the police have reason to believe were committed.

► Index offenses   The FBI's *Uniform Crime Reports* of the occurrences of the eight crimes considered most serious: murder and nonnegligent manslaughter, forcible rape, robbery, aggravated assault, burglary, larceny-theft, motor vehicle theft, and arson. In June 2004, the FBI discontinued publishing data according to index offenses because of the misrepresentation of crime in an area that can be caused by a very high (or low) volume or rate of crime of only one of these serious crimes in that area.

► Crimes known to the police
All serious criminal offenses that have been reported to the police for which the police have sufficient evidence to believe the crimes were committed.

► Crime rate   The number of crimes per 100,000 population.

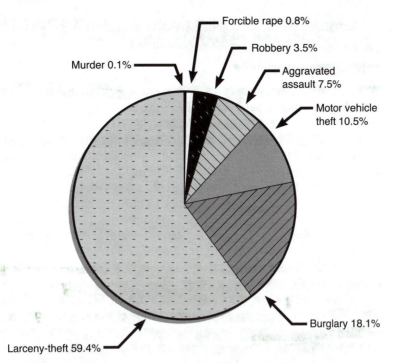

Murder 0.1%

Forcible rape 0.8%

Robbery 3.5%

Aggravated assault 7.5%

Motor vehicle theft 10.5%

Burglary 18.1%

Larceny-theft 59.4%

Figure 2-2
Percent Distribution for Crime Index Offenses for 2002
Source: Federal Bureau of Investigation, *Crime in the United States: Uniform Crime Reports 2002* (Washington, D.C.: U.S. Government Printing office, 2003), p. 11.

that might lead to an arrest. Murder is the crime most likely to be cleared by arrest; burglary is least likely, but motor vehicle theft and larceny-theft have low clearance rates, too.

Arrest information in the *UCR* is presented in two forms: (1) the total estimated numbers of arrests by crime for each of the recorded offenses and (2) the number of arrests made during one year for each of the serious offenses per 100,000 population. The *UCR* does not report the number of persons arrested each year because some individuals are arrested more than once during the year. The actual number of arrested persons, therefore, is likely to be smaller than the total number of arrests.

In addition to data on crimes reported and arrest information for Part I offenses, the *UCR* publishes the number of arrests for less serious, Part II offenses. Examples of these offenses are other assaults (simple), forgery and counterfeiting, fraud, embezzlement, stolen property, vandalism, prostitution and commercialized vice, other sex offenses, drug abuse violations, driving under the influence (DUI), drunkenness, and disorderly conduct. Although some of the offenses included in Part II are felonies, others are misdemeanors, and they receive little attention in criminal justice texts, but they are important in criminal justice systems.

Recall that Chapter 1 noted that misdemeanors are the less serious criminal offenses, whereas felonies are more serious. Perhaps this is why so little attention is paid to misdemeanors in most textbooks. But, in terms of their impact on criminal justice systems and victims, misdemeanors can be extremely important. They occur more frequently than felonies, and attempts to apprehend offenders who commit misdemeanors often lead to a violation of suspects' constitutional rights.

Chapter 1 also pointed out that some offenses may be misdemeanors the first time they are committed but classified as felonies for subsequent offenses. Chapter 1's discussion of whether the criminal law should be used to cover consenting sexual behavior between adults in private, child pornography, substance abuse, the use of marijuana for medicinal purposes, or even fetal abuse points to one of the reasons that misdemeanors are important. Attempts to enforce statutes covering the possession of small amounts of marijuana for one's own use or such offenses as some consensual, private sexual acts, may lead to the infringement of constitutional rights, such as the right to privacy. Attempts to enforce statutes regulating vagrancy and loitering may lead to violations of a person's right to be governed by statutes that are clear, concise, and not too broad. Arrests in violation of constitutional rights offend our sense of fairness and justice and force our citizens to expend money and energy fighting criminal justice systems.

The lack of focus on misdemeanors is one problem with the *UCR*, but the FBI's reporting system has other limitations as well.

Limitations of the *UCR*

The most serious limitation of the *UCR* is that it does not include all crimes that are committed. Some scholars have argued that *UCR* data are significantly lower than the actual incidence of crime. The *UCR* does not record all criminal activity for several reasons.

First, not all crimes are reported; in fact, most crimes are not reported to police. There are many reasons for not reporting a crime. Some victims think police will not do anything; others are embarrassed or believe they will be blamed for the crime. For example, rape victims may think that they will be suspected of encouraging the crime, particularly if the rape was committed by an acquaintance. Rape victims may not want to go through a trial in which they must face the alleged rapist and submit to questions by the defendant's attorney. They may be too embarrassed to relate the details of the crime to police or to their own families.

A second factor affecting crime data is the delay in reporting crimes. Delay may be caused by an inability to decide whether to report the crime. There are three reasons for this indecisiveness. Some citizens want to verify that a crime has been committed. Others take some actions to cope with the crime before calling the police. Still others experience conflict about calling the police, so they try to avoid making a quick decision. Once the decision to call the police has been made, there may be further delays. A phone may not be available. The caller may not know the police number. The caller may have difficulty communicating with the police department dispatcher.[5]

Another factor affecting the *UCR* is police decisions. Crimes are included in the *UCR* only if the police decide there is sufficient evidence to believe that a crime has been committed. Police have wide discretion in making that decision, and factors such as the seriousness of the crime, the relationship between the complainant and the alleged offender, the desire for informal disposition of the case, and deference shown the police may influence police decisions regarding arrest.

Police individually, or as a department, may want to downplay the amount of crime in their areas; consequently, they do not record all reported crimes even when there is sufficient evidence that a crime has been committed. In a 1974 analysis of police reporting of thefts, investigators concluded that official crime data were misleading. Because they are used as official data by people who are under pressure to have certain results, the data can be, and are, manipulated to show higher or lower crime rates.[6]

In June 2003, the New York City police commissioner, Raymond W. Kelly, acknowledged that he had ordered a major investigation into allegations that in one precinct 203 out of 811 felonies were improperly reduced to misdemeanors, giving that jurisdiction a crime rate *decrease* of 7.42 percent over the previous year, compared with what would have been a 15.7 percent *increase* had the crimes been recorded as felonies. A second precinct was also being investigated for the same improper actions. A spokesperson for the Patrolman's Benevolent Association (PBA) stated that the PBA believed that downgrading crimes happens "to a far greater extent than just one precinct" but that police officers are afraid to report this. The spokesperson referred to cases in which punitive action was taken against officers who refused to downgrade a reported crime and concluded, "We believe this is systemic, retaliations are swift, and because of that most cops will not come forward." In contrast, a professor of police studies at the John Jay College of Criminal Justice suggested that "cooking the books" is not common in New York City police stations because swift punishments result when an officer is caught in such violations. The announcement of the 2003 investigation came shortly after the police commissioner and the mayor had held a news conference to cite declining rates of serious crimes in the city for the previous 11 years and to declare New York City "the safest big U.S. city."[7]

UCR crime data are also affected by the fact that some crimes are not included within the list of crimes for which data are collected. As noted already, some misdemeanors are not included. Furthermore, some very serious crimes, such as those categorized as **white-collar**

▶ **White-collar crime**
The illegal actions of corporations or individuals, committed while pursuing their legitimate occupations. Examples are consumer fraud, bribery, and embezzlement.

crimes, are handled informally, or they are handled by administrative agencies rather than by criminal courts and thus are not counted as crimes.

Other kinds of crimes that might be considered serious but that are not recorded as either Part I or Part II offenses are computer crimes, organized crime, and corporate crimes, yet the economic impact of these crimes, along with white-collar crimes, is extensive, resulting in far greater total financial damage to the society than the theft crimes included in the *UCR*.

NIBRS: The New Approach

The FBI recognizes that more data are needed. In 1988, the FBI published details of its new approach: **National Incident-Based Reporting System (NIBRS).** NIBRS views crime, along with all its components, as an incident and recognizes that the data constituting those components should be collected and organized for purposes of analysis. The FBI refers to *elements* of crimes, among which are the following:

1. Alcohol and other drug influence
2. Specified location of the crime
3. Type of criminal activity involved
4. Type of weapon used
5. Type of victim
6. Relationship of victim to offender
7. Residency of victim and arrestee
8. Description of property and their values[8]

The NIBRS collects data on additional crime categories beyond the 8 included as Part I offenses and the 21 included as Part II offenses in the *UCR*. Among other differences, the NIBRS reports data on the number of rapes reported with male victims, whereas the *UCR* reports only female victims. The NIBRS is expected to improve the knowledge of crime, but it will take 10 to 15 years to implement the system completely.

2-1b   National Crime Victimization Survey (NCVS)

The existence of unreported crime, often called the *dark figure of crime*, which never becomes part of official crime data, has led to the establishment of another method of measuring crime. It was thought that, if victims do not report crimes to the police, perhaps they will do so on questionnaires submitted to samples of the general population.

Victimization surveys conducted by the Bureau of Justice Statistics (BJS) are called the **National Crime Victimization Survey (NCVS).** The NCVS is based on the results of interviews conducted each six months with persons in about 60,000 households. Household members are questioned about whether they have been the victims of rape, robbery, assault, household burglary, personal and household larceny, and motor vehicle theft. In addition, the NCVS conducts research on large samples in 20 of the largest cities in the country, along with 8 impact cities. These surveys include questions on business as well as personal victimizations.

The NCVS is a valuable supplement to the *UCR*. In addition to disclosing some crimes that are not reported to police, the surveys relate the reasons people give for not reporting crimes. However, the data are dependent on victim recall and perception, which may not be accurate. Despite this problem, victimization studies add to our knowledge of criminal activity. Following an evaluation of the NCVS by the National Academy of Sciences, efforts have been made to redesign it. This project began in 1979.

In 1997, the Bureau of Justice Statistics (BJS) reported that, as a result of the changes in the design for collecting victimization data, the survey resulted in higher estimates of crime victimizations. Specifically, the rates for the following crimes were higher: "personal crimes (44% higher), crimes of violence (49%), rapes (157%), assaults (57%), property crimes (23%), burglaries (20%), and thefts (27%). A statistically significant difference could not be found for robbery, personal theft, and motor vehicle theft."[9]

▶ **National Incident-Based Reporting System (NIBRS)** A reporting system used by the FBI in collecting crime data. In this system, a crime is viewed along with all of its components, including the type of victim, type of weapon, location of the crime, alcohol/drug influence, type of criminal activity, relationship of victim to offender, and residence of victims and arrestees, as well as a description of the property and its value. This system includes 22 crimes, rather than the 8 that constitute the FBI's Part I Offenses of serious crimes.

▶ **National Crime Victimization Survey (NCVS)** Crime data collected by the Bureau of Justice Statistics (BJS) and based on surveys of people to determine who has been victimized by crime.

There are concerns, however, about the traditional independence of the BJS and its reports. There were allegations that persons within the BJS and the National Institute of Justice (NIJ), the statistical and the research agencies, respectively, of the U.S. Department of Justice (DOJ) were pressured by subordinates of Attorney General John Ashcroft with regard to the data they gather, analyze, and report. It was not known what position, if any, the new attorney general, Alberto Gonzales, would take on this issue, but historically, the BJS and the NIJ, created by Congress, have been independent of the DOJ officials, releasing reports and awarding grants without interference from the DOJ. Persons (including employees, former employees, and scholars) making these allegations regarding political pressures placed by DOJ officials on BJS and NIJ employees state that the new involvement by the DOJ (which must clear releases and grant awards, thus delaying some by months) state that the change came as a result of the October 2002 passage of the **USA Patriot Act.** That legislation, which is discussed later in the text, encompasses sweeping antiterrorism measures, some of which erode the traditional independence of the BJS and the NIJ.[10]

2-1c Self-Report Data (SRD)

In addition to the *UCR* data and surveys of the population that report how many people have been victimized, self-report studies are used to gather data on the extent and nature of criminal activity. **Self-report data (SRD)** are acquired by two methods: (1) the interview, in which a person is asked questions about illegal activities, and (2) the questionnaire, usually anonymous. Until recently, self-report studies were conducted mainly with juveniles, but increasingly the method is being used to study adult career criminals.

SRD have been criticized on several grounds. The first problem is that of accuracy. Some respondents, especially juveniles, overreport their involvement in illegal activities, whereas others do not report some or all of their criminal activities. Other criticisms of SRD are that the surveys include too many trivial offenses and sometimes omit serious crimes, such as burglary, robbery, and sexual assault. Furthermore, self-report studies include too few minorities.

Taken together, these criticisms raise serious questions. White respondents tend to report greater involvement in less serious crimes that occur more frequently, and African Americans tend to report illegal acts that are less frequent but more serious. One study found that African American male offenders fail to report known offenses three times more often than white male offenders.[11]

Differences by gender have been reported, but such findings do not invalidate the use of self-reports. However, they do suggest that it may be necessary to compare these results with other measures and to develop more sophisticated methods for data analysis.

2-2 Crime and Offenders: An Overview

Before looking at crime data, it must be understood that all methods of counting and compiling crimes have problems. How crime is defined and how crimes are counted affect the results of all the methods. Crime is recorded and counted according to the policy used to determine whether one or more crimes occurred during the interaction between the offender and his or her victim. Frequently, the issue arises in sex crimes. For example, in one rape case a defendant was convicted of three counts of forcible genital penetration. The defendant argued that he should have been convicted of only one count because each act lasted only a few seconds and all three occurred during a brief period, 7 to 10 minutes. The court disagreed, stating that the statute's prohibition of "penetration, however slight, of the genital or anal openings of another person by any foreign object, substance, instrument, or device" against the victim's will means that *each penetration* is a separate act. A "violation is *complete* the moment such 'penetration' occurs." The court emphasized that the purpose of the statute is to punish those who commit the "outrage to the person and [violate] feelings of the victim" and that this outrage occurs "each time the victim endures a new, unconsented sexual insertion."[12] Another issue is that a sex crime that meets the definition of **rape** might be charged in one jurisdiction by another name, such as sexual battery, or

USA Patriot Act The United and Strengthening America by Providing Appropriate Tools Required to Intercept and Obstruct Terrorism Act of 2001, enacted in fall 2001 in response to the 9/11/01 terrorist attacks. The act expands the powers of the federal government to deal with terrorism. Some of those powers involve the expansion of wiretaps on terrorist suspects' email, telephone conversations, and use of the Internet.

Self-report data (SRD) The process of collecting crime data by asking people about their criminal activity, usually by use of anonymous questionnaires.

Rape Historically, unlawful vaginal intercourse with a woman; it is called *forcible rape* if engaged in against the will of the woman by the use of threats or force; it is called *statutory rape* if the sexual intercourse was consensual between a man and a woman who was under the age of consent. More recently some rape statutes have been rewritten to include male victims, as well as penetration of any body opening by any instrument, including but not limited to the male sexual organ.

might be reduced to a lesser charge, such as lewd behavior. With these caveats, we will look at some crime data.

In the foreword to the 1982 *UCR,* the director of the FBI announced with cautious optimism that the rate of serious crime was down 3 percent from 1981. The cautiousness of his optimism stemmed from the fact that, in the 1970s, crime rates dropped twice, only to turn back upward shortly thereafter. In the 1984 *UCR,* the director announced that crime had declined for the third straight year, with fewer serious offenses reported to law enforcement that year than in any year since 1978. He cautioned that the unprecedented three-year period of decline might be coming to an end because there had been a slight increase in crime during the last quarter of 1984.[13]

The number of crimes reported to the police, along with the crime rate, began climbing in 1984, leading the director of the FBI to say, "There are few social statements more tragic than these."[14] The increase in the number of crime offenses continued through 1991 but began dropping between 1991 and 1992. The numbers continued to decline and by 1999 had fallen for the eighth consecutive year, but they leveled off in 2000, 2001, and 2002, with only small changes in 2003, as already noted.

Experts do not agree on the explanations for the changes in the volume and rates of crime in recent years. For example, the attempts to explain the changes in the crime rates in New York City are illustrated by a *New York Times* article in November 2002 headlined "Reasons for Crime Drop in New York Elude Many." The article quoted criminologist Jeffrey A. Fagan, professor of law and public health at Columbia University, as saying, "It is the mystery of the ages." Two of the most reliable crime figures are those of murder and motor vehicle thefts, and murder rates in New York City decreased by 12.7 percent between 2001 and 2002, with motor vehicle thefts decreasing by 5.3 percent. New York City Police Commissioner Raymond W. Kelly cited the city's efforts to increase law enforcement personnel over the previous decade, focusing on serious as well as quality-of-life criminal violations.[15] Others were not so sure and referred to the manipulation of data in some parts of the city.

The FBI's division of serious crimes into two categories—*violent crimes* (murder and nonnegligent manslaughter, forcible rape, robbery, and aggravated assault) and *property crimes* (burglary, larceny-theft, motor vehicle theft, and arson)—is used for further analysis of crime data. We begin with serious violent crimes.

2-2a   Violent Crimes

Most of the reported serious crimes in the United States are property crimes, not violent crimes against persons, as noted in Figure 2-2, which graphs the specific serious crime offenses (with the exception of arson) in terms of their percentage of the total crimes reported in 2002, as noted, the last year the FBI published data by the index offenses. (See again Figure 2-2.)

Violent crimes in the *UCR* include murder and nonnegligent manslaughter, forcible rape, robbery, and aggravated assault. The number of violent crimes in the United States, estimated at 1,423,677 in 2002, decreased by 3 percent between 2002 and 2003, to 1,381,259. Figure 2-3 graphs the changes in the volume and rate of violent crime in the United States between 1999 and 2003, with the rate dropping 9.2 percent during that period. The FBI's preliminary figures for 2004, released in June 2005, showed a 1.7 percent decrease in violent crimes.[16]

The crime of **murder** (which, in the FBI compilation includes nonnegligent **manslaughter**) is defined as the "willful (nonnegligent) killing of one human being by another." In 2003, an estimated 16,503 murders occurred, representing a 1.7 percent increase over 2002 and a 6.3 percent rise over 1999. The murder rate for 2003 was approximately the same as that for 2002, representing 5.7 murders per 100,000 of the population (compared with 5.6 in 2002). Murder and nonnegligent manslaughter account for less than 1 percent of all serious crimes.[17]

The second serious violent crime is **forcible rape,** defined by the *UCR* as "the carnal knowledge of a female forcibly and against her will. Assaults or attempts to commit rape by force or threat of force are included; however, statutory rape (without force) and other sex

Violent crimes   Crimes defined by the FBI's *Uniform Crime Reports* as serious crimes against a person. They include murder and nonnegligent manslaughter, robbery, forcible rape, and aggravated assault.

Murder   The unlawful killing of another person with either express or implied malice aforethought.

Manslaughter   The unlawful killing of a human being by a person who lacks malice. Manslaughter may be *involuntary* (or negligent), the result of recklessness while committing an unlawful act (such as driving while intoxicated), or *voluntary,* an intentional killing committed in the heat of passion.

Forcible rape   *See* **rape.**

Figure 2-3
Trends in U.S. Violent Crime, 1999–2003
Source: Federal Bureau of Investigation, *Crime in the United States, Uniform Crime Reports 2003* (Washington, D.C.: U.S. Government Printing Office, 2004), p. 11.

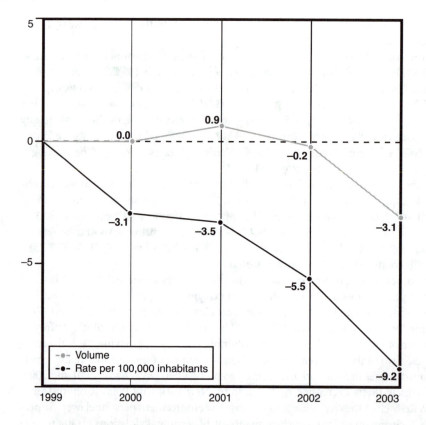

▶ **Robbery** The use of force or fear to take personal property belonging to another against that person's will.

▶ **Aggravated assault** Technically an assault is a threat to commit a battery, but often the term is used to refer to a battery. Aggravated assault involves a battery inflicted by use of a deadly weapon.

offenses are not included in this category." Data for 2003 disclose that forcible rapes decreased (after three years of increasing), showing a 1.9 percent decrease over 2002. The forcible rape volume for 2003 was 4.5 percent higher than the volume for 1999, but it was 8.6 percent lower than the 1994 figures. As noted in Figure 2-2, rape represented only .8 percent of serious violent crimes in 2002.[18]

The third violent crime, **robbery,** is often used to refer to an act that constitutes theft rather than robbery. Since property is taken in both crimes, what is the difference? Robbery involves the same elements as larceny-theft but adds two elements that make it a violent crime: (1) taking the property from the person or in the presence of the person *and* (2) using force or threatening to use force. The FBI defines robbery as "the taking or attempting to take anything of value from the care, custody, or control of a person or persons by force or threat of force or violence and/or by putting the victim in fear."

An estimated 413,402 robberies occurred in 2003, representing a 1.8 percent decrease from 2002, a 1 percent increase from 1999, and a 33.2 percent decrease from 1994. As Figure 2-2 indicates, robbery constituted 3.5 percent of all serious crimes in 2002; it constituted 29.9 percent of all violent crimes in 2003.[19]

In some cases, the line between larceny-theft and robbery is a fine one, and not all scholars agree on how or where to draw that line. Thus, a crime such as purse snatching, which occurs so quickly that the victim does not have time to offer resistance or to be scared, may be classified as larceny-theft rather than robbery. But the fear that the victim suffers *after* the incident may be greater than the concern a victim has after a burglary or larceny-theft. It is this fear of violence, as well as the possibility of violence, that places robbery in the violent personal crime category.

The fourth violent crime, **aggravated assault,** is defined by the FBI as "an unlawful attack by one person upon another for the purpose of inflicting severe or aggravated bodily injury. . . . Attempts involving the display or threat of a gun, knife, or other weapon are included because serious personal injury would likely result if the assault were completed." Although some aggravated assaults are conducted without a weapon, many involve the use of a deadly weapon. In 2003, an estimated 857,921 aggravated assaults occurred, representing the tenth consecutive year of declines in the volume of this crime. Aggravated assaults declined 3.8 percent over 2002 and 5.9 percent over 1999. In 2003, aggravated assaults represented 62.1 percent of all serious violent crimes.[20] As Figure 2-2 shows, aggravated assaults constituted 7.5 percent of all serious crimes in 2002.

2-2b   Property Crimes

Most of the serious crimes committed in the United States are not violent personal crimes; they are crimes against property. These crimes involve taking money or property that belongs to others, but they do not involve force against the victims. Four **property crimes** are included within the FBI's Part I, or serious crimes: burglary, larceny-theft, motor vehicle theft, and arson. The FBI reported 10,445,523 property crimes in 2003, representing a 0.2 percent decrease over 2002. But the 2003 volume of property crimes was 2.2 percent higher than that of 1999 and 14 percent lower than property crimes in 1994.[21] Figure 2-4 graphs the changes in the volume and rate of property crime in the United States between 1999 and 2003.

The crime of **burglary** is defined by the FBI as "the unlawful entry of a structure to commit a felony or theft. The use of force to gain entry is not required to classify an offense as burglary." Burglary in the *UCR* is "categorized into three subclassifications: forcible entry, unlawful entry where no force is used, and attempted forcible entry." For 2003, the FBI reported an estimated 2,153,464 burglaries, representing a 0.1 percent increase over 2002. The number of burglaries decreased 2.5 percent between 1999 and 2003 and 20.6 percent between 1994 and 2003. Burglary accounted for 20.6 percent of all property crimes in 2003. In June 2005, the FBI announced that property crimes for the year 2004 declined overall by 1.8 percent.[22]

The most frequently committed property offense is **larceny-theft,** which is defined as the "unlawful taking, carrying, leading, or riding away of property from the possession or constructive possession of another. It includes crimes such as shoplifting, pocket-picking, purse snatching, thefts from motor vehicles, thefts of motor vehicle parts and accessories, bicycle thefts, etc., in which no use of force, violence, or fraud occurs." In the *UCR*, larceny-theft "does not include embezzlement, con games, forgery, and worthless checks. Motor

▶ **Property crimes**   Crimes aimed at the property of another person rather than at the person. Serious property crimes include larceny-theft, burglary, motor vehicle theft, and arson.

▶ **Burglary**   The illegal or forcible entering of any enclosed structure in order to commit a crime, usually theft. Some jurisdictions require that the intent be to commit a felony rather than a less serious crime.

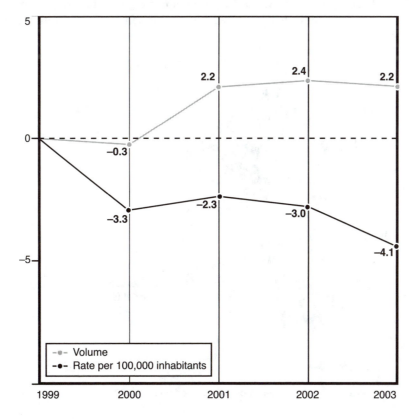

Figure 2-4
Trends in U.S. Property Crimes, 1999–2003
Source: Federal Bureau of Investigation, *Crime in the United States, Uniform Crime Reports 2003* (Washington, D.C.: U.S. Government Printing Office, 2004), p. 41.

Larceny-theft   (page 37) The unlawful removal of someone else's property with the intention of keeping it permanently. Historically small thefts were categorized as *petit larceny* and large thefts as *grand larceny*. The latter was punished by the death penalty, a punishment no longer permitted for larceny in the United States. Some modern theft laws do not distinguish between the two types of larceny.

Motor vehicle theft   The stealing of an automobile, in contrast to the stealing of an automobile part or larceny-theft from an automobile.

Arson   The willful and malicious burning of the structure of another with or without the intent to defraud. Burning of one's own property with the intent to defraud is included in some definitions. Many modern statutes carry a more severe penalty for the burning of a dwelling than of other real property.

vehicle theft is also excluded from this category inasmuch as it is a separate . . . [Part I, or serious] offense." The number of reported larceny-thefts in the United States in 2003 was 7,021,588, representing a decrease of 0.5 percent over 2002, with an estimated $4.9 billion cost to victims. As Figure 2-2 shows, larceny-theft accounted for 59.4 percent of all serious, Part I offenses in 2002; it represented 67.3 percent of all property crimes in 2003.[23]

Motor vehicle theft, defined as "the theft or attempted theft of a motor vehicle," does not include thefts of items from within a motor vehicle; those are counted as larceny-theft. In 2003 there were approximately 1,260,471 motor vehicle thefts in the United States, representing a 1.1 percent increase from 2002, a 9.4 percent increase from 1999, and an 18.1 percent decrease from 1994.[24] As Figure 2-2 notes, motor vehicle thefts constituted 10.5 percent of all serious crimes in 2002.

The final serious property crime is **arson,** defined by the FBI as "any willful or malicious burning or attempt to burn, with or without intent to defraud, a dwelling house, public building, motor vehicle or aircraft, personal property of another, etc. Only fires determined through investigation to have been willfully or maliciously set are classified as arsons. Fires of suspicious or unknown origins are excluded." Arson did not become a Part I offense until 1979; thus, trend data are available for this crime as for other Part I offenses. Data are not available for all reporting agencies, and the FBI warns that, as a result, caution must be used in interpreting arson data. During 2003, an estimated 71,319 arsons occurred.[25]

This completes the overview of the four violent and four property crimes that constitute Part I offenses in the *UCR*. But beginning with the report on the 1996 data, the FBI has included a section on hate crimes, which is discussed briefly here.

2-2c   Hate Crimes

The *Uniform Crime Reports'* definition of **hate crime** is as follows: "A hate crime, also known as a bias crime, is a criminal offense committed against a person, property, or society which is motivated, in whole or in part, by the offender's bias against a race, religion, disability, sexual orientation, or ethnicity/national origin." Hate crimes may be aimed at property or at persons, but most of them are aimed at persons. The percent distribution of types of hate crimes in 2003 is graphed in Figure 2-5.[26]

In 2003, in *Virginia* v. *Black,* the U.S. Supreme Court considered a Virginia statute that stated as follows: "It shall be unlawful for any person or persons, with the intent of intim-

Figure 2-5

Hate Crimes: Percent Distribution 2003

Source: Federal Bureau of Investigation, *Crime in the United States, Uniform Crime Reports 2003* (Washington, D.C.: U.S. Government Printing Office, 2004), p. 65.

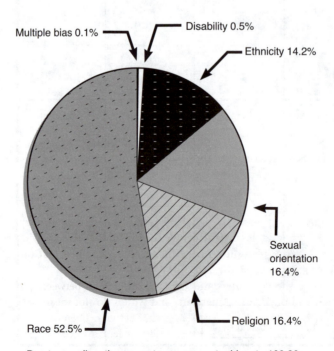

Due to rounding, the percentages may not add up to 100.00.

idating any person or group of persons, to burn, or cause to be burned, a cross on the property of another, a highway, or other public place." The second part of the statute provided that "Any such burning of a cross shall be prima facie evidence of an intent to intimidate a person or group of persons." Three separate cases were joined for purposes of the appeal. Barry Black led a Ku Klux Klan rally, in which 25 to 30 people gathered on private property, talked about their beliefs, including negative comments about African Americans and Mexicans, and finally, burned a cross. Black was tried before a jury that was instructed that they must prove that the defendant intended to intimidate, which means to put in fear, but that the intent could not be inferred by the fact of cross burning.[27]

In a separate incident, Richard Elliott and Jonathan O'Mara, along with another individual, attempted to burn a cross on the yard of an African American, James Jubilee. Jubilee, who lived next door to Elliott, had inquired of Elliott's mother about shots that were fired from behind the Elliott home. Elliott's mother responded that her son shot firearms as a hobby and that he did so in his back yard. In an apparent attempt to "get back" at Jubilee for his complaint about the firearms, Elliott and O'Mara drove a truck onto Jubilee's property, planted a cross, and attempted to burn it. Jubilee saw the partially burned cross the next morning. He said he was "very nervous" because "a cross burned in your yard . . . tells you that it's just the first round."

In considering these three cases, the justices of the U.S. Supreme Court were not in agreement on several of the issues, some of which are procedural and beyond the scope of this text. Relevant here is that a majority of the Court held that it is not unconstitutional to ban cross burning with the intent to intimidate, but for a conviction to be upheld under this statute, prosecutors must prove beyond a reasonable doubt that the cross burning was for the purposes of intimidation rather than as an expression of symbolic speech, which would violate the First Amendment (see Appendix A). The Court reversed Black's conviction because the jury was instructed that the required intent could be inferred from the fact of cross burning. That instruction was not at issue in O'Mara's case, because he entered a guilty plea to both charges against him, attempted cross burning and conspiracy to commit cross burning. In the trial of Elliott on both of those charges, the jury instruction concerning inferring intent was not given. The cases of Elliott and O'Mara were vacated and remanded for further proceedings.

Justice Clarence Thomas wrote a scathing dissent, in which he characterized cross burning as a unique symbol of racial hatred and discrimination.

2-2d   Characteristics of Offenders

The FBI data on criminal offenders comes from arrests. In 2003, law enforcement officials throughout the United States reported that they had made an estimated 13.6 million arrests (excluding traffic infractions). Violent crimes accounted for 4.4 percent of these arrests, while the largest number of arrests for any offense were for drug abuse violations, accounting for 1.7 million arrests. The total arrests in 2003 represented a decrease of 2.8 percent over arrests in 1994.[28]

A thorough study of crime includes not only an analysis of the number and type of crimes but also information on the characteristics of those who commit crimes. In this section, after a general overview of sources, data on offenders are discussed by age, race, and gender.

Before the collection of self-report data, most studies of criminals were based on the *UCR* data, which revealed that a higher percentage of the arrestees were young African Americans from the lower socio-economic class. Many people concluded that persons with these characteristics were more likely to commit crimes, whereas others argued that the data represented discrimination against these individuals.

When looking at the data, we should understand that the differences between the crime rates of men and women and of African Americans and whites do not mean that gender or race *causes* the criminal activity or the reaction to that activity. There is some evidence that it is not age, race, or gender that influences official reaction to the alleged offender but, rather, the seriousness of the offense committed and the degree of the

> **Hate crime** (page 38) As defined in the federal criminal code, a crime "that manifests evidence of prejudice based on race, religion, disability, sexual orientation, or ethnicity, including where appropriate the crimes of murder, non-negligent manslaughter, forcible rape, aggravated assault, simple assault, intimidation, arson, and destruction, damage or vandalism of property."

offender's involvement in that offense. There is evidence, too, that the differences in crime rates between the SRD and *UCR* data may be explained by the fact that only a small number of African Americans were sampled in the self-report studies. Furthermore, some studies show that African Americans and whites differ in their tendencies to report certain crimes, but it may be argued that the differences in crime rates by race are too great to be explained in any way other than discrimination.[29]

Age

Age is a factor most often associated with crimes, most of which are committed by young people. Adults (those over the age of 18) constituted 83.7 percent of the total arrestees in 2003. Almost one-third of arrestees were under 21, whereas 46.3 percent were under the age of 25. The crime for which juveniles were most often arrested was larceny-theft; adults were most frequently arrested for driving under the influence.[30]

Race

Another factor often associated with crime is race, although there is no general agreement on the impact of race on crime. In 2003, most arrestees were white (70.6 percent, compared with 27 percent for African Americans), with whites accounting for 60.5 percent of arrests for violent crimes and 68.2 percent of property crimes, whereas African Americans were arrested for 37.2 percent of violent crimes and 29.1 percent of property crimes. Whites were most often arrested for driving under the influence, African Americans for drug abuse violations.[31]

While analyzing these data, we must realize that, even in cases in which the arrest rates are higher for whites than for African Americans, they may still be disproportionate, as African Americans constitute only approximately 11 percent of the total population. Second, we must consider not only arrest data but also the fact that official and unofficial crime data show differences between African Americans and whites at all levels of criminal justice system activity.

Gender

A third demographic factor associated with crime is gender. Historically, crime rates for men have been significantly higher than those for women, with the exception of those crimes that, by definition, are committed predominantly by women, such as prostitution. Males constituted 76.8 percent of the 2003 arrestees, 82.2 percent of all violent crimes, and 69.2 percent of all property crimes. The number of female arrests, although small overall, increased by 1.9 percent over those of 2002, whereas arrests of males decreased by 0.4 percent during that period. The crime for which women were most frequently arrested was larceny-theft; for men it was drug abuse violations, followed by driving under the influence.[32]

2-3   Crime Victims

Historically the study of victims was not an important focus among social scientists. This has changed in the past decade, with more attention being given to studying the characteristics and problems of victims as well as to improving the responses of criminal justice systems to victims' needs. Professional societies such as the National Organization for Victim Assistance (NOVA) have been instrumental in passing federal and state legislation concerning victims. NOVA has provided assistance to thousands of victims and works directly with local organizations to improve services at that level. Workshops on **victimology** have increased our knowledge and understanding of the problems. Job opportunities have been developed in victimology, as illustrated by Professions 2-1.

▶ **Victimology**   The discipline that studies the nature and causes of victimization, as well as programs for aiding victims and preventing victimization.

Concern with victims' needs has led to national legislation on their behalf. In response to the Victim and Witness Protection Act of 1982,[33] a federal statute, the U.S. Attorney General's office issued detailed guidelines concerning the treatment of crime victims and witnesses by prosecutors and investigators in the Department of Justice. These guidelines are designed to protect the privacy of victims and witnesses and to provide medical, social,

Professions 2-1

Careers in Victimology

In recent years, Congress and most states have enacted legislation to provide assistance to crime victims, creating numerous job opportunities in victimology. Provisions for financial assistance require qualified persons to administer the programs. Counseling of crime victims necessitates providing specialized training, especially in the treatment of victims of rape and other sex crimes. Many jurisdictions have established rape crisis centers, whereas others have concentrated on training police and prosecutors to understand the trauma suffered by sex crime victims. Schoolteachers must be informed regarding what to expect, especially from children who have become crime victims.

Background checks for employees in many jobs are important in order to avoid the negligent hiring of persons who might victimize those with whom they come into contact during work. All individuals who work with victims must be sensitized to the privacy requirements regarding the victims' crime records. Preparing victim impact statements for courts is a new area of crucial paperwork required of probation officers and others. Requirements that victims be notified of pending court and other important hearings create jobs for persons charged with these responsibilities.

Although we have a long way to go before victims receive sufficient assistance in our criminal justice systems, we have made progress at the national, state, and local levels, and interesting and challenging job opportunities exist for those who wish to work with crime victims.

and counseling services. Notification of court proceedings, restitution, and other programs available for the assistance of victims and witnesses are also provided. Some states have gone beyond the federal provisions and have enacted additional legislation to aid victims, and in the 1994 crime bill Congress included some provisions to enhance victims' rights, with a major focus on domestic violence victims.[34]

Special legislation was also provided to compensate the victims of the 11 September 2001 terrorist attacks. Within 11 days of the attacks Congress enacted the Air Transportation Safety and System Stabilization Act of 2001, to provide financial compensation for victims who agreed not to sue the airlines or others for negligence. During the first year of operation, the fund administrators settled 202 claims, ranging from $1.4 million to $6 million. Some victims chose to forego damages from this fund and sue; those lawsuits could take years. In June 2004, the Victim Compensation Fund was ended, with 97 percent of the 2,973 eligible families taking part in its provisions.[35]

Victim compensation programs, however, do not solve all of the problems of victims. Many of these programs are not adequately funded and thus do not provide sufficient money to satisfy reasonable claims. Further, a study of prosecutors' offices, published in 2002, noted that such programs place heavy burdens on prosecutors, who are primarily responsible for their implementation. Prosecutorial offices must hire additional staff and develop policies and programs that require financial and other resources.[36] Even supervising restitution required by law to be paid by offenders to their victims can be a significant financial burden on prosecutorial offices. Finally, many of the state laws are not written clearly or are not enforced widely.[37]

> **Victim compensation programs** Plans for assisting crime victims in making social, emotional, and economic adjustments.

2-3a   Characteristics of Victims

The NCVS data include information on the demographic characteristics of crime victims. For many years, analyses of victimization data have shown differences in the rates of victimization of specific groups within the population. The most frequent violent crime victims are young people, men (except for rape and sexual assault), African Americans, Hispanics, divorced or separated people, the unemployed, the poor, and residents of central cities.

Age

In general, the younger the person, the more likely he or she is to become a crime victim. The BJS found that, in 2003, persons between 12 and 24 were more frequently violent crime victims than persons of all other ages, but, "Beginning with the 20–24 age category, the rate at which persons were victims declined significantly as the age category increased."[38]

Race

Victimization data show that African Americans suffer higher rates of violent and household crimes than whites, and generally violent crimes against African Americans are more serious than those committed against whites. Offenders who victimize African Americans are more likely to use weapons; violent crimes against African Americans involve a gun in twice as many cases as compared with whites. African American victims are more likely than whites to be attacked physically during the crime's commission.[39]

The BJS reported that, in 2003,

- "Per every 1,000 persons in that racial group, 28 blacks, 23 whites, and 15 persons of other races sustained a violent crime.
- Black and white persons experienced statistically similar rates of simple assault.
- Black, white, and other races experienced similar rates of rape/sexual assault and robbery."[40]

Victimization data distinguish Hispanic victims as well. Earlier analyses of data disclosed that Hispanics, whose growth is expanding more rapidly than any other racial group in the United States, were more often victimized by violent crimes than were non-Hispanics. They also endured a higher rate of household crimes.[41]

BJS trend data for 1993–2002, however, reveal that crime victimization of Hispanics fell 56 percent. For 2003, BJS reported the following with regard to ethnicity:

- "733,000 Hispanic persons age 12 or older were victims of rape, sexual assault, aggravated assault, and simple assault.
- Violence against Hispanics age 12 or older most often took the form of simple assault (67%).
- Hispanic persons age 12 or older experienced 14% of all violent crimes [up from 12 percent in 2002] and made up 13% of the population.
- Hispanics were victims of overall violence at about the same rate as non-Hispanics.
- Hispanics were significantly more likely to be victims of aggravated assault than non-Hispanics.
- There were no differences between Hispanics and non-Hispanics for simple assault and robbery."[42]

Gender

Overall, men are more likely than women to be victimized by crime, especially violent crime, although trend data show that the rates are getting closer. Women have higher violent crime victimization rates than men in only the categories of forcible rape and other sexual assaults.

Violent crime rates for both female and male victims decreased between 1973 and 2003, as Figure 2-6 shows. The BJS victimization data on which that figure is based include the crimes of homicide, forcible rape, robbery, and both simple and aggravated assault.

2-3b   The Relationship between Victims and Offenders

Social interaction between offenders and their victims is an important factor in some crimes. Normally violence in the form of assault or murder is preceded by social interaction, and physical violence is more likely if both the offender and the victim define the situation as one calling for violence. If only one is prone toward physical violence, generally the altercation will not become a physical one. In this sense, the victim may contribute to his or her own injury or death, but that does not mean the victim *caused* or is responsible for the crime.

The extent of violence committed by those who know each other, especially within the domestic setting, is difficult to estimate. These crimes are not always reported by the victims or by other family members because of fear, embarrassment, or for other reasons, such as a hope that the situation will improve. To improve data collections, NCVS officials spent 10 years redesigning their survey instruments. For example, the new techniques involve asking about a broader scope of sexual assaults, ranging from a completed rape to a threat of sexual violence by a domestic partner.

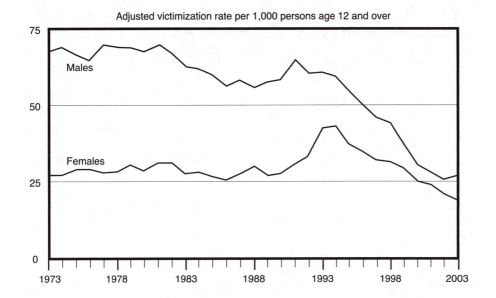

Adjusted victimization rate per 1,000 persons age 12 and over

Figure 2-6
Violent Crime Victimization Rates by Gender of Victim, 1973–2003
Source: Bureau of Justice Statistics, U.S. Department of Justice, *Violent Crime Trends by Gender of Victim,* www.ojp.usdoj.gov/bjs/glance/vsx2.htm (retrieved 12 June 2005.)

Many violent crime victims, especially murder victims, know their assailants, but recent data also show a decline in the homicide of intimates (defined as spouses, ex-spouses, boyfriends or girlfriends), especially male victims. For example, the Bureau of Justice Statistics (BJS) reported that between 1976 and 2000 the number of men who were murdered by intimates dropped by 68 percent. The number of women who were murdered by intimates declined in 1993 through 1995 (after being stable for two decades) and then stabilized through the year 2000. Intimates remain a significant factor in homicides, however, with the latest BJS data reporting through the year 2002, showing the following:

- "Spouses and family members made up about 15 percent of all victims.
- About one third of the victims were acquaintances of the assailant.
- In 14 percent of all murders, the victim and the offender were strangers.
- The victim/offender relationship was undetermined in about one third of homicides."[43]

The BJS also reports that female, as compared with male, murder victims, are much more likely to be victimized by their intimates and that, in recent years,

- "About one third of female murder victims were killed by an intimate.
- About 4 percent of male murder victims were killed by an intimate.
- Of all female murder victims, the proportion killed by an intimate was relatively stable until 1995 when the proportion began increasing.
- Of male murder victims, the proportion killed by an intimate has dropped."[44]

One final area of victim abuse involving close associations is that of the abandonment or killing of newborns. In Houston, Texas, for example, an increase in this crime led to the enactment of an ordinance that encourages mothers to turn over their newborns to hospitals or fire stations rather than abandon them. The mothers are provided legal protection if they take this route. But it is also a growing concern that some mothers in the maternity wards of hospitals are abandoning drug-addicted babies, along with those infected with HIV.[45] Provisions for protecting mothers (or fathers) who abandon their newborn children in ways that will protect those infants are called **Baby Moses laws** and are becoming more common in the United States as well as some other countries.

2-3c Fear of Crime and Citizens' Reactions

Another victimization focus is on the fear of random violence. The fear of violent crime by strangers, who often pick their victims randomly, led U.S. Supreme Court Chief Justice Warren E. Burger to refer in 1981 to the "reign of terror in American cities." One privately funded study of crime concluded that "the fear of crime is slowly paralyzing American society."[46]

▶ **Baby Moses laws** Provisions for protecting mothers (or fathers) who abandon their newborn children in ways that will protect those infants; these laws are becoming more common in the United States as well as in some other countries. Normally the laws permit new parents to leave the babies in safe places and avoid prosecution.

The fear of crime may not always be realistic in terms of the probability that crimes will occur, but fear leads to lifestyle changes for many, especially the elderly. A purse snatching may have a far more serious effect on an elderly person than it would have on a younger victim. The elderly are more likely to be injured seriously in any altercation with an assailant. Such direct contact may be much more frightening to an elderly person, and the loss of money may be more serious to a person living on a fixed income. For many elderly, the fear of crime leads to significant lifestyle changes; some even refuse to leave their dwellings.

Women may adjust their lifestyles to decrease their chances of becoming crime victims. They may be advised by police and others to do so. In various cities, police have reported that a high percentage of forcible rapes are committed against female victims who have been careless—walking alone at night, hitchhiking, sleeping in apartments with unlocked doors or windows, or going out with someone they met at a bar. Other women, because of their fear of crime, may avoid going to places they would like to go in order to reduce the probability that they will be victimized. But they deprive themselves of a lifestyle they prefer. For them, one cost of crime is diminished personal freedom.

One venue in which young women fear personal violence, especially rape, is on college and university campuses. Research shows that women in this venue are more likely to become rape victims than their cohorts who are not in college. In a recent study of college women, researchers found that their fear of rape shadows their fear of other crimes, especially face-to-face crimes, and that women fear rape even more than murder.[47] Others disagree that women's fear of rape so shadows their fear of other crimes that it accounts for the greater fear of crime among women than among men. Although clearly "the magnitude of fear [of crime] for women is greater than it is for men," say other researchers, "the patterns of variables that predict fear are similar for both men and women." It is argued that a "generalized fear of personal harm may be the more important predictor, rather than a specific fear of rape." This latter study measured fear of gang violence, and that fear extended to both men and women.[48]

Women and the elderly are not the only ones who make lifestyle changes as a result of a concern with crime. Many people install expensive burglar alarm systems or move to another, and hopefully safer neighborhood. Others refrain from going out at night or from traveling to certain areas. As two scholars have concluded, "Left unchecked, [fear] can destroy the fabric of civilized society, causing us to become suspicious of each other, locking ourselves in our homes and offices, and relinquishing our streets to predators."[49]

Our fear of crime has been enhanced by the events of 11 September 2001, which made it clear that thousands of innocent persons can be subject to catastrophic injury, property damage, and even death. The reach of those terrorist acts, along with the bombing of the federal building in Oklahoma City, school shootings, and numerous other highly publicized criminal acts, has resulted in increased security not only at airports and in large cities and major events but in schools as well. The inconvenience and time consumption of some of these security measures (such as long waits at airports) provide constant reminders that we are all subject to random violence.

2-3d Criminal Justice Systems and Crime Victims

Research in the 1980s and 1990s provided information on how victims react to crime. The findings of this research have led to significant changes in criminal justice systems. It has not been an easy journey for crime victims; nor are all of their problems solved. Victim reaction, however, has been a key factor in these changes.

In 1982, President Ronald Reagan established the President's Task Force on Victims, which was followed in 1984 by the Attorney General's Task Force on Family Violence. Both commissions interviewed crime victims and others. Most of the victims spoke negatively about their treatment in criminal justice systems.

The criminal justice systems' reaction to some crime victims means that they are victimized twice: once by the criminal and once by the system in a variety of ways. First, the victim may be blamed for the crime. Particularly in the case of sexual assault, the response of the system may be that the victim asked for it by being in a questionable place, such as a bar; by hitchhiking on the highway; by having a questionable reputation; or by wearing provocative clothing. This is referred to as **victim precipitation.**

In addition to being blamed for the crime, victims may perceive that police and others will not be sympathetic to crimes committed by persons known to the alleged victim, that they view those actions as domestic problems, not violence. Some rape victims have complained about the reactions of police and prosecutors, alleging that they have not tried to understand the problems suffered by the victims.

Third, some victims (and others) complain that U.S. criminal justice systems favor defendants over victims. This response should be analyzed in light of later discussions in this text of defendants' rights, but basically the position is that criminal justice systems have gone too far in protecting defendants to the exclusion of victims.

Some changes designed to benefit victims have been made within criminal justice systems. Many departments now train police and prosecutors to be sensitive to the needs of adult rape and domestic violence victims, as well as young children who are abused in any way by their family, their friends, or strangers. Other departments have special units of officers designated to handle allegations by these or other types of victims.

Police departments have changed their arrest policies in response to victims who have complained that often police do not arrest the offenders and that, if they do, some prosecutors will not file charges. Police response to that complaint has been that most victims will not cooperate and, without their cooperation, most prosecutions of domestic violence cases will not be successful. Victims respond that they are afraid that, if they cooperate, the alleged offenders will retaliate.

In an attempt to remove the responsibility (and thus the increased chances of retaliation by the accused) from the victim, some police departments have instituted a policy of mandatory arrests in domestic battery cases. Mandatory arrests remove from police the discretion to avoid the situation, mediate, or recommend civil action only. If called to the scene of a domestic battering, police must arrest if they have probable cause to believe that battering has occurred.

Legislative and administrative changes in the roles of prosecutors and judges have also been made. Training programs for prosecutors have given them greater understanding of the unique problems suffered by rape, domestic abuse, or child abuse victims. The provision of counseling services for victims; court-ordered counseling for those found guilty of rape, domestic violence, or child abuse; greater restrictions on pretrial release of suspects; and many other changes have occurred.

A final way in which some criminal justice systems have responded to victims' needs is through victim compensation programs. Beginning in 1965 with California, the first state to adopt a victim compensation program, the trend toward adoption of these programs moved quickly. Unfortunately, many states have not provided adequate funding, leaving victims with an illusion that they will receive financial aid, medical care, and counseling assistance for the injuries and losses they have suffered as the result of crime. The provisions of state victim compensation programs vary considerably. The state plans also differ in the methods of application, eligibility requirements, and minimum and maximum awards.

Despite their popularity, state victim compensation programs have been criticized severely. The passage of legislation in this area gives the impression that something is being done for victims. But, for many reasons, many crime victims are not compensated adequately, if at all. Also, it is not clear that the programs meet other goals, such as increased crime reporting.

Some jurisdictions have enacted legislation to benefit witnesses as well as crime victims. Congress passed a victim compensation bill that applies to victims and witnesses involved in federal crimes, the Victim and Witness Protection Act of 1982 (VWPA), which has been amended subsequently. The act contains various provisions designed to prevent harassment of victims and witnesses. It establishes guidelines for fair treatment of crime victims and witnesses in criminal justice systems. It requires victim impact statements at sentencing, contains more stringent bail requirements, and provides that the sentencing judge must order defendants to pay restitution to victims or state reasons for not doing so.[50]

▶ **Victim precipitation**
Concept that a criminal act may have been brought on by the alleged victim's actions.

Congress also passed the Victims of Crime Act of 1984 (VOCA), which authorizes that federal funds be distributed by the Office of Justice Programs through its Office for Victims of Crime and Bureau of Justice for state victim compensation and assistance programs. VOCA originally provided that federal funds would stop after 30 September 1988, but Congress reauthorized the program to continue. The money for the fund comes from fines, penalties, and the sale of forfeited goods. The fund is distributed to local agencies and has been used for hiring counselors to work with victims, to compensate victims, and even for technology, such as computers, used to assist victims.[51]

In recent years, additional attempts have been made to compensate victims and to increase their participation in criminal justice systems. Although a proposed amendment to the U.S. Constitution was withdrawn by its sponsors, who stated that they knew they could not get the necessary support for passage, a new federal bill was pased by the U.S. Congress and signed by president George W. Bush in late 2004. In part, the Crime Victims' Rights Act provides the following:

1. The right to be reasonably protected from the accused.
2. The right to reasonable, accurate, and timely notice of any public court proceeding, or any parole proceeding, involving the crime or of any release or escape of the accused.
3. The right not to be excluded from any such public court proceeding, unless the court, after receiving clear and convincing evidence, determines that testimony by the victim would be materially altered if the victim heard other testimony at that proceeding.
4. The right to be reasonably heard at any public proceeding in the district court involving release, plea sentencing, or any parole proceeding.
5. The reasonable right to confer with the attorney for the Government in the case.
6. The right to full and timely restitution as provided in law.
7. The right to proceedings free from unreasonable delay.
8. The right to be treated with fairness and with respect for the victim's dignity and privacy.[52]

Chapter Wrap-Up

This chapter provided an overview of data on crime, offenders, and crime victims and discussed how those data are secured. The three basic methods for collecting crime data were described and analyzed. The official data of the *Uniform Crime Reports (UCR)* report the amount of crime as recorded by police departments and reported to the FBI.

In recent years, the FBI has recognized the limitations of its method of collecting and recording crime data. Its most significant change, the National Incident-Based Reporting System (NIBRS), is in operation in many states. NIBRS views crime as an incident that involves many elements, including alcohol and drug abuse; the types of victims, weapons, and criminal activity; the victim's and arrestee's residency; the relationship between victims and offenders; and a description of property and property values. The collection of these additional elements of criminal acts will significantly enhance our ability to analyze crime.

The second source of crime data is the National Crime Victimization Survey (NCVS). It is valuable because it reveals that many victims do not report their victimizations to the police. The NCVS provides data on why people do not report victimizations. It does not give any information on arrests, and it is dependent on the accuracy of perception and reporting of crime victims.

The third major source of crime data—self-report data (SRD)—contains data that are not secured by either of the official methods. Through this method we get information on characteristics of people who say they have committed crimes. SRD provide valuable information for social scientists who study why crimes are committed, as well as for officials who must make decisions concerning the use of resources aimed at crime control and prevention. SRD allow the study of repeat offenders. The major problem with this approach is that respondents may underreport or overreport crimes.

All the data sources can be used to analyze the nature and extent of crime, but it is important to analyze carefully the time periods and the definitions of crimes being measured before comparing data from the various sources. Data in this chapter come primarily from the *UCR*, with victimization data coming from the NCVS. The data on criminal offenders are analyzed by three major variables: age, race, and gender.

Following the look at data, the chapter explored the recently developed and rapidly expanding study of victimology. It discussed the characteristics of crime victims, along with the problems those victims face in criminal justice systems. The chapter noted that, although they are the most frequently studied, women, the elderly, and children are not the most frequent crime victims. Most violent crimes are committed against African American men, and men are more frequent crime victims than women. Brief mention was made of the smallest victims—newborns who are abandoned by their mothers—and the Baby Moses laws designed to encourage mothers to give those infants a chance at life and adoption.

The chapter noted some of the specific problems crime victims face within criminal justice systems. It closed with a discussion of efforts to assist crime victims, mentioning such measures as victim compensation, revised court procedures, and victim participation in criminal justice processes.

Like most changes in the system, recognizing the rights of victims creates other needs, such as training programs for profession-als within the system and financial backing for those programs as well as for victim compensation plans. Furthermore, victims' rights and defendants' rights may come into conflict. Nevertheless, changes made in the system to help victims may produce positive results, such as increased crime reporting and more arrests and convictions. But what appear to be positive results could create problems for the system and society because of the increased need for jails and prisons. Thus, a study of crime victims provides another example of the need to assess the effect that changes in one aspect of the system have on the rest of the system and on society.

This completes the introductory chapters. We turn now to a look at policing, the criminal justice component through which many people enter criminal justice system processing.

Key Terms

aggravated assault (p. 36)
arson (p. 38)
Baby Moses laws (p. 43)
burglary (p. 37)
crime rate (p. 30)
crimes known to the police (p. 30)
forcible rape (p. 35)
hate crime (p. 39)
index offenses (p. 30)
larceny-theft (p. 38)

manslaughter (p. 35)
motor vehicle theft (p. 38)
murder (p. 35)
National Crime Victimization
    Survey (NCVS) (p. 33)
National Incident-Based Reporting
    System (NIBRS) (p. 33)
property crimes (p. 37)
rape (p. 34)

robbery (p. 36)
self-report data (SRD) (p. 34)
Uniform Crime Reports (UCR) (p. 30)
USA Patriot Act (p. 34)
victim compensation programs (p. 41)
victimology (p. 40)
victim precipitation (p. 45)
violent crimes (p. 35)
white-collar crime (p. 32)

Apply It

1. Describe and contrast the major sources of crime data.
2. Why should attention be paid to misdemeanors?
3. What are the limitations of the *UCR*?
4. Explain and evaluate the FBI's NIBRS of data reporting.
5. Why are some crimes not reported by victims? If you were a crime victim, would you call the police? Would it depend on the nature of the crime?
6. What are the advantages and disadvantages of self-report studies?
7. What have been the major changes in the amount of crime in the United States in the past decade?
8. What are the major differences between violent crimes and property crimes? List and define the four crimes in each of these categories.
9. What is *hate crime?* Discuss. How does the recent U.S. Supreme Court case on cross burning relate to hate crimes?
10. Discuss the relationship between crime and each of the following: age, race, and gender.
11. What progress has been made recently in the study of victims?
12. Discuss the characteristics of crime victims.
13. Define *Baby Moses laws* and discuss their impact.
14. What lifestyle changes might you consider because of the risk of crime?
15. What, if any, effect did the 9/11/01 terrorist attacks have on your view of crime?
16. Is the fear of crime realistic?
17. What changes have been made in criminal justice systems to improve the plight of crime victims?

Endnotes

1. Federal Bureau of Investigation, *Crime in the United States: Uniform Crime Reports 1999* (Washington, D.C.: U.S. Government Printing Office, 2000), pp. 6–50.
2. *Crime in the United States, 2000,* News Release, Federal Bureau of Investigation (22 October 2001), p. 1.
3. "The Nation: Crime Falls Slightly in 2002, FBI Reports," *Los Angeles Times* (17 June 2003), p. 25; "FBI Reports 0.2 Percent Drop in Crime," United Press International Press Release (16 June 2003); FBI press release (28 October 2003).
4. Federal Bureau of Investigation, *Crime in the United States: Uniform Crime Reports 2003* (Washington, D.C.: U.S. Government Printing Office, 2004), pp. 11, 41.
5. William Spelman and Dale K. Brown, *Calling the Police: Citizen Reporting of Serious Crime* (Washington, D.C.: National Institute of Justice, October 1984), pp. xxiv–xxvii.
6. David Seidman and Michael Couzens, "Getting the Crime Rate Down: Political Pressure and Crime Reporting," *Law and Society Review* 8 (Spring 1974): 457–493.
7. "Precinct Altered Statistics: Kelly Admits Felonies Downgraded by Cops," *Newsday* (New York) (21 June 2003), p. 6.
8. See Federal Bureau of Investigation, *Uniform Crime Reporting: National Incident-Based Reporting System,* vol. 1, *Data Collection Guidelines* (Washington, D.C.: U.S. Department of Justice, 1 July 1988).

9. Bureau of Justice Statistics, National Crime Victimization Survey, *Effects of the Redesign on Victimization Estimates* (Washington, D.C.: U.S. Department of Justice, Office of Justice Programs, April 1997), p. 2.

10. "Some Experts Fear Political Influence on Crime Data Agencies," *New York Times* (22 September 2002), p. 23.

11. Michael J. Hindelang, Travis Hirschi, and Joseph G. Weis, "Correlates of Delinquency: The Illusion of Discrepancy between Self-Report and Official Measures," *American Sociological Review* 44 (December 1979): 995–1014.

12. People v. Harrison, 768 P.2d 1078, 1081, 1082 (Cal. 1989).

13. Federal Bureau of Investigation, *Crime in the United States: Uniform Crime Reports 1984* (Washington, D.C.: U.S. Government Printing Office, 1985), p. iii.

14. Federal Bureau of Investigation, *Crime in the United States: Uniform Crime Reports 1985* (Washington, D.C.: U.S. Government Printing Office, 1986), p. iii.

15. "Reasons for Crime Drop in New York Elude Many," *New York Times* (29 November 2002), p. 28.

16. *Uniform Crime Reports 2003*, p. 11; "FBI: Violent Crimes Decreased in the U.S.," UPI Press Release (8 June 2005).

17. *Uniform Crime Reports*, 2003, p. 15.

18. Ibid., p. 27.

19. Ibid., p. 31.

20. Ibid., pp. 11, 37.

21. Ibid., p. 41.

22. Ibid., p. 45; "FBI: Violent Crimes Decreased in the U.S."

23. *Uniform Crime Reports*, 2003, p. 49.

24. Ibid., p. 55.

25. Ibid., p. 61.

26. Ibid., p. 61.

27. Virginia v. Black, 538 U.S. 343 (2003).

28. *Uniform Crime Reports 2003*, p. 268.

29. See, for example, William Wilbanks, *The Myth of a Racist Criminal Justice System* (Monterey, Calif.: Brooks/Cole, 1987) and Joan Petersilia et al., *Racial Equity in Sentencing* (Santa Monica, Calif.: Rand, February 1988).

30. *Uniform Crime Reports 2003*, pp. 268, 280.

31. Ibid, pp. 268–269.

32. Ibid., pp. 268, 287.

33. U.S. Code, Title 18, Section 3663 (2005).

34. See, for example, Title IV, Violence against Women, of the Violent Crime Control and Law Enforcement Act of 1994, Public Law 103-322 (13 September 1994).

35. The Air Transportation Safety and System Stabilization Act of 2001, as amended in 2002, Pub. Law No. 107-72 (2002). See also "9/11 Fund Closes Its Doors," *New York Times* editorial (18 June 2004), p. 30.

36. "Victim Rights Impose Burdens on Prosecutors, Study Shows," *Criminal Justice Newsletter*, Vol. 32, No. 10 (5 June 2002): 3.

37. "States Closing Loopholes in Victim Restitution Laws," *Criminal Justice Newsletter* (16 January 2003), p. 4.

38. Bureau of Justice Statistics, *Victim Characteristics*, Summary Findings, www.ojp.usdoj.gov/bjs/cvict_v.htm (retrieved 11 June 2005), based on 2003 data.

39. Bureau of Justice Statistics, *Black Victims* (Washington, D.C.: U.S. Department of Justice, April 1990), p. 1.

40. Bureau of Justice Statistics, *Victim Characteristics*.

41. Bureau of Justice Statistics, *Hispanic Victims* (Washington, D.C.: U.S. Department of Justice, January 1990), p. 1; Bureau of Justice Statistics, *Criminal Victimization 1994*, p. 4.

43. Bureau of Justice Statistics, *Victim Characteristics*.

43. Bureau of Justice Statistics, U.S. Department of Justice Office of Justice Programs, "Homicide Trends in the U.S.: Intimate Homicide," www.ojp.usdoj.gov/bjs/homicide/intimates.htm (retrieved 24 March 2005).

44. Ibid.

45. "A Flurry of Baby Abandonment Leaves Houston Wondering Why," *New York Times* (21 December 1999), p. 12.

46. "The Curse of Violent Crime: A Pervasive Fear of Robbery and Mayhem Threatens the Way America Lives," *Time* (23 March 1981), p. 16.

47. Bonnie S. Fisher and John J. Sloan III, "Unraveling Fear of Victimization among College Women: Is the 'Shadow of Sexual Assault Hypothesis' Supported?" *Justice Quarterly* 20, no. 3 (September 2003): 633–659.

48. Jodi Lane and James W. Meeker, "Women's and Men's Fear of Gang Crime: Sexual and Nonsexual Assault as Perceptually Contemporaneous Offenses," *Justice Quarterly* 20, no. 2 (June 2003): 337–371; quotation is on p. 366.

49. Hubert Williams and Anthony M. Pate, "Returning to First Principles: Reducing the Fear of Crime in Newark," *Crime & Delinquency* 33 (January 1987): 53.

50. U.S. Code, Title 18, Section 3663 (2005).

51. U.S. Code, Title 42, Section 10601 *et seq.* (2005).

52. Crimes Victims' Rights Act, U.S. Code, Title 18, Section 3771(a) (1)-(8) (2005).

Entry into Criminal Justice Systems: Policing

The President's Commission on Law Enforcement and Administration of Justice emphasized in its 1967 report that police occupy the front line. Our ability to do what we want, free from the fear of crime, depends on the police. But despite the responsibilities and powers granted to the police, they cannot deal effectively with crime without the assistance of victims and witnesses, and that cooperation is not always given. However, police are blamed if crime rates increase and if reported crimes are not solved.

Part 2 explores the nature, organization, function, and problems of policing in an attempt to place this important aspect of criminal justice systems in proper perspective. Chapter 3 covers the history of policing and explains how formal police systems emerged. It differentiates the levels of public police systems in the United States, looks briefly at international policing, and reviews the nature and problems of private policing. The organization and administration of police systems are considered, with a focus on community-oriented policing.

Chapter 4 describes what police actually do, ranging from performing many services within the community to engaging in the dangerous job of apprehending criminals. Police functions are discussed in the context of legal requirements and empirical social science research. Part 2 closes with Chapter 5, which focuses on the major problems and issues in policing.

The Emergence and Structure of Police Systems

3

Policing is one of the most important functions in criminal justice systems. As stated by a noted expert on policing, "The strength of a democracy and the quality of life enjoyed by its citizens are determined in large measure by the ability of the police to discharge their duties."[1] However, the ability of U.S. police to function effectively and properly has come into serious question in recent years, as when television cameras around the world replayed an amateur photographer's recording of police officers beating an African American suspect, Rodney King. The acquittal of four white officers in their state trial was followed by rioting. Subsequently, two of the officers were convicted and two were acquitted in federal trials. King settled his suit with the Los Angeles Police Department (LAPD), but the problems of that department continued, as Spotlight 3-1 notes (see page 52).

This chapter and the following two chapters discuss policing: its past, present, and future. The discussion begins with a history of policing to explain the reason for the formal systems of present-day public policing. The history is traced from its informal beginnings in other countries to today's formal systems in the United States. The decentralized systems of U.S. policing are examined by their major categories: local, state, and federal policing systems, with the discussion on the federal level giving particular attention to the FBI and the newly created Departments of Homeland Security (DHS) and Transportation Security Administration (TSA). Relevant recent federal legislation creating these new agencies and others is discussed. Brief attention is given to international policing, followed by a section on private policing and security.

The chapter then focuses on the organization and administration of police departments and closes with a discussion and an analysis of two policing models: the professional model and community-oriented policing.

LEARNING OBJECTIVES

After reading this chapter, you should be able to do the following:

- **Discuss the history of U.S. policing, paying special attention to the contributions of the British police**
- **Explain the meaning of decentralized policing**
- **Distinguish among local, state, and federal policing systems**
- **State and evaluate the role, function, and recent reorganization of the FBI**
- **Evaluate recent scandals within the FBI**
- **Comment on the major recent federal legislation designed to combat terrorism**
- **Discuss the purpose of the Department of Homeland Security**
- **Analyze the function and problems of the Transportation Security Administration**
- **Explain the difference between private and public policing and discuss their comparative growth and importance**
- **Note early reform efforts in the organization and administration of policing systems**
- **Distinguish the professional model from the community-oriented policing model and evaluate each**

3-1   The History of Policing

Although formal policing is a relatively modern development, some form of policing has existed for centuries. When societies were small and cohesive, with most members sharing goals and activities, it was usually possible to keep order without a formal **police** structure. The rules and regulations of the society were taught to new members as they were socialized, and most people observed the rules. Others could be coerced into observing those rules by informal techniques of social control. If that did not work and if rules were violated, crime victims might have handled the situation informally. The victim might also have been permitted to take private revenge against the offender.

In some countries informal policing was organized beyond the immediate family or individual concerned. England had the **frankpledge system,** in which families were organized into a **tithing** (10 families) and a **hundred** (10 tithings) for purposes of protecting each other, as well as for enforcing laws. The frankpledge was a system of mutual pledge or mutual help, with all adult members responsible for their own conduct and that of others in the system. If the group failed to apprehend a lawbreaker, the English Crown fined all members.

Individual private policing had its limits, however, and, as societies grew in size and complexity, public policing was needed. The appointment of constables in England in the twelfth century signaled the beginning of public policing in that country. An unpaid **constable** was responsible for taking care of the weapons and the equipment of the hundred, as well as keeping the peace by enforcing laws.

A second kind of police officer emerged when hundreds were combined to form **shires,** which were analogous to counties. The king appointed a shire-reeve to supervise each shire. The shire-reeve was the forerunner of the **sheriff.** Originally the shire-reeve was responsible only for ensuring that citizens performed their law enforcement functions adequately, but later the duties were expanded to include apprehending law violators. The shire-reeve, the only paid official, was assisted in his duties by constables.

During the reign of Edward I (1272–1307), the **watch system,** the immediate forerunner to modern police systems, emerged in England. The watch system was developed as a

---

Police   A government official authorized to enforce the law and to maintain order, using physical, including deadly, force if necessary.

Frankpledge system   In old English law, a system whereby the members of a tithing had corporate responsibility for the behavior of all members over 14 years old. Ten tithings formed a hundred, and hundreds were later combined to form shires, similar to counties, over which a sheriff had jurisdiction.

Tithing   In English history, a system of 10 families who had responsibility for the behavior of members over the age of 14. Tithings were also important in protecting the group from outsiders.

Hundred   In English law, a combination of 10 tithings as part of the frankpledge system. *See also* **tithing** and **frankpledge system.**

Constable   An officer of a municipal corporation who has duties similar to those of a sheriff, such as preserving the public peace, executing papers from the court, and maintaining the custody of juries.

Shires   *See* **Frankpledge system.**

Sheriff   The chief law enforcement officer in a county, usually chosen by popular election.

Watch system   A system charged with the duties of overseeing, patrolling, or guarding an area or a person. Watchmen were prominent in the early watch system of policing.

Spotlight 3-1   The Los Angeles Police Department under Scrutiny

In September 1999, an officer of the Los Angeles Police Department (LAPD) was apprehended for stealing cocaine from an evidence room. This incident led to criminal allegations against the officer, Rafael Perez, and an investigation that resulted in the firing of numerous officers. The report, issued in March 2000, included a list of 108 recommendations for changes. The department was criticized for a lack of training and supervision of officers, a lack of attention to citizen complaints, a "startling lack" of internal auditing, a "near universal ignorance" of the department's policies concerning the use of informants, and the framing and shooting of innocent persons.

The 350-page report concluded that mediocrity flourished within the LAPD, with internal policies often ignored by officers and others. The report began with an investigation of the anti-gang unit but was expanded to include other units. Police Chief Bernard C. Parks, in issuing the report, stated that many of the problems resulted from "people failing to do their jobs with a high level of consistency and integrity. . . . Unfortunately, we found this to be true at all levels of the organization, including top managers, first-line supervisors, and line personnel." Parks concluded, "Clearly, pride in one's work and a commitment to do things correctly the first time seem to have waned."[1]

In February 2000, Perez was sentenced to five years in prison for stealing cocaine. Part of his plea bargain was that he would not be charged with other crimes to which he admitted, such as framing innocent persons by planting evidence on them and lying about these cases in court hearings, but that plea bargain does not prohibit federal prosecutors from charging Perez with any federal crimes he may have committed. In April 2001, Perez was released after serving only part of his five-year sentence after the judge ruled that he had met the terms of his plea agreement and that he had been treated unfairly by being incarcerated in jail rather than in prison. Prison time, in contrast to jail time, may result in obtaining more days off a sentence due to good behavior.

In November 2000, the city of Los Angeles settled for $15 million (the largest settlement for police abuse in that city to that date) with Javier Francisco Ovando, a former gang member who is paralyzed from the waist down after being shot by Perez and officer Nino Durden, who then planted a gun on Ovando and claimed that he was threatening the officers.

Ovando was an innocent man who served nearly 3 years (of a 23-year sentence) but was freed as a result of the investigation into police corruption in the Los Angeles Police Department. In April 2001, Durden, the former partner of Rafael Perez, pleaded guilty to federal charges stemming from the framing of Ovando and other crimes he, Perez, and other LAPD officers had committed.[2] Durden was sentenced to five years in prison.

In November 2000, Los Angeles officials agreed to enter into a consent decree to avoid an investigation by the U.S. Department of Justice. The decree mandated reforms in the LAPD. In late 2001, an independent monitor, appointed in June of that year, concluded that those reforms were on schedule.[3] In early 2003, the district attorney announced that his office was completing its investigation of the Rampart scandal and would not be prosecuting any additional officers, stating that Durden had implicated only himself and Perez. The *Los Angeles Times* concluded otherwise after obtaining copies of secret debriefings of Durden. In an article published on 1 March 2003, the *Times* stated as follows:

> As a result of the [Rampart] investigation, more than 100 convictions were overturned and taxpayers have paid more than $40 million to settle lawsuits. Eight officers were charged with on-duty crimes. Four officers, including Durden, pleaded guilty or no contest to crimes. Three other officers were convicted of corruption-related offenses by a jury, but the judge in the cases overturned the jury's verdict. [The district attorney] is appealing the judge's decision. One officer was acquitted of wrongdoing.[4]

In December 2004, prosecutors dropped charges against those three officers.

The problems of the LAPD led to the resignation of Bernard Parks and the appointment of a new chief in October 2002. William J. Bratton had formerly served as the police commissioner in New York City and prior to that, in Boston. Although Bratton is not a minority (the two previous chiefs were African American; neither was appointed to a second five-year term), it was predicted that he would be accepted by the minority community, but some residents were skeptical. As one alleged, "The problem here is nobody trusts the police. . . . It is no secret that the L.A.P.D. is racist, that they profile black people, and they

means of protecting property against fire and for guarding the walls and gates of the cities. Watchmen were responsible for maintaining order and monitoring public behavior and manners. The London watchmen carried clubs and swords. They did not wear uniforms and could be distinguished from other citizens only by the lanterns and staffs they carried. Originally they were to patrol the streets at specified intervals during the night, announcing that all was well. As the city grew, a day shift was added.

In 1326, Edward II supplemented the shire-reeve supervised mutual pledge system by creating an office of justice of the peace. The justices were appointed by the king, and their initial function was to assist the shire-reeve with policing the counties. Later the justices assumed judicial functions. As the central government took on greater responsibility for law enforcement in England, the constables lost their independence as officials of the pledge system and were under the authority of the justices, who were assisted by volunteers.

plant evidence. How does one man change a community's mind? No one has that answer."[5]

Other problems have surfaced in the LAPD. A July 2002 videotape shows two white police officers beating an African American teenager whom they had handcuffed after stopping him for an alleged traffic violation. The officers were pictured slamming the youth's face against a patrol car and hitting him in the jaw. Jeremy J. Morse and Bijan Darvish were tried in the summer 2003. The jurors could not reach a verdict on the charges against Morse, who was retried, and that trial also ended in a hung jury. Darvish was acquitted.

In April 2003, the Los Angeles County Bar Association released the details of a study conducted by a 20-member panel. The panel issued numerous recommendations aimed at preventing another Rampart-type scandal in the LAPD.[6] And in June 2003 the LAPD police chief announced that the issues in the Rampart cases needed another review. The fifth Rampart inquiry was headed by civil rights attorney Connie Rice, but in September 2003 the former LAPD police chief, Bernard Parks, then a member of the city council, refused to participate in the study, declaring that another review was not needed.[7]

By November 2003, little had been done on the investigation because of a lack of funding. Only about 25 percent of the needed funding had been secured. By December 2004, the *Los Angeles Times* had reported that funding remained a problem in meeting all of the requirements of the Rampart agreements. Funding for more officers was particularly a problem, with Los Angeles having only 9,241 officers for 1,000 population, compared with 14,075 in Chicago and 39,779 in New York City. Also by December 2004, the media had announced that the investigation into the June 2004 beating scandal was almost complete. Officer John J. Hatfield was videotaped (by a camera in an overhead police helicopter during a vehicle chase) apparently striking an African American suspect 11 times with a flashlight. Officer Hatfield said he thought the young man was armed and was trying to subdue him so that he could be handcuffed. The suspect, Stanley Miller, entered a guilty plea to evading arrest and joyriding. He faced up to five years in prison but was given a three-year sentence.[8]

Prosecutors declined to prosecute Hatfield, but in April 2005, Chief Bratton reported (without giving names) that two officers would face serious disciplinary action and that four others would be suspended for 4 to 15 days. The media reported that Hatfield and another officer were relieved of their duties pending Board of Rights hearings. In February 2005, LAPD Officer Steve Gardia shot and killed an African American, Devin Brown, age 13, who was driving a car with a 13-year-old passenger. According to John Mack, president of the Los Angeles Urban League, the police fired 10 rounds at the car when Brown began backing it toward their squad car. The editorial claimed that the officers had gotten out of their car and were in no danger of being hit; it noted that the boys had no business being on the street late at night; and Brown should not have been driving at all. Mack alleged that LAPD officers too often stereotype young African Americans as gang members.

> The LAPD has a long-standing institutional culture in which some police officers feel that they have the tacit approval of their leadership, especially at the mid executive level, to brutalize and even kill African American boys and men. They believe—and they've often been proved right—that heads will turn the other way....
>
> The LAPD is, again, on trial in the minds of many. And the jury is still out.[9]

1. "Los Angeles Police's Report Cites Vast Command Lapses," *New York Times* (2 March 2000), p. 14; "LAPD Issues Self-Critical Report, but Others Seek Outside Control," *Criminal Justice Newsletter* 30 (20 March 2000): 2.
2. "Los Angeles Settles Lawsuit against Police," *New York Times* (22 November 2000), p. 18; "Perez's Ex-Partner Pleads Guilty," *Los Angeles Times* (3 April 2001), p. 2B.
3. "LAPD Reforms Are on Track, Independent Monitor Says," *Criminal Justice Newsletter* 31, no. 21 (24 November 2001): 3.
4. "Transcripts on Rampart Belie D.A.," *Los Angeles Times* (1 March 2003), p. 1, Part 2.
5. "Naming of New Police Chief Raises Minorities' Hopes," *New York Times* (4 October 2002), p. 21.
6. "Bar Association's Task Force Releases Rampart-Related Report," *City News Service* (22 April 2003).
7. "Council to Decide on Blueprint for Rampart Panel," *City News Service* (18 November 2003).
8. "Man Hit by Police Is Sent to Prison," *Los Angeles Times* (9 December 2004), p. 3B; "Bratton's Biggest Goal Still Elusive," *Los Angeles Times* (30 November 2004), p. 1.
9. John Mack, "Commentary: The LAPD Is on Trial Once Again," *Los Angeles Times* Home Edition (13 February 2005), p. 5.

Constables performed functions such as supervising night watchmen, taking charge of prisoners, serving summonses, and executing warrants. The justices performed judicial functions, thus beginning the separation of the functions of the police and the judiciary. This distinction between the police functions of the constable and the judicial functions of the justices, with the constables reporting to the justices, remained the pattern in England for the next 500 years.

The mutual pledge system began to decline, however, as many citizens failed to perform their law enforcement functions within the system. The early police officials were not popular with citizens; nor were they effective. Citizens were dissatisfied with the watch system and its inability to maintain order and prevent crime. English life was characterized by rising levels of crime, a perceived increase and greater severity of public riots, and an increase in public intoxication resulting from a rise in drinking among the lower classes.

Public drunkenness became a serious problem, resulting in a significant increase in violent street crimes and thefts. The government responded by improving city lighting, increasing the number of watchmen, and increasing the punishment for all crimes. But the watchmen were not able to control the frequent riots that occurred; neither could they protect citizens and their possessions. The public responded by refraining from entering the streets at night without a private guard and by arming themselves. The rich moved to safer areas, leaving behind them the residential segregation characteristic of contemporary society.[2]

The rise of industrialization in England contributed to the need for a formal police force. As more people moved to cities and life became more complex, maintaining law and order became more difficult, and the less formal system of policing was not sufficient.

3-1a Modern Policing: The London Beginning

Although scholars debate how and why formal police systems emerged, usually the beginning is traced to England, where Londoners protested the ineffectiveness of the watch system and agitated for a formal police force. Some believed that a police force constantly patrolling the town would reduce and eventually eliminate street crime. Others feared that the concentration of power necessary for a formal police force would lead to abuses, especially if the force were a national one. Eventually the tension between these two positions was resolved by the establishment of local police systems.

Dissatisfaction with the constable system led the English to experiment with other systems. In the mid-eighteenth century John Fielding and Henry Fielding, London **magistrates,** instituted a system called the **Bow Street Runners.** The Fieldings selected constables with a year of experience and gave them police powers of investigation and arrest. The constables were given some training and were paid a portion of the fines in the cases they prosecuted successfully.

Increased concern about safety and security in London led to pressures from citizens to improve police protection. Between 1770 and 1828, a total of six commissions appointed by the English Parliament investigated policing and made suggestions, but an attempt in 1785 to establish a metropolitan police force was defeated by the opposition of powerful commercial interests. None of the English efforts were successful in establishing a satisfactory police force until 1829.[3]

In 1829, the first modern police force, the Metropolitan Police, was founded in London by Sir Robert Peel. The men employed by the force were called *Peelers* or *Bobbies* after the founder. Working full-time and wearing special uniforms, the officers' primary function was to prevent crime. They were organized by territories, and they reported to a central government. Candidates had to meet high standards to qualify for a job as a police officer in London. The system has been described as follows:

> Peel divided London into divisions, then into "beats." The headquarters for the police commissioners looked out upon a courtyard that had been the site of a residence used by the Kings of Scotland and was, therefore, called "Scotland Yard." . . . [I]n 1856 Parliament required every borough and county to have a police force similar to London's.[4]

London set the example; the rest of England was slow to follow, but other countries began establishing modern, formal police systems. Some countries developed a centralized police system, but a decentralized system developed in the United States. Most European countries followed the British practice of not arming the police, but the amount of violence led the British to change that tradition in 1994, when some specially trained Bobbies began carrying guns.

Despite its historical reputation for professional and successful policing, Scotland Yard faced a crisis in 1999, when an investigation concluded that it was infected with "institutional racism." The force had a poor record of minority recruitment, hiring, retention, and promotion. Only 3 percent of the police officers were minority, but 25 percent of the city's ethnic population was minority. Police were criticized for their overall investigation of the slaying of an 18-year-old black man, Stephen Lawrence, who was stabbed to death by a group of whites in 1993. According to the report, police were insensitive to minorities'

Magistrate A judge in the lower courts of the state or federal court system. Usually magistrates preside over arraignments, preliminary hearings, bail hearings, and minor offenses.

Bow Street Runners The mid-eighteenth-century London system that gave the police powers of investigation and arrest to constables, who were given some training and paid a portion of the fines in successfully prosecuted cases.

rights. Charges of racial profiling were cited, along with rising crime rates. Police argued that they were understaffed and underpaid, citing the high cost of living in London (one of the highest in the world) and their comparatively low salaries.[5]

In spring 2003, on the tenth anniversary of Lawrence's death, England's prime minister, Tony Blair, in a letter to the Lawrence family, wrote that, although progress had been made, "There is still a great deal more to do if we are to build a genuinely fair and inclusive society. . . . [There is a] genuine commitment, shared by all our public institutions, to ensure they are really representative and responsive to all the people and communities they serve. One of Britain's great strengths is that it is a country of many races, many cultures and many faiths." Blair continued, "The diversity of our society is respected and celebrated."[6] Despite his comments, the fact is that Britain, like many countries, including the United States, has not been successful in recruiting sufficient minorities into policing.

In October 2004, dozens of Britain's most senior constables converged on Parliament to warn that the country was in danger and that, if more funds were not provided for law enforcement, hundreds of jobs would have to be cut. According to the media, "That would mean fewer bobbies on the beat—which would be devastating for Tony Blair at a time when gun and knife crime is soaring." In November, over 125 of Scotland Yard's Specialist Firearms Squad were threatening to refuse to carry arms in protest over the suspension of two colleagues who shot dead a suspect who was carrying a table leg, which they apparently thought was a gun. These threats came "at a time when security is meant to be at an all-time high to combat the threat of terrorist attacks." Some officers did turn in their guns, but most resumed firearms duties. Not all of Britain's police are licensed to carry guns.[7]

3-1b   The Emergence of Policing in the United States

People in the United States saw a variety of policing systems in the early days. Immigrants brought many aspects of the English system to this country. The constable was in charge of towns, and the sheriff had jurisdiction over policing counties. Before the American Revolution, these positions were filled by governors appointed by the British Crown, but subsequently most constables and sheriffs obtained their positions by popular elections.

The English watch system was adopted by many of the colonies. The New York City system was said to be an example. Bellmen walked throughout the city, ringing bells and providing police services. Later they were replaced by a permanent watch of citizens and still later by paid constables.

One of the most familiar kinds of policing, still in use in some rural areas today, was the **posse.** Under the posse system, a sheriff could call into action any number of citizens over a certain age if they were needed to assist in law enforcement.

In some early U.S. systems, law enforcement officials were paid by local government. Others were paid by private individuals. "By the early nineteenth century, American law enforcement had become a hodgepodge of small jurisdictions staffed by various officials with different powers, responsibilities, and legal standing. There was no system, although there were ample precedents for public policing."[8]

It did not take long, however, for Americans to realize that these methods of policing did not produce the efficiency and expertise necessary to control the urban riots and increasing rates of crime and violence that accompanied the industrialization, increased complexity, and growth of American cities. A professional police system was needed, and by the late 1880s most American cities had established municipal police forces, although the county sheriff system continued to provide policing services in rural areas. State police systems were added gradually, followed by the federal system. The state and federal systems, however, were not to supercede the local systems.[9]

One final type of policing that should be mentioned is **vigilantism,** which means *watchman* and refers to the acts of a person who is alert, cautious, suspicious, and ready to take action to maintain and preserve peace. Vigilantism is based on the belief that laws aid persons who are vigilant and who do not sleep on their rights. In colonial days people (usually only men) formed vigilante committees to stop rebellions and other problems and to

> **Posse**   The rural police system in which the sheriff may call into action any number of citizens over a certain age if they are needed to assist in law enforcement.

> **Vigilantism**   Literally, "watchman"; action by a person who is alert and on guard, cautious, suspicious, ready to take action to maintain and preserve peace; actions of citizens who take the law into their own hands in an effort to catch and punish criminals.

Spotlight 3-2   Vigilantism in the Air

Passengers say they will take action; pilots have encouraged them to do so if necessary. Another 9/11/01 will not happen on my flight! That appears to be the reaction of many pilots and passengers after the Attack on America. The would-be shoe bomber found out the hard way.

Richard Reid, 29, a British citizen, attempted to bomb a flight from Paris to Miami. The flight was carrying 197 people in December 2001, when Reid attempted to light a fuse protruding from his shoe. Passengers overpowered Reid, whose shoe carried concealed plastic explosives. Reid entered a guilty plea, stating that he hated the United States and was a follower of Osama bin Laden. On 30 January 2003, when Reid, who had converted to Islam, was to be sentenced, he yelled at the judge, "You will be judged by Allah! Your government has sponsored the torture of Muslims in Iraq and Turkey and Jordan and Syria with their money and weapons." In part, federal judge William Young responded as follows:

We are not afraid of any of your terrorist co-conspirators, Mr. Reid. We are Americans. We have been through the fire before. You are a terrorist. You are not a soldier in any war. To give you that reference, to call you a soldier gives you far too much stature....

You hate our freedom. Our individual freedom. Our individual freedom to live as we choose, to come and go as we choose, to believe or not believe as we individually choose.

Here, in this society, the very winds carry freedom. They carry it from sea to shining sea. It is because we prize individual freedom so much that you are here in this beautiful courtroom....

See that flag, Mr. Reid? That's the flag of the United States of America. That flag will fly there long after this is all forgotten. That flag stands for freedom. You know it always will.[1]

Reid was sentenced to the maximum term for his crime: life in prison. The issue of vigilantism, however, goes far beyond this case and raises the possibility that, if airline passengers are willing to take physical action against suspected terrorists, what might the results be? For example, in September 2002, passengers aboard a Southwest Airlines flight from Phoenix to Salt Lake City beat and kicked to death a young man who charged the cockpit door.[2] Subsequent to the 9/11 Attack on America cockpit doors were made more secure, and, along with other security precautions, they are locked during flights.

1. Quoted in "At Sentencing, Judge Lets Shoe Bomber Know What America Stands For," *St. Louis Post-Dispatch* (17 April 2003), p. 2.
2. The information on the Southwest flight came from a paper published on the last day of 2000, and the focus of that article was whether cockpit doors should be locked to protect pilots from attack. "Should Plane Cockpit Doors Be Locked?" *The Straits Times* (Singapore) (31 December 2000), pp. 1, 2.

catch and punish criminals. These groups operated outside the law, but apparently they viewed themselves as preserving law.

Vigilante committees and groups continue to operate within our society, and often they aim their efforts at the suppression of racial and other minority groups, thus constituting a serious threat to the rights of these people. They may, however, also be very helpful, as indicated in Spotlight 3-2, which relates the events of an attempted terrorist act on an airplane.

3-2   Decentralized Policing: U.S. Systems

In the United States formal police systems are decentralized, operating at local, state, and federal levels.

3-2a   Local Policing

Local policing includes police agencies at the rural, county, and municipal levels. Most studies of police focus on municipal policing. Few criminal justice texts discuss rural policing, and usually only slight attention is given to county police systems, leaving the impression that these levels of policing are not important. This conclusion is erroneous because local and county levels of policing cover significant geographical areas of the country. In fact, the majority of police agencies in the United States are located in small towns, villages, or boroughs.

Rural Policing

Throughout the United States, but particularly in southern and western regions, many towns and villages are too small to support a police department. Some of these areas depend on the county police system for protection. Others have their own systems, usually consisting of an elected official. This official may be called a *constable,* who has policing duties similar to those of the county sheriff. Constables might not be trained in law or policing. However, they have the power to enforce laws, to arrest, to maintain order, and to execute processes from the magistrate's courts, which are courts of limited jurisdiction, often called *justice of the peace courts.*

Rural policing is very important but often plagued with financial and personnel problems. One officer cannot police even a small area for 24 hours a day. Frequently, citizens are without police protection; local police officers are overworked; and in many jurisdictions funds are not available for the support services necessary for adequate policing.

Many rural officers do not have sufficient resources for investigating criminal activity. They are more isolated from other officers. Quick backup services from other officers may be a scarce luxury rather than a daily reality. Working conditions of rural police may be less desirable than those of police officers at other levels. Most salaries are low and not necessarily compensated for by a lower cost of living. Initial training is more limited and may not be geared to the unique problems of rural policing. Most officers must train in urban settings because in many areas there are not enough rural police to justify separate training centers. As a result, those officers may have unrealistic expectations of rural policing. In addition, many rural officers do not have the opportunity for continued education and training.

Budget planning and other activities concerning policing in rural areas might be town projects, with police officers involved in heated discussions from which their urban counterparts might be shielded by police administrators. This high visibility and total immersion in local problems and politics might affect the social life of the officer, who finds it impossible to go anywhere in the area without being viewed as a police officer. For rural officers, long periods of inactivity may lead to boredom and a lowered self-concept. In comparison with urban police, rural police may face greater citizen expectations for a variety of services not connected with law enforcement.

On the positive side, some rural officers enjoy their involvement in community activities with local citizens. The lower crime rates, particularly the lower rates of violence, may increase police security. The lack of complexity in the police system might be seen as a positive rather than a negative factor. Problems associated with a lack of security, when only one officer is assigned to an area, might be eliminated or greatly reduced by cooperation from the next level, county policing. In many areas, rural police are limited to traffic functions and some ministerial duties, with the major law enforcement activities being handled by the county sheriff and county police officers. The county may contract with the rural community to provide these services.

County Policing

Some county police agencies are rural, but the county system is larger and usually employs a sheriff as the primary law enforcement officer. The county sheriff may have numerous other functions unrelated to law enforcement, such as acting as the county coroner, collecting county taxes, or supervising any number of county government activities. If the department is large enough, the county police department might have a deputy sheriff and law enforcement officers assigned to patrol the county and enforce order.

The sheriff is considered the most important law enforcement officer in the county, but in practice the functions of the sheriff's office usually are limited to the unincorporated areas of the county, with law enforcement in the incorporated areas handled by the municipal police in the larger cities. Most sheriffs are elected officials. Previously, most sheriffs served for very long periods, but it is becoming difficult, if not impossible, for long sheriff tenures to continue. In many jurisdictions, political activists have been successful in unseating sheriffs who have served for years.

Larger county police departments may contract their services to smaller county or rural departments. The county department may employ a county **marshal,** a sworn officer whose primary function is to perform civil duties for the courts, such as delivering papers to initiate civil proceedings or serving papers for the arrest of criminal suspects.

▶ **Marshal** A sworn law enforcement officer who performs the civil duties of the courts, such as the delivery of papers to begin civil proceedings. In some jurisdictions marshals serve papers for the arrest of criminal suspects and escort inmates from jail to court or into the community when they are permitted to leave the jail or prison temporarily.

Larger county police departments have investigative units that service the district attorneys who bring the prosecutions in the county. These departments are staffed by sworn officers and support personnel. Departments too small for investigative units may contract for such services from the municipal or urban police departments in the area or from the Federal Bureau of Investigation (FBI).

The movement of drugs into the rural areas of U.S. communities has changed the nature of both county and rural policing. In one feature article on this issue, the sheriff of Jefferson Davis County, Mississippi, noted the increase in violence and related problems in rural areas due to the influx of drug dealers, who have become wealthy dealing in the prescription painkiller Oxycontin, as well as illegal drugs, such as crack and powder cocaine and marijuana. According to the sheriff, the office has received calls from teachers warning that students in their classrooms who deal in drugs have threatened to kill each other and from an elderly woman stating that her crack-addicted son's life has been threatened by a drug dealer. A 13-year-old was shot and killed when he was standing outside his home. His assailant was a drug dealer who was looking for the teen's brother with whom he had had a fight. The sheriff noted the problems in trying to apprehend drug dealers. For example, the officers cannot go under cover to buy drugs because the department does not have the money; successful undercover work would be impossible, anyway, because everyone knows everyone.[10]

Municipal Policing

Most studies of policing focus on municipal departments; consequently, the discussions in the following two chapters apply primarily to municipal policing. In this chapter, we examine the differences between municipal, or urban, policing and policing at the other local levels.

Municipal police departments differ from other local police agencies mainly in their size, organization, complexity, and services. Although they may service smaller geographical areas than rural or county systems, most municipal police systems have more employees and provide more extended services. The complexity of the departments leads to greater problems in staffing, organization, and fulfillment of the public's needs. Many municipal departments have more resources, which may be shared with rural and county systems on a contract basis. On the other hand, citizens' expectations for services from municipal police departments may be greater than expectations at the rural or county level, where the department's mandate may be less defined and more open-ended.

Municipal departments, in contrast to departments at other levels, may encounter more difficult political problems with their governing bodies. The municipal police department competes with other agencies for funding. The costs of policing are highest in urban areas, where population changes may present more problems. Many large cities have experienced significant changes in the numbers of people who live in the city, compared with the number who commute daily to work. The residential tax base goes down as the need for services, order maintenance, and law enforcement increases.

Generally, crime rates are much higher in urban than in rural or county areas. The composition of the urban population may present greater policing problems. Urban areas have a more heterogeneous population, as well as a greater number of unemployed people, transients, and those who have been in trouble with the law.

3-2b   State Policing

State police patrol highways and regulate traffic. They have the primary responsibility for enforcing some state laws and providing services such as a system of criminal identification, police training programs, and a communications system for local law officials. The organization and services provided by state police vary from state to state. No national or central control exists, except for some standards of the U.S. Department of Justice and the U.S. Department of Transportation.

This lack of centralization stems from the historic distrust of national police systems, as well as from the different law enforcement needs of the individual states. For example, in 1835, the Texas Rangers, a group of uneducated and untrained men, were recruited and given authority to protect the Texas border from the Mexicans. After Texas was admitted to the Union, the Rangers were retained, along with their primary duty of patrolling the southern border of Texas.

The Texas Rangers became the first state-supported organization of police in the United States. As police functions expanded, the role of the Texas Rangers was enlarged, as was their training.

The industrialization and expansion of the country led to many problems that could not be handled adequately at the local level, and, although Texas had the first state police agency, Pennsylvania's system became the early model for state police in the United States. In the late 1870s, a powerful secret organization, the **Molly Maguires,** responded to anti-Irish riots in Pennsylvania by forming Irish labor unions, which used violence to terrorize the state's coal-producing regions. The Molly Maguires controlled all hiring and firing. Some employers who ignored their mandates were killed. The terrorists threatened the growing Pennsylvania economy, which was heavily dependent on mineral wealth. The state was settled sparsely, and local police authorities could not control the Molly Maguires. "The Pinkerton Detective Agency, a private national organization, was eventually brought in to infiltrate the Molly Maguires, and twenty of its members were convicted of murder and other crimes."[11]

▶ **Molly Maguires** A powerful secret police organization in the 1870s in Pennsylvania.

In 1905, Pennsylvania's governor succeeded in convincing that state's legislature to appropriate funds for a constabulary to help prevent future disasters, such as those caused by the Molly Maguires. The movement toward state policing did not happen quickly, however, for many still feared that the next step would be national police and political repression. But the use of automobiles and increased problems with traffic on state roads and highways in the twentieth century created an obvious need for state police.

State police are similar to the state patrol. Both have uniformed, sworn officers who carry weapons. They differ primarily in their law enforcement powers. Most state patrol officers engage primarily in traffic control. Although they may be empowered to enforce criminal laws violated in their presence, on the highway, or within sight of or adjacent to the highway, they do not have general powers of law enforcement for all state laws, as state police have. State police, in contrast to state patrol, may have their own investigative units as well as a forensic science laboratory.

State police and state patrol also differ in that many state police systems include specialized forms of policing, such as control over fishing and gaming laws, regulation of gambling and horse racing, and regulation of alcohol sales. The Alcohol Board of Control is a state agency responsible for investigating requests for liquor licenses and has the power to establish rules concerning the conditions under which liquor is sold. This board is in charge of enforcing state laws enacted to regulate the sale of dangerous drugs.

3-2c Federal Policing

Enforcement of criminal laws in the United States historically has been viewed as the function of states, although states may and do delegate some of their powers to local police agencies. The federal constitution does not provide for a central police agency. It gives the federal government specific power to enforce only a limited number of crimes. The Constitution also provides that all powers not delegated to the federal government are reserved to the states. The federal Constitution gives Congress the power to pass laws that are "necessary and proper" for the exercise of congressional powers. Over the years Congress has passed statutes on federal crimes. The U.S. Supreme Court has upheld the power of Congress to do so.

Federal law enforcement includes federal prosecutors and federal police agencies. The federal policing level is complex and encompasses more than 50 enforcement agencies, which are located within various departments, but some of which have been transferred to the newly created Department of Homeland Security, discussed later in this chapter. One agency is that of the U.S. Marshals Service, which is featured in Professions 3-1.

In addition to the U.S. Marshals Service, the Department of Justice encompasses other major investigative agencies, the largest of which is the Federal Bureau of Investigation.

Professions 3-1

U.S. Marshals Service

The U.S. Marshals Service, located within the Department of Justice, is the oldest federal law enforcement agency, with more than 4,500 employees celebrating the organizations 215th anniversary on 24 September 2004. The service consists of one person from each federal judicial district. The marshals are appointed by the U.S. president, with the advice and consent of the Senate. The marshals are assisted by deputy marshals.

The primary function of U.S. marshals is to transport federal inmates between prison and court and to escort them to homes or jobs when they have temporary leaves. The marshals provide protection for federal jurors, judges, prosecutors, attorneys, and witnesses. They are in charge of seizing and auctioning property that has been taken by officers under federal court orders. As sworn police officers, U.S. marshals may make arrests for federal offenses and perform other police functions, such as controlling riots and executing federal fugitive warrants.

In marking the 215th year of the U.S. Marshals, President George W. Bush wrote the following in a letter to the organization's employees:

> U.S. Marshals have contributed to the safety of our Nation by providing security for our courts and witnesses, capturing fugitives, assisting with prisoner transportation, and responding to emergency situations.[1]

Each year U.S. Marshals capture approximately 34,000 federal fugitives, arresting more of them than all other federal agencies combined. In 2003, task forces led by U.S. Marshals also arrested over 27,000 state and local fugitives. Additional information about the U.S. Marshal Service and employment opportunities within this agency can be found at www.usmarshals.gov.

1. News Release, United States Marshals Service (24 September 2004).

The Federal Bureau of Investigation (FBI)

On 26 July 1908, President Theodore Roosevelt directed the U.S. Attorney General to issue an order creating the agency now known as the Federal Bureau of Investigation (FBI). In 1924, J. Edgar Hoover was appointed director of the organization and remained in that position until his death in May 1972. The FBI is the primary agency charged with enforcing all federal laws not assigned to other special agencies. The FBI headquarters are located in Washington, D.C. Field officers are located in major cities throughout the United States and in San Juan, Puerto Rico. The director of the FBI is appointed by the president of the United States, by and with the consent of the Senate.

The investigative work of the FBI is performed by special agents, who are trained at the FBI Academy, located on the U.S. Marine Corps Base in Quantico, Virginia. In addition to special agents, the FBI employs individuals who perform such investigative functions as fingerprint examinations, clerical and receptionist duties, computer programming, and laboratory work. Attorneys, accountants, and other professionals are also employed.

The FBI is not a national police force. Primarily, it is an investigative agency. FBI agents may investigate crimes over which the federal government has jurisdiction by statute; they may investigate state and local crimes when requested by those agencies. There is no charge for these services.

The training facilities of the FBI Academy are used by other agencies for training law enforcement officers; some foreign officers are accepted into the program. The academy provides continuing education and training for officers. Another important function of the FBI is the collection of national data on crimes known to the police and on arrests, as discussed in Chapter 2.

Throughout its history, particularly during the long years it was headed by J. Edgar Hoover, the FBI was criticized severely as well as praised highly. During most of its existence, the FBI has had only loose directives from Congress. A strong leader such as Hoover was able to take advantage of that situation and build a powerful, extremely influential organization, which allegedly held extensive control even over the presidents under whom Hoover served.

In recent years the FBI has experienced charges of scandals, corruption, favoritism, discrimination against minorities and women, sexual harassment, and other problems. In 1993, President Bill Clinton appointed Judge Louis J. Freeh to head the FBI. Freeh's appointment followed the resignation of the former director, William Sessions, who was plagued by allegations of ethics violations. Freeh was criticized but remained in office until June 2001.

Other problems have arisen recently. In its August 1999 annual statement the FBI reported that it had fired 32 employees for misconduct in 1998, compared with only 18 the previous year. The agency's spokesperson emphasized that the increased firings for misconduct did not necessarily represent a trend. An increase in the number of agents assigned to investigate employees resulted in greater efficiency and speed in the investigative process. Agents were fired for a variety of acts, including extortion, lying to internal investigators, unprofessional conduct, drunk driving, drug abuse, theft or embezzlement of government property, unauthorized disclosures, and sexual harassment.[12]

In spring 2001, FBI officials admitted that the agency had withheld documents from the attorneys of Timothy McVeigh, who was convicted of capital murder in the 1995 bombing of the federal building in Oklahoma City, Oklahoma. McVeigh's execution was postponed as a result, but after the trial judge refused to grant a second delay, McVeigh did not appeal, and he was executed on 11 June 2001. Also in 2001, a former FBI agent accused of spying for Moscow, Robert P. Hanssen, pleaded guilty to 15 counts of espionage, attempted espionage, and conspiracy. As a result of Hanssen's plea bargain, some charges against him were dropped and he was spared the death sentence, but he will serve life in prison. The Hanssen case, coupled with reports in the spring 2001 that the FBI could not account for 449 weapons and 184 laptop computers, led some legislators to proclaim that the agency could "no longer manage its basic operations," and that "lax administrative controls over sensitive materials like these cannot be tolerated." Vermont Senator Patrick J. Leahy commented, "There are some very, very serious management problems at the F.B.I."[13]

In summer 2001, Robert S. Mueller III was confirmed as the new FBI director. In the fall of that year, the Bush administration announced its plan to revamp the FBI, focusing the agency's efforts on counterterrorism, which would require a deemphasis on some of the agency's traditional targets, such as drug enforcement, bank robbery, and some violent crime investigations. In fact, within hours after the 9/11/01 terrorist attacks, thousands of FBI agents were reassigned to counterterrorism. And in October 2001, one senior White House official was quoted as saying, "12 months from now, the F.B.I. is not going to be the organization it was on Sept. 10."[14]

Significant changes were made in the FBI, and the June 2003 reports of two investigative groups, constituting the most thorough study of the changes at the FBI, gave encouraging but cautious comments. One report was the work of the General Accounting Office (GAO), which is the investigative agency of Congress. The other was conducted by the National Academy of Public Administration, with the investigation headed by the former U.S. Attorney General, Richard Thornburgh. Both reports stated that the FBI had made significant progress in its reorganization efforts but that important challenges remained. Specifically, the reports considered the efforts of the FBI to update its technology systems, develop programs for sharing intelligence information with other government agencies, and maintain full law enforcement on traditional areas (such as drug trafficking) while focusing on counterterrorism. In particular, the GAO report noted an approximately 15 percent decrease in drug trafficking referrals made by the FBI, compared with the previous year. Approximately 400 FBI agents were transferred from units investigating drugs to those concerned with terrorism. Another concern was the lack of independence of the newly created Terrorism Threat Integration Center. The purpose of this agency is to filter intelligence information concerning terrorism across government agencies, but, noted several lawmakers to whom the reports were presented, the Central Intelligence Agency (CIA) runs the Terrorism Threat Integration Center. Some feared that the CIA would not be willing to share some of the terrorism information with other agencies.[15]

The 9/11 Commission Report, the *Final Report of the National Commission on Terrorist Attacks upon the United States* (the commission was established by the U.S. Congress and President George W. Bush in November 2002) was quite critical of the FBI. Consider, for example, the following statement from that report:

> Responsibility for domestic intelligence gathering on terrorism was vested solely in the FBI, yet during almost all of the Clinton administration the relationship between the FBI Director

and the President was nearly nonexistant. The FBI Director would not communicate directly with the President. His key personnel shared very little information with the National Security Council and the rest of the national security community. As a consequence, one of the critical working relationships in the counterterrorism effort was broken.[16]

The chairman of the commission, Thomas H. Kean, said that reports of the FBI's work both before and after the 9/11 attacks was an "indictment of the F.B.I. It failed and it failed and it failed and it failed. . . . This is an agency that does not work. It makes you angry. And I don't know how to fix it."[17] Some changes in the FBI were made in 2005 as this text went to press. The bureau, under pressure from the Bush White House, had agreed to accept some of the recommendations of a presidential commission. Specifically, the FBI had agreed to permit the newly appointed and first Director of National Intelligence, John Negroponte, to assist in the selection of the FBI's intelligence chief, the third-ranking official of the FBI. It will be the first time in history that the FBI has given an outsider a significant role in the selection of one of its top officials.

The FBI, like other federal law enforcement agencies, should be viewed as a supplement to, not a replacement of, state and local agencies. The agency is assisted by other federal agencies. All are aided by recent legislative enactments.

Recent Federal Legislative Enactments

After 11 September 2001, President George W. Bush proposed and Congress enacted several pieces of legislation to create new federal agencies and to empower those agencies and others in the fight against terrorism.

The USA Patriot Act (United and Strengthening America by Providing Appropriate Tools Required to Intercept and Obstruct Terrorism Act of 2001) was passed by Congress and signed by President Bush in fall 2001 in response to the 9/11/01 terrorist attacks. The act basically expands the powers of the federal government to deal with terrorism. Some of those powers involve the expansion of wiretaps on terrorist suspects' email, telephone conversations, and use of the Internet. Tighter controls are placed on immigration and on money laundering.[18] The USA Patriot Act has been lauded by many and criticized by others, who claim that it invades the constitutional rights of privacy, due process, and free speech and gives the government, in effect, the power to spy on Americans and others. Lawsuits were filed quickly after the enactment of the act. In January 2004, a federal court in California held a portion of the USA Patriot Act unconstitutional. That court held that the act's ban (along with that of an earlier statute aimed at terrorist acts) against providing "expert advice or assistance" to terrorists is vague and thus violates the First Amendment.[19] The USA Patriot Act is discussed in greater detail in Chapter 4 of this text.

The National Homeland Security and Combating Terrorism Act of 2002 coordinates the federal agencies involved in domestic preparedness; all the federal agencies that are involved in activities for domestic preparedness; and the agencies that coordinate plans for natural and person-made crises and emergency planning. The legislation provides for the creation of a White House Office of Combating Terrorism, empowered to oversee governmentwide antiterrorism policies and coordinate threats, be in charge of a national strategy to combat terrorism, and exercise control over the budget for counterterrorism. A subtitle of the Homeland Security legislation, the Homeland Security Information Sharing Act, contains provisions for requiring the federal government to share classified information, along with unclassified but sensitive information, with state and local law enforcement agencies.[20]

Another recent piece of legislation designed to assist the federal government in fighting terrorism is the Enhanced Border Security and Visa Entry Reform Act of 2002. This is an extensive act designed to provide greater security with regard to granting foreigners permission to enter the United States.[21]

Still another piece of legislation important to combating terrorism is the Public Health Security and Bioterrorism Response Act of 2002, which authorized $4.6 billion to fund measures to protect the United States against bioterrorist attacks. Among other provisions of this act are those aimed at increasing the ability of law enforcement officers to respond quickly and efficiently to bioterrorist attacks and funding for public health preparedness. The act funds measures to increase the protection of the nation's supplies of food, drugs, and drinking water. It also provides funds to state and local governments to assist officers at those levels to improve their preparation for potential bioterrorist attacks.[22]

Despite these acts and others, a study published by the International Association of Chiefs of Police (IACP) in 2003 disclosed that officials at most police departments throughout the United States were not confident of their abilities to prevent or respond to terrorist attacks. Only 4 percent of the respondents said they were adequately prepared to respond to terrorism, whereas 52 percent said they felt somewhat prepared. Only 10 percent said that since 9/11 they had secured additional funding to combat terrorism, and 82 percent responded that what they most needed was technical equipment—in particular, chemical protective equipment.[23]

Two new federal agencies designed to combat terrorism in the United States are the Department of Homeland Security and the Transportation Security Administration.

The Department of Homeland Security (DHS)

One of the major proposals of the Bush administration after the 9/11/01 terrorist attacks was the creation of the **Department of Homeland Security (DHS).** The administration's wish to make the DHS into a cabinet-level position was approved by Congress. DHS employs approximately 170,000 persons and combines 22 former federal agencies (not including the CIA and the FBI, which remain independent agencies). The new department began with a $37.5 billion budget and was headed by Tom Ridge, Pennsylvania's former governor. Ridge resigned after the reelection of President George W. Bush, who in early December 2004 named Bernard B. Kerik, a former New York City police commissioner, to succeed Ridge; however, Kerik withdrew his name after one week, stating that the nomination was the "honor of a life time" but that, in going through his personal financial records in preparation for the confirmation hearing, he noted that he had previously hired a nanny without proper immigration papers and may not have paid required taxes on her behalf. It would have been impossible for Kerik's name to go forward after that information surfaced, if for no other reason than the fact that the head of DHS oversees immigration procedures and policies.[24] In February 2005, Michael Chertoff was confirmed by the U.S. Senate as the new head of the Department of Homeland Security.

The creation of DHS constituted the most extensive federal government reorganization in 50 years. DHS is the third largest federal agency (after the Defense Department and the Department of Veterans Affairs). Spotlight 3-3 details the major components of the Homeland Security Act of 2002.

▶ **Department of Homeland Security (DHS)** The cabinet-level department created after the 9/11/01 terrorist attacks; its creation constituted the most extensive federal government reorganization in 50 years; it combines 22 federal agencies and constitutes the third largest federal agency.

The Transportation Security Administration (TSA)

Another agency created since 9/11 is the **Transportation Security Administration (TSA),** which was created by the Aviation and Transportation Security Act (ATSA), enacted in November 2001. The TSA was developed to take on the screening functions for all commercial flights. This job had been performed by the Federal Aviation Administration (FAA), which was restructured by the statute. The TSA is a part of DHS and is devoted to securing modes of transportation. By the end of its first year in operation, the TSA had hired and trained 44,000 federal screeners (for which it had over 1.4 million applications) and deployed them to 429 commercial airports, along with 158 federal security directors.[25] In 2003, the TSA reduced its workforce for financial reasons. But in October 2004, Congress approved a bill for the 2005 TSA budget; it was signed by President Bush on 18 October. The bill limited the number of TSA agents to no more than 45,000 and provided $32 billion for the agency's operations and activities for the year 2005, which was $496 million above President Bush's request and $1.1 billion above the 2004 level. The major change was that the legislation required the TSA to triple the amount of cargo inspected at airports.[26]

▶ **Transportation Security Administration (TSA)** A federal agency created by the Aviation and Transportation Security Act (ATSA), enacted two months after the 9/11/01 terrorist attacks. The TSA was developed to take over the security screening functions for all commercial flights in the United States.

Other Federal Law Enforcement Agencies

Prior to the changes in federal agencies since the 9/11/01 terrorist attacks, in addition to the FBI, the U.S. Department of Justice (DOJ) contained two other major law enforcement agencies: the Drug Enforcement Administration (DEA) and the Immigration and Naturalization Service (INS). The DEA previously was part of the Treasury Department and called

| Spotlight 3-3 | Federal Law Enforcement and the Homeland Security Act of 2002 |

On November 25, 2002, President George W. Bush signed into law the Homeland Security Act, creating the Department of Homeland Security (DHS), a new Cabinet-level Department that will plan, coordinate, and integrate U.S. Government activities related to homeland security.

The legislation creates a new Office of Inspector General, and transfers all or part of 22 existing agencies to DHS. (For more information, see the DHS website, www.dhs.gov.) Most transfers had occurred by March 1, 2003, with full integration during the following months. Several agencies employing officers with arrest and firearm authority are now part of DHS.

The following are transferred as distinct entities reporting directly to the DHS secretary:

U.S. Coast Guard—Transferred from the Department of Transportation. In times of war, or on direction of the President, the Coast Guard will still be attached to the Department of Defense, U.S. Navy.

U.S. Secret Service—Transferred from the Department of the Treasury.

In addition to agencies or components that report directly to the Secretary, DHS includes five Directorates: Border and Transportation Security, Emergency Preparedness and Response, Information Analysis and Infrastructure, Science and Technology, and Management.

The Directorate of Border and Transportation Security includes the following:

Federal Law Enforcement Training Center—transferred from the Department of the Treasury.

Federal Protective Service—transferred from the General Services Administration.

U.S. Customs Service (except for some revenue functions)—transferred from the Department of the Treasury.

Immigration and Naturalization Service—The INS is terminated, and its functions are transferred from the Department of Justice.

Transportation Security Administration (TSA)—TSA, which was created in November 2001 and includes the Federal Air Marshals program, is transferred from the Department of Transportation.

The Directorate of Border and Transportation Security will include two major new bureaus with law enforcement duties: The Bureau of Customs and Border Protection (CBP), with about 30,000 employees, will primarily perform border protection and inspections functions. It combines Customs Service and INS inspection services, the Border Patrol, and the Agricultural Quarantine Inspection program. CBP is directed by the Customs commissioner.

The Bureau of Immigration and Customs Enforcement (BICE) will enforce immigration and customs laws within the U.S. interior. Its 14,000 employees are comprised primarily of Customs Service and INS special agents, INS detention and deportation officers, the INS Immigration Litigation Section, and Federal Protective Service (FPS) employees. Customs air and marine interdiction functions, and intelligence components of INS, Customs, and FPS are also included.

Immigration and citizenship services formerly handled by the INS will reside with the new Bureau of Citizenship and Immigration Services (BCIS). BCIS will report directly to the DHS Deputy Secretary.

the *Bureau of Narcotics*. It was shifted to the DOJ in 1973. The FBI has some drug enforcement powers, too, and engages in some cooperative work with the DEA, although the drug enforcement of the FBI has declined since the bureau was reorganized.

The INS was in charge of policing the borders of the United States (trying to prevent the entrance of illegal aliens) and admitting foreigners who qualify for U.S. citizenship. The agency gained international and national attention in 2000, when its agents entered the home of the Miami, Florida, relatives of a Cuban boy, Elian Gonzalez; forcibly took him from their care; and returned him to his father, who had come from Cuba to retrieve his son. Elian had survived an escape attempt from Cuba in November 1999. His mother had died in that attempt, and Elian had been living with relatives during the custody fight between them and his father. After months of legal proceedings, Elian, his father, and other relatives and friends were permitted to return to Cuba in June 2000.

The INS drew intense criticism after 9/11, and the agency as such was replaced on 1 March 2003 by the Bureau of Citizenship and Immigration Services (BCIS). In June 2003, Eduardo Aguirre's nomination to head the BCIS was confirmed unanimously by the U.S. Senate. The BCIS is a new office within the DHS. A Bureau of Border Security (BBS) also became part of the DHS's Directorate of Border and Transportation Security (BTS).[27]

Some federal law enforcement agencies are part of the U.S. Treasury Department. The U.S. Customs Service handles inspections at entry points into the United States. The Internal Revenue Service (IRS) is in charge of laws regulating federal income tax and its collection. The

The Directorate for Emergency and Preparedness Response includes:

Federal Emergency Management Agency (formerly independent).

Also affected by the Homeland Security Act:

Bureau of Alcohol, Tobacco and Firearms (ATF)—Law enforcement functions transferred from the Department of the Treasury to the Justice Department. Revenue functions remain at Treasury. Legislation incorporates the Safe Explosives Act, creating new ATF enforcement powers related to explosives. The agency name has changed to Bureau of Alcohol, Tobacco, Firearms and Explosives, though ATF initials will still be used.

Figure 1

As of June 2002, agencies in the Justice (55%) and Treasury (23%) Departments were the largest employers of Federal officers with arrest and firearm authority; however, the Homeland Security Act made the Departments of Homeland Security (38%) and Justice (37%) the major employers in 2003.

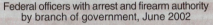
Federal officers with arrest and firearm authority by branch of government, June 2002

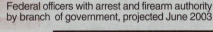
Federal officers with arrest and firearm authority by branch of government, projected June 2003

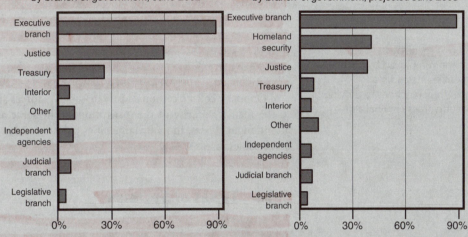

Percent of federal officers in each year, excluding the CIA, federal Air Marshals, and Armed Forces

Source: Bureau of Justice Statistics, *Federal Law Enforcement Officers, 2002* (Washington, D.C.: U.S. Department of Justice, August 2003), p. 5.

Secret Service is responsible for protecting the president and vice president (and their immediate families), as well as former presidents, their spouses and minor children, and during an election campaign qualified presidential and vice presidential candidates and their spouses. The Secret Service also protects visiting heads of state. In addition, the agency is in charge of investigating forged government checks, other securities, and counterfeiting activities.

The Bureau of Alcohol, Tobacco, and Firearms (ATF) has jurisdiction over laws and licensing requirements regarding the sale of alcohol and other drugs and over federal gun control laws, as well as over the collection of taxes connected with these areas. As Spotlight 3-3 notes, this agency was transferred from the Treasury to the Justice Department, and its name was changed to Bureau of Alcohol, Tobacco, Firearms and Explosives, although it retains the initials ATF.

Other federal agencies are concerned with law enforcement, licensing, or both. The Food and Drug Administration oversees the enforcement of the vast number of laws regulating the sale and distribution of pure food and drugs. The Department of Agriculture has an office that investigates fraud in the areas of food stamps, aid to disaster victims, subsidies to farmers and rural homebuyers, and other activities over which the department has administrative authority. Additional criminal law enforcement divisions are found in the Securities and Exchange Commission, the Department of Labor, the U.S. Postal Service, and other federal agencies.

3-2d   The International Level

The functions that federal agencies may provide for local and state police are illustrated by the participation of the federal government in **INTERPOL,** a world police organization established for cooperation among nations involved in common police problems. INTERPOL was founded in 1923 but did not function actively until after its reorganization in 1946. The United States became a member in 1938. INTERPOL is to "track and apprehend criminal fugitives, thwart criminal schemes, exchange experience and technology, and analyze major trends of international criminal activity. A police official of any member country may initiate a request for assistance on a case that extends beyond his country's territory."[28]

▶ **INTERPOL**   A world police organization that was established for the purpose of cooperation among nations involved in common policing problems.

3-3   Private Police and Security Forces

In addition to public policing, an important development all over the world is the growth of private policing. Retail businesses employ security guards to protect their premises from shoplifting and to secure the personal safety of employees and shoppers. Security guards are employed to escort female employees from their places of work to their automobiles at night, particularly in high-crime areas. Apartment owners have increased their use of **private security forces,** as have neighborhood associations. Increasingly common are guard gates, at which drivers entering an association's area are required to stop and present adequate identification before being granted permission to enter the premises.

▶ **Private security forces**   Persons employed by private agencies instead of governmental ones to provide security from criminal activity.

On many college campuses private security forces are hired for night work in addition to the regular security of the institution. Some serve as escorts for female students who attend night classes. In many large cities private security forces are hired to patrol housing and business areas. The demand for private security and private police has risen as citizens have felt a lack of sufficient security provided by public police.

3-3a   Types of Systems

Private security may be *proprietary* or *contractual.* In the case of proprietary, organizations or individuals have their own private investigators and security personnel. For those who cannot afford this approach or who choose not to do so, contracts may be made with professional agencies to provide private security. Regardless of the type of system, a variety of components exist, including security managers, uniformed officers, undercover agents, and electronic specialists or equipment.

The oldest and largest of the firms providing investigative and security services is Pinkerton's, founded in 1850 by Allan Pinkerton. Pinkerton was the first detective of the Chicago Police Department. Local, state, and federal agencies, as well as private companies and individuals, have employed the services of Pinkerton's. "The term 'private eye' had its source in the unblinking eye that was Pinkerton's trademark for many years." The primary business of Pinkerton's, headquartered in New York City, is to supply private security guards, but the firm also provides private consultants, electronic surveillance devices, and some investigation services.[29]

Private security is also provided by alarm companies. The most frequently used security program is alarm systems; increasing numbers of systems are being installed in private residences and in businesses. Fire and burglar alarm systems are most common, but alarm companies also install access control systems, fixed security equipment, and perimeter security systems. Most alarm systems are installed by relatively small companies, although some companies have services available nationally. The most sophisticated systems monitor covered premises constantly for increased protection and may be extensive and very expensive.

Private security is provided by armored vehicles with armed guards for transporting precious jewels, money, and other valuables. Courier services provide fast delivery of valuables and papers that must be transported quickly and safely. Private security services may be employed for emptying cash machines, delivering money from businesses to bank drops after hours, and providing many other activities in which business persons or private citizens feel a need for added security. Other services include security training courses, screening of personnel for businesses, technical countersurveillance to determine whether bugging devices have been installed, security consultation, and drug detection. Some people who want access to their valuables after regular banking hours use private security vaults.

The private employment of public police for additional security is also used. Sociologist Albert J. Reiss Jr. has emphasized the increased use of public police for private security. In fact, while on patrol with the police, Reiss remarked that it was impossible to tell which officers were performing as public employees and which off-duty public employees were working in a private capacity. Reiss researched the problems and issues of off-duty police employment with special emphasis on the particular departments noted in Spotlight 3-4, which also enumerates the three models for off-duty police employment.

Some police departments place restrictions on off-duty employment. Reiss found that generally officers were forbidden to take any assignments that involved a "conflict of interest between duties as a police officer and duties for the outside employer" and those that constituted "threats to the status or dignity of the police," as well as those that posed an "unacceptable risk of injury that would disable an officer for regular duty." In addition, police departments may limit the jurisdiction in which officers work, the compensation received, and the number of hours worked.[30]

3-3b Public and Private Policing Compared

Some attempts have been made to study the relationships between public law enforcement and private security systems. A national government study highlighted some of the problems between the two systems as well as the progress in solving those problems. It was found that the two systems share many goals, such as recovering stolen property, protecting life and property, and deterring and discovering criminal activity. In addition, the study

---

Spotlight 3-4 **Models of Off-Duty Police Employment**

Officer Contract Model

- Each officer finds own secondary employment.
- Officer independently contracts conditions of work, hours, pay.
- Officer then applies for permission to accept off-duty job.
- Department grants permission provided job meets minimum standards.
- Employer pays office in cash (work is "called cash detail").

Departments in Atlanta, Charlotte, Cincinnati, Minneapolis, and Omaha generally follow this mode differing on what work is permitted.

Arlington County permits uniformed employment only by permission of the police chief and only at activities funded or sponsored by the county, state, or U.S. government. Any other work must be nonpolice in nature.

In Peoria, most secondary employment is independently contracted, but the department itself contracts for civic center jobs, lets department heads broker other work, and permits officers to broker work for other officers.

In Cincinnati, work for private parties is independently contracted, but the department contracts work for city, county, or state agencies.

Union Brokerage Model

- Union, guild, or association finds paid details.
- Union assigns officers who have volunteered.

- Union sets assignment conditions for paid details.
- Union bargains with the department over status, pay, and condition of paid details.

Most off-duty employment of Seattle police is coordinated by the Seattle Police Officers' Guild, although the officers act as independent contractors. For privately sponsored special events at the Seattle Center complex, off-duty officers are employed by the center's security officer and paid through an outside accounting firm.

Department Contract Model

- Police agency contracts with employers.
- Agency assigns officers and pays them from reimbursements by employers.
- Agency assigns off-duty employment coordinator to receive employer requests, issue off-duty work permits, and assign officers to paid details.
- Agency negotiates with union or guild on pay, conditions, and regulations governing employment.

Boston, Colorado Springs, New Haven, and St. Petersburg fit this model. Metro Dade contracts for police-related work (including, unlike most departments, work for private security firms) but lets officers contract for nonpolice jobs, each of which requires a permit.

Source: Albert J. Reiss Jr., *Private Employment of Public Police* (Washington, D.C.: U.S. Department of Justice, December 1988), p. 3.

disclosed that public law enforcement officials rated private security personnel as poor in almost every area of their work and that they did not have a high regard for the ability of private security officers to prevent crime.

The study concluded that there was a "climate of suspicion and distrust between private security and law enforcement," although some progress toward cooperative efforts had been made. There was evidence of a willingness to cooperate and to transfer some responsibilities from public law enforcement to private security. Some efforts had been made to integrate the activities and increase the understanding between private security personnel and public law enforcement officers.[31]

Other issues have arisen concerning private police protection. Despite recent legislation in many states, some still do not have licensing requirements for private security. In those jurisdictions, there are few, if any, checks on the quality of security services or on the recruitment or training of security personnel.

Some states have enacted statutes providing for the regulation of private security, but issues remain, such as statutes that are not broad enough to include all types of private security. Increased reliance on private security forces also raises the moral and ethical question of whether society can afford to have a system in which necessary police protection is available only to those who can pay for it.

A study published in 1991 cited evidence that in some jurisdictions the age, experience, and training of private security officers was approaching that of public officers, with private policing showing greater growth in diversity by hiring more minorities and women than public policing.[32] But in 2003, with the significant recent growth in private security since 9/11, one news article disputed that earlier finding, stating that many private security guards earn low wages, have few if any benefits, and are not well trained.[33] And a 2001 news article cited numerous lapses in security by the leader in airport security services at that time, Argenbright Security. Less than two months after the 9/11/01 terrorist attacks, for example, a passenger got through security at Chicago's O'Hare Airport with a bag of knives, Mace, and other weapons.[34]

Perhaps it is ironic that private security has grown because people fear they are not adequately protected by public security, yet so little attention is paid by many to the type of training required of private security guards. Obviously the federal government was not pleased with private security at airports, as illustrated by the development of the TSA. But serious breaches of security have also occurred since the TSA took over U.S. airport security.

3-4   The Organization, Administration, and Management of Police Systems

The organization, administration, and management of any large department presents numerous challenges and problems, but these may be particularly acute in publicly supported police departments. The police department is the largest and most complex agency in many criminal justice systems, with patrol officers exercising immense authority over citizens. The functions performed by these people are varied and complex, although the training for the job is focused primarily on only one of those functions—law enforcement.[35]

Despite the importance of police administration, until recently little attention was given to the issues and problems of organization or administration. Indeed, in contrast to the well-planned development of the English police system, the development of U.S. policing was preceded by little planning because of a basic mistrust of a professional police force. Early systems were characterized by corruption and inefficiency.

3-4a   Early Reform Efforts

Widespread corruption, inefficiency, and a realization of the often negative impact of partisan politics on police systems gave rise in the early 1900s to a study of the role of organization and administration in improving the quality of policing and to the increased use of private security guards. These early efforts were assisted by the work of the major reformer August Vollmer, often referred to as the father of modern police management systems or the dean of American chiefs of police. As chief of the Berkeley, California, Police Department, Vollmer instituted a summer program in criminology at the University of California at Berkeley and began an emphasis on the importance of educating police formally.

In 1931, the School of Criminology was founded at Berkeley. In 1933, it granted the first police degree, an A.B. degree with a minor in criminology. In 1930, the first two-year college police program was begun at the San Jose (California) Junior College, but the first grants to such programs were not offered until 1966. These programs comprised courses in liberal arts, behavioral sciences, public administration, law, and government. Many changes have occurred in criminal justice education, with other programs developing and some, such as Berkeley's, being abolished.

Others who were influential in the development of earlier criminal justice programs were Bruce Smith, who contributed to police professionalism through his writings and as a professional police consultant, and O. W. Wilson. Wilson was influential as a police chief who emphasized advanced training for officers in Wichita, Kansas, in the late 1920s. He was dean of the School of Criminology at Berkeley and authored a widely acclaimed text on police administration. Perhaps he is best known for his contributions in the 1960s as Chicago's police superintendent.

Vollmer, Smith, and Wilson influenced the emergence of a professional model for policing, which included not only the use of management skills at the administrative levels of policing but also the application of modern technology in improving police work. The result was a model characterized by "a tight quasi-military organization; rigorous discipline; a streamlined chain of command; higher recruitment standards; a lengthy period of preservice training; the allocation of available personnel according to demonstrated need; and extensive use of vehicles, communications, and computer technology."[36]

3-4b   Policing Models

The organization and management of police departments received considerable attention from the President's Commission on Law Enforcement and Administration of Justice (the President's Commission). Some of the commission's conclusions, stated in its 1967 report on police, were the lack of qualified leadership; resistance to change; the lack of trained personnel in research and planning, law, business administration, and computer analysis; the inefficient use of personnel; and departmental organization that did not incorporate "well-established principles of modern business management."[37]

A Professional Model of Policing

The President's Commission graphed one model of departmental organization—the traditional, or professional, model, characterized by a hierarchical structure, with the police chief as the central authority in the organization. Heads of departments, such as internal investigation, community relations, administration bureau, operations bureau, and services bureau, report directly to the chief. Each of these heads has subordinate administrators reporting directly to him or her. Under this model, the police department is organized around specialized functions, such as patrol, traffic, personnel and training, and data processing, all of which are subunits of the major divisions of administration, operations, and services. This model has major units concerned with internal investigations and community relations. Some departments have a unit specializing in crime prevention.

The chain of command in the professional model is clear. Subordinates in each unit report directly to their division heads, who report to the police chief. This model involves many rules and regulations, with little input from subordinates in developing them. It may be a very efficient model for making quick decisions, for prescribing safety measures, and for internally controlling subordinates. Often the professional model results in high production output.

The professional model of policing gained momentum with the reports of the 1967 President's Commission and the National Advisory Commission on Criminal Justice Standards and Goals in 1973. According to the 1981 report of the U.S. Commission on Civil Rights, "These two commissions, in particular, gave added impetus to some specific suggestions, such as the more effective use of police personnel and, most emphatically, the requirement that police officers have some college education."[38]

The need for professional police systems became obvious in the 1960s, when television brought into American homes the violent clashes between police and minorities, including the young as well as racial and ethnic groups. The urban riots of the 1960s demonstrated the need to train police in handling orderly protests as well as violence and law enforcement.

During the 1960s, police and other elements of criminal justice systems became the focus of the federal government. In 1965, President Lyndon Johnson appointed the President's Commission on Law Enforcement and Administration of Justice, as noted earlier. This commission issued several reports in 1967. In 1965, Congress established the Office of Law Enforcement Assistance and, in 1968, the **Law Enforcement Assistance Administration (LEAA).** Until its demise in 1982, LEAA provided over $7 billion for research, development, and evaluation of various programs in criminal justice, some of which went for hardware in police departments (a source of criticism of the LEAA). Money was provided for police education through the **Law Enforcement Education Program (LEEP).** The result was the development of criminal justice departments throughout the country. Most of them focused on police education or training, discussed in Chapter 4.

The professional model is criticized for being too authoritarian and for establishing policing units that are too specialized. For example, if a police officer assigned to the patrol division encounters a problem with a juvenile, under the professional model that person should be turned over to the juvenile division, even though the patrol officer in that district may have more knowledge of the individual juvenile and his or her background. Controlling traffic and issuing traffic citations are the specialty of the officers in the traffic division; they should be called for handling these problems in the patrol officer's district. The officer may arrest a suspect for violating a crime, but the investigation of that crime will be conducted by a detective in another division. There may be overlap in the record-keeping of these various divisions, in addition to the obvious fragmentation of functions.

Community-Oriented Policing

Dissatisfaction with the professional model has led to an emphasis on a problem-solving approach to policing, which focuses on the community. The popular term is *community-oriented policing.* The problem-solving nature of this approach focuses on a less extensive division of labor, fewer rules and regulations, and few levels of authority. The emphasis is on solving problems, and power comes from the ability of employees to succeed in that goal, not from the titles of their positions. Its emphasis is on gaining knowledge and using that knowledge to adapt to new situations. This model provides greater flexibility, which may be necessary for some decisions, while permitting more involvement of subordinates in the police force. It is based on the belief that police effectiveness may be increased if the expertise and creativity of line officers are utilized to develop innovative methods for solving the underlying problems that cause or influence criminal behavior.

Since much of police work requires officers to make on-the-spot decisions, the community-oriented model may be more effective than the professional model in developing the ability to make decisions effectively. Community-oriented policing can focus on underlying problems in any or all of the three traditional areas of policing: order maintenance, law enforcement, and community service (all discussed in Chapter 4; Section 4-3, "Police Functions"). It is designed to enhance the effectiveness of policing by identifying underlying problems and attempting to solve those problems.

The problem-solving approach to policing has been emphasized in the writings of Herman Goldstein, who developed his earlier published ideas in a 1990 book. Among other examples, Goldstein discussed a Philadelphia case involving a police sergeant who noted that many noise complaints (505 separate calls in a six-month period) about the same bar had been made to police, who responded to all of these complaints. The officers did not find the noise to be in violation of the city ordinance. After some time, however, officers discovered that the noise about which the neighbors complained was coming from the vibration of the jukebox located at the common wall. The jukebox was moved to another wall, and the noise complaints stopped.[39]

Law Enforcement Assistance Administration (LEAA)
The agency established by Congress in 1965. It provided funding for the development of police departments, police techniques, police education, and police training. It was abolished in 1982. Money for education was provided through the Law Enforcement Education Program (LEEP).

Law Enforcement Education Program (LEEP) *See* **Law Enforcement Assistance Administration (LEAA).**

A focus on community-oriented policing does not mean that police will not respond to calls for service, but the demands created by these calls may lead administrators to rationalize that they do not have the personnel to engage in innovative policing, such as problem-solving approaches. It is necessary to integrate the traditional calls for service with problem-solving policing, and this cannot be done without better management of police time.

Goldstein responded to the time issue by stating,

> A common reaction to problem-oriented policing is that the agency has no time available for it. . . . This type of reaction assumes that problem-oriented policing is an add-on. It fails to recognize that the concept raises fundamental questions about how police currently spend their time, both in responding to calls for assistance and in the intervals between calls.[40]

It is argued that the time that police may waste in patrol under the professional policing model can be used more effectively if the police are involved in problem-solving approaches. For example, give police daily assessments of specific problems in their patrol areas and let them work on those problems. As one authority noted, "Many of the citywide crime problems would appear more manageable if officers could deal with them at the neighborhood level."[41]

Community-oriented policing is based on the concept that officers should become less anonymous and more integrated into the communities they patrol. Returning to foot patrol or using horses or bicycles assists officers in this effort. Police become more visible and more accountable to the public, and they are encouraged to view citizens as partners in crime prevention. Furthermore, more decision making at the patrol level means that those who are best informed of the problems in the community are the ones making important policing decisions.

Criminologist Gary W. Cordner has analyzed community-oriented policing and concluded, "In less than two decades, community policing has evolved from a few small foot patrol studies to the preeminent reform agenda of modern policing. . . . [It has become] the dominant strategy of policing."[42]

The measure of Cordner's statement is underscored by the support given to community-oriented policing at the national level, especially by President Bill Clinton's administration. In early 1994, the administration announced the "down payment" on its campaign promise to put 100,000 more police on the street by offering federal grants for hiring police. Later that year Congress enacted a new crime bill that contained a provision for the 100,000 promised officers.[43]

Despite opposition by Republicans to President Clinton's Community-Oriented Policing Services (COPS) program, by fall 1998 money had been appropriated for over two-thirds of the promised 100,000 additional officers, and the Clinton administration was proclaiming that the program was a success. However, the U.S. Department of Justice's inspector general issued a report that contained sharp criticism of the program. The report questioned whether the funds were being used for the intended purpose (putting more officers on the streets and assigning them to community-oriented policing tasks). The auditors reported insufficient controls over how the grants were allocated and spent, concluding that the COPS office "accepts virtually any activity related to law enforcement as community policing." This created confusion concerning the meaning of community-oriented policing. The report raised doubt that the goal of adding 100,000 officers would be met because some agencies were using the grant money to fund current rather than new officers.[44]

President George W. Bush requested that funding for COPS be eliminated from the 2003 budget, but that did not occur. Restoring adequate funding to the COPS program was an issue promoted by Senator John Kerry in the 2004 presidential election, and in September 2004 the Senate Appropriations Committee unanimously passed its appropriations act, providing $756 million for the COPS program in 2005. That was roughly $714 million more than President Bush had proposed and $100 million more than the House had proposed. In the final budget, however, Democrats were unable to rescue the COPS program. The 2005 budget slashed funds for the COPS program, and the president's proposed budget for 2006 would virtually eliminate this federal program.[45]

Chapter Wrap-Up

Earlier chapters introduced the subject of social control and explored the differences between informal and formal methods of control. This chapter illustrated those differences, with reference to the need for a formal police system. The history of informal and formal policing methods in England and the United States was examined. Many factors contributed to the need for formal policing, but in both countries the increasing complexity that resulted when society became industrialized was a crucial factor. The rising levels of criminal activity, public unrest, and riots that accompanied industrialization demonstrated the inability of informal methods of policing to provide adequate protection.

The formal system of policing that has evolved in the United States, a decentralized system having local, state, and federal levels, results in overlaps and gaps among levels. It also permits states and localities to experiment with methods that might be effective in light of the problems that distinguish their policing needs from those of the federal government. The various levels of policing cooperate in some functions, such as investigation and training. Numerous law enforcement agencies exist at the federal level, and they are available to assist states and local agencies as well. These federal agencies have undergone dramatic changes in recent years, especially since the 9/11/01 terrorist attacks. The changes, such as the development of two new agencies, the Department of Homeland Security and the Transportation Security Administration, have not been without controversy; nor has the legislation that created and empowered these agencies.

Formal, public policing systems have been the object of criticism for a long time; some citizens have reacted by employing private police or by having security devices installed in their homes or businesses. Conflict between public and private policing developed and continues, although there is some evidence of cooperation between the two. Some states have established minimum requirements for licensing private security firms.

The type of police organization and administration may have a significant effect on policing. The chapter discusses early reform efforts in police organization and administration and then focuses on differentiating the two major models of policing: the professional model and community-oriented policing. The choice of model affects the way people perform their jobs; thus, this chapter provides a framework in which to examine the nature and functioning of policing, the focus of Chapter 4.

Key Terms

Bow Street Runners (p. 54)
constable (p. 51)
Department of Homeland Security (DHS) (p. 63)
frankpledge system (p. 51)
hundred (p. 51)
INTERPOL (p. 66)
Law Enforcement Assistance Administration (LEAA) (p. 70)

Law Enforcement Education Program (LEEP) (p. 70)
magistrate (p. 54)
marshal (p. 57)
Molly Maguires (p. 59)
police (p. 51)
posse (p. 55)
private security forces (p. 66)

sheriff (p. 51)
shires (p. 51)
tithing (p. 51)
Transportation Security Administration (TSA) (p. 63)
vigilantism (p. 55)
watch system (p. 51)

Apply It

1. Why do we have a formal system of policing?
2. Explain the meaning of the following to the development of modern policing: Bow Street Runners; Peelers, or Bobbies; posse; and Molly Maguires.
3. Define vigilantism and discuss its advantages and disadvantages with regard to air travel today.
4. Compare local, state, and federal police systems. What are the advantages and disadvantages of decentralized policing?
5. What are some of the unique problems of rural law enforcement?
6. What is the role of the county sheriff in most jurisdictions?
7. What is the function of U.S. marshals?
8. Discuss the strengths and weaknesses of the FBI and comment on the reorganization and reputation of this agency since the 9/11/01 terrorist attacks. What do you think should be the role of the FBI with regard to counterterrorism efforts?

9. What impact have illegal drugs had on rural and county policing in recent years?
10. Discuss two of the recent pieces of federal legislation designed to combat terrorism.
11. Describe the Department of Homeland Security and the Transportation Security Administration.
12. What is the role of private police agencies? Evaluate.
13. How would you describe the administration of early police systems in the United States?
14. Evaluate the traditional, authoritarian model of organizational structure of police departments.
15. Trace the development of the professional model of policing.
16. Describe and analyze the concept of community-oriented policing.

Endnotes

1. Herman Goldstein, *Policing in a Free Society* (Cambridge, Mass.: Ballinger, 1977), p. 1.
2. Jonathan Rubinstein, *City Police* (New York: Ballantine Books, 1973), p. 5.
3. David H. Bayley, "Police: History," in *Encyclopedia of Crime and Justice,* vol. 3, ed. Sanford H. Kadish (New York: Free Press, 1983), pp. 1122–1123.

4. Louis B. Schwartz and Stephen R. Goldstein, *Law Enforcement Handbook for Police* (St. Paul, Minn.: West, 1970), p. 34.

5. "Scotland Yard Confounded by Crisis of Confidence," *USA Today* (25 August 1999), p. 8.

6. "10 Years after Their Son Was Killed, Blair's Message to the Lawrences: Still Too Much Racism," *Evening Standard* (London) (22 April 2003).

7. "Bobbies Face .350m Beating," *Western Daily Press* (21 October 2004), p. 14; "Police 'Strike' Is Over," *Daily Star* (4 November 2004), p. 19; "Sweeney Cops Join Growing Gun Crisis," *The Sun* (3 November 2004).

8. Bayley, "Police: History," p. 1124.

9. Ibid.

10. "As Drug Use Drops in Big Cities, Small Towns Confront Upsurge," *New York Times* (11 February 2002), p. 1.

11. Robert Borkenstein, "Police: State Police," in *Encyclopedia of Crime and Justice,* vol. 3, ed. Kadish, p. 1133.

12. "F.B.I. Reports More Dismissals," *New York Times* (8 August 1999), p. 18.

13. "Senators Criticize F.B.I. for Its Security Failures," *New York Times* (19 July 2001), p. 16.

14. "Focus of F.B.I. Is Seen Shifting to Terrorism," *New York Times* (21 October 2001), p. 1B.

15. "F.B.I. Is Retailoring to Meet New Threats but Stretched Thin, Reports Say," *New York Times* (19 June 2003), p. 15.

16. *The 9/11 Commission Report: Final Report of the National Commission on Terrorist Attacks upon the United States,* Authorized Edition (New York: W.W. Norton & Company, 2004), p. 358.

17. "F.B.I. Is Assailed for Its Handling of Terror Risks," *New York Times* (14 April 2004), p. 1.

18. The USA Patriot Act is Public Law 107–56 (2005).

19. Humanitarian Law Project v. Ashcroft, 2004 U.S. Dist. LEXIS 926, *reprinted as amended,* 309 F.Supp. 2d 1185 (C.D. Cal. 2004). The section of the USA Patriot Act in question was U.S. Code, Title 18, Sections 2339A and 2239B (2005).

20. The Homeland Security Act of 2002 is codified as Public Law 107–296 (2005).

21. Enhanced Border and Visa Entry Reform Act of 2002, U.S. Code, Title 8, Section 7101 *et seq.* (2005).

22. Public Health Security and Bioterrorism Response Act of 2002, Public Law 107–188 (2005).

23. "Law Enforcement Not Confident on Terrorism, Survey Shows," *Criminal Justice Newsletter* (1 August 2003), p. 4.

24. "Kerik Withdraws As Bush's Nominee for Security Post," *New York Times* (11 December 2004), Late edition, p. 1.

25. "TSA Meets Deadline; Deploys More Than 44,000 Feds to Airports," *Federal Human Resources Week* 9, no. 32 (5 December 2002): 1.

26. "Congress Retains Screener Cap in New Security Budget," *Airport Security Report* 11, no. 21 (20 October 2004).

27. "Anarchy, Amnesty, and the Demise of INS," *New York Law Journal* (17 March 2003).

28. Michael Fooner, "INTERPOL," in *Encyclopedia of Crime and Justice,* vol. 3, ed. Kadish, p. 912.

29. James S. Kakalik and Sorrel Wildhorn, *The Private Police: Security and Danger* (New York: Crane Russak, 1977), p. 68.

30. Albert J. Reiss Jr., *Private Employment of Public Police* (Washington, D.C.: U.S. Department of Justice, December 1988), pp. 2–3.

31. William C. Cunningham and Todd H. Taylor, "Ten Years of Growth in Law Enforcement," *Police Chief* 1 (June 1983): 32.

32. William C. Cunningham et al., *Private Security: Patterns and Trends* (Washington, D.C.: National Institute of Justice, August 1991), p. 4.

33. "Private Security Guards: Homeland Defense's Weak Link," *USA Today* (23 January 2003), p. 23.

34. "Leader in Security at Airports Has a Long History of Lapses," *New York Times* (9 November 2001), p. 1.

35. The basis for this discussion is the article by Herman Goldstein, "Police Administration," in *Encyclopedia of Crime and Justice,* vol. 3, ed. Kadish, pp. 1125–1131.

36. Ibid., p. 1126.

37. The President's Commission on Law Enforcement and Administration of Justice, Task Force on the Police, *Task Force Report: The Police* (Washington, D.C.: U.S. Government Printing Office, 1967), p. 44.

38. United States Commission on Civil Rights, *Who Is Guarding the Guardians? A Report on Police Practices* (Washington, D.C.: U.S. Government Printing Office, 1981), p. 6.

39. Herman Goldstein, *Problem-Oriented Policing* (New York: McGraw-Hill, 1990), p. 81 (n. 6).

40. Ibid., p. 151.

41. David A. Kessler, "Integrating Calls for Service with Community- and Problem-Oriented Policing: A Case Study," *Crime and Delinquency* 39 (October 1993): 506.

42. Gary W. Cordner, "Community Policing: Elements and Effects," in *Critical Issues in Policing: Contemporary Readings,* 5th ed., ed. Roger G. Dunham and Geoffrey P. Alpert (Long Grove, Ill.: Waveland Press, 2005), pp. 401–418; quotation is on p. 401.

43. Violent Crime Control and Law Enforcement Act of 1994, Public Law 103-322 (13 September 1994).

44. "Audit Cites Many Problems in Monitoring of COPS Grants," *Criminal Justice Newsletter* 29 (15 December 1998): 3–4; "COPS Grant Progress Overstated, Justice Department Auditor Says," *Criminal Justice Newsletter* 30 (16 March 1999): 4.

45. "Local Government's Priorities Are Tested in FY 2004 Appropriations," *Nation's Cities Weekly* 26, no. 37 (15 September 2003): 1; "Senate Public Safety Appropriations A Mixed Bag for Cities," *Nation's Cities Weekly* 27, no. 39 (27 September 2004), p. 3; "Congress Cut Back the Bush . . ." *The Washington Post* (7 December 2004), p. 23; "Cuts To Hit L.A. Hard; COPS, Women's Program's Slashed," *Daily News of Los Angeles* (8 February 2005), p. 1N.

Policing in a Modern Society

4

Police in the United States are expected to prevent crime, apprehend and arrest criminals, enforce traffic ordinances and laws, maintain order in domestic and other kinds of disputes, control or prevent disturbances, and perform numerous miscellaneous services. Police must perform these functions in the context of political, legal, and societal expectations, which may be unrealistic and conflicting.

Some of the functions assigned to police are shared by other persons or agencies, which often results in conflict concerning police roles. But police are given greater discretion and power in performing their tasks than are other agencies. Why? The possibility that disorder, or even violence, will occur convinces us that the police should handle the situation. Therefore, we are willing to grant police the power to act when intervention is necessary.

This chapter focuses on what police do in a modern society, but those functions should be examined in the context of the extensive discretion police have in performing their jobs. The importance of discretion and the possibility of its abuse require that high standards be maintained by those who occupy policing roles. The chapter's discussion of discretion is thus preceded by a look at preparing for policing.

The chapter's discussion of police functions focuses first on order maintenance and community service before devoting substantial coverage to law enforcement, which begins with an overview of constitutional issues. Particular attention is given to the USA Patriot Act and its potential for limiting civil rights and liberties in an attempt to counter terrorist acts.

The specifics of law enforcement begin with an analysis of traffic stops and other attempts to enforce traffic ordinances. The investigatory stop by police is examined in terms of racial profiling and issues regarding stop and frisk. The arrest, search, and seizure of suspects is examined by a look at warrants and the meaning of probable cause, along with a summary of the laws regarding home, automobile, and person searches. The final two sections cover the interrogation and investigation of suspects.

LEARNING
OBJECTIVES

After reading this chapter, you should be able to do the following:

- **Describe the importance of police recruitment and selection**
- **Discuss the role of higher education in policing**
- **Analyze the importance of police training**
- **Explain the meaning of discretion in policing**
- **List the three major areas of police functions and explain each**
- **Present an overview of the U.S. constitutional provisions that govern policing**
- **Discuss the implications of the USA Patriot Act**
- **Discuss recent U.S. Supreme Court decisions regarding traffic stops and searches**
- **Explain the difference between an investigatory stop and an arrest**
- **Assess the meaning and importance of racial profiling**
- **Discuss the meaning of probable cause and explain the purpose of requiring a warrant for most searches**
- **Explain what police can and cannot do in searching a home, an automobile, and a person**
- **Compare the police role of interrogation with that of investigation**
- **Explain and evaluate the *Miranda* rule and its exceptions**

4-1   Preparing for Policing

The importance of policing demands that careful attention be given to the recruitment and selection, as well as the training, of persons who will become police officers. Part of the preparation involves education. Attention is given in this section to these areas.

4-1a   Recruitment and Selection

One difficulty in the recruitment and selection of police is that desirable qualities and characteristics are usually not defined in acceptable and measurable terms. Perhaps the problem is that in the past the focus was on the recruits and their qualities, the assumption being that, if different types of people were attracted to policing, the profession would improve. Some researchers reported that certain types, for example, authoritarian and cynical people, are attracted to policing. Others argued that policing *creates* these personalities.[1]

Successful recruitment of police officers requires more research into the characteristics most highly associated with effective policing. Good policing requires many qualities, including intelligence and the ability to think independently, to perform different roles and functions, to comprehend and accept other cultures and subcultures, and to understand the importance of freedom and the dangers of abusing authority.

It is crucial for police departments to recruit people who have high moral and ethical standards and who have not been engaged in previous infractions with the law. Chapter 5 discusses corruption in policing; avoiding that problem requires recruiting persons who will not succumb to the temptations facing law enforcement officers. This is difficult to do, however, as police officials throughout the country have discovered. Officers are recruited from a generation of young people who have grown up in a culture in which it may be considered acceptable to engage in some law violations, such as using illegal drugs. Trying to recruit persons who have never used drugs may be an impossible task, especially in some of the larger cities. Of course, recruiting ethical candidates for jobs is important in most jobs, but, as one authority on police ethics notes, it is particularly crucial in policing. The cover page of his text notes as follows: "Few occupations make as significant moral demands on their practitioners as policing. Yet no occupation has been as poorly prepared for the moral demands laid on it."[2]

It is also important to give police recruits an understanding of the context in which policing occurs, as well as the nature of the job. This information might alleviate the stress caused by recruits' unrealistic expectations.

The success of efforts to recruit persons with high moral and ethical standards into policing and to encourage them to maintain those standards may be analyzed in terms of the subsequent behavior of recruits. In that respect, the New York City Police Department is often the focus of attention. For example, a major investigation into policing in that city occurred upon the arrest of four police after a brutal attack on Abner Louima, a Haitian immigrant at a Brooklyn station house on 9 August 1997. In testimony before the New York City Council, Frank Serpico, a former New York City police officer, stated, "We must create an atmosphere where the crooked cop fears the honest cop, and not the other way around." Serpico testified against other officers in the early 1970s, turning in those who engaged in corrupt or other forms of illegal behavior. He almost lost his life in his fight against the problems of the department, and his story became a best-selling book and movie, *Serpico*.[3]

Recruiting well-qualified candidates for policing has become a serious problem in some areas, which have experienced a decline in the number of persons taking the qualifying exams for officers. In 2002, the New York City Police Department (NYPD) attempted another approach to recruitment: it recruited at Ivy League schools, such as Harvard, Yale, and Columbia. At the recruitment effort at Columbia in March 2002, interest by students was slight. Only 35 students signed up to take the qualifying exams, and some students, when asked about becoming police officers said, "Absolutely not" or "Never." The New York City police chief said that he knew it would be difficult to recruit candidates for policing from Ivy League schools. After all, the annual starting salary of a New York City police officer at that time ($31,305) was less than the cost of one year of schooling at Columbia. Despite that issue, the NYPD was attempting to recruit bright students from diversified backgrounds. The department was also recruiting at military bases, churches in minority neighborhoods, and train stations.[4]

In 2001, the NYPD faced another problem in recruiting. In addition to the increased fear potential recruits might face after the 9/11/01 terrorist attacks, the demands on NYPD officers were such that, by the end of the fiscal year 2002, many of them had doubled their income through overtime pay, creating an incentive to retire while their salaries reflected those increases. Police with 20 years in the NYPD may retire at one-half the pay of their last 12 months of service.[5] Heavy retirements, which had already risen significantly over the previous year, made recruitment difficult but increased the problems of adjustment on the police force. As one police chief stated, "When there is a sudden intrusion of new rookies, they overwhelm the organization. . . . They are able to impose their values on the organization. They can be resistant to positive mentoring."[6]

Another aspect of recruiting police officers is that some young people who are well qualified to enter other professions have become law enforcement officers. The NYPD recruited one of these young people: Adam Kasanof, who scored 1410 on the SAT and attended Columbia University to study Latin but subsequently became a police officer. Although the department does not keep records on where its officers attended college, the estimate is that a few dozen attended elite universities. A Cornell graduate who became a police officer a few years after graduation said that many people think he is wasting his time, but he does not feel that way. According to Sgt. Andrew Hatki, "I feel like I'm doing what I want to do."[7]

It is possible, however, for an applicant to be "too smart" to be selected for policing. In the fall 1996, Robert Jordan, 46, wished to be interviewed for a police job with the New London (Connecticut) Police Department. The city manager told him he would not be interviewed because "he didn't fit the profile." Jordan suspected age discrimination and filed a complaint with the Commission on Human Rights and Opportunities. The city's response was that Jordan was not interviewed because he scored a 33 on the qualifying test and that was too high! In order to prevent significant turnover from officers who become bored, the city would not interview anyone who scored over 27 on the test. Jordan filed a civil rights action in the federal district court, which dismissed his complaint. On appeal, the lower court decision was upheld, stating that the city's use of an "upper cut" did not violate the equal protection clause of the U.S. Constitution.[8]

The amount, if any, of higher education that should be required of police officers continues to be debated, and one of the arguments against requiring college courses is that officers will become bored and either become ineffective or resign, creating high turnover. Others argue that officers should have a broad educational background; thus, some departments require higher education for officers. The importance of educating our law enforcement officers was underscored by a retired 25-year veteran of policing, who, with regard to recruiting more officers, stated in 2003, "We don't need numbers, we need more highly educated officers, who understand the art of working with people to solve issues before they become problems. We need supervisors and executives who understand community-based problem-solving tactics and the value of formal education."[9]

If the police are recruited from the educated (or officers are supported to obtain higher education), it is imperative that the education be of high quality. The Massachusetts Board of Education announced in spring 2003 that it would close some of the units that had been providing criminal justice education for police in that state, which was facing a $3 billion deficit. Under the Massachusetts Quinn Bill, cities and towns pay one-half of the cost of higher education expenses for police, while the state pays the other half. Police salaries are increased with each level of higher education obtained (10 percent for an associate degree, 20 percent for a bachelor's degree, and 25 percent for a master's degree; pension costs also increase), and some taxpayers do not believe the expenditure is worth the cost, about $100 million annually. The state proposed to cut some of the so-called cop shops that "specialize in quickie criminal justice diplomas." In 2004, the Quinn bill was still in effect but had been overhauled by the Board of Education, which instituted new and stricter testing and curriculum standards, "and officers can no longer receive credit for 'life experience' and required police academy training." Additional requirements have been placed on the colleges that offer police education, which are now required to hire more professors with advanced degrees in criminal justice or related fields. Perhaps as a result of the Quinn bill (and as a result of overtime pay), police in Boston, Massachusetts, are among the highest paid law enforcement officers in the country.[10]

4-1b   Education

Most would agree that education is important for police officers, but there is disagreement over the amount and type of education that should be required. The dispute over whether any college education should be mandated is significant. As far back as 1917, a college education for police received significant attention from August Vollmer, when he recruited part-time police officers from students at the University of California. Despite his emphasis on the importance of higher education and his reputation as an outstanding police administrator, Vollmer did not succeed in convincing many police departments to follow his lead. During the Great Depression, when jobs were scarce, college-educated men were recruited by police departments, but that practice ceased with the end of the Depression.

In 1967, when the average police officer had only slightly more than a high school diploma, the President's Commission recommended that the "ultimate aim of all police departments should be that personnel with general enforcement powers have baccalaureate degrees."[11] The federal government provided financial incentives and support for the development of programs for higher education of police officers.

Professions 4-1

Police Personnel and Pay: Local Departments

Following is information published in 2003 by the Bureau of Justice Statistics concerning local police departments higher education requirements for officers.

Figure 1

Local police officers in departments with a college education requirement for new recruits, 1990 and 2000

*Nondegree requirements only.

Source: Bureau of Justice Statistics, *Local Police Departments, 2000* (Washington, D.C.: U.S. Department of Justice, January 2003), p. 6.

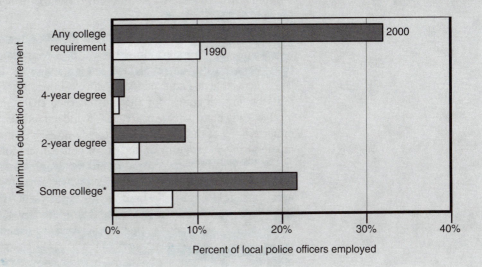

As noted in Chapter 3 one of the provisions of the 1994 crime control bill was to put more police on the streets. The money provided by Congress for community-oriented policing, the COPS program, was used in some jurisdictions for enhanced training and education of police. The 1994 statute provided funds for the development in six states (Maryland, North Carolina, Oregon, Nevada, Arkansas, and South Carolina) of programs that were modeled after the military's Reserve Officers Training Corps (ROTC). For college graduates who agreed to serve four years in policing, the program reimbursed up to $30,000 in educational costs. But, also as noted in Chapter 3, the Bush administration was not supportive of the COPS program, and funding cuts essentially gutted the COPS program.

There has been some improvement in the college education of police recruits, with 9 percent of police officers in 2002 (the latest data available) being employed by departments that require some type of college education. This compares with 3 percent in 1990. But as Professions 4-1 notes, only a small percentage required a college degree.

Those who do not favor college education for police cite several reasons. First, there is concern that raising educational requirements might discriminate against minority applicants. Second, there is concern that the applicant pool may be too small. Third, there is concern that some police unions are opposed to higher educational requirements.[12] Finally, many of the criminal justice programs that have provided police education have come under attack. Critics argue that there is too much emphasis on technical skills at the expense of a broad educational background.[13]

Others cite the advantages of higher education for police. For example, in 1989 the Police Executive Research Forum (PERF) released a study of police education in which it noted the perceived advantages and disadvantages of having police officers with higher education. The authors concluded that, overall, college-educated officers were more responsible and made better decisions than their less educated counterparts. As such, officers with some college education were not only more effective in performing their jobs but also more efficient in that costs associated with lost personnel time were lower.[14]

Finally, the authors of an analysis of higher education and policing concluded the following:

> We find that higher education has two important roles to play. One is to carry education beyond the classroom in ways that encourage broad reform. The other is to help make improvements in police training and education in ways that, at least will produce higher levels of civility, and might even encourage a more humanistic police professionalism.[15]

4-1c Training

In its 1967 report, the Task Force on Police of the President's Commission on Law Enforcement and Administration of Justice emphasized the importance of adequate police training, noting that the problem was particularly acute in small police departments. Many larger departments had expanded police training, but the task force concluded that "current training programs, for the most part, prepare an officer to perform police work mechanically but do not prepare him to understand his community, the police role, or the imperfections of the criminal justice system." Few of the programs reviewed by the commission provided training on the use of police discretion.[16]

The President's Commission recommended that police training include instruction on "subjects that prepare recruits to exercise discretion properly and to understand the community, the role of the police, and what the criminal justice system can and cannot do." The commission recommended "an absolute minimum of 400 hours of classroom work spread over a four-to-six month period so that it can be combined with carefully selected and supervised field training." In-service training at least once a year, along with incentives for officers to continue their education, should be provided.[17] In 1973, the National Advisory Commission on Criminal Justice Standards and Goals put police training into perspective with some harsh comments: "Perhaps no other profession has such lax standards or is allowed to operate without firm controls and without licensing."[18]

In 1981, the U.S. Commission on Civil Rights emphasized the need for formal police training and concluded that most of the examined programs "do not give sufficient priority to on-the-job field training, programs in human relations, and preparation for the social service function of police officers, including intervening in family-related disturbances." The commission found that in many jurisdictions even firearms training was inadequate and "subject to the ambiguities found in statutes and departmental policies." Because of this ambiguity, the commission concluded that it is imperative that police training expose recruits to situations in which the use of firearms might or might not be appropriate. Alternatives to deadly force should also be demonstrated. Finally, the Civil Rights Commission recommended that police receive training in the social services they are expected to perform.[19]

Basic police training includes many areas of expertise, ranging from firing weapons to understanding the ordinances and laws that govern a particular jurisdiction. Much of the training is standard and cannot be detailed here, but it is important to go beyond the traditional, standard training. Let's consider just a few examples. A 2003 publication of a five-year study of drug-related deaths of suspects in police custody concluded that approximately one-third of those deaths could have been prevented had police been adequately trained for significant intervention. But prevention requires more than "just an officer standing outside [the cell] and seeing if someone is sleeping; it requires a more active process of rousing and checking." The study found that jailers and medical examiners need more training in recognizing drug problems. Police and correctional officers must be constantly vigilant to prevent cell deaths.[20]

Another area in which police need special training is patrolling in and around schools. With the increase in violence on school grounds and inside school buildings, security has become increasingly important. In Troy, Michigan, a special force of police officers on bicycles patrol school grounds as well as parks and special events within the city. These officers must be specially trained. They receive 40 hours of classroom and practical training, which includes instruction on how to repair and maintain a bicycle. They must be in excellent physical condition, for, as one of these special officers said, "You've got to be able to pedal quick and under control."[21]

Despite the special training needed for policing in and around schools, a 2001 poll of school resource officers revealed that they were not required to have any special training beyond that required of all police officers. The executive director of the National Association of School Resource Officers stated as follows: "Because policing a school is so tremendously different than policing the street, the need for training is very [important]. . . . Administrators need to commit to making sure officers are specially trained."[22]

Another important area of police training is in the skills needed to dissect crime scenes for relevant evidence, especially when the evidence is buried. For example, a course entitled Skeletal Remains in Homicide Investigations, initiated by one sheriff's department in 1994 to train its own officers, now trains other local law enforcement agents as well as FBI agents in the craft of sifting through graves to find evidence. The work is described by one FBI agent as "bringing archaeology to a forensic site. The key is slow and mechanical digging and then tagging all the evidence." The importance of the training was emphasized by one detective. "Here, you can make a mistake. . . . In the field, a mistake could lose you a whole case if it's a homicide."[23]

It is, of course, expensive to train law enforcement officers, and most departments do not have the resources to train their officers in all areas. Some departments take advantage of the courses at other local departments, as noted in the previous paragraph, whereas others send their officers to the FBI academy for advanced or specialized training. To illustrate, according to a news release on 4 June 2003, an officer in Owasso, a small town near Tulsa, Oklahoma, received education and certification in "how to properly clean-up a clandestine meth lab site" by attending the Drug Enforcement Administration (DEA) course at the DEA's training academy. The police officers in Owasso had seized about eight suspected labs in the six months prior to the news release.[24]

In addition to helping train police in other departments, police may help other professions train to assist law enforcement in preventing crimes, such as terrorism. In Indiana, for example, the state police began a program in June 2003 to train truckers to assist law enforcement in spotting national security and highway safety threats on the state's roads. The project is financed by a federal grant.[25]

Increased training for law enforcement officers, along with additional equipment and other resources, is expensive, and some local departments do not have the funds to finance these ventures. In addition to grants provided by the federal government, some local law enforcement agencies take advantage of the offerings of local colleges and universities. The East Haven, Connecticut, Police Department, for example, saved about $80,000 in 2003 by taking advantage of the reduced rates provided by the state's community college system. Police and administrators were provided training and permitted to purchase computers and other equipment at the college's bulk rate price. At the successful completion of the training, the officers received college credit and certificates.[26]

The importance of adequate police training was emphasized by a 1989 U.S. Supreme Court decision, *City of Canton, Ohio* v. *Harris,* in which the Court held that inadequate police training may result in civil liability for the municipality under which the police department operates. The Supreme Court placed limitations, stating that liability may exist "only where the failure to train amounts to deliberate indifference to the rights of persons with whom the police come into contact."[27] The case is discussed in Spotlight 4-1. Examples of civil liability for negligent hiring are discussed in Chapter 5.

Other forms of **negligence,** in addition to negligence in training, may lead to police liability. These include negligence in hiring, assignment, supervision, direction, entrustment, and investigation or discipline.

▶ **Negligence** In law, an act that a reasonable person would not do, or would not fail to do under similar circumstances. Negligence does not require a criminal intent.

Spotlight 4-1   **The Importance of Adequate Police Training: The U.S. Supreme Court Speaks**

[In 1989, the U.S. Supreme Court emphasized the importance of police training. Portions of the case *City of Canton, Ohio* v. *Harris* explain.]

In this case, we are asked to determine if a municipality can ever be liable . . . for constitutional violations resulting from its failure to train municipal employees. We hold that, under certain circumstances, such liability is permitted. . . .

In April 1978, respondent Geraldine Harris was arrested by officers of the Canton Police Department. Harris was brought to the police station in a patrol wagon.

When she arrived at the station, Harris was found sitting on the floor of the wagon. She was asked if she needed medical attention, and responded with an incoherent remark. After she was brought inside the station for processing, Mrs. Harris slumped to the floor on two occasions. Eventually, the police officers left Mrs. Harris lying on the floor to prevent her from falling again. No medical attention was ever summoned for Mrs. Harris. After about an hour, Mrs. Harris was released from custody, and taken by an ambulance (provided by her family) to a nearby hospital. There, Mrs. Harris was diagnosed as suffering from several emotional ailments; she was hospitalized for one week, and received subsequent outpatient treatment for an additional year.

Some time later, Mrs. Harris commenced this action alleging many state law and constitutional claims against the city of Canton and its officials. Among these claims was one seeking to hold the city liable . . . for its violation of Mrs. Harris' right, under

the Due Process Clause of the Fourteenth Amendment, to receive necessary medical attention while in police custody. . . .

We hold today that the inadequacy of police training may serve as the basis for liability only where the failure to train amounts to deliberate indifference to the rights of persons with whom the police come into contact. . . . Only where a municipality's failure to train its employees in a relevant respect evidences a "deliberate indifference" to the rights of its inhabitants can such a shortcoming be properly thought of as a city "policy or custom" that is actionable. . . .

Moreover, for liability to attach in this circumstance the identified deficiency in a city's training program must be closely related to the ultimate injury. Thus in the case at hand, respondent must still prove that the deficiency in training actually caused the police officers' indifference to her medical needs. Would the injury have been avoided had the employee been trained under a program that was not deficient in the identified respect? Predicting how a hypothetically well-trained officer would have acted under the circumstances may not be an easy task for the factfinder, particularly since matters of judgment may be involved, and since officers who are well-trained are not free from error and perhaps might react very much like the untrained officer in similar circumstances. But judge and jury, doing their respective jobs, will be adequate to the task.

Source: City of Canton, Ohio v. Harris, 489 U.S. 378 (1989), footnotes and citations omitted.

4-2 Police Discretion

Chapter 1 includes a discussion of discretion and notes that wide discretion exists in criminal justice systems. That discretion is extreme and critical in policing. Police have wide discretion in determining whether to begin the formal processing of criminal justice systems. When they see a person who appears to be violating the law, police may refuse to acknowledge that action. Or they may investigate the situation and decide that they do not have sufficient reason to think a crime has been committed. They might also decide that a crime has been committed but not by the suspect, or that the suspect may have committed the crime but for some reason should not be arrested.

How the officer exercises discretion is determined by a number of factors. Consider this hypothetical scenario: A police officer, while out on patrol at midnight on a Friday night, observed a car weaving down the highway, going 5 miles over the speed limit. The officer turned on the car siren and lights and directed the driver to stop. After checking the operator's driver's license, the officer inquired where the person was going and why she was speeding. The driver replied that she did not realize she was speeding but that she was in a hurry to get home because a contact lens was causing pain. Something apparently had flown into her eye and blurred her vision temporarily. She considered it unsafe to stop by the side of a busy highway. She was trying to get to her home only a mile away.

When asked where she had been, the driver replied that she was an *A* student in a criminal justice program and had been at a friend's house, studying, since the library closed at 11 P.M. When asked whether she had been drinking, the driver replied that she had drunk one beer. The driver answered all questions politely and nondefensively.

What would you do if you were the police officer? Would you ticket the driver for speeding? Would you believe her response about the contact lens? Would you believe what she told you about drinking only one beer? Would it make any difference in your decision if you had stopped her at 3 A.M. rather than at midnight? You could, of course, give the driver a verbal warning and let her go. You could give her a speeding ticket. If you had sufficient reason to think that she had been drinking to the point that she was legally drunk, you could ask her to get out of the car and perform some simple tests. Or you might arrest her and take her to the police station to begin official processing through the criminal justice system.

Now, think about the results of your decision. If the driver is telling the truth and you decide to arrest her, what have you accomplished by your action? Is it not possible that the negative effect of the arrest and subsequent experiences she has in the criminal justice system will outweigh any benefit that society will get from this arrest? On the other hand, if she has been drinking too much, is it not possible that an arrest will cause her to think before she gets into a car again after drinking? Or will it have no effect on her behavior? What about the behavior of her friends, who will certainly hear about your actions?

Perhaps by now you have decided what action you would take. Let's add some factors to the scenario. Suppose that, when you begin to talk to the driver, she curses you and tells you to mind your own business. Would this affect your decision to write a speeding ticket or give her roadside tests for intoxication?

Police must make such decisions as these daily. Selective enforcement of laws is necessary because our system cannot process all cases of law violations, even if we choose to do so. Police discretion is important because police are the primary persons responsible for the initial entry of someone into the criminal justice system. The necessity to exercise discretion without adequate guidelines puts tremendous pressure on police.

In recent years attention has been given to the need to prepare police for the appropriate use of discretion. The need for guidelines is recognized, although there is no agreement on what those guidelines should be or which agency should formulate them. Legislatures enact statutes for general guidance and delegate to police departments, as administrative agencies, the power to develop more specific rules. Courts have the responsibility for interpreting the guidelines, statutes, and policies in terms of state and federal constitutions.

Numerous studies have been made of police discretion, with most of them emphasizing that, in some circumstances, discretion is exercised on the basis of extralegal rather than legal factors. For example, one study of the reasons police exercise their discretion to report rather than to ignore alleged child abuse found that the most significant reason to report the behavior was the officer's definition of the act as serious, and the definition was "*not out of line with societal standards and definitions concerning child abuse.*" The study also found that race was a factor in some cases, with white families more likely than African American families to be reported. These findings on race differ from some others that show police taking action more frequently against African Americans than against whites. It is important to note that in this study the race of the victim and that of the alleged suspect were the same. It is possible, concluded the authors, that police are more willing to accept violence among African American families than among whites.[28]

4-3 Police Functions

Although in the popular image police may spend most of their time apprehending and arresting criminals, these functions constitute a very small, though significant, part of the daily lives of police officers. Police also perform a variety of functions not directly related to law enforcement. These functions have been categorized as *order maintenance* and *community service*, which we will discuss prior to our analysis of law enforcement.

There appears to be agreement that law enforcement, order maintenance, and community service are the three basic areas of police functions, but there is no agreement on whether they *should* be. Nor is there agreement on how police time and resources should be allocated among the three areas. It is clear, however, that the areas are not discrete; there is considerable overlap. Attention to an order maintenance problem or provision of a particular service may prevent a situation from escalating into criminal behavior. Engaging in order maintenance functions and services may alert the police to criminal law violations. Finally, police are expected to prevent crime, and that may occur while they are performing any of their three main functions.

Before we analyze police functions in more detail, it is important to emphasize that all involve an enormous amount of paperwork, which consumes considerable police time, a fact that is rarely mentioned in discussions on policing. Perhaps this oversight is typical of other professions, and those who enter have no prior concept of the incredible detail expected of them in filing reports. With police, however, expectations are particularly important because, if the paperwork is not done properly, cases may be dropped or evidence may be excluded. The defendant may be acquitted or civil actions may be brought against the police. Reports must be filed immediately to preserve accuracy, and police rarely have access to sufficient staff assistance in writing and filing their reports. Thus, paperwork is a tedious and time-consuming, but very important, police function.

4-3a   Order Maintenance

Police are charged with maintaining order, particularly in areas in which crime might erupt. James Q. Wilson, a noted authority on the subject, defined order as the absence of disorder, by which he meant behavior that tends to disrupt the peace and tranquility of the public or that involves serious face-to-face conflict between two or more persons. Wilson believed that the key to order maintenance is the management of conflict situations to bring about consensual resolution. In his view, order maintenance is the primary police function, and it is important because police encounter more problems in this area than in community service or law enforcement (with the exception of traffic violations). According to Wilson, the maintenance of order, "more than the problem of law enforcement, is central to the patrolman's role for several reasons."[29]

First, many police departments receive more calls for help in order maintenance than in law enforcement. Some of these complaints result in arrests, but most do not. Police may be called to quiet down noisy neighbors or to intervene in disputes between friends and associates who cannot solve their differences and who appear to be on the brink of fighting. Public drunks wandering around the city alarm some people, who call the police to handle the situation. Some of these activities violate local ordinances, but many of the situations involve activities that are not criminal, although they may be obnoxious to those who call the police.

Order maintenance is an important police function for a second reason. Maintaining order may subject the police and others to physical danger. A large protest group may turn into a riot. Some domestic disputes lead to violence between the participants or against the police, and many domestic problems occur late at night, when other resources and personnel are not available to the complainant.

A third reason listed by Wilson as underscoring the importance of order maintenance is that, in this area, police exercise

> substantial discretion over matters of the greatest importance (public and private morality, honor and dishonor, life and death) in a situation that is, by definition, one of conflict and in an environment that is apprehensive and perhaps hostile.[30]

Not all scholars and practitioners agree on the emphasis that should be placed on order maintenance. George L. Kelling analyzed order maintenance in the context of earlier policing reforms. He found that, as professionalism in policing was emphasized, the evaluation of individual police and of police departments focused on tangibles, such as arrests and quick response time of police to citizen calls. Police departments did not recognize or reward police behavior that did not lead to arrests. Police concentrated on crime prevention, arrests, and apprehension of criminals, thus emphasizing law enforcement over order maintenance or provision of services. This approach, said Kelling, decreased police corruption and improved the internal management of policing, but it resulted in less emphasis on order maintenance.[31]

Kelling argued that the focus on law enforcement had not lowered crime rates significantly but that a decreased involvement of police in order maintenance had had negative effects. His position was that increased police attention to order maintenance improves relationships between the police and the community, which results in greater cooperation of citizens with the police. Citizen fear of crime is reduced, community support of the police is improved, police feel less isolated from the community, and crime detection and prevention increase.[32] Kelling, along with Wilson, advocated a significant enlargement in the time allocated to order maintenance in policing. Neither believed this approach would endanger law enforcement.[33]

The Kelling and Wilson position was challenged by Carl B. Klockars, who argued that American police, historically and today [1981], maintain "an extraordinarily strong crime-fighting mandate," seen by them and others as the primary mission of policing. To reduce that emphasis by increasing resources for order maintenance is undesirable. It would not reduce crime significantly because the police do not have control over many of the factors that produce crime. The financial cost would be much greater and would be at the sacrifice of a reduction in the number of calls for service to which police could respond quickly.

Klockars suggested that one solution might be to use foot patrols in high-density areas, particularly business areas. The increased costs might be financed partially by voluntary, tax-deductible contributions by businesspeople, who stand to gain the most from the increased presence of police in the area. The problem with that suggestion, warned Klockars, is that one study of a foot patrol experiment in Newark disclosed that commercial residents perceived "a deterioration in their neighborhoods: more activity on the street, more crime-related problems, reduced safety, more victimization, poorer police service, and greater use of protective devices." Klockars was not arguing against order maintenance but only against an extended and more systematic and costly approach, which would require significant changes in the administrative structure of police departments.[34]

4-3b Community Service

In addition to law enforcement and order maintenance, police perform a variety of other services for the community. Wilson maintained that these services are expected of police as a result of historical accident and community convenience; there is no good reason for police to perform these services; and the services should "be priced and sold on the market."[35]

Removal of unnecessary community service does not mean that the police should not continue to be involved in community services either directly or indirectly related to crime prevention or order maintenance. For example, many police departments provide the equipment and officers to visit community groups and individual homes to assist residents in marking their possessions so that stolen items may be identified more quickly and easily. Officers give talks on crime prevention, emphasizing to residents what they can do to diminish the possibility that they will become crime victims. Educating women on rape prevention is a frequent topic of these sessions. Visiting with schoolchildren to educate them in crime prevention is another type of police community service.

One way to solve police time commitment problems is to train and assign special officers for community service. Community service officers generally have less training, less education, and lower salaries than other officers. The community service program, however, provides career opportunities for qualified young people who cannot or do not wish to fulfill all of the assignments required of police officers.

4-3c Law Enforcement

The third major area of police functions is law enforcement. Police are empowered to detect and prevent crime, even if to do so means using force, although there are limitations on the force that may be used. The ability of police to handle crime is limited, however, and they are dependent on citizens for assistance, although they do not always get that assistance.

The law enforcement function of policing cannot be understood adequately except in the context of the legal requirements that must be observed by police officers performing this function. Thus, before discussing particular law enforcement activities, it is necessary to look at the legal context of law enforcement.

Constitutional Provisions

Any discussion of law enforcement must consider it in the context of the federal and state constitutions under which it operates. The legal right to use coercive force to intervene in the daily lives of people is a tremendous police power, and it cannot be unrestricted.

An Overview   Earlier in the text, we discussed the constitutional concepts of due process and equal protection. This chapter considers the application of these constitutional rights to the police functions of stopping and questioning suspects; arresting and conducting searches of the person, home, or automobile of a suspect; and the practices of custodial interrogation and initial investigation. That discussion begins with a brief look at traffic control, an area of law enforcement in which many police officers engage and one that may lead to the detection of serious crimes. But first it is important to look briefly at the constitutional issues raised by one of our most recently enacted laws, the USA Patriot Act, which was passed quickly after the 9/11/01 terrorist attacks.

The USA Patriot Act   The USA Patriot Act, a major piece of legislation that was enacted to provide law enforcement officers with the necessary tools for combating terrorism, was introduced in Chapter 3. In that discussion it was noted that the act has been challenged.

The USA Patriot Act contains 157 sections. Many of those sections are not controversial, although they have been criticized for the methods employed. For example, the USA Patriot Law provides financial assistance to terrorism victims, as well as increased benefits for public safety workers, but there is disagreement over how that assistance is to be processed.

In the minds of some critics, the USA Patriot Act was not debated sufficiently prior to its passage. It has been suggested that the lack of debate was appropriate; we needed to act quickly. But now, with time for reflection, Congress, the American Civil Liberties Union (ACLU), and others are questioning several provisions of the legislation. As of this writing, the legal challenges are still in process, but they center around a few key provisions, involving such actions as delaying informing suspects that their property has been searched and items seized pursuant to a warrant; permitting the government to obtain some records and other items in order to protect against international terrorism or espionage, which has been interpreted by some to permit the government to monitor the reading habits of everyone by obtaining copies of their library records, bookstore sales, and so on; and detaining aliens indefinitely for minor visa violations and without judicial authorization. Critics note that the last action is permitted only when there are "reasonable grounds to believe" that the suspects entered the United States for illegal purposes to commit terrorist or related acts. In July 2004, the U.S. House of Representatives deadlocked 210 to 210 and thus defeated an attempt to curb the scope of the USA Patriot Act by banning the government from demanding records from libraries and booksellers when investigating terrorists.[36]

The first constitutional challenge to the USA Patriot Act was filed in July 2003 by the ACLU and six Muslim groups. The suit claimed that the act violates the constitutional rights of privacy, due process, and free speech. A spokesperson for the ACLU stated, "There are basically no limits to the amount of information the F.B.I. can get now—library book records, medical records, hotel records, charitable contributions—the list goes on and on, and it's the secrecy of the whole operation that is really troublesome." The Department of Justice response was that the USA Patriot Act gives law enforcement the tools needed to fight terrorism and does not trample on civil rights.[37]

In August 2003, U.S. Attorney General John Ashcroft began a campaign to increase support for the USA Patriot Act by giving speeches throughout the country. His efforts received mixed reactions. And even the chair of the American Conservative Union stated, "Among conservatives, more and more people are saying that the Patriot Act oversteps the powers that government needs. . . . The mood in Congress has clearly changed since the law was passed after 9/11, and I think the attorney general is trying to reverse that trend."[38]

The USA Patriot Act has been challenged in court, and in January 2004 a federal court held a portion of the act unconstitutional. According to the decision of U.S. District Court Judge Audrey B. Collins (Los Angeles), the act's ban (along with that of an earlier statute aimed at terrorist acts) against providing "expert advice or assistance" to terrorists is vague and thus violates the First Amendment.[39] Additional and more recent information concerning the constitutionality of the USA Patriot Act is included in Chapter 7. The USA Patriot Act was scheduled to expire in 2005. The Bush administration was pushing for it to be extended; the American Bar Association and many members of Congress were opposing that position.[40]

The USA Patriot Act is aimed at terrorist acts, but attempts to counteract terrorism may also involve other law enforcement acts, beginning with traffic stops.

Traffic Control and the Enforcement of Traffic Laws

Traffic control is an important aspect of law enforcement. Police enforce state and local ordinances governing the operation of motor vehicles. This function includes enforcing requirements that vehicles be licensed and inspected, as well as ticketing motorists who commit moving violations. Normally violations of this type involve a simple procedure in which the police officer signs a statement, noting the violation, and gives a copy to the driver, explaining that the ticket, if unchallenged, may be handled by mail or in person at the police station. Court appearances are not required unless the motorist decides to challenge the ticket, and most people do not do so. The officer may decide not to issue a ticket; a verbal or written warning may be given instead.

The enforcement of statutes and ordinances designed to regulate the flow of traffic and to create safe conditions for drivers and pedestrians is also an important police function. Driving with excessive speed on any street or highway, speeding in school zones or failing to stop for school buses, and driving under the influence of alcohol or other drugs are dangerous. The apprehension of people who violate traffic ordinances may lead to disorder and violence. Thus, it is important that trained police officers be in charge of such apprehensions, which may lead police to evidence of criminal activity, such as stolen automobiles, violations of substance abuse laws, escaped felons, wanted persons, burglaries, and other crimes.

Some aspects of police discretion concerning moving violations have, however, been questioned. One example is the stopping of drivers who are not wearing seat belts in jurisdictions in which there is a statute requiring drivers and passengers to wear seat belts. A controversial case involving this issue occurred in Texas, which permitted police to stop and arrest drivers who were not buckled up (a misdemeanor in that state), in contrast to some jurisdictions that permit a stop and arrest for failure to wear a seat belt *only* if the driver has committed a moving violation.

In *Atwater* v. *City of Lago Vista,* the police stopped Gail Atwater, who was driving her two children, ages four and six, home from soccer practice in a town near Austin, Texas, in 1997. The children were not seat belted as required by law. The officer had stopped Atwater on a prior occasion, thinking her son was not seat belted, but he actually was. Atwater alleged that when she was stopped this second time and arrested, the officer yelled at her, frightening her children. A friend took the children home, but Atwater was handcuffed and taken to the police station, where she was booked, photographed, and kept for about one hour before she was released on $310 bond. Eventually the case was settled by a $50 fine, the maximum permitted. Atwater sued the arresting officer, the police chief, and the city. The defendants won a summary judgment (dismissal on the grounds that insufficient facts are presented to sustain the allegation) at the trial court level, and that was upheld by the Fifth U.S. Circuit Court of Appeals. The U.S. Supreme Court affirmed, holding that the officer's actions were reasonable.[41]

The U.S. Supreme Court acknowledged that "Atwater's claim to live free of pointless indignity and confinement clearly outweighs anything the city can raise against it specific to her case." The Court agreed that Atwater suffered "gratuitous humiliations imposed by a police office who was [at best] exercising extremely poor judgment." But the U.S. Supreme Court recognized the problems involved with a scenario in which "every discretionary judgment in the field [is] converted into an occasion for Constitutional review." And if changes are to be made concerning the authority of the police to arrest for minor offenses, those changes should be made by legislators and police officials, not by the courts. The Supreme Court noted that even Atwater's attorney did not cite examples of any other "comparably foolish" arrests. The Court concluded that "the country is not confronting anything like an epidemic of unnecessary minor-offense arrests." Accordingly, the U.S. Supreme Court concluded the following:

> [W]e confirm today what our prior cases have intimated. . . . The standard of probable cause applies to all areas, without the need to balance the interests and circumstances involved in particular situations. If an officer has probable cause to believe that an individual has committed even a very minor criminal offense in his presence, he may, without violating the Fourth Amendment, arrest the offender.[42]

The Investigatory Stop

The problem arises when police go too far in making the so-called pretextual traffic stop (a stop allegedly for a traffic offense but actually conducted as a pretext to look for a more serious offense, such as the possession of illegal drugs). In recent years the U.S. Supreme Court has decided several important cases involving traffic stops and the protections of the Fourth Amendment prohibition against unreasonable searches and seizures (see Appendix A).

In 1996, the Court decided *Whren* v. *United States,* an automobile search case based on a pretextual traffic stop. In *Whren* the initial stop was made by District of Columbia Metropolitan Police plainclothes vice-squad officers, who were traveling in an unmarked car in an area known for high levels of illegal drug trafficking. The officers observed two young African American males in a dark Nissan Pathfinder truck waiting for an unusually long time at a stop sign, with the driver looking into the lap of his passenger. When the officers made a U-turn to follow the vehicle, the driver turned without signaling and took off at what the officers considered an unreasonable speed. The officers overtook the truck when it was stopped behind traffic at a signal. One officer got out, approached the truck, and told the driver to put the vehicle in park. The officer saw the passenger holding two large plastic bags of what appeared to be crack cocaine. The driver and the passenger were arrested, and quantities of various illegal drugs were seized. Both men were charged with four counts of violating federal drug laws. On appeal, the petitioners "challenged the legality of the stop and the resulting seizure of the drugs. They argued that the stop had not been justified by probable cause to believe, or even reasonable suspicion, that the petitioners were engaged in illegal drug-dealing activity; and that [the officer's] asserted ground for approaching the vehicle—to give the driver a warning concerning traffic violations—was pretextual." The defense further argued that, if police are permitted to search in such situations, they might harass persons (such as, in their case, minorities) for whom they otherwise could not make a stop for lack of reasonable suspicion that a violation had occurred. The U.S. Supreme Court held that an officer who is suspicious of the behavior of the occupants of a motor vehicle but does not have grounds for stopping them may do so when a traffic violation occurs. That stop may then be used to pursue the other suspicions of illegal acts.[43]

In another 1996 case the U.S. Supreme Court examined the issue of whether police must tell drivers detained for alleged traffic violations that they are free to leave before they ask them for permission to search their vehicles. In *Ohio* v. *Robinette,* decided by a vote of 8-to-1, the justices held that "sweet-talking" drivers into consenting to a vehicle search is permitted and that police are not required to tell the drivers that they are free to leave and thus do not have to consent to the search. After all, drivers should know enough to resist pressure from police. This might be questioned when it is understood that the officer does have the power to write a ticket for the alleged traffic violation.[44]

In 1997, in *Maryland* v. *Wilson,* the U.S. Supreme Court held that during a routine traffic stop police may order occupants of the car (as well as the driver) out of the car without any reason to suspect them of wrongdoing. In *Wilson* a police officer signaled a stop to a driver whose car was traveling at a speed of 64 in a 55-mile-per-hour area. The driver initially refused to stop and, during the 1 1/2-mile pursuit, the officer noticed three passengers in the car, each turning from time to time to look at the officer. After the car stopped, the driver exited and walked back to the officer's car. The driver was trembling and appeared very nervous, but he produced a valid state driver's license. The officer instructed the driver to return to the car and retrieve the rental papers. When the driver complied, followed by the officer, the officer noted that one of the passengers was sweating and appeared to be nervous. The officer asked that passenger to exit the vehicle and, when he did, a quantity of crack cocaine fell to the ground. The passenger was arrested, charged with possession of cocaine with intent to distribute, tried, and convicted. The U.S. Supreme Court held that the evidence was properly admitted at trial. As part of its reasoning the Supreme Court stated:

> [D]anger to an officer from a traffic stop is likely to be greater when there are passengers in addition to the driver in the stopped car. While there is not the same basis for ordering the passengers out of the car as there is for ordering the driver out, the additional intrusion on the passenger is minimal. We therefore hold that an officer making a traffic stop may order passengers to get out of the car pending completion of the stop.[45]

A law professor has stated that, as a result of these three cases, motorists are left "to fend for themselves when confronted with the authority and power of the police."[46] Others argued that, in all of these cases, the officer in question observed facts that supported a reasonable belief that additional law infractions were being committed.

Another issue arises when, in stopping motorists, police take actions that are not based on individualized suspicion. In November 2000, the U.S. Supreme Court held that, when this allegedly occurs, the officer's *purpose* in making the stop should be considered in deciding whether the action was legitimate. The case of *City of Indianapolis* v. *Edmond* was brought by motorists in Indianapolis, Indiana, who asked the federal court to prohibit police from stopping them for the purpose of detecting illegal drugs. In *Edmond*, while police were checking driver's licenses and car registrations, other officers circled the cars with their canines around them to search for illegal drugs. Although the U.S. Supreme Court refused to uphold this practice, in which police admitted that the primary purpose was to detect motorists with illegal drugs, the issue of whether it would be permissible to make suspicionless stops if drug offenses were a secondary purpose was not answered.[47]

The U.S. Supreme Court distinguished *Edmond* from an earlier case, in which the Court had held that police may make suspicionless stops of motorists to check for drivers under the influence of alcohol. In *Michigan Dept. of State Police* v. *Sitz,* the Supreme Court emphasized that the stops were brief and for the purpose of enabling officers to detect and remove drunk drivers from the highways, a purpose that, according to the Supreme Court, was clearly aimed at protecting public safety. In contrast, according to Justice Sandra Day O'Connor, who wrote the majority opinion, the stops in *Edmond* were "ultimately indistinguishable from the general interest in crime control."[48]

In September 2003, the U.S. Supreme Court again entertained the issue of when the police may stop motorists about whom they have no reason to suspicion illegal acts. *Illinois* v. *Lidster* involved a fatal hit-and-run accident in Chicago, Illinois. One week after the accident, police stopped all motorists at the same intersection at the same late hour and handed them a flier describing the accident and requesting information concerning any witnesses to it. One driver nearly hit the officer with his car and was given a sobriety test, arrested for drunk driving, tried, and convicted. In a 4-to-3 vote, the Illinois Supreme Court held that the roadblock was an unconstitutional stop, not a valid investigatory tool, and overturned the conviction. The justices' questions during the oral arguments on this case raised many issues. Justice Antonin Scalia asked one counselor if it would be reasonable for the police to stop every car to ask, "Sir, or Madam, have you seen any crime committed in the last six months?" The attorney responded that normally that would be bad, but it might be reasonable in a city with "rampant lawlessness," many unsolved crimes, and a population of persons afraid of law enforcement. In *Lidster* the police roadblock did not uncover any additional witnesses, but a local television station's coverage of the road-block did produce a witness who was able to identify a suspect. This might suggest that television coverage would suffice and that such police roadblocks are ineffective as well as intrusive. The U.S. Supreme Court upheld the roadblock, however, ruling that it is consti-tutional for the police to establish "information-seeking checkpoints" in their efforts to combat crime.[49]

Whatever the case, the apprehension of traffic violators and their passengers, as well as of persons suspected of having committed crimes in other environments, begins with the investigatory stop, which may or may not lead to an arrest. One issue in the initial stop is racial profiling.

Racial Profiling   In the area of traffic and other stops, police have been accused of engaging in **racial profiling,** in which persons are stopped by police who have stereotyped them as law violators because of their race or ethnicity. Traffic stops of African Americans have been referred to by some cities as *driving while black.* Police in New Jersey were accused of racial profiling after they shot three unarmed men during a traffic stop in April 1998. The white officers had stopped a van carrying African American and Latino men and subsequently claimed that they had stopped the van because their supervisors had taught them that minorities were more likely to be involved in drug offenses. The officers claimed that they shot the men in self-defense. A study in New Jersey found that state troopers were engaging in racial profiling in many of their stops and that, in comparison with troopers' treatment of whites, African Americans and other minorities were treated in a discrimina-tory manner after they were stopped. In December 1999, state officials and the U.S. Department of Justice entered into a consent agreement on the issue. Included in that agreement was the provision of an independent monitor to report on whether troopers were following the terms of the consent agreement. Race as a reason for stopping a driver is permitted only if it is relevant to a description of a crime suspect for whom they are looking.[50]

In 2002, the troopers involved in the shooting of the three unarmed men in the 1998 shooting were permitted to plead guilty to misdemeanor charges of obstructing the inves-tigation and lying about the facts shortly after the incident. They avoided prison time and were fined $280 each. The officers had already lost their jobs. The judge noted that one of the officers had been involved in a previous shooting and had returned to work too quick-ly and without adequate counseling. The judge also noted that the men were following the policies they had been taught. To the officers the judge said, "You are victims not only of your own actions but of the system which employed you." Both officers, John Hogan and James Kenna, signed statements that they would never again seek employment as law enforcement officers.[51]

A 1999 study in New York City reported that police stopped African Americans and Hispanics at a rate much higher than stops of whites. The difference could not be explained entirely by higher crime rates in the areas of those stops, according to the report issued by the state's attorney general. More than one-half of the stops were of African Americans. The New York City police commissioner criticized the report as "critically flawed in many of its analyses."[52]

In 2001, the U.S. Department of Justice released a study (conducted by the Bureau of Justice Statistics [BJS] and mandated by a 1994 law requiring the publication of data on the use of force by police) of approximately 80,000 U.S. residents age 16 and over. The study reported that African American motorists are more likely than white motorists to be stopped by police, to be stopped more than once in the same year, to be given a ticket, to be handcuffed, to be subjected to a search of the person and of the vehicle, to be subjected to force, and to be arrested. The BJS emphasized that the data could reflect actual violations rather than profiling and thus did not *prove* racial profiling.[53] More information published by the BJS on drivers and police is reported in Spotlight 4-2.

The lack of such studies to prove racial profiling does not, however, mean that profiling is not an important issue. A study published in 2001 by the Police Executive Research Forum

▶ **Racial profiling** The reaction by law enforcement officers to potential suspects based solely on their race or ethnicity.

Spotlight 4-2   Characteristics of Drivers Stopped by Police

General characteristics of drivers stopped by police in 1999 . . .

- Among drivers age 16–24, blacks (17.1%) did not differ significantly from either whites (20.1%) or Hispanics (15.5%) in the probability of being stopped. White drivers age 16–24 were somewhat more likely than their Hispanic counterparts to be pulled over.
- The average number of stops was greater for young black males (2.7%) than young white males (1.7%) and marginally greater than for young Hispanic males (1.8%).

Drivers' opinions of the legitimacy of the stops

- Both blacks (74.0%) and Hispanics (81.6%) were less likely than whites (86.0%) to feel they were stopped by police for a legitimate reason.
- Of drivers stopped more than once, whites (84.4%) were more likely than both blacks (70.2%) and Hispanics (70%) to feel the stop was legitimate.
- Among male drivers age 16–24, blacks (75.7%) were not significantly less likely than whites (83.2%) or Hispanics (76.0%) to feel the stops were legitimate.

Reason for traffic stop

- Few drivers were not informed of the reason for being stopped by police. No significant differences were found between white (1.5%), black (2.0%), or Hispanic (1.2%) drivers in the likelihood of being informed by the officer of the reason for the traffic stop.
- Males stopped for speeding were more likely to be ticketed (70.3%) than females (66.5%).
- Drivers age 16–24 who were stopped for speeding were ticketed (73.6%) more often than drivers over 24 (66.8%).
- Among drivers stopped for speeding, blacks (75.7%) and Hispanics (79.4%) were more likely than whites (66.6%) to be ticketed.

Searches conducted by police during traffic stops

- In 1999, 6.6% of traffic stops involved a search of the driver, the vehicle, or both.
- Police were more likely to conduct a search of the vehicle and/or driver in traffic stops involving black male drivers (15.9%) or Hispanic male drivers (14.2%), compared to white male drivers (7.9%).
- Of the nearly 1.3 million searches of vehicles and/or drivers conducted following traffic stops in 1999, 37% were accompanied by an arrest of the driver.

Police use of force in traffic stops and in other situations

- Approximately 422,000 persons age 16 or older said the police used or threatened to use force against them at least once during 1999.
- Traffic stops accounted for 139,000 police use of force incidents, 33% of the 422,000 incident total.
- Of the 139,000 force contacts that occurred during a traffic stop, the majority involved a male driver (98.2% of

those contacts). Males accounted for 81.4% of the remaining 282,00 force contacts that occurred at times other than a traffic stop.
- Persons under 25 were involved in just over half of all force contacts with police in 1999.
- Most (76.1%) of the 422,000 people involved in a police use of force incident said the force was excessive.

Characteristics of drivers stopped by police . . .
Driver race/ethnicity

Whites were 76.7% of licensed drivers and 77% of drivers stopped by police in 1999. Blacks were 9.8% of licensed drivers, but 11.6% of stopped drivers, while Hispanics accounted for 9.9% of licensed drivers and 8.4% of stopped drivers. An additional 3.6% of licensed drivers were persons of other races, who were also 3% of drivers stopped by police.

Driver gender, age, and race/ethnicity

Young white males (those age 16–24) were 5.2% of licensed drivers and 12.3% of the 19.3 million drivers pulled over by police. . . . Young black males accounted for 0.8% of licensed drivers and 1.6% of traffic stops, while young Hispanic males were 1.1% of licensed drivers and 2% of stopped drivers. Young males of other races formed 0.4% of persons with a license and 0.6% of drivers involved in a traffic stop.

Likelihood of drivers being stopped . . .
Driver race/ethnicity

Black drivers were somewhat more likely than white drivers to be stopped at least once (12.3% of blacks versus 10.4% of whites). Blacks were significantly more likely than both Hispanics (8.8%) and drivers of other races (8.7%) to be stopped at least once. There was also some indication that black drivers (3.0%) were more likely than both white drivers (2.1%) and Hispanic drivers (2%) to be stopped more than once.

Driver gender, age, and race/ethnicity

Among persons age 16–24—
- blacks (17.1%) did not differ significantly from either whites (20.1%) or Hispanics (15.5%) in the probability of being stopped. . . .
- whites (20.1%) were somewhat more likely than Hispanics (15.5%) to be pulled over.
- no significant differences by race were found in the probability of being stopped more than once.

Among persons over age 24—
- blacks (11.2%) were significantly more likely than whites (8.9%) to be pulled over and somewhat more likely than Hispanics (7.8%). . . .
- blacks (2.2%) were significantly more likely than Hispanics (1.3%) and somewhat more likely than whites (1.5%) to be stopped more than once by police.

Source: Erica Leah Schmitt et al., Bureau of Justice Statistics, *Characteristics of Drivers Stopped by Police, 1999* (Washington, D.C.: U.S. Department of Justice, March 2002), pp. 1, 2, 3.

(PERF) revealed that there is a difference between the way police see their actions and the public's perception of them. The public believes that racial profiling exists and that it damages the ability of police to work effectively in areas characterized predominantly by minority populations. The PERF report contained numerous recommendations for improving policing and its effect on minorities and concluded that racial and ethnic differences should never be the sole justification for police action; race and ethnicity do not support probable cause or even reasonable suspicion.[54]

In April 2000, the Ninth Circuit Court of Appeals held that it is not permissible to use ethnicity as a factor in deciding whether to stop an individual suspected of a crime. The court noted the large number and rapid growth rate of Hispanics in California and concluded that, despite a 25-year-old U.S. Supreme Court decision ruling that racial appearance was an appropriate factor for deciding whether a person should be stopped by police, this practice is not currently acceptable. "Hispanic appearance is, in general, of such little probative value that it may not be considered as a relevant factor where particularized or individualized suspicion is required." The case of *United States* v. *Montero-Camargo* involved three Mexicans who were stopped by the U.S. Border Patrol in 1996, about 115 miles east of San Diego. The agents, responding to a tip, gave five factors they considered in their decision to stop the suspects, one of which was their Hispanic appearance. The U.S. Supreme Court refused to review the case, thus permitting the decision to stand.[55]

Charges of racial profiling continue, however, as illustrated by the May 2003 resignation of two New Jersey officers in another racial profiling scandal in that state. The acting state police superintendent publicly rebuked Kevin Goldberg and Howard Parker for stopping African American drivers, using racial epithets, and stomping on drugs rather than preserving them as evidence. The evidence against the officers came in the form of a recently discovered video made in 1991. The attorney for the two officers said they resigned because they did not think they could get a fair disciplinary hearing. The seven-year statute of limitations for official misconduct in office had passed, so the officers could not be charged with that crime.[56]

Recent research by criminologists suggests that police can do something about perceptions of racial profiling. Police can offer legitimate reasons for stops. "Several studies have shown that citizens, and blacks especially, are much more likely to cooperate with officers when they are given a reason for the stop, and that people put a premium on officers being polite, listening to citizens, and explaining their actions." It is also possible that, if officers are required to explain to motorists why they were stopped, police officers will be less likely to engage in racial profiling.[57]

Another recent study of racial profiling by police concluded with the observation that requiring police to attend sensitivity training will not "have much impact on a practice that reflects the values of the community to which the police are accountable."[58]

Both George W. Bush and Al Gore stated in their presidential campaigns in the year 2000 that they would work to eradicate racial profiling. In June 2003, President Bush announced his guidelines for eliminating racial profiling, but his policy exempted acts suspected to be related to terrorism and national security. In those cases, officers could use race in "narrow circumstances" only for the purpose of identifying terrorist threats and to "stop potential catastrophic attacks." The guidelines applied to federal but not to state or local law enforcement persons.[59]

Finally, in February 2003, the California Highway Patrol settled a three-year lawsuit by agreeing to discontinue using traffic stops as a pretext to search for drugs. The lawsuit was brought by a Latino lawyer, Curtis Rodriguez, who was stopped and searched by the highway patrol in 1998. Rodriguez claimed that prior to being pulled over he saw other Latino motorists who had been stopped by the highway patrol on the same highway. According to the American Civil Liberties Union, California was the first state to announce that it would discontinue asking motorists for permission to search their cars when they are stopped for traffic violations. The agreement also specified that the highway patrol would compile and analyze extensive data collected about each highways stop. The agency also agreed to pay over $800,000 in attorney fees for the plaintiff in this case.[60]

Stop and Frisk The police may be notified or they may observe a situation that gives them a reasonable basis for stopping a pedestrian or a driver. At this initial stop, police have wide discretion. They can decide not to make the stop. They can stop but not arrest the suspect. They can release the suspect with a verbal or written warning. The police must make important judgment calls at the stage of stopping and questioning suspects, for it would be an inefficient use of police time and a violation of suspects' constitutional rights for police to arrest persons when there is no probable cause to believe they are violating the law. Spotlight 4-3 discusses the *Lawson* case, which illustrates police abuse of the discretion to stop and question a suspect. For several reasons this case is very important, despite the fact that it was decided in 1983. First, it is still good law. Second, it was decided by the U.S. Supreme Court. Third, it stands against the recent decisions, discussed earlier, in which the Supreme Court has refused to restrict police in stopping and searching, especially in the area of traffic control. Finally, it is argued by some that the stop in *Lawson* represented a case of racial bias, which is not permitted.

The *Lawson* case makes it clear that police may not use a vague statute for purposes of stopping, questioning, and otherwise harassing individuals. But the case also makes it clear that police may stop and question individuals. How can the police tell when they can go beyond initial questioning and make an arrest?

Some discretion must be allowed the police officer who, based on experience, perceives that a crime might have been committed and that the suspect may be armed, thus constituting a threat to the life or health of the officer and others who are present. It is permissible for the police to conduct pat-down searches, or **frisk** the suspect in some cases, as illustrated by the following example.

In *Terry* v. *Ohio*, Detective Martin McFadden of the Cleveland, Ohio, Police Department noticed two men standing on a street corner in front of several stores. The men made many trips up and down the street, peering into store windows. They talked to a third man, whom they followed up the street after his departure. McFadden, who had 39 years of experience as a police officer, suspected that the men were casing the stores for a robbery. He approached the men, identified himself as a police officer, and asked their names. The men mumbled responses, at which point the detective spun one of the men, Terry, around and patted his breast pocket. Officer McFadden removed the pistol that he felt and then frisked the second man, on whom he also found a pistol. The third man was frisked but did not have a weapon.[61]

> ▶ **Frisk** An action by a law enforcement officer or a correctional officer consisting of patting down or running one's hands quickly over a person's body to determine whether the suspect or inmate has a weapon or other contraband. This is in contrast to a body search, which is a more careful and thorough examination of the person.

Spotlight 4-3 **The *Lawson* Case and the Abuse of Police Discretion to Stop and Question**

Thirty-six-year-old Edward Lawson—tall, black, muscular, and longhaired—walked almost everywhere he went. Lawson was stopped by police approximately 15 times between March 1975 and January 1977. Police in California were relying on a California statute that prohibited a person from loitering or wandering

> upon the streets or from place to place without apparent reason or business and who refuses to identify himself and to account for his presence when requested by any peace officer to do so, if the surrounding circumstances are such as to indicate to a reasonable man that the public safety demands such identification.[1]

Each time he was stopped, Lawson refused to identify himself. He was arrested five of the times he was stopped, convicted once, and spent several weeks in jail. The *Lawson* case illustrates the tension between the police claim that in order to combat crime they must be able to stop and question people

who look suspicious and the right of citizens to be free of unreasonable intrusions into their privacy.

Lawson appealed his convictions to the U.S. Supreme Court, which reversed them on the grounds that the statute under which Lawson was convicted was vague. The problem with the California statute was not the initial police stop. According to the Court, "Although the initial detention is justified, the State fails to establish standards by which the officers may determine whether the suspect has complied with the subsequent identification requirement." The U.S. Supreme Court held that giving a police officer such discretion "confers on police a virtually unrestrained power to arrest and charge persons with a violation" and therefore "furnishes a convenient tool for 'harsh and discriminatory enforcement by local prosecuting officials against particular groups deemed to merit their displeasure.'"[2]

1. Cal. Penal Code, Section 647(e) (1977).
2. Kolender et al. v. Lawson, 461 U.S. 352, 360, 361 (1983).

In *Terry* the U.S. Supreme Court emphasized that even brief detention of a person without probable cause for an arrest is a seizure of that person. These stops constitute a serious intrusion that can lead to strong resentment. But police officers are injured and killed in the line of duty. They cannot be expected to take unreasonable risks; thus, they may conduct a search that is limited in time and scope.

In *Terry* the U.S. Supreme Court looked at the totality of the circumstances, holding, that if during the pat-down search the police feel an object that might be a weapon, they may continue the search until they are satisfied that it is not a weapon. The Supreme Court did not, however, answer the question of whether they could seize a **contraband** item that is not a weapon. In 1993, the Supreme Court decided that issue. In *Minnesota* v. *Dickerson* the Court held that, if during a *Terry* search and before an officer has concluded that the suspect is not armed the officer feels an item "whose contour or mass makes its identity immediately apparent," that item may be seized without a warrant. The discovery of the contraband would not constitute any greater invasion of privacy than had occurred during the permissible weapons search and thus is acceptable. The Supreme Court referred to this as the *plain feel* doctrine. But officers may not go beyond the permissible scope of the weapons search to examine the item suspected of being contraband but not a weapon.[62]

The totality of the circumstances rule articulated by the U.S. Supreme Court in the *Terry* case was emphasized again in 2002, when the Court, in *United States* v. *Arvizu,* upheld a border patrol agent's search. Agent Clinton Stoddard was working at a checkpoint about 30 miles north of a border town when he was notified that a magnetic sensor had been triggered on a back road near his location. Agent Stoddard concluded that a motorist might be trying to avoid the main road checkpoint because he or she was smuggling illegal drugs or immigrants. Stoddard drove to the road in question and pulled over to get a good look at an oncoming minivan as it passed him. Based on his observations and his knowledge, he concluded that the driver might be smuggling. Stoddard signaled the van driver to pull over and stop. Stoddard's suspicions were based on a number of factors:

- The car was a minivan, a type of car often used by smugglers.
- The car was on a back road often used by smugglers.
- The time was during shift changes, when detection might be interrupted.
- The driver slowed down sharply as he approached Stoddard's car, did not look at Stoddard, and appeared stiff and rigid.
- Three children in the minivan waived mechanically, as if they might have been told to do so.
- The knees of the children were unusually high, as if they might have their feet resting on objects.
- There were no picnic grounds in the area, so it was unlikely the family was on an outing for recreational purposes.[63]

Stoddard signaled the van to pull over and asked for permission to search the car. He was granted permission; he found 130 pounds of marijuana. At his trial Arvizu asked the court to exclude the marijuana. The court refused, but the Ninth Circuit Court of Appeals reversed, stating, among other comments, that, if every strange act of a child "could contribute to a finding of reasonable suspicion, the vast majority of American parents might be stopped regularly." The U.S. Supreme Court reversed, holding that the totality of the circumstances and the agent's experience should be considered in making a determination whether the officer had reason to pull over a car and request permission to search it. According to a unanimous Supreme Court, "This process allows officers to draw on their own experience and specialized training to make inferences from and deductions about the cumulative information available to them that 'might well elude an untrained person.'"[64]

Law enforcement officers might also have reason to stop a motorist if the driver takes flight. In a unanimous 2000 opinion in *Illinois* v. *Wardlow,* the U.S. Supreme Court held that under some circumstances the flight of a person who sees a law enforcement officer provides reasonable grounds for the officer to stop and search. But the justices disagreed on

▶ Contraband Any item (such as weapons, alcohol, or other drugs), possession of which is illegal or violates prison rules.

how the facts of a Chicago case should be analyzed in light of that principle. In *Wardlow* the defendant fled when he saw several police cars in an area of the city known for heavy trafficking in illegal narcotics. One officer chased Wardlow down an alley and found that he was carrying a loaded gun. In a controversial 5-to-4 decision, Chief Justice William H. Rehnquist, writing for the majority, concluded that, in an area of that type, an unprovoked flight constituted grounds for a stop and search. According to Rehnquist, "The determination of reasonable suspicion must be based on common sense judgments and inferences about human behavior." Rehnquist also stated, "Headlong flight—wherever it occurs—is the consummate act of evasion; it is not necessarily indicative of wrongdoing, but it is certainly suggestive of such."

Justice John Paul Stevens stated in his dissenting opinion that these facts did not justify the search. "Among some citizens, particularly minorities and those resident in high crime areas, there is also the possibility that the fleeing person is entirely innocent, but, with or without justification, believes that contact with the police can itself be dangerous, apart from any criminal activity associated with the officer's sudden presence."[65]

Arrest, Search, and Seizure

The process of stopping and questioning suspects may lead to an **arrest,** which is a crucial step in criminal justice proceedings because most cases are initiated by arrest. **Search and seizure** may accompany arrest, but a clear understanding of these processes requires a brief introduction to the Fourth Amendment of the U.S. Constitution. That amendment prohibits only *unreasonable* searches and seizures (see Appendix A). This provision of the U.S. Constitution is pertinent to our discussion because under some circumstances stopping and arresting a person may constitute a seizure of the person and therefore must follow proper procedures or be ruled unreasonable by the courts.

Warrants and Probable Cause With some exceptions, arrests and searches may not be made until the police secure a **warrant.** A 1948 decision emphasized the purpose of the **search warrant,** but the principle also applies to arrests. According to the U.S. Supreme Court,

> The point of the Fourth Amendment, which often is not grasped by zealous officers, is not that it denies law enforcement the support of the usual inferences which reasonable men draw from evidence. Its protection consists in requiring that those inferences be drawn by a neutral and detached magistrate instead of being judged by the officer engaged in the often competitive enterprise of ferreting out crime. . . . When the right of privacy must reasonably yield to the right of search is, as a rule, to be decided by a judicial officer, not by a policeman or government enforcement agent.[66]

The Fourth Amendment requires that a warrant shall not be issued except upon a finding of **probable cause.** Probable cause is required as well in those exceptions in which arrest, search, and seizure are permitted without a warrant. To constitute probable cause, the facts of the situation must be such that, upon hearing those facts, a reasonable person would conclude that in all probability a crime had been committed.

How is probable cause established? Facts sufficient to lead a reasonable person to conclude that a crime has been committed by a particular person or that a particular kind of contraband may be found at a specified location may be secured in various ways. One of the most controversial ways occurs when the facts come from an **informant,** who may have a history of criminal activity, or from an anonymous source. The U.S. Supreme Court considered the latter in *Illinois* v. *Gates.* In *Gates* the police received an anonymous letter alleging that two specified people, a husband and wife, were engaging in illegal drug sales and that on 3 May 1978 the wife was going to drive their car to Florida. The letter stated that the husband would fly to Florida to drive the car to Illinois with the trunk loaded with drugs and that the couple had about $100,000 worth of drugs in the basement of their Illinois home.

After receiving this information, a police detective secured the couple's address. The officer found that the husband had a reservation to fly to Florida on 5 May 1978. The flight

---

▶ **Arrest** The act of taking an individual into custody in order to make a criminal charge against that person.

▶ **Search and seizure** The examination of a person or a person's property and the taking of items that may be evidence of criminal activity; it generally requires a search warrant. Unreasonable searches and seizures are prohibited.

▶ **Warrant** A court-issued writ authorizing an officer to arrest a suspect or to search a person, personal property, or a place.

▶ **Search warrant** *See* **warrant.**

▶ **Probable cause** In search warrant cases a set of facts and circumstances that leads to the reasonable belief that the items sought are located in a particular place. In arrest cases the facts and circumstances lead to the reasonable belief that the suspect has committed a crime.

▶ **Informant** A person who gives information to law enforcement officials about a crime or planned criminal activity.

was put under surveillance, which disclosed that the suspect took the flight. It was confirmed that he spent the night in a motel room registered to his wife and that the next morning he left in a car with a woman. The license plate of the car was registered to the husband suspect. The couple was driving north on an interstate highway used frequently for traffic to Illinois.

The police detective in possession of these facts signed a statement under oath concerning the facts and submitted that statement to a judge, who issued a search warrant for the couple's house and automobile. The police were waiting for them when they returned to their Illinois home. Upon searching the house and car, the police found drugs, which the state attempted to use against the couple at trial. The Gateses' motion to have the evidence suppressed at trial was successful, and the Illinois Supreme Court upheld the lower court on this issue.

The U.S. Supreme Court disagreed and looked at the totality of the circumstances, holding that, in this case, independent police verification of the allegations from the anonymous source provided sufficient information on which a magistrate could have probable cause to issue the warrants. The Supreme Court emphasized that probable cause is a fluid concept based on probabilities, not certainties. All of the circumstances under which information is secured must be considered and weighed in determining whether probable cause exists for issuing a warrant.[67]

The U.S. Supreme Court has established rules that must be followed when police secure information from known informants. There must be underlying circumstances that would lead a reasonable person to conclude that the informant is reliable and credible in what he or she is saying, and there must be underlying circumstances that provide a basis for the conclusions drawn by the informant. If the informant is a police officer, credibility might not be questioned, although it is necessary to show why that person has reason to have such information. When the informant is a known or suspected criminal, as is frequently the case, establishing credibility is more difficult.

Although the U.S. Supreme Court upheld the use of an informant in the *Gates* case, the Court ruled against such use in a 2002 case, *Florida* v. *J.L.* This case involved an anonymous call to the Miami-Dade, Florida, police, who were told that a young African American male, wearing a plaid shirt and carrying a gun, was standing at a particular bus stop. Police went to the stop and found three African American males, one of whom was wearing a plaid shirt. That young man made no suspicious or threatening movements; no gun was obvious. The police had no reason—except for the anonymous tip—to suspect any of the three young men of illegal activity. The police frisked all three suspects and found a gun in the pocket of J.L., who was wearing the plaid shirt. J.L. was only 15, so his name was not used because he was a juvenile, and their names are kept confidential. J.L. was charged with possessing a firearm while under the age of 18 and carrying a concealed weapon. The trial court granted the defendant's motion to exclude the gun; an intermediate appellate court reversed; the Florida Supreme Court upheld the trial court, and Florida appealed. Florida sought review in the U.S. Supreme Court because other courts had held that such evidence is admissible. The U.S. Supreme Court agreed to hear the case to settle the dispute.

The U.S. Supreme Court referred to its holding in *Terry* v. *Ohio,* noting the differences between the two cases. In *J.L.* the officers did not observe any behavior that was suspicious. They had no reason, other than the anonymous tip, to believe that any of these young men were armed and dangerous. According to the Supreme Court, the anonymous tip alone was not sufficient to warrant the search and thus the evidence secured by means of that illegal search was properly excluded from trial. Police may not search for weapons without reasonable suspicion, as established in *Terry.*[68]

Some searches and seizures are permissible without a warrant, without probable cause, and without consent. One exception to the warrant requirement is a search that occurs when an officer makes a lawful arrest. The U.S. Supreme Court has emphasized, however, that the right to search the person without a search warrant or the suspect's consent, even when the arrest is proper, is a limited privilege.

Exigent Circumstances and Warrantless Searches

Police are permitted to conduct warrantless searches in limited cases, including those with exigent circumstances. In a 1994 California case the court refused to suppress evidence seized in a warrantless search of a home by police who were responding to an anonymous call concerning domestic violence. Police were greeted at the door by a woman who said she was alone and safe. But police saw a man in the house, and the woman appeared to have been hit recently. The woman told police she had just fallen down the stairs.

Police entered the home and seized the illegal drugs that were in plain view. The California court held that the officers entered the home under exigent circumstances. They knew that the woman had lied about being alone, and they had reason to suspect she had been hit recently, perhaps by the man they saw in the home. For her protection, they had a right to enter. While they were in the home legally, police were justified in seizing illegal drugs that were in plain view.[1]

1. People (California) v. Higgins, 26 Cal.App.4th 247 (4th Dist. 1994), *review denied,* 1994 Cal. LEXIS 5620 (Cal. Oct. 13, 1994).

After an arrest, some warrantless searches, such as searches of possessions or of the person when the suspect is booked into jail (inventory searches), are proper. Routine searches at the border are also permitted. Inspections and searches of regulated industries are permitted, too, as are searches at certain fixed checkpoints, such as checks for drivers under the influence of controlled substances. As Spotlight 4-4 notes, warrantless searches are permissible under exigent circumstances.

Warrantless searches may also be conducted legally when a person consents to the search. This consent may be given prior to arrest, at the time of arrest, or later at the police station. It may involve searching possessions, automobiles, homes, or persons. The critical factor is whether the consent is made knowingly and voluntarily. In some circumstances, consent to a search may be given by a third party, but these circumstances are limited.

In 1996 in *Ornelas* v. *United States,* the U.S. Supreme Court held that, when judges are confronted with a warrantless search, they are to consider the facts that led to the stop or search and then determine whether those facts "viewed from the standpoint of a reasonable police officer" constitute probable cause. The decisions of trial judges on this matter are to be reviewed by appellate judges only for clear error, and during that review due weight must be given to the consideration of the facts by local law enforcement officers and trial judges. Appellate review of such cases should be undertaken *de novo* (from the beginning). Again, the U.S. Supreme Court emphasized its "strong preferences for searches conducted pursuant to a warrant."[69]

Under some circumstances, arrests may be made without a warrant. Historically, under English common law, police were permitted to make lawful arrests without a warrant if they had probable cause to believe that a *felony* had been committed and that it had been committed by the person to be arrested. Today, either by court decisions or by statutes, this rule exists in most jurisdictions. But historically, under the common law, in cases of less serious offenses, *misdemeanors,* police were permitted to arrest without a warrant only if the act constituted a breach of peace that occurred within the presence of the officer.

Today most jurisdictions permit police to make a warrantless arrest for any misdemeanor committed in their presence. If the offense is not committed in the officer's presence, however, most jurisdictions require a warrant for an arrest of a suspected misdemeanant, even if the officer has overwhelming evidence that the suspect committed the offense. "Committed in the presence of the officer" does not mean that the officer must have seen the crime committed; usually it is interpreted to mean that the officer has probable cause to believe that the misdemeanor was committed in his or her presence.

An arrest without a warrant is a serious matter, however, and the U.S. Supreme Court has placed restrictions on this procedure. Persons arrested without a warrant are entitled to a prompt judicial determination of whether probable cause exists. The Court has interpreted *prompt* to be 48 hours under most circumstances. If a weekend is involved and the judicial determination of probable cause will not be held within 48 hours, the state has the burden of showing that the delay beyond that period is reasonable.[70]

The U.S. Supreme Court has held that investigation of a homicide is not one of the recognized exceptions to the requirement of a warrant before a search. In *Flippo* v. *West Virginia*, decided in 1999, the police were called by a minister, James M. Flippo, to a cabin he was occupying with his wife. Flippo told officers that he and his wife had been attacked; the wife was dead when police arrived. Flippo was taken to the hospital for treatment of injuries that he claimed had occurred during the attack. The area outside the cabin was searched for signs of forced entry and footprints. Police reentered the cabin when a police photographer arrived. They processed the crime scene and conducted a search. Inside a briefcase they found a photograph of a man, later identified as a member of Flippo's congregation, who appeared to be taking off his pants. Prosecutors used that photograph at the trial, arguing that Flippo was having a sexual relationship with another man and that, when his wife found out and objected, he had a motive to kill her. Flippo argued that the evidence should have been excluded.

The U.S. Supreme Court agreed with Flippo, ruling that a homicide scene is not an exception to the warrant requirement before a search is executed. The Supreme Court did not, however, rule on whether the admission of the tainted evidence constituted **harmless error** or **reversible error.** Nor did the Court rule on the issue of whether Flippo consented to a search by virtue of calling 911 and asking the police to come to the cabin. Consent, said the Supreme Court, is a fact to be determined by the lower court, as it is a factual (in contrast to a legal) question.[71]

Home Searches   The U.S. Supreme Court has said that the "physical entry of the home is the chief evil against which the wording of the Fourth Amendment is directed."[72] The Supreme Court recognizes a difference between searches and seizures within a home or an office and the search of a person's property in other places.

An example of an unreasonable entry into and search inside of a home occurred in *Mapp* v. *Ohio.* Police had received information that a person wanted for questioning in a bombing was hiding out in a two-family dwelling. Mapp and her daughter by a previous marriage lived on the top floor of the home. When police arrived at the home and knocked on the door, Mapp called her attorney and then denied entrance to the officers without a warrant. The police advised their headquarters of that response and put the house under surveillance. About three hours later, with more officers on the scene, police attempted entry again. When Mapp did not come to the door quickly, the officers forced their way into the house. Mapp's attorney arrived, but the police would not let him enter the house or see Mapp.[73]

Mapp demanded to see a search warrant. The officers produced a paper they claimed to be a search warrant. Mapp grabbed that paper (which was not a warrant) and tucked it into her bosom. The officers retrieved the paper and handcuffed Mapp for being belligerent. Mapp complained that the officers were hurting her. The officers took the complaining and handcuffed suspect to her bedroom, where they conducted a search. They searched other rooms as well and found obscene materials in a basement trunk.

The seized evidence was used against Mapp at trial, and she was convicted of "knowingly having had in her possession and under her control certain lewd and lascivious books, pictures, and photographs." The U.S. Supreme Court ruled that the evidence seized in Mapp's home could not be used against her in a state trial. The Court referred to the seizure as a "flagrant abuse" of the "constitutional . . . right to privacy free from unreasonable state intrusion."[74]

Even if police have a right to search a home, there is an issue of the permissible scope of that search. Several factors must be considered. In *Chimel* v. *California*, police officers searched a house thoroughly after they entered with an arrest warrant but without a search warrant. The U.S. Supreme Court reversed the defendant's conviction and limited the areas that may be searched for weapons, if necessary, to protect the life of the officer and others. The suspect may be searched to the extent necessary to prevent the destruction of evidence.

▶ **Harmless error**   A minor or trivial error not deemed sufficient to harm the rights of the parties who assert the error.   Cases are not reversed on the basis of harmless errors.

▶ **Reversible error**   An error in a legal proceeding, such as a trial, that is considered sufficient to require the reversal of a conviction or a sentence.

The officer may search the area "within the immediate control" of the arrestee, such as a gun lying on a table near the suspect.[75]

In 1971, the U.S. Supreme Court held that police may seize evidence without a warrant while they are within the home to execute a lawful arrest, provided that evidence is in plain view.[76] In 1987, the Court held that probable cause is required to invoke the **plain view doctrine**.[77]

In 1990, the U.S. Supreme Court held that an officer who is executing an arrest warrant within a private dwelling may search rooms other than the one in which the arrest is made. The Court called this a *protective sweep* search, but there are limitations. Although the search does not require probable cause or even reasonable suspicion, it is permitted only for the purpose of locating another person who might pose danger. Thus, the officers may "look in closets and other spaces immediately adjoining the place of arrest from which an attack could be immediately launched." To go further, the officers must have "articulable facts which, taken together with the rational inferences from those facts, would warrant a reasonably prudent officer in believing that the area to be swept harbors an individual posing a danger to those on the arrest scene." The Supreme Court emphasized that this warrantless search is permissible only for the protection of those present and cannot extend to a full search of the premises, "but [it] may extend only to a cursory inspection of those spaces where a person may be found." The protective sweep must be brief; it may last "no longer than is necessary to dispel the reasonable suspicion of danger and in any event no longer than it takes to complete the arrest and depart the premises."[78]

The U.S. Supreme Court has elaborated on the scope of the lawful search of a home's **curtilage.** The Court has held that a barn 60 yards from a house and outside the area surrounding the house enclosed by a fence is not part of the curtilage. The Court stated that

> curtilage questions should be resolved with particular reference to four factors: the proximity of the area claimed to be curtilage to the home, whether the area is included within an enclosure surrounding the home, the nature of the uses to which the area is put, and the steps taken by the resident to protect the area from observation by people passing by.[79]

The U.S. Supreme Court has ruled that the Fourth Amendment does not prohibit warrantless searches and seizures of garbage that is left outside a home's curtilage. The Court reasoned that, since the garbage is readily accessible to the public, its owner has no reasonable expectation of privacy.[80] The Court left unanswered the issue of whether the Fourth Amendment prohibits warrantless searches of garbage left within the curtilage, but in 1991 a lower federal appellate court ruled that such a search would not be unlawful, provided the garbage was left under circumstances in which it was readily accessible to the public. That test was interpreted to include garbage left on a driveway 50 feet south of the house and 20 feet from the unattached garage, 25 to 30 feet west of the street, and 18 feet west of the public sidewalk. The garbage in question was halfway up the driveway, a bit closer to the sidewalk than to the garage and technically within the curtilage. The Seventh Circuit Court of Appeals ruled that, despite that location, the garbage was abandoned and exposed to the public; consequently, its owner had no reasonable expectation of privacy with regard to its contents. The U.S. Supreme Court refused to review the case, thus allowing the Seventh Circuit's ruling to stand.[81]

The U.S. Supreme Court has also held that police may prevent a person outside his or her home from entering that home while police secure a search warrant. In 2001 in *Illinois* v. *McArthur,* the Court approved the decision of police to prevent Charles McArthur from reentering his home after police received a tip from McArthur's wife, Tera McArthur, that "Chuck has dope in there." Tera McArthur had summoned the police to keep the peace while she removed her personal belongings from the trailer in which she had lived with her husband. After she finished, Tera told police about the drugs. By that time, Charles McArthur was on the porch. Police asked him for permission to search the trailer; he refused. Police then told McArthur that he could not reenter the trailer unless he was accompanied by a police officer. Approximately two hours later the police, with a search warrant, entered the trailer, found less than 2.5 grams of marijuana, and arrested McArthur. McArthur moved to have the drugs excluded as evidence, arguing that they were seized during an improper

▶ **Plain view doctrine** The legal doctrine that permits a law enforcement officer who is legally searching a place for particular items to seize those that are in plain view but not listed on a search warrant.

▶ **Curtilage** The enclosed ground and buildings immediately around a dwelling.

search. The trial court granted the motion; the U.S. Supreme Court ruled 8-to-1 that the seizure was proper. The Court held that the restriction on McArthur's freedom to return unaccompanied to the inside of the trailer was reasonable because

- The police had probable cause to believe that illegal drugs were inside the trailer.
- The police had good reason to fear that McArthur might destroy the drugs if he returned to the inside unaccompanied.
- The police made reasonable efforts to reconcile the need to protect McArthur's right to privacy while maintaining good law enforcement.
- The police limited the restraint to a reasonable time period, approximately two hours.[82]

State constitutions, statutes, and courts may provide *greater* protection than the federal Constitution requires. For example, the New Jersey Supreme Court has held that police need a search warrant to open and examine garbage bags left at curbside for collection.[83]

Another type of search regarding the home and its curtilage is the aerial search. The U.S. Supreme Court has held that aerial searches may be conducted without a warrant.[84] But in a 5-to-4 decision in 2001, the Court held that it is unconstitutional to use a thermal imaging device (from a public street) to detect heat radiating from the external surface of a private home to determine whether marijuana is being grown within the home.[85]

Another issue concerning searches of the home is the long-standing principle of "knock and announce," meaning that police who arrive at a dwelling to search with or without a warrant must knock and announce their presence prior to entering. In 1995, the U.S. Supreme Court elevated that principle to a constitutional dimension.[86] The rule may be relaxed under exigent circumstances, such as if there is reason to believe the evidence sought will be destroyed or the suspects are armed and dangerous. The Court left it to lower courts to devise rules under which the principle could be waived. However, in 1997 in *Richards* v. *Wisconsin,* the Supreme Court struck down a blanket exception to the knock-and-announce rule. In this case the rule applied to felony drug investigations. The lower court had held that police are never to knock and announce before entering if they have a search warrant for felony drug investigations, the assumption being that they already have reasonable cause to believe that exigent circumstances exist in such cases. The Supreme Court upheld the no-knock in this case because it found that the officers' decision not to knock and announce was reasonable under the circumstances of that case, but the Court rejected the blanket rule permitting no-knock in all cases involving alleged felony drug violations. The Court held that a case-by-case analysis was required.[87]

In 1998, the U.S. Supreme Court answered the question of whether damage to property during a no-knock entry of a home should be considered in determining whether the entry was reasonable. In *United States* v. *Ramirez,* in order to prevent a suspect from having access to weapons thought to be stored in a garage, police broke a window in the attached garage before they announced their presence to the suspect in the house. When the suspect was told that the forced entry was caused by police, not burglars, he surrendered. The Supreme Court held that under these circumstances it was reasonable for police to break the window without first announcing their presence.[88]

In 1999 in *Minnesota* v. *Carter,* the U.S. Supreme Court held that individuals who are paying a short-term visit to a home for commercial purposes do not have the reasonable expectation of privacy that is protected by the Fourth Amendment. In *Carter* the officer peered through a gap in a blind at a window in an apartment and saw three people bagging cocaine. The suspects were arrested and convicted of state drug offenses. The trial court ruled that the officer's observations did not constitute a search under the Fourth Amendment and that the respondents did not have a reasonable expectation of privacy; thus, the search was reasonable. The U.S. Supreme Court agreed, noting that the expectation of privacy that one has in a commercial setting is less than that in one's home or even during an overnight stay as a social guest in a friend's home.[89]

One final case concerning home searches is one in which the U.S. Supreme Court considered the time that police must wait for forcible entry after announcing their presence and intent. In *United States* v. *Banks,* Las Vegas, Nevada, police arrived at an apartment to execute a search warrant for drugs. They knocked and yelled, "Police search warrant." When the resident, LaShawn L. Banks, did not answer the door within 15 to 20 seconds, the police entered forcibly and found crack cocaine, three guns, and $6,000 in cash.[90]

The *Banks* case was appealed by the government from the decision by the Ninth Circuit Court of Appeals, which held that the search was unconstitutional and thus the evidence should have been excluded from Banks's federal trial on drug charges and weapons violations. According to the Ninth Circuit, the 15 to 20 seconds the police waited before entering forcibly was an insufficient amount of time in light of the fact that the search warrant was one week old and there were no exigent circumstances requiring such quick action and destruction of property. When police knocked, Banks was in the shower. The Ninth Circuit did not suggest how long police should have waited before a forced entry. The government, arguing on appeal that the wait was reasonable, emphasized that drugs can be disposed of very quickly. Banks's attorney agreed to that statement, noting that "the modern marvel of indoor plumbing does give the opportunity to destroy evidence." But, added the attorney, that plumbing also permits one to shower in the privacy of his own home. Justice Antonin Scalia queried, "What does a shower have to do with it? Is it your contention that a reasonable time is how long it takes to complete a shower?" When Banks's attorney began his reply by stating, "We don't know how long Mr. Banks would have continued showering," Justice Scalia interrupted by stating, "We don't know and we don't care." Justice David H. Souter stated that there might be many reasons that a suspect cannot answer a door quickly when the police arrive with a warrant, but the test for the time permitted before the police enter forcibly should be the time reasonable under the circumstances known to the police. But what is that time? The U.S. Supreme Court did not answer that question but did uphold the police action in this case. The Supreme Court remanded the case to the Ninth Circuit for further action; that court remanded it to the lower court for action consistent with the U.S. Supreme Court's holding.

Automobile Searches Some of the rules concerning warrantless automobile searches were discussed earlier in connection with traffic violation stops, but the U.S. Supreme Court has decided a number of cases that go beyond that scenario.

In *Carroll* v. *United States,* the U.S. Supreme Court held that, when police stop an automobile and have probable cause to believe it contains contraband, it is not unreasonable to search that vehicle. However, the Court did not deal with the *scope* of that permissible search. In *Chambers* v. *Maroney,* the Supreme Court held that a search warrant is not necessary "where there is probable cause to search an automobile stopped on the highway; the car is moveable; the occupants are alerted; and the car's contents may never be found again if a warrant must be obtained." Each case must be judged on its facts, for the Court has made it clear that not all warrantless car searches are lawful.[91]

In 1991, the U.S. Supreme Court clarified some of the procedural problems in *Carroll, Maroney,* and other cases, holding that "the police may search an automobile and the containers within it where they have probable cause to believe contraband or evidence is contained."[92]

In 1981 in *Robbins* v. *California,* the U.S. Supreme Court held that, when police stopped a car for proceeding erratically, smelled marijuana smoke as the door was opened, searched the car, and found two packages wrapped in opaque plastic, they went beyond the scope of a legitimate search without a warrant when they opened the packages.[93] One year later in *United States* v. *Ross,* the Supreme Court reconsidered its position by examining the extent to which police officers, who have stopped an automobile legitimately and who have probable cause to believe that contraband is concealed somewhere within it, may conduct a probing search of compartments and containers within the vehicle if its contents are not in plain view. "We hold that they may conduct a search of the vehicle that is as thorough as a magistrate could authorize in a warrant 'particularly describing the place to be searched.'" The U.S. Supreme Court emphasized that such searches must be based on probable cause.[94]

In 1985, the U.S. Supreme Court held that a warrantless search of packages held for three days after seizure by customs officials was not unreasonable. Customs officials had been observing what appeared to be a drug-smuggling operation. They saw several packages removed from two small airplanes, which had landed in a remote section of the airport. The packages were loaded onto two pickup trucks. The customs officers approached the trucks, smelled marijuana, and saw packages that were wrapped in plastic bags and sealed with tape. Some of the individuals were arrested, and the packages were seized and placed in a Drug Enforcement Agency (DEA) warehouse. Three days later, without a search warrant, officers opened the packages and found marijuana. In ruling that the search was proper even without a warrant, the U.S. Supreme Court held that the warrantless search of a vehicle need not occur contemporaneously with the lawful seizure of the items. The Court emphasized, however, that officers may not hold vehicles and their contents indefinitely before they complete a search.[95]

As noted earlier, in some cases police may conduct warrantless vehicle searches. This may be done to protect the police from danger; to protect the owner's property while the police have custody of the vehicle; and to protect police against claims that items were stolen from the vehicle while it was in police custody.[96] Furthermore, the U.S. Supreme Court held that, when a driver who was stopped for an illegal turn consented to a search of his car, police could legally examine the contents of a closed container within that car.[97]

The search of vehicles may include buses. In 1991, the U.S. Supreme Court held that when police board long-distance buses and, without reasonable suspicion that anyone on those buses is smuggling drugs, ask passengers for permission to search their luggage for narcotics, they are not violating those passengers' constitutional rights per se.[98] In 2002, the U.S. Supreme Court ruled that, when police board a bus to check for drugs or for other purposes, they are not required to tell passengers that they have a right to refuse to cooperate. Reasonable people understand that they are free to leave the bus or to answer questions; thus, when the police board the bus, that action does not constitute a seizure, ruled the Court. Among the three dissenters, Justice David Souter wrote that the "officers took control of the entire passenger compartment" and that "no reasonable passenger could have believed" that he or she was free to refuse to cooperate.[99]

In an earlier decision in 2000, however, the U.S. Supreme Court ruled by a 7-to-2 margin that police do not have the right to feel the personal bags that passengers take onto buses. In *Bond* v. *United States,* the Supreme Court emphasized that when passengers board buses "for whatever reason" they may take personal items in bags that are placed in the overhead racks. In *Bond* the petitioner was a passenger on a Greyhound bus that left California headed for Little Rock, Arkansas. As required by law, the bus stopped at a permanent border patrol checkpoint in Sierra Blanca, Texas, where a border agent boarded the bus to check passengers' immigration status. As the agent walked the aisle, he squeezed the soft luggage in the overhead bins. He felt a "brick-like" object in the soft bag in the rack over Bond's head. Bond acknowledged that was his bag and consented to a search. The agent found a "brick" of methamphetamine. Bond was arrested, charged, and convicted of illegal drug possession.[100]

In 1999, the U.S. Supreme Court held that an officer who has probable cause to conduct a warrantless search of an automobile may search all containers that might hold the object of the search. This includes containers that belong to a passenger. In *Wyoming* v. *Houghton,* a police officer who stopped an automobile noted that the driver had a hypodermic syringe in his shirt pocket. The driver, David Young, was stopped for speeding and driving with a defective brake light. Young admitted that he used the syringe to take drugs. Two passengers were also in the front seat. The officer searched the car, including a purse on the back seat. The respondent in this case, Sandra K. Houghton, claimed the purse, which contained her driver's license with her correct identification. When questioned before this search, Houghton had told the officer that she was Sandra James and that she had no identification. When asked why she had lied, Houghton told the officer she did that "in case things went bad." Upon further search the officer found a brown pouch, which Houghton denied was hers. She admitted ownership of the black, wallet-type container. Officers found illegal drugs and drug paraphernalia and a syringe in each, but the amount of drugs in the syringe within the black container (60 cc of methamphetamine) was not sufficient to support the felony conviction in this case. Fresh needle marks were noticed on

Houghton's arms. She was arrested and charged with felony possession of methamphetamine in a liquid amount greater than three-tenths of a gram. Her motion to have the contraband excluded was denied; she was convicted. A divided Wyoming Supreme Court reversed the conviction, stating that the officer should have known that the purse did not belong to the driver and there was no probable cause to search the possessions of the passengers. Thus, the evidence against Houghton should have been excluded, as the search violated the Fourth and Fourteenth Amendments. By a 6-to-3 vote the U.S. Supreme Court reversed, holding that the police had probable cause to search the car and thus were permitted to search the appellee's belongings that might have contained the items for which the police were searching.[101]

In *Maryland* v. *Pringle,* decided in 2003, the U.S. Supreme Court considered the following fact pattern. The appellant was a passenger in the front seat of a car; another passenger was in the back seat. The police had probable cause to stop the driver of the car because he was speeding. The driver and the passengers consented to a search, during which the police found cocaine in the back seat armrest and a significant amount of cash in the glove compartment. None of the occupants claimed possession of the drugs or the cash. All three occupants of the car were arrested and charged with the possession of illegal drugs. Joseph Pringle argued successfully to a Maryland appellate court that the police did not have probable cause to arrest him and thus the illegal drugs and questionable cash should not have been admitted as evidence against him, although he acknowledged that those items were his property. The U.S. Supreme Court disagreed and held that the arrest was proper. According to the Supreme Court, a reasonable officer could have thought any or all of the car's occupants were responsible for the contraband; thus, the officers had probable cause to arrest all three occupants.[102]

Finally, we consider the issue of whether police violate a suspect's constitutional rights when they use a drug-detecting dog to sniff a vehicle after they signal the driver to pull over in a routine traffic stop. In *Illinois* v. *Caballes,* police stopped Roy Caballes because he was driving 71 miles per hour in a 65-mile-per-hour zone on Interstate 80. Upon request, Caballes provided police with his driver's license, vehicle registration, and proof of insurance. Caballes was asked to join the police officer in his squad car; when he did, a warning ticket for speeding was issued. Caballes refused to grant the officer's request to search his car. The officer asked Caballes if he had ever been arrested, and he replied in the negative. But the police dispatcher informed the officer that Caballes had been arrested twice on suspicion of distributing marijuana. While the officer was writing the ticket, another officer arrived with a dog trained to sniff for drugs; the dog smelled drugs; Caballes's car was searched; marijuana was found; and Caballes was arrested for drug trafficking. The U.S. Supreme Court agreed to review the case to determine whether the Fourth Amendment (see Appendix A) prohibition against unreasonable searches and seizures requires police to have a reasonable suspicion before they use drug-sniffing dogs during a legitimate traffic stop. In January 2005, the Supreme Court ruled in the *Caballes* case, holding that a well-trained narcotics-detection dog used, as in this case, to sniff only the outside of the vehicle during a legitimate traffic stop, is permitted by the Fourth Amendment.[103]

Body Searches   The search of body cavities is the most controversial search and seizure issue. Some body cavity searches are permitted, but there are limitations on the type, time, place, and method of search. The classic case involving body searches was decided in 1949 when three deputy sheriffs of Los Angeles County, relying on some information that a man named Rochin was selling narcotics, went to Rochin's home and entered the home through an open door. The officers forced open the door of the second-floor bedroom, where they found Rochin, partially clothed, sitting on the bed where his wife was lying. The officers saw two capsules beside the bed, and asked, "Whose stuff is this?" Rochin grabbed the capsules and swallowed them. The officers, applying force, tried to remove the capsules and, when they were unsuccessful, handcuffed Rochin and took him to the hospital. They ordered his stomach pumped, and the drugs were used as evidence in the subsequent trial, at which Rochin was convicted. In *Rochin* v. *California,* the U.S. Supreme Court stated why this search and seizure was illegal.[104]

Rochin v. California

[T]he proceedings by which this conviction was obtained do more than offend some fastidious squeamishness or private sentimentalism about combating crime too energetically. This is conduct that shocks the conscience, illegally breaking into the privacy of the petitioner, the struggle to open his mouth and remove what was there, the forcible extraction of his stomach's contents—this course of proceeding by agents of government to obtain evidence is bound to offend even hardened sensibilities. They are methods too close to the rack and the screw to permit of constitutional differentiation.

Body cavity searches are permitted under some circumstances. Safety and security within jails and prisons are sufficient reasons for strip searching prison inmates, but a distinction can be made between prison inmates and detained suspects. Thus, the Ninth Circuit Court of Appeals invalidated a blanket policy of strip searching all felony arrestees.[105]

The Ninth Circuit held that it was illegal to conduct a strip and visual search of the vagina and anus of each of three women who were arrested for shoplifting rings. No rings were found, and no charges were filed. The court noted that, even if the women had secreted rings in their body cavities, they were in no danger to themselves. Furthermore, officials could have monitored their behavior until a search warrant was secured. Thus, no exigent circumstances existed for conducting a warrantless body cavity search.[106]

Earlier we noted that border searches are permissible. Body cavity searches may also be conducted at the borders into the country whenever customs officials have reason to believe a person is smuggling contraband by carrying the contraband, usually illegal drugs, therein. This crime is referred to as *alimentary canal smuggling*. Probable cause is not required for the search of body cavities in these cases; customs officials need only have a reasonable suspicion that a traveler is committing the crime of alimentary canal smuggling to conduct the search.

The U.S. Supreme Court has decided a case on this issue. *United States* v. *Montoya de Hernandez* involved a woman who arrived in Los Angeles from Bogota, Colombia. Customs officials became suspicious when, while examining her passport, they noted that she had made numerous recent trips to Miami and Los Angeles. She was carrying $5,000 in cash and told officers that she planned to purchase goods for her husband's store, but she had made no hotel reservations or any appointments with merchandise vendors. Customs officials suspected that she was smuggling drugs within her body. A patdown search by a female officer disclosed that the suspect's abdomen was firm and that she was wearing plastic underpants lined with a paper towel.[107]

Officials asked the suspect to consent to an X ray, which at first she agreed to do, but subsequently she withdrew her consent. At that point she was given three choices. She could return to Colombia on the next available flight, submit to an X ray, or remain in detention until she produced a bowel movement, which would be monitored. She chose to return to Colombia, but no flight was available, so she was detained for 16 hours. During that time she refused to use the toilet facilities provided for her (a wastebasket placed in a restroom). She refused to eat or drink. Officials obtained a court order for an X ray and a body search of her rectum. They found a cocaine-filled balloon. During the next four days of detention, the suspect excreted numerous balloons filled with cocaine, totaling more than half a kilogram of the drug.

In upholding the body search as legal, the U.S. Supreme Court stated that the right to privacy is diminished at the border. The suspect's rights are important, but the government has an interest in preventing drug smuggling. The test used by the Court for border searches is whether, after considering all of the facts involved, customs officials reasonably suspect that the traveler is smuggling contraband in his or her alimentary canal.

In contrast is a case involving proposed surgery to remove a bullet from a suspect who refused to consent to the surgery. The U.S. Supreme Court held that this search and seizure would be unreasonable. The prosecution claimed that the bullet would link the suspect to the crime. Initial investigation had shown that the surgery would involve only a minor incision, which could be conducted with a local anesthetic; on the basis of that evidence, the lower court granted the request to conduct the surgery. Further evidence indicated that the bullet was embedded deeply and that removal would require a general anesthetic.

The U.S. Supreme Court noted that the interest of individuals in their right to privacy, as well as health and life, must be considered against the government's interest in combating crime. A surgical procedure to remove evidence may be unreasonable and therefore illegal if it "endangers the life or health of the suspect . . . and [intrudes] upon the individual's dignitary interest in personal privacy and bodily integrity." In this case the Supreme Court said there was considerable medical uncertainty regarding the safety of the procedure.[108]

One example of illegal body searches does not involve an appeal because the case was settled out of court. In New York City 50,000 or more people were eligible to share in a settlement of $50 million for damages sustained when they were strip searched after arrests for such minor offenses as disorderly conduct, loitering, and subway violations. The searches were conducted by jail guards in Manhattan and Queens over a 10-month period in 1996 and 1997. The individual awards ranged from $250 to $22,500. The higher awards were available to plaintiffs who could prove significant emotional damages.[109]

The settlement ended those claims, but in October 2003 a judge ruled that the allegations brought by 20 persons of illegal strip searches by New York police in Brooklyn were sufficient to state a cause of action for trial. Those persons and others with similar claims could sue the police department for searching them (after arrests on minor charges) even when there was no reason to suspect that they were concealing illegal drugs or other contraband. One Haitian man, Paul G. Brumaire, who was arrested on a misdemeanor charge evolving from a dispute with a tenant, said he was forced to undress and bend over in front of laughing officers. One officer was holding a metal wand, normally used as a metal detector. Brumaire said he began to think of Abner Louima, the Haitian who was sodomized by New York police, resulting in the criminal trials of several officers.[110]

An interesting body search and seizure case was decided by the Texas Court of Criminal Appeal in April 2003. On 20 December 1997, a Houston police officer received a call from a "concerned citizen" that a man named McGee and two other men were selling crack cocaine at a particular intersection and that McGee was hiding the drugs between his buttocks. The officer went to the intersection, found three men who matched the description, smelled marijuana, and saw blue smoke surrounding the men. Based on his experience, the officer decided the smoke came from marijuana. He asked for identification and confirmed the names with those given by the caller. The officer checked for weapons and found none. McGee admitted that someone smoked marijuana but that he did not do so. The police found a cigar containing marijuana on the ground. The men were handcuffed and transported to a nearby fire station. The Texas court noted the following additional facts.[111]

McGee v. Texas

At the fire station, Officer Rowan took McGee to a secluded area of the station and compelled Mcgee to drop his pants, bend over, and spread his buttocks. Officer Rowan proceeded to perform a visual search of McGee's anal region. The officer testified that he saw several rocks of crack cocaine wrapped in red plastic in plain view lodged between McGee's buttocks. He further testified that the crack cocaine was not inside McGee's anus, but that when the cocaine was exposed, McGee attempted to push it into his anus. Officer Rowen testified that he was able to retrieve the drugs before McGee pushed them into his anus without digitally probing the anus. McGee was then charged with possession of cocaine.

Before trial, McGee presented his motion to suppress evidence, which the trial court denied after a hearing. McGee then pled guilty to the charge of possession of cocaine weighing less than one gram and was sentenced to 90 days' confinement. . . . [McGee appealed, arguing that the evidence should have been excluded because it was the result of an illegal search and seizure and that the arrest was illegal. The court of appeals agreed. The state sought review by the Texas Court of Criminal Appeals, which reversed the lower appellate court. Among other comments, the court stated the following.]

The [U.S.] Supreme Court has upheld the use of visual body cavity searches based on suspicion short of probable cause.... [In this case] the arresting officer had probable cause to believe that McGee was engaged in illegal activity. Probable cause is the highest level of justification employed by the courts. While we do not create a per se rule that probable cause always justifies a body cavity search, in this instance we find from the totality of the circumstances that Officer Rowan had sufficient justification to believe that a search was necessary....

The Court of Appeals was incorrect in holding that the cocaine should have been suppressed. We reverse the judgment of the Court of Appeals and reinstate the judgment of the trial court.

One final strip search case does not involve a criminal but, rather, a civil issue, but it is included here to illustrate the allegation that searches may be racist—and to show how long it might take to settle a civil case. The case began in 1991, when Rhonda Brent, a Houston, Texas, woman, who is African American, arrived at the Miami International Airport on her way home from a vacation in Nigeria. On her flight from Rome, Brent met a Nigerian man. She was walking through customs with him when agents began to question him and she indicated her disapproval of the agents' actions. She began to walk away but was stopped and questioned by an agent. She was detained for 10 hours, thus missing her flight. During the detention she was strip searched. Brent claimed she was victimized because she is African American; the agents responded that they had searched her because she appeared nervous and they had evidence that African American males were using African American females to transport illegal drugs. Brent and her Nigerian acquaintance were the only black passengers on the flight. In November 2003, Brent accepted a settlement offer of $350,000 from the U.S. government.[112]

Interrogation

Another important law enforcement function of policing is interrogation. Police must be able to question suspects, but that need to question must be balanced with the Fifth Amendment provision that no person "shall be compelled in any criminal case to be a witness against himself" (see Appendix A). For much of our history, it was assumed that most decisions regarding police interrogation and the admission of evidence obtained by those interrogations were governed by state, not federal, law. Jurisdictions recognized various police practices, and coercion of confessions was not uncommon. In 1964, the U.S. Supreme Court declared that "today the admissibility of a confession in a state criminal prosecution is tested by the same standard applied in federal prosecutions since 1897," which meant that the Fifth Amendment's prohibition against self-incrimination was applicable to the states.[113]

In 1964 in *Escobedo* v. *Illinois,* the U.S. Supreme Court spoke of "the right of the accused to be advised by his lawyer of his privilege against self-incrimination." Although *Escobedo* concerned the Sixth Amendment right to counsel (see Appendix A), it was considered important in the movement toward interpreting the Fifth Amendment as constituting a right not to testify against oneself.[114]

In 1966, the U.S. Supreme Court decided *Miranda* v. *Arizona* by a 5-to-4 decision, which set off a flurry of reaction from liberals and conservatives but established the constitutional rights of the accused concerning interrogation. The Supreme Court engaged in a lengthy examination of police manuals, which stated, among other things, how to use psychological coercion to elicit the suspect's confession. The Court examined the facts of the *Miranda* case. Briefly stated, Ernesto Miranda was arrested, taken into custody, and identified by a complaining witness. He was held and interrogated for two hours by police, who admitted that they did not tell him he had a right to have an attorney present. The police obtained from Miranda a written confession, which said that his confession was voluntary, that he had made it with full knowledge that it could be used against him, and that he fully understood his legal rights. That confession was admitted into evidence at the trial, and Miranda was convicted.

The Arizona Supreme Court upheld the conviction, emphasizing that Miranda did not ask for an attorney. The U.S. Supreme Court reversed the conviction in a lengthy decision discussing the dangers of establishing psychological environments in which the accused, even if innocent, would confess. To protect suspects from impermissible psychological interrogation, the Court handed down the **Miranda warning,** which consists of the following:

- The right to remain silent.
- The right to notice that anything said by the suspect may and will be used against him or her at trial.
- The right to the presence of an attorney, who will be
- Appointed (that is, paid for by the government) if the suspect is indigent.[115]

The suspect may waive the right to an attorney, but that waiver must be made voluntarily, knowingly, and intelligently. If the suspect indicates a willingness to talk but subsequently wishes to remain silent, police should not continue their interrogation.

The U.S. Supreme Court has decided numerous cases interpreting *Miranda*. For example, in *Davis* v. *United States* the Court voted 5-to-4 to uphold a defendent's conviction of murdering a fellow serviceman on naval grounds. After he received the *Miranda* warnings, the suspect signed a waiver of his right to counsel and began talking. Later he stated, "Maybe I should see a lawyer." At that point officers stopped questioning him about the crime and began inquiring whether he wanted counsel. The suspect said he did not wish to speak with an attorney, and interrogation was resumed. The suspect's statements were used against him, and he was convicted. On appeal, the Supreme Court upheld the admission of this evidence. In the opinion written for the majority, Justice Sandra Day O'Connor stated that the Court was not willing to go beyond previous cases and hold that police may not question a suspect who *might* want an attorney. The suspect must request an attorney.[116] This case is not to be confused with the Court's previous holdings that once a suspect has invoked the right to counsel the police must cease interrogation.[117]

By far the most important of the recent decisions concerning *Miranda* was *Dickerson* v. *United States,* decided by the U.S. Supreme Court in 2000. In this case, decided by a 7-to-2 vote, the Court reaffirmed *Miranda,* with Chief Justice William H. Rehnquist writing the opinion and calling the decision a part of American culture. The case involved a 1968 congressional statute, which provided that, in determining whether a confession is voluntary, courts should weigh several factors, only one of which is whether the *Miranda* warning was given. The issue before the Supreme Court in the *Dickerson* case was whether the federal statute was an unconstitutional attempt by Congress to overrule *Miranda.* It had been assumed that *Miranda* establishes an irrebuttable presumption that a confession is not voluntary if it is made prior to the giving of the *Miranda* warning. The argument was that the U.S. Constitution does not require this presumption; thus, Congress has the power to reverse the rule by statute, which it did in this 1968 law.[118]

Section (b) of the federal statute provides as follows:

(b) The trial judge in determining the issue of voluntariness shall take into consideration all the circumstances surrounding the giving of the confession, including (1) the time elapsing between arrest and arraignment of the defendant making the confession, if it was made after arrest and before arraignment, (2) whether such defendant knew the nature of the offense with which he was charged or of which he was suspected at the time of making the confession, (3) whether or not such defendant was advised or knew that he was not required to make any statement and that any such statement could be used against him, (4) whether or not such defendant had been advised prior to questioning of his right to the assistance of counsel; and (5) whether or not such defendant was without the assistance of counsel when questioned and when giving such confession.[119]

▶ **Miranda warning** The rule stemming from *Miranda* v. *Arizona,* which stipulates that anyone in custody for an offense that might result in a jail or prison term must be warned of certain rights before any questioning by law enforcement officials occurs. These rights include the right to remain silent, to be told that anything said can and will be held against the suspect, the right to counsel (which will be appointed if the suspect cannot afford to retain private counsel), and the right to cease talking at any time. If the warning is not given or is given and violated, any information obtained from the suspect may be inadmissible as evidence at trial. The rights may be waived if done so willingly and knowingly by one who has the legal capacity to waive them.

The presence or absence of any of the previously mentioned factors to be taken into consideration by the judge need not be conclusive on the issue of the voluntariness of the confession. Federal prosecutors had made little or no effort to enforce this statute until the *Dickerson* case.

In *Dickerson* the U.S. Supreme Court ruled that the *Miranda* rule is constitutional; it rests on the principles of due process as guaranteed by the Fourteenth Amendment and the Fifth Amendment's (see Appendix A) privilege against self-incrimination. Thus, Congress did not have the power to reverse the requirement by statute. Reversal would have required a constitutional amendment.

Dickerson did not answer all the *Miranda* questions, however, and in December 2003 the U.S. Supreme Court heard oral arguments in three cases involving the issue of whether police may question suspects first and then issue the *Miranda* warning after those suspects have confessed. The case of *Missouri* v. *Seibert* involved a mother who was accused of conspiring for her 17-year-old retarded son to die in a fire in their mobile home in order to cover up evidence that a younger son had died by neglect. Five days after the fire, when Patrice Seibert was sleeping in the waiting room at the hospital, police interrogators awakened her and questioned her about the fire, using repeatedly the phrase, "Donald was also to die in his sleep." The interrogators said they were instructed to question the suspect and get a confession before giving her the *Miranda* warnings. Seibert confessed, was tried, and convicted. The Missouri Supreme Court reversed the conviction on the grounds that Seibert's constitutional rights were violated when she was not first given the *Miranda* warning; thus, her confession could not be used at her trial. The legal issue was whether her confession could be used because it was voluntary. The U.S. Supreme Court affirmed the Missouri Supreme Court's ruling, holding that questioning a suspect first tended to thwart the purpose of the *Miranda* warning and thus the confession violated Seibert's constitutional rights.[120]

In the second case, *United States* v. *Fellers*, John Fellers was convicted of drug charges. The police had gone to Fellers's home; told him they were there to discuss his involvement in drug distribution; and asked to talk with him. Fellers invited the police into his home, after which they told him that a grand jury had indicted him on drug charges and that they had a warrant for his arrest. The police named four of the persons with whom the indictment stated Fellers had conspired. Fellers told the officers that he knew the four and had used drugs with them. Fellers was arrested and taken to the county jail, where he was given his *Miranda* warning for the first time. Fellers then repeated his earlier statement. Subsequently Fellers petitioned the court to exclude these statements from his trial; the statements made at his home were excluded; those made at the jail were admitted; and he was convicted. On appeal Fellers argued that the jailhouse statements should have been excluded as the "forbidden fruits" (evidence obtained as the result of an illegal search or an illegal interrogation) of the statements made in his home in violation of his constitutional rights. The U.S. Circuit Court of Appeals for the Eighth Circuit held that Fellers's jailhouse statements were properly admitted at his trial because they had been made voluntarily and thus were not tainted by the failure of the arresting officers to give the *Miranda* warnings *before* the statements were made. The U.S. Supreme Court found that the police had deliberately elicited the statements from Fellers at his home, in violation of Fellers's Sixth Amendment right to counsel. The High Court sent the case back to the Eighth Circuit court for a determination of whether the testimony secured as the result of the police violation of Fellers's constitutional right at his home tainted the testimony elicited from Fellers at the jailhouse, thus requiring that the jailhouse confession also be excluded. The Eighth Circuit held that there was no evidence that the police used the illegally secured testimony of Fellers at his home to elicit his jailhouse confession. The policies that support excluding from trial any evidence that is illegally obtained were, according to the court, fulfilled by the exclusion of the testimony Fellers made at his home. The exclusion of his jailhouse testimony would not promote the fairness of the trial process, because it was not unfair to Fellers; thus, it was properly used against him. The Eighth Circuit upheld the convictions but sent the case back to the trial court for resentencing, noting that the court had erred in its determination of Feller's sentence.[121]

The third case on the *Miranda* warning and part of the U.S. Supreme Court's docket in December 2003, *United States* v. *Patane,* involved the use of physical evidence secured before the police gave the *Miranda* warning. Colorado Springs, Colorado, police went to the home of Samuel Patane to arrest him, a felon accused of violating a domestic restraining order. After Patane was arrested and handcuffed, one officer began reading him the *Miranda* warning, but Patane stopped the officer. When the police later asked him about a gun, Patane told them where it could be found. That weapon, secured from Patane before he had heard his full *Miranda* rights, was admitted at his trial. Patane was convicted of being in possession of a firearm, which is illegal for felons. On appeal, the Tenth Circuit Court of Appeals held that the gun should not have been admitted as evidence because it was obtained during a search that violated the suspect's *Miranda* rights. The U.S. Supreme Court reversed and remanded the case, stating that the fruits of an unwarned but voluntary statement from a suspect may be admitted against that person at trial.[122]

These three cases, along with another one, *Yarborough* v. *Alvarado*[123] (which involved the *Miranda* warnings as they apply to juveniles and is discussed in Chapter 12), decided by the U.S. Supreme Court during its 2003–2004 term, gave the Supreme Court an opportunity to refine further the implications of the *Miranda* decision.

The issues of police interrogation continue. In a 2003 article, Yale Kamisar, noted law professor and author of numerous scholarly publications on police interrogation (and other topics), wrote a special piece for the *National Law Journal.* In this article Kamisar spoke about the importance of tape recording police interrogations. Referring to the *Miranda* decision statement that the secrecy surrounding police interrogation "results in a gap in our knowledge as to what in fact goes on in the interrogation rooms," Kamisar noted, "37 years later, we know little more about actual police interrogation practices than we did at the time of Miranda. The 'swearing contest' between police and suspect as to what was said [a contest usually won by the police] has not let up." Kamisar noted that police often tape confessions but not interrogations prior to those confessions. He referred to a narrowly defeated bill in Illinois that would have required police to videotape or audiotape all police interrogations. That bill died after the law enforcement community successfully lobbied against it, complaining that it would increase the defendants' rights and hinder public security. Said Kamisar, "Why making a complete record of what happened during interrogations would expand the rights of the accused was not made clear. Illinois has, however, . . . passed a new bill to take effect in two years that will require videotaping of interrogations in murder cases." Kamisar concluded his article with this statement:

> It is not because a peace officer is more dishonest than the rest of us that we should demand an objective recording of the critical custodial events. Rather, it is because we are entitled to assume that the police are no less human—and equally inclined to reconstruct and interpret past events in a favorable light—that we should not permit them to be the judges of their own cause.[124]

Finally, it is important to understand that *Miranda* applies only to a *custodial* interrogation. Police are free to ask questions in noncustodial circumstances without giving the required warning. The question often is, however, what constitutes a custodial situation. In a 2003 Texas case the U.S. Supreme Court refused to uphold a decision in which police had gone to the home of Robert Kaupp, 17, who was awakened at 3 A.M. and told, "[W]e need to go and talk." Kaupp was convicted for a 1999 murder and sentenced to 55 years in prison. The U.S. Supreme Court rejected the lower court's decision that Kaupp was not under arrest, as he was free to refuse to cooperate with the officers. Thus, his answers to police questions were admissible in court. The Supreme Court stated that a "group of police officers rousing an adolescent out of bed in the middle of the night with the words 'we need to go and talk' presents no option but 'to go.' . . . It cannot seriously be suggested that when the detectives began to question Kaupp, a reasonable person in his situation would have thought he was sitting in the interview room as a matter of choice, free to change his mind and go home to bed." The U.S. Supreme Court vacated the lower appellate court's decision, sent the case back for reconsideration, and instructed the court that Kaupp's confession should be excluded "unless . . . the state can point to testimony undisclosed on the record before us, and weighty enough to carry the state's burden despite the clear force of the evidence shown here."[125]

Investigation

Crime scene investigation has become a popular topic in the United States, capturing the attention of millions on television shows such as *CSI: Crime Scene Investigation,* and *CSI: Miami,* the number one and number two shows for 16–22 June 2003, as well as many other weeks, although by the end of November 2004 *CSI: Miami* had slipped to number three, with *Desperate Housewives* in the number two slot.[126] A popular board game based on the TV series enables players to serve as interns assigned to solve a horrible Las Vegas crime, and *CSI: Crime Scene Investigation—the Complete First Season* is available on DVD. Further, with the assistance of a $2 million federal grant, the University of New Haven has established the nation's first national crime scene investigation training center, located in the university's Henry C. Lee Institute of Forensic Science. Dr. Lee is an internationally known forensics expert, who stated that this center "is going to provide a real CSI training center for the country." According to a legal account, "At the school crime lab workers, lawyers and other law enforcement officials will take intensive, hands-on, week long classes about the basics of processing crime scenes and protecting evidence. The school will also offer specialized classes on other investigative tools, from ballistics tests to the science of blood stains."[127]

Searching and seizing, along with interrogation, illustrates the investigative function of policing. The success or failure of the prosecution of a suspect for a particular crime often depends on the investigative abilities of the police before, during, or after the suspect's arrest. Evidence may be destroyed quickly or never found. Without physical evidence, it may be impossible to link the alleged criminal activity with the suspect.

In large police departments, criminal investigations may be the responsibility of specialists, and police officers may not be closely involved in the process. In many cases, however, the police officer who makes the arrest is a critical element in the investigative process. In some police departments, the patrol officer's investigative function is limited. Most of this work, at least in serious cases, is conducted by specialized officers in the criminal investigation unit of the department. These investigators conduct various kinds of activities, ranging from the maintenance of field activity records to total crime scene management, including such other activities as collecting body fluids, photographing crime scenes, following up on investigations, sketching crime scenes, obtaining search/arrest warrants, conducting interviews/interrogations, and attending autopsies.

Police use many investigative techniques. Fingerprinting is one of the most effective methods. This technique has been available in the United States since it was first used around 1900 by London's Scotland Yard. The use of computers to assist with fingerprint identification has increased investigative techniques in this area.

Another technique is the use of deoxyribonucleic acid, or DNA, "which carries the genetic information that determines individual characteristics such as eye color and body size." Some argue that DNA is close to 100 percent accurate, compared with traditional blood and semen tests, which are only 90 to 95 percent accurate. Advocates call this process *DNA genetic fingerprinting.*[128]

DNA results have been used to free inmates who were convicted and have served years in prison. The results have been used to win acquittals for defendants as well as to convict others. But the use of DNA remains controversial; courts do not agree on whether testimony regarding DNA should be admitted, although the trend is toward admitting the evidence. Some courts have admitted certain methods of DNA testing while excluding others or have instructed trial courts to examine the testing methods more carefully. Lawyers may also challenge the methods of collecting and analyzing DNA evidence.

Chapter Wrap-Up

This chapter is the second of three on policing, and it began with a discussion of preparing for policing, which looked at the issues surrounding the recruitment, selection, education, and training of police.

Police exercise wide discretion in criminal justice systems, and the chapter devoted a section to the explanation and analysis of why discretion is necessary and how it might be abused. Discretion cannot be abolished; thus, controlling it is a necessity. The primary focus of the chapter, however, was on the functions that police must perform in an increasingly complex society. Those functions are numerous, but they are categorized as law enforcement, order maintenance, and community service. In the chapter the last two were discussed briefly before greater attention was given to law enforcement.

The controversy over the importance of order maintenance was noted within the context of the contributions of several experts on policing. Order maintenance may be a crucial function of policing, as the absence of order may lead to law violations, even serious criminal acts, such as the violent crimes of aggravated assault and murder. Likewise, the community service function of policing may prevent or reduce actions that might lead to law violations. Furthermore, many of the activities police are called upon to perform occur after hours, when other organizations have closed for the day.

The discussion of law enforcement began with a brief overview of the constitutional limitations on policing, for it is clear that police could make more arrests and conduct more thorough investigations if they did not have to observe defendants' due process rights. U.S. criminal justice systems place great emphasis on the right of individuals to be free from unreasonable governmental intrusion. This does not mean that police cannot arrest, search and seize, interrogate, and investigate but only that these functions must be performed within the limits of state and federal statutes, constitutions, and court decisions. Those limits are being challenged in many cases, but particular attention was given in this chapter to recent cases questioning the USA Patriot Act.

The Fourth Amendment's prohibition against unreasonable search and seizure and the Fifth Amendment's provision that a person may not be forced to incriminate him- or herself are the key constitutional bases of what police may and may not do in law enforcement. The investigatory stop, brief detention, arrest, and searching and seizing are important police activities regulated by constitutional requirements, court interpretations of those requirements, and departmental policies.

A look at a few key cases on the law of stop, arrest, search, and seizure should make it obvious that it is impossible to state what *the law* is in these areas. The facts of a particular case must be analyzed carefully in light of previous court decisions, statutes, and constitutional provisions. Reasonable minds may differ as to the conclusion in any given case. It is important to analyze case law carefully, looking at the rule of a case as well as the reasons for that rule.

In some situations police are permitted to stop, arrest, search, and seize without a warrant, although the U.S. Supreme Court prefers warrants. Again, it is impossible for police to know in every case whether they face exceptions to the warrant requirement. Frequently, law enforcement is ambiguous, leaving considerable discretion to the individual officer, who may be second-guessed by the courts. Despite the need to analyze individual cases in terms of their unique facts, there are some general principles of constitutional law governing the law enforcement function of policing. Those were discussed in the chapter, with attention paid to some of the major U.S. Supreme Court cases governing each aspect of law enforcement, from the initial stop to the searching and seizing of homes, automobiles, and persons.

Interrogation is another important law enforcement function. The U.S. Supreme Court has decided many cases in this area. The *Miranda* warning must be given in cases in which a person might be deprived of his or her liberty, but it is not always clear when interrogation has begun and the warning must be given. Failure to comply with *Miranda* requirements may result in the exclusion of evidence from the trial, an issue to be discussed in Chapter 5.

Investigation was the final police function discussed in this chapter. Traditionally police have spent considerable time investigating crimes at the scene of their occurrence without significant effectiveness. Recently investigative techniques have been improved by the use of forensic science, especially DNA. Some continue to question its reliability or challenge the scientist's work on DNA.

Policing has changed in many ways in recent years. This chapter touches on only a few areas in which changes have been attempted. Chapter 5 focuses on the primary problems and issues of policing.

Key Terms

arrest (p. 95)

contraband (p. 94)

curtilage (p. 99)

frisk (p. 93)

harmless error (p. 98)

informant (p. 95)

Miranda *warning* (p. 107)

negligence (p. 81)

plain view doctrine (p. 99)

probable cause (p. 95)

racial profiling (p. 90)

reversible error (p. 98)

search and seizure (p. 95)

search warrant (p. 95)

warrant (p. 95)

Apply It

1. If you were in charge of recruiting persons into policing, what characteristics would you emphasize? What emphasis would you place on higher education and why? What type of training would you require and why? How would you assess the ethical and moral standards of recruits? What standards would you require for policing and what efforts would you suggest for maintaining those standards within police forces?

2. What effect do you think the Attack on America has had on policing? What types of training would prepare police for such terrorist acts?

3. Discuss the importance of discretion in policing.

4. What is meant by *order maintenance* in policing?

5. What should be the role of police with regard to service functions within the communities they serve?

6. Explain briefly the constitutional provisions that govern policing.

7. Describe the origin and purpose of the USA Patriot Act and note the constitutional issues regarding this expansive act.

8. What functions do police have in traffic control and enforcement of traffic laws and ordinances? Discuss the recent U.S. Supreme Court cases in this area.

9. Under what circumstances may police stop, question, and arrest a suspect? When may police frisk?

10. Explain racial profiling and its implications.

11. Why are warrants usually required for arrest and search?

12. Under what circumstances may police search without a warrant? Arrest without a warrant?

13. What is the meaning of *probable cause* and how may it be established?

14. When may police search a home? How much of the home may be searched? Explain the plain view doctrine and define curtilage.

15. After knocking and announcing, how long must police wait before entering a home forcibly to execute a search warrant?

16. Do you believe police should be permitted to use drug-sniffing dogs at the scene of a normal traffic stop?

17. Explain the *plain feel* doctrine.

18. Under what circumstances may an automobile be searched?

19. Under what circumstances may body searches be conducted?

20. What is the *Miranda* warning? Why is it important? What did the U.S. Supreme Court hold in the *Dickerson* case? What right-to-counsel issues has the U.S. Supreme Court decided recently?

21. What is DNA testing and why is it controversial?

Endnotes

1. See Arthur Niederhoffer, *Behind the Shield: The Police in Urban Society* (Garden City, N.Y.: Anchor Books, 1969), pp. 109–160.

2. John Kleinig, *The Ethics of Policing* (New York: University of Cambridge, 1996), front cover, as cited in a review of the text by Richard N. Holden, *Criminal Justice Review* 22 (September 1997): 113.

3. "Ex-Cop Serpico Testifies on NYPD," *Miami Herald* (24 September 1997), p. 8.

4. "At Columbia, Low Turnout for Police Recruiting Efforts, but It's No 1968," *New York Times* (28 March 2002), p. 24.

5. "New York Police Overtime Soars: Extra Pay May Speed Retirement," *New York Times* (2 November 2002), p. 1.

6. "Los Angeles Police Officials Admit Widespread Lapses," *New York Times* (19 February 2000), p. 12, quoting Edward A. Flynn, police chief of Arlington County, Va.

7. "Ivy Leaguers with a P.D.: Choice of Police Work Brings Skepticism from Both Sides," *New York Times* (17 January 1999), p. 23.

8. Jordan v. City of New London, 2000 U.S. App. LEXIS 22195 (2d Cir. 2000).

9. "Give Police Officers the Training They Need to Excel," *Fresno Bee* (California) (17 May 2003), p. 9B.

10. "A Costly Gift to Police," *Boston Globe* (29 April 2003), p. 20; "Proposed Police Standards Raise Opposition in House," *Providence Journal* (16 March 2004), p. 1C; "Boston Police among Highest Paid in Nation," *Boston Globe* (29 March 2004), p. 1. The so-called Quinn bill is codified at ALM GL Chapter 41, Section 108L (2004).

11. The President's Commission on Law Enforcement and Administration of Justice, *The Challenge of Crime in a Free Society* (Washington, D.C.: U.S. Government Printing Office, 1967), p. 109.

12. See Patrick Murphy, foreword to David L. Carter et al., *The State of Police Education: Policy Direction for the 21st Century* (Washington, D.C.: Police Executive Research Forum, 1989), pp. iii–iv.

13. For an analysis of higher education and policing, see Agnes L. Baro and David Burlingame, "Law Enforcement and Higher Education: Is There an Impasse?" *Journal of Criminal Justice Education* 10 (Spring 1999): 57–74.

14. Carter et al., *The State of Police Education*, p. 15.

15. Baro and Burlingame, "Law Enforcement and Higher Education: Is There an Impasse?" p. 70.

16. The President's Commission on Law Enforcement and Administration of Justice, *Task Force Report: The Police* (Washington, D.C.: U.S. Government Printing Office, 1967), p. 138.

17. The President's Commission on Law Enforcement and Administration of Justice, *The Challenge of Crime in a Free Society*, pp. 112–113.

18. National Advisory Commission on Criminal Justice Standards and Goals, *A National Strategy to Reduce Crime* (Washington, D.C.: U.S. Government Printing Office, 1973), p. 83.

19. The U.S. Commission on Civil Rights, *Who Is Guarding the Guardians? A Report on Police Practices* (Washington, D.C.: U.S. Government Printing Office, October 1981), p. 155.

20. "Training Could Prevent Many Police Cell Fatalities," *Birmingham Post* (11 June 2003), p. 6.

21. "Bike Cops Get Road-Ready: Training Helps Officers Learn Skills and Stamina to Patrol on Two Wheels," *Detroit News* (25 June 2003), p. 1K.

22. "Ensure School-Based Officers Are Trained to Work on Campus," *School Violence Alert* 7, no. 12 (27 November 2001).

23. "Cops Get Grisly Lesson in Unearthing Clues: County Police Training Program Draws Officers from Across Nation," *Asbury Park Press* (29 May 2003), p. 1B.

24. "Owasso Police Officer to Train with DEA," *Tulsa World* (4 June 2003), p. 1ZE.

25. "Homeland Security," *Indianapolis Star* (13 June 2003), p. 3B.

26. "Community College/Police Training Partnership," *Public Management* 85, no. 2 (1 March 2003): 22.

27. City of Canton, Ohio v. Harris, 489 U.S. 378 (1989).

28. Cecil L. Willis and Richard H. Wells, "The Police and Child Abuse: An Analysis of Police Decisions to Report Illegal Behavior," *Criminology* 26 (November 1988): 695–715.

29. James Q. Wilson, *Varieties of Police Behavior: The Management of Law and Order in Eight Communities* (Cambridge, Mass.: Harvard University Press, 1968), pp. 16, 17, 21.

30. Ibid., p. 21.

31. George L. Kelling, "Order Maintenance, the Quality of Urban Life, and Police: A Line of Argument," in *Police Leadership in America: Crisis and Opportunity*, ed. William A. Geller (Chicago: American Bar Foundation, 1985), p. 297.

32. Ibid., p. 308.

33. See James Q. Wilson and George L. Kelling, "Police and Neighborhood Safety: Broken Windows," *Atlantic Monthly* 249 (March 1982): 29–38.

34. Carl B. Klockars, "Order Maintenance, the Quality of Urban Life, and Police: A Different Line of Argument," in *Police Leadership in America,* ed. Geller, p. 316, quoting *The Newark Foot Patrol Experiment* (Washington, D.C.: Police Foundation, 1981), p. 88.

35. Wilson, *Varieties of Police Behavior,* p. 5.

36. "Effort to Curb Scope of Antiterrorism Law Falls Short," *New York Times* (9 July 2004), p. 16.

37. "Suit Challenges Constitutionality of Powers in Antiterrorism Law," *New York Times* (31 July 2003), p. 15.

38. "Administration Plans Defense of Terror Law," *New York Times* (19 August 2003), p. 1.

39. Humanitarian Law Project v. Ashcroft, 2004 U.S. Dist. LEXIS 4411 (C.D. Cal. 2004), *reprinted as amended,* 309 F. Supp. 2d 1185 (C.D. Cal. 2004). The section of the USA Patriot Act in question was U.S. Code, Title 18, Sections 2339A and 2239B (2005).

40. "Judge Opposes 'Vagueness' in Antiterror Laws," *American Bar Association Journal Report* (30 January 2004), on the Internet at www.abanet.org/journal/ereport/j30patriot.html.

41. Atwater v. City of Lago Vista, 533 U.S. 924 (2001).

42. Atwater v. City of Lago Vista, 533 U.S. 924 (2001).

43. Whren v. United States, 517 U.S. 806 (1996).

44. Ohio v. Robinette, 519 U.S. 33 (1996).

45. Maryland v. Wilson, 519 U.S. 408 (1997).

46. Tracey Maclin, "Open Door Policy: Court Rulings on Traffic Stops Undercut Fourth Amendment Protections," *American Bar Association Journal* 83 (July 1997): 46.

47. Indianapolis, Ind. v. Edmond, 531 U.S. 32 (2000).

48. Indianapolis, Ind. v. Edmond, 531 U.S. 32 (2000), referring to Michigan Dep't. of State Police v. Sitz, 496 U.S. 444 (1990). See also United States v. Martinez-Fuerte, 428 U.S. 543 (1976), permitting suspicionless stops of motorists for the purpose of intercepting illegal immigrants.

49. Illinois v. Lidster, 747 N.E.2d 419 (Ill. 2d Dist. 2001), *aff'd.,* 779 N.E.2d 855 (Ill. 2002), *rev'd.,* 540 U.S. 419 (2004). The comments from the justices are reported in "When Can Drivers Be Halted? Justices Take Up Issue Anew," *New York Times* (6 September 2003), p. 25.

50. "New Jersey Enters into Consent Decree on Racial Issues in Highway Stops," *Criminal Law Reporter* 66 (5 January 2000), p. 251.

51. "New Jersey Troopers Avoid Jail in Case That Highlighted Profiling," *New York Times* (15 January 2002), p. 1.

52. "New York Police Stop Minorities Disproportionately, Study Finds," *Criminal Justice Newsletter* 30 (1 July 1999): 1–2.

53. Bureau of Justice Statistics, *Contacts between Police and the Public: Findings from the 1999 National Survey* (Washington, D.C.: U.S. Department of Justice, 2001), reported in "Survey Shows Harsher Treatment of Minorities in Traffic Stops," *Criminal Justice Newsletter* 31, no. 8 (14 March 2001): p. 4.

54. "Racially Biased Policing: A Principled Response," available on the Internet at www.policeforum.org or in print from the Police Executive Research Forum, 1120 Connecticut Avenue NW, Suite 930, Washington, D.C., 20036.

55. United States v. Montero-Camargo, 208 F.3d 1122 (9th Cir. 2000), *cert. denied,* 531 U.S. 889 (2000).

56. "2 New Jersey Troopers Resign in New Race Profiling Scandal," *New York Times* (10 May 2003), p. 7.

57. Ronald Weitzer and Steven A. Tuch, "Perceptions of Racial Profiling: Race, Class, and Personal Experience," *Criminology* 40 (May 2002): 435–456; quotation is on p. 452. See also Lorie Fridell et al., *Racially Biased Policing: A Principled Response* (Washington, D.C.: Police Executive Research Forum, 2001).

58. Albert J. Meehan and Michael C. Ponder, "Race and Place: The Ecology of Racial Profiling African American Motorists," *Justice Quarterly* 19, no. 3 (September 2002): 399–430; quotation is on pp. 426–427.

59. "Bush Issues Racial Profiling Ban but Exempts Security Inquiries," *New York Times* (18 June 2003), p. 1.

60. "California Ending Searches during Minor Traffic Stops," *New York Times* (28 February 2003), p. 16.

61. Terry v. Ohio, 392 U.S. 1 (1968).

62. Minnesota v. Dickerson, 508 U.S. 366 (1993).

63. United States v. Arvizu, 534 U.S. 266 (2002).

64. United States v. Arvizu, 534 U.S. 266 (2002).

65. Illinois v. Wardlow, 528 U.S. 119 (2000).

66. Johnson v. United States, 333 U.S. 10, 13–14 (1948).

67. Illinois v. Gates, 462 U.S. 213 (1983); United States v. Miller, 925 F.2d 695 (4th Cir. 1991), *cert. denied,* 502 U.S. 833 (1991).

68. Florida v. J.L., 529 U.S. 266 (2000).

69. Ornelas v. United States, 517 U.S. 690 (1996).

70. County of Riverside v. McLaughlin, 500 U.S. 44 (1991).

71. Flippo v. West Virginia, 528 U.S. 11 (1999).

72. United States v. U.S. District Court, 407 U.S. 297 (1972).

73. Mapp v. Ohio, 367 U.S. 643 (1961).

74. Mapp v. Ohio, 367 U.S. 643 (1961).

75. Chimel v. California, 395 U.S. 752 (1969).

76. Coolidge v. New Hampshire, 403 U.S. 443 (1971).

77. Arizona v. Hicks, 480 U.S. 321 (1987).

78. Maryland v. Buie, 494 U.S. 325 (1990).

79. United States v. Dunn, 480 U.S. 294 (1987).

80. California v. Greenwood, 486 U.S. 35 (1988).

81. United States v. Hedrick, 922 F.2d 396 (7th Cir. 1991), *cert. denied,* 502 U.S. 847 (1991).

82. Illinois v. McArthur, 531 U.S. 326 (2001).

83. State v. Hempele, 576 A.2d 793 (N.J. 1990).

84. See California v. Ciraolo, 476 U.S. 207 (1986); Florida v. Riley, 488 U.S. 445 (1989).

85. Kyllo v. United States, 533 U.S. 27 (2001). For a discussion of this case, see Thomas W. Hughes, "Thermal Imaging and the Fourth Amendment: Kylo v. U.S.," *American Journal of Criminal Justice* 26, no. 1 (Fall 2001): 43–60.

86. Wilson v. Arkansas, 514 U.S. 927 (1995).

87. Richards v. Wisconsin, 520 U.S. 385 (1997).

88. United States v. Ramirez, 523 U.S. 65 (1998).

89. Minnesota v. Carter, 525 U.S. 83 (1999).

90. United States v. Banks, 282 F.3d 699 (9th Cir. 2002), *rev'd., remanded,* 540 U.S. 31 (2003), *and rev'd., remanded,* 355 F.3d 1188 (9th Cir. 2004).

91. Carroll v. United States, 267 U.S. 132 (1925); Chambers v. Maroney, 399 U.S. 42 (1970). See also Florida v. Myers, 466 U.S. 380 (1984) *(per curiam),* upholding the warrantless search by police of a car that was impounded and had been subjected to a previous legitimate inventory search.

92. California v. Acevedo, 500 U.S. 565 (1991).

93. Robbins v. California, 453 U.S. 420 (1981).

94. United States v. Ross, 456 U.S. 798 (1982).

95. United States v. Johns, 469 U.S. 478 (1985).

96. See Colorado v. Bertine, 479 U.S. 367 (1987); Florida v. Wells, 495 U.S. 1 (1990).

97. Florida v. Jimeno, 500 U.S. 248 (1991).

98. Florida v. Bostick, 501 U.S. 421 (1991).

99. United States v. Drayton, 536 U.S. 194 (2002).

100. Bond v. United States, 529 U.S. 334 (2000).

101. Wyoming v. Houghton, 526 U.S. 295 (1999).

102. Maryland v. Pringle, 540 U.S. 366 (2003).

103. Illinois v. Caballes, 125 S.Ct. 834 (2005).

104. Rochin v. California, 342 U.S. 165 (1952), *overruled as stated in* Lester v. Chicago, 830 F.2d 706 (7th Cir. 1987).

105. Fuller v. M.G. Jewelry, 950 F.2d 1437 (9th Cir. 1991).

106. Fuller v. M.G. Jewelry, 950 F.2d 1437 (9th Cir. 1991).

107. United States v. Montoya de Hernandez, 473 U.S. 531 (1985).

108. Winston v. Lee, 470 U.S. 753 (1985).

109. "New York to Pay $50 Million over Illegal Strip-Searches," *New York Times* (10 January 2001), p. 1; "New York Judge OKs $50 Million Illegal Strip Search Settlement," *Jet* (2 July 2001), p. 38.

110. "Suit Accuses Brooklyn Police of Improper Strip-Searches in Minor Cases," *New York Times* (Final Edition) (30 October 2003), p. 1.

111. McGee v. Texas, 105 S.W.3d 609 (Tex. Crim. App. 2003).

112. "Houston Woman Settles in '91 Strip-Search Case," *Houston Chronicle* (13 November 2003), p. 6.

113. Malloy v. Hogan, 378 U.S. 1 (1964).

114. Escobedo v. Illinois, 378 U.S. 478 (1964).

115. Miranda v. Arizona, 384 U.S. 436, 478-479 (1966).

116. Davis v. United States, 512 U.S. 452 (1994).

117. See Edwards v. Arizona, 451 U.S. 477 (1981); Minnick v. Arizona, 498 U.S. 146 (1990).

118. Dickerson v. United States, 530 U.S. 2326 (2000).

119. U.S. Code, Chapter 18, Section 3501 (2005).

120. Missouri v. Seibert, 2002 Mo. App. LEXIS 401 (Mo. Ct. App. 2002), *aff'd.,* 540 U.S. 519 (2004).

121. United States v. Fellers, 285 F.3d 721 (8th Cir. 2002), *rev'd., remanded,* 540 U.S. 519 (U.S. 2004), *and aff'd. in part and remanded in part,* 397 F.3d 1090 (8th Cir. 2005).

122. United States v. Patane, 304 F.3d 1013 (10th Cir. 2002), *rev'd., remanded,* 124 S.Ct. 2620 (2004).

123. Yarborsough v. Alvarado, 541 U.S. 562 (2004).

124. Yale Kamisar, "Interrogating Suspects," *National Law Journal* 25, no. 84 (9 June 2003): 43.

125. Kaupp v. Texas, 538 U.S. 626 (2003).

126. "Improved Numbers Shelter CBS from the Fallout," *New York Times* (25 November 2004), p. 1C.

127. "Prosecution and Defense," *Connecticut Law Tribune* 28, no. 44 (4 November 2002): 12.

128. Debra Cassens Moss, "DNA—The New Fingerprints," *American Bar Association Journal* 74 (1 May 1988): 66.

Problems and Issues in Policing

5

Policing is a job that arouses great controversy. Police may use deadly force, and in some circumstances they would be negligent if they did not do so. Police are expected to stop and question persons who appear to have violated laws, but they may be criticized for doing so. Police are expected to obey all laws, but not all police meet that expectation. Police are expected to be well trained and have enough education to use reasonable judgment and discretion, but they may be stressed and bored if they are too highly educated or trained. They are expected to be alert on the job, but the dull aspects of many patrol assignments may make it difficult to remain alert at all times. In short, policing is stressful.

In considering the problems in policing, we must realize that no problem is pervasive. The purpose of this chapter is to discuss issues that arise in policing, not to suggest that all police, or even most police, encounter the problems and do not resolve them successfully. Policing, like all jobs, has some persons who are corrupt, incompetent, or in some other way unprofessional; however, many police officers work very hard to serve the public, and they do an excellent job. And many police officers find their work to be challenging and rewarding.

Policing presents officers and administrators with some serious dilemmas. Conflicts arise over allocation of the officer's time; investigations may compromise the officer's integrity or lead the public to question the officer's investigative techniques. Processing domestic violence calls, confronting the drug scene, and dealing with the reality that some suspects or victims may have communicable diseases, are situations that, among others, create serious problems for police.

Role conflicts, the threat of danger, methods of evaluating job performance, job satisfaction, and other problems create stressful situations that lead to professional and personal problems. The dangers of terrorism, especially since the 9/11/01 terrorist attacks, concern all of us, but police must face the possibility of rescue and investigation, including people whose lives depend on their success. Some police react in the same way many people react to stress: they confront the issues and deal with them successfully. They may become involved in a police subculture in which they feel comfortable and accepted while off duty. Others may become involved in corruption or overzealous law enforcement or they may succumb to the use of illegal drugs or even drug trafficking. A few turn to brutality against crime suspects. The line between appropriate and excessive use of deadly force is not easy to draw, but court decisions give some guidelines. When the line is crossed, civil liability attaches, and civil lawsuits against police are increasing. The control of policing is not easy but is

After reading this chapter, you should be able to do the following:

- **Explain the meaning of dilemmas in policing**
- **Summarize the external political pressures of policing**
- **Explain time allocation pressures in policing**
- **Define proactive and reactive policing and discuss each in the context of domestic violence**
- **Assess the impact of various stressors in policing**
- **State what we can do to decrease domestic violence among police**
- **Explain and analyze the impact of police subcultures**
- **Discuss the nature and extent of police misconduct**
- **Explain the proper use of deadly force in the context of fleeing felons and vehicle pursuits**
- **Discuss the nature and implications of police brutality**
- **Discuss violence against police**
- **Explain how police activities may be controlled by police departments**
- **Explain and evaluate the exclusionary rule**
- **Suggest ways in which federal regulations might improve policing**
- **Discuss the control of policing by community relations and through civil actions**
- **Explain the legal actions that citizens may take if they are mistreated by negligently trained police officers**
- **Discuss the impact that affirmative action programs have had on policing and what might be expected in the future.**

attempted through police department regulations, federal regulations, courts, and community relationships.

The final section of the chapter focuses on affirmative action policies. The efforts of police departments to recruit minority and female applicants have increased the representation of these groups. Court cases had chipped away at affirmative action policies, but on the last day of its 2002–2003 term, the U.S. Supreme Court upheld some affirmative action policies. These cases are discussed.

5-1   Dilemmas in Policing

In any work environment it is necessary to make adjustments to conflicting demands and pressures, but conflicts may be greater in policing than in most jobs or professions. We expect the police to solve and prevent crimes. We want them to respond cheerfully, quickly, and efficiently to a host of public services. At the same time, police are expected to be polite, even when being attacked verbally or physically, and to be effective in securing evidence of crimes without violating suspects' constitutional rights. They must use violence when necessary, not when unnecessary, and the line between those two is not clearly articulated. Police should report ethical and legal violations of their colleagues, but frequently internal pressures are against such reportings. All of the dilemmas police face are enhanced by external political pressures.

5-1a   External Political Pressures

Although external political pressures impact many if not all work environments, policing may involve greater pressures than most. Many of these pressures are legal, but they create serious problems for police administrators and line officers, who are more visible than workers in most other jobs and professions. In addition, police may experience greater and more varied demands for their services than is required of most other people. Failure in policing is highly visible, and the consequences may be more severe to police and to the public than is failure in other work environments. Accountability is difficult, and temptations are great for those who wield so much power over our daily lives.

Police are accountable to local, state, and federal agencies. Legal restrictions may be placed on police by any of these levels. This chapter's discussions of U.S. Supreme Court decisions demonstrate the role that federal courts play in policing at all levels. Furthermore, police departments must compete with other public agencies for funding, and, to be competitive, they must show that, although they are using their existing resources efficiently and prudently, local, state, and federal problems have grown beyond their ability to cope without additional resources.

The wide discretion police have in law enforcement may create political problems. Police are supposed to enforce laws that are violated; however, if they arrest a prominent, influential citizen, they may find that strict enforcement is not expected or even tolerated. Failure to enforce laws whenever prominent, influential citizens are involved creates political pressures from those against whom those laws are enforced. Political pressure to control the poor and minorities leads to allegations that policing is for the purpose of protecting the majority's status quo, with little regard for the rights of all people. A police administrator might find it impossible to be responsive to the needs of all of his or her constituents because of political influences that could cause the administrator to lose the job. Political pressures from local, state, and federal levels permeate policing and cannot be ignored. The fact that these external pressures may conflict with internal pressures makes the situation even more difficult and stressful for police.

The internal values of a police department may be at odds with those of the external constituency. To make the situation even more complicated, both the external and internal values and pressures may not be suitable for the current challenges of policing. One issue that creates conflict within and outside of the police department is how police time should be allocated.

5-1b   Allocation of Police Time

There is little agreement on how police should allocate their time among law enforcement, order maintenance, and community service, the three major functions of policing discussed in Chapter 4. Part of this conflict could be solved if recruits were informed about the time pressures of policing. Studies of why people call police departments illustrate this time pressure. Earlier studies of police time allocation gained considerable attention. James Q. Wilson sampled calls to the Syracuse (New York) Police Department in 1966 and found that only 10.3 percent of those calls related to law enforcement, compared with 30.1 percent for order maintenance. Requests for services dealing with accidents, illnesses, and lost or found persons or property constituted 37.5 percent (the largest category of calls), whereas 22.1 percent of the calls were for information.[1]

In another study, published in 1971, Albert J. Reiss Jr. analyzed calls to the Chicago Police Department. His findings were similar to those of Wilson in one respect: 30 percent of the calls were for noncriminal matters. But Reiss found that 58 percent of the calls were related to law enforcement matters.[2] In 1980, Richard J. Lundman, published the results of his study of police activities in five jurisdictions. Lundman found law enforcement to be the most frequent category of functions in which police engaged, consuming slightly less than one-third of all police time.[3]

The inconsistent findings of these studies may be attributed to the different methodology used for assessing police time allocation. Wilson and Reiss analyzed calls made to police departments; Lundman observed officers on patrol. Perhaps a more important variable in explaining the difference lies in the failure to specify carefully which activities would be included in each category.

Carefully defined, narrow categories may produce a more accurate picture of police time allocation. Eric J. Scott categorized more than 26,000 calls to police departments. According to Scott's 1981 publication, 21 percent of the calls were for information; 17 percent concerned

Spotlight 5-1   Intimate Partner Violence, 1993–2001

According to estimates from the National Crime Victimization Survey (NCVS), there were 691,710 nonfatal violent victimizations committed by current or former spouses, boyfriends, or girlfriends of the victims during 2001 (table 1). Such crimes—*intimate partner violence*—primarily involve female victims. About 588,490, or 85% of victimizations by intimate partners in 2001 were against women.

Intimate partner violence—by current or former spouses, boyfriends, or girlfriends—made up 20% of all nonfatal violence against females age 12 or older in 2001.

- The number of violent crimes by intimate partners against females declined from 1993 to 2001. Down from 1.1 million nonfatal violent crimes by an intimate in 1993, women experienced about 588,490 such crimes in 2001.
- In 1993 men were victims of about 162,870 violent crimes by an intimate partner. By 2001 that total had fallen to an estimated 103,220 victimizations.

TABLE 1   Violence by Intimate Partners by Type of Crime and Gender of Victims, 2001

	Intimate Partner Violence					
	Total		Female		Male	
	Number	Rate per 1,000 Persons	Number	Rate per 1,000 Females	Number	Rate per 1,000 Males
Overall violent crime	691,710	3.0	588,490	5.0	103,220	0.9
Rape/sexual assault	41,740	0.2	41,740	0.4	—	—
Robbery	60,630	0.3	44,060	0.4	16,570	0.1
Aggravated assault	117,480	0.5	81,140	0.7	36,350	0.3
Simple assault	471,860	2.1	421,550	3.6	50,310	0.5

Note: The difference in male and female intimate partner victimization rates is significant at the 95%-confidence level within each victimization category presented.
—Based on 10 or fewer sample cases.

nonviolent crimes; 12 percent were for assistance; 22 percent were for public nuisances; 9 percent were for traffic problems; 8 percent were citizens offering information; and 7 percent were concerned with interpersonal conflict. Other categories were violent crimes (representing only 2 percent of the calls), medical assistance, dependent persons, and calls regarding internal operations. Each of the categories was subdivided into more specific categories. For example, the category *assistance* included animal problems, property checks, escorts and transports, utility problems, property discoveries, assistance to motorists, fires, alarms, crank calls, unspecified requests, and other.[4]

According to Scott, the failure of other investigators to define each category carefully was a serious problem because "the addition or subtraction of a particular call from some categories can cause a large change in the percentage of calls attributable to that category."[5] Scott was concerned with the problem of coding calls as crime or noncrime. Many police activities involve a little of each and cannot be coded accurately into two discrete categories. As a result, the various studies are not comparable, as it is not possible to determine how specific types of calls in the various studies were coded.

These studies of the allocation of police time have important implications for police recruitment, as well as for understanding the role conflicts of those already in policing. If people are attracted to policing because they think most of an officer's time is spent in exciting chases of dangerous criminals and have no concept of the often dull periods of waiting for action, they might be unhappy as police officers. If they have no concept of the community functions of policing and are not trained to perform those functions, life on the beat might come as an unpleasant surprise.

- Intimate partner violence made up 20% of all nonfatal violent crime experienced by women in 2001. Intimate partners committed 3% of the nonfatal violence against men.
- For intimate partner violence, as for violent crime in general, simple assault was the most common type of crime.

- 1,247 women and 440 men were killed by an intimate partner in 2000. In recent years an intimate killed about 33% of female murder victims and 4% of male murder victims.

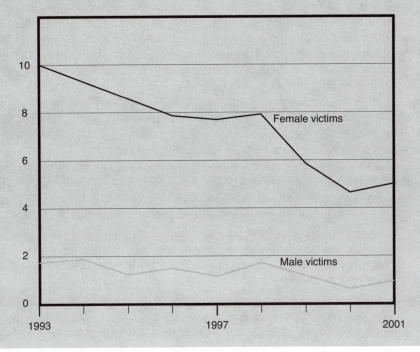

Exhibit 1
Rate of victimization by an intimate partner per 1,000 persons of each gender

Source: Callie Marie Rennison, Bureau of Justice Statistics, *Intimate Partner Violence, 1993–2001* (Washington, D.C.: U.S. Department of Justice, February 2003), p. 1.

An additional problem is that police officers may encounter supervisors who do not give equal credit to successful performance of the three police functions. Catching dangerous criminals might result in a faster promotion than performing order maintenance or community service functions successfully. Police officers may experience a similar response from their colleagues and from the community.

5-1c Proactive versus Reactive Policing

Regardless of how police activities are categorized, it is clear that police do not spend most of their time engaging in the stereotype held by many: catching dangerous criminals. In fact, many police officers spend very little time in actual crime detection. Most police work is **reactive,** not **proactive;** that is, police are dependent on the assistance of victims, witnesses, and others to report crimes.

There have been some changes in recent years. In Chapter 3 we examined community-oriented policing, whereby police identify and try to eliminate problems that may be creating a criminal situation. Police have become proactive in other areas, too, such as identifying and arresting domestic violence offenders.

Police and Domestic Violence

In recent years more attention has been paid to **domestic violence,** which involves spouses abusing each other, parents abusing children, and children abusing each other or their parents. Some studies include courtship violence, also referred to as *intimate partner violence,* as noted in Spotlight 5-1, which reports that the number of violent crimes against intimate

▶ **Reactive** In policing, depending on the reports of citizens to find criminal suspects, rather than working independently; it is important because police are not in a position to observe most criminal behavior.

▶ **Proactive** In policing, preparing for, intervening in, or taking the initiative in finding criminals, rather than depending on the reports of others.

▶ **Domestic violence** (page 119)
The causing of serious physical harm or the threatening of such harm to a member of one's family or household, including spouses, ex-spouses, parents, children, persons otherwise related by blood, persons living in the household, or persons who lived there formerly. May include relationships of persons who do not live together but who have had intimate relationships, such as courtship.

partners was down in 2001, as compared with 1993. The data in Spotlight 5-1 are based on interviews with victims of intimate partner violence. Data show that intimate partner violence also exists among police. First, we look at police intervention in domestic and intimate partner violence cases in general.

In earlier times, violence within the family was considered a domestic problem, not a crime, and if police intervened at all they did so mainly as mediators, not as law enforcement officers. Rarely were arrests made. The federal Violence against Women Act of 1984 provides some protection for victims of domestic violence, sexual assault, and stalking. In 1996, the Department of Justice published its final rules covering federal grants authorized by this legislation. Included are provisions for programs that train police for handling domestic violence cases, develop policies providing sanctions for officers who refuse to arrest in such cases, develop guidelines for when to arrest in domestic violence cases, and so on.[6] After the passage of that act, many states enacted statutes giving police discretion to arrest in misdemeanor cases they had not witnessed. Many police departments began training officers in how to handle domestic violence, and some jurisdictions instituted a policy of mandatory arrests in domestic violence cases. But the evidence on the results of police arrests in domestic violence cases is contradictory.

Under a mandatory arrest policy, the police officer must arrest the alleged perpetrator of domestic violence if there is sufficient evidence that violence has occurred. This approach has resulted in more arrests in domestic violence cases in which police act on their own, without waiting for victims to insist on pressing charges.

Some of the earlier evaluations of higher arrest rates in domestic violence cases show that this approach—as compared with a nonarrest policy—is more successful in preventing further domestic violence. In assessing the results of the Minneapolis Domestic Violence Experiment, Lawrence W. Sherman and Richard A. Berk concluded that

> arrest was the most effective of three standard methods police use to reduce domestic violence. The other police methods—attempting to counsel both parties or sending assailants away—were found to be considerably less effective in deterring future violence in the cases examined.[7]

Such findings led the Attorney General's Task Force on Family Violence (appointed in 1984) to recommend that, "to provide the most effective response, operational procedures should require the officer to presume that arrest, consistent with state law, is the appropriate response in cases of family violence."[8]

The Minneapolis findings were not replicated in a similar study in Omaha, Nebraska, however, leading its authors to suggest that their findings

> will undoubtedly cast some doubt on the deterrent power of a mandatory or even presumptory arrest policy for cases of misdemeanor domestic assault. At this point, researchers and policymakers are in the awkward position of having conflicting results from two experiments and no clear, unambiguous direction from the research on this issue.[9]

Other studies report that the first time an offender is apprehended by police after a domestic violence call is the most potent one and that arrest is most effective at that time. Arrest is more effective if followed by court-mandated treatment. Subsequent monitorings of these offenders reveal that, the more educated an offender, the more likely it is that he or she will not repeat domestic violence offenses.[10]

Lawrence W. Sherman examined what is known or not known about domestic violence, particularly the effect of arrest, and concluded that,

> after more than a decade of evaluating arrest for misdemeanor domestic violence, we still have much to learn. The jigsaw puzzle of diverse results in different cities has not been put together, and too many pieces are still missing.[11]

Another study regarding policing spousal violence reported that, although police were not likely to arrest in such cases (arrests were not made in 76 percent of the cases), arrests were no more likely in other types of violence cases.[12] And an analysis of police responses to domestic violence in the past few decades concluded that authorities had yet to develop a set of tools or responses that "work well across a variety of situations in reducing the likelihood of future violence" within domestic environments.[13]

In another analysis, criminologists Richard B. Felson and Jeff Ackerman examined arrests for domestic and other assaults. These researchers emphasized the importance of looking at the types of violence and the degree of seriousness and suggested that "moral outrage" about domestic violence could lead some researchers to overlook these important variables. The fact that police refuse to arrest in a situation involving minor domestic violence does not mean that police are treating that situation differently than a minor assault against a nonspouse or an intimate. In short, domestic violence should not be examined in isolation but, rather, in the general context of violence. Felson and Ackerman concluded that police decisions regarding arrests are affected by the relationship between the suspect and the victim. In particular,

> the police are less likely to arrest strangers than nonstrangers for assault because they are often unable to identify them. On the other hand, when the police are able to identify the suspect, they show lenience when the suspect knows the victim. Their leniency is not due to a tolerance for intimate violence or violence against women; they are more likely to make an arrest in incidents involving intimate violence than in incidents involving other nonstrangers. Rather, leniency in nonstranger incidents is due to the reluctance of victims to sign complaints, the absence of witnesses, and the unwillingness of the police to arrest suspects for minor acts of violence against people they know.[14]

These and other studies suggest that we need to continue evaluating the best ways to handle domestic violence, a situation that remains one of conflict for police. Even where mandatory arrest policies are in effect, police encounter alleged victims who refuse to cooperate. Many spouses do not want their partners arrested; if police insist and make the arrest, the complaining partner may become hostile, belligerent, even violent. Thus, what appears to be a positive change in policing may result in greater role conflict for police officers, including violence against them. Mandatory arrests may also increase the number of cases beyond a reasonable level for some prosecution offices. Researchers who studied the situation in Milwaukee, Wisconsin, after the adoption of a mandatory arrest policy in domestic violence cases in 1987 concluded the following:

> Good intentions do not always result in good public policy. Arresting more batterers does not necessarily result in more prosecutions. Our results show that prosecuting more domestic violence cases can increase court delay, increase pretrial recidivism, and lower conviction rates. The domestic violence literature is becoming filled with examples of how well-intended policies regarding domestic violence can backfire.... Good intentions of policy makers need to be balanced with a realistic view of how the criminal justice system functions and what the actual effects of new policies are likely to be.[15]

There is some recent research evidence, however, that most laws do have the effect of reducing domestic violence, although fewer of those laws "appear to influence police involvement and none relate to more arrests. This suggests that laws may deter would-be offenders from harming family and partners."[16]

Other variables that should be considered in analyzing domestic violence and policing are those involving reasons that victims do or do not report the violence. Richard B. Felson, quoted previously, and three of his colleagues analyzed the reasons for reporting or not reporting domestic violence. They found several reasons domestic violence victims are less likely than other victims to report violence: privacy concerns, fear of reprisal, and the desire to protect their assailants. But they also found that domestic violence victims are *more* likely to report violence than are other victims because they see the violence as more serious, as it occurs in the home. The researchers concluded, "As a result of these and other offsetting factors, victims of domestic violence are just as likely as other victims of assault to call the police."[17]

One final area of domestic violence and policing that is gaining more attention is police violence against their own intimate partners. In November 1999, it was reported that complaints of *serious* domestic violence allegedly committed by police officers in New York City had increased by 35 percent, whereas less serious offenses had increased by 16 percent. Officials thought these data might represent an increase in reporting rather than an increase in actual violence; still, it is significant that domestic violence by police in that city was a serious problem. It has received more attention since 1998, when Manhattan police

Spotlight 5-2   Police Suicides

Suicide is always a shock to the family and friends of the person who chooses to end his or her life, but the suicide of a police officer is perhaps less expected and thus even more shocking. When that officer has been accused of domestic abuse and kills his or her spouse before committing suicide, the reaction is rage as well as shock, especially as details are released that show the possibility that at least some people should have known of the difficult situations and perhaps even intervened.

On 26 April 2003, David Brame, police chief in Tacoma, Washington, fatally shot his wife, Crystal, and then killed himself. Two young children (ages eight and five) witnessed the killings. Records show that in 1981 two psychologists concluded that Brame should not be hired as a rookie officer. A woman claimed that in 1988 Brame had raped her. In 2001, a city human resource official reported that Brame's past might embarrass the city, and there were reasons to take his gun from him the day before Brame killed his wife and himself. After she filed for divorce in early 2003, Crystal spoke to her family and others about years of alleged domestic violence by her spouse. There is some evidence that police officials knew about the allegations, and investigations are ongoing. Crystal's family filed a $75 million lawsuit against the police department and the city.[1]

In the adjacent state of Oregon, at midnight on 26 April 2003, a 32-year-old detective Benjamin Crosby went to the Sherwood Police Department holding cell while off duty and shot himself. He left a note outside, warning that his body was inside. In an apparent effort to reduce questions, he left several letters about his action, stating, "This is a suicide, not a homicide." He had left a letter for his 7-year-old son. Detective Crosby had been depressed; his wife declined comment.[2]

The bombing of the federal building in Oklahoma City in 1995, resulting in the deaths of 168 persons, also claimed at least one police officer who was on duty during the tragedy. In 1996, Sgt. Terrance Yeakey, 30, took his own life. He left no note, but friends suggested that, although he had saved four people in the Oklahoma City disaster, he may have felt guilty about not saving more. Sgt. Yeakey was one of the first officers to arrive on the scene, but after he rescued the four persons he fell two stories in the building, injuring his back.[3]

Like all other professionals, police react to stress in a variety of ways. One reaction to stress is violence against others or against oneself. According to a study conducted by the Fraternal Order of Police, in many cities the number of law enforcement officers who take their own lives exceeds the number killed by others while on duty. In San Diego, for example, between 1992 and 1998 five officers committed suicide; none were killed in action. In New York City between 1985 and 1998 a total of 87 officers committed suicide, whereas 36 were killed in the line of duty. According to the National P.O.L.I.C.E Suicide Foundation, approximately 300 officers commit suicide each year.[4]

Police suicides are not limited to the United States. In a 2003 Hong Kong, China, report, two police suicides were noted, with the comment that police commit suicide for the same reasons as many other people: depression, marital stress, and work problems. One of the examples cited was an officer who had killed himself after losing his pension savings through gambling. Another was suffering from psychosis. One of the writers stated, "Every profession has working problems; it depends on how you face them." He noted, however, the importance of training people to understand and accept those problems.[5] In June 2003, a Singapore news source reported the increase in police suicides in India and noted that "at least five stressed-out policemen a day seek premature retirement."[6]

1. Summarized from multiple media sources.
2. "Sherwood Officer Remembered for His Caring," *The Oregonian* (29 April 2003), p. 1B.
3. "Policeman in Bombing Rescue in Oklahoma City Is a Suicide," *New York Times* (11 May 1996), p. 9.
4. Reported in "Suicide on the Force: Nation's Cops Falling at Alarming Rate," *USA Today* (1 June 1999), pp. 1, 2.
5. "Tragic Police Suffer Like the Rest of Us," *Hong Kong Imail* (26 June 2003).
6. "Cops on the Edge," *The Straits Times* (Singapore).

officer Patrick Fitzgerald killed his wife, his two children, and then himself. Leeanne Fitzgerald's family alleged that their daughter had complained frequently to police supervisors of her husband's abusive behavior, but they had refused to intervene.[18]

Similar allegations will be made in the civil lawsuit filed by the family discussed in Spotlight 5-2, which looks at police violence in the context of suicide as a reaction to stress. The Spotlight also discusses the Tacoma, Washington, police chief who murdered his wife (after abuse allegedly known to at least some members of the police department) in front of their children in April 2003.

5-1d Stress

In recent years increasing attention has been given to stress and the effects it has on people in various occupations and professions. A variety of harmful physical results occur when individuals do not handle stress successfully. Although all people may be affected in some way by on-the-job stress, studies have found evidence of particularly high stress rates in some jobs; policing has been called the most stressful.

Stress in policing is not confined to patrol officers. Undercover officers may experience the same stresses as patrol officers, along with some other stressors, such as the need for secrecy, unique to undercover work. Police administrators may experience stress for the following reasons:

- Dependence on others, such as staff, to get the work done (after being trained to be relatively independent as line officers)
- Concerns for personnel and their needs
- Lack of resources
- Increased community demands and pressures
- Impact of the external bureaucracy
- Political and sedentary nature of the job
- Lack of preparation (special programs for police chiefs and other administrators are relatively recent developments and still not sufficiently available)
- Conflict with employee organizations
- Difficulty in effecting lasting change
- Separation from the police subculture[19]

This discussion may imply that stress in policing is no different from stress in other occupations and professions. But there is one major difference; police are trained to injure or kill, and, if the situation requires, they are expected to do so. Indeed, they may be sanctioned for not using their weapons. It is this requirement, say some officers, that is unique in creating stress in policing.

A psychologist notes that, in war, military officers may cope by defining the opposition as bad. But that is not true of police officers, who may be highly criticized, even sanctioned, for a killing. Officers who kill may be isolated socially from their colleagues. Routine procedure is to suspend officers pending investigation of a shooting. Said one officer, "I felt as alone as I ever had in my whole life. They take you out of a group and make you stand alone." Another officer spoke of the nightmares, the flashbacks, and the social isolation that he felt after he had killed a person while on patrol. "I consider myself part of a class of people other people don't understand."[20]

Professors at Michigan State University have found that officers who kill in the line of duty suffer postshooting trauma, which may lead to severe problems, perhaps even ending their careers as police officers. Some police departments have recognized the need for psychological counseling as part of the professional assistance provided for police. In one Florida county, for example, police and firefighters who are involved in "crisis calls" are required to undergo debriefings after those calls. These sessions do not focus on what went wrong and what went right but, rather, on how the professionals *felt* about seeing human pain and death.[21] And in New York City after the 9/11/01 terrorist attacks, all 55,000 employees of the police department were required to attend mental health classes to help them cope with the attacks on the Twin Towers of the World Trade Center. Similarly, all rescue workers were required to attend classes after the 1995 bombing of the federal building in Oklahoma City.[22]

Long before these tragic and shocking terrorist events, the U.S. Commission on Civil Rights emphasized the need to provide stress management programs and services for police. The commission noted that unfortunately, most police departments lack such programs, despite the emphasis on stress as "an important underlying factor in police misconduct incidents."[23]

Police and Suicide

One reaction to stress is to take one's own life. Suicides among police have been given more attention in recent years, especially as some of the suicides have involved violence against others. For example, in 2002 Edward Lutes, a 17-year veteran of the Seaside Heights (New Jersey) Police Department, killed five people and injured his boss before killing himself. Lutes was angry at his neighbors, one of whom was tried but acquitted of sexually molesting

Lutes's daughter. The neighbor and his wife took care of the daughter each morning after Lutes left for work and before the daughter went to school. Lutes killed both neighbors and then crossed the street and killed another couple and their son. He then drove 20 miles to the police chief's home and shot and wounded him before shooting himself. Lutes was found dead in his car. These shootings occurred shortly after a retired Newark (New Jersey) police officer was arrested and indicted for killing his granddaughter and three neighbors not far from the neighborhood in which Lutes and his murder victims lived.[24] In October 2003, John W. Mabie, 71, dropped his defense of diminished capacity and entered guilty pleas to the murder counts.

The Impact of AIDS

A second major source of stress for police is the fear of contracting the human immunodeficiency virus (HIV), which causes acquired immune deficiency syndrome (AIDS). AIDS is a deadly disease that affects the immune system, leaving the body unable to fight infections. It can be acquired through exchanges of body fluids, including sexual activity with an infected person, through use of an unsterile needle, and by means of a transfusion of tainted blood. The virus can also be transmitted by a pregnant woman to her fetus.

One other issue of concern is police officers who have AIDS. Although there is no evidence that AIDS is transmitted by casual contact, many people are concerned about contacts with persons infected with AIDS. Colleagues may react negatively to an officer who has AIDS.

In August 2000, a news article focused on New York City police officers with AIDS who had come to the attention of a retired officer who counseled them and shared his own experiences with the disease. Stephen P. Yurcik described his counselees, who did not even know each others' names, as follows:

> To their fellow officers, they are indistinguishable from the rest of the 40,000 men and women who police New York City, but in their own minds, AIDS has set them a world apart. For many, it weighs them down not only with the fear of death, but also with a secret they are desperate to keep from their fellow officers.[25]

In 2003, the Village of Westmont, Illinois, settled a suit with a plaintiff who claimed he was refused a job with the police department because he is HIV positive. The applicant, who received $125,000 in the settlement, was a police academy graduate who had worked in another police department. The Westmont department required medical examinations of its applicants, but in the settlement, the department agreed that it would no longer test its applicants for HIV. The department also agreed that medical exams would be limited to issues relevant to policing. The plaintiff in this case, who refused to reveal his name, called the settlement "an encouragement for people who have been discriminated against, that they do have rights and they can stand up for them." A federal district court had refused to dismiss the case. The settlement ended the litigation.[26]

The Impact of Terrorism

Perhaps the greatest stressors police face as a group are those related to terrorism. This is not to suggest that police have any greater concern or fear for themselves personally but that the demands placed on law enforcement by the 9/11/01 terrorist attacks have created significant problems for law enforcement officers. Not only the FBI but also many local departments reassigned officers from their usual jobs to terrorist task forces. Some officers were required to leave their jobs and serve in the war in Iraq. Others were killed in the 9/11/01 terrorist attacks; many retired. Police departments were required to answer and investigate many calls concerning substances that might be deadly Anthrax or that might be related to suspected terrorists. Local departments located in cities with airports faced the need to provide those facilities with added security.

A little over a month after the 9/11/01 terrorist attacks officials expressed their concern that the diversion of FBI agents to terrorism task forces and a deemphasis on drug-related offenses and bank robberies placed increasing pressure on local departments to provide law enforcement in these areas. And most departments were already facing budget problems as a result of terrorism and other problems. Even the canine patrol was overworked in many cities, with the added calls for bomb checks. In Los Angeles, for example, officers received 44 bomb threat calls on one day; none were substantiated. Crime prevention may suffer, for as the chief of the Seattle Police Department stated, "Historically, every budget cut for the last 25 years has almost always started with crime prevention, because it's difficult for anyone to evaluate the crime reduction impact of those programs."[27]

5-2 The Police Subculture

One way of handling dilemmas, role conflicts, and stress is to withdraw into a more comfortable situation. If sufficient numbers of a group do so, a subgroup, or **subculture,** is formed. The subculture has values and expectations that distinguish it from the dominant culture and that solidify its members.

▶ **Subculture** A group of significant size whose behavior differs significantly from the behavior of the dominant groups of society.

Police can become isolated from people who might be their friends if it were not because of the officers' authority and responsibility to regulate the daily lives of citizens. Traffic violations and laws regulating the use of alcohol and other drugs are examples. It would be difficult to form an intimate relationship with someone who was expected "to arrest you for common and petty violations which intimates would ordinarily know about."[28]

Earlier studies suggested that police were a homogeneous group who formed subcultures and manifested a distinct personality type. They were said to be authoritarian, cynical, punitive, rigid, physically aggressive, assertive, and impulsive risk takers.[29] Police were viewed as people who looked for negatives and who stereotyped situations, making quick judgments whenever they thought crime was involved. Such attitudes may lead to violence.

It was assumed that the best way to alleviate police cynicism was to increase their professionalism, but some studies reported that, although "commitment to a professional ideology reduces cynicism among police," the relationship between these two variables was more complex than earlier researchers had thought.[30] Thus, it is necessary to look more carefully at the dimensions of each of the variables: cynicism and professionalism.

There is some evidence of a relationship between professionalism and cynicism among police chiefs, although there are some differences when comparing chiefs with other police officers. Also, there are differences based on the duration of service. For example, cynicism "is highest for police chiefs during their early years and gradually declines with experience." Cynicism varies according to the size of the chief's police agency, with those in larger agencies showing less cynicism.[31]

There is some evidence that police officers, like police chiefs, become less cynical as their length of service increases.[32] Taken as a whole, research on police cynicism underscores the importance of looking carefully at all variables that might account for cynicism and analyzing those variables in their full complexity. It is not sufficient to find cynicism and professionalism (or any other trait) among police officers or chiefs and draw the conclusion that the relationship is a simple one. On the other hand, professionalism is important in policing, as it is in other occupations and professions.

Studies of police subcultures are related to what is often called the *blue code of silence,* meaning that police will not testify against each other or even report any improper behavior. In a 2001 lawsuit, a female officer was awarded $3 million in her claim against the Cook County (Chicago) Forest Preserve Department of Law Enforcement. Officer Cynthia Spina, one of approximately 100 officers in the department, only 9 of whom were women, complained about sexual harassment for four years. She alleged that she had been touched inappropriately; that sexual materials had been mailed to her home; and that she had often been subjected to sexual comments and stories. She had reported the behavior but nothing was done. According to Spina's lawyer, Monica E. McFadden, the key witness in her client's successful case was Penny Harrington, the former police chief of Portland, Oregon, and the head of the National Center for Women in Policing. Harrington "explained police culture and practices, what the 'code of silence' is and what breaking it means for a police officer and why Spina is essentially unemployable as a police officer due to her courage in confronting this harassment and retaliation." McFadden stated that Harrington explained how officers shun and isolate those among them who complain to officials about the behavior of other officers. A clinical forensic psychiatrist testified that Spina suffered from "an adjustment disorder brought on by the stress of the harassment and the department's failure to respond." A federal judge, stating that $3 million for years of sexual harassment was "monstrously excessive," gave the plaintiff the option of accepting $300,000 or going to trial again on the issue of damages only. The case was settled in March 2003 for $1.525 million, $375,000 for Spina and $1.15 million in lawyers' fees.[33]

5-3 Police Misconduct

Police officers have many opportunities for engaging in improper behavior, and they have the power to coerce individuals to comply. One area of misconduct that has received some attention lately is sexual misconduct, but in recent years most reported police misconduct has involved *corruption,* defined as follows:

> A public official is corrupt if he accepts money or money's worth for doing something that he is under a duty to do anyway, that he is under a duty not to do, or to exercise a legitimate discretion for improper reasons.[34]

The possibility for corruption varies, with the greater opportunities available in larger cities, but corruption can be found in all types of police departments.

James Q. Wilson analyzed police corruption according to the type of organization in a police department. He defined three types of law enforcement styles and found those styles to be related to the degree of police corruption.[35] According to Wilson, most police corruption is found in departments characterized by the *watchman style,* in which police are expected to maintain order, not regulate conduct. Low salaries and the expectation that police will have other jobs increase the probabilities that police will be involved in corruption.

Corruption is found to a lesser degree in departments characterized by the *legalistic style,* with its emphasis on providing formal police training, recruiting from the middle class, offering greater promotional opportunities, and viewing law as a means to an end, rather than an end in itself. Formal sanctions are used more frequently than informal ones, with police giving less attention to community service and order maintenance than to law enforcement.

Corruption is not a serious problem in the third type of style, the *service style.* In this management style, law enforcement and order maintenance are combined, with an emphasis on good relationships between the police and the community. Police command is decentralized, with police on patrol working out of specialized units. Higher education and promotional opportunities are emphasized, and police are expected to lead exemplary private lives.

Lawrence W. Sherman analyzed police corruption according to types. The first, the *rotten apples,* refers to a department characterized by a few police officers who accept bribes and engage in other forms of corruption. Generally, those people are uniformed patrol officers, but they are loners who will accept bribes for overlooking traffic violations, licensing ordinances, or crimes. Some work in groups, termed *rotten pockets,* accepting bribes for nonenforcement of the law. Many members of the vice squad are found in this type.[36]

The second type of corruption, according to Sherman, is *pervasive organized corruption,* describing the highly organized hierarchical organization of the political processes of the community, which goes beyond the police force. Some police departments are characterized by widespread but unorganized corruption, labeled as *pervasive unorganized corruption.*[37]

5-3a The Knapp Commission and Its Aftermath

In 1970, in response to allegations of corruption in New York City, Mayor John V. Lindsay issued an executive order establishing the Knapp Commission. The 1972 commission's report disclosed widespread police corruption. Rookies were initiated into the system quickly, many became corrupt, and some grew cynical. The commission found that police were involved with organized crime (the most lucrative form of corruption); payoffs from citizens, especially for traffic citations; and the acceptance of money for overlooking violations of licensing ordinances.[38]

New York City Police Department officials contend that only a very small percentage of police officers are involved in corruption. They say that undercover tests of integrity, whereby some officers are assigned to make secret reports on the behavior of other officers, have eliminated most corruption. Others contend that corruption has not been eliminated in the New York City Police Department or any other; they hold that corruption is inevitable. According to one authority,

> corruption is endemic to policing. The very nature of the police function is bound to subject officers to tempting offers. . . . Solutions, so far, seem inadequate and certainly are not likely to produce permanent results.[39]

There is evidence that, even after the Knapp Commission report, corruption continued in the New York City Police Department. Consider, for example, the following information concerning the Mollen Commission.

5-3b   The Mollen Commmission

In the fall of 1993, the Mollen Commission, headed by former judge Milton Mollen, began a study of police corruption in New York City. In referring to the commission's interim report, published in December of that year, a *New York Times* editorial stated these findings:

> [P]ockets of police corruption and brutality exist because the ingrained culture of the Police Department tolerates wrongdoing, even protects the wrongdoer. The panel recommends shaking up the department's anti-corruption bureaucracy, and appointing an outside panel to conduct investigations.[40]

The final report of the commission was issued in July 1994. This report concluded that corruption was less common in New York City than it was during the Knapp Commission study but that its nature had changed. In 1994, more officers sought opportunities to move beyond bribery to violating other laws. Some officers stole routinely from drug dealers after stopping them for traffic violations, and some used violence to carry out their thefts. The commission found that corruption flourished in some parts of New York City because of opportunities but also because the police culture placed a greater emphasis on loyalty than on integrity. The majority of New York City's officers were not involved in corruption, but they feared reporting those who were.[41]

Finally, the Mollen Commission coined a new word to characterize the pervasive falsifications they found by police: *testilying*. That word was used in the spring 2003, when the Houston (Texas) Police Department was under fire for corruption for falsifying information in its crime lab, although in reference to this scandal, a state representative, Harold Dutton, said, "We have a name for that in Texas, and that is perjury." Noted defense attorney and long-time Harvard Law School professor Alan M. Dershowitz has stated that testilying occurs because too many people focus on guilt or innocence rather than on the process itself. Dershowitz told the U.S. House of Representatives Judiciary Committee that,

> clearly, the most heinous brand of lying is the giving of false testimony that results in the imprisonment or even execution of an innocent person. Less egregious, but still quite serious, is false testimony that results in the conviction of a person who committed the criminal conduct but whose rights were violated in a manner that would preclude conviction if the police were to testify truthfully.[42]

Finally, with regard to corruption in the New York City Police Department, a more recent commission appointed by the mayor to monitor the police department's anticorruption efforts reported that the department's internal system for processing discipline problems was not effective. In June 2000, the commission concluded that the monitoring and disciplining system is so slow that police officers have little confidence in it.[43]

5-3c   Drugs and Policing

The nation's declared war on drugs presents criminal justice systems and police with one of their most frustrating problems. The escalation of drug trafficking has resulted in violence, distorted and ruined lives, enormous expense, and a crushing blow to all elements of criminal justice systems. Jails and prisons are overcrowded, due in large part to drug offenders, many of whom are creating a new underworld within prisons, with the result that some prison correctional officers have been corrupted.[44] Civil cases are backed up for years to enable courts to process the drug cases.

Police face the difficulty of confronting the massive drug problem without sufficient resources, whereas drug offenders have resources to tempt officers who earn relatively low salaries in highly stressful jobs. In 1997 in Chicago, 124 narcotics cases were dismissed because the primary witness for the prosecution in each case was one of the police officers apprehended the previous year for extorting and robbing undercover officers who were posing as drug dealers. The police department's superintendent, Matt Rodriguez, resigned in November after the disclosure that he had violated department policy by maintaining a close friendship with a convicted felon.[45] The problem of police corruption by drugs and drug offenders has led some law enforcement departments to implement random drug testing.[46]

5-4   Violence and the Police

Historically, police have been viewed as agents who are necessary for establishing law and order, often by applying justice on the spot. Although violence between police and citizens had been reported earlier, the violence and unrest that occurred in the 1960s led to demands for larger and better-trained police forces. During that decade predominantly white police and minority citizens clashed in hot, crowded cities. Many student protesters found themselves in conflict with the police, and the police experienced disillusionment with a system that they did not believe protected their interests. They, too, became more active. Police unions were established; these were viewed by many as a representation of hostility by the police.

In short, the decade of the 1960s brought open violence between police and citizens, and the 1970s brought more cases of police violence and corruption. Meanwhile, crime rates began to rise and citizens demanded greater police protection. Demands for a more professionalized police force were heard, along with allegations of police misconduct.

Police are, however, entitled to use force. The issue is under what circumstances.

5-4a   Police Use of Deadly Force

> **Deadly force**   Force likely to cause serious bodily injury or death.

The use of **deadly force** by police has been defined as "such force as under normal circumstances poses a high risk of death or serious injury to its human target, regardless of whether or not death, serious injury or any harm actually result."[47] Police officers may use deadly force under some circumstances. If they use deadly force improperly, the officers (and the police department) may be liable to the injured person (or, in the event of death, to the family of the deceased) in a civil suit. Most rules for the use of deadly force come from federal statutes and administrative decisions.

Excessive use of force may occur while police are chasing suspects either on foot or in vehicles, or it may occur when suspects are already apprehended. We will consider first the use of force in attempts to apprehend suspects.

Fleeing Felon Rule

> **Fleeing felon rule**   The common law rule that permitted police to shoot at any fleeing felon. The rule has been modified to require circumstances involving (1) the threat of serious injury to or death of an officer or others, (2) the prevention of an escape if the suspect threatens the officer with a gun, or (3) the officer's having probable cause to believe that the suspect has committed or has threatened to commit serious bodily harm.

In the past, shooting any fleeing felon was permitted. Because all felonies were punishable by death, it was assumed that any felon would resist arrest by all possible means. The **fleeing felon rule** developed during a time when apprehending criminals was more difficult than it is today. Police did not have weapons that could be used for shooting at a long distance; nor did they have communication techniques that would enable them to quickly notify other jurisdictions that a suspect had escaped arrest. Therefore, if fleeing felons were not apprehended quickly, it was possible for them to escape and begin a new life in another community without fear of detection by the local police.

As more efficient weapons were developed, it became easier for police to apprehend escaping felons, and many did so by use of deadly force, even though the fleeing felons were not dangerous. Such actions were not necessary to protect the officer and others; nor were they necessary to apprehend felons. Despite these developments, however, most states adopted the common law rule that permitted police officers to use deadly force in apprehending fleeing felons. This practice was condemned by many commentators and scholars, but it was not prohibited by the U.S. Supreme Court until 1985, when that Court ruled that Tennessee's fleeing felon statute was unconstitutional under the facts of the case.

Tennessee v. *Garner* involved an unarmed teenager who was killed by a police officer as the youth fled from an unoccupied house. The officer could see that the fleeing felon was a youth and apparently unarmed. But the officer argued that he knew that, if the suspect got over the fence, he could escape, so he fired at him. The Tennessee statute allowed an officer to shoot a suspect if it appeared to be necessary to prevent the escape of a felon.[48]

In *Garner* the U.S. Supreme Court emphasized that the use of deadly force by police officers must be reasonable to be lawful. Deadly force is reasonable under the following circumstances:

- To prevent an escape when the suspect has threatened the officer with a weapon
- When there is a threat of death or serious physical injury to the officer or others
- If there is probable cause to believe that the person has committed a crime involving the infliction or threatened infliction of serious physical harm and, where practical, some warning has been given by the officer

A statute that permits an officer to shoot a fleeing felon may be constitutional in some instances; however, used against a young, slight, unarmed youth who was suspected of burglary, deadly force is unreasonable and therefore unlawful.

Vehicle Pursuits

A second area in which police may be involved in deadly force is in vehicle pursuits. High-speed chases may end in injury or death to the suspect, the police pursuer, or innocent bystanders. Earlier studies report some data suggesting that these pursuits are not worth the results in property damage, human injuries, and deaths. Likewise, some courts have held police departments liable for the consequences of such pursuits. Consequently, police departments restrict the types of cases in which vehicle pursuits are permitted or forbid hot pursuits entirely.

The Los Angeles Police Department (LAPD) provides an example of recent policy changes, which took effect in May 2003. Los Angeles had more police pursuits than any other city, and almost 60 percent of those were the result of traffic violations or other minor infractions. In 2002, Los Angeles had 721 police vehicle pursuits, with 200 of those resulting in crashes that injured 63 people. In 2001, the department had 781 pursuits, which caused 6 deaths and 139 injuries. Under the new policy, police may engage in vehicle pursuits only in serious cases and with a helicopter tracking them. According to one LAPD commander, "We're balancing protecting the public by apprehending criminals while at the same time trying not to endanger the public. . . . The pursuit is probably one of the most dangerous activities involved in law enforcement."[49]

In a national study of 1,200 police departments published in 1997, Geoffrey P. Alpert found that 90 percent had written policies governing police vehicle pursuits. Although some of those policies were old, dating back to the 1970s, one-half had been revised or drafted within the previous two years. Most of the changes involved making the policies more restrictive. Alpert reported "strikingly effective" results after changes were made in policies. For example, in Miami, Florida, a change in policy in 1992, stating that only violent felonies warrant pursuits, was followed by an 82 percent drop in pursuits. Omaha, Nebraska's, policy, however, was changed to a more permissive one in 1993 and was followed by an increase in pursuits of over 600 percent the following year.[50]

Over one-half of all traffic accidents that occur during police high-speed chases occur within the first two minutes of the chase, according to a study by the Pursuit Management Task Force, a panel composed of local, state, regional, and federal law enforcement agencies. The most common and most effective technique for stopping the vehicle being pursued is the "spike strip," which is placed in the road. The strip deflates the tires of the pursued vehicle. Other techniques are being developed.[51]

Spotlight 5-3   Police Brutality: The 1990s and Beyond

Allegations of police brutality in recent years have focused on several highly publicized cases. In Spotlight 3-1, recent allegations of police violence in Los Angeles were discussed. Here we look at the Rodney King case in that city as well as examples of brutality in other cities.

Los Angeles: 1991

The brutality of white police officers against an African American suspect might have gone unnoticed, but an eyewitness taped the actions of 3 March 1991. National television brought the details of a police beating into our homes as we saw Rodney King, a 25-year-old African American suspect, fired on by a white police officer carrying a 50,000-volt Taser stun gun. Three other officers kicked and beat the suspect on his head with their nightsticks, causing injuries to his neck, legs, and kidneys. King suffered multiple skull fractures, a broken ankle, a crushed cheekbone, internal injuries, severe bruises, and some brain damage.

All four officers in the King incident were charged with assault with a deadly weapon and excessive force by an officer under color of authority (acting in their capacity as federal, state, or local employees). Two were charged with filing a false police report, and one was charged with being an accessory after the fact. In the spring of 1992, the officers were tried by a jury in Simi Valley, California, a predominantly white community to which the trial had been moved when defense attorneys successfully argued that their clients could not get a fair trial in Los Angeles. All of the officers were acquitted of the assault and secondary charges, but the jury could not reach a verdict on the excessive force charge against one officer. The judge declared a mistrial on that charge. The prosecutor announced plans to retry the officer, and the judge ruled that the trial would be held in Los Angeles.

The reaction in Los Angeles was violent. The resulting rioting and looting led to 60 deaths, although later reports indicated that approximately 15 of those were not related to the rioting. Still, it was the "most deadly U.S. disturbance in the twentieth century."[1]

All four police officers were tried on federal charges of violating Rodney King's civil rights. Two officers, Timothy Wind and Ted Briseno, were acquitted. Officer Laurence Powell and Sgt. Stacey Koon were found guilty and sentenced to prison for two-and-one-half years. A federal appeals court upheld the convictions but ordered the trial court to reconsider the sentences, ruling that they were too short. The case was appealed to the U.S. Supreme Court, which upheld some but not all of the reasons for the trial court judge's sentence. The case was sent back for reconsideration by the trial judge in light of the Supreme Court's analysis of federal sentencing guidelines. On reconsideration, the original sentence was not changed.[2]

New York City Trials: 1999, 2000

Before the end of his trial in May 1999, New York City police officer Justin A. Volpe entered a guilty plea to sodomizing Abner Louima, a Haitian immigrant, with a stick, which he then brandished in Louima's face to humiliate him. The act occurred in the police stationhouse in 1997. Volpe also admitted that he threatened to kill Louima if he told anyone about the incident. Volpe admitted his guilt only after several other officers testified against him and it appeared that he would be convicted. A conviction could have resulted in a life sentence; Volpe was sentenced to 30 years in prison.

The New York City trial continued for the other officers who were tried with Volpe. After an 18-hour deliberation the jury acquitted Thomas Bruder and Thomas Wiese of beating Louima in a patrol car but convicted Charles Schwarz of holding Louima while Volpe sodomized him. In March 2000, Schwarz, Bruder, and Wiese were found guilty of conspiracy to obstruct justice in their attempts to cover up the brutalizing of Louima.[3] An appellate court reversed those charges in March 2002. That summer Schwarz was retried and found guilty of perjury, but the jury could not reach an agreement on the other charges against him, including two civil rights charges. The prosecutors announced that they would try Schwarz again, but the prosecution and the defense reached a plea agreement shortly before the scheduled trial. Schwarz entered a guilty plea to perjury and was sentenced to up to four years in prison. Louima settled his civil suit against the police for $8.7 million.

In 1999 an Albany, New York, jury acquitted four white New York City police officers who fired 41 times in the shooting death of Amadou Diallo, an unarmed West African immigrant.

Police Brutality

In a classic and frequently cited article on police brutality published in 1968, sociologist Albert J. Reiss Jr. began his discussion with a 1903 quotation by a former New York City police commissioner:

> For three years, there has been through the courts and the streets a dreary procession of citizens with broken heads and bruised bodies against few of whom was violence needed to affect an arrest. Many of them had done nothing to deserve an arrest. In a majority of such cases, no complaint was made. If the victim complains, his charge is generally dismissed. The police are practically above the law.[52]

During the summer of 1966, Reiss conducted a study of police-citizen interactions in Boston, Chicago, and Washington, D.C. In discussing the results of that study, Reiss pointed out the difficulty of defining police brutality, but he emphasized the importance to the citi-

An anonymous juror reportedly stated that the prosecution did not prove its case beyond a reasonable doubt.[4]

Detroit, Michigan: 2003

Years of complaints of misconduct by police in Detroit, Michigan, led the city's mayor to request the U.S. Department of Justice (DOJ) to investigate, beginning in 2000. Several police shootings were the focus of the inquiry, but the allegations also included mistreatment of prisoners. In 2002, the DOJ made 175 recommendations for changes; more were presented to the city in March 2003. In 2003, the DOJ and the city agreed to a monitor to oversee the department. It was estimated that the changes required for the Detroit Police Department to meet the federal mandate could exceed $100 million, with a cost of $50 million alone for remodeling the holding cells at the jail. Providing adequate screening for medical problems of inmates, along with proper care for those who are sick, is another major expense. Improved training of officers will be expensive and may require overtime pay. No longer will inmates receive bologna on two slices of bread for lunch. Rather, their food must come from a menu approved by a dietician. The federal monitor, Sheryl Robinson, and her staff may cost between $5 million and $10 million. Police must conduct a campaign to inform citizens on how to make complaints and buy new video cameras for holding cells and squad cars. The costs could be even more expensive, given the time constraints ordered for some changes. The city encountered these costs just as it laid off employees in the face of budget and funding cuts. Some civil rights activists, however, claimed that the consent decrees were not strong enough and that the DOJ was entering into them because it wished to settle the cases rather than file lawsuits against police departments. DOJ officials pointed out that they could still sue if the federal monitors determined that police departments were not in compliance.[5]

In October 2004, the federal monitor reported that few changes had been made and that the Detroit Police Department had failed to improve. Specifically, Sheryl Robinson said that the department had complied with only 2 of the 98 consent requirements, although she did acknowledge that the greatest improvement had come in the previous three months. It was estimated that it would cost the city at least $98 million to bring the police department into compliance with the federal consent agreements.[6]

Benton Harbor, Michigan: 16 June 2003

The death of Terrance Shurn, a 28-year-old African American, after he lost control of his motorcycle and crashed into a wall during a high-speed chase by white police officers on 16 June 2003, led to two nights of rioting in Benton Harbor, Michigan. Rumors that police had bumped the motorcycle spread quickly, but police investigations denied that. Benton Harbor, with its predominantly African American population, had a history of poverty, high unemployment, and racial tensions. Shortly after the riots, an 18-year-old teen, Coleman Tavon Edwards, shot a police officer. Edwards was convicted of assault with intent to murder and sentenced to 18 to 45 years in prison as well as two years on a weapons charge. A committee appointed to investigate the riots made its report in October 2003, urging improved relationships between the police and the community and "eradicating substandard housing in the city, where poverty and joblessness are rife."[7]

1. "One-Fourth of L.A. Riot Deaths Found Unrelated to Violence," *St. Petersburg Times* (2 June 1992), p. 4.
2. "Court Recommends Longer Sentences in Beating of King," *New York Times* (20 September 1994), p. 1. The case is United States v. Koon, 34 F.3d 1416 (9th Cir. 1994), *aff'd. in part, rev'd. in part, remanded,* 518 U.S. 81 (1996).
3. "Three Are Guilty of Cover-Up Plot in Louima Attack," *New York Times* (7 March 2000), p. 1.
4. "Pressed on Not-Guilty Verdicts, Diallo Juror Points to Prosecution," *New York Times* (27 February 2000), p. 1.
5. "Detroit Reform Tab May Top $100 Million," *Detroit News* (29 June 2003), p. 1; "Detroit Agrees on Monitor for the Police," *New York Times* (12 June 2003).
6. "Detroit Police Fail to Improve: Federal Monitor Says Department Has Made Little Progress in First Year of Sweeping Overhaul," *Detroit News* (19 October 2004), p. 1B.
7. "Cops Out in Force in Benton Harbor As Governor Vows Help," *Chicago Sun-Times* (20 June 2003), p. 3; "National Briefing Midwest: Michigan: Recommendations by Panel on Rioting," *New York Times* (22 October 2003), p. 18; "Teen Draws 20-Year Sentence: State Trooper Shot Week after June Riots," *South Bend Tribune* (21 October 2003), p. 1.

zen of the status degradation aspect of police behavior, "the judgment that [inmates] have not been treated with the full rights and dignity among citizens in a democratic society."[53] Police brutality may cause serious injury or even death, and police use of deadly force is at the root of most of the controversy surrounding questionable police behavior. Some of the most publicized allegations of police brutality of recent years are discussed in Spotlight 5-3. Also, refer back to Spotlight 3-1, which relates some of the incidents of police brutality in Los Angeles.

Allegations of police brutality such as those discussed in Spotlight 5-3 draw widespread media attention. Some of the attention is justified and, in some cases, police are found guilty of crimes for their use of force toward citizens. But it is important to put these incidents into perspective and note that most people who have encounters with police report that those interactions do not include violence. The Bureau of Justice Statistics (BJS) reports that less than 1 percent of persons who come into contact with police reported that officers threatened to use or did use force against them. During the years studied by the BJS, one in five respondents had some contact with police. Of those, one-third were seeking help or offering assistance; another one-third were reporting that they had been victims of or witnesses to crimes; less than one-third reported that the police had initiated the contact. But, as one authority pointed out, the report "probably doesn't really speak to the strained relations between the police and minority communities in America."[54]

A second type of violence involving police occurs when citizens engage in violence *against* the police.

5-4b   Violence against the Police

A 2001 BJS publication reported that law enforcement officers are at a higher risk of workplace violence than are other types of employees. Correctional officers were second, with cab drivers third.[55] In 1995, the number of felonious killings—that is, killings caused by the criminal acts of others—of law enforcement officers reached a six-year high, but in 1996 the number of officers killed in the line of duty was the lowest it had been since 1960. The 117 federal, state, and local officers killed feloniously in 1996 represented a 30 percent decrease over the number killed in 1995.[56]

In 1998, 9 fewer law enforcement officers were killed feloniously than in 1997, for a total of 61 officers, but 16 more officers died accidentally in the line of duty in 1998, compared with 1997. In 1999, the number of police killed in the line of duty decreased by 19 over 1998. The number of officers killed accidentally decreased by 16. In 2001, 72 officers were killed in the 9/11/01 terrorist attacks; another 70 were killed feloniously at other times during the year; and another 77 were killed accidentally. But even if the 72 are excluded, the total of police officers killed in 2001 exceeded those in 2000 by 37 percent. In 2002, a total of 56 law enforcement officers were killed feloniously while in the line of duty. In 2003, the number was 52, but an additional 80 officers were accidentally killed in the line of duty in 2003, up from 76 in 2002.[57]

It is important to understand that not all police deaths in the line of duty are felonious deaths. Approximately 40 percent of police deaths are the results of accidents. Furthermore, not all police who are confronted with violence by others are killed, although some of those are seriously injured, and police also encounter hostility that may result in verbal abuse. It is debatable which comes first and which causes which, but there are indications that both verbal and physical violence against police officers are accompanied by violence by police officers. In their report of a Police Foundation study focusing on police use of deadly force, the authors stated that they were "acutely aware of the interrelationship between acts committed *by* the police and acts committed *against* them."[58]

Violence against police has serious repercussions. Officers who survive may have physical injuries or psychological problems that preclude further work as police officers. Families and friends of those who are killed are also victims of such violence. There is evidence that these family members develop feelings of hostility and fear; they have difficulty making decisions; they feel alone in social situations; they have emotional problems; they develop sleep disorders; and they may have guilt feelings about their interactions with the deceased prior to his or her death.[59]

5-5   The Control of Policing

Although only a minority of police officers may be guilty of misconduct, any misconduct is serious and should be subject to discipline. Policies and programs should be developed to avoid as much misconduct as possible. Police misconduct may be controlled from within the department or by outside agencies.

5-5a   Regulation by Police Departments

Regulation of police conduct is not easy, given the number of persons involved, the extent of the potentially compromising situations, and limitations on funding for recruitment and training, but the efficient operation of any department requires internal discipline of employees. In the case of police departments, it is important that the public's image of internal operations also be positive. The U.S. Commission on Civil Rights emphasized that it is essential that police departments have an effective system of internal discipline that will "include clear definition of proper conduct, a reliable mechanism for detecting misconduct, and appropriate sanctions, consistently imposed, when misconduct has been proven." Policies must be clearly articulated.[60]

Police departments should enforce their written policies actively and fairly. If officers believe that they will not be reprimanded for violating departmental policies, those policies may be ineffective in curbing police abuse of discretion. The Commission on Civil Rights recommended that "every police department should have a clearly defined system for the receipt, processing, and investigation of civilian complaints." Once a violation of policy is found, "discipline imposed should be fair, swift, and consistent with departmental practices and procedures."[61] Police departments should take measures to identify violence-prone officers in an attempt to avert problems.

A recent publication based on a study funded by the federal Office of Community Oriented Policing Services (COPS) and conducted by the Police Executive Research Forum (PERF) stated that approximately one-fourth of the larger law enforcement agencies have an *early warning system,* which is designed to detect officers who might abuse their power. According to PERF, there is evidence that these systems, which are expected to be in force in many more departments within the near future, are successful in reducing problem behaviors. The early warning systems analyze citizen complaints, officer firings, high-speed chases, reports of the use of force, and other criteria to identify officers who are potential problems. Generally the first reaction will be for the officer's immediate supervisor to talk with him or her and document what the officer is told and his or her response. This information should be reviewed by a higher-ranking commander. Some departments involve the higher-ranking person directly; some require the identified officers to attend special training classes. Officers who are identified early as potential problems may never become problems. Another advantage of early intervention is to alert supervisors to their role in identifying and preventing problem behavior. The researchers emphasize that, for early intervention programs to be successful, they must involve accountability of supervisors and higher-up commanders. Examples of potential identifiers are frequent traffic stops of women or minorities.[62]

5-5b Federal Regulations

Another method for regulating local and state police is for federal agencies to be involved. We have noted that federal monitors are being used in several cities (for example, see again the discussion in Spotlight 5-3). These monitors are appointed after federal investigations, often with federal courts ordering the monitoring system.

Various federal statutes have enacted measures designed to improve local and state policing. Some of these statutes provide funds for increasing the number of police—although, as we noted earlier, some of these funds were cut significantly for 2005 (see again, for example, the discussion in Chapter 3 of the COPS program), with more cuts proposed for 2006, or for assisting police departments with training or acquiring the necessary equipment to improve their programs. And the FBI's academy at Quantico, Virginia, is used for training officers from non-FBI agencies.

Professions 5-1 presents information on one federal agency, the Drug Enforcement Administration (DEA), that has a wide variety of job opportunities.

5-5c Regulation by Courts

Police departments do not control themselves sufficiently, and the courts must be used for some types of control. Courts have two major ways of controlling policing: excluding evidence and providing a forum for civil lawsuits against police officers and their departments.

Professions 5-1

U.S. Drug Enforcement Job Opportunities

DEA regularly has many other positions available, ranging from lab technicians to assistants, to budget analysts, to attorneys. Please visit www.usajobs.opm.gov/a9dea.htm for more information.

DEA requires that all applicants complete a drug questionnaire as part of their application process. Please complete the following questionnaire and submit it with your application package (found at the previously mentioned OPM site) to the address identified with the respective vacancy announcement.

DRUG QUESTIONNAIRE

OMB No. 1117-0043
EXP. DATE: 10/2007

Privacy Act Statement

<u>Authority:</u> Executive Order 12564, September 15, 1986, the Drug Enforcement Administration's Drug-Free Workplace Plan and Title 5, United States Code. <u>Purpose:</u> DEA is charged with enforcement of the Controlled Substance Act; therefore, drug abuse by DEA employees would be intolerable and totally unacceptable. To be considered for employment with the DEA, it is mandatory that all applicants being considered for positions complete this form prior to the interview. Noncompliance with this requirement may result in non-consideration for employment. Applicants who are found, through investigation or personal admission, to have experimented with or used narcotics or dangerous drugs, except those medically prescribed, will not be considered for employment with the (DEA). Exceptions to this policy may be made for applicants who admit to limited youthful and experimental use of marijuana. Such applicants may be considered for employment if there is no evidence of regular, confirmed usage and the full-field background investigation and result of the other steps in the process are otherwise favorable. <u>Routine Uses:</u> Information contained in this form may be disclosed to other federal agencies for assistance in completing the security clearance process.

Name: Last_____ First_____ Middle_____
         (Please Print)

SSN: _____ Date of Birth _____

Please indicate the date, if any, on which you last used any of the following substances. Do not include instances in which the substance was prescribed, administered or dispensed for you by a duly authorized physician for treatment of a legitimate medical condition. Additionally, do not volunteer any information other than what is requested. Neither your truthful responses nor information derived from your response will be used as evidence against you in a subsequent criminal proceeding.

Substance	Approximate Month/Year You Last Used/Tried/ or Experimented with this Substance	Please Initial if Never Used/ Tried/Experimented
Marijuana	____/____	_____
Hashish/Hash Oil	____/____	_____
Cocaine/Crack	____/____	_____
PCP	____/____	_____
Heroin	____/____	_____

_____
Initials

Name _____ SSN: _____ Date of Birth_____

Substance	Approximate Month/Year You Last Used/Tried/ Experimented This Substance	Please Initial if Never Used/Tried/Experimented
Opium	____/____	_____
LSD	____/____	_____
Methamphetamine	____/____	_____
Ecstasy	____/____	_____
Any Other Illegal Substance identify	_____ ____/____	_____

I certify that the information provided on this questionnaire is correct and complete to the best of my knowledge. I further certify that I was not asked any information concerning use of the substances listed on this questionnaire other than that contained in the questionnaire. I understand that any misstatement of fact or omission of information may subject me to disqualification for further consideration in the hiring process.

_____

Signature of Applicant   Date

PAPERWORK REDUCTION ACT NOTICE: See Title 44 United States Code, Chapter 35. This form asks you to disclose your personal history, if any, of use of illegal drugs. This information will be used by DEA to determine your qualifications for employment. We try to create forms and instructions that are accurate, can be easily understood, and which impose the least possible burden on you to provide us with information. The estimated average time to complete and file this form is five minutes. If you have comments regarding the accuracy of this estimate, or suggestions for making this form simpler, you can write to: Human Resources Division, Drug Enforcement Administration, 2401 Jefferson Davis Highway, Alexandria VA 22301. Under the Paperwork Reduction Act, an agency of the United States government may not conduct or sponsor, and a person is not required to respond to, a request for collection of information unless it contains a currently valid OMB control number.

Revised 10/04   DEA Form No. 341

Source: DEA, U.S. Drug Enforcement Administration Web page, http://www.usdoj.gov/dea/resources/job_applicants.html retrieved 2 April 2005.

The Exclusionary Rule and Its Exceptions

Exclusionary rule Evidence secured as a result of illegal actions by law enforcement officers should be excluded from a trial.

If police seize evidence illegally or secure confessions improperly, the evidence may be excluded from trial. This procedure is the result of the U.S. Supreme Court's **exclusionary rule.** In 1914, the Supreme Court held that the Fourth Amendment (which prohibits unreasonable searches and seizures; see Appendix A) would have no meaning unless courts prohibited the use of illegally seized evidence. Consequently, when the police conducted an illegal search, the evidence they seized could not be used in *federal* cases. In 1961, the Court held that the exclusionary rule also applies to the states.[63]

The exclusionary rule is controversial, mainly because it applies after the fact. When illegally seized evidence is excluded from a trial, we know who the suspect is and may believe that guilt is obvious. Thus, for instance, when a judge rules that a gun allegedly used in a murder cannot be admitted at the suspect's trial because the evidence was obtained illegally by the police, and the suspect goes free because there is not enough legal evidence for a conviction, there may be strong public reaction of disbelief and outrage.

The exclusionary rule serves a symbolic purpose. According to one scholar, it is "a symbol of our system of criminal procedure. It is lauded as a crowning achievement of a free society."[64] If police violate individual rights to obtain evidence to convict alleged criminals, the government, in a sense, is supporting crime. When this occurs, the government becomes a lawbreaker, and, in the words of a noted jurist, "it breeds contempt for law; it invites . . . anarchy."[65]

The second reason for the exclusionary rule is a practical one: it is assumed that the rule prevents police from engaging in illegal searches and seizures. According to the U.S. Supreme Court, the exclusionary rule "compels respect for the constitutional guarantee in the only effectively available way—by removing the incentive to disregard it."[66] It is difficult to know whether that statement is true, because most illegal searches conducted to harass or punish take place in secret and may not be reported. Research on the issue is inconclusive. There is evidence, however, that the rule has led some police departments to increase the quantity and quality of police training, thus educating officers in what they may and may not do regarding search and seizure.[67]

In recent years the exclusionary rule has come under severe attack, with many people calling for its abolition or modification. Most of their arguments are the reverse of the arguments in favor of the rule. First is the argument of the symbolism of abolition, based on the view that, when people see guilty persons going free as a result of a technicality, they lose respect for law and order and criminal justice systems are weakened. The public's perception of letting guilty people go free is crucial.

Second, the abolitionists contend that the exclusionary rule should be eliminated because it results in the release of guilty people. The rule "is attacked as one of the chief technical loopholes through which walk the guilty on their way out of the courthouse to continue their depredations."[68] It makes no difference how many: one is too many, argue the abolitionists.

Third, the possibility of having evidence excluded from trial because it was not properly seized leads defendants to file numerous motions to suppress evidence, which consumes a lot of time and contributes to court congestion. In criminal cases, objections to search and seizure are the issues raised most frequently.

Good faith exception The provision that illegally obtained evidence will not be excluded from a subsequent trial if it can be shown that the police secured the evidence in good faith, meaning that they had a reasonable belief that they were acting in accordance with the law.

The U.S. Supreme Court has recognized some exceptions to the exclusionary rule. Under the **good faith exception,** illegally obtained evidence is not excluded from trial if it can be shown that police secured the evidence in good faith; that is, they had a reasonable belief that they were acting in accordance with the law. In *Massachusetts* v. *Sheppard* the Supreme Court held that when police conduct a search in good faith, even if the technical search warrant is defective, the seized evidence should not be excluded from the trial.[69] In 1995, the Supreme Court ruled that an unconstitutional arrest resulting from errors made by a court's clerical employee may be admitted against the accused at trial.[70]

The U.S. Supreme Court has interpreted the U.S. Constitution to permit the use of evidence seized by officers who had a warrant to search one apartment but searched the wrong apartment and found illegal drugs. In *Maryland* v. *Garrison* the Supreme Court reasoned that, because the search was in good faith and excluding its use in such cases would not deter police, who thought they were searching an apartment included in the warrant, nothing positive would be gained by applying the exclusionary rule in this fact pattern.[71]

The U.S. Supreme Court has held that a defendant's federal constitutional rights are not violated when police officers lose or destroy evidence that might have been used to establish the defendant's innocence, provided the officers' actions were made in good faith. The case *Arizona* v. *Youngblood* involved Larry Youngblood, who had been convicted of the kidnapping, molestation, and sexual assault of a 10-year-old boy. The police had failed to refrigerate the victim's semen-stained clothing or to make tests capable of showing whether the semen had come from Youngblood. The results of such tests might have shown that Youngblood was not the offender. William H. Rehnquist, writing for the majority, argued that the omission could "at worst be described as negligent."[72]

Since the U.S. Supreme Court adopted the good faith exception to the exclusionary rule, some state courts have held that it does not apply under their state constitutions and thus all illegally seized evidence must be excluded at trial, regardless of the motivation of the officer who seized the evidence. Because this involves enlarging, not reducing, a U.S. Supreme Court interpretation of the federal Constitution, as it decreases the amount of evidence that can be used against a defendant, such lower court rulings are permissible.

The U.S. Supreme Court has also recognized a second major exception to the exclusionary rule: the **inevitable discovery rule.** According to this rule, illegally seized evidence will be admitted at trial if it can be shown that eventually the evidence would have been discovered by legal methods. Writing for the Supreme Court in *Nix* v. *Williams,* Chief Justice Warren E. Burger said, "Exclusion of physical evidence that would inevitably have been discovered adds nothing to either the integrity or fairness of a criminal trial."[73]

> ▶ **Inevitable discovery rule**
> Evidence secured illegally by police will not be excluded from the suspect's trial, provided it can be shown that the evidence would have been discovered anyway under legal means.

In a 1990 case the U.S. Supreme Court further demonstrated its relaxing of the exclusionary rule. In 1980, the Court had held that the Fourth Amendment prohibits police from entering a suspect's home without a warrant and without the suspect's consent to make a felony arrest. The Court stated that its reason for this rule was to protect the physical integrity of the home. In 1990, the Court ruled that even a violation of this earlier case does not invalidate a statement made by the accused *after* the warrantless entry of the home if the accused makes a statement to police *outside* the home. It is not necessary to exclude the statement despite the illegal entry into the home. The prohibition against the warrantless entry of the home is to protect the home's physical integrity, "not to grant criminal suspects protection for statements made outside their premises where the police have probable cause to make an arrest."[74]

In 1991, a sharply divided U.S. Supreme Court permitted the use of coerced confessions in some circumstances. In 1967, the Supreme Court had articulated the *harmful error rule,* which holds that, if a confession is coerced, it must be excluded at trial. But in *Arizona* v. *Fulminante* the Court held that the Constitution does not require the *automatic* exclusion of the coerced confession. Rather, a coerced confession is to be considered like any other trial error; it is to be analyzed under the circumstances, and the trial court is to make a decision regarding whether it is a harmful error beyond a reasonable doubt. If so, it must be excluded; if not, it is a harmless error, and the evidence may be used against the suspect.[75]

In addition to the exclusionary rule, courts assist in the regulation of police actions through civil cases, as noted in the following discussion.

Civil Actions

The use of civil lawsuits to bring actions against police (or other authorities) who violate suspects' civil rights is thought to be an effective deterrent for such illegal actions. Even if these lawsuits do not deter other violations, civil actions permit abuse victims (or their survivors) to recover monetary damages for their physical injuries (or death) and for emotional, psychological, and economic damages.

Civil actions are brought under the Civil Rights Act of 1964 and are commonly called *1983 actions,* after the section of the U.S. Code in which the provision for such actions is codified.[76] Section 1983 actions may be brought by persons who are injured as a result of police negligence, as in high-speed chases that result in injuries (or death) to bystanders. Suits may also be brought for police mistreatment. Civil actions against police represent a growing body of civil law and increasing expenses for the municipalities that are legally responsible for those actions.

Civil suits against police may be brought not only for intentional or malicious conduct. *Negligence* is also a basis for liability, especially negligence in hiring and training. In 1989, for example, the U.S. Supreme Court held that inadequate police training may result in civil liability for the municipality under which the police department operates. Spotlight 4-1 discussed the case of *City of Canton, Ohio* v. *Harris.*[77] As that spotlight noted, the case involved civil liability for the misconduct of police. Some examples are pertinent here. In 2003, the Mississippi Supreme Court held that police who engage in high-speed chases through densely populated areas may be held responsible in civil actions for any injuries or deaths they cause. In *Jackson* v. *Brister,* police were summoned to a bank in which a customer was attempting to cash a forged check. When the customer saw the police she fled the bank in her car, followed by the police. The high-speed chase ended when the customer's car hit another car, killing the driver. The driver's estate sued for civil damages, and the court ruled that the usual immunity provided to police for civil damages does not apply when officers act recklessly in disregard for human life. The police department policy permits such pursuits only when the officer knows the suspect has committed a felony and it is reasonable to assume that the suspect is more dangerous to the community than is the risk of a high-speed chase. In this case, the officers could have gotten the license plate number, tracked down the suspect, and arrested her. The high-speed chase was not necessary.[78]

5-5d   Community Relations

Another method of controlling police activities is through community involvement and improved police-community relationships. It is vital that relationships between police and the community be improved. Police are not able to apprehend most criminals without the support of citizens. The U.S. Commission on Civil Rights emphasized that the men and women who are authorized to make arrests depend to a great extent on the cooperation of the public. "Perhaps the most valuable asset these officers can possess is credibility with the communities they serve."[79]

The importance of these contacts is emphasized by studies showing that citizens who have positive images of the police are more likely to report crimes than are those with negative images. Those most likely to have negative images of the police are members of the lower socio-economic class, African Americans, and other nonwhites—persons who feel a general alienation from the political process and those who perceive an increase in crime in their neighborhoods.

As noted earlier, community-oriented policing (COPS) is in vogue today. Earlier studies disclosed that some positive results, such as crime reduction, follow COPS.[80] Crime prevention programs are also important. Police educate the community about various approaches to crime prevention. Community organization activities in which police and the community work together to identify community problems are helpful. Herman Goldstein, who has written extensively about numerous criminal justice issues, concluded that full development of the overall concept of community policing, including a "concern with the substance of policing as well as its form," could "provide the integrated strategy for improving the quality of policing."[81]

We have already noted that violence by the police may evoke violence against the police. Earlier commissions underscored police violence as a catalyst for urban rioting in the 1960s.[82] But they also noted the impact of race in explaining violence by and against the police. For example, the U.S. Commission on Civil Rights emphasized the importance of hiring more racial minorities and upgrading their positions on police forces when it cited the study of the National Minority Advisory Council on Criminal Justice, which stressed the far-reaching effects of police brutality.[83] Efforts to increase diversity in policing deserve analysis.

5-6   Affirmative Action Recruitment and Hiring

Diversity in police departments is increasingly being recognized as one way to improve the services police offer to the community, as well as to improve the community's perception of police.

The need to recruit women and racial minorities was emphasized by the U.S. Commission on Civil Rights, which concluded,

> Serious underutilization of minorities and women in local law enforcement agencies continues to hamper the ability of police departments to function effectively in and earn the respect of predominantly minority neighborhoods, thereby increasing the probability of tension and violence.
>
> While there has been some entry of minorities and women into police service in recent years, police departments remain largely white and male, particularly in the upper-level command positions. Utilization figures for women hardly approach tokenism, although studies have indicated that as a rule women perform at least as well as men on the force.

In light of that finding, the commission recommended that "[p]olice department officials should develop and implement affirmative action plans so that ultimately the force reflects the composition of the community it serves."[84]

The U.S. Commission on Civil Rights found that efforts by police departments to recruit women and racial minorities may be hindered by the community's perceptions that the department is not committed to such recruitment. Such perceptions are created in different ways. For example, newspaper reports of the way police handle cases involving women and racial minorities, complaints of former members of the police force, and the treatment received by women and minorities who applied but were turned down as recruits by the police department may affect perceptions. Perceptions of race and gender discrimination are created by the lack of advancement opportunities for women and racial minorities within police departments, as well as by the high rates of attrition during training. The commission concluded that, in addition to an emphasis on recruitment, "minorities and women, through the implementation of equal opportunity programs, should hold positions that lead to upward mobility in the ranks, allowing them to compete for command positions."[85]

Recruitment of women and minority officers has had some help from the courts, with both groups having filed successful affirmative action cases under federal statutes. Women have successfully argued that they were discriminated against in hiring, on-the-job assignments, and promotions. After a decade of decisions on affirmative action policies concerning minorities and women, in 1987 the U.S. Supreme Court held that it is permissible for employers to give preferential treatment in jobs on the basis of gender and race. *Johnson* v. *Transportation Agency* involved a white man who argued that he was discriminated against when his employer promoted a white woman to a position for which he, too, was qualified.[86]

In *Johnson* the U.S. Supreme Court upheld the voluntary affirmative action plan of the transportation agency. Under this plan, in making promotions to positions in which women and minorities traditionally have been excluded or underrepresented, the agency was authorized to consider gender and race as a reason for a promotion. No quota was mentioned, but the policy did call for short-range goals of actively promoting women and minorities.

In 1987 in *United States* v. *Paradise*, the U.S. Supreme Court upheld an Alabama affirmative action plan that established a one-for-one racial quota for promotions. The Court said that this action is permissible because of the long history of excluding African Americans from employment as state troopers.[87]

Some have argued, however, that affirmative action discriminates against whites, and in recent years the programs designed to increase diversity have come under fire. The cases are complicated, and they involve settings other than policing, but several are significant.

In 1995, the U.S. Supreme Court decided *Adarand Constructors, Inc.* v. *Pena.* Although the Court did not use the words *affirmative action,* by a 5-to-4 decision the Court held that *federal government* programs that classify persons by race are presumably unconstitutional.

To survive, such programs must pass a test of "strict scrutiny" and be "narrowly tailored" to meet a purpose in which the government has a "compelling state interest." The case involved federal government contracts, but it has implications for affirmative action hiring by federal agencies, as it severely restricts the leeway the government has in minority (and, by analogy, gender) hiring. The case created considerable controversy, and within two weeks after its announcement, a spokesperson stated that the Federal Communications Commission was making plans to scale back a program that gave preferences to women and minorities in the awarding of wireless communication licenses.[88]

In 1995, the California Board of Regents ended affirmative action in that state's colleges and universities, and in 1996 a federal court in Texas refused to uphold the affirmative action policies of the University of Texas Law School. The U.S. Supreme Court declined to review the case, thus letting the decision stand.[89] The Court did agree, however, to hear a New Jersey affirmative action case during its 1997–1998 term.

The New Jersey case, *Piscataway Township Board of Education* v. *Taxman,* involved the dismissal of a white teacher rather than a similarly situated African American teacher when school district officials thought it necessary to cut back the payroll. The case was settled out of court prior to a decision by the U.S. Supreme Court, and in December 1997 the Supreme Court dismissed the case. Thus, the issue remained unresolved by the highest Court.[90] Subsequently some universities and some states abolished affirmative action programs within their colleges and universities, and it was possible that remaining programs would be held unconstitutional.

In 2003, the U.S. Supreme Court looked at two admissions policies from the University of Michigan. One involved a law school admissions policy; the second involved undergraduate admissions. The law school admissions policy was upheld; the undergraduate policy was rejected.

In the undergraduate case, *Gratz* v. *Bollinger* the University of Michigan used a 150-point scale for admissions. An applicant needed 100 points for guaranteed admission. Applicants from underrepresented minority groups were given 20 points for that fact alone. The U.S. Supreme Court ruled that using race as an admissions factor in that way—that is, using a mechanical formula—is unconstitutional.[91] The law school, however, used race as only one factor among others, such as grade point average, score on the law school admission test, teacher recommendations, alumni connections, and personal essays. In *Grutter* v. *Bollinger,* the U.S. Supreme Court upheld this practice.[92] Although one could argue that both systems are race-conscious and that the real differences are only symbolic, some legal scholars believe that the important difference is public perception.

According to a Harvard University constitutional law professor, "The fact that people psychologically treat the 20-point add-on as tantamount to a quota and therefore tend to resent it means a good bit." Other legal scholars differ. According to a University of Texas law professor, "There is a principled difference between saying you've got to look at everyone individually and saying you're just going to award points for race."[93] University of Texas law dean, Bill Powers, said, "We wholeheartedly agree with the Supreme Court's emphasis on the importance of making legal education accessible to 'talented and qualified individuals of every race and ethnicity.'"[94]

Justice Sandra Day O'Connor, who wrote the majority opinion upholding the Michigan Law School's policy (and who also voted in the majority rejecting the undergraduate admission policy), stated the importance of affirmative action in this comment: "In order to cultivate a set of leaders with legitimacy in the eyes of the citizenry, it is necessary that the path to leadership be visibly open to talented and qualified individuals of every race and ethnicity." According to O'Connor (who also stated that she hopes affirmative action will not be necessary in 25 years), the law school policy represents a "highly individualized, holistic review of each applicant's file" and does not use race in a "mechanical way." Further, the policy utilizing race must be narrowly tailored so that race is used as only one "plus

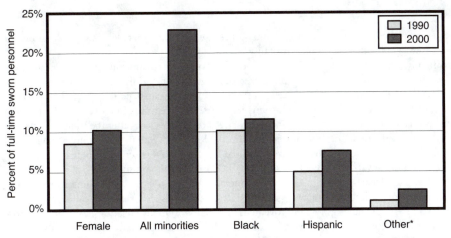

Figure 5-1
**Female and Minority Local Police
Officers, 1990–2000**
Source: Matthew J. Hickman and Brian A.
Reaves, Bureau of Justice Statistics, *Local Police
Departments 2000* (Washington, D.C.: U.S.
Department of Justice, January 2003), p. iii.

factor," permitted by the 1978 U.S. Supreme Court case involving a white applicant to a California medical school, the *Baake* case, in which Justice Lewis Powell Jr. wrote for the majority that "student body diversity is a compelling state interest that can justify the use of race in university admissions."[95]

The importance of diversity in many areas of life was emphasized by the members of over 300 organizations who signed 60 briefs submitted to the U.S. Supreme Court in support of the University of Michigan affirmative action policies prior to the hearing of those cases. The briefs provided compelling reasons to uphold affirmative action. For example, one submitted by the military (including General Norman Schwarzkopf, who commanded the allied forces during the first Persian Gulf War) insisted that the United States cannot be properly defended without diversity in the troops. Businesses (such as Coca-Cola, General Electric, and Microsoft) included in their statements that diversity in education admissions is crucial to their recruiting of a diverse workforce, which they believe is necessary for their significant contributions to the international marketplace. According to the comments of the senior vice president and general counsel at Merck, a pharmaceutical company, "Diversity creates stronger companies. . . . The work we do directly impacts patients of all types around the globe. Understanding people is essential to our success."[96]

Not everyone agrees with the U.S. Supreme Court's upholding of affirmative action policies. In his dissent in the law school admission case, U.S. Supreme Court Justice Clarence Thomas, the only African American on the Court, stated the following:

> I believe blacks can achieve in every avenue of American life without the meddling of university administrators. Because I wish to see all students succeed whatever their color, I share, in some respect, the sympathies of those who sponsor the type of discrimination advanced by the University of Michigan Law School. The Constitution does not, however, tolerate institutional devotion to the status quo in admissions policies when such devotion ripens into racial discrimination.[97]

These recent decisions by the U.S. Supreme Court will have an impact on police hiring. Clearly some form of affirmative action is still considered constitutional; clearly a mechanical system is not acceptable. And there is a practical issue: if minorities believe that their representation in a given police force will be too small, they may not apply. But both women and minorities have been involved in policing for a long time, although they represent a small percentage of law enforcement officers, and most hold subordinate roles. Still, their numbers have been increasing, as noted in Figure 5-1, and these latest decisions may increase their representation.

Chapter Wrap-Up

This chapter focused on some problems and issues connected with policing in a complex society. Political pressures from within the department, along with pressures from the community and other outside forces, create problems. Problems may be related to the role conflicts of policing. Most officers receive more training in law enforcement than in order maintenance and performance of community services. Many of them view policing primarily as law enforcement; superiors may evaluate them by their work in that area. However, studies reveal that officers spend less time in law enforcement than in other police functions. Nor are the lines always clear regarding law enforcement. For example, today most departments view domestic violence as a law enforcement issue, not a social problem, but not all police administrators, officers, or the public agree. But domestic violence among police has also become an issue.

Police encounter numerous stressors on their jobs. Some are due to the nature of the job and varying citizen expectations, and many citizens have no hesitation in complaining if all police functions are not performed quickly, efficiently, and adequately. The real problem may lie in our unrealistic expectations of police. In theory, we want them to enforce all laws; however, in reality, we will not tolerate full enforcement—police will not and cannot do that, anyway. We expect the police to prevent crime, but that is not always possible, either. We think that they should be authoritarian in enforcement situations yet maintain a supportive and friendly approach in others. We authorize them to handle all kinds of emergencies, yet we do not provide them with the resources or authority for these functions. No matter what police do, they encounter conflicts.

Most important, we cannot separate policing and its context from the rest of our society. As one authority on policing concluded, the actions of the police "mirror the social relations of American society. Until those relations change we will continue to have a police problem."[98]

Stress may become a major issue for police, some of whom commit suicide as a result. The spread of AIDS has created stress for officers who are infected as well as for those who do not know how to react to AIDS-infected colleagues. The concern with and planning for the prevention of terrorist attacks has placed stress on law enforcement officers and administrators. The development of a subculture is one way police cope with these and other stressors.

Police misconduct is another problem and has been widely studied. Reports vary as to the pervasiveness and nature of misconduct, but it is clear that at least some police are involved in drug transactions and other illegal acts. Departmental efforts to eradicate this illegal behavior are not always successful. Police use of deadly force has become a critical issue in some departments. Police are permitted to use some force, but the *abuse* of that responsibility is a focus of concern. Court decisions have required changes in the use of deadly force, for example, and some police departments have responded with a greater emphasis on proper training in the use of deadly force. In addition, some have established more detailed departmental policies on the use of vehicular pursuits. Despite these changes, some police use excessive force, leading to allegations of police brutality.

Violence and brutality by police came into national focus in the widely publicized beating of Rodney King, an African American, by white police officers. Violence against police and police violence against citizens lead to serious repercussions, as illustrated by the deadly and destructive Los Angeles riots after the state acquittals of the officers tried in the King case. Recent allegations of police violence have refocused attention on this serious problem of policing. Violence against police is also an important concern in today's world.

Efforts to control improper policing have come from department regulations, court decisions, civil actions against police, and the improvement of community-police relations. The most controversial of these efforts has been the U.S. Supreme Court's exclusionary rule, whereby evidence obtained by police in violation of a suspect's constitutional rights may be excluded from that individual's trial. The Court has created some exceptions to the exclusionary rule, such as good faith and inevitable discovery. Civil actions against police may serve as a deterrent to improper police behavior, and an increasing number of these suits are being filed under the federal code.

Further problems and issues in policing surround affirmative action programs aimed at employing more women and racial minorities. These groups argue that the police cannot understand their problems and gain the support of their members unless the groups are represented adequately among police officers and administrators. Others argue that recruitment efforts have lowered standards or that court decisions upholding affirmative action programs for increasing the number of women and racial minorities on a police force are unfair and create internal problems for police. Changes in affirmative action policies in some states were followed by significant decreases in the university enrollments of African Americans and other minorities. The U.S. Supreme Court's upholding of some affirmative action policies in 2003 may give a green light to universities and businesses—including law enforcement agencies—to attempt to achieve greater diversity in admissions and hiring.

Despite problems in policing, many officers are satisfied with their profession. Problems exist in any profession, and perhaps it is good that we are never free of the opportunities for improvement that problems present. Policing is not for everyone; however, for those who enjoy a challenging, exciting job in which there is opportunity for service as well as hard work, policing is a viable choice.

Joseph Wambaugh, a former police officer and an author of best-selling novels, in assessing his life in both professions, said he did not miss the tedium and bureaucracy of policing, but he did miss the loyalty and camaraderie of his former police colleagues. "I find a lot of disloyalty in show business. In police work, it's totally different. . . . For the period of time that you're working together [in policing] you are absolutely loyal to each other." Wambaugh concluded, "Being a cop was a good life."[99]

Key Terms

deadly force (p. 128)
domestic violence (p. 120)
exclusionary rule (p. 136)

fleeing felon rule (p. 128)
good faith exception (p. 136)
inevitable discovery rule (p. 137)

proactive (p. 119)
reactive (p. 119)
subculture (p. 125)

Apply It

1. What external political situations might affect policing?
2. How should police spend most of their time? Why?
3. What is meant by *proactive* and *reactive* policing, and what changes are being made in the former?
4. What is the relationship between domestic violence and policing?
5. What are the major stressors in policing?
6. What is meant by a *subculture*? How does that concept apply to policing?
7. Discuss the extent and result of police corruption, with particular reference to the influence of drugs.
8. What is the *fleeing felon rule*? Contrast its historical meaning with the U.S. Supreme Court's ruling currently in effect.
9. Analyze the reasons for and concern with police vehicle pursuits.
10. Discuss police brutality in the context of a recent example.
11. What is the relationship between violence against the police and violence by the police?
12. Distinguish between police department regulations and civil lawsuits as methods of controlling policing.
13. How have changes in federal regulations affected law enforcement?
14. State the purpose of the *exclusionary rule* and analyze whether that purpose is being met. What exceptions has the U.S. Supreme Court permitted?
15. Discuss civil liability that may result from inadequate training of police.
16. What has been the result of efforts to recruit women and racial minorities into policing? What would you recommend for the future?

Endnotes

1. James Q. Wilson, *Varieties of Police Behavior: The Management of Law and Order in Eight Communities* (Cambridge, Mass.: Harvard University Press, 1968), p. 19.
2. Albert J. Reiss Jr., *The Police and the Public* (New Haven, Conn.: Yale University Press, 1971), pp. 63, 64, 71.
3. Richard J. Lundman, "Police Patrol Work: A Comparative Perspective," in *Police Behavior: A Sociological Perspective*, ed. Richard J. Lundman (New York: Oxford University Press, 1980), p. 55.
4. Eric J. Scott, *Calls for Service: Citizen Demand and Initial Police Performance*, National Institute of Justice (Washington, D.C.: U.S. Department of Justice, July 1981), pp. 24–30.
5. Ibid., p. 27.
6. Violence against Women Act of 1994, U.S. Code, Title 42, Chapter 136, Section 1381 (2005). The final rule is published in the *Federal Register*, Volume 61, Section 40727-34 (6 August 1996).
7. Lawrence W. Sherman and Richard A. Berk, *The Minneapolis Domestic Violence Experiment* (Washington, D.C.: Police Foundation, 1984), p. 1.
8. *Attorney General's Task Force on Family Violence*, Final Report (Washington, D.C.: U.S. Department of Justice, 1984), p. 20.
9. Franklyn W. Dunford et al., "The Role of Arrest in Domestic Assault: The Omaha Police Experiment," *Criminology* 28 (May 1990): 204.
10. Maryann Syers and Jeffrey L. Edleson, "The Combined Effects of Coordinated Criminal Justice Intervention in Woman Abuse," *Journal of Interpersonal Violence* 7 (December 1992): 490–502.
11. Lawrence W. Sherman, "The Influence of Criminology on Criminal Law: Evaluating Arrests for Misdemeanor Domestic Violence," *Journal of Criminal Law and Criminology* 83 (Spring 1992): 1–45; quotation is on pp. 44–45.
12. David A. Klinger, "Policing Spousal Assault," *Journal of Research in Crime and Delinquency* 32 (August 1995): 308–324.
13. Robert C. Davis and Barbara Smith, "Domestic Violence Reforms: Empty Promises or Fulfilled Expectations?" *Crime & Delinquency* 41 (October 1995): 541–552; quotation is on p. 541.
14. Richard B. Felson and Jeff Ackerman, "Arrest for Domestic and Other Assaults," *Criminology* 39, no. 3 (August 2001): 655–676; quotation is on p. 672.
15. Robert C. Davis et al., "Increasing the Proportion of Domestic Violence Arrests That Are Prosecuted: A Natural Experiment in Milwaukee," *Criminology and Public Policy* 2, no. 2 (March 2003): 263–282; quotation is on p. 280.
16. Laura Dugan, "Domestic Violence Legislation: Exploring Its Impact on the Likelihood of Domestic Violence, Police Involvement, and Arrest," *Criminology and Public Policy* 2, no. 2 (March 2003): 263–283; quotation is on p. 283.
17. Richard B. Felson et al., "Reasons for Reporting and Not Reporting Domestic Violence to the Police," *Criminology* 40: 3 (August 2002): 617–648; quotation is on p. 617.
18. "Rise in Claims of Wife Abuse against Police," *New York Times* (14 November 1999), p. 39.
19. James D. Sewell, "The Boss As Victim: Stress and the Police Manager," *FBI Law Enforcement Bulletin* 57 (February 1988): 15–19.
20. Quoted in Anne Choen, "I've Killed That Man Ten Thousand Times," *Police Magazine* (July 1980), pp. 17–23.
21. "Stress Therapy Ordered for Cops on Crisis Calls," *Miami Herald* (2 May 1989), p. 2.
22. "New York Police Officers Face Counseling on Sept. 11 Events," *New York Times* (30 November 2001), p. 1.
23. The U.S. Commission on Civil Rights, *Who Is Guarding the Guardians? A Report on Police Practices* (Washington, D.C.: U.S. Government Printing Office, October 1981), p. 156.
24. "Ex-Cop Indicted in Killing of Ken, 3 Neighbors," *The Record* (Bergen County, NJ) (4 September 2002), p. 3.
25. "A Silent Fraternity: Officers with H.I.V.," *New York Times* (2 August 2000), p. 23.
26. "Westmont Settles Job Bias Suit; Police Applicant is HIV-Positive," *Chicago Tribune* (30 May 2003), p. 4 Metro. The case is Roe v. Village of Westmont, 2003 U.S. Dist. LEXIS 245 (N.D. Ill. 2003).
27. "Focus on Terror Creates Burden for the Police," *New York Times* (28 October 2001), p. 1.

28. Rodney Stark, *Police Riots: Collective Violence and Law Enforcement* (Belmont, Calif.: Focus Books, 1972), p. 93.

29. See Arthur Niederhoffer, *Behind the Shield: The Police in Urban Society* (Garden City, N.Y.: Doubleday, 1969).

30. Eric D. Poole and Robert M. Regoli, "An Examination of the Effects of Professionalism on Cynicism among Police," *Social Science Journal* 16 (October 1979): 64.

31. John P. Crank et al., "Cynicism among Police Chiefs," *Justice Quarterly* 3 (September 1986): 343–352.

32. Dennis Jay Wiechman, "Police Cynicism toward the Judicial Process," *Journal of Police Science and Administration* 7 (September 1979): 340–345.

33. "Police Officer Subjected to 'Code of Silence' for Complaining about Harassment Wins Substantial Verdict," *Criminal Law Reporter* 45 (April 2002): 113; "Judge Slashes $3 Million Jury Award," *Chicago Daily Law Bulletin* (3 June 2002). The case is Spina v. Forest Pres. Dist., 2001 U.S. Dist. LEXIS 19146 (N.D. Ill. 2001). "Law Discriminates against Victims of Discrimination," *Newsday* (New York) (22 May 2003), p. 40.

34. Lawrence W. Sherman, ed., *Police Corruption: A Sociological Perspective* (Garden City, N.Y.: Doubleday, 1974), p. 6.

35. Wilson, *Varieties of Police Behavior,* Chs. 5–7, pp. 140–226.

36. Sherman, ed., *Police Corruption,* pp. 7–8.

37. See ibid., pp. 1–39.

38. *The Knapp Commission Report on Police Corruption* (New York: Braziller, 1972).

39. Herman Goldstein, *Policing a Free Society* (Cambridge, Mass.: Ballinger, 1977), p. 218.

40. "Pursuing Corrupt Cops," *New York Times* (30 December 1993), p. 12.

41. "Police Corruption in New York Found Rarer but More Virulent," *Criminal Justice Newsletter* 25 (15 July 1994): 1–2.

42. "A Choice Word for Crime Lab Mess," *Houston Chronicle* (26 April 2003), p. 31.

43. "Panel Finds Police Department Ineffective at Disciplining Officers," *New York Times* (29 June 2000), p. 25.

44. "Explosive Drug Use in Prisons Is Creating a New Underworld," *New York Times* (30 December 1989), p. 1.

45. "Drug Cases Are Upended by the Police in Chicago," *New York Times* (27 December 1997), p. 6.

46. See Thomas J. Hickey and Sue Titus Reid, "Testing Police and Correctional Officers for Drug Use after *Skinner* and *Von Raab*," *Public Administration Quarterly* 19 (Spring 1995): 26–41. The cases are Skinner v. Railway Labor Executives' Association, 489 U.S. 602 (1989), upholding drug testing among railway workers; and National Treasure Employees Union v. Von Raab, 489 U.S. 656 (1989), upholding a drug testing program in the U.S. Customs Service for employees who sought promotions to positions involving such activities as carrying firearms or interdiction of illegal drugs.

47. Catherine H. Milton et al., *Police Use of Deadly Force* (Washington, D.C.: Police Foundation, 1977), p. 41.

48. Tennessee v. Garner, 471 U.S. 1 (1985).

49. "New Pursuit Rules Held a Week: Police Intend to Work Out Kinks before Changing Policy," *Daily News of Los Angeles* (3 May 2003), p. 3N.

50. Geofrey P. Alpert, National Criminal Justice Reference Service, *Police Pursuit: Policies and Training* (Washington, D.C.: U.S. Department of Justice, 1997), as cited in "Police Tightening Policies on High-Speed Chases, Study Finds," *Criminal Justice Newsletter* 28 (1 July 1997): 6.

51. "Most Police Chase Accidents Occur in First Two Minutes, Study Finds," *Criminal Justice Newsletter* 29 (3 August 1999): 7.

52. Albert J. Reiss Jr., "Police Brutality," *Transaction Magazine* 5 (1968), reprinted in *Police Behavior: A Sociological Perspective,* ed. Richard J. Lundman (New York: Oxford University Press, 1980), pp. 274–275.

53. Ibid., p. 276.

54. "In Study of Contact with Police, Less Than 1% Cite Use of Force," *New York Times* (23 November 1997), p. 14.

55. Bureau of Justice Statistics, *National Crime Victimization Survey: Violence in the Workplace* (Annapolis Junction, Md.: 2001), p. 1.

56. "Number of Slain Police Officers Is Lowest since 1960," *New York Times* (1 January 1997), p. 7.

57. Federal Bureau of Investigation, *Crime in the United States: Uniform Crime Reports 1998* (Washington, D.C.: U.S. Department of Justice, October 1999), p. 291; Federal Bureau of Investigation, *Crime in the United States: Uniform Crime Reports 1999* (Washington, D.C.: U.S. Department of Justice, October 2000), p. 291; *Law Enforcement Officers Killed and Assaulted, 2001,* a 109-page report by the FBI, available at www.fbi.gov, cited in "Killings of Officers Increased Last Year, FBI Announces," *Criminal Justice Newsletter* 32, no. 22 (5 December 2002): 6; *Uniform Crime Reports* 2002, p. 323; *Uniform Crime Reports* 2003, p. 365.

58. Milton et al., *Police Use of Deadly Force,* p. 3.

59. Frances A. Stillman, National Institute of Justice, *Line-of-Duty Deaths: Survivor and Departmental Responses,* (Washington, D.C.: U.S. Department of Justice, January 1987), pp. 2, 3.

60. U.S. Commission on Civil Rights, *Who Is Guarding the Guardians?* p. 35.

61. Ibid., pp. 157, 159. See also pp. 58–79.

62. *Early Warning Systems: Responding to the Problem Police Officer* (Rockville, Md., 2001), as cited in "Police Creating Warning Systems for Potential Problem Officers," *Criminal Justice Newsletter* 31, no. 17 (19 September 2001): 4.

63. Weeks v. United States, 232 U.S. 383 (1914); Mapp v. Ohio, 367 U.S. 643 (1961).

64. Lawrence Crocker, "Can the Exclusionary Rule Be Saved?" *Journal of Criminal Law & Criminology* 84 (Summer 1993): 310–351; quotation is on pp. 310–311.

65. Olmstead v. United States, 277 U.S. 438, 485 (1928), Justice Brandeis, dissenting.

66. Elkins v. United States, 364 U.S. 206, 217 (1960).

67. See Stephen H. Sachs, "The Exclusionary Rule: A Prosecutor's Defense," *Criminal Justice Ethics* 1 (Summer/Fall 1982).

68. Crocker, "Can The Exclusionary Rule Be Saved?" p. 311.

69. Massachusetts v. Sheppard, 468 U.S. 981 (1984). See also United States v. Leon, 468 U.S. 897 (1984) (decided the same day).

70. Arizona v. Evans, 514 U.S. 1 (1995).

71. Maryland v. Garrison, 480 U.S. 79 (1987).

72. Arizona v. Youngblood, 488 U.S. 51 (1988).

73. Nix v. Williams, 467 U.S. 431 (1984).

74. New York v. Harris, 495 U.S. 14 (1990), referring to the previous case, Payton v. New York, 445 U.S. 573 (1980).

75. Arizona v. Fulminante, 499 U.S. 279 (1991).

76. U.S. Code, Chapter 42, Section 1983 (2005).

77. City of Canton, Ohio v. Harris, 489 U.S. 378 (1989).

78. Jackson v. Brister, 838 So.2d 274 (Miss. 2003).

79. U.S. Commission on Civil Rights, *Who Is Guarding the Guardians?* p. 2.

80. See Jerome H. Skolnick and David H. Bayley, *The New Blue Line: Police Innovation in Six American Cities* (New York: Free Press, 1986); Albert J. Reiss Jr., *Policing in a City's Central District: The Oakland Story* (Washington, D.C.: National Institute of Justice, 1985).

81. Herman Goldstein, "Toward Community-Oriented Policing: Potential, Basic Requirements, and Threshold Questions," *Crime & Delinquency* 33 (January 1987): 28.

82. *Who Is Guarding the Guardians?* p. vi.

83. National Minority Advisory Council on Criminal Justice, *The Inequality of Justice: A Report on Crime and the Administration of Justice in the Minority Community* (October 1980), pp. 15–16, as quoted in U.S. Commission on Civil Rights, *Who Is Guarding the Guardians?* p. 2.

84. *Who Is Guarding the Guardians?* p. 2.

85. Ibid., p. 154.

86. Johnson v. Transportation Agency, 480 U.S. 616 (1987).

87. United States v. Paradise, 480 U.S. 149 (1987). For a discussion of the legal issues in affirmative action, see Thomas J. Hickey, Sue Titus Reid, and K. Lee Derr, "Legal Issues in Affirmative Action Policy Development," *International Journal of Public Administration* 19, no. 1 (January 1996): 123–149.

88. See Adarand Constructors, Inc., v. Pena, 515 U.S. 200 (1995), sending a Colorado case back to the lower federal court for retrial under the test articulated by the Court. The case applies only to federal contracts, for the facts involved a federal agency. The U.S. Supreme Court had previously held that state and local agency policies involving racial classifications should be analyzed under strict scrutiny. See Richmond v. J.A. Croson Co., 488 U.S. 469 (1989).

89. Hopwood et al. v. Texas, 78 F.3d 932 (5th Cir. 1996), *cert. denied,* 518 U.S. 1033 (1996).

90. Taxman v. Board of Education, 91 F.3d 1547 (3d Cir. 1996), *cert. granted,* Piscataway Township Board of Education v. Taxman, 521 U.S. 1117 (1997), and *cert. dismissed,* 522 U.S. 1010 (1997).

91. Gratz v. Bollinger, 539 U.S. 244 (2003).

92. Grutter v. Bollinger, 539 U.S. 306 (2003).

93. Both quoted in "Affirmative Action Proponents Get the Nod in a Split Decision," *New York Times* (24 June 2003), p. 23.

94. "Where Hopwood Failed, Grutter Succeeds: U.S. Supreme Court Upholds Race-Conscious Admissions Policy," *Texas Lawyer* 19, no. 17 (30 June 2003): 6.

95. Grutter v. Bollinger, 539 U.S. 306 (2003); Regents of the University of California v. Baake, 438 U.S. 263 (1978).

96. "300 Groups File Briefs to Support the University of Michigan in an Affirmative Action Case," *New York Times* (18 February 2003), p. 14.

97. Grutter v. Bollinger, 539 U.S. 306 (2003).

98. Michael K. Brown, *Working the Street: Police Discretion and the Dilemmas of Reform* (New York: Russell Sage, 1981).

99. Quoted in Claudia Dreifus, "A Conversation with Joseph Wambaugh," *Police Magazine* (May 1980), pp. 37–38.

Processing a Criminal Case: Criminal Court Systems

The processing of a criminal case involves a complex series of stages that center on the criminal courts. The chapters in Part 3 examine the pretrial, trial, and appellate procedures of criminal court systems. Chapter 6 explores the structure of courts, how they are administered, what role judges play in the court system, and what might be done about the current crisis in courts created by the increase in cases at the trial and appellate levels.

Attorneys play important roles in the trial of criminal cases. Prosecutors and defense attorneys are seen popularly as fighting their battles in the drama of criminal courtrooms. Their roles are far more complex, however, than the media portray. Chapter 7 looks at the differences between the prosecution and the defense and analyzes their roles in criminal justice systems. Particular attention is given to prosecutorial discretion. Chapter 7 also covers pretrial procedures, including the frequently used and highly controversial process of plea bargaining.

Chapter 8 focuses on the trial of a criminal case, examining each step of the trial and explaining the roles of defense, prosecution, and judges in the criminal trial. But perhaps the most controversial process in criminal justice systems is the sentencing of persons who are found guilty. Chapter 8 examines recent trends in sentencing, along with the sentencing process and an analysis of issues raised by sentencing. The chapter closes with a discussion of appeals.

Criminal Court Systems

The importance of courts in American criminal law cannot be overemphasized. Courts supervise most aspects of criminal justice systems. The actions that occur within courts affect all other aspects of criminal justice systems. However, a 1999 survey published by the American Bar Association revealed that most of the respondents had limited knowledge of U.S. criminal courts. Only 17 percent of the respondents knew the name of the Chief Justice of the U.S. Supreme Court (this might be higher now, as millions saw Chief Justice William H. Rehnquist preside over the Senate impeachment trial of President Bill Clinton and, in 2004–2005, were exposed to significant media attention to Rehnquist's health problems). Over one-third thought that defendants must prove their innocence in criminal trials. Ninety percent of the respondents thought that affluent people have an advantage in criminal courts, whereas 47 percent believed that criminal justice systems treat minorities and the poor unfairly. Of those who had used the services of a lawyer in the previous five years, 53 percent were very satisfied, whereas another 22 percent were somewhat satisfied. Only 8 percent expressed strong confidence in the news media, but 50 percent reported that they had strong confidence in the U.S. Supreme Court. Finally, compared with a similar study in 1978, the 1999 survey revealed an increase in "public confidence in all levels of the judicial system" but a decline in the public's "confidence in doctors, organized religion, public schools and Congress, as well as the news media." Further, a majority of the respondents rejected the statement that "the courts are just puppets of the political system."[1]

This chapter begins with an introduction to some legal concepts that must be understood for an adequate explanation of courts. It examines court structures, pointing out the distinctions between federal and state court systems. Both systems have trial and appellate courts; those types are discussed and distinguished. The highest court in the United States, the U.S. Supreme Court, is examined in more detail.

The next major section of the chapter examines the judge's role. The final section focuses on court congestion and discusses solutions to this major problem.

L E A R N I N G

OBJECTIVES

After reading this chapter, you should be able to do the following:

- **Discuss the judicial branch of government; define basic legal terminology regarding courts; and distinguish between trial and appellate courts**
- **Diagram the levels of state and federal court systems and explain what happens at each level**
- **Discuss the history and purpose of the U.S. Supreme Court and explain and evaluate its functions and operations**
- **Describe the role of judges in criminal trials**
- **Explain and evaluate the sentencing role of trial judges**
- **Contrast the role of an appellate judge with that of a trial judge**
- **List and explain two methods for selecting judges**
- **Explain briefly the training, retention, and control of judges**
- **Describe court congestion and suggest remedies**

6-1   The Judicial Branch of Government

The framers of the U.S. Constitution established three branches of government at the national level—legislative, executive, and judicial—and provided for the establishment of one supreme court. They envisioned a separation of the powers of these three branches, although there is some overlap. Federal **judges** and justices of the U.S. Supreme Court are appointed by the president, representing the executive branch, and confirmed by the Senate, representing the legislative branch. Because courts have limited enforcement powers, they rely on the executive branch for enforcement of their decisions. The court system must depend on the legislative branch of government for financial appropriations.

In U.S. criminal justice systems, a separate judicial branch is viewed as necessary for assuring that the constitutional and statutory rights of citizens are not controlled by political pressures. In practice, however, political pressures may enter into the selection of judges, as well as into the organization and administration of courts and the judicial decision-making process.

> **Judge**   An elected or appointed officer of the court who presides over a court of law; the final and neutral arbiter of law who is responsible for all court activities.

6-1a   Definitions of Legal Terms

For a complete understanding of criminal court systems, it is necessary to understand some legal terms and concepts. *Jurisdiction* refers to a court's power to hear and decide a case. This power is given by the constitution or statute that created that court. A court's jurisdiction may be limited to a certain age group (e.g., juvenile courts, with jurisdiction over juvenile delinquency, child custody, and adoption proceedings) or to a particular type of law (e.g., criminal, civil, bankruptcy). Some courts have jurisdiction only over minor offenses, or *misdemeanors*. Others hear only the more serious kinds of offenses, called *felonies*. Some courts hear only civil cases, others only criminal cases. This chapter is concerned primarily with courts that have jurisdiction over criminal law, although at appellate levels most courts hear both criminal and civil cases.

It is important to distinguish original from appellate jurisdiction. *Original jurisdiction* refers to the jurisdiction of the court that may hear a case first—that is, the court that may try the facts. *Appellate jurisdiction* refers to the jurisdiction of the court that may hear the case on appeal. When more than one court may hear a case, those courts have *concurrent jurisdiction.* When only one may hear a case, that court has *exclusive jurisdiction.*

The subject of jurisdiction arose in a highly publicized case in January 2000, after Michael Skakel, a nephew of the late Senator Robert F. Kennedy, was arrested and charged with the murder of Martha Moxley, age 14, almost 25 years earlier. Skakel, a neighbor and friend of Moxley's, was 15 at the time of her murder, which would have given the juvenile court jurisdiction over him at that time. That jurisdiction would have ended when Skakel reached 21. The defense argued that no court had jurisdiction over Skakel in the year 2000. The prosecutor argued that the adult criminal court had jurisdiction because Skakel was 39 at the time of his arrest. The trial judge ruled that the adult criminal court had jurisdiction to try the case.

In June 2002, Skakel was convicted of Moxley's murder; he was sentenced to 20 years-to-life in prison and must serve 11 years before he is eligible for parole. In November 2003, attorneys for Skakel filed an appeal, asking the Connecticut superior court to overturn his conviction. The appeal alleged that "prosecutors engaged in pervasive misconduct, including falsely claiming a powerful family cover-up."[2] The defense alleged that the prosecution used improper statements in its closing argument, stating without any evidence that Skakel masturbated on the victim's body and further, calling the defendant a killer and a spoiled brat. The appeal also alleged that the juvenile court, not the adult criminal court, should have had jurisdiction of the Skakel case and that the case was tried 19 years after the statute of limitations expired. The prosecution filed a 114-page brief in response to Skakel's appellate brief. Skakel is incarcerated in the MacDougall Correctional Institution in Suffield, Connecticut. In late 2004, Leonard Levill, who worked on the case for years, published a book, *Conviction: Solving the Moxley Murder,* in which he quoted Skakel's priest as quoting Skakel's counselor as saying that Skakel told him there was "blood all over the place." But in January 2005, Brian Wood, a retired police officer and one of the jurors who convicted Skakel, said that he was no longer convinced that Skakel was guilty and that he was now working with Skakel's defense team.[3] Also in January 2005 the Connecticut Supreme Court heard oral arguments on Skakel's appeal, but no decision had been made as of this writing.

Another limitation on courts is that they hear only actual cases and controversies. Courts do not decide hypothetical issues, and normally they do not give advisory opinions. Only when a dispute involves a legal right between two or more parties will a court hear the case. If the controversy ends before the completion of the trial or the appeal, usually the court will not decide the case, as the issue is **moot,** meaning that it is no longer a real case because no legal issue between the parties remains to be resolved. Thus, if a defendant has appealed the exclusion of evidence at trial but the case is decided on a plea bargain, there is no reason for the appellate court to hear the appeal on the evidence issue: that issue is moot once the defendant and the prosecution have agreed to a plea, which has been accepted by the trial court judge.

Because law needs stability, courts follow the rule of *stare decisis* ("to abide by, or adhere to, decided cases"), whereby previous decisions become precedents for current and future decisions. But law is flexible, and courts may overrule (specifically or by implication) their previous decisions, although this is not done often.

It is important to distinguish between the rule of the court and the dicta of the judges or justices. **Dicta** are judicial comments on issues that are not part of the court's ruling. These comments, even if they represent the opinion of a majority of the court, must be recognized as dicta and not confused with the holding or rule of law of the court. For this reason it is necessary to read cases carefully.

Most appellate court judges and justices issue written opinions that are recorded in official reports. Decisions of the U.S. Supreme Court are recorded officially in the *United States Reports,* but this official printing may take a year or longer. When recent U.S. Supreme Court cases are cited in this text, endnotes reference those cases as printed in the *Supreme Court Reporter* (S.Ct.); the *U.S. Law Week* (USLW); or a legal computer service, such as Lexis-Nexis, which also provides access to important information, such as the prior decisions in those cases, as well as any subsequent court action. Today U.S. Supreme Court cases are also available on the World Wide Web shortly after announcement, thus making them available almost immediately to anyone with access to the Internet.

Decisions of the U.S. Supreme Court are binding on all lower federal courts. They are also binding on state courts when applicable—that is, where *federal* statutory or constitutional rights are involved.

6-1b   Trial and Appellate Courts

It is important to distinguish trial from appellate courts. Both exist at the state and federal levels. Both are involved in making and interpreting laws, but generally it is said that trial

---

▶ **Moot**   The term used to describe a controversy that has ended or evolved to the stage at which a court decision on that case is no longer relevant or necessary; this is a limitation on the power of courts to decide a case.

▶ *Stare decisis*   Literally, "let the decision stand." The doctrine that courts will abide by or adhere to the rulings of previous court decisions when deciding cases having substantially the same facts.

▶ **Dicta**   The written portions of a judge's opinion that are not part of the actual ruling of the court and are not legally binding precedents for future court decisions.

courts try the facts of the case and appellate courts are concerned only with law. There are exceptions.

Trial courts are the major fact finders in a case. The trial jury (or judge if the case is not tried before a jury) decides the basic questions of fact. In a criminal trial, for example, the trial jury decides whether the accused committed the crime for which he or she is being tried; whether a defense (such as insanity) was proved; and so on. In making these findings, the jury considers evidence presented by both the defense and the prosecution. Because the trial judge and jury hear and see the witnesses, it is assumed that they are in a better position than the appellate court to decide whether those witnesses are credible. Thus, it is argued, the appellate court should be confined to issues of law and not be permitted to reverse a trial court's decision regarding ultimate fact issues, such as guilt or innocence.

After the judge or jury has made a decision at the trial level, the defendant, if found guilty, may **appeal** that decision. In a criminal case, the defendant has a right of appeal in state and federal court systems, although he or she does not (except in a few specific cases, such as those involving the death penalty) have the right to appeal to the jurisdiction's highest court.

At the appellate level, the **appellant,** the defendant at trial, alleges errors in the trial court proceeding (for example, admission of an illegal confession or exclusion of minorities from the jury) and asks for a new trial. The **appellee,** the prosecution at trial, argues that either errors did not exist or they did not prejudice the appellant and therefore a new trial should not be granted.

Appeal cases are heard by judges or justices rather than juries. The appellate court looks at the trial court record, considers written briefs submitted by attorneys who use them to establish and support their legal arguments, and may hear oral arguments from counsel for the defense and the prosecution regarding alleged errors of law during the trial. The appellate court makes a ruling on those issues. The court may hold that no errors were committed during the trial, in which case the appellate court *affirms* the lower court's decision. It may hold that there were errors but that they did not prejudice the defendant, and thus the conviction stands. The court may hold that there were errors and that one or more of those errors prejudiced the defendant, which means that the defendant could not have received a fair trial. In that case, the appellate court may reverse the case and send it back for another trial with instructions concerning the errors. This process is referred to as *reversed and remanded.* The court may reverse the case *with prejudice,* meaning that no further trials may be permitted on those charges.

In essence, appellate courts are assessing the work of trial courts. This system allows appellate courts to exercise some administrative control over trial courts, thus achieving more uniformity among courts than would exist otherwise. Trial court judges and juries exercise considerable power in criminal justice systems, however, as many cases are not appealed. In cases that are appealed and retried, frequently the lower court reaches the same decision on retrial.

In addition to the power to hear and decide cases appealed on facts of law in criminal trials, appellate courts have the power of **judicial review** over acts of the legislative and executive branches of government if those acts infringe on freedoms and liberties guaranteed by the state statutes and state constitutions (in state cases) and by the U.S. Constitution or federal laws (in federal cases). This power of judicial review represents the great authority of courts. The U.S. Supreme Court also has the power to declare acts of the president or of Congress unconstitutional.

The highest court of each state determines the constitutionality of that state's statutes in relation to its constitution. The U.S. Supreme Court is the final decision maker in the process of judicial review of federal statutes and U.S. constitutional issues.

6-2   The Dual Court System

The United States has a dual court system consisting of state and federal courts, as diagrammed in Figure 6-1. State crimes are prosecuted in state courts, and federal crimes are tried in federal courts. State crimes are defined by state statutes, federal crimes by Congress.

▶ **Appeal**   The stage in a judicial proceeding in which a higher court is asked to review a decision of a lower court.

▶ **Appellant**   The loser in a court case, who seeks a review of the decision by a higher appellate court.

▶ **Appellee**   The winning party in a lower court, who argues on appeal against reversing the lower court's decision.

▶ **Judicial review** The authority of an appellate court to check the decisions of lower courts as well as those within the executive and legislative branches of government within its jurisdiction to determine whether any of those acts are in violation of statutes or conditions.

Figure 6-1
The U.S. Dual Court System
Note: Arrows indicate avenues of appeal generally; there may be some exceptions. State court systems are explained in more detail in Spotlight 6-1.

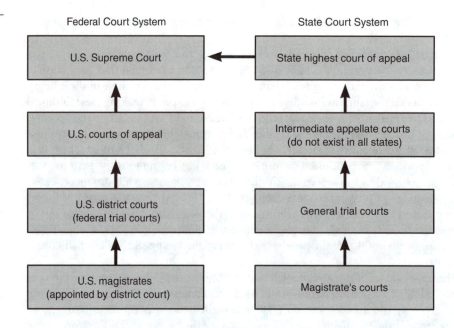

Some acts violate both federal and state statutes, in which case the defendant may be tried in a state or a federal court or both. For example, the four Los Angeles police officers who were acquitted of charges in a California state court (review Spotlight 5-3) were tried in a federal court for the violation of Rodney King's *federal* civil rights; two were convicted. Lower federal and state courts constitute separate systems. Cases may not be appealed from a state court to a federal court, except to the U.S. Supreme Court, and then only when a federal statutory or constitutional right is involved. Federal and state courts may hear only cases over which they have jurisdiction. Many of the cases brought in federal courts by state inmates are appropriate to those courts because the inmates are alleging that federal rights have been violated.

A closer look at the structure and organization of state and federal court systems facilitates understanding of the subsequent material in this chapter, as well as the analysis of pretrial and trial processes in subsequent chapters. This discussion begins with the state court systems, since most criminal cases are tried in state and local courts.

6-2a   State Courts

Considerable variation exists in the organization of state court systems. Differences exist within states, too, leading to problems that have prompted some states to move toward a unified court system. Despite the variety in systems, it is possible to make some general observations that provide an overview of state court systems. This discussion focuses on courts that process criminal cases (although they may also process civil cases). The main aspects of the structure, function, and jurisdiction of state courts are summarized in Spotlight 6-1.

Courts of Limited Jurisdiction

In discussions about courts, frequent references are made to lower courts. These are the courts of limited jurisdiction, so-called because legally they are entitled to hear only specific types of cases. Usually jurisdiction is limited to minor civil cases and criminal misdemeanors. Jurisdiction over criminal cases may be limited to certain kinds of misdemeanors, such as those that carry a jail or short prison term or some other, less serious sanction.

Jurisdiction may be limited to certain activities of the courts. The judge or magistrate who presides over courts of limited jurisdiction may conduct some pretrial procedures, such as issuing warrants for searches or arrests, deciding bail, appointing counsel for indigent defendants, or presiding over the initial appearance or preliminary hearing.

Spotlight 6-1	Structure and Jurisdiction of State Court Systems

Court	Structure	Jurisdiction
Highest state appellate court (usually called the supreme court)	Consists of five, seven, or nine justices, who may be appointed or elected; cases decided by this court may not be appealed to the U.S. Supreme Court unless they involve a federal question, and then there is no right of appeal except in limited cases.	If there is no intermediate appellate court, defendants convicted in a general trial court have a right of appeal to this court; if there is an intermediate appellate court, this court has discretion to limit appeals with few exceptions, such as in capital cases.
Intermediate appellate court (also called court of appeals; exists in approximately half of the states)	May have one court that hears appeals from all general trial courts or may have more than one court, each with appellate jurisdiction over a particular area of the state; usually has a panel of three judges.	Defendants convicted in general trial court have right of appeal to this level.
General trial courts (also called superior courts, circuit courts, district courts, court of common pleas)	Usually state is divided into judicial districts, with one general trial court in each district, often one per county; courts may be divided by function, such as civil, criminal, probate, domestic.	Jurisdiction to try cases usually begins where jurisdiction of lower court ends, so this court tries more serious cases; may have appellate jurisdiction over cases decided in lower courts.
Courts of limited jurisdiction (also called magistrate's courts, police courts, justice of peace courts, municipal courts)	Differ from state to state; some states divide state into districts, with each having the same type of lower court; in other states, courts are located in political subdivisions, such as cities or townships, in which case the structure may differ from court to court; may not be a court of record, in which case the system will permit trial *de novo* in general trial court; particularly in rural areas, magistrates may not be lawyers and may work only part-time.	May be limited to specific proceedings, such as initial appearance, preliminary hearing, issuing of search and arrest warrants, setting of bail, appointing of counsel for indigent defendants; jurisdiction of cases is limited to certain types, usually the lesser criminal and civil cases; some jurisdictions may hear all misdemeanor; others are limited to misdemeanors with minor penalties.

Lower courts, which are called by various names, as noted in Spotlight 6-1, should not be considered unimportant due to their limited jurisdiction. Certainly the power to grant or deny bail or some other method of pretrial release is a tremendous power. Despite the importance of lower courts, many are underfinanced and staffed by part-time judges with limited staff and resources.

General Trial Courts

General trial courts are called by various names, as noted in Spotlight 6-1. Usually these courts have a wider geographical base than lower courts. In large areas, the general trial court may be divided by functions: traffic cases; domestic cases; civil cases (excluding domestic and traffic cases); probate; estates and wills; and criminal cases. Smaller jurisdictions may have fewer divisions. A civil and a criminal division is one model used frequently.

In most systems the jurisdiction of general trial courts begins where the jurisdiction of the lower courts ends and includes the more serious cases. If the lower court is not a court of record, meaning that the court does not make provision for a transcript of the proceedings, a case appealed from the lower court to the general trial court may be tried *de novo*. In that instance, the evidence will be presented again. Over time, however, evidence may be destroyed, and witnesses may die or forget. Thus, the probability of being convicted when a case is tried *de novo* at this level may be lower than the probability of conviction in the lower court.

> **De novo** Literally "anew" or "fresh." A trial *de novo* is a case that is tried again, as if no decision had been rendered previously. In some jurisdictions a first appeal from a lower court may be a trial *de novo*. The term may be used to refer to other proceedings, such as hearings.

Professions 6-1

Careers in Criminal Court Systems

A wide variety of positions exist in criminal court systems. Not all require a law degree, but those of lawyers and judges generally do.

Lawyers perform various functions in court systems. Prosecutors represent the government and prosecute cases, but lawyers also serve as attorneys for those who are accused of violating the criminal law. Lawyers must receive a law degree (usually a three-year program) and pass the bar. Although some states are reciprocal and permit attorneys from other states to be admitted to practice through a petitions process, many states require that the bar be taken in that state. Some permit attorneys from other states to become members of the bar by taking only part of the exam, provided they have passed the bar of another state and engaged in some years of practice.

Most *judges* are lawyers. Some of them have practiced law; others have not. Judges may or may not have received special training for their new roles, although it is becoming more common to provide judicial training.

Paralegals may perform some legal functions in criminal court systems, but they are not recognized as lawyers and generally must be supervised by attorneys. They have some legal training, but it is not as extensive as that required for a law degree. *Legal assistants* and *law clerks* may assist attorneys, but they, too, must be supervised. Although the position of law clerk (generally held by law students) usually does not pay well, that is not the case with legal assistant and paralegal positions, which, in some jurisdictions, are relatively high-paying.

The *court clerk,* normally a position that does not require formal legal training, is the court officer charged by statute or court rules with the responsibility of maintaining all court records. The court clerk files the pleadings and motions and records any decisions made by the court. These are very important functions because judgments are not enforceable if they have not been filed properly. The court clerk is assisted by a staff, which in large jurisdictions may include a deputy for each of the court's divisions (such as traffic, probate, civil, and crimi-

nal). Various personnel may be employed to handle the paper work of the court.

The *bailiff,* perhaps best known for pronouncing, "Hear ye, hear ye, this court of the Honorable Judge Smith is in session; all rise" before the judge's entry into the courtroom, has a variety of functions associated with keeping order in the courtroom. The bailiff may eject or otherwise discipline people who do not observe proper courtroom behavior. The bailiff may transport defendants to and from the court, pass papers and exhibits to and from attorneys and the judge, run errands for the judge, and guard the jury during its deliberations. In some courts a deputy sheriff performs the bailiff's functions. In federal courts a deputy marshal may serve as bailiff. And in state courts the bailiff's position may carry a different title, such as *court service officer.*

In courts of record, a verbatim account of all proceedings is kept by a *court reporter.* The proceedings are not transcribed unless one or both of the parties request it, in which case there is a fee. If a criminal defendant is indigent, the state pays for the transcript when it is required for an appeal. Court reporters also record proceedings outside of court when attorneys are securing evidence for trial by questioning witnesses. Court reporters must have extensive training, and generally the pay is very good. Many court reporters have their own businesses; others are employed by the courts.

The *minute clerk* is an employee of the court who records an outline of what happens during the proceedings but does not maintain a verbatim account. The minute clerk might record the charges against the defendant, summarize the process of selecting the jury, perhaps note the time spent in that process, list the names of the jurors and alternates, summarize the presented evidence, and record the court's decision.

In larger court systems other professionals are employed. *Counselors* or *social workers* may be available, along with *psychologists, statisticians, probation officers,* and clerical personnel.

Both of the court levels discussed thus far are at the trial level. Before considering state appellate courts, it is important to note the personnel and their functions in trial courts. The positions and their functions may vary among jurisdictions, but most are fairly common and are noted in Professions 6-1. Some of these positions are also characteristic of appellate courts.

Intermediate Appellate Courts

All states provide for at least one appeal from an adverse decision in a criminal trial, but only about half of the states have an intermediate appellate court, usually called a *court of appeals.* In states that have an intermediate appellate court, only one court may hear all appeals, or courts in various districts may hear appeals from their respective geographical areas. Defendants who have been convicted in general trial courts have a right to appeal to this court where it exists. If it does not exist, they have a right of appeal to the highest court; however, if the state has an intermediate appellate court, the defendant may not have a right to appeal to more than one appellate court, except in capital (death penalty) cases. Thus, the defendant who loses an appeal at the intermediate appellate level may have no other appeal unless he or she has other legal issues that might be raised—for example, in a federal court.

Highest State Appellate Courts

If the state does not have an intermediate appellate court, cases may be appealed from the general trial courts to the highest court, which in most states is called the *state supreme court.* Justices of this court are either elected or appointed, and the court may have five, seven, or nine justices. In states having intermediate appellate courts, except in a few types of cases, the highest appellate court has the power to limit the cases it hears and decides. This court has the final decision on cases that involve legal issues pertaining to the constitution or statutes of the state in which the case is brought. If the case involves any federal issues, the defendant may appeal to the U.S. Supreme Court, although that Court hears only a limited number of the cases for which review is requested.

Other states have two final appellate courts. For example, both Texas and Oklahoma have a final court of appeals for criminal cases and a second one for civil cases. Cases may not be appealed from one of these courts to the other.

6-2b   Federal Courts

In the federal court system, U.S. magistrates, judicial officers appointed by the district court (as was noted in Figure 6-1), may have full jurisdiction over minor offenses along with jurisdiction over some of the pretrial steps of more serious offenses. The basic trial courts in the federal system are the U.S. district courts. These courts hear cases in which individuals have been accused of violating federal criminal laws. They try civil cases that meet specified criteria. Each state has at least one federal district court, and some states have several. In the federal district courts, cases are prosecuted by U.S. attorneys and presided over by federal trial judges. These are appointed positions.

Cases appealed from federal district courts go to the appropriate intermediate federal appellate courts. These courts, referred to as *circuit courts,* are called the United States Court of Appeals for the First (Second, and so on) Judicial District. Decisions of the federal appellate courts are not binding on state courts unless they involve federally created procedural rights that have been held to apply to the states or federally protected constitutional rights, such as the right to counsel. The decision of one court of appeals is not binding on another federal appellate court. If circuit courts decide similar cases differently, the resulting conflict may be resolved only by the U.S. Supreme Court, the final appellate court in the federal system. The importance of that Court warrants a closer look, but first it is appropriate to note some improvements in the federal court system.

Each year the U.S. Supreme Court chief justice gives a "state of the judiciary" report on the federal court system. In his January 2003 report, released for publication on New Year's Day, Chief Justice William H. Rehnquist made his annual plea for higher salaries for the federal judiciary. According to Rehnquist, "There will always be a differential between government and private sector pay for excellent lawyers. . . . But the judiciary, in particular, will be compromised if there is too wide a gap. At the present time there is not just a gap, there is a chasm." The chief justice repeated those concerns in his 2004 report. The yearly salaries in 2004 were as follows:

- District judges—$158,100
- Appellate judges—$167,600
- Associate justices of the U.S. Supreme Court—$194,300
- Chief justice of the U.S. Supreme Court—$203,000[4]

In his annual 2003 report on the state of the judiciary, Rehnquist alleged that recruiting and retaining highly qualified lawyers as judges had suffered because of the low salaries in the federal judiciary. Rehnquist also called for provisions for more federal judges and faster confirmation of nominees for vacant judgeships. For example, Rehnquist noted that there had been no increases in the number of bankruptcy judges since 1992 and that the average caseload for the bankruptcy judges had risen from 2,998 in 1992 to 4,777 in 2003. With regard to filling vacancies, the chief justice proclaimed that it was of no concern to the judiciary "which political party is in power. . . . We simply ask that the president nominate qualified candidates with reasonable promptness and that the Senate act within a reasonable time to confirm or reject them."[5]

A law professor who analyzed federal judicial salaries and tenure spoke in favor of increased salaries because federal judges deserve them ("compensation ought to bear some relationship to a job's value") but emphasized that, despite relatively low salaries, many lawyers still apply for federal judgeships. Federal judges are appointed for life; they retire at full pay; they do not have the pressures of private lawyers to bill enough hours to meet the firm's demands; they do not face civil liability for their actions; and they enjoy great prestige. Steven Luber of Northwestern University continued with these comments:

> Meanwhile, practicing lawyers report extraordinary levels of job dissatisfaction, sometimes bordering on outright despair. Those high salaries come at an equally high cost, exacting their toll in time and stress. It is hardly surprising, therefore, that lawyers are abandoning private practice at a far greater rate than federal judges are leaving the bench.[6]

In March 2003, President George W. Bush signed legislation that gives all federal judges a cost-of-living raise each year. Prior to the enactment of this legislation, federal judges did not receive this raise automatically; Congress was required to determine their raises. Almost all other federal employees, however, already received cost-of-living raises.[7]

A final concern often expressed by Chief Justice Rehnquist is the trend toward federalizing crimes. Rehnquist has encouraged Congress to avoid criminalizing acts that are already covered by state laws. In 1999, he stated his position clearly:

> The pressure in Congress to appear responsive to every highly publicized societal ill or sensational crime needs to be balanced with an inquiry into whether states are doing an adequate job in these particular areas and, ultimately, whether we want most of our legal relationships decided at the national rather than local level. . . . While there certainly are areas in criminal law in which the federal government must act, the vast majority of localized criminal cases should be decided in the state courts which are equipped for such matters.[8]

6-3 The United States Supreme Court

The U.S. Supreme Court is the only specific court established by the federal Constitution, which designates a few cases in which the Supreme Court has original jurisdiction. The Court has appellate jurisdiction under such exceptions and regulations as determined by Congress. In the debates of the Constitutional Convention, it was recognized that the Supreme Court would have the power to review state court decisions whenever those decisions affect *federal* rights.

The basic function of the U.S. Supreme Court is to interpret federal laws and the federal Constitution. In fulfilling this judicial review function, the Court is often accused of making law or of reshaping the Constitution. In response to this allegation, a constitutional law expert said, "Like a work of artistic creation, the Constitution endures because it is capable of responding to the concerns, the needs, the aspirations of successive generations."[9]

If the U.S. Supreme Court is to interpret the Constitution according to these guidelines, it will be subjected to criticism because these are issues on which reasonable minds differ. Technically, then, the Court does not make but, rather, interprets law. A former member of the Court said that the justices "breathe life, feeble or strong, into the inert pages of the Constitution and of statute books." One constitutional lawyer pointed out that "it matters who does the breathing."[10]

Nine justices sit on the U.S. Supreme Court. The Court began its 2002–2003 term with seven men, one of whom is African American, and two women. William H. Rehnquist is the chief justice and presides over the Court. Professions 6-2 contains pertinent information concerning what one might expect to see and hear during a Supreme Court session.

Professions 6-2

The United States Supreme Court

General Procedures

Welcome to the Supreme Court of the United States.

This is your Supreme Court and we hope you find your visit here enjoyable, interesting and informative. However, we do ask you to recognize our restrictions and requirements for visitors. In order to maintain the atmosphere one might expect in the nation's highest court, we would appreciate your cooperation.

Please refrain from smoking and restrict food and beverages to the cafeteria, snack bar, and vending machine alcove.

Be as quiet as possible. There are Court employees working in their offices near the public areas of the building who would appreciate not being disturbed.

Oral Argument

You are about to attend an oral argument. A case selected for argument usually involves interpretations of the U.S. Constitution or federal law. At least four Justices have selected the case as being of such importance that the Supreme Court must resolve the legal issues.

An attorney for each side of a case will have an opportunity to make a presentation to the Court and answer questions posed by the Justices. Prior to the argument each side has submitted a legal brief—a written legal argument outlining each party's points of law. The Justices have read these briefs prior to argument and are thoroughly familiar with the case, its facts, and the legal positions that each party is advocating.

Beginning the first Monday in October, the Court is scheduled to hear up to four one-hour arguments a day, three days a week, in two week intervals, (with longer breaks in December and February), concluding the oral argument portion of the term in late April. Typically, two arguments are held in the mornings beginning at 10 A.M. and two in the afternoons beginning at 1 P.M. on Monday, Tuesday, and Wednesday. In the recesses between argument sessions, the Justices are busy writing opinions, deciding which cases to hear in the future, and reading the briefs for the next argument session. They grant review in approximately 100–120 of the more than 7,000 petitions filed with the Court each term. No one knows exactly when a decision will be handed down by the Court in an argued case, nor is there a set time period in which the Justices must reach a decision. However, all cases argued during a term of Court are decided before the summer recess begins, usually by the end of June.

During an argument week, the Justices meet in a private conference, closed even to staff, to discuss the cases and to take a preliminary vote on each case. If the Chief Justice is in the majority on a case decision, he decides to write it himself or he may assign that duty to any other Justice in the majority. If the Chief Justice is in the minority, the Justice in the majority who has the most seniority assumes the assignment duty.

Draft opinions are privately circulated among the Justices until a final draft is agreed upon. When a final decision has been reached, the Justice who wrote the opinion announces the decision in a Court session and may deliver a summary of the Court's reasoning. Meanwhile, the Public Information Office releases the full text of the opinion to the public and news media.

Participants in the Courtroom

Justices. The Justices enter the Courtroom through three entrances behind the Bench. The Chief Justice and two senior Associate Justices enter through the center, and three Associate Justices enter through each side. They also sit on the Bench in order of seniority with the Chief Justice in the middle, and the others alternating from left to right, ending with the most junior Associate Justice on the far right, as you face the Bench.

Clerk. The Clerk of the Supreme Court or his representative sits to the left of the Bench. His responsibilities in the Courtroom include providing the Justices with materials about the case if the Justices desire additional documents and notifying the appropriate Court personnel when an opinion can be released to the public. He also swears in new members of the Supreme Court Bar.

Marshal. The Marshal or his representative sits to the right side of the Bench. His roles are to call the Court to order, maintain decorum in the Courtroom, tape the audio portions of argument, and time the oral presentations so that attorneys do not exceed their one-half hour limitations.

Marshal's Aides. Marshal's aides are seated behind the Justices. They often carry messages to the Justices or convey messages from a Justice to a member of his or her staff.

Attorneys. The attorneys scheduled to argue cases are seated at the tables facing the Bench. The arguing attorney will stand behind the lectern immediately in front of the Chief Justice. On the lectern there are two lights. When the white light goes on, the attorney has five minutes remaining to argue. The red light indicates that the attorney has used all the allotted time.

Attorneys who are admitted as members of the Supreme Court Bar may be seated in the chairs just beyond the bronze railing. Any member of the Supreme Court Bar may attend any argument, space permitting.

Others

Law Clerks. Each Justice has the option of employing up to four law clerks as assistants. These clerks are law school graduates who have previously clerked for a federal judge on a lower court. The clerks often listen to oral arguments. They are seated in the chairs flanking the Courtroom on the right.

Special Guests. Guests of Justices are seated in the benches to the right of the bench and are seated in order of the seniority of the Justice who invited them. The row of black chairs in front of the guest section is reserved for retired Justices and officers of the Court, such as the Reporter of Decisions or the Librarian, who attend oral argument from time to time.

News Media. Members of the Supreme Court press corps sit to the left of the Bench in the benches and chairs facing the guest section. The press enter the Courtroom from the hallway on the left.

Source: Free Pamphlet available at the U.S. Supreme Court, Washington, D.C.

There was speculation that one or more justices (most probably Sandra Day O'Connor and William H. Rehnquist) would retire in June 2004, but that did not happen, so the Court began its 2004–2005 term with the same justices it has had for 10 years, the second longest stretch in U.S. history without changes.[11] However, in fall 2004 Rehnquist was diagnosed with thyroid cancer. He reduced his work schedule, remained on the Court, and participated in some decisions from his home. In early 2005 he returned to the bench. In June 2005 O'Connor announced her retirement.

▶ **Writ of *certiorari*** *Certiorari* literally means "to be informed of." A writ is an order from a court giving authority for an act to be done or ordering that it be done; a writ of *certiorari* is used by courts that have discretion to determine which cases they will hear. It is used most commonly today by the U.S. Supreme Court when cases are appealed to that Court from lower courts.

A case gets before the U.S. Supreme Court if the Court grants a **writ of *certiorari*** on an appealed case. A *writ* is an order from a court authorizing or ordering that an action be done. *Certiorari* literally means "to be informed of." When the Supreme Court grants a writ of *certiorari*, in effect it is agreeing to hear the case appealed from a lower court and is ordering that court to produce the necessary documents for that appeal. If the Court denies *certiorari*, it is refusing to review the case. In those instances, the decision of the lower court stands. Four of the justices must vote in favor of a writ in order for it to be granted. If an even number of justices is sitting and there is a tie vote, the decision being appealed is affirmed. In an average term, the Court hears only about 3 percent of the cases filed.

In recent years the U.S. Supreme Court has decreased the number of cases it decides. During the term that ended in June 2003, the Court decided only 84 cases, of which 15 were decided by a 5-to-4 vote.[12] During its 2003–2004 term the Supreme Court decided 79 cases. In previous terms the Court has decided as many as 150 cases.

One of the reasons for limiting the number of cases is the time required for oral arguments as well as for the deliberations and opinion writing of the justices. The second reason the U.S. Supreme Court hears only a percentage of the cases filed was emphasized by a former chief justice of the Court:

> To remain effective, the Supreme Court must continue to decide only those cases which present questions whose resolution will have immediate importance far beyond the particular facts and parties involved.[13]

The U.S. Supreme Court may hear cases when lower court decisions on the issues in question have differed. The Court's decision becomes the final resolution of the issue, unless or until it is overruled by a subsequent U.S. Supreme Court decision, by a constitutional amendment, or by congressional legislation.

Cases that are accepted for review by the U.S. Supreme Court must be filed within a specified time before oral arguments. The attorneys who argue before the Court are under considerable pressure. They may be interrupted at any time by a justice's question. Attorneys are expected to argue their cases without reading from the prepared briefs. Each is limited to 30 minutes (sometimes an hour) for oral arguments.

▶ **Concurring opinion** A judge's written opinion agreeing with the result in a case but disagreeing with the reasoning of the majority opinion.

Most U.S. Supreme Court decisions are announced in written opinions, which represent majority opinions in many cases. A **concurring opinion** may be written by a justice who voted with the Court but disagreed with one or more of its reasons; who agreed with the decisions, but for reasons other than those in the Court's opinion; or who agreed with the Court's reasons but wishes to emphasize or clarify one or more points. Thus, in some cases, the opinion of the Court represents the views of a plurality of the justices. Opinions concurring in part, dissenting in part, and dissenting entirely may also be written.

Judicial opinions, especially those of U.S. Supreme Court justices, are a very important part of U.S. legal systems. These opinions are read carefully by lawyers, who use the reasoning and conclusions of law in future cases. The justices circulate among themselves drafts of their opinions, which are printed in secret and remain secret until the Court announces its decision in the case. In this way the entire Court participates in formulating an opinion; rarely is a written opinion the sole product of the justice whose name appears as the author.

Decisions of the U.S. Supreme Court are handed down on opinion days, usually three Mondays of each month of the term, although at times the Court also issues opinions on other days. The announced decisions are public, and the media pick up those portions of the decisions thought to be of greatest interest. Decisions of the U.S. Supreme Court are also available on the World Wide Web.

6-4   Judges in Criminal Court Systems

Historically judges have been held in high esteem by the U.S. public. In recent years, however, the position of judge has come under severe criticism. In their decisions on pretrial releases, judges have been accused of releasing dangerous persons who prey on the public, commit more crimes, and terrorize citizens. In their sentencing decisions, judges have been accused of coddling criminals. Judges are easy scapegoats, and some critics are taking the opportunity to accuse them of causing most of the critical problems in the handling of criminals. Although some of the criticism is justified, much of it is not.

Judges begin their participation in criminal justice systems long before the trial occurs. They determine when there is probable cause to issue a search or an arrest warrant. After arrest, a suspect must be taken before a neutral magistrate or judge, who will determine whether there is probable cause to hold the alleged offender. Judges determine whether the accused is released on bail or some other pretrial procedure or is detained in jail, awaiting trial.

Judges hear and rule on motions made by attorneys before trial. They approve plea bargains made between the prosecution and the defense. Judges play a critical role in the criminal trial. They hear and rule on motions made before, during, and after the trial, and in most cases they determine the sentences of convicted offenders. Judges (or justices) at the appellate level determine whether cases should be reversed or affirmed.

6-4a   Trial Judges

At a trial, judges are referees. Theoretically they are neither for nor against a particular position or issue but, rather, are committed to the fair implementation of the rules of evidence and law. They are charged with the responsibility of ensuring that attorneys follow the rules.

In the role of referee, the judge has immense power. If the defense makes a motion to have some important evidence suppressed on the grounds that it was allegedly obtained illegally, the judge's decision whether or not to grant that motion might be the deciding factor in the case. Without the evidence, the prosecution might not be able to prove its case. Likewise, the judge's decision to admit evidence offered by the defendant, such as the testimony of a psychiatrist regarding the defendant's mental state, may be the deciding factor in the ability of the defense to convince the jury of its position.

Although trial judges' decisions may be appealed, most are not. Many decisions that are appealed are not reversed, and, even if the defense wins on appeal, considerable time is lost—time that might have been spent by the accused in jail. Furthermore, the U.S. Supreme Court has emphasized that it is important to *prevent* problems at trial whenever possible and that responsibility lies with the trial judge.

Another important responsibility of the trial judge is to rule on whether **expert witness** testimony may be admitted. Many issues in criminal cases are beyond the common knowledge of jurors, so it is necessary to submit expert testimony. In addition to deciding whether the area of expertise is acceptable, the judge must determine whether the offered expert is qualified to testify about that evidence. Generally judges make these decisions after hearing oral arguments from the defense and the prosecution, and some judges require written motions by attorneys prior to those arguments.

Another responsibility of the trial judge is to decide whether there is sufficient evidence to send a case to the jury for a decision on the evidence presented or whether the case should be dismissed for lack of evidence. Even if the judge sends the case to the jury and the jury finds the defendant guilty, the trial judge may reverse that decision if he or she believes the evidence is not sufficient to determine guilt beyond a reasonable doubt. This power is given to judges so they can serve as a check on jurors who might be influenced by passion or prejudice despite the evidence in the case.

The role of the trial judge in deciding whether to accept a jury verdict is illustrated by the trial and conviction of au pair Louise Woodward, discussed in Spotlight 6-2.

▶ **Expert witness**   A person with extensive training or education in a particular field, such as medicine, who testifies at depositions or at trials concerning a critical issue of that case, such as what caused the death of the deceased.

Spotlight 6-2   Judicial Power in Question: The Au Pair Case

In a case that gained international media attention in 1997, Louise Woodward, age 19, was convicted of second-degree murder in the death of Matthew Eappen, 8 months old. Woodward was a British au pair whom Matthew's parents had hired to take care of the baby and his older brother. Woodward was charged with murder after she called 911 on 4 February to report that Matthew was not responsive. The prosecution argued that Woodward had shaken the baby and knocked his head against a wall or the tub. The defense claimed that Matthew died of a skull injury he had incurred several weeks prior to his death.

The defense asked the judge to instruct the jury on murder charges only, taking the gamble that, if the jury had to choose between murder and acquittal for Woodward, it would choose acquittal. The defense was wrong. After deliberating for 27 hours, the jury found Woodward guilty of second-degree murder; she faced life in prison.

At a subsequent hearing, the trial judge, Hiller B. Zobel, listened to arguments from both the defense and the prosecution, took a few days to contemplate, and then announced his decision: Louise Woodward's conviction for second-degree murder was not supported by the evidence. "Having considered the matter carefully, I am firmly convinced that the interests of justice . . . mandate my reducing the verdict to manslaughter. I do this in accordance with my discretion and my duty."[1]

The judge ruled that, had the jury been instructed on manslaughter, it might have chosen that option, which he believed was one rational conclusion based on the evidence. He did not believe the evidence supported a murder conviction. At a subsequent hearing the judge sentenced Woodward to the time she had already served and set her free.

The Woodward case illustrates the power of the judge to change a jury's decision if he or she believes such is required by the evidence. Some argue that is a plus in the system; others suggest that it is unreasonable and unfair. After the Woodward decision, the Massachusetts Society for the Prevention of Cruelty to Children published a letter signed by 49 child abuse specialists, stating that the prosecution's expert evidence at trial was overwhelmingly supportive of the theory that Woodward had shaken the baby and thus had caused his death. The case appeared to turn on the controversial scientific evidence, and perhaps one result of the case was a closer look at the presentation of such evidence in criminal trials.[2]

After serving only 279 days in prison, Woodward returned to her home in England, and in 2002 she received a law degree from London's South Bank University. Subsequently she won a coveted place on the Legal Practice course at the Manchester Metropolitan University, becoming "the first convicted killer to be allowed on such a top course." Some of the students were furious when they discovered her identity. One said, "Louise is a convicted killer who uses a different name. Nobody told us she was on the course. We all found out by accident and were speechless." The student continued, "She may have paid her debt in America for what she did, but many of us still find it goes against the grain to have her sitting alongside us, on probably the best law course you can get."[3]

In 2003, Louise Woodward fell in love with a man who said he understood and accepted her past. She was hoping to marry and have children, and she was given permission to practice law.[4] In fall 2004, Woodward gave interviews to several media stations in the United States. She proclaimed her innocence, stating that she was haunted by Matthew's death; she did not know what had happened to him; she only knew what had not happened—she had not shaken him violently. Three other updates on the Woodward case are interesting. Her parents were charged with dishonesty in withdrawing money from the trust that was established with the money donated for Woodward's defense fund, and one of her lawyers, Elaine Whitfield Sharp, was ordered to pay over $200,000 in a civil case. Sharp charged that, when a state trooper arrested her for drunk driving, he told her that he would not arrest her if she had sex with him. The officer stated in his written report that Sharp said she was drinking because she then believed Louise Woodward was guilty of murder in the Matthew Eappen case. Sharp, who entered a plea of no contest to the drunk driving charge, denied that she made that statement to the arresting officer. She was found liable for defaming him. Shortly after her arrest Sharp left the Woodward defense team. She said she quit; the other lawyers said they fired her.[5] And in March 2005 Woodward quit her job as a lawyer to become a dance instructor.[6]

Matthew Eappen's family moved from the home in which Matthew died. The parents and brother were joined by two more children. An attempt has been made to enact legislation to require that nannies be trained and certified, including training in first aid.[7]

1. "Excerpts from the Judge's Decision Reducing Conviction of AuPair," *New York Times* (11 November 1997), p. 16.
2. "Pediatric Experts Express Doubt on Au Pair's Defense," *New York Times* (12 November 1997), p. 14.
3. "Killer Nanny Is Training to Be Legal Eagle," *Daily Star* (1 February 2003), p. 27.
4. "Why I Long for a Baby of My Own," *Daily Mail* (London) (27 September 2003), p. 8.
5. "Woodward Claim False," *Daily Record* (15 August 2002), p. 23; "Louise Woodward Lawyer Loses Case against Trooper," *Boston Herald* (9 October 2002), p. 15.
6. "Baby Killer Woodward Leaves Law for Dance," *UPI Press release* (29 March 2005).
7. "Matthew's Law to Make Nannies Safe," *The Mirror* (14 November 2002), p. 30.

▶ **Acquittal**   Legal verification of the innocence of a person in a criminal trial.

After hearing the evidence in a case, a judge may direct the jury to return a verdict of **acquittal.** This may occur before the judge hears all the evidence as well as after a jury verdict of guilty. Once the verdict of acquittal has been entered, however, the defendant may not be retried on the same issue; to do so would violate the defendant's constitutional right not to be tried twice for the same offense.

Another role of the judge is to instruct the jury regarding the law in the case it must decide. In addition, the judge must monitor all activities of the trial, ensuring that the defendant's constitutional and statutory rights are protected, that all rules and regulations are followed, and that all participants and spectators (including the media) behave appropriately.

The role of the trial judge at sentencing is one of the most important of all judicial functions. Despite the tremendous importance of sentencing, until recently little attention was paid to preparing judges for this decision. Nor was there any emphasis on the importance of thorough presentence reports by probation or other officers of the court to assist judges in making the decision. Likewise, little attention was given to appellate review of judicial sentencing.

Concern with the extensive power of judges over sentencing, along with other sentencing issues, has led to sentence reform, which is discussed in Chapter 8. Clearly the purpose of most of the reform efforts has been to reduce judicial sentencing power, thought to cause sentence disparity. Some of the alleged disparity results from a consideration of legally acceptable factors, such as the defendant's prior record and the nature of the current charge(s). However, some of the differences may be the result of unacceptable factors, such as the gender, age, or race of a defendant, as well as the result of the personalities, backgrounds, and prejudices of the sentencing judges. Therefore, before concluding that judicial sentencing differences are unfair, unreasonable, or unconstitutional, it is important to consider all the variables involved in the decision-making process.

The sentencing decision is a difficult one; it may be impossible to achieve justice at this stage. As one judge concluded, "I am sure that I speak for my many colleagues when I state that the imposition of a criminal sentence is the most delicate, difficult, distasteful task for the trial judge."[14]

In all of these and other activities at trial, not only the decision but also the demeanor and attitude of the judge are important. The judge's behavior may influence the attitudes and decisions of jurors, witnesses, and victims at the trial, as well as the general public's image of criminal justice systems. In addition, the judge influences the flow of cases through the criminal courts. Poor management of a caseload contributes to court congestion and risks impairing the rights of defendants to a speedy trial.

6-4b Appellate Judges

We have noted that the decisions of trial judges may be reversed on appeal. In most cases, however, appellate courts defer to trial courts on issues in which trial judges have an advantage because of their direct observation of the events that occurred at trial. Only a fraction of cases are reversed on appeal, but those cases are important not only to the individual defendants but to the justice system as well.

Frequently appellate judges and justices are faced with interpreting the laws and constitutions of their jurisdictions in ways that will have an effect on more than the parties before the court. In that respect, their decisions have a much broader impact than the decisions of trial courts. Usually their decisions, in contrast to those of trial courts, are accompanied by written opinions, thus placing an even greater responsibility on judges to articulate why they decided a specific issue in a particular way.

6-4c Judicial Selection, Training, and Retention

The first issue in deciding how to select, train, and retain judges is to decide what qualities are desired. Historically judges have been white, male, and Protestant, with conservative backgrounds. Only recently have more women and minorities joined the judiciary, and scholars continue to debate whether race and gender impact judicial decision making.

Judges should be impartial and fair. They should be able to approach a case with an objective and open mind concerning the facts. If for any reason a judge cannot be objective in a case, he or she should withdraw from that case, a process known as **recusal**. Objectivity enables the judge to be fair, to insist that attorneys play by the rules of the game, and to see that due process is not violated. Judges should be well educated in substantive law, procedural rules, and evidence. Judges should be able to think and write clearly. Their opinions are of great importance to attorneys and other judges, who use them to analyze how future

▶ **Recusal** The removal of oneself from a proceeding, such as by a judge who has a conflict of interest in a case.

cases might be argued and decided. Judges should have high moral and ethical standards, enabling them to withstand political and economic pressures that might influence decisions. They should be in good physical, mental, and emotional health. They should be good managers, because they have considerable power over the court system. They should be able to assume power sensibly, without abuse, and to exercise leadership in social reform where necessary and desirable.

The late Irving R. Kaufman, a federal judge on the Second Circuit, addressed the issue of the qualities and characteristics that should be considered in the selection of federal judges, but his suggestions are also applicable to state and local judges. According to Kaufman,

> a judge's comportment must at all times square with the ideals of justice and impartiality that the public projects on us in our symbolic role. A judge must be reflective, perhaps even a bit grave, but must always demonstrate an openness consistent with our tradition of giving each side its say before a decision is rendered. [A judge should be able to] separate the dignity of the office from a sense of self-importance.[15]

Finding persons with the desired judicial qualifications is not always easy. Several methods have been used for selecting judges in the United States. During the colonial period, judges were appointed by the king, but after the Revolution this practice ceased. In a majority of the colonies, judges were appointed by the legislators. In some colonies, the appointment was made by the governor, with or without the required approval of his council.

As the colonies became states, they gradually began to select judges by popular election, but that method came under criticism, with frequent allegations that undue political influence led to the selection of incompetent and corrupt judges. Today most states use the election process for some of their judges. Another method of selecting judges, the merit plan, is traced to Albert M. Kales, one of the founders of the American Judicature Society. The plan was first adopted by Missouri in 1940. It is referred to as the *Missouri plan* or, less commonly, the *Kales plan* or *commission plan.*

Merit selection plans vary extensively from state to state, but most plans include a non-partisan commission, which solicits, investigates, and screens candidates when judicial openings occur. The commission sends a select number of names (usually three to five) to the executive branch, where an appointment is made. The new judge may serve a probationary period (usually a year) and may be required to run unopposed on a general election retention ballot. Voters are polled with a yes or no vote to decide whether this judge should be retained in office. A judge who receives a majority of votes (which is usually the case) will be retained. A merit selection plan does not assure that politics will not enter into the selection process, but arguably the prescreening by a nonpartisan commission places only qualified candidates in a position for election. Criticisms remain, however, and politics plays an important role.[16]

In an effort to avoid public pressures on judicial decision making, federal judges are appointed and hold their jobs for life. Technically they are appointed by the president of the United States and confirmed by the Senate, but usually the recommendations to the president are made by the attorney general or the deputy attorney general, and the president accepts those recommendations. Members of the U.S. House of Representatives and the U.S. Senate are influential in nominating these judges. The constitutional provision for the appointment of federal judges and justices has been interpreted to mean that they hold their appointments for life. They may be removed only for bad behavior, but the process is very difficult and is not often undertaken, even when there are reasons to do so.

Most U.S. jurisdictions do not have required formal training for judges, although training is mandatory in many other countries. Despite the lack of requirements for judicial training, we are making progress in providing training programs for newly appointed or elected judges. Most states provide some training, and many are offering continuing education courses for judges already on the bench.

Recruiting the right kind of attorneys and giving them proper training in the judiciary is important, but retention of our best judges is becoming a serious problem. In the past a judicial appointment, especially to the federal bench, was the ultimate aim of many lawyers. But the increasing number of resignations of federal judges has led some to refer to the revolving door of the federal judiciary, with some of the best candidates refusing nominations or accepting them, staying a few years, and then leaving. For those who do stay, morale may be affected as they realize the substantial pay cut they take by leaving private practice to accept an appointment to the bench.

Judicial salaries vary significantly from state to state. Although generally salaries are higher in the federal system, the level of compensation of federal judges was described by Judge Kaufman in an open letter to President Ronald Reagan: "And as you know, we receive for our services little more than those fresh-faced lads a few years out of Harvard at the larger New York firms."[17] Salaries of federal judges have been increased since Judge Kaufman made that statement, and, as noted earlier, they now get cost-of-living raises, but judicial salaries will never compete with those in private practice and some highly qualified attorneys will not be attracted to judicial positions.

Added to the problems of low pay (compared with the income of attorneys of their comparable experience in private practice) and heavy workloads is the stress that judges experience. Judges handle issues that are very important and highly controversial but must be decided. As Judge Kaufman said, "Much tension accompanies the job of deciding the questions that all the rest of the social matrix has found too hard to answer."[18]

In addition to stresses faced by any professional person, judges face several stressors not common to other professions. There is a lonely transition from the practice of law to a position about which they may know very little except as outside observers. Usually at the peak of their legal careers when they become judges, they must give up many of their positions and even their friendships. Additional stresses on judges come from the judicial code of conduct that places limitations on their financial and social lives. For example, contacts that might compromise a judge's decisions must be avoided; close associations with attorneys who might appear before them must be restricted; and they are limited in terms of when and with whom they may discuss cases.

One final area of stress is the increased violence encountered by judges, as courtrooms in some parts of the country have been invaded by the violence that threatens peace and safety in the rest of American society, as illustrated by the shootings in an Atlanta courtroom on March 2005, when a man entered the courtroom of Superior Court Judge Rowland W. Barnes and shot and killed him and his court reporter, Julie Ann Brandau. The alleged gunman, Brian Nichols, 33, was a defendant in a criminal trial presided over by Judge Barnes. It was alleged that Nichols overpowered his guard, Cynthia Hall, who was critically injured, took her weapon, and went to the judge's chambers, where he overpowered another deputy, handcuffing him and stealing his gun. After killing Barnes and Brandau, Nichols allegedly went to the parking garage, overpowered and pistol whipped a reporter, and stole his car. Outside the courthouse a third murder victim, Sgt. Hoyt Teasley, was shot in the abdomen and killed. Other acts of violence were attributed to Nichols after he left the courthouse area and before he was captured.

These acts of violence at the Fulton County courthouse and in the city of Atlanta occurred less than two weeks after violence in Chicago that was associated with judges. Upon arriving home one day, Judge Joan Humphrey Lefkow of the United States District Court, who had previously been the target of death threats for which a suspect, Matthew Hale, was convicted, found her husband, Michael F. Lefkow, 64, and her mother, Donna Humphrey, 89, both dead of gunshot wounds. Judge Lefkow was under federal protection until Hale's conviction, at which time she and the U.S. Marshals decided it was not necessary to continue that protection. A suspect was arrested and charged with the murders.

Many courthouses do provide security checks on all persons who wish to enter, and in high-profile cases it is now customary to have extra courthouse security, such as metal detectors and additional security personnel, but it would be prohibitive to provide round-the-clock protection to all judges.

6-4d   Judicial Control

At the opposite extreme of the problem of how to retain good judges is the delicate issue of how to get rid of bad ones. Like all other professions, the judiciary is characterized by some who engage in questionable behavior in their professional and personal lives. Their shortcomings may affect their abilities to function effectively as judges. Although the sexual behavior of most adults may be considered their private business as long as it is private consensual, and does not involve minors, the public consider it their business when judges engage in illicit sexual behavior. Sexual harassment by anyone is unacceptable, but sexual harassment by a judge is even more shocking. Excessive drinking may be tolerated in some circles, but excessive drinking by a judge, particularly one charged with driving while intoxicated, is unacceptable.

How do we control improper judicial behavior? It is not easy to unseat judges even after they have been convicted of a crime. Usually they are asked to resign, but if they do not do so it may take months or even years to go through disciplinary channels to unseat them. Elected judges may be unseated by a recall vote. When judges are appointed, however, the process is more difficult. At the federal level, where judges serve for life and may be removed only by impeachment and conviction by Congress, legislation provides some avenues for disciplining judges. The Judicial Councils and the Judicial Conduct and Disability Act of 1980 provide several sanctions: certify disability, request the judge to retire, strip the judge of his or her caseload "on a temporary basis," and censure or reprimand privately or publicly.[19]

Another method for controlling judicial misconduct and compensating those who are victimized by judges is to permit federal civil rights charges to be brought against judges. In 1997, the U.S. Supreme Court considered a case appealed from a lower federal court, which had held that the federal civil rights statute involved in a Tennessee case did not provide notice that it covered simple or sexual assault crimes. The Supreme Court held that the statute need not specify the *specific* conduct covered and sent the case back for the lower court to reconsider the issue in light of the Supreme Court's holding that the rule is "whether the statute, either standing alone or as construed [interpreted], made it reasonably clear at the relevant time that the defendant's conduct was criminal."[20]

This case, *United States* v. *Lanier,* involved allegations that Judge David Lanier sexually assaulted five women in his judicial chambers. Judge Lanier had presided over the divorce and custody hearings of one of the complainants. It was alleged that, when the woman interviewed for a secretarial position at the courthouse in which he worked, Judge Lanier suggested to her that he might have to reexamine her daughter's custody case. The woman charged that as she left the interview the judge "grabbed her, sexually assaulted her, and finally committed oral rape."[21]

Judge Lanier was convicted in 1992 and served two years of his 22-year sentence before a federal appeals court released him on his own recognizance after its decision that the statute did not apply to the facts of his case. After the U.S. Supreme Court heard the case, ruled that the statute in question applied, and sent the case back to the lower court, that court ordered Judge Lanier to appear on 22 August 1997 for a hearing. He did not appear; the court issued a warrant for his arrest and subsequently dismissed his appeal. The judge was located and arrested two months later in Mississippi, where he was living under an assumed name. In December 1997, he entered a plea of guilty to eluding arrest to avoid prison. The judge is back in prison, now serving a 25-year sentence.

6-5   Crisis in the Courts

Numerous problems exist in our criminal courts, some of which are mentioned in the discussions in this chapter. But by far the most serious problem is the pressure placed on courts, on defendants, and on society by the increased number of cases tried and appealed. This increase has led to a crisis in our courts, and the crisis continues, despite additional judges in both the state and the federal court systems.

The greatest number of criminal offenses in federal criminal courts fall into the categories concerned with drugs, leading to recommendations that most drug cases be tried in state courts. In addition to drug cases, the federal court caseload has grown because of the increased number of crimes that have been made *federal* offenses by statute. Over a decade ago Chief Justice William H. Rehnquist warned against this trend of "one new federal statute after another," but his warnings have not been heeded.[22]

In some federal jurisdictions the problem is particularly significant. For example, in summer 2000, five years after the Clinton administration and Congress began a massive attempt to reduce the flow of drugs and illegal immigration from Mexico into the United States, the five federal judicial district courts in the Southwest were facing severe overload, with some handling twice or four times the average caseload of federal district courts in other parts of the country. Senior judges (semiretired judges) were being called in to hear cases, along with judges from states as far away as Vermont.[23]

Part of the problem was a backlog of judicial appointments, and this was particularly significant during the first term of President George W. Bush. Senate Democrats blocked some of Bush's appointments. In May 2004, the White House and those Democrats reached an agreement; the senators agreed to permit 25 of the president's nominees to go forward, and the president agreed to stop making recess appointments to the bench, thus bypassing the Senate. Democratic senators did not, however, agree not to block the confirmation of 7 appointees, whom they "deemed extreme ideologues."[24] The problems continued, however, and in early 2005 President Bush renominated 12 of those lawyers nominated previously but not confirmed, as Democrats and Republicans continued to argue over judicial nominations and appointments. By June 2005 only one of those 12, Janice Rogers Brown, justice on the California Supreme Court, had been confirmed by the Senate. Four other nominees had been approved by the Senate Judiciary Committee, but the full Senate had not taken action on them.

Shifting federal cases to state courts might ease the problem in federal courts, but state courts also face case backlogs. In 2000, U.S. Supreme Court Chief Justice William H. Rehnquist emphasized that the crises in state courts were greater than those in federal courts, with many systems facing serious funding cuts. Rehnquist concluded, "It seems likely for the foreseeable future that a regime of fiscal austerity will predominate at the national and state levels."[25]

Unfortunately, Rehnquist's predictions were accurate. A survey of state budget problems published in December 2003 reported that the economy was improving and "the wrenching budget-cutting that states went through in recent years may be winding down." However, the report concluded, "The good times haven't yet begun to roll into statehouses across America." According to the report, during 2003, 40 states—the largest number for any year during the 23 years of the survey of state budgets—cut a total of $11.8 billion from their budgets. The total cut by 38 states in 2002 was $13.7 billion, the largest cuts in any year in the survey's history. Approximately 30 percent of state budgets are allocated for health care costs, which keep rising.[26] In some states, budget cuts have resulted in delayed trials as personnel and resources have been reduced or cut. Lawsuits have resulted as in 2004 and 2005 further budget cuts have occurred in some states.

Some local courts have also faced problems due to budget cuts. In 1999, although the number of most major crimes in New York City had declined, the mayor's efforts to clear the streets of minor offenders resulted in a crush of cases in the city's courts. Since the early 1990s, in that city the number of judges in the city's courts had remained relatively stable, while the number of cases had increased by 85 percent. Prosecutors, judges, defense attorneys, and court administrators, who often disagree on issues, were said to be uniform in concluding that "this latest burden on a system that has long been stretched to capacity is hampering the judicial process."[27] The rapid increase in court caseloads raised serious questions, such as whether public safety is jeopardized when the outcome of criminal cases can be delayed for many months or even longer and when, in order to accommodate criminal cases, courts delay civil cases for years.

Court congestion results in delayed trials. It is argued that justice delayed is justice denied. That concept is based on the belief that, when a trial is delayed for a significant time, there is a greater chance for error. Witnesses may die or forget. Crowded court dockets have created pressures that encourage plea bargaining and mass handling of some cases. Delayed trials may deny defendants their constitutional right to a speedy trial.

For the accused who are not released before trial, court congestion may mean a long jail term in already overcrowded facilities. Because their court-appointed attorneys are so busy with other cases, defendants may not see them during that period. The accused are left with many questions, no answers, and a long wait, often under crowded conditions in local jails. Those who are incarcerated before trial face more obstacles in preparation for trial.

Spotlight 6-3 **Federal Criminal Case Processing, 2002**

Highlights

- During 2002 U.S. attorneys initiated investigations involving 121,818 suspects for possible violations of Federal law. Almost a third (31%) of those investigated were suspected of a drug violation.

- Between 1994 and 2002, investigations initiated by U.S. attorneys have increased 25%—from 99,251 to 121,818. Investigations for immigration violations increased from 5,526 to 16,699; for drug offenses, investigations increased from 29,311 to 38,150.

- U.S. attorneys declined to prosecute a smaller proportion of those investigated, as declinations of matters concluded decreased from 36% during 1994 to 27% during 2002.

- During 2002, 124,074 suspects were arrested by Federal law enforcement agencies for possible violation of Federal law. Just over 27% of all arrests were for drug offenses, 21% for immigration offenses, 18% for supervision violations, 14% for property offenses, 6% for weapon offenses, 4% for violent offenses, and 3% to secure and safeguard a material witness.

- Between 1994 and 2002, the number of defendants charged in criminal cases filed in U.S. district court increased 41%, from 62,327 to 87,727. The number of defendants charged with an immigration offense increased from 2,453 to 13,101, while the number charged with a drug offense increased from 20,275 to 30,673.

- During 2002 criminal cases involving 80,424 defendants were concluded in U.S. district court. Of these, 89% were convicted. Almost all (96%) of those convicted pleaded guilty or no contest.

- Drug prosecutions have comprised an increasing proportion of the Federal criminal caseload—from 21% of defendants in cases terminating in U.S. district court during 1982 to 36% during 2002.

- Since implementation of the Sentencing Reform Act of 1984, the proportion of defendants sentenced to prison increased from 54% during 1988 to 75% during 2002. The proportion of drug offenders sentenced to prison increased from 79% to 91%.

- Prison sentences imposed increased slightly from 55.1 months during 1988 to 57.1 months during 2002. For drug offenses, prison sentences increased from 71.3 months to 76.0 months; for weapon offenses, sentences imposed increased from 52.3 mnths to 83.8 months.

- Time expected to be served in prison, on average, increased from 26.9 months for offenders admitted during 1988 to 46.1 months for offenders admitted during 2002. For drug offenses, the amount of time an incoming offender could expect to serve increased from 39.3 months to 62.4 months; for weapon offenses, expected time served increased fom 32.4 months to 64.5 months.

- During 2002, the U.S. Court of Appeals received 11,569 criminal appeals, of which 9,764 were guidelines-based appeals. Fifty-eight percent of these appeals challenged both the conviction and the sentence imposed.

- During 2002, 107,367 offenders were under Federal community supervision. Supervised release has become the primary form of supervision in the Federal system: 68% of offenders were on supervised release compared to 28% on probation, and 3% remaining on parole.

- On September 30, 2002, 143,031 offenders were serving a prison sentence in Federal prison; 57% were incarcerated for a drug offense; 11% for an immigration offense; 10% for a violent offense; 9% for a weapon offense; 7% for a property offense; and 6% for all other offenses.

Obvious injustices are created by overcrowded courts that must decide cases presented by overworked prosecutors and defense attorneys. The image of inefficiency and injustice that the crowded court dockets and delayed trials project colors public perceptions of criminal justice systems.

Empirical data on the federal system's processing of criminal cases is included in summary form in Spotlight 6-3. That information is based on 2001 data but also includes trend data. Notice, for example, that between 1994 and 2001 investigations by U.S. attorneys increased by 23 percent, while the number of suspects charged in federal courts increased by 33 percent. A careful reading of those highlights also shows the impact of drug laws on the federal court systems. Recall Chief Justice Rehnquist's recommendation that too many offenses have been placed in the federal system. Some argue that decriminalizing drugs would ease the burdens of an already overcrowded system. The diagram that follows the highlights in Spotlight 6-3 dramatizes the effect of drugs on the system; it was the top offense for which suspects were investigated in 2001, but in 1983 it was considerably below property offenses in frequency of investigation. One of the suggestions for reducing the number of drug offenses in the federal system is to have special drug courts, discussed later in Chapter 11.

Figure 1
Number of suspects in criminal matters investigated by U.S. attorneys, by selected offenses, 1982–2002

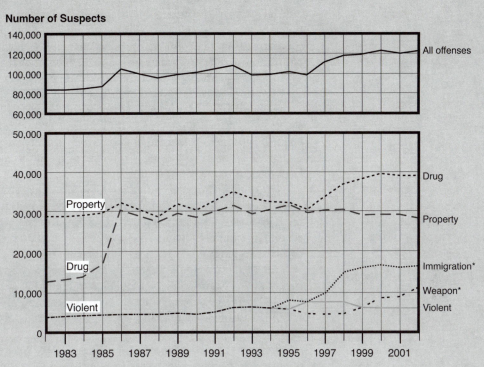

Number of Suspects

Note: Data for 1982 through 1993 are estimated from calendar year data; see *Methodology*. Beginning in 1994, data are reported on the federal fiscal year running from October 1 through September 30.

*Figure 1 displays data for weapon and immigration offenses beginning in 1994. Public-order offenses are not shown.

Source: Bureau of Justice Statistics, *Federal Criminal Case Processing, 2002, with Trends 1982–2002* (Washington, D.C.: U.S. Department of Justice, January 2005), pp. 1, 8.

In addition to the overcrowded court dockets, there are other reasons for court delays. One is the use of a **continuance,** or postponement. The purpose of granting continuances is to guarantee a fair hearing. The defense or the prosecution may need more time to prepare; additional evidence might have come to light and need evaluating; additional witnesses may need to be located.

A second reason for congestion in criminal courts is that courts must handle some cases that perhaps should be processed in some other way. The criminal law is used in an effort to control behaviors such as some types of alcohol and other drug abuse, consenting sexual behavior between adults in private, prostitution, and gambling. This is not to suggest that we should be unconcerned with these activities but only to question the reasonableness of using the criminal law to regulate them. Removal of some or all of these actions from the criminal court system would reduce the number of cases in those courts.

A third reason for court congestion may be the filing of frivolous lawsuits. This occurs in civil cases, but some inmates have filed numerous and frivolous lawsuits as well. Some of these lawsuits involve allegations of violations of federal constitutional rights in prison, but some of them are civil cases. For example, one inmate filed five products liability lawsuits

> **Continuance**
> The adjournment of a trial or another legal proceeding until a later date.

in one year in New York. He alleged that a scoop of yogurt contained glass, which cut his mouth and paralyzed his lip; his head was burned by Revlon's Flex protein conditioner; a can of shaving cream exploded in his face; a television set caught fire and burned his clothes; and a Nuprin tablet caused severe kidney damage and left him comatose. The judge dismissed the cases, stating that the court "cannot tolerate this type of cynical abuse of the judicial process." The judge also ordered the removal of the inmate's word processor, computer, printer, and any other instruments used in filing the frivolous claims. The inmate was barred from filing any new products liability cases with the court without the judge's permission, and he was ordered to pay a $5,000 fine to the court clerk.[28]

Many suggestions have been made for solving court congestion. The first is to reduce the number of offenses covered by criminal law. Building new court facilities and expanding the number of judges, prosecutors, defense attorneys, and support staff are other possible solutions. Better management of court proceedings and court dockets may also be helpful. Court personnel need to update their equipment and make use of improved technology. Some courts are using computers to speed up the paperwork. Other courts have been reorganized for greater efficiency.

Other suggestions are to use lay judges, volunteers who would handle misdemeanor cases, such as disorderly conduct, petit larceny, prostitution, and criminal mischief, as a method of relieving pressures in the regular court system. Volunteers may be used as prosecutors in some cases, while special courts, such as drug courts, are "better than standard courts at keeping addicts from repeating their crimes."[29]

Another suggestion is the use of alternatives to courts, based on the assumption that in many cases courts could be avoided. Although most of the alternatives, such as arbitration and mediation, apply primarily to civil cases, some are also used in criminal cases. The expanded use of plea bargaining, whereby defense and prosecution reach an agreement out of court, is an example.

The costs of these proposals must be evaluated. We are not talking only about the cost of enlarging the judiciary. Expanding courts and increasing the number of judges involve the direct cost of the expansions along with support staff and an increase in the number of prosecutors, defense attorneys, courtrooms, other facilities, and police and correctional personnel and facilities.

Chapter Wrap-Up

An understanding of the nature and structure of criminal court systems is necessary for a study of the activities taking place within those systems. Terminology is also important. If a court does not have jurisdiction, it cannot hear and decide a case. Cases must be brought before the proper court, and this is determined by the seriousness of the offense, the type of offense, or both. Some courts hear criminal cases; others hear civil; some hear both. Some hear petty offenses or misdemeanors, whereas others have jurisdiction over felony cases.

Trial courts must base their decisions on facts, which may or may not establish whether the defendant committed the alleged criminal act or acts. Usually appellate courts are concerned only with questions of law. They ask, "During the trial, did the trial court commit any serious errors in law, such as the admission of evidence that should have been excluded, and, if so, was that error prejudicial to the defendant's right to a fair trial?" If so, the case is reversed and sent back for retrial. The appellate court might find less serious errors in law and not reverse the case.

Criminal cases may be appealed, but not necessarily to the highest court. Cases in the state system may not be appealed to the lower federal appellate courts. If a federal constitutional right is involved in a state case, the U.S. Supreme Court may hear that case. Cases decided in state courts must be followed in the states in which they are decided but are not binding on other states' courts.

Decisions at one level or jurisdiction may be used by other courts as reasons for their decisions if the judges choose to do so. Decisions of the U.S. Supreme Court are binding on state and lower federal courts. However, because the Supreme Court hears only a few of the cases it is asked to hear, many issues remain unsettled, for courts in different jurisdictions decide similar cases differently.

The primary figure in court efficiency and administration is the judge. Despite the importance of judges in U.S. court systems, some who become judges are not trained in judicial decision making or trial and appellate procedures. Some have had limited experience as trial lawyers, yet they are given vast powers in criminal justice systems. Most perform admirably; some need to be disciplined or removed, but the system is not very well equipped for those processes.

Today courts are criticized for being in a state of crisis as a result of the large backlog of cases, criminal and civil, at both the trial and appellate levels. Some steps must be taken to reduce this backlog; lawyers and judges have a great responsibility to solve this problem. But the role of the public is important, too.

Significant changes cannot be made in court systems without public support, especially financial support. It is imperative to realize that changes must be made in all areas of criminal justice systems. Significant changes in the courts have an effect on the other elements of criminal justice systems. If we create more courts, so

that we can try, convict, and sentence more people to prison, yet do not build adequate facilities to accommodate that increase, we push the problems from one area of the systems to another. Courts must be analyzed and altered in the total social context in which they operate.

Key Terms

acquittal *(p. 160)*
appeal *(p. 151)*
appellant *(p. 151)*
appellee *(p. 151)*
concurring opinion *(p. 158)*

continuance *(p. 167)*
de novo *(p. 153)*
dicta *(p. 150)*
expert witness *(p. 159)*
judge *(p. 149)*

judicial review *(p. 151)*
moot *(p. 150)*
recusal *(p. 161)*
stare decisis *(p. 150)*
writ of certiorari *(p. 158)*

Apply It

1. Distinguish the judicial from other branches of government.
2. What is meant by *jurisdiction?* How does it apply to the dual court system?
3. What is the difference between trial and appellate courts?
4. What is the relationship between state and federal courts?
5. What are the levels of courts in each of the two main court systems, state and federal?
6. What is the purpose of the U.S. Supreme Court, and how does a case get before that Court? What happens to a case that is appealed to but not accepted by that Court? What changes would you suggest in the operation of the Supreme Court in order to handle the increasing workload it faces?
7. What are the main roles of judges in trial courts? In appellate courts?

8. How are judges and justices selected? What are the advantages and disadvantages of each method?
9. Should an effort be made to recruit more female and minority judges? Why or why not? What methods do you suggest if you think more should be recruited?
10. What actions do you think should be sufficient to disqualify a person for a state judgeship? A federal judgeship? Appointment to the U.S. Supreme Court?
11. To what extent, if any, should public opinion be permitted to influence judicial appointments? Judicial retention?
12. How would you suggest that the current caseload crisis in trial and appellate courts be resolved?

Endnotes

1. "47 in Poll View Legal System as Unfair to Poor and Minorities," *New York Times* (24 February 1999), p. 12.
2. "Kennedy Cousin Appeals His Murder Conviction," *Los Angeles Times* (25 November 2003), p. 9.
3. "Skakel: If I've Appealed It Once, I've Appealed It a Million Times," *The Hotline* (27 August 2004); "Book Hits at Skakel," *Sunday Mirror* (7 November 2004), p. 23; "Skakel Prosecutors Urge Conviction Be Upheld," *CNN.com*, no page number. "Skakel Juror Now Working for Killer's Defense Team," *Boston Herald* (16 January 2005), p. 12.
4. Tony Mauro, "Rehnquist to Bush: Judges Need Raises," *Legal Times* (6 January 2003), p. 9; "Rehnquist Scolds Congress over New Sentencing Law," *Western Massachusetts Law Tribune* 5, no. 2 (February 2004): 8.
5. Mauro, "Rehnquist to Bush," Ibid.
6. Steven Luber, "Judging Pay," *The American Lawyer* (March 2003), no page no.
7. "President Signs Legislation Authorizing Judicial COLA," *Federal Human Resources Week* 9, no. 43 (3 March 2003): no page number.
8. From the annual report of the chief justice, reprinted in part in "Chief Justice Criticizes Federalization of Crimes Already Covered by State Law," *Criminal Law Reporter* 64 (6 January 1999): 256.
9. Paul A. Freund, *On Law and Justice* (Cambridge, Mass.: Harvard University Press, 1986), p. 54.
10. "Court at the Crossroads," *Time* (8 October 1984), p. 28, referring to a remark by Floyd Abrams in response to the

earlier remark by former U.S. Supreme Court Justice Felix Frankfurter.
11. Erwin Chemerinsky, "Supreme Court Review: Elections, Religion, and Federalism Top Court's Docket in New Term," *Trial* 39, no. 12 (November 2003): 78.
12. Ibid.
13. Chief Justice Fred M. Vinson, quoted in Ronald L. Carlson, *Criminal Justice Procedure,* 2d ed.(Cincinnati, Ohio: Anderson, 1978), p. 243.
14. United States v. Wiley, 184 F.Supp. 679 (D.Ill. 1960).
15. Irving R. Kaufman, "An Open Letter to President Reagan on Judge Picking," *American Bar Association Journal* 67 (April 1981): 443.
16. See, for example, "ABA Judicial Ratings Draw Fire," *American Bar Association Journal* 80 (November 1994): 38.
17. Kaufman, "An Open Letter," p. 444.
18. Quoted in "By and Large We Succeed," *Time* (5 May 1980), p. 70.
19. Judicial Councils Reform and Judicial Conduct and Disability Act of 1980, Public Law No. 96-458, incorporated into Complaints of Judicial Misconduct or Disability, USCS Ct. App. Fed. Cir. R 51 (1994).
20. United States v. Lanier, 520 U.S. 259 (1997).
21. United States v. Lanier, 520 U.S. 259 (1997).
22. "Troubling Review: Rehnquist Sees Rough Times Ahead of Federal and State Courts," *American Bar Association Journal* (January 1994): 94.
23. "Expanded Border Policing Clogs the Courts and Jails," *New York Times* (1 July 2000), p. 7.

24. "Deal Ends Impasse over Judicial Nominees," *New York Times* (19 May 2004), p. 17.

25. Ibid.

26. "States Getting a Grip on Their Financial Problems," *Legal Ledger* (St. Paul, Minn.) (8 December 2003), Section: News.

27. "A Glut of Minor Cases Swamps City's Courts," *New York Times* (2 February 1999), p. 19.

28. "Judge Ensures Frivolous Suits Will Stop," *St. Petersburg Times* (30 March 1994), p. 9.

29. Michael Higgins, "Drug War on the Cheap," *American Bar Association* 83 (August 1997): 24.

Prosecution, Defense, and Pretrial Procedures

The adversary philosophy that characterizes U.S. criminal justice systems applies not only to the trial and appeal of a criminal case but also to many activities that occur prior to a trial. The purpose of this chapter is to discuss those critical pretrial procedures, but first it is necessary to examine the role that lawyers play. Underlying the adversary philosophy is the belief that the best way to obtain the facts of a criminal case is for each side to have an advocate, or attorney, to present evidence and cross-examine the witnesses on the opposing side.

Attorneys are important figures at various stages in criminal justice systems. This chapter examines the important functions of each side and then focuses on the pretrial procedures in which they engage, along with the judge and other participants in criminal cases. The chapter begins with a general overview of lawyers and the legal profession.

LEARNING
OBJECTIVES

After reading this chapter, you should be able to do the following:

- Discuss briefly the historical background of the legal profession
- Explain the organization and structure of prosecution systems
- Recognize the importance and problems of prosecutorial discretion regarding whether to prosecute
- Explain the role of the defense attorney
- Explain and analyze the right to be represented by defense counsel
- Discuss the reasons for private defense counsel in contrast to public defense counsel
- Distinguish among public defender systems, assigned counsel, and contract systems for defense counsel
- Explain the meaning of effective assistance of counsel and the right to refuse counsel
- List and explain the major steps in the criminal justice process before trial
- Explain the importance of bail to defendants
- List and explain the ways in which a defendant may be released pending trial
- Explain the process of entering a plea in a criminal case
- Discuss the arguments for and against plea bargaining

7-1   Lawyers and the Legal Profession

Lawyers have created controversy historically throughout the world. One of Shakespeare's characters in *Henry VI* exclaimed, "The first thing we do, let's kill all the lawyers," and English poet John Keats said, "I think we may class the lawyer in the natural history of monsters." According to a popular news magazine, lawyers have been "charged with the practice of witchcraft, demagoguery, corrupting justice, hypocrisy, charging outrageous fees, pleading unjust causes, and misusing language."[1]

During the seventeenth century, the American colonies operated under a legal system without lawyers. Lawyers were so distrusted and scorned that most people handled their own cases. The Puritans preferred to keep law and religion as one. Their law was the Bible, and many of their criminal laws were taken verbatim from that source. In Massachusetts it was illegal for a lawyer to take a fee for his work. For 70 years after Pennsylvania was settled, the colony had no lawyers.[2]

As legal matters became more complicated, people began to recognize the need for experts trained in law, and the legal profession developed into one of power and wealth. In the 50 years before the American Revolution, the profession flourished. Of the 55 men who served in the Continental Congress, 31 were lawyers; 25 of the original signers of the Declaration of Independence were lawyers.

Between 1830 and 1870, as a result of the rejection of anything English and out of fear of a legal aristocracy, the American bar fell into disfavor again. During this frontier era, with its dislike for specialists, practicing law was considered a natural right. Michigan and Indiana permitted any male voter of good moral character to practice law. After 1870, there was a move toward professionalism, which resulted in the improvement of legal education, along with higher law school admission standards, the licensing of lawyers, and the beginning of a strong bar association.[3]

The public view of lawyers improved in the United States, and in the 1900s public opinion polls revealed that generally lawyers were accorded high prestige.[4] In 1975, however, a Louis Harris public opinion poll found that "the public had more confidence in garbage collectors than in lawyers, or doctors or teachers."[5]

The image of the legal profession in the United States was tarnished by the criminal activities of high-level politicians during the administration of President Richard M. Nixon. Prosecution of some of those politicians in the Watergate scandal led to prison terms. (The Watergate scandal was so-called because of the illegal entrance into the offices of the Democratic National Headquarters in Washington, D.C.'s Watergate, a building containing condominiums as well as offices and businesses.) Many of the people involved in Watergate were attorneys. In addition to violating the law and the ethics of the legal profession, they violated the ethical principles of many Americans. According to one writer, the result was that "the pedestal on which lawyers traditionally have been placed is crumbling faster than at any other time in history."[6]

During the years since the Watergate scandal, the image of the legal profession has remained tarnished. The highly publicized and internationally televised trial of O. J. Simpson, acquitted of murder in the deaths of his ex-wife and her friend, also exacerbated that tarnished image.

Attacks on lawyers have also come from within the legal profession. The 1977 criticisms by U.S. Supreme Court Chief Justice Warren Burger were widely publicized. Burger warned that society was moving toward excessive litigation, and he predicted that if we did not stop that trend and devise "substitutes for the courtroom process . . . we may well be on our way to a society overrun by hordes of lawyers hungry as locusts competing with each other, and brigades of judges in numbers never before contemplated." Justice Burger recognized the great contribution lawyers had made in the United States but warned that "unrestrained, they can aggravate the problem."[7]

A lack of understanding of the adversary system may influence the public's image of lawyers, especially of those who practice in criminal justice. The public's image of justice may be confused with the attorney's obligation to protect the adversary system. It is said that on one occasion a federal judge drove Supreme Court Justice Oliver Wendell Holmes in a horse-drawn carriage to a session of the U.S. Supreme Court. The judge said, "Well, sir, good-bye. Do justice." Justice Holmes turned and scowled, "That is not my job. My job is to play the game according to the rules."[8]

Law and lawyers play a critical role in the administration of justice in any society. The terrorist acts of 11 September 2001 caused some U.S. lawyers to renew their commitment to their chosen profession, as illustrated by the excerpts (reprinted in Professions 7-1) from a letter sent by the president of the American Bar Association (ABA) to all of the association's members.

The terrorist attacks in 2001 were preceded and followed by a decline in the economy due to a weakening of the high-technology market and other reasons. The decline in the U.S. economy affected some law firms as well as other businesses. For example, a May 2003 publication reported that one large law firm had cut more than 30 lawyers from its Chicago, Illinois, headquarters, cut its number of summer associates in half, and withdrawn 8 of 15 job offers to 2003 graduates. In addition, the income per partner was predicted to be down about 14 percent that year. A spokesperson stated that the law partners were trying to focus "on right-sizing the firm in response to what's going on in the economy generally." The firm, one of the 10 or 12 most profitable in the nation, was expected to remain in that category even with the cutbacks. The firm had about 320 lawyers and, in addition to its U.S. offices, had 10 offices overseas. Despite these predictions, however, the firm had collapsed by the end of 2003 as did another large Chicago law firm, Peterson and Ross, which was 110 years old and employed 50 lawyers. An even larger law firm to collapse in 2003 was in San Francisco: Brobeck, Phleger & Harrison, with approximately 500 attorneys. According to a December 2003 legal journal, "The collapse [of the two Chicago firms] . . . showed that even the most venerable firms were not immune to the pressures of a changing market and a struggling economy." The publication went on to note the following:

> In early 2003, Altheimer & Gray was snapping up new attorneys for its new San Francisco office; by June, the firm announced its demise. Even in the last months of the firm's existence, it employed about 300 attorneys worldwide, about 130 of whom worked in Chicago.[9]

Professions 7-1

An Open Letter to American Lawyers

[Reprinted here is part of an open letter written to members of the American Bar Association (ABA) via e-mail on 10 September 2002 by the ABA president, Alfred P. Carlton, Jr.]

The seasons have now cycled since that moment when we saw a blue September sky turn the darkest of gray. One year ago, forces from outside our imagination attacked innocent and earnest people for no other reason than they were workaday participants in the wondrous journey that is America.... [Carlton discusses many of the values that are important to Americans and to the world before he continues.]

Such an allegiance to these ideals is not just rhetorical. It is written into, and facilitated by, our laws. It is our law, above all else, that binds us all to a common moral code. Our law protects us from tyranny, rewards our creativity, punishes our corruptness. Our law facilitates that which is the greatest moral concept our species has ever had the temerity to develop—the concept of justice. As lawyers, you and I see justice every day. Fair hearing, due process, and presumption of innocence are the foundations on which everything else

rests. It is you and I, the American lawyer, whose calling it is to ensure that justice is done.

Most of us become lawyers because of a desire to be involved in the operation of the social construct. As officers of the court, we seek to ensure that our vast universe of human endeavor moves with the grace of justice. We are sworn to pursue this calling with our common oath to "uphold, defend and protect the Constitution and the laws of the United States of America."

I hope all lawyers have felt, as I have, a renewed passion for our chosen profession in these new times. No matter how far removed your daily work seems from the founding principles of this nation we know that it is not. Justice exists every day, each a fair hearing, each served by due process. The law is, and always will be, our collective shelter from the storm.

Source: Email to this text author and all other members of the American Bar Association, 13 September 2002.

The economic slump has found more lawyers looking for employment, with the unemployment rate in the legal profession at 1.2 percent in 2003 (representing 11,000 unemployed out of 940,000 lawyers). Although that figure was much less than the overall unemployment rate of white-collar professionals (about 9 percent, according to the U.S. Department of Labor), it was the highest unemployment rate for lawyers since 1997 and represented a sharp rise from the 1999 rate of 0.6 percent. Not all lawyers are suffering economically, however. The most vulnerable areas are those that were among the most profitable in the 1990s—for example, high-tech areas. The most profitable in 2003 were bankruptcy, patent prosecution, and litigation.[10]

Despite the sour economy in 2002 and beyond, some law firms were thriving and even expanding. The 10 largest law firms with offices in the state of Illinois, for example, expanded by 632 lawyers firm-wise, including 85 lawyers practicing within that state.[11]

Our discussion of the roles lawyers play in the prosecution and defense of criminal cases begins with the prosecution.

7-2 Prosecution

Prosecution The process that occurs when the state (or federal government) begins the formal process in a criminal case. The action is taken by a **prosecuting attorney.**

Defendant The person charged with a crime and against whom a criminal proceeding has begun or is pending.

The **prosecution** of a criminal case is the process by which formal charges are brought against a person accused of committing a crime. Formal prosecutions are a modern phenomenon. In the American colonies, although an attorney general or a prosecutor had the authority to initiate prosecutions, many criminal prosecutions were left to the alleged victims. There was considerable abuse of the system, with some victims initiating criminal prosecutions in order to pressure a **defendant** to make financial settlements with them. Because the penalties for many criminal offenses were severe, it was not uncommon for the accused to settle financially—thus, in effect, buying freedom from criminal prosecution.

Such abuses led to the exercise of the power of public prosecution by the colonial attorney general. Soon it became evident that one attorney general and one colonial court could not handle all the prosecutions in a colony. Gradually a system developed by which prosecutors in each county brought local prosecutions in the emerging county courts. These county prosecutors were viewed as local and autonomous, not as arms of the colonial government.[12]

The system of public prosecution differed from colony to colony. Some counties distinguished between violations of state statutes and violations of local ordinances and had a separate prosecution system for each. Today all states have local and state prosecution systems. Local jurisdictions may have local ordinances applicable only to those jurisdictions, and local prosecutors are responsible for prosecuting violations of those ordinances. Serious offenses are designated by state statutes, although generally they are prosecuted in local courts by local prosecutors. The federal criminal justice system also has prosecutors, referred to as *U.S. attorneys*.

7-2a   The Organization and Structure of Prosecution Systems

Most local and state prosecutors are elected officials, although the elected prosecutor may appoint other attorneys to serve as deputy (or assistant) prosecutors within the office. Election means that prosecutors may be subject to the pressures of local and state politics, but it is argued that the election of this important official makes the prosecutor more accountable to the people. Prosecution systems may be categorized as local, state, or federal.

Local prosecution systems exist at the rural, suburban, and urban levels. The advantages of rural prosecution are numerous. Generally small towns and rural areas have lower crime rates, and case processing may be more informal. Caseloads are lighter, so rural district attorneys may have more time to prepare cases. Most prosecutors are acquainted with the other lawyers, judges, and court personnel on a professional as well as a social level. Cases are usually handled individually, and most personnel, from the judge to the probation officer, may give each case considerable attention.

In rural areas, most cases are settled by guilty pleas. Since rural judges and juries tend to give harsher sentences, defense attorneys are less likely to advise their clients to go to trial, and more defendants are willing to plead guilty without a trial. Rural prosecutors handle a different type of population and different types of cases than do urban prosecutors. Violent crimes, such as armed robbery or murder, are rare.

One disadvantage of rural prosecution is that salaries are low; many prosecutors maintain a private law practice in order to survive financially. Another disadvantage is that many rural prosecutors must function without a full-time staff, adequate office equipment, or resources to investigate crimes. Criminal justice systems may be affected, too: when the sole prosecutor has an unexpected illness or emergency, the court cannot process cases. Suburban prosecutors usually have more funds and resources than those in rural offices. The land development, population increases, and growth in the tax base in suburban areas provide greater resources for their criminal justice systems.[13]

The third type of local prosecution system is urban prosecution, which is more complex than rural and suburban prosecution because the volume of crime is higher in most large urban areas and the types of crime include the more serious violent personal crimes, such as armed robbery and murder. Caseloads are also heavier. Some urban prosecutors are so busy that they may not see the files of cases involving less serious offenses until a few minutes before they arrive in court to prosecute the cases.

Generally the salaries of urban prosecutors are not competitive with those of attorneys in private practice, and for that reason it is difficult to attract the most qualified attorneys to prosecution. Many who do become prosecutors may not stay long because of low salaries or job burnout or because they view the job only as a training ground. On the positive side, most salaries for urban prosecutors are higher than those in suburban and rural areas. Offices are better equipped and better staffed, and some attorneys find the variety in the types of crime prosecuted in large cities to be a challenge not found in other areas of legal work.

Urban prosecution offices may include programs not available in smaller offices. In recent years many urban prosecution offices have added programs for crime victims and witnesses. Special prosecutors may be trained to work with adult rape victims, as well as with children who are victims of sexual and other forms of abuse.

A second major type of prosecution occurs at the state level. These systems differ from state to state, but most are headed by a state attorney general, usually an elected official, who is the chief prosecutor for the state. The state attorney general has jurisdiction throughout the state for prosecuting violations of state statutes, although some of that responsibility may be delegated to local levels. The attorney general may issue opinions on the constitutionality of state statutes. He or she may appoint assistant attorney generals.

Many young attorneys view the office of the state attorney general as an excellent place to gain experience in a legal career. It is excellent preparation for other types of law practice and provides young lawyers with valuable contacts in the legal profession.

The final type of prosecution system occurs at the federal level and was provided for by the Judiciary Act of 1789. Federal prosecutors, or U.S. attorneys, are appointed by the president (who often accepts the recommendations of the members of the U.S. Senate and the U.S. House of Representatives from the area in which the U.S. attorney will work) and are approved by the Senate. These officials and their assistant U.S. attorneys, along with other lawyers in the U.S. Department of Justice, have jurisdiction for prosecuting alleged violations of federal statutes. Additional information on federal prosecutors is featured in Professions 7-2.

The U.S. Department of Justice (DOJ) is headed by the attorney general, an attorney who is appointed by the president and confirmed by the Senate. During the first term of

Professions 7-2

Federal Prosecutors

At the federal level, cases are prosecuted by attorneys who are called *United States attorneys* or U.S. attorneys. The chief prosecutor is the U.S. attorney general. The positions are political appointments and require a law degree. Special prosecutors may be appointed by the attorney general. An example was the appointment of Kenneth Starr to head the investigation of allegations of impropriety by President Bill Clinton; his wife, Hillary Rodham Clinton; and their associates in the failed Whitewater venture. Although Starr was criticized for taking his investigations further and delving into allegations of sexual improprieties by the president, he was given permission by Attorney General Janet Reno to extend his investigation into those allegations.

Some of the functions of U.S. attorneys, along with their method of appointment, are described in this excerpt:

The United States Attorneys serve as the chief Federal law enforcement officers within their respective districts. They are appointed by the President, confirmed by the Senate, and report to the Attorney General through the Deputy Attorney General. Each United States Attorney is responsible for establishing law enforcement priorities within his or her district. Each United States Attorney is also the chief litigator representing the United States in civil judicial proceedings in the district. The United States Attorneys, too, carry out the important role of liaison with Federal, state and local law enforcement officers and members of the community on programs such as the Attorney General's Anti-Violent Crime Initiative, juvenile violent crime and drug demand reduction, and the Weed and Seed Program. . . .

Assistant United States Attorneys constituted 54 percent of all Department of Justice attorneys and about 60 percent of those Department attorneys with prosecution or litigation responsibilities. Most new Assistant United States Attorneys have prior litigation experience with a prosecuting attorney's

office, a law firm, or another government agency. In addition to their prior legal experience, Assistant United States Attorneys nationwide have an average of eight years' experience in United States Attorneys' offices.

While the civil caseload is larger numerically, about 75 percent of the United States Attorneys' personnel were devoted to criminal prosecutions and 25 percent to civil litigation. Ninety percent of all attorney work hours spent in the United States District Court were devoted to criminal prosecutions and ten percent to civil litigation. . . .

The United States Attorneys continued to make the best use of resources during Fiscal Year 1996 by promoting coordination and cooperation among Federal, state and local law enforcement through continued use of their Law Enforcement Coordinating Committees (LECC). The LECCs bring together Federal agencies such as the Federal Bureau of Investigation, Drug Enforcement Administration and Bureau of Alcohol, Tobacco and Firearms, along with state and local prosecutors' offices, state police agencies, and local sheriffs' and police departments, thereby enhancing the effectiveness of the criminal justice system. . . .

The United States Attorneys, their Assistants, Victim-Witness Coordinators and other members of their staffs worked with community, business, and social service representatives to provide assistance to the victims and witnesses of crime, to identify and address the particular violent crime problems within their local communities, to develop and implement prosecution and redevelopment strategies for selected neighborhood sites under the Weed and Seed program, and to encourage and initiate local activities to deter both drug use and violent crime among America's children.[1]

1. *United States Attorneys Annual Statistical Report* (Washington, D.C.: U.S. Department of Justice, 1997), pp. 1–3.

President George W. Bush, John Ashcroft served as U.S. attorney general. Ashcroft resigned in early 2005 and Alberto R. Gonzales was appointed and confirmed. U.S. attorneys are responsible to the attorney general, to whom they report through the deputy attorney general, but generally they are free to develop their own priorities within the guidelines provided by the DOJ. This freedom may result in greater job satisfaction for the attorneys who occupy these positions and provide the needed flexibility for federal prosecutions to be concentrated on the types of crime characteristic of specific areas. But it may also result in different types of law enforcement throughout the federal system, which in turn may lead to charges of unjust practices.

7-2b The Prosecutor's Role

According to the American Bar Association, the duty of the **prosecuting attorney** is to "seek justice, not merely to convict."[14] In a criminal case the prosecutor is responsible for bringing charges against persons accused of committing crimes, assessing the evidence and deciding whether to plea bargain a case, recommending to the judge that the charges be dropped, or if the case goes to trial developing and presenting the evidence against the accused. Prosecutors also participate in the sentencing phase of a criminal case. Most of these functions are discussed in this chapter; the importance of this section is to assess the role of discretion in prosecutorial decisions whether to charge or proceed with a case.

> **Prosecuting attorney**
> A government official responsible for representing the state or federal government against an offender in criminal proceedings.

The prosecutor in most jurisdictions has extensive discretion in deciding whether to bring formal charges against the accused. Statutes vary among the states, but generally they provide that the prosecutor or assistant prosecutors of a particular jurisdiction shall appear at all trials and shall prosecute all actions for crimes committed in their jurisdictions. These statutes have been interpreted to mean that prosecutions must be brought by prosecutors or their assistants and not that prosecutors must file charges in *all* crimes brought to their attention. Consequently, prosecutors have the discretion to refuse to prosecute; this discretion is virtually unchecked, as noted by a New Jersey appellate court:

> A decision to prosecute or not to prosecute is to be accorded judicial deference in the absence of a showing of arbitrariness, gross abuse of discretion or bad faith. . . . It is fundamental that the mental processes of public officials by means of which governmental action is determined are generally beyond the scope of judicial review.[15]

The decision to prosecute may also be highly criticized. A Florida case is illustrative. In November 2001, Terry King was beaten to death with a baseball bat while he slept in a recliner in the livingroom of his home. King's sons, Alex, 12, and Derek, 13, confessed to the slaying and to burning the house to destroy the evidence. Subsequently they recanted their statements and alleged that a family friend, Ricky Chavis, committed the murder to cover up a sexual relationship with Alex. Prosecutors first tried Chavis on the basis of the boys' allegations and then the teenage brothers, on the basis of their prior confessions, thus representing two different and contradictory theories: either Chavis committed the murder or the boys did so. Either the boys were lying when they said Chavis committed the murder or they were lying when they confessed. Chavis was acquitted, but that fact was withheld until the brothers were tried and convicted of second-degree murder. The boys filed a motion for a new trial, and the judge reversed their convictions, reasoning that the trial of the boys and of Chavis under the contradictory theories denied the boys due process. The trial judge ordered mediation, rarely ever done in murder cases, to avoid another trial. The King teens entered pleas to third-degree murder. Derek received a sentence of 8 years, Alex of 7.

Although Chavis was acquitted of sexually molesting Alex King, he was convicted of falsely imprisoning him (Chavis hid the King boys in his trailer for two days after their father's murder). Chavis was sentenced to 5 years in prison on that charge. Subsequently he was found guilty of trying to cover up the King murder, witness tampering, and being an accessory after the murder. He was sentenced to 30 years on the accessory charge and 5 years for witness tampering. The sentences are being served consecutively, and Chavis must spend at least 29 years in prison before he is eligible for parole.[16]

The King boys are serving time in separate Florida juvenile detention centers, having been moved there 29 days after being sent to the Florida reception center for adult offenders. The prosecutors were furious with that decision, with one stating, "The lady of justice has been beaten, gang-raped, and left for dead. . . . This serves as a warning to all juveniles that if they commit murder, they could possibly serve 29 days in state prison. . . . That should strike fear in all their hearts."[17]

The King case raised legal questions concerning the transfer of the juveniles to an adult criminal court (discussed in Chapter 12), but for purposes of this discussion, it has resulted in criticism of the prosecutorial decision to try the teens and Chavis under two different and contradictory theories. Consider the possibility that all had been convicted under the contradictory theories! According to one media analysis,

> instead of figuring out which [theory] was true, prosecutors decided to give each of the contradictory theories a shot. It was an outrageous move. . . . The prosecutors had an obligation to decide on a single theory of the case before going to trial. It was an abdication of their role, and perhaps an ethical violation, for them to ask jurors to find defendants guilty beyond a reasonable doubt when the prosecutors themselves were so uncertain about who committed the crime. . . . In the future, prosecutors should decide who they think is guilty and then ask a jury to convict, and not the other way around.[18]

The potential abuse of prosecutorial discretion has led to suggestions that limits be placed on that power. It is clear that most people accused of crimes are not prosecuted, and there may be rational reasons for this practice, such as limited time and resources. Of those who are prosecuted, most do not proceed through all stages of a criminal justice system.

What influences decisions whether or not to prosecute? It is, of course, possible that extralegal factors, such as race or gender, influence prosecutorial decisions. If so, the accused may have legal recourse, but it is difficult to win these cases. In 1996, the U.S. Supreme Court decided an important case on prosecutorial discretion. In *United States* v. *Armstrong* the Court held that a defendant who alleges racial bias regarding a prosecutorial decision must show that similarly situated persons of other races were not prosecuted. In *Armstrong* African American defendants argued that because of their race they were selected for prosecution for alleged crack cocaine violations. The U.S. Supreme Court held that they had not met the requirements for proving race discrimination.[19] In an earlier case involving alleged prosecutorial discrimination, the Supreme Court said, "The conscious exercise of some selectivity in enforcement is not in itself a federal constitutional violation."[20]

It is important to understand that practical reasons, such as the lack of resources, may lead to a refusal to prosecute, especially in cases that involve a lot of time, resources, and expense. Other reasons are summarized in Spotlight 7-1. These reasons may also apply to a prosecutor's decision to request a dismissal after a case has been filed.

U.S. Attorney General John Ashcroft imposed limits on prosecutorial discretion at the federal level in the fall 2003, when he established guidelines that generally prosecutors should bring the most serious charges possible in a given case. The former U.S. attorney general, Janet Reno, had given federal prosecutors wide discretion in making decisions concerning charges. Ashcroft emphasized that it is the duty of federal prosecutors to "be fair, uniform, and tough," and continued with these words: "It is the policy of the Department of Justice that federal prosecutors must charge and pursue the most serious, readily provable offense or offenses that are supported by the facts of the case except in limited, narrow circumstances." According to Ashcroft, the *most serious offense* means the one that will, upon conviction, result in the most severe sentence under the federal sentencing guidelines. A charge that is not *readily provable* is one in which the prosecutor has a "good faith doubt, for legal or evidentiary reasons, as to the government's ability readily to prove a charge at trial." In other words, prosecutors should not file weak charges in order to gain an advantage in plea bargaining.[21]

Once the prosecutor decides to prosecute, he or she must decide the appropriate charge(s) to bring. Many criminal statutes overlap. Some offenses are defined by degrees of seriousness, such as first- or second-degree murder. There may be evidence that the suspect has committed more than one crime. The prosecutor must decide which charges to make in

| *Spotlight 7-1* | **Reasons for Prosecutorial Rejection or Dismissal of Some Criminal Cases** |

Many criminal cases are rejected or dismissed because of

- *Insufficient evidence* that results from a failure to find sufficient physical evidence that links the defendant to the offense
- *Witness problems* that arise, for example, when a witness fails to appear, gives unclear or inconsistent statements, is reluctant to testify, is unsure of the identity of the offender or where a prior relationship may exist between the victim/witness and offender
- *The interests of justice,* wherein the prosecutor decides not to prosecute certain types of offenses, particularly those that violate the letter but not the spirit of the law (for example, offenses involving insignificant amounts of property damage)

- *Due process problems* that involve violations of the Constitutional requirements for seizing evidence and for questioning the accused
- *A plea on another case,* for example, when the accused is charged in several cases and the prosecutor agrees to drop one or more of the cases in exchange for a plea of guilty on another case
- *Pretrial diversion* that occurs when the prosecutor and the court agree to drop charges when the accused successfully meets the conditions for diversion, such as completion of a treatment program
- *Referral for other prosecution,* such as when there are other offenses, perhaps of a more serious nature in a different jurisdiction, or deferral to Federal prosecution

Source: *Report to the Nation on Crime and Justice,* 2d ed. (Washington, D.C.: U.S. Department of Justice, 1988), p. 73.

each case, and there is no requirement that the suspect be charged with all possible crimes. In jurisdictions in which separate charges may not be prosecuted in the same trial, or for other reasons, prosecutors may decide to bring charges only on the more serious charges.

Once the prosecutor has decided on specific charges, formal charges must be made. The law specifies where and how those charges are to be filed with the court. The prosecutor prepares an **information,** a document that names a specific person and the specific charge(s) against that individual. The information is only one method by which formal charges are made, however. Another method is an **indictment** by a **grand jury.** There are cases in which the law *requires* a formal grand jury indictment, but even then the prosecutor may have considerable influence over the grand jury's decision. Although the grand jury is viewed as a safeguard against unfounded criminal charges, and thus serves as a check on the prosecutor, most grand juries follow prosecutors' recommendations, especially in urban jurisdictions faced with a large number of alleged criminal violations, many of which may be serious crimes. In smaller jurisdictions, especially in rural areas, grand juries may have more time to consider cases and thus be less influenced by prosecutors.

When charging decisions are made, most prosecutors have scant evidence about the defendant or the alleged crime. Charging decisions may be based on intuition, personal beliefs about the usefulness of punishment, the relation of the crime to the possible penalty, and even personal bias or prejudice. Most prosecutors must make charging decisions without adequate guidelines or established goals. Where goals and guidelines exist, they differ from one jurisdiction to another. However, some general goals of prosecution are commonly accepted.

One goal of charging decisions is crime reduction. Prosecutors attempt to control crime by prosecuting and, therefore, incapacitating offenders and presumably deterring potential criminals. Charging practices may be affected by decisions to concentrate on cases involving repeat offenders and the use of habitual criminal statutes with enhanced penalties. Thus, defendants who are convicted of multiple specified crimes may be given longer prison terms than they could receive for each crime individually or for all of them cumulatively. In addition, crime control efforts may focus on high-rate, dangerous offenders.

Another goal of charging decisions is the efficient use of resources in the prosecutor's office. Funds and staff limit the number of cases that can be processed. The cost of prosecuting some cases may be too great, and charging decisions must emphasize early case disposition in offices that cannot afford many trials.

▶ **Information** A formal written document used to charge a person with a specific offense. Prosecutors issue informations, in contrast to indictments, which are issued by grand juries.

▶ **Indictment** The written accusation of a grand jury, formally stating that probable cause exists to believe that the suspect committed a specified felony.

▶ **Grand jury** A group of citizens, convened by legal authority, who evaluate evidence to ascertain whether a crime has been committed and whether there is sufficient evidence against the accused to justify prosecution. If so, the grand jury may return an indictment. In some jurisdictions grand juries are empowered to conduct investigations into alleged criminal activities.

Still another goal may be the rehabilitation of the defendant. The prosecutor may set the level of charge for a defendant with the goal of diverting that person into an alternative treatment program, such as job training or alcohol or other drug rehabilitation, rather than incarceration in prison.

Prosecutors have even more discretion than police. The arrest power of the police may be minimized by prosecutors who refuse to file formal charges against arrestees. Although the prosecutor has no direct control over the police, this power to decline prosecution may affect the way police operate. If the prosecutor repeatedly refuses to prosecute certain types of offenses, the police may stop making arrests when suspects appear to have committed those offenses. Vigorous prosecution of some crimes might encourage police to be more diligent in arresting for those crimes.

Prosecutorial discretion cannot be eliminated, but it can be subjected to some controls. One method is for the prosecutor's office to establish guidelines and policies. This has been done in some offices, as prosecutors have realized the need for innovative practices. Another method is the establishment of statutory guidelines, as the U.S. Department of Justice and some states have done.

A third way to control prosecutorial discretion is by the exercise of judicial review. Defendants who think they have been treated unfairly might appeal their convictions on the basis of prosecutorial misconduct. This is possible but difficult, as noted in the discussion earlier in this chapter concerning the *Armstrong* case.

The landmark case using the equality principle to overturn a prosecutor's decision is over a century old. In 1886, the U.S. Supreme Court held that, if the prosecutor uses a law that is fair and impartial as written and applies it with "an evil eye and an unequal hand," so that the prosecutor creates discrimination, the defendant has been denied equal protection of the laws, and the decision may be overturned.[22]

Overcharging is another type of prosecutorial abuse for which judicial review may be a remedy. Prosecutors abuse their discretion when they file charges that are not reasonable in light of the evidence available at the time the charges are filed. Overcharging may be done on purpose to coerce the defendant to plead guilty to a lesser charge.

Allegations of overcharging are difficult to prove. Prosecutors may legally charge a suspect with any crime for which there is sufficient evidence to connect that person. If the prosecutor decides not to file the most serious charge(s) that could be filed, and if the defendant refuses to plead guilty to the lesser charge(s), the prosecutor may file the more serious charge(s). This is not an abuse of discretion.

Prosecutorial misconduct may involve withholding evidence that would be favorable to the defense. A landmark 1963 Supreme Court case held that prosecutors who suppress evidence favorable to defendants are violating the due process rights of those defendants.[23]

Prosecutorial misconduct can occur in or out of court by the manner in which the prosecutor talks or acts. Spotlight 7-2 mentions one case. There is a fine line, however, between prosecutorial misconduct and questionable judgment. To illustrate, prosecutors may reprosecute defendants after a mistrial, although it is reasonable to question numerous reprosecutions of the same defendant. For example, in 1998 after the fifth trial of Curtis Kyles for the 1984 murder of Delores "Dee" Dye in a New Orleans supermarket parking lot after a botched robbery attempt ended in a hung jury, the prosecutor decided not to retry the man who had endured five trials over a 14-year period. One of Kyles's defense attorneys concluded that the prosecution in these cases was more concerned about its own reputation than about justice. Fourth and fifth prosecutions are rare, but a few have occurred.[24] Recall also our earlier discussion of the grounds articulated on appeal by Michael Skakel.

In June 2003, the Center for Public Integrity, a research firm located in Washington, D.C., and concerned with ethics and accountability in governments, published a report on prosecutorial misconduct. The study included 11,453 cases in which appellate courts had reviewed allegations of prosecutorial misconduct since 1970. In 2,103 of those cases the appellate judges reversed; allegations of misconduct were not addressed by the appellate judges in 731 cases. In 8,709 of the cases the judges found that prosecutors had behaved inappropriately but concluded that the behavior in question did not warrant reversals of the convictions. Some of the types of misconduct were as follows:

Spotlight 7-2 **Prosecutorial Misconduct**

All attorneys who serve the courts should be held to a high standard of conduct. This includes how they act and what they say, both in and out of court. Defense and prosecution attorneys may be placed under a complete or restricted gag order by the judge. If they violate the order and discuss the case with anyone other than those working on the case, such as the press, they may be sanctioned. Attorneys may also be sanctioned for making improper comments during court proceedings. When their statements or actions are challenged by the opposing side, courts analyze the questioned statements in the context in which they were made and consider whether the effect of the words was to deny the defendant a fair trial.

Consider the case of *Darden* v. *Wainwright*. Among other questionable comments, the prosecutor stated that the defendant "shouldn't be out of his cell unless he has a leash on him and a prison guard at the other end of that leash. I wish [Mr. Turman] had had a shotgun in his hand when he walked in the back door and blown [sic] his [Darden's] face off. I wish I could see him sitting here with no face, blown away by a shotgun."[1]

The crime involved in *Darden* was a particularly heinous one. Darden was attempting an armed robbery of Mrs. Turman in a furniture store in 1973. When Mrs. Turman's husband unexpectedly came in the back door, Darden shot him. As Mr. Turman was dying, Darden attempted to force Mrs. Turman into a sexual act. A young neighbor entered the store and tried to help Mr. Turman but was shot three times by Darden, who fled after the assault. In his rush to escape, Darden had an automobile accident. A witness to that accident testified that Darden was zipping his pants and buckling his belt. Officers traced the car and, with this evidence, charged Darden with the crimes against the Turmans.

During the trial, in addition to the comment quoted earlier in this Spotlight, the prosecutor said repeatedly that he wished Darden had used the gun to kill himself. The U.S. Supreme Court held that, although the prosecutor's comments were improper, they were not sufficient to deny Darden a fair trial. Four justices dissented. In 1988, Darden was executed in Florida's electric chair.

1. Darden v. Wainwright, 477 U.S. 168 (1986).

- Failing to disclose evidence that would aid the defense
- Tampering with evidence or using false or misleading evidence
- Making inflammatory remarks in front of the jury
- Characterizing the evidence to the jury in an unfair and misleading way
- Making attempts to introduce evidence that is not admissible
- Charging suspects when the prosecutors have no credible evidence against them[25]

The following example of prosecutorial misconduct is an actual case cited by the study by the Center for Public Integrity. A 17-year-old woman alleged that she had been sexually assaulted by a 19-year-old man, who said the sexual act was consensual. The alleged victim was examined at a hospital, and the evidence supported the defendant's account rather than hers. When the alleged victim appeared before the grand jury to testify, the prosecutor asked her if she had been examined by a gynecologist at the hospital. The woman answered yes. The prosecutor did not present any evidence concerning the findings of that physician, thus misleading the grand jury, which indicted the defendant, who was convicted. An appellate court overturned the conviction and chastised the prosecutor with this statement:

> The results of the exam were not given to the grand jurors [even though the prosecution conceded that the evidence would have been helpful to the defense] . . . It is essential that the jurors be informed of the relevant facts. [The medical report] directly contradicts the victim's claim of anal and vaginal penetration and does not support her claim of a one-and-a-half-hour struggle. The grand jurors . . . were skillfully misled. . . . The state treated this grand jury as a rubber stamp, its playtoy. . . . Given the nature of the medical report, the failure to present it can be termed an intentional subversion of the process.[26]

Finally, prosecutors may be blamed for their failures to gain convictions. After the acquittal of the New York City police officers in the shooting death of unarmed suspect Amadou Diallo (see again Spotlight 5-2), prosecutors were blamed for not being sufficiently aggressive in their prosecution, for lacking passion, and for not presenting the evidence in a way that appealed to the jurors. Some critics blamed the prosecutors for the acquittals.[27]

7-3   Defense

One of the most effective ways to control prosecutorial misconduct is to provide adequate defense counsel for those accused of crimes. This section focuses on the role of the attorney as defense counsel in U.S. criminal justice systems, giving particular attention to the right to counsel.

7-3a   The Defense Attorney's Role

Defense attorney The counsel for the defendant in a criminal proceeding, whose main function is to protect the legal rights of the accused.

The **defense attorney** is charged with the responsibility of protecting defendants' constitutional rights at all stages of the legal proceedings, which begin long before trial. The first encounter that a defense attorney usually has with a client is at the jail. Normally after arrest and booking a suspect is permitted one phone call. That call is usually to a lawyer or to a friend, requesting that the friend call a lawyer. If the suspect cannot afford an attorney, counsel is appointed by the judge at the first court appearance. Usually defendants who can afford to retain counsel are visited by their attorneys before that court appearance.

The first responsibility of the defense attorney is to interview the client and obtain as many facts as possible. The attorney must gain the confidence of the client, so that the defendant is willing to disclose all facts. The attorney should explain that this information is confidential between the attorney and the defendant. The defense attorney may begin an investigation by interviewing witnesses or friends, going to the scene of the alleged crime, and securing physical evidence. The attorney will talk to the prosecutor to see what information the police and prosecution have secured against the defendant.

The initial interview with the defendant is a very important one. Defendants may be confused about the law. They may have little or no recognition of their constitutional rights. They may not understand the importance of certain facts to the defense. The attorney must be able to elicit the needed information while maintaining a sense of perspective and understanding.

As soon as the defense attorney has enough information, he or she should advise the defendant concerning the strategy that could be used in the case. It might be reasonable for the defendant to plead guilty rather than go to trial. Negotiating pleas before trial is a frequent and very important procedure. The defense attorney should explain to the defendant the pros and cons of pleading guilty, but the attorney must be careful about encouraging a guilty plea when there is evidence that the defendant is not guilty. Even in those cases, a particular defendant, because of his or her prior record or the nature of the alleged offense, might be advised to plead guilty to a lesser offense rather than risk conviction on a more serious charge. All of these issues involve trial strategy, which includes knowing what to expect from the prosecutor as well as trying to predict what the judge and jury will do, should the case go to trial.

In some cases defense attorneys talk to their clients' families and inform them of what to expect during the initial stages of the criminal justice process. Families and friends might also be valuable sources of information for the attorney in preparing a defense, as well as in sentencing recommendations if the defendant is found guilty. Getting the facts from defendants and their families and friends is a difficult task in many cases. It is emotionally draining as well, and it is a process for which many defense attorneys are not trained. Defense attorneys devise strategies to elicit information from clients. Some use sworn police statements to shock the defendant into being honest. Others appear nonjudgmental and use hypothetical questions to allow clients to save face. Some attorneys admit that they browbeat their clients by being tyrannical. Others try to be friendly, but they may resent the time required to discover the facts.

The defense attorney must keep track of the scheduled procedures for the remainder of the time the case is in the criminal justice system. Defense attorneys are criticized for missing deadlines, being unprepared for hearings, and attempting to delay the proceedings by asking for a continuance. Sometimes continuances are justified because there has not been sufficient time to prepare for the hearing. At other times the requested delays are unreasonable and should be denied by the trial judge.

Some private defense attorneys have attempted to delay proceedings because they have not been paid by their clients. It is difficult to collect fees after a case has ended, particularly when the defendant is not pleased with the result. Some attorneys handle this problem by requiring that defendants pay in advance. They require a retainer fee, and, when that amount of money has been exhausted by the time and expenses of the attorney, another fee is required before the attorney continues with the case.

Even while obtaining facts and other forms of evidence from defendants and others, most defense attorneys begin preparing the case for trial, should that occur. Trial strategy is important, and an unprepared attorney does a disservice to the defendant. If the case results in a trial and the defendant is convicted, the defense attorney must be prepared to file an appeal if the case warrants one and to present evidence at sentencing.

7-3b Defense and the Right to Counsel

The defense of a criminal case is extremely important in an adversary system. If the prosecutor tries to prove the case against the defendant by introducing evidence that has been seized or a confession that has been elicited in violation of the defendant's rights, the defense attorney may ask the court to exclude that evidence. If the prosecutor files charges for which there is insubstantial evidence, the defense attorney may petition the court to dismiss those charges.

The primary job of a defense attorney is to protect the legal rights of the defendant and thereby preserve the adversary system. It is not the function of the defense attorney to judge the guilt or innocence of the defendant; that is a factual question to be decided by the jury (or the judge if the case is not tried to a jury). The defense attorney gathers and presents evidence and witnesses that support the defense and examines the evidence and witnesses introduced by the prosecutor.

It is important to understand this basic defense function. The adversary system requires that, for a person to be convicted of a criminal offense, all of the elements of that offense be proved by the prosecutor and the question of guilt decided by a jury or judge. The evidence must be strong enough to determine the defendant's guilt beyond a reasonable doubt, a much tougher burden than that required in a civil case. The prosecution may fail in this burden, as illustrated by the high-profile case of Terry Nichols, who, along with Timothy McVeigh (who was convicted of murder and executed), was charged with the *federal* crimes associated with the bombing of the federal building in Oklahoma City in April 1995. Nichols was found guilty of manslaughter (along with the conspiracy charges), but not of murder, and he was sentenced to life in prison. Some of the jurors, who spoke after they had deadlocked on the penalty issue, said the government did not prove beyond a reasonable doubt that Nichols was guilty of murder or that he should be given the death penalty. Oklahoma subsequently tried Nichols for murders under its *state* statute. He was convicted and sentenced to life.

The most important aspect of the defense of a criminal case is that the accused has a **right to counsel.** The drafters of the U.S. Constitution recognized that in a criminal trial the state's powers are immense, compared with those of the defendant. The Sixth Amendment to the U.S. Constitution provides that, "in all criminal prosecutions, the accused shall enjoy the right . . . to have the Assistance of Counsel for his defense" (see Appendix A). Many scholars consider the right to counsel to be the most important of all the defendant's constitutional rights. The use of counsel by those who can retain private attorneys has been accepted, but the right to have counsel appointed at the expense of the state (or federal government in a federal trial) has been the subject of considerable litigation.

It is important to an understanding of the right to counsel to note that the Bill of Rights, the first 10 amendments of the U.S. Constitution, was included to restrain the federal government's power. Today most of those rights have been applied to the states through the due process clause of the Fourteenth Amendment, which specifies that states may not deny life, liberty, or property without due process of law (see Appendix A). It took the U.S. Supreme Court over a century, however, to rule that most of the rights contained

> **Right to counsel** The right to be represented by an attorney at crucial stages in the criminal justice system. Indigent defendants have the right to counsel provided by the state.

in the Bill of Rights also apply to the states. The evolution of the right to appointed counsel is an example.

Appointed Counsel

The right to appointed counsel, which means counsel provided at government expense, has not always been recognized in the United States. In 1932 in *Powell* v. *Alabama,* the U.S. Supreme Court gave limited recognition to the right.[28] In *Powell,* a state case, nine African American youths were charged with the rape of two white Alabama women. Eight of the defendants were convicted and sentenced to death. Several issues were raised on appeal; two of them pertained to the lack of counsel.

In *Powell* the U.S. Supreme Court focused on the issue of whether appointed counsel should have been provided for defendants because they could not have afforded to retain counsel even if they had been given the opportunity to do so. In discussing the right to counsel, the Supreme Court emphasized that the right to be heard would have little meaning unless accompanied by a right to counsel. The Court held that there is a right to appointed counsel but limited that right to the facts of *Powell,* in which the crime committed carried the death penalty. At the time *Powell* was decided, almost half the states already provided appointed counsel in capital cases. In federal trials appointed counsel was provided by a congressional statute.

In a 1938 *federal* case the U.S. Supreme Court held that there is a right to appointed as well as to retained counsel and that this right is not limited to capital cases.[29] In 1942, the Supreme Court refused to apply the right to appointed counsel to state cases. In *Betts* v. *Brady* the Supreme Court established a fundamental fairness test, holding that an indigent defendant in a state trial would be entitled to appointed counsel in a noncapital case only where it could be shown that circumstances necessitated appointed counsel for the defendant to receive a fair trial.[30] *Betts* v. *Brady* was a controversial case, but it remained the law until 1963, when it was overruled, as the following discussion explains.

On 8 January 1962, the U.S. Supreme Court received a large envelope from Florida inmate number 003826. Clarence Earl Gideon, a pauper who had been in and out of prison most of his life, had printed his request in pencil. He was not a violent man, but he had committed several nonviolent crimes. In this case he was charged with breaking and entering a poolroom with the intent to commit a misdemeanor, a felony under Florida law. Gideon requested that the state appoint an attorney for him. The judge responded that he was sorry but that the laws of Florida did not provide for appointed counsel except in capital cases. Gideon responded, "The United States Supreme Court says I am entitled to be represented by Counsel." Gideon conducted his own defense. He was convicted and sentenced to five years in the state prison.

Gideon appealed to the U.S. Supreme Court, which agreed to hear the case and appointed a prestigious law firm in Washington, D.C., to defend Gideon. The result was one of the few occasions in which the Supreme Court has overruled an earlier decision by name. In *Gideon* v. *Wainwright* the Court reversed its ruling in *Betts* v. *Brady* and applied the right to appointed counsel to state cases. According to the Court,

> In our adversary system of criminal justice, any person haled into court, who is too poor to hire a lawyer, cannot be assured a fair trial unless counsel is provided for him. This seems to us to be an obvious truth. . . . [The Court quoted *Powell:*] "He lacks both the skill and knowledge adequately to prepare his defense, even though he may have a perfect one. He requires the guiding hand of counsel at every step in the proceedings against him. Without it, though he be not guilty, he faces the danger of conviction because he does not know how to establish his innocence."[31]

Gideon was convicted of a felony; consequently his case extended the right to appointed counsel only to felony cases. In 1972, the U.S. Supreme Court held that the right to appointed counsel also extends to misdemeanors for which a conviction might result in the "actual deprivation of a person's liberty." In *Argersinger* v. *Hamlin* the Supreme Court held that, without a "knowing and intelligent waiver, no person may be imprisoned for any offense, whether classified as petty, misdemeanor, or felony unless he was represented by counsel at his trial."[32]

The U.S. Supreme Court clarified *Argersinger* in *Scott* v. *Illinois,* decided in 1979. Scott was fined but not given a prison sentence, although the statute under which he was convicted for shoplifting provided for either punishment. In ruling that Scott was not entitled to appointed counsel, the Supreme Court emphasized the difference between actual imprisonment and any other form of punishment.[33]

Gideon, Argersinger, and *Scott* concern the right to appointed counsel at trial. In 1967, the U.S. Supreme Court held that the Sixth Amendment right to counsel applies during "critical stages" in criminal proceedings.[34] The right applies when the court begins adversarial judicial proceedings, and it is not necessary for the defendant to ask for an attorney. At the stage when the right to counsel begins, if an attorney is not provided, any further judicial proceedings are improper and will result in the reversal of a conviction.

In 2002, the U.S. Supreme Court extended the right to appointed counsel in a case in which the defendant was not actually incarcerated but, rather, received a suspended sentence. In *Alabama* v. *Shelton,* the defendant, LaReed Shelton, was convicted of a third-degree assault, a misdemeanor, for his role in a fight occurring after a traffic accident. Shelton was told repeatedly that in representing himself he might commit errors that would harm his case, but he was never told that he had a right to an appointed attorney. After his conviction the court sentenced Shelton to 30 days in the county prison, but the sentence was suspended and Shelton was placed on unsupervised probation for two years. He was ordered to pay restitution in the amount of $516.69, along with a $500 fine. Shelton appealed to the Alabama Supreme Court, which agreed with him; the U.S. Supreme Court affirmed (by a 5-to-4 vote), with Justice Ruth Bader Ginsburg writing the following:

> Deprived of counsel when tried, convicted, and sentenced, and unable to challenge the original judgment at a subsequent probation revocation hearing, a defendant in Shelton's circumstances faces incarceration on a conviction that has never been subjected to the crucible of meaningful adversarial testing. The Sixth Amendment does not countenance this result.[35]

The general right to counsel does not apply to all pretrial stages, although it has been applied to most. The right to appointed counsel applies to some but not to all appeals. States may extend constitutional rights beyond those mandated by U.S. Supreme Court interpretations of the federal Constitution, and some have done so.

The right to counsel involves a right to refuse counsel. Defendants may choose to give up their right to counsel and decide to represent themselves. The **waiver** of the right to counsel must be made voluntarily and knowingly. Judges know that the trial process is complicated, and they guard against the possibility that defendants will create an unfair disadvantage by appearing *pro se* (representing themselves). Judges question defendants carefully about their knowledge of criminal law and procedure and their understanding of the advantages of having counsel present. Some judges require standby counsel to be present with the defendant to explain the basic rules, formalities, and etiquette in the courtroom.

Private Defense Counsel

Many defendants prefer to retain (hire) their own defense counsel, and they must do so if they are not eligible for an attorney provided at public expense. It is a common belief that the defense attorney with the best reputation for winning cases is one who works privately and charges very high fees, but this is not always the case. In many jurisdictions the attorneys who try cases regularly and are familiar with the local prosecutors and judges may have a better chance of gaining an acquittal in a difficult case.

Finding a competent, affordable defense attorney may be difficult. Few standards exist for measuring the competency of attorneys in criminal defense work. Some are selected by references from former clients. Others are selected from advertising on radio or television. In some cities the local bar association makes referrals on request. Defendants should choose an attorney who is a competent trial lawyer and negotiator, but the personality and style of the attorney might be important as well. It is wise to avoid attorneys who guarantee results or who have a reputation for plea bargaining all or most cases rather than going to trial. On the other hand, an attorney who insists on a trial might not provide the best representation for some clients.

Waiver   The giving up of one's rights, such as the right to counsel or to a jury trial. Waivers must be knowing and intelligent; that is, the defendant must understand what is being relinquished. Some rights may not be waived.

Pro se   Literally, "on behalf of self"; acting as one's own attorney.

Whether defendants have private or appointed counsel, they are entitled to effective counsel, although the nature and meaning of that right are not clear.

The Right to Effective Assistance of Counsel

The right to effective assistance of counsel is not mandated by the U.S. Constitution, but it has been held to be implied by that document. After all, the right to counsel would have little or no meaning without effective counsel. The U.S. Supreme Court used the concept of "effective and substantial aid" in *Powell* v. *Alabama,* discussed earlier, and in several subsequent cases the U.S. Supreme Court has referred to the effective assistance of counsel.

The definition and application of the term *effective assistance of counsel* has, for the most part, been left to the lower courts. In 1945, the District of Columbia Court of Appeals articulated the standard that representation would not be considered ineffective unless counsel's actions reduced the trial to a "farce or mockery of justice." Other lower courts adopted this standard; some courts developed higher standards, such as "reasonably effective assistance."[36] In 1984, the U.S. Supreme Court adopted the "reasonably effective assistance" standard then used by all the lower federal courts and stated that no further definition was needed than the establishing of a two-prong test, explained in *Strickland* v. *Washington* as follows:

> First, the defendant must show that counsel's performance was deficient. This requires showing that counsel made errors so serious that counsel was not functioning as the "counsel" guaranteed the defendant by the Sixth Amendment. Second, the defendant must show that the deficient performance prejudiced the defense. This requires showing that counsel's errors were so serious as to deprive the defendant of a fair trial, a trial whose result is reliable.[37]

Although a court may conclude that counsel was ineffective based on a single error, *Strickland* requires the court to consider the *totality of circumstances* of the case, and there is a strong presumption that counsel provided effective assistance. The problem comes in deciding which facts are sufficient to constitute ineffectiveness. Let's consider some examples.

The first case was emphasized by Massachusetts Senator Edward M. Kennedy, in his comments on March 2003, recognizing the 40th anniversary of the *Gideon* decision. In August 2002, Wallace M. Fugate III was executed in Georgia. Fugate, who had no prior record when he was charged with the capital murder of his former wife, was represented by lawyers who, according to Senator Kennedy, admitted that they were not familiar with "the most basic criminal and death penalty precedents. They did not ask for plea negotiations or request funds for an investigator. They filed only three motions, none exceeding two pages in length." They did not present any mitigating circumstances, and the sentencing hearing lasted only 27 minutes.[38]

Senator Kennedy cited a second case, also in 2002, in which the U.S. Supreme Court refused to hold that an appellant had received ineffective assistance of counsel. According to Kennedy, in *Bell* v. *Cone* (see Spotlight 7-3) the Supreme Court upheld "the performance of a lawyer who failed to interview witnesses, present mitigating evidence or even plead for his client's life at the sentencing hearing." The senator continued:

> The [U.S. Supreme] Court's constitutional jurisprudence on this fundamental issue has now deteriorated to the point that it is unclear whether a defendant is "prejudiced" when a defense lawyer sleeps through substantial portions of his capital trial. In 2000, a panel of the 5th U.S. Circuit Court of Appeals ruled in *Burdine* v. *Johnson* that he is not. Fortunately, that ruling was overturned by the full 5th Circuit. But five of the judges dissented.[39]

The *Burdine* case involved the appeal of Calvin Jerold Burdine. After spending 16 years on death row for a 1984 murder, Burdine filed a writ of *habeas corpus,* claiming that he should be released from prison because he was prejudiced at his trial when his attorney fell asleep. The Fifth Circuit Court of Appeals agreed with Burdine and ordered a new trial. The U.S. Supreme Court refused to hear the case of the Texas sleeping counsel, thus allowing the Fifth Circuit decision to stand. A federal district court ordered Burdine released from death row after the prosecution failed to meet the deadline for procedures concerning a new trial, but a federal appellate court reversed.[40] Burdine remained in prison, awaiting a new trial, which was scheduled for March 2003. However, in June 2003 the prosecution offered and the defense accepted a plea bargain that will keep Burdine off death row, but he will serve most if not all of the rest of his life in prison. Under the terms of the agreement, Burdine pleaded guilty to aggravated assault with a deadly weapon, felony possession of a weapon, and capital murder. He was given a life sentence for each charge, with the sentences running consecutively.[41]

In 2002, the U.S. Supreme Court upheld the conviction and death sentence of a man whose appeal was based on his argument that his assistance of counsel was ineffective because his court-appointed lawyer had previously represented the victim in another case. A bitterly divided Supreme Court held 5-to-4 in *Mickens* v. *Taylor* that the appellant did not show that he was prejudiced in the case.[42] Recall that showing prejudice is one of the *Strickland* requirements.

In a 1988 case the Nevada Supreme Court held that a defense attorney's efforts to further his own career rather than pursue the best interests of his client constituted ineffective assistance of counsel. The defendant was charged with first-degree murder for killing her sleeping husband, who had previously abused her. Counsel advised her to plead not guilty on the grounds of self-defense, allegedly believing that an acquittal on that basis would enhance his own career. Technically self-defense does not apply in such cases; however, the defense has been permitted in some battered person syndrome cases, in which the defendant (usually a woman) had been abused previously (and frequently) by her intimate partner but was not threatened at the time she committed the otherwise criminal act. Considerable publicity is given to cases in which that defense is used successfully. Counsel's advice to his client concerning the case implied his own professional motives, leading the appellate court to reverse the defendant's conviction for first-degree murder.[43] Spotlight 7-3 contains more information about ineffective assistance of counsel, as it discusses the latest U.S. Supreme Court cases on the issue.

Defense Systems for Indigents

Court-appointed counsel for indigent defendants represents a critical part of U.S. criminal justice systems. Approximately 80 percent of jail inmates and 75 percent of prison inmates are represented by appointed rather than retained counsel. In recent years, funding of indigent defense programs has been threatened, while demand for these defense services has increased. Underfunding of public defender systems at all levels may have a greater impact on minorities than on white defendants, leading to allegations of racism.

Defense counselors' caseloads are too high; salaries are too low to attract many of the brightest law graduates; and capital case appeals have increased and are complicated, with an insufficient number of well-trained attorneys to handle them. The situation in New York City was described in a series of newspaper articles in 2001, with the conclusion that the heavy caseloads for appointed defense attorneys were pushing the criminal justice system to the "breaking point" and that "lawyers often fail New York's poor." The paper's editorial page, in discussing these articles, ran the headline "Drive-by Legal Defense."[44]

There are other examples of serious problems with indigent defense programs. For example, a defendant in Marks (Quitman County), Mississippi, reported that her appointed defense attorney, who first met with her in the company of eight other defendants, told her that she was facing 60 years in prison for charges of assault, drunk driving, and leaving the scene of an automobile accident and that she should accept the prosecution's offer to plead guilty in exchange for a 10-year prison sentence. The attorney gave Diana Brown only 5 minutes to make a decision, and she accepted the plea bargain. Quitman County officials had sued the state of Mississippi, which is one of the few states that does not provide funds for the defense of indigents in noncapital cases. The county officials claimed that they cannot afford anything other than assembly-line justice for the defendants in their jurisdiction.[45]

Quitman County officials were not successful in their legal attempts to force the state to provide appointed counsel for indigent defendants. In November 2003, a Quitman County judge ruled that the state law requiring counties, not the state, to pay for the cost of appointed counsel was not unconstitutional; thus, the counties must provide the services.[46]

Spotlight 7-3   Ineffective Assistance of Counsel: A U.S. Supreme Court Update

Since it decided *Strickland* v. *Washington* in 1984 and established the requirement of reasonably effective assistance of counsel, as discussed in the text, the U.S. Supreme Court has given more insight into what it means to have effective assistance of counsel. In 2001, the Court stated, "Authority does not suggest that a minimal amount of additional time in prison cannot constitute prejudice." To the contrary, ruled the justices, "our jurisprudence suggests that any significant jail time has Sixth Amendment [which establishes the right to counsel; see Appendix A] significance." The case, *Glover* v. *United States,* involved a defendant who argued on appeal to the U.S. Supreme Court that he had ineffective counsel for the following reason. The federal sentencing guidelines provide for a grouping of certain crimes, and that grouping results in a shorter sentence. Paul Glover's crimes were not grouped together, placing him in a sentencing range between 78 and 97 months in prison. Had his crimes been grouped, his sentence would have been in the range of 63 to 78. The result was that his sentence was 6 to 21 months longer than it would have been otherwise. He appealed to the lower federal courts and lost the appeal, with both courts refusing to reach the issue of ineffective assistance of counsel on the grounds that an increase of 6 to 21 months was not sufficiently significant to constitute prejudice to Glover. The U.S. Supreme Court disagreed; the case was reversed and remanded to the lower federal court, which sent it back to the district (trial) court, which scheduled a new sentencing hearing.[1]

In June 2003, the U.S. Supreme Court decided, by a 7-to-2 vote in *Wiggins* v. *Smith,* that the failure of Kevin Wiggins's trial lawyer to conduct a "reasonable investigation" into his client's social background denied Wiggins his Sixth Amendment right to the effective assistance of counsel.[2]

Writing for the majority in *Wiggins,* Justice Sandra Day O'Connor pointed out that the *Strickland* case requires an appellant to show that the attorney's behavior prejudiced the client's defense. According to *Strickland,* a "defendant must show that there is a reasonable probability that, but for counsel's unprofessional errors, the result of the proceeding would have been different. A reasonable probability is a probability sufficient to undermine confidence in the outcome."

Justice O'Connor continued with these words:

In assessing prejudice, we reweigh the evidence in aggravation against the totality of available mitigating evidence. In this case, our review is not circumscribed by a state conclusion with respect to prejudice, as neither of the state courts below reached this prong of the Strickland analysis.

The mitigating evidence counsel failed to discover and present in this case is powerful. As Selvog [a licensed social worker] reported based on his conversations with Wiggins and members of his family, Wiggins experienced severe privation and abuse in the first six years of his life while in the custody of his alcoholic, absentee mother. He suffered physical torment, sexual molestation, and repeated rape during his subsequent years in foster care. The time Wiggins spent homeless, along with his diminished mental capacities, further augment his mitigation case. Petitioner thus has the kind of troubled history we have declared relevant to assessing a defendant's moral culpability. [As stated in *Penry* v. *Texas*] "evidence about the defendant's background and character is relevant because of the belief, long held by this

---

In June 2005 Montana legislators, facing a lawsuit from the American Civil Liberties Union, passed a statute revamping the state's public defender law. Under the previous system, some accused waited in jail longer than the maximum sentence that could be imposed for the crimes for which they were charged. A study had branded Montana's public defender system as "ineffective, inefficient, unethical, [and] conflict-ridden."[47]

Indigent defense systems also exist at the federal level; those systems differ widely among the various districts, but a study published in 2003 by the Vera Institute reported that some federal districts had made significant efforts to improve their systems.[48]

Three models have been used for organizing the provision of defense counsel for indigent defendants: the public defender, the assigned counsel, and the contract models. Each is defined briefly in Spotlight 7-4. Most public defender systems are public law firms whose mission is to provide counsel in criminal cases for defendants who cannot afford to retain private counsel. Most public defender systems are located in metropolitan areas. They are supported publicly and administered by an attorney, usually called the **public defender.**

Like prosecutors, public defenders have the advantage of specializing in criminal cases. This increases their expertise and efficiency, but it may contribute to professional burnout. Like prosecutors, many public defenders work with tremendous caseloads, leaving them insufficient time to devote to any particular case. In addition, inadequate budgets result in a lack of support staff and equipment.

Better recruitment and more intensive training of attorneys would improve public defender programs. Training programs should include an emphasis on efficiency and ethical standards as well as negotiation and trial skills. If the office does not have a formal training program, efforts might be made to assign new personnel to a more experienced

▶ **Public defender** An attorney retained and paid by the government to represent indigent defendants in criminal proceedings.

society, that defendants who commit criminal acts that are attributable to a disadvantaged background ... may be less culpable than defendants who have no such excuse."[3]

In contrast, in 2002 the U.S. Supreme Court upheld the death sentence of a Tennessee death row inmate, Gary Cone, who argued that he had received a death sentence rather than life in prison because his attorney did not give him effective assistance of counsel. Cone was convicted of brutally murdering an elderly couple in their home. The previous day Cone had robbed a jewelry store and shot a bystander and a law enforcement officer who attempted to apprehend him. Cone alleged that because his attorney did not present mitigating evidence during the sentencing hearing, did not put Cone on the stand to testify, and did not present a final argument in the case, his representation constituted ineffective assistance of counsel. It was also noted that Cone's attorney was treated for mental illness and subsequently committed suicide.

The U.S. Supreme Court held that the allegations by Cone against his attorney were too minor to constitute ineffective assistance of counsel; indeed, the defense counsel may have had strategic reasons for the choices he made in representing Cone. The Court emphasized the *Strickland* test, which requires the appellant to prove that "there is a reasonable probability that, but for counsel's unprofessional errors, the result of the proceeding would have been different" and that counsel's representation "fell below an objective standard of representation." Cone's case failed to meet those tests.[4]

Finally, on 20 June 2005, in *Rompilla* v. *Beard,* the U.S. Supreme Court reversed the death penalty sentence of Ronald Rompilla. The Pennsylvania case, decided by a 5-to-4 vote, involved public defenders who did not search the records (located in the same courthouse) of their client's rape conviction 14 years earlier despite the fact that the prosecution had informed the defense that they planned to use that case as evidence of the defendant's prior act of violence, an aggravating factor supporting the death penalty. According to Justice David Souter, who wrote the majority opinion, "no reasonable lawyer would forgo examination of the file" under the circumstances. The file indicates that Rompilla is of limited mental capacity, was an abused child, and most probably suffered from fetal alcohol syndrome and schizophrenia. Subsequent investigations by Rompilla's appellate lawyers uncovered evidence that their client and his brother were locked in a small dog pen that was "filthy and excrement filled" by their father; that they went to school in rags; and that Rompilla dropped out in the ninth grade. According to Justice Souter, a competent lawyer would have uncovered this information and presented it to the jury; such information might have resulted in a result different from the death penalty. A noted law professor, citing the cases discussed in this Spotlight, declared, "The basic themes of fundamental fairness in the administration of the death penalty have penetrated the Supreme Court as well as the general public."[5]

1. Glover v. United States, 531 U.S. 198 (2001), *on remand, remanded,* 2001 U.S. App. LEXIS 4258 (7th Cir. 2001), *on remand, summ. judgment granted,* 149 F.Supp. 2d 371 (N.D. Ill. 2001).
2. Wiggins v. Smith, 539 U.S. 510 (2003).
3. Wiggins v. Smith, 539 U.S. 510 (2003), footnotes omitted.
4. Bell v. Cone, 535 U.S. 685 (2002).
5. Rompilla v. Beard, 125 S.Ct. 2456 (2005). "Justice Overturn a Death Sentence, Citing an Inadequate Defense Counsel," *New York Times,* Late Edition-Final (21 June 2005), p. 16.

attorney for a period of observation or to contract with private agencies or other public defender offices for training programs.

The burden of improving public defender services rests in two places. Both the legal profession and society must assume the responsibility for protecting constitutional guarantees. Criminal defendants will never be popular, but the public must provide the money and resources necessary to make the system work as a protective device to ensure that no one is denied the constitutional right to be defended by counsel.

The second method of providing counsel for indigents is the **assigned counsel** system. Under this model, attorneys are assigned to defend particular indigent defendants. Normally assignments are made by the judge scheduled to preside over the trial, but some jurisdictions have moved to a more formal and organized system in an attempt to coordinate assignments throughout a jurisdiction. Most assignments are made from lists of attorneys who have volunteered to participate in the program, although in some jurisdictions all attorneys are expected to participate in the assigned counsel program. A minority of jurisdictions have some procedures for assessing the qualifications of attorneys who participate in assigned counsel cases, but the majority have no qualifications beyond a license to practice law. Most areas that have assigned counsel systems do not have formal provisions for removing names from the list of participating attorneys.

Assigned counsel are paid on a fee schedule determined by state statute or by local bar regulations. These fees are usually too low, however, to attract a sufficient number of lawyers. And in recent years overall funding has been a problem. As noted previously, most states have faced budget shortfalls in recent years, with most cutting their budgets, including

▶ **Assigned counsel** An attorney appointed by and paid for by the court to represent a defendant who does not have funds to retain a private attorney.

Spotlight 7-4 Indigent Defense: Types of Delivery Systems

Although the U.S. Supreme Court has mandated that the states provide counsel for indigents accused of crime, the implementation of how such services are to be provided has not been specified. The states have devised various systems, rules for organizing, and funding mechanisms for indigent defense programs. As a consequence, each state has adopted its own approach for providing counsel for poor defendants.

Three systems have emerged throughout the country as the primary means to provide defense services for indigent defendants.

Public defender programs are public or private nonprofit organizations with full- or part-time salaried staff. Local public defenders operate autonomously and do not have a central administrator.

By contrast, under a statewide system, an individual appointed by the governor, a commission, council, or board is charged with developing and maintaining a system of representation for each county of the state. In thirty states a public defender system is the primary method used to provide indigent counsel for criminal defendants.

Assigned counsel systems involve the appointment by the courts of private attorneys as needed from a list of available attorneys. Assigned counsel systems consist of two types. Ad hoc assigned counsel systems are those in which individual private attorneys are appointed by an individual judge to provide representation on a case-by-case basis. Coordinated assigned counsel systems employ an administrator to oversee the appointment of counsel and to develop a set of standards and guidelines for program administration.

Contract attorney systems involve governmental units that reach agreements with private attorneys, bar associations, or private law firms to provide indigent services for a specified dollar amount and for a specified time period.

Source: Steven K. Smith and Carol J. DeFrances, Bureau of Justice Statistics Selected Findings, *Indigent Defense* (Washington, D.C.: U.S. Department of Justice, February 1996), pp. 1–2.

staff as well as programs. For example, in Missouri state funding for legal services fell from over $1 million in 1999 to $50,000 in 2002.[49] While these state budget cuts were occurring, states and localities were getting less money from the Legal Services Corp., a federal agency that provides funds for state and local legal aid clinics. Some states were considering other ways to finance legal aid.[50]

In general, the money received by assigned counsel is less than the average fees paid to private defense attorneys and in most jurisdictions is considerably less. In some systems maximum fees are established, making it impossible for assigned counsel to be paid an adequate fee for all hours worked in a complicated case.

The third model is the *contract system,* which is not used widely. Most of the counties that utilize this method are small (fewer than 50,000 people). In the contract system, a bar association, a private law firm, or an individual attorney contracts with a jurisdiction to provide legal assistance for indigent defendants.

In conclusion, legal representation for indigent defendants at trial and for convicted inmates on appeal (especially for death row inmates) is in significant need of attention and funding. Providing competent counsel is also an issue. A study of legal representation of Texas death row inmates illustrates. The study, named "Lethal Indifference," was published in 2002 by an advocacy group, Texas Defender Service. According to the study, death row inmates in Texas who have assigned counsel often have lawyers who are not qualified for the intricacies of death row appeals. According to the executive director of the group, "The overall message of the study is that our post-conviction system is broken in Texas."[51]

The May 2003 issue of the *National Law Journal* reported its study of all 50 states and their respective proposed budget cuts affecting judicial systems. Many of the states had frozen hiring, eliminated positions, and cut budgets. Some had closed state law libraries; others had closed some prisons. Several of the changes might be viewed as positive, however. For example, Hawaii changed its sentencing laws in 2002 to mandate probation and drug treatment rather than incarceration for nonviolent, first-time drug offenders. This change was made to reduce prison crowding and costs.[52]

There are some bright spots in the area of defending indigent defendants. A study published in 2002 and sponsored by the Bureau of Justice Statistics (BJS) and several other organizations found that many public defenders saw themselves in a wider role than the traditional one of addressing only the legal issues of their clients. According to the report, the new "holistic" model of representation is "client-focused, interdisciplinary, and community-based," with lawyers viewing their clients' legal needs as only a starting point. For example, a legal aid lawyer whose female client has been charged with armed robbery might look beyond that charge and discover that she is in an abusive relationship with a male and that she has a serious drug problem. These last two problems might be addressed along with the legal issues of the arrest, detainment, and forthcoming trial.[53]

An encouraging sign for funding indigent defense came in late 2004, when Congress passed and President Bush signed, the Justice for All Act of 2004, which contains a provision known as the Innocence Protection Act. This act includes grants to states to improve the quality of legal representation in capital cases. As of this writing, however, the Bush administration had not funded the act in its proposed 2006 budget. However, in his State of the Union address in January 2005, the president indicated his support for improving indigent defense services for capital cases."[54]

The prosecution and the defense begin playing their respective roles and interacting with each other during a series of important pretrial procedures, the focus of the rest of this chapter.

7-4   Pretrial Procedures

This section explores the important processes and procedures that occur prior to the trial of a criminal case. It is important to understand, however, that the stages in the criminal justice process of any trial are not discrete. They do not always happen one after the other; some stages overlap. Nor are the functions of the police, prosecutors, defense attorneys, and judges limited to particular stages. Citizens—as victims, witnesses, or members of a jury—function at different levels as well.

7-4a   Steps in the Criminal Justice Process

Figure 1-1 in Chapter 1 diagrams the steps in the criminal justice process. References to that figure are made in this chapter to help you visualize the processes. The specific stages occurring before trial are enumerated in Spotlight 7-5 for easy reference in this chapter.

The stages in the criminal justice process are very important for two reasons. First, most people who are arrested are not tried in a criminal court. After the initial investigation, there may not be sufficient evidence for an arrest. There may be sufficient evidence, but the police may not be able to locate the suspect, or for some other reason the police may not arrest. Those who are arrested may not be prosecuted, for any number of the reasons discussed previously. Second, after the prosecutor files charges, those charges may be dismissed by the judge or dropped by the prosecutor. This action may occur during any of the court sessions before or after the trial begins.

The procedures listed in Spotlight 7-5 begin with the report of an alleged crime, which may be followed by a formal arrest and **booking.** In the second step, the alleged crime must be investigated. Early investigation of a reported crime is very important—evidence may be lost or destroyed or witnesses may disappear. Thus, police prefer to question potential witnesses at or near the scene of a crime as soon as possible. Police use various methods in investigating an alleged crime. Defense attorneys may use the same methods or even retain private investigators to search for evidence that would assist in the defense of the case. They

> ▶ **Booking**   The official recording of the name, photograph, and fingerprints of a suspect, along with the offense charged and the name of the officer who made the arrest.

Spotlight 7-5   **Steps in the Criminal Justice Process before Trial**

1. Report of a crime
2. Investigation prior to arrest
3. Arrest
4. Booking
5. Postarrest investigation
6. Prosecutor's decision to charge suspect with a crime
7. Initial appearance
8. Preliminary hearing
9. Grand jury review
10. Arraignment
11. Pretrial motions
12. Pretrial conferences

check for physical evidence by analyzing the victim's clothing and looking for hair, blood, or other evidence that might associate the accused with the reported crime. They look for a weapon or weapons that might have been used in the crime. They question all parties who might know something about the alleged crime or the suspect, looking for information such as motive as well as any evidence linking a specific individual with the crime.

Securing physical evidence that a crime has occurred may involve searching the suspect's automobile, home, or office. It may involve securing physical evidence from the accused as well. For example, police may obtain body fluids or hair samples from the suspect. Police cannot compel suspects to testify against themselves, however; that would be a violation of the Fifth Amendment (see Appendix A), but the U.S. Supreme Court has held that some forms of evidence may be secured from suspects without violating their due process rights. Thus, samples of hair, fiber, blood, and saliva may be seized and tested for deoxyribonucleic acid, or DNA, a genetic code by which individuals may be identified and connected to a crime.

The results of tests on evidence may lead the prosecution to decide not to file charges or to drop charges already filed. In earlier stages the police may decide not to arrest after conducting a preliminary investigation. For example, a person suspected of driving under the influence may be given a field test for alcohol and perform so well that the officer decides not to pursue the matter.

Police may be required to file detailed reports, even if they decide not to pursue the investigation, and this is true especially if the reported crime is a felony. Usually the reports are filed on a printed form that contains questions about the offense, location, description of any vehicle, weapons, injuries, and location of the injured parties or damaged property.

These initial investigations at the time of a crime or shortly after a crime has been reported may be followed by more intensive investigations by the police or prosecution. Investigations may continue throughout the case and for a very long time before a case is settled—even before an arrest. In the case of the Unabomber, the investigation went on for 17 years before Theodore "Ted" Kaczynski was arrested. Kaczynski, age 53 at the time of his arrest in 1996, was suspected of carrying out 16 mail bombings, which killed 3 people and wounded 23 others over a 17-year period. Kaczynski is a former math professor who received his Ph.D. from the University of Michigan at Ann Arbor and taught at the University of California at Berkeley.

Examinations may be required of violent crime victims to secure physical evidence of the alleged crime. Psychological examinations of victims may be given to obtain evidence that might be useful to the prosecution. A psychological or psychiatric examination of a defendant may be ordered at some point before trial in order to determine whether the defendant is mentally competent to stand trial. In the Unabomber case the trial was postponed after the judge ordered that the suspect be examined to determine whether he was competent to stand trial. Kaczynski had previously been declared competent, but his actions shortly before and during the week the trial was to begin led the judge to order the competency examinations.

During investigations both sides look for testimonial as well as for physical evidence. Both sides may use the services of an expert witness to testify regarding a crucial element of the case. An expert witness is an individual who has specialized knowledge in a recognized area, such as medicine. Both the prosecution and the defense also look for eye witnesses to the crime. One frequently used method of obtaining eye-witness identification of a suspect is to conduct lineups. A **lineup** involves several people. The witness (who may also be the alleged victim) is asked to look at all of the people in the lineup and decide whether he or she can identify the person(s) who allegedly committed the crime. Lineups are permissible, provided they are conducted properly.

It is improper in most instances to ask a witness to identify the suspect in a **showup**, which involves only that suspect. This kind of identification procedure has been condemned by courts but allowed under limited circumstances. Pictures may be shown to witnesses for identification of suspects, although restrictions are placed on this procedure. It must be shown that the witnesses had a good opportunity to see the suspect. The pictures must be viewed soon after the alleged crime while the memory of the witnesses is clear.

▶ **Lineup**   A procedure in which a group of people are placed together in a line to allow the complainant or an eyewitness to point out the alleged offender.

▶ **Showup**   An identification procedure during a police investigation; it involves showing the alleged victim only one person rather than several, as in a lineup; it is permitted only in extraordinary circumstances.

Multiple witnesses may not view the pictures in the company of each other. The police may not make suggestive comments regarding the pictures and the suspect. Usually it is not permissible to offer the witness only one photograph, that of the accused.

If the investigation convinces the prosecutor that sufficient evidence is available to lead a reasonable person to think that a particular suspect committed a crime, and if the prosecutor decides to file formal charges against the suspect, in most cases that suspect must be taken before a magistrate for an **initial appearance.** The initial appearance is for the purpose of having the court determine whether there is probable cause to charge the suspect with the crime.

A suspect who has been retained in custody must be taken before the magistrate without unreasonable delay. The time involved in processing the suspect at the police station usually means that the initial appearance cannot take place until the following day. If the suspect is booked on a weekend, the initial appearance cannot take place until the following Monday, unless special provisions have been made. In some metropolitan areas, because of the high volume of weekend arrests, magistrates' courts hold special sessions on weekends to permit initial appearances earlier than usual and thus decrease the amount of time suspects must spend in jail before their initial appearances.

Most initial appearances are brief. Magistrates verify the names and addresses of the defendants and inform them of the formal charges and of their constitutional rights. Although the procedures differ among jurisdictions, at this stage in many areas the process of appointing counsel is started. Most defendants who have retained counsel have their attorneys with them at their initial appearances.

If the defendant is charged with a minor offense, such as a misdemeanor, he or she may enter a plea at the initial appearance. Many defendants enter guilty pleas at this stage. Defendants who do not plead guilty are informed of the next stage in the proceeding. Defendants charged with felonies may not enter a plea at the initial appearance. In some felony cases the defendant is not required to appear in court at this stage, although defense counsel will do so. For defendants who have been detained in custody to this point, magistrates make determinations whether to release them pending trial. If defendants have been released by the police after booking, at the initial appearance magistrates review the terms of those releases and decide whether they were properly made under the circumstances.

In some jurisdictions, the initial appearance is followed by a **preliminary hearing,** at least in cases involving felonies. Normally the preliminary hearing occurs between one and two weeks after the initial appearance. During the interval between these two stages, some or all of the charges may be dropped as prosecutors discover that there is insufficient evidence to proceed. If the charges are not dropped, a preliminary hearing is held to determine whether there is probable cause to continue with those charges. A preliminary hearing is not required in all jurisdictions. If it is not required, prosecutors may take the case directly to a grand jury where that is required. If a grand jury is not required, prosecutors may proceed on their own.

At the preliminary hearing, the prosecution and the defense must present sufficient evidence to enable the magistrate to decide the issue of probable cause. Normally the preliminary hearing is open because of the First Amendment right (see Appendix A) of the press to cover and of the public to know about such hearings. The hearing may be closed if a defendant shows that he or she cannot get a fair hearing without closure. Defendants may waive the preliminary hearing and many choose to do so, but the waiver must be a knowing and intelligent one.

In the United States an official criminal charge begins in one of two ways. First, the prosecutor may initiate the proceedings by returning an information. That may be done in cases not requiring action by the grand jury or when the grand jury review is waived. Second, the case may begin with a grand jury indictment, which some states require in felony cases, although the states differ in the crimes for which an indictment is required. Some states limit the requirement to serious felonies. In federal courts, grand jury indictments are required for the prosecution of capital or otherwise infamous crimes, with the exceptions noted in the Fifth Amendment (see Appendix A).

The grand jury is composed of private citizens, usually 23 persons, although some states have reduced the number. Originally a majority vote was required for a decision, but

▶ **Initial appearance** The first appearance of the accused before a magistrate; if the accused is detained in jail immediately after arrest, he or she must be taken quickly to a magistrate for the initial appearance. At that point the magistrate decides whether there is probable cause to detain the suspect and, if so, tells the suspect of the charges and of his or her constitutional rights, including the right to an attorney.

▶ **Preliminary hearing** An appearance before a lower-court judge to determine whether there is sufficient evidence to submit the case to the grand jury or to the trial court. Preliminary hearings may include the bail decision.

▶ **True bill** The prosecutor's indictment returned with the approval of the grand jury. After hearing the prosecutor's evidence, the grand jury determines that the indictment is accurate; that is, it is a true bill.

▶ **Presentment** A document issued by a grand jury that states that probable cause exists to believe that the suspect committed the crime. Presentments are issued without the participation of the prosecutor. *See also* **indictment.**

▶ **Arraignment** A hearing before a judge, during which the defendant is identified, hears the formal reading of the charges, is read his or her legal rights, and enters a plea to the charges.

▶ *Nolo contendere* Literally, "I will not contest it." In a criminal case this plea has the legal effect of a guilty plea, but the plea cannot be used against the defendant in a civil action based on the same act. The plea might be used in a case involving a felony charge of driving while intoxicated. A guilty plea could be used as evidence of liability in a civil action of wrongful death filed by the family of the victim who died in the accident, whereas a *nolo* plea requires that the plaintiff in the civil action prove liability.

▶ **Motion** A document submitted to the court, asking for an order or a rule.

▶ **Discovery** A legal motion requesting the disclosure of information held by the opposing counsel and intended for use in the forthcoming trial.

today some states, particularly those with grand juries smaller than 23, require more than a majority vote. The grand jury review differs from the initial appearance and the preliminary hearing in that evidence in this review is presented only by the prosecutor. The defendant does not have a right to present evidence or to be present. The grand jury is not bound by all the evidence rules that are required at a trial. The deliberations are secret.

The basic function of the grand jury is to hear the evidence presented by the prosecutor and to decide whether there is probable cause to return the indictment presented by the prosecutor. An indictment returned by a grand jury is called a **true bill.** The *indictment* is the official document stating the name of the accused, the charge, and the essential facts supporting that charge. In returning that indictment, the grand jury is not bound by the magistrate's decision at the preliminary hearing. Generally a grand jury indictment is not required in misdemeanor or petty offense cases. Those are begun officially when the prosecutor returns an information.

Once it is in session, the grand jury may initiate investigations. This may be done, for example, when there are allegations of widespread corruption in public agencies. The grand jury may also be used to investigate organized crime. When the grand jury begins an official prosecution in this manner—that is, by action on its own knowledge without the indictment presented by the prosecutor—it returns a **presentment,** which is an official document, an accusation asking for the prosecutor to prepare an indictment.

In theory, the grand jury serves as a check on prosecutorial discretion. The U.S. Supreme Court recognized this important function when it said that the grand jury serves the significant function of standing between the accuser and the accused, whether the latter is an individual, a minority group, or another entity, to determine whether a charge is founded on reason or was dictated by an intimidating power or by malice and personal ill will.[55]

In many cases, however, the grand jury is an arm of the prosecution. In fact, in most cases presented by prosecutors to grand juries, the indictment is returned as a true bill. Of course, some procedures must be observed by the grand jury, and the body of case law is extensive and at times conflicting. Like the selection of trial juries, the selection of the grand jury may not involve systematic exclusion because of race or other suspect categories, such as gender.

After the indictment or information is officially filed with the court, an **arraignment** is scheduled. At that hearing, judges or magistrates read the indictments or informations to the defendants, inform them of their constitutional rights, and ask for pleas to the charges. If a defendant pleads not guilty, a date is set for trial. If a defendant pleads guilty, a date is set for formal sentencing, unless that takes place at the arraignment, as is often the case with less serious offenses.

In some jurisdictions a defendant is permitted to plead *nolo contendere,* which literally means "I do not contest it." That plea in a criminal case has the legal effect of a guilty plea. The difference is that the plea may not be used against that defendant in a civil case. Thus, if the defendant pleads *nolo contendere* to felony charges of driving while intoxicated and leaving the scene of an accident, that plea may not be used in a civil case filed by a victim who suffered injuries and property damage in the accident.

Throughout the pretrial proceedings both sides may file motions. A **motion** is a document submitted to the court, asking for a rule or an order. Some motions are inappropriate before trial; a motion for a new trial is an example. Other motions may be made before the trial begins. The defense may make a motion to suppress evidence on the allegation that the evidence was secured in violation of the defendant's rights. Defendants may make motions to dismiss the case because of insufficient evidence. There could be other reasons: the defense might attack the technical sufficiency of the charging document, question the composition of the grand jury, or claim prosecutorial misconduct.

It is common for the defense to file a motion requiring the prosecutor to produce evidence, a process called **discovery.** Discovery procedures are defined by court rules and procedural statutes, but the nature of discovery rules varies from permitting extensive discovery to allowing rather limited discovery. Discovery is a two-way street. The prosecution and the defense are entitled to certain information that the other side plans to use at trial. Lists of witnesses, prior statements obtained from those witnesses, and the nature of physical evidence are the kinds of information that the prosecution and defense might obtain. Prosecutors and defense attorneys may be sanctioned for violating discovery rules.

Under some circumstances both the prosecution and the defense may obtain oral statements from witnesses outside of court and before trial. These statements are called **depositions.** They are taken under oath, are recorded verbatim (usually by a court reporter), and may be used in court. They are permitted when there is a court order or rules of procedure that allow depositions. Attorneys for both sides are present. Witnesses or other parties may also be given **interrogatories,** a series of questions that are to be answered truthfully, with the respondents signing notarized statements of oath that the answers are correct.

Discovery is very important in criminal as well as in civil cases. The deposition is one of the best tools for gathering information (although it is not permitted in criminal cases in all jurisdictions). Although we are accustomed to movies and television shows in which surprise witnesses appear unexpectedly in court and change the nature of the case, or known witnesses blurt out an incriminating fact to the surprise of everyone, normally this does not occur in actual cases.

Another motion the defense might file is for a change of **venue,** which is the place of trial. If the case has received considerable media attention, the defense may succeed with the argument that the defendant could not get a fair trial in that jurisdiction, and therefore a change of venue should be granted.

Changing the venue of a trial is usually controversial. An example occurred in New York City in 1999. On 4 February 1999, four New York City police officers were accused of firing 41 bullets and killing Amadou Diallo, who was unarmed. Their trial was scheduled to begin on 3 January 2000, but the Supreme Court Appellate Division in New York ruled that the trial should be moved from the Bronx, where the crime occurred, to Albany County. Reactions were mixed. The prosecutors, along with friends and family members of the deceased, were outraged with the change, which caused a delay of the trial. An editorial in the *New York Times* argued that no evidence had been presented that the people of the Bronx would be biased against the defendants. Furthermore, moving the trial to Albany, which was predominantly white, could have increased the suspicions that minorities had about the criminal justice system. The *Times* suggested that the trial could have been moved, if at all, to Manhattan, Queens, or Brooklyn. But Alan Dershowitz, Harvard law professor and private defense attorney, argued that the venue had to be changed to secure a fair trial. Dershowitz emphasized that *the community* has no constitutional rights involved in a fair trial: those belong to defendants. If the trial had occurred in the Bronx, it might have become a trial of longstanding feelings about the police, rather than one focused on the facts of the Diallo case.[56] As noted in Spotlight 5-3, the officers were acquitted.

Although many defense motions might be filed before trial, these motions do not usually result in dismissals. The prosecutor might file motions, too, including a motion to drop the case or change the charges. In some jurisdictions, once formal charges have been filed, prosecutors may not drop or change those charges without the court's permission. Frequently the prosecutor files a motion to drop or lower charges as a result of plea bargaining.

In addition to motions that the prosecution and defense might wish to make individually, or other issues they want to discuss with the judge, there are times when both sides want to meet with the judge to ask for more time to secure evidence, to prepare pretrial motions, to negotiate a plea, or to handle any other pretrial matters. In some instances these arrangements are made between the attorneys and do not require the presence or approval of the judge. In other cases the judge might keep a tight hold on the management of the case and not permit any changes (such as an extension of the discovery period) without judicial approval.

Pretrial conferences can also be referred to as *status conferences.* They may be informal, with the prosecution and the defense discussing the status of the case, enumerating the issues on which they agree, so that no court time is wasted on arguing issues that are not in dispute. The judge may ask each attorney to estimate the time he or she expects to take to present the case. The answer is important for time management in courts, and the defense and prosecution might be limited by their predictions during these conferences;

> **Deposition**   Oral testimony taken from the opposing party or a witness for the opposing party. Depositions are taken out of court but under oath. They are recorded verbatim, usually by a court reporter. Attorneys for both sides are present. Depositions may be used when the deposed is not able to appear in court. They may also be used to impeach the testimony of a witness in court.

> **Interrogatories**   A set of questions given to a party thought to have pertinent information that may be used at a trial or other legal proceedings. The party completing the interrogatories must sign an oath that the statements are correct.

> **Venue**   The location of a trial; a change of venue is the removal of a trial from the location where it would be held normally to another location, either to avoid public pressure or to obtain an impartial jury.

thus, the estimates should be made only after close scrutiny of the evidence each attorney thinks should be presented.

Both the prosecution and the defense use the pretrial period to prepare for trial. Preparation includes further investigating and testing physical evidence, repeatedly attempting to locate witnesses who have not yet been found, interviewing witnesses, obtaining depositions of expert and other witnesses, and reviewing those depositions and all other information pertinent to the trial. Attorneys spend time with their own witnesses, ensuring that they know what information the witnesses will give at trial and preparing them for the questions that might be asked by opposing counsel.

Attorneys are involved in keeping records of the expenses of trial preparation, which include costs of their own time (even if they are public defenders paid by the case and not by the hour or prosecutors on salary, most keep an hourly record of their activities), as well as out-of-pocket costs for investigations, depositions, interrogatories, and expenses for expert witnesses and other matters. Most attorneys who require retainers in advance for criminal cases in all probability still keep an annotated record of the time they spend on the case.

Lists of witnesses who will be called for trial must be prepared, and the proper papers for notifying those witnesses must be filed. If the witnesses do not want to appear, the attorney may request a court order to subpoena them. A **subpoena** is an order to appear in court at a particular time and place and to give testimony on a specified subject or issue. As a precautionary measure, subpoenas might be issued to all potential witnesses to make it more difficult for them to change their minds and refuse to appear in court or at a deposition to testify. Witnesses may also be ordered to produce documents or papers that are important to the trial.

Pretrial conferences are very important to attorneys as they assess and prepare their cases. For example, the prosecutor may decide that the defense position is strong enough that a guilty verdict is unlikely. The attorneys may offer and accept (or reject) plea bargains for a plea to the charge(s) or to lesser charges. Many issues may be discussed during these pretrial conferences.

7-4b   Release or Detention: Bail or Jail?

Once a person has been charged with a crime and arrested, the decision whether to release or detain that individual pending trial is an important one. According to the U.S. Supreme Court, for the defendant it is a time "when consultation, thoroughgoing investigation and preparation . . . [are] vitally important."[57] During this period the defendant retains an attorney or is assigned counsel. The defense counsel and the prosecutor negotiate and consider plea bargaining. Witnesses are interviewed, and other attempts are made by both sides to secure evidence for the trial. Uncovering additional evidence may change the nature of the case and may even result in dropping or reducing charges before trial.

The Bail Decision

For society the issue of whether the defendant is released or detained before trial is critical. Public outcries, accusing courts of coddling criminals, are common when persons charged with serious crimes are released. When those releasees commit additional crimes, the responses are even more critical.

The procedures by which the **bail** decision is made vary among jurisdictions, but a hearing is required and the defendant is entitled to the benefit of counsel at that hearing. In the federal system, the hearing must take place within 24 hours of arrest. In some jurisdictions there are statutes specifying what types of offenses are bailable. In others there are specifications concerning what the magistrate may consider in making the decision. In many cases, however, the magistrate has wide discretion in the bail decision, and there is virtually no check on this discretion.

The magistrate has wide latitude in setting the amount of bail. In the federal system, the factors most closely related to the level of bail, in order of importance, are the seriousness of the current charge, the district in which the bail hearing occurs, and the criminal record of the alleged offender.[58]

> **Subpoena**   A command issued by a court, ordering a person to appear in court (or another designated place) at a specified time and place for the purpose of giving testimony on a specified issue. Persons may be ordered to bring documents pertinent to the case; that order is called a subpoena *duces tecum*.

> **Bail**   Money or property posted by the defendant (or a surety) to guarantee that he or she will appear for trial, sentencing, or imprisonment. If the defendant does not appear, the court may require that the money or property be forfeited.

A defendant who is detained may petition the court to reduce the amount of bail or to grant bail if it had been previously denied. Some judges grant these motions, particularly when the defense has had more time to gather evidence that favors the defendant's pretrial release.

The Eighth Amendment to the U.S. Constitution prohibits requiring excessive bail (see Appendix A). This provision has been interpreted to mean that, when bail is set, its amount may not be excessive, but there has been no clear definition of what that means. In 1951 in *Stack* v. *Boyle*, the U.S. Supreme Court considered this issue and stated that bail set at a "figure higher than an amount reasonably calculated to fulfill this purpose [assuring the presence of the defendant at trial] is 'excessive' under the Eighth Amendment."[59]

Until recently the only legitimate purpose of bail was to secure the presence of the accused at trial. In 1970, with the passage of the District of Columbia Court Reform and Criminal Procedure Act, **preventive detention** was recognized as a legitimate purpose of bail. The statute was upheld in 1981.[60] It permits judges to deny bail to defendants charged with dangerous crimes if the government has clear evidence that the safety of others would be endangered if the accused were released. In addition, bail can be denied in cases involving persons who had been convicted of violent crimes while on probation or parole. Other jurisdictions followed the District of Columbia in passing statutes or changing their constitutions to permit the denial of bail for preventive detention. And in 1984 in *Schall* v. *Martin,* the U.S. Supreme Court upheld the preventive detention of juveniles.[61]

The most controversial changes in bail, however, occurred in the Bail Reform Act of 1984, a federal statute that permits judges to deny bail if they have sufficient reason to think a defendant poses a dangerous threat to the community. The defendant is entitled to a prompt hearing on that issue, but, if the hearing is not prompt, the government is not required to release a defendant who otherwise meets the criteria for detention. If there is sufficient evidence to charge the defendant with drug or certain other serious offenses, there is a presumption of dangerousness. This means that bail may be denied unless the defendant can prove to the court that he or she is not dangerous. This burden is a difficult one to sustain.[62]

In 1987, the U.S. Supreme Court decided a case challenging the Bail Reform Act's provision for the preventive detention of dangerous persons. *United States* v. *Salerno* involved the detention of defendants charged with numerous acts associated with organized crime. At the **pretrial detention** hearing the government presented evidence that both defendants were in high positions of power in organized crime families. The government contended that the only way to protect the community was to detain these persons pending trial.[63]

Most recently, the preventive detention of suspects was questioned in relation to the detainees suspected of ties to terrorist acts. In November 2003, the U.S. Supreme Court agreed to hear a case involving the issue of whether foreigners suspected of terrorism may be held indefinitely at the U.S. Naval Base at Guantanamo Bay, Cuba. After the 9/11/01 terrorist attacks, the Bush administration took the position that, in the country's efforts to combat terrorist acts, it was permissible under the USA Patriot Act to detain indefinitely those labeled by the administration as *enemy combatants.* Over 650 persons were held indefinitely at Guantanamo Bay under rather secret circumstances. The Bush administration argued that military tribunals, rather than U.S. courts, must hear the claims of these foreign nationals, who were captured by U.S. troops who were fighting in Afghanistan to disarm al-Qaida, the terrorist group held responsible for the Attack on America. The detainees argued that their cases should be heard by U.S courts because the military base on which they were held is controlled by the United States, even though it is located in Cuba.

In 2004, in *Rasul* v. *Bush,* the U.S. Supreme Court ruled that all persons in U.S. custody, even foreign nationals, have a right to know why they are being detained, a right to consult with an attorney, and a right to a hearing before a neutral judge. According to the Supreme Court, this also applies to the foreigners captured during the war on terror and held at the U.S. Military Base in Guantanamo Bay, Cuba.[64] Thus, the detainees may have hearings to challenge their respective detentions, and many were in the process of doing so. The following are the brief facts about two of the so-called enemy combatants, a designation that has no specified termination point.

Preventive detention *See* **pretrial detention.**

Pretrial detention The detention of a defendant in jail between arrest and trial, either because the judge has refused bail or the defendant cannot meet the requirements of bail. Generally the purpose is to assure the presence of the accused at trial. Also, *preventive detention* of defendants who are detained because they are thought to present a danger to themselves, to others, or to both if released pending trial.

Yaser Esam Hamdi, who was born in Louisiana but moved to Saudi Arabia as a child, was a suspected terrorist whose Taliban unit surrendered in Afghanistan in November 2001. Hamdi was held, often in isolation, for over two years without charges being filed against him. In June 2004, in *Hamdi* v. *Rumsfeld,* eight justices of the U.S. Supreme Court ruled that Hamdi was entitled to an attorney and his day in court, stating that "a state of war is not a blank check for the president." The Supreme Court justices did not, however, agree on what should be done with Hamdi, who was being held at a military brig in South Carolina. The Court remanded the case to the lower court for resolution.[65] Subsequently Hamdi was released to return to Saudi Arabia without ever being charged with a crime by U.S. officials. As part of the agreement for his release, Hamdi was required to give up his U.S. citizenship and not sue the U.S. government for his detention.

José Padilla, an American citizen who was born in New York and grew up in Chicago, was suspectd of plans to detonate a so-called dirty bomb to attack the United States. These bombs are conventional explosives designed to spread radioactive material. Padilla was seized at Chicago's O'Hare Airport and was detained for almost two years without being charged with a crime; during that time he was not permitted to see a judge, an attorney, or even his own family. After the decision in *Hamdi,* it was logical that Padilla would win his case as he was arrested on American soil. In February 2005 U.S. District Judge Henry F. Floyd, in Spartanburg, South Carolina, ruled that within 45 days, Padilla must be either charged with a crime, released from detention, or the judge's order appealed. Padilla was released without being charged with a crime.[66]

The Bail System

The bail system developed for practical reasons. It began in England, probably before A.D. 1000. Before urbanization and the development of modern courts, judges traveled from one jurisdiction to another to hold court sessions. They could not get to any one place often; consequently, it was necessary to devise a way of detaining the accused before the judges arrived. The bail system developed because the detention facilities were recognized as horrible places of confinement and were expensive.

An opportunity to make money in the bail system resulted in the development of the bail **bond** system. In return for a fee, the bail bondsman/woman posts bond for the defendant. If the defendant does not appear at trial, theoretically the bond money must be forfeited to the court. In reality the forfeiture provision is rarely enforced; however, since some bondsmen/women post bond without having the money available, some jurisdictions require them to prove that they can pay the forfeiture, should that be necessary. Abuses of the bail bond system led to alternative methods for pretrial release, as defined in Spotlight 7-6.

> ▶ **Bond** A written document indicating that the defendant or his or her sureties assure the presence of that defendant at a criminal proceeding and that, if the defendant is not present, the court may require that the security posted for the bond be forfeited.

7-4c   The Guilty Plea

The guilty plea is very important in U.S. criminal justice systems because approximately 90 percent of defendants plead guilty. Although many guilty pleas are entered after plea bargaining begins, defendants may choose to plead guilty without any negotiation between the prosecution and the defense. Various reasons account for this decision. Some defendants are guilty and see no reason to go to trial, thinking that they have no chance of an acquittal or a conviction on a lesser offense. They may not want to engage in any kind of plea bargaining because, as in a trial, that might take more time than they are willing to devote to the process. Some defendants want a quick decision. This may be true particularly if they have been denied bail and must wait in jail until a plea bargain is reached or the trial occurs. Still other defendants may not want to experience the public exposure of the evidence the prosecution will present at trial.

In cases involving minor offenses, most defendants are placed on probation. That means they do not have to serve time in jail or prison. They might prefer to plead guilty and get on with their lives. Pleading guilty may save the family money in the case of defendants who do not qualify for publicly supported counsel. Getting back to work enables

Spotlight 7-6	**Methods of Pretrial Release**

Both financial bonds and alternative release options are used today.

Financial Bond

Fully secured bail The defendant posts the full amount of bail with the court.

Privately secured bail A bondsman signs a promissory note to the court for the bail amount and charges the defendant a fee for the service (usually 10 percent of the bail amount). If the defendant fails to appear, the bondsman must pay the court the full amount. Frequently, the bondsman requires the defendant to post collateral in addition to the fee.

Deposit bail The courts allow the defendant to deposit a percentage (usually 10 percent) of the full bail with the court. The full amount of the bail is required if the defendant fails to appear. The percentage bail is returned after disposition of the case, but the court often retains 1 percent for administrative costs.

Unsecured bail The defendant pays no money to the court but is liable for the full amount of bail should he or she fail to appear.

Alternative Release Options

Release on recognizance (ROR) The court releases the defendant on the promise that he or she will appear in court as required.

Conditional release The court releases the defendant subject to his or her following specific conditions set by the court, such as attendance at drug treatment therapy or staying away from the complaining witness.

Third party custody The defendant is released into the custody of an individual or agency that promises to assure his or her appearance in court. No monetary transactions are involved in this type of release.

Citation release Arrestees are released pending their first court appearance on a written order issued by law enforcement personnel.

Source: Bureau of Justice Statistics, *Report to the Nation on Crime and Justice: The Data,* 2d ed. (Washington, D.C.: U.S. Department of Justice, 1988), p. 76.

defendants to continue supporting their families and to reduce the stress placed on everyone by an indecisive situation.

Defendants who plead guilty may be familiar with the court process and the reputation of the prosecutor in that jurisdiction. If the prosecutor has a reputation for recommending stricter sentences for defendants who insist on trials, compared with those who plead guilty, the defendant may be willing to enter a guilty plea. If juries in that jurisdiction have a reputation for being tough on defendants, that information might lead the defendant to plead guilty.

The defense attorney may encourage the defendant to plead guilty. In many cases, this is the best advice that the attorney can give the defendant and should not be viewed as a dereliction of the defense attorney's duty to the client. It may be bad advice in some cases, however; if the defendant has little chance of an acquittal, the defendant is entitled to know that. In addition, most attorneys will explain what may be expected financially and otherwise if the case goes to trial. In all cases, however, the final decision whether to plead guilty should be made by the defendant.

In deciding whether to plead guilty, the defendant may consider carefully the implications of studies showing that defendants who plead guilty are less likely to be sentenced to prison than defendants who go to trial and are convicted. Many who plead guilty receive shorter sentences than those who go to trial. The difference may be related to the nature of the offense or to other factors that are not in themselves related to whether guilt is determined by a guilty plea or by a trial.

Jurisdictions vary in the processes by which defendants plead guilty, but generally the plea is entered in open court and recorded on a form signed by the defendant and defense counsel. By signing this form, defendants swear that they are of sound mind, that they are not under the influence of alcohol or other drugs, that they understand fully that they are waiving the rights associated with a trial, and that nothing has been promised in return for their signatures on this form. The form contains the sentence recommended by the prosecutor. The judge is not required to follow that recommendation but usually does.

After the form is completed, the defendant, the defense attorney, and the prosecutor appear before the magistrate or judge for formal entering of the plea. At that time the judge questions the defendant. Before the plea is accepted, the judge must be convinced that the plea is a knowing and intelligent one and was made voluntarily. The U.S. Supreme Court has made it clear that, because a defendant who pleads guilty gives up several constitutional rights, including the right to a trial by an impartial jury, a guilty plea requires "an intentional relinquishment or abandonment of a known right or privilege" and must be declared void if it is not a knowing and intelligent plea.[67]

If the judge decides that the plea is a knowing and intelligent one, he or she may accept that plea, in which case a formal record is made with the court. Generally the form specifies how long the defendant has for an appeal on a sentence imposed by the court. Defendants who change their minds and wish to withdraw their guilty pleas may petition the court to do so. If that request is made prior to sentencing, the judge may grant it; usually motions to withdraw a guilty plea after sentencing are not granted. There is no absolute right to withdraw a guilty plea at any time.

7-4d   Plea Bargaining

> **Plea bargaining**   The process of negotiation between the defense and the prosecution before or during the trial of a defendant. The process may involve reducing or dropping some charges or a recommendation for leniency in exchange for a plea of guilty on another charge or charges.

One of the most controversial practices in U.S. criminal justice systems is **plea bargaining**, the process in which the prosecution and the defense attempt to negotiate a plea. The negotiation may involve reducing charges, dropping charges, or recommending a sentence. Plea bargaining became a part of U.S. criminal justice systems after the Civil War but was not practiced widely until the 1990s. Little attention was paid to the process until crime commissions began their studies in the 1920s.

It was not until the 1970s that the U.S. Supreme Court recognized plea bargaining as appropriate and even essential to criminal justice systems. In 1971, the Court approved plea bargaining as a means of managing overloaded criminal dockets, referring to the process as "an essential component" of the criminal process, which "properly administered . . . is to be encouraged."[68] The plea bargaining process may not involve threatened physical harm or mental coercion that might result in an involuntary plea by the defendant.

On 19 January 2001, the day before he was leaving office, President Bill Clinton and the special prosecutor's office entered into a plea arrangement by which Clinton agreed to some admissions regarding his behavior with a White House intern, and the special prosecutor agreed not to charge him with any crimes. Clinton also agreed to surrender his law license for five years. Many felt this arrangement was best for the country. It avoided the possibility of a long, expensive, and emotional trial. It permitted the new president, George W. Bush, to begin his administration without the cloud of Clinton's problems, and it allowed Clinton to move forward with his life.

Plea bargains may be rejected by defendants to their detriment. Perhaps the best-known recent example is that of Lionel Tate, who, at age 14, was sentenced to life without parole after he was convicted in a Florida adult criminal court for murder (during aggravated child abuse) in the 1999 death of Tiffany Eunick, when Tate was 12 and she was 6. Prior to the trial, the prosecutor offered Tate a plea bargain consisting of 3 years in a juvenile prison, followed by a year of house arrest and probation for 10 years. Tate rejected the plea bargain offer and went to trial. The jury did not believe Tate's testimony that he accidentally killed Eunick while he was imitating pro wrestlers, and Tate was convicted. Under Florida law, a conviction for first-degree murder carries an automatic sentence of life without parole. Florida Governor Jeb Bush considered but rejected Tate's first request for clemency, stating, "We must never forget that the life of a 6-year-old girl has been lost." The governor also stated at that time, "I am not sure it is right to consign such a young child to a life without any hope, even when that child is guilty of a truly horrendous crime." In quoting Bush and reviewing the case in a 2 July 2003 article, a Florida newspaper called for the state clemency board to grant clemency to Tate at that time. Here were some of the reasons:

- Tate was thought to be the youngest person sentenced to life without parole.

- Tate had not been given a competency hearing prior to his trial.

- Florida law provides that an adult with the mental capacity of a 12-year-old is not competent to stand trial, so why should a 12-year-old be tried in an adult criminal court?

The editorial did not call for a pardon but, rather, a change in the sentence to time served and a release under supervision.[69]

In December 2003, a three-judge panel of Florida's Fourth District Court of Appeals reversed Tate's conviction and life sentence and ordered a new trial. Of the issues on appeal, the appellate court ruled that one required reversal, holding that the defense request to have Tate's mental competency evaluated post-trial should have been granted. The appellate court did state that the "evidence was clear that the victim was brutally slain" and that it would have taken "tremendous force to inflict" the injuries Eunick sustained.[70] It was not stated why the defense had not requested a competency hearing earlier in the process. Tate was to remain incarcerated for at least 15 days, during which time the state could request a hearing of the appeal. If the state did not do so, Tate's defense lawyers planned to file a motion that their client be released pending the results of his new trial.[71]

Rather than retry Tate, the prosecution offered him the same plea deal they had offered before his trial: 3 years in a juvenile institution followed by a year of house arrest and 10 years on probation. Tate accepted the plea bargain and was released in January 2004 to the custody of his mother, as he had already served the required time. Under the terms of the plea deal, Tate was also required to undergo psychiatric counseling and to perform 1,000 hours of community service. Tate was released from prison four days prior to his seventeenth birthday.[72]

In September 2004, Tate was accused of violating the terms of his probation by staying out late at night. For a month he was placed in another home, but the family found the visitations by probation officers to be stressful and requested that Tate be moved. A judge permitted Tate to return to his mother's home.[73] In June 2005, Tate was again apprehended, accused of robbing a pizza deliveryman at gunpoint; he was jailed without bail. A few weeks later, the teen who accused Tate, recanted and said it was not Tate. Investigations were pending as of the time of this writing.

There is no legal right to a plea bargain. According to the U.S. Supreme Court, the states and Congress may abolish plea bargaining; however, where it does exist, it is not improper to offer leniency "and other substantial benefits" to defendants in exchange for a guilty plea.[74] In 1984, the U.S. Supreme Court upheld a prosecutor's withdrawal of an offer that had been accepted by a defendant. After he had accepted the prosecutor's offer, the defendant was told that the offer was a mistake and was being withdrawn. He appealed; the federal appellate court agreed with the defendant that the withdrawal was not permissible. However, the Supreme Court disagreed, reversed the lower federal court, and stated that an agreement to a plea bargain is an "executory agreement that does not involve the constitutional rights of the accused until it is embodied in the formal pleas." In upholding the prosecutor's withdrawal of the plea, the Court said, "The Due Process Clause is not a code of ethics for prosecutors" but, rather, is concerned "with the manner in which persons are deprived of their liberty."[75]

The reasons for allowing plea bargaining, as well as some of the prosecutorial activities permissible in the process, were articulated by the U.S. Supreme Court in *Bordenkircher* v. *Hayes*, decided in 1978. This case involved a defendant who was indicted by a grand jury on the charge of uttering a forged instrument (passing a hot check), an offense carrying a prison term of 2 to 10 years. After the defendant's arraignment on the charge, the prosecutor offered to recommend a 5-year sentence if the defendant would plead guilty to the indictment. If the defendant did not do so, the prosecutor said that he would return to the grand jury and ask for an indictment under the Kentucky Habitual Criminal Act (since repealed). Conviction under that act would have resulted in a life term in prison because the defendant had two prior felony convictions.

Defendant Hayes did not plead guilty. The prosecutor secured the indictment under the Habitual Criminal Act. The jury found Hayes guilty of uttering a forged instrument and in a separate proceeding found that he had two prior felony convictions. As required by statute, upon conviction under that act, he was sentenced to life in prison. The U.S. Supreme Court noted the need for plea bargaining; acknowledged that it is not a right; and held that, although one may not be punished for exercising constitutional rights, the give-and-take of plea bargaining leaves the defendant free to accept or reject an offer. "To hold that the prosecutor's desire to induce a guilty plea is an 'unjustifiable standard,' which, like race or religion, may play no part in his charging decision, would contradict the very premises that underlie the concept of plea bargaining itself."[76] Four justices dissented in *Bordenkircher,* arguing that the facts of the case constituted prosecutorial vindictiveness, which the U.S. Supreme Court had held was impermissible.

In 1995, the U.S. Supreme Court decided a plea bargaining case that might reduce the use of this practice. Although the Court was interpreting a federal statute, the principle of the case may be used in other situations. *United States* v. *Mezzanatto* involved a statute specifying that incriminating statements made by a defendant in the course of a plea bargain may not be used against him or her at trial. The defendant agreed to the prosecutor's demand during plea bargaining that, if the informal process was not effective and the case went to trial, he would not invoke that provision. Thus, the issue was whether the defendant should be permitted to waive the statutory provision. The U.S. Supreme Court held that the exclusionary provision of the federal rule could be and was waived by the defendant. Lower federal courts had split in their decisions on the issue.[77] It is possible that some defendants will be less candid in plea bargaining sessions as a result of this decision.

Plea bargaining may occur during any stage of the criminal process, but most defense attorneys begin negotiations as soon as possible. The longer a defendant has been in the system, the less likely prosecutors are to plea bargain because of the time and effort already spent on the case. The prosecutor may want to initiate plea bargaining early to dispose of a heavy caseload. On the other hand, he or she might stall on the process, thinking that defendants will be more cooperative the longer they have to wait, especially if they are being detained in jail.

Plea bargaining may be initiated by either the prosecution or the defense. The prosecutor may refuse to discuss any kind of bargain and insist on a trial. Likewise, the defendant may refuse to bargain and insist on a trial, but a defendant who enters a guilty plea cannot withdraw it merely because he or she chose the wrong strategy.

Normally plea bargaining begins early in the pretrial procedures and is completed before the date set for trial. A high-profile murder case illustrates the use of plea bargaining very early in the criminal justice process. In November 2003, the prosecution in King County (Seattle) Washington offered a plea deal to Gary L. Ridgway, who was accused in the murders of 48 young women in the Green River area of Seattle. Many of the victims were prostitutes or runaways. This case, which baffled police for 20 years, is unusual in that normally plea bargains are not offered in cases involving multiple murders, but the prosecution's position was that the plea deal was the only way to bring closure to all of the cases. Ridgway, showing no emotion, entered a guilty plea to all 48 cases, making him the deadliest serial killer in U.S. history. A statement made previously by Ridgway was read in court: "I killed the 48 women. . . . In most cases, when I murdered these women I did not know their names. Most of the time I killed them the first time I met them, and I did not have a good memory for their faces. I killed so many women, I have a hard time keeping them straight." When asked in court whether that statement was true, the defendant said, "Yes, it is." The statement continued as follows:

> I placed most of the bodies in groups which I called clusters. I did this because I wanted to keep track of all the women I killed. I liked to drive by the clusters around the county and think about the women I placed there.[78]

Ridgway had been charged with only seven of the Green River killings and was scheduled to go on trial in 2004; the prosecution was asking for the death penalty. By entering guilty pleas Ridgway spared his own life. He had sexually assaulted and strangled most of the women and teens. Ridgway was sentenced to one prison life term for each murder.

In April 2005, another controversial plea bargain was announced. Eric Rudolph pleaded guilty to multiple terrorist acts in the 1990s. Rudolph's bombings at Atlanta's Olympic games in 1996, in 1997 at an Atlanta office building (an abortion clinic inside that building was thought to be the target), at an Atlanta bar frequented by gays and lesbians, and at an abortion clinic in Birmingham, Alabama, in 1998. These terrorist acts resulted in the deaths of two persons, including a police officer, and injuries to over 100 others. Rudolph was a fugitive and listed on the FBI's 10 Most Wanted, but he eluded law enforcement officials until his capture in 2003 near Murphy, North Carolina, while he was scavenging for food. Rudolph was to be tried first in Alabama, where prosecutors were seeking the death penalty. After jury selection began, the prosecution announced that they had struck a plea bargain with Rudolph. He would plead guilty to all of the bombings in return for a life sentence. In an 11-page statement released by his attorneys, Rudolph made no apologies, but lashed out at what he called a morally corrupt government, which permits abortions and makes accommodations for gays and lesbians. Some victims were angry that Rudolph did not get the death penalty; others were relieved that there would not be a trial and they had some explanation for his terrorist acts.

It is possible for the parties to negotiate a final plea after the trial has begun. In the case of Ted Kaczynski, a few weeks before the scheduled date of the trial the defense offered to plead guilty in exchange for a sentence of life without parole. The U.S. Department of Justice, however, recommended that the plea be rejected, and it was. This decision was questioned by some, who pointed out the irony that, after the defendant's alleged attempt at suicide, "having insisted on the death penalty, the Government is now engaged in the bizarre exercise of trying to prevent Mr. Kaczynski from killing himself so that it can continue to spend enormous amounts of money and court time trying to execute him." The *New York Times* editorialist concluded that pressing a capital trial in this case "will only prolong this costly legal farce." The amount of evidence suggesting that the defendant was mentally ill probably would have been sufficient to trigger a successful appeal if he had been convicted.[79] A plea was accepted in this case, and the defendant was sentenced to life without parole. Kaczynski, who was representing himself at the time of the plea, subsequently claimed that the plea was involuntary. He appealed his conviction, but it was upheld by the federal appellate court, and the U.S. Supreme Court refused to hear the case, thus permitting the conviction to stand.[80]

Once a plea bargain is reached, the defense and prosecution submit formal papers to the judge, who must accept or reject the agreement. The judge is not required to abide by any promise made by the prosecution. Thus, after plea negotiations, it is possible for the defendant to enter a guilty plea with the understanding that a particular sentence will be imposed and subsequently be faced with a different, even harsher sentence.

Generally judges may not participate in plea negotiations in federal cases, although some state and local jurisdictions permit this practice. When judges participate in plea bargaining, they may suggest directly or indirectly the sentence that might be imposed in the case, encourage defense attorneys and prosecutors to reach a settlement, nudge defendants to accept the plea negotiation decision, or intervene actively in the negotiations.

Some jurisdictions permit victims to be a part of the plea negotiations if they choose to do so. Some victims do not want to participate; others may be too vindictive or too lenient, but at a minimum victims should be kept informed of the proceedings at all stages in the pretrial procedures. Whether they should participate actively in plea negotiations is controversial. Some argue that it would give defendants a chance to begin the rehabilitation process by being confronted by the victim. It would give victims an opportunity to see the defendant as a whole person. Others take the position that the participation of victims would be disruptive to the system and would have a negative impact on victims.

One final issue regarding plea bargaining is important. Recall that earlier in this chapter we discussed the directive issued by U.S. Attorney General John Ashcroft concerning prosecutorial discretion. Ashcroft was calling for charging suspects with the most serious crimes in most cases. At the same time, the attorney general all but called for the elimination of plea bargaining. This directive was certain to increase the number of federal trials at a time when federal court dockets are already overcrowded. One sentencing expert stated, "If even just a small fraction of the 96 percent of all defendants who currently plead guilty end up going to trial, the courts will be overrun in no time." The federal directive came at a time when, primarily because of budget cuts, many states were looking for ways to reduce the number of trials and the amount of time offenders serve in prison. The result could be significantly longer prison terms for federal than for state offenders convicted of the same or similar crimes.[81] As noted earlier, Ashcroft resigned as attorney general in late 2004; perhaps the charging policies will change as a result.

Chapter Wrap-Up

This chapter discussed the attorneys who prosecute and defend in criminal cases and continued through an overview of the pretrial procedures in which they engage. It began with a historical overview of the legal profession before turning to the prosecution of a criminal case. In its analysis of the prosecution, the chapter looked briefly at the historical emergence of public prosecution, contrasting that approach with the method of private prosecution that was its predecessor in the United States and that still exists in some other countries.

U.S. public prosecution systems are varied. Although most prosecutors are elected officials, their functions and the structures of their offices differ, depending on the size of the jurisdiction and the complexities of local needs. State systems of prosecution, like those at the federal level, may be quite large. They differ from local systems in some respects. State and federal prosecutors may issue opinions on the constitutionality of their respective state and federal statutes. In addition, they are charged with the prosecution of state and federal crimes, and, like local prosecutors, they must make important decisions on which cases to prosecute and which charges to bring in each case.

This authority to determine whom to prosecute and which charges to bring when there are several options gives prosecutors tremendous power. Generally a decision not to prosecute ends the case. Once the initial decision to prosecute has been made, prosecutors may drop charges. Charges may be dropped for a lack of evidence or for political or personal reasons. This power is virtually unchecked. Even when the prosecutorial decision to drop charges occurs after the defendant has made a court appearance and the judge must approve the prosecutor's decision, the prosecutor has immense power in the final determination. Frequently judges defer to prosecutors, who may insist that they are overworked, that their resources are limited, and that there is not enough evidence to continue the prosecution.

Such extensive power may lead to abuse. Prosecutors may abuse their discretion in many ways. They may charge defendants with crimes for which they have little or no evidence in order to coerce the defendants to plead guilty to crimes for which they have sufficient evidence. This avoids trials and reduces the prosecutors' caseloads while providing them with "victories."

The second focus of the chapter was on the defense of a criminal case. It began with an overview of the defense attorney's role, followed by a discussion of the right to counsel. The evolution and current status of the right to appointed counsel for indigent defendants was explored, culminating with the critical *Gideon* decision in 1963, in which the U.S. Supreme Court held that the right to appointed counsel for indigents is not limited to capital cases but applies to other felonies as well. In 1972, the right to appointed counsel for indigents was extended. In *Argersinger* v. *Hamlin* the Supreme Court held that no one may be sentenced to incarceration, even for a short time or for a petty offense, without having had benefit of counsel at trial.

The right to appointed counsel does not exist at all pretrial and post-trial stages, although it does exist at critical stages. The right to counsel also involves a right to refuse counsel. Defendants may serve as their own attorneys, provided their waivers of counsel have been made knowingly and intelligently. They may retain private counsel if they prefer and can afford to do so.

The right to counsel implies a right to effective counsel, which has been defined by the U.S. Supreme Court in *Strickland* v. *Washington* as involving a two-prong test. The defendant must show that counsel was deficient and that deficiency resulted in prejudice to the defendant, who as a result did not get a fair trial. This standard is very difficult to prove, but the courts must consider the totality of the circumstances in making their decisions concerning whether a defendant had effective assistance of counsel. The chapter updated the issue of effective assistance of counsel by looking at cases decided since *Strickland*.

The discussion of defense closed with an explanation of the three major systems by which appointed counsel are provided: the public defender system, the assigned counsel system, and the contract system, noting how they differ from each other and from the use of privately retained defense counsel.

The interaction of the defense attorney and the prosecutor is important during criminal proceedings. The pretrial procedures that are the focus of their interaction were the subject of the final section of the chapter. These procedures include some of the most critical issues and most difficult procedures in criminal justice systems. All of the pretrial court hearings are crucial, for at any stage failure to find probable cause must result in the release of the defendant. If any rights of the accused are violated during arrest, interrogation, investigation, or search and seizure, the evidence secured as a result of those violations may be excluded from the trial. Without the illegally seized evidence, many cases must be dismissed for lack of probable cause. The initial appearance, the preliminary hearing, the grand jury review, and the arraignment are concerned with the issue of determining whether there is sufficient evidence to continue the case.

The critical roles of the prosecution and the defense in these stages cannot be overemphasized. Prosecutorial discretion to drop the charges after the police have arrested a suspect may negate police crime control efforts. However, that discretionary power may serve as a check on overzealous police officers. Even after the formal charges are filed with the court, either through a prosecutorial information or a grand jury indictment, the prosecutor has considerable influence in getting those charges dismissed. This dismissal may be done for good reasons, such as lack of evidence, or for bad reasons, such as discrimination or political pressure. Prosecutors have great power at the stage of grand jury review, because grand juries usually return a true bill on indictments submitted by the prosecution.

The role of the defense attorney is to protect defendants' rights at all pretrial stages and to plan the defense strategy, should the case go to trial. The role of the judge is important as well. He or she presides over all formal court hearings and has the power to grant or deny motions, to grant or deny bail in most cases, and to accept or reject guilty pleas. To a great extent, the judge controls the timing of all the stages, as he or she sets dates for the court hearings and for the trial. If a guilty plea has been accepted, usually the judge has the power to impose sentencing at that time.

Two critical procedures discussed in this chapter raise controversial issues in our criminal justice systems: the decision whether to release or to detain defendants pending trial and the practice of plea bargaining. The decision whether to release a defendant on bail or to allow another alternative requires the judge to predict whether that person would appear for trial if released prior to trial. With recent legislation in some jurisdictions permitting pretrial detention for preventive purposes, some judges have the power to detain if they think the defendant is a danger to society. These are not easy decisions in a world in which predicting human behavior is inaccurate, yet the decision to detain imposes great burdens on defendants, who are inconvenienced and may lose their jobs, suffer the indignities and embarrassments of a jail term, and in some cases suffer physical attacks by other inmates. For those who are acquitted of the crimes for which they are charged, pretrial detention is an incredible injustice. For society, pretrial release may mean more crime; however, pretrial detention creates the need for more facilities, thus increasing the cost of criminal justice systems.

Plea bargaining is another procedure that raises many issues. The practice is necessary as long as we have high crime rates and insufficient facilities and personnel to try all cases. The practice allows the flexibility necessary if the system is to respond with any degree of concern for the circumstances of individual cases. But that flexibility may lead to abuse of discretion, resulting in bitter defendants, some of whom have reasonable justification for believing that they have been treated unfairly by the system. Plea bargaining may entice defendants to plead guilty to crimes they did not commit rather than risk their constitutional right to trial. Such a choice might, and usually does, result in conviction.

As with other chapters, Chapter 7 discussed issues relating to the 9/11/01 terrorist attacks. Such issues include prosecutorial discretion and plea bargaining, as well as the detention of foreign nationals for unlimited periods of time at the U.S. Naval Base in Guantanamo, Cuba, without formal charges or access to attorneys. In 2004, the U.S. Supreme Court held that this policy violates the constitutional rights of those detainees.

Many of the subjects discussed in this chapter are important to Chapter 8 as well. Attorneys and judges are the major professionals in the trial, as well as during pretrial procedures. Plea bargaining may continue. Many of the motions made at pretrial may be made during the trial. The issue of whether a detained defendant should be released from jail may be reconsidered; likewise, the decision to release a defendant pending trial may be revoked when changes in the circumstances warrant that decision. Both prosecution and defense may continue the investigation to secure more evidence to present at trial, particularly during a long trial. The stages in criminal justice systems are not separable. Some procedures and issues, however, are peculiar to the criminal trial, the focus of Chapter 8, which also discusses the stages of sentence and appeal.

Key Terms

arraignment *(p. 194)*
assigned counsel *(p. 189)*
bail *(p. 196)*
bond *(p. 198)*
booking *(p. 191)*
defendant *(p. 174)*
defense attorney *(p. 182)*
deposition *(p. 195)*
discovery *(p. 194)*
grand jury *(p. 179)*
indictment *(p. 179)*

information *(p. 179)*
initial appearance *(p. 193)*
interrogatories *(p. 195)*
lineup *(p. 192)*
motion *(p. 194)*
nolo contendere *(p. 194)*
plea bargaining *(p. 200)*
preliminary hearing *(p. 193)*
presentment *(p. 194)*
pretrial detention *(p. 197)*
preventive detention *(p. 197)*

pro se *(p. 185)*
prosecuting attorney *(p. 177)*
prosecution *(p. 174)*
public defender *(p. 188)*
right to counsel *(p. 183)*
showup *(p. 192)*
subpoena *(p. 196)*
true bill *(p. 194)*
venue *(p. 195)*
waiver *(p. 185)*

Apply It

1. Contrast the current with the historical views held by the public about U.S. lawyers.
2. Why did a system of public prosecution develop, and what is the difference between public and private prosecution? Which system do you think is better?
3. Compare local, state, and federal prosecution systems.
4. What is the main function of a prosecutor? Why is the prosecutor allowed so much discretion in fulfilling that role? What are the problems with allowing such discretion?
5. How can prosecutorial discretion be kept within reasonable limits? Evaluate one example of prosecutorial misconduct discussed in the chapter.
6. What is meant by the *right to counsel?* Describe briefly what that right means today, compared with its historical meaning in the United States.
7. What is the importance of the *Gideon* case?
8. What is the scope of the right to appointed counsel? Should it be expanded? Should it apply to the detention of those suspected of terrorist acts? If not, why not? If so, under what circumstances?
9. Do you think a defendant should have the right to refuse counsel? Explain your answer.

10. What does the U.S. Supreme Court mean by *effective assistance of counsel?* If you had the opportunity to define that term for the Court, what would you include?
11. Enumerate and explain the three major systems by which appointed counsel are provided.
12. How would you suggest improving the availability and quality of legal defense counsel?
13. Would you prefer to be a defense attorney or a prosecuting attorney? Why?
14. Define each of the major steps in the criminal justice process before trial.
15. What restrictions are placed on the securing of physical evidence from a suspect?
16. Describe the main purposes of the *initial appearance, preliminary hearing,* and *arraignment.*
17. What is a *grand jury indictment?* How does that process differ from a prosecutor's *information?*
18. Distinguish between *depositions* and *interrogatories.*
19. What should be considered in deciding whether to release a defendant prior to trial?
20. What is the *bail bond system,* and why is it controversial today?
21. Which of the alternatives to a bail bond system do you think is most feasible? Why?

22. What should be the goals and purposes of detention prior to trial? Should foreign nationals be treated differently than others? Should it make a difference where they are detained? What do you think of the U.S. Supreme Court ruling in this case?

23. Describe the process of pleading guilty before trial. Does it make any difference whether the plea is a negotiated one?

24. Do you think plea bargaining should be abolished? Why? If it is, what might result?

25. Evaluate some of the recent high-profile cases involving plea bargaining.

26. What do you think about the directive by John Ashcroft that essentially eliminates plea bargaining in the federal system?

Endnotes

1. Quoted in "Those #*X!!! Lawyers," *Time* (10 April 1978), p. 66.

2. Alexis de Tocqueville, "The Temper of the Legal Profession in the United States," in *Before the Law: An Introduction to the Legal Process*, ed. John J. Bonsignore et al. (Boston: Houghton Mifflin, 1974), p. 151.

3. James Willard Hurst, *Growth of American Law* (Boston: Little, Brown, 1950), p. 6.

4. See Peter H. Rossi, "Occupational Prestige in the United States, 1925–1963," *American Journal of Sociology* 70 (November 1964): 286–302.

5. Bailey Morris, "Lawyers' Images of Yesteryear Are Crumbling Fast," *Washington Star* (13 September 1976), p. 1A.

6. Ibid.

7. "Burger Warns about a Society Overrun by Lawyers," *New York Times* (28 May 1977), p. 1.

8. Whitney North Seymour Jr., *Why Justice Fails* (New York: Morrow, 1973), p. 7.

9. "Tough Market? Just Ask Altheimer & Gray How Tough," *Chicago Daily Law Bulletin* (8 May 2003), p. 1; "Law Firms Collapse, Others Merge in Whirlwind 2003," *Chicago Lawyer* (December 2003), p. 12.

10. "The Attorney, Unemployed," *Broward Daily Business Review* 44, no. 101 (2 May 2003): 8.

11. "Firms Remain Stable in Illinois, Grow Outside of State," *Chicago Lawyer* (May 2003), p. 8.

12. See Abraham S. Goldstein, "Prosecution: History of the Public Prosecutor," in *Encyclopedia of Crime and Justice*, vol. 3, ed. Sanford H. Kadish (New York: Macmillan, 1983), pp. 1286–1289.

13. Joan E. Jacoby, *The American Prosecutor: A Search for Identity* (Lexington, Mass.: D.C. Heath, 1980), pp. 55–61, 64–65, 71–74, 275, 277, 278.

14. *ABA Standards for Criminal Justice: The Prosecution Function*, Standard 3-1.2, approved by the ABA House of Delegates February 1992.

15. State v. Mitchell, 395 A.2d 1257 (Sup.Ct.App.Div. N.J. 1978).

16. "Man Guilty of Concealing Boys' Killing of Father," *New York Times* (6 March 2003), p. 20.

17. "Kings Sent to Juvenile Facilites," *Pensacola News Journal* (17 December 2002), p. 1.

18. "Prosecutorial Outrage in Florida," *New York Times* (21 October 2002), p. 22.

19. United States v. Armstrong, 517 U.S. 456 (1996).

20. Oyler v. Boles, 368 U.S. 448, 456 (1962).

21. "Ashcroft Imposes New Limits on Prosecutors' Charging Discretion," *Criminal Justice Newsletter* (1 October 2003), p. 7.

22. Yick Wo v. Hopkins, 118 U.S. 356 (1886). In the *Yick Wo* case, a public board that was authorized to issue laundry licenses denied licenses to Chinese applicants and granted licenses to most white applicants.

23. Brady v. Maryland, 373 U.S. 83 (1963).

24. "Tried and Tried Again: Defense Lawyers Say the D.A. Went Too Far Prosecuting a Louisiana Man Five Times for Murder," *American Bar Association Journal* 84 (April 1998): 38.

25. "Report Cites Convictions Reversed Due to Prosecutorial Misconduct," *Criminal Justice Newsletter* (15 July 2003), p. 4. The report, *Harmful Error: Investigating America's Local Prosecutors*, is available on the Internet at www.publicintegrity.org.

26. State v. Gaughran, 615 A.2d 1293 (N.J. Superior, 1992).

27. See, for example, "Prosecution in Diallo Case Now Finds Itself Accused," *New York Times* (28 February 2000), p. 19.

28. Powell v. Alabama, 287 U.S. 45 (1932). See also Wayne R. LaFave and Jerold H. Israel, *Criminal Procedure* (St. Paul, Minn.: West, 1985), pp. 473–475. This source was used for the historical background discussion of the right to counsel.

29. Johnson v. Zerbst, 304 U.S. 458 (1938).

30. Betts v. Brady, 316 U.S. 455 (1942), *overruled*, Gideon v. Wainwright, 372 U.S. 335 (1963).

31. Gideon v. Wainwright, 372 U.S. 335 (1963).

32. Argersinger v. Hamlin, 407 U.S. 25, 37 (1972).

33. Scott v. Illinois, 440 U.S. 367 (1979).

34. United States v. Wade, 388 U.S. 218 (1967).

35. Alabama v. Shelton, 535 U.S. 654 (2002).

36. Diggs v. Welch, 148 F.2d 667 (D.C.Cir. 1945); *cert denied*, 325 U.S. 889 (1945).

37. Strickland v. Washington, 466 U.S. 668 (1984).

38. Edward M. Kennedy, "Sen. Kennedy: George Case Mocks Gideon Promise," *Fulton County Daily Report* 3, no. 25 (25 March 2003): no page number. The case is Wallace M. Fugate III v. Head, 261 F.3d 1206 (11th Cir. 2001), *cert. denied*, 535 U.S. 1104 (2002).

39. Kennedy, ibid.

40. Burdine v. Johnson, 66 F.Supp. 2d 854 (S.D. Tex. 1999), *stay denied, mot. granted, in part, denied, in part*, 87 F.Supp. 2d 711 (S.D. Tex. 2000), *vacated, remanded*, 231 F.3d 950 (5th Cir. 2000), *and on reh'g., aff'd.*, 262 F.3d 326 (5th Cir. 2001), *cert. denied*, 535 U.S. 1120 (2002).

41. "Burdine Pleads Guilty, Gets Three Consecutive Life Sentences," *Texas Lawyer* 19, no. 16 (23 June 2003): 8.

42. Mickens v. Taylor, 535 U.S. 162 (2002).

43. Lawson v. State, 766 P.2d 261 (Nev. 1988).

44. "Lawyers Often Fail New York's Poor," *New York Times* (8 March 2001), p. l; "Caseloads Push System to Breaking Point," *New York Times* (9 March 2001), p. 1; "Appeals for the Poor Don't Pay for the Lawyers Assigned to the Case," *New York Times* (10 March 2001), p. l.

45. "County Says It's Too Poor to Defend the Poor," *New York Times* (15 April 2003), p. l.

46. "Judge Rules Counties, not State, Must Pay for Poor People's Lawyers," *Commercial Appeal* (Memphis, Tenn) (11 November 2003), p. 4B.

47. "Montana Aims to Fix Public Defender System," *Chicago Tribune*, Final Edition (21 June 2005), p. 11.

48. For details of the study, see *Good Practices for Federal Panel Attorney Programs: A Preliminary Study of Plans and Practices,* a 39-page report available on the Internet at www.vera.org; the report is summarized in "Some Successes Identified in Bolstering Indigent Defense," *Criminal Justice Newsletter* (16 August 2003), p. 2.

49. "Romney Vetoes $201M in Spending Local Aid," *Boston Globe* (1 July 2003), p. 1.

50. "Aiding Legal Aid," *American Bar Association Journal* 88 (June 2002): 28.

51. "Texas Death Row Appeals Lawyers Criticized," *New York Times* (3 December 2002), p. 24.

52. "The 50 States Make Tough Decisions on Cuts," *National Law Journal* 25, no. 81 (19 May 2003): 10.

53. See *Cultural Revolution: Transforming the Public Defender's Office,* available from the National Criminal Justice Reference Service, P.O. Box 6000, Rockville, MD 20849-6000, cited in "Public Defenders See Wider Role in Helping Clients Outside Court," *Criminal Justice Newsletter* 32, no. 20 (6 November 2002): 4–5.

54. Justice for All Act of 2004, Public Law 108-405 (2005).

55. Wood v. Georgia, 370 U.S. 375, 390 (1962).

56. "Four Officers' Trial Moved to Albany," *New York Times* (17 December 1999), p. 1; "Why Justice Had to Get Out of Town," *New York Times* (17 December 1999), p. 31.

57. Powell v. Alabama, 287 U.S. 45, 57 (1932).

58. See U.S. Code, Title 18, Section 3142(c)(1) (2005).

59. Stack v. Boyle, 342 U.S. 1 (1951).

60. United States v. Edwards, 430 A.2d 1321 (D.C.Ct.App. 1981), *cert. denied,* 455 U.S. 1022 (1982).

61. Schall v. Martin, 467 U.S. 253 (1984).

62. The Bail Reform Act can be found in U.S. Code, Chapter 18, Sections 3141 et.seq. (2005).

63. United States v. Salerno, 481 U.S. 739 (1987).

64. Rasul v. Bush, 124 S.Ct. 2633 (2004) footnotes omitted.

65. Hamdi v. Rumsfeld, 316 F.3d 450 (4th Cir. 2003), *vacated, remanded,* 124 S.Ct. 2633 (2004), *on remand, remanded* 378 F. 3d 426 (4th Cir. 2004).

66. Padilla v. Hanft, 2005 U.S. Dist. LEXIS 2921 (D.S.C.) (28 February 2005).

67. Johnson v. Zerbst, 304 U.S. 458 (1938).

68. Santobello v. New York, 404 U.S. 257, 260–61 (1971).

69. "Grant Clemency to Lionel Tate," *Sun-Sentinel* (Ft. Lauderdale, Fla.) (2 July 2003), p. 24.

70. Tate v. State, 864 So.2d 44 (Fla.Dist.Ct.App. 4th Dist. 2003).

71. "New Trial for Boy with Life Term in Killing of Playmate in Florida," *New York Times* (11 December 2003), p. 1.

72. "Florida Youth Who Got Life Term for a Killing Is Freed at 16," *New York Times* (27 January 2004), p. 12.

73. "National Briefing South: Florida: Teenager Can Serve Probation at Home," *New York Times* (30 November 2004), p. 16.

74. Corbitt v. New Jersey, 439 U.S. 212 (1978).

75. Mabry v. Johnson, 467 U.S. 504 (1984).

76. Bordenkircher v. Hayes, 434 U.S. 357, 360–365 (1978).

77. United States v. Mezzanatto, 513 U.S. 196 (1995).

78. "In Deal for Life, Man Admits Killing 48 Women," *New York Times* (6 November 2003), p. 1.

79. "The Unabomber Travesty," *New York Times* (10 January 1998), p. 24.

80. United States v. Kacynski, 239 F.3d 1108 (9th Cir. 2001), *cert. denied,* 535 U.S. 933 (2002).

81. "New Plea Bargain Limits Could Swamp Courts, Experts Say," *New York Times* (24 September 2003), p. 1.

Trial, Sentencing, and Appeal

Chapter 7 noted that most cases are not tried, and in 2003 yet one more study confirmed this fact in the federal system, pointing out that since 1962 both civil and criminal trials had decreased. The study reported that between 1962 and 2000 the number of federal criminal cases going to trial fell from 5,096 to 3,574. In percentages, this means that in 1962 approximately 15 percent of federal criminal cases went to trial, compared with 5 percent in 2000. The percentage of federal civil cases going to trial in 2000 was 1.8, compared with 11.5 percent in 1962. One federal judge described these changes as follows: "What's documented here . . . is nothing less than the passing of the common law adversarial system that is uniquely American."[1]

The reason we have fewer trials despite the larger number of cases is that more cases are resolved out of court. In the civil arena more cases are settled through negotiations that might include mediation or arbitration; in the criminal area more are resolved through plea bargains. In both the civil and the criminal venues these changes may be occurring because of the increased complexity and the high cost of trials. Another reason might be the changes in sentencing practices, which are discussed in this chapter.

For the cases that do proceed to trial, however, especially in the criminal area, it is important to know the rules and constitutional principles that govern the processes involved. This chapter begins with a discussion of defendants' constitutional rights at trial and explains the major processes that occur during criminal trials.

Sentencing, which may occur even in cases that are not tried, is a critical part of criminal justice systems and is discussed at some length in this chapter. The concept and process of sentencing is explained; types of sentences are discussed, with particular emphasis on the death penalty; and significant attention is given to current sentencing issues. These issues include sentence disparity and the recent approaches of three strikes and you're out and truth in sentencing—both punitive approaches that have dominated sentencing in recent years. But the chapter also pays attention to the recent diminishing of sentences through a treatment approach.

Finally, the chapter turns to the procedures through which convictions and sentences are challenged, by discussing appeals and writs.

OBJECTIVES

After reading this chapter, you should be able to do the following:

- **State an overview of defendants' constitutional rights**
- **Explain the defendant's right to a speedy, public trial by an impartial jury**
- **Discuss the variables of gender, race, age, and disability in jury selection**
- **List and explain the stages in the trial and appeal of a criminal case in the United States**
- **Explain how evidence is presented in a criminal trial and discuss the various types of evidence and objections to evidence**
- **Distinguish the prosecution's case from the case of the defense**
- **Discuss the role of the jury in deciding a criminal case**
- **Explain and analyze the concept and process of sentencing and sentencing strategies**
- **Discuss the sentencing hearing and decision**
- **List and define the major types of sentences**
- **Describe the use of sentencing guidelines by states and the federal government**
- **Explain the difference between indeterminate and determinate sentencing and evaluate each**
- **Explore the meaning, causes, and consequences of sentence disparity**
- **Discuss the meaning and impact of three strikes and truth in sentencing legislation**
- **Consider the impact of a treatment approach to sentencing**
- **Describe appeals and writs**

8-1   Constitutional Issues at Trial

This analysis of constitutional issues at trial is not meant to be exclusive. It must be understood in the context of the discussions in earlier chapters, but it focuses on the constitutional issues and rights that pertain primarily to a trial in a U.S adult criminal court.

8-1a   Speedy Trial

> **Trial**   In criminal law, court proceedings during which a judge, a jury, or both listen to the evidence as presented by the defense and the prosecution and determine whether the defendant is guilty beyond a reasonable doubt.

The right to a speedy **trial** is embodied in the Sixth Amendment (see Appendix A) to the U.S. Constitution. The U.S. Supreme Court has held that this right "is as fundamental as any of the rights secured by the Sixth Amendment."[2]

In 1974, Congress passed the Speedy Trial Act, which, with its subsequent amendments, provides that, for suspects in federal cases, an indictment or an information charging the suspect must be filed within 30 days of the arrest or of the time when the suspect is served with a summons on the charge. That period may be extended for 30 days in a felony charge if the grand jury was not in session during that time. It is possible for the defendant to be tried so quickly that there would not be adequate time for preparing a defense. The Speedy Trial Act provides that, without the consent of the defendant, "the trial shall not commence less than thirty days from the date on which the defendant first appears through counsel or expressly waives counsel and elects to proceed pro se [on his or her own]."[3]

Some delays are permissible under the Speedy Trial Act. Several are listed in the act, including the obvious ones, such as those delays caused by examinations to determine whether the defendant is competent to stand trial; delays caused by the defendant's mental incompetence to stand trial; and delays caused by deferred prosecution when that is agreed upon by the prosecutor, the defendant, and the court. The act permits delays caused by continuances requested by the defense or the prosecution when they are granted to serve the ends of justice.

The Speedy Trial Act applies only to prosecutions in federal courts, but most states have constitutional provisions for the right to a speedy trial. For example, a New York statute provides for a speedy trial as well as a trial by an impartial jury. The statute, entitled *Rights of persons accused of crime,* is as follows:

> In all criminal prosecutions, the accused has a right to a speedy and public trial, by an impartial jury, and is entitled to be informed of the nature and cause of the accusation; to be confronted with the witnesses against him; and to have compulsory process for obtaining witnesses in his favor.[4]

In addition, most states have procedural or statutory rules denoting how many days may elapse between arrest and trial. Texas, for example, provides as follows:

> Insofar as is practicable, the trial of a criminal action shall be given preference over trials of civil cases, and the trial of a criminal action against a defendant who is detained in jail pending trial of the action shall be given preference over trials of other criminal actions.[5]

The Texas rules of criminal procedure provide specifically that an adult trial court shall entertain a motion to set aside an indictment, an information, or a complaint if the state is not prepared to go to trial within a specified time after these methods of beginning criminal cases have begun. The time permitted is 180 days for a felony case; 90 days for a misdemeanor punishable by more than 180 days in prison; and 60 days for a misdemeanor punishable by less than 180 days in prison or by a fine only.[6]

8-1b Public Trial

The Sixth Amendment guarantees the right to a public trial. This right does not mean that the defendant may be tried by the media. If it can be shown that the defendant cannot get a fair trial because of publicity in the jurisdiction in which the case is to be tried, the trial should be moved to another jurisdiction.

Media publicity in criminal cases raises a delicate problem: the conflict between the First Amendment (see Appendix A) free speech right of the press and the public's right to know and the defendant's right to a trial by an impartial jury not biased by media information.

The U.S. Supreme Court has had several occasions to consider the conflict between the defendant's right to a fair trial and the First Amendment rights of the press. In a 1966 case, the Court overturned the conviction of Dr. Sam Sheppard, who had served 10 years in prison after his conviction for murdering his wife. On retrial Sheppard was acquitted. In overturning Sheppard's conviction the Supreme Court said,

> Murder and mystery, society, sex and suspense were combined in this case in such a manner as to intrigue and captivate the public fancy to a degree perhaps unparalleled in recent annals. Throughout the preindictment investigation, the subsequent legal skirmishes and the nine-week trial, circulation-conscious editors catered to the insatiable interest of the American public in the bizarre. . . . In this atmosphere of a "Roman holiday" for the news media, Sam Sheppard stood trial for his life.[7]

In subsequent cases the U.S. Supreme Court has continued to wrestle with the rights of defendants versus those of the press and the public. The Court has held that under some circumstances the former must give way to the latter. For example, in *Globe Newspaper Co. v. Superior Court* the Court invalidated a Massachusetts statute that had been interpreted to mean exclusion of the press from *all* trials when sexual offense victims under the age of 18 were testifying. The Court ruled that each case must be examined in terms of its own facts, such as "the minor victim's age, psychological maturity and understanding, the nature of the crime, the desires of the victim, and the interests of parents and relatives."[8]

In some highly publicized cases it has been argued that the defendant cannot get a fair public trial in any jurisdiction. Thus, Timothy McVeigh, who was tried on capital charges and convicted for the murders resulting from the bombing of the federal building in

Oklahoma City, Oklahoma, on 19 April 1995, argued unsuccessfully that he could not get a fair trial. In addition to immense publicity about the bombing and its victims, the media carried articles stating that McVeigh had confessed to his attorneys. After two of these articles were published, McVeigh's attorneys asked the court to dismiss the charges against their client—or, in the alternative, grant a long continuance. The district court denied the motions, and the federal appellate court affirmed. The venue of the trial was moved from Oklahoma to Denver, Colorado—an action, claimed the appellate court, that significantly lessened the chance of prejudice in the selection of a jury. Members of the jury pool were subjected to numerous questions in an attempt to secure jurors who could analyze the evidence objectively, and the appellate court was not convinced that McVeigh did not have fair jurors.[9] McVeigh was scheduled to be executed in May 2001, but after it was discovered that the Federal Bureau of Investigation had failed to disclose over 3,000 pages of documents to the defense, that execution was postponed. McVeigh was executed in June 2001.

8-1c   Trial by Jury

The Sixth Amendment (see Appendix A) guarantees the defendant in a criminal case the right to a trial by **jury.** Technically the jury that sits in a trial is called the **petit jury.** The word *petit* means minor, small, or inconsequential, but in this context it is used to distinguish the trial jury from the larger grand jury, not to carry the connotation of inconsequential.

The importance of the right to a jury trial, along with a brief history of its evolution, was emphasized by the U.S. Supreme Court in 1968 in *Duncan v. Louisiana*. This case involved a defendant who was charged with simple battery, a misdemeanor punishable by a maximum of two years' imprisonment and a $300 fine. Duncan's request for a trial by jury was denied by a Louisiana trial court. At that time, the Louisiana constitution granted jury trials only in cases in which convicted defendants could be sentenced to imprisonment at hard labor or to capital punishment. Duncan was convicted of the crime charged, sentenced to 60 days in the parish prison, and fined $150. The Louisiana Supreme Court denied his request for an appeal. Duncan appealed to the U.S. Supreme Court, alleging that he had been denied his constitutional right to a jury trial. That Court agreed, as illustrated by the following brief excerpt.[10]

> **Jury**   In a criminal case, a group of people who have been sworn in at court to listen to a trial and to decide whether the defendant is guilty or not guilty. In some jurisdictions, juries may determine or recommend sentences.

> **Petit jury**   *Petit* literally means "small, minor, or inconsiderate"; a trial jury, in contrast to a grand jury. *See also* **jury.**

Duncan v. Louisiana

A right to jury trial is granted to criminal defendants in order to prevent oppression by the Government.... Providing an accused with the right to be tried by a jury of his peers gave him an inestimable safeguard against the corrupt or overzealous prosecutor and against the compliant, biased, or eccentric judge.... [T]he jury trial provisions in the Federal and State Constitutions reflect a fundamental decision about the exercise of official power—a reluctance to entrust plenary powers over the life and liberty of the citizen to one judge or to a group of judges.... The deep commitment of the Nation to the right of jury trial in serious criminal cases as a defense against arbitrary law enforcement qualifies for protection under the Due Process Clause of the Fourteenth Amendment, and must therefore be respected by the States.

Although it held that Duncan was entitled to a trial by jury, the U.S. Supreme Court did say in passing "that there is a category of petty crimes or offenses which is not subject to the Sixth Amendment jury trial provision." Further, the right to a jury trial may be waived, provided it is done knowingly, intelligently, voluntarily, and in writing and it is accepted by the trial court judge.

The U.S. Constitution does not specify how many jurors must be present in order for the defendant's right to a jury trial to be legal. Although 12 is the usual number of petit jurors, the U.S. Supreme Court has upheld the use of smaller juries in some cases. But there must be at least 6 jurors, and a jury that small must be unanimous. A unanimous vote is required in all federal jury trials.

The Sixth Amendment provides for the right to trial by an *impartial* jury, which means a number of things, including the right to a jury not prejudiced unduly by media publicity. We have noted that in some cases it is necessary to move the location of the trial to eliminate the impact of extensive publicity in the area in which the crime occurred. However, that might not be possible because of extensive national publicity. In those instances the trial judge may order the jury sequestered for the trial, but a very long sequestration might work against the defense (or the prosecution, if the sequestration is perceived as prolonging the trial unnecessarily) and certainly is disruptive to the lives of the jurors, their families and friends, and their employers.

Some states have mandatory requirements for sequestration in serious cases. In 2001, the New York legislature unanimously enacted a statute deleting its 100-year-old requirement that all juries that deliberate for more than a day be sequestered (since 1995, exceptions had been made for some low-level criminal cases). The bill was signed by the governor within hours and became effective immediately. New York had the strictest sequestration requirements in the country. Under the present law juries may be sequestered only upon orders of the trial judge.[11]

The Sixth Amendment provides for a trial by a jury of the defendant's peers, which has been interpreted by the U.S. Supreme Court to involve implications for the exclusion of people from the jury on the basis of specific characteristics, such as gender, race, and religion. Despite the acceptance of the process of excusing some potential jurors, our statutes and court decisions establish guidelines on exclusions that may be made in the composition of juries.

> Juries must be representative of the community, but that does not mean that juries must mirror the community and reflect the various distinctive groups in the population. Defendants are not entitled to a jury of any particular composition, but the jury wheels, pools of names, panels, or venires [lists of persons summoned to serve in the jury pool for a particular case] from which juries are drawn must not systematically exclude distinctive groups in the community and thereby fail to be reasonably representative thereof.[12]

It is not clear what is meant by *the community*, but exclusions based on race and gender are not permitted. It is the *systematic exclusion* of particular groups of persons from the jury pool or jury selection that constitutes a constitutional issue, illustrated primarily by the U.S. Supreme Court's rulings regarding the exclusion of African Americans from juries. In 1880, the Supreme Court held that a statute permitting only white men to serve on juries was unconstitutional. In 1965, the Court held that it was permissible to exclude individual African Americans by using a **peremptory challenges** (a challenge that does not require the attorney to state a reason), but the Court left open the issue of systematic exclusion of African Americans.[13]

Other decisions were made in the intervening years, but the key decision did not come until 1986 in *Batson* v. *Kentucky*, in which the defendant proved that he was a member of a cognizable racial group whose members were excluded from the jury under circumstances that raised an inference that they were excluded because of race. Portions of *Batson* are included in Spotlight 8-1.

In *Batson* the U.S. Supreme Court articulated a three-prong test to use when analyzing an allegation that the peremptory challenge was used to eliminate a potential juror because of race:

- A defendant must show a *prima facie* (on its face) case that a peremptory challenge was based on race.

- If the defendant makes that showing, the prosecution must give a race-neutral explanation for why the juror in question was challenged.

- The trial court judge must consider the evidence submitted for the preceding two reasons and determine whether the defendant has shown purposeful discrimination based on race.[14]

▶ **Peremptory challenge** A challenge that may be used by the prosecution or the defense to excuse a potential juror from the jury panel. No reason is required. Each attorney gets a specified number of peremptory challenges. Peremptory challenges are distinguished from *challenges for cause,* which are unlimited and based on a reason for disqualification, such as a conflict of interest in the case.

Spotlight 8-1   Race and Jury Selection: The *Batson* Rule

[In *Batson* v. *Kentucky,* the U.S. Supreme Court held that it is unconstitutional to exclude African Americans from juries when there is evidence that the exclusion is based on race. The Court stated:]

Petitioner, a black man, was indicted in Kentucky on charges of second-degree burglary and receipt of stolen goods. The prosecutor used his peremptory challenges to strike all four black persons on the venire, and a jury composed only of white persons was selected....

Exclusion of black citizens from service as jurors constitutes a primary example of the evil the Fourteenth Amendment was designed to cure....

The Equal Protection Clause guarantees the defendant that the State will not exclude members of his race from the jury venire on account of race, or on the false assumption that members of his race as a group are not qualified to serve as jurors.... Racial discrimination in selection of jurors harms not only the accused whose life or liberty they are summoned to try. Competence to serve as a juror ultimately depends on an assessment of individual qualifications and ability impartially

to consider evidence presented at a trial. A person's race simply "is unrelated to his fitness as a juror."...

The harm from discriminatory jury selection extends beyond that inflicted on the defendant and the excluded juror to touch the entire community. Selection procedures that purposefully exclude black persons from juries undermine public confidence in the fairness of our system of justice....

Although a prosecutor ordinarily is entitled to exercise permitted peremptory challenges "for any reason at all, as long as that reason is related to his view concerning the outcome" of the case to be tried, the Equal Protection Clause forbids the prosecutor to challenge potential jurors solely on account of their race or on the assumption that black jurors as a group will be unable impartially to consider the State's case against a black defendant.

[The Court discussed procedures for contesting the peremptory challenges and concluded that the conviction in this case should be reversed.]

Source: Batson v. Kentucky, 476 U.S. 79 (1986), citations and footnotes omitted.

Since *Batson,* lower courts and the U.S. Supreme Court have dealt with variations in fact patterns in which the case might apply, including holding that a criminal defendant does not have to be of the same race as the excluded juror to object to race-based exclusions because excluded jurors have a constitutional right not to be excluded from juries based on their race; holding that *Batson* applies equally to the removal of white as well as African American potential jurors and to the defense, as well as to the prosecution; holding that a defendant may challenge a prosecutor's race-based exclusion of a potential juror regardless of whether the defendant and the excluded juror are of the same race; and holding that *Batson* applies to civil as well as to criminal cases.

In 2003, the U.S. Supreme Court again considered the issue of jury selection and racial bias. The case came from Texas and involved a death-row inmate, Thomas Miller-El, an African American who was within one week of his scheduled execution when the U.S. Supreme Court agreed to review his case. Miller-El argued that his conviction was a violation of his constitutional rights because the prosecution eliminated 10 of 11 African Americans from the jury pool. The prosecution claimed that it did so because those potential jurors had indicated that they would hesitate to impose the death penalty. Miller-El presented compelling evidence of a larger pattern of racial discrimination in jury selection in that county. His motion to strike the jury (prior to his conviction) had been rejected, and he was convicted by a jury consisting of only one African American. He was sentenced to death. Miller-El's appeal was rejected by the lower appellate courts, and he asked the U.S. Supreme Court to hear his case. That Court heard the case and decided *Miller-El* v. *Cockrell* by an 8-to-1 vote, holding that Miller-El should have been granted a hearing by the federal circuit court of appeals. The Supreme Court chastised the lower federal court (the Fifth Circuit Court of Appeals), urging that court to rethink its "dismissive and strained interpretation of the proof in the case and to give more serious consideration to the significant evidence pointing to unconstitutional discrimination against black jurors during the jury selection process." Instead of following the orders of the U.S. Supreme Court, the Fifth Circuit gave no relief and quoted extensively from the one dissenting vote in the U.S. Supreme Court's decision, that of Justice Clarence Thomas. One journalist referred to this as "something akin to plagiarism," whereas a former federal judge proclaimed that the lower federal court "just went out of its way to defy the Supreme Court." In a subsequent appeal to the U.S. Supreme court, Miller-El was again successful. In June 2005 the Court, by a 6-to-3 vote, in an opinion written by Justice David Souter, detailed the various tactics and "trickery" that the prosecution had used to exclude African Americans from Miller-El's jury. The tactics included asking different questions of whites and of African Americans (in an apparent attempt to encourage African Americans to disqualify themselves by stating opposition to the death penalty) as well as shuffling the jury pool when too many African Americans appeared in the front of the panel. Justice Souter stated that the prosecution's explanation of their use of their peremptory challenges to exclude African Americans because they were opposed to the death penalty "reeks of afterthought." Justice Clarence Thomas, in a dissenting opinion longer than that of the majority, concluded that the prosecution's position was "eminently reasonable."[15]

Gender is another important category in jury selection. Men and women have a right to serve on juries, and defendants have a right to have both genders as jurors. Thus, in 1994 the U.S. Supreme Court's decision in *Batson* was extended to include gender. *J.E.B.* v. *Alabama ex. rel. T.B* was a civil rather than a criminal case, but it is likely that the holding will apply to criminal cases as well.[16] In this case, Alabama sued J.E.B. to establish paternity and award child support to T.B. (the real names are omitted to protect the child), who alleged that J.E.B. was the father of her minor child. During jury selection, the state used most of its peremptory challenges to remove men from the jury pool, whereas the defense used most of its peremptory challenges to remove women from the pool. An all-female jury was empaneled. The U.S. Supreme Court held that the use of peremptory challenges by the prosecution to exclude men from the jury was unconstitutional because the prosecution did not show "an exceedingly persuasive justification" for doing so. One of the dissenting opinions noted that for every man excluded by the prosecution, the defense excluded a woman; thus, men were not singled out for discriminatory treatment.

Two other categories that might be the basis for exclusion or failure to include are age and disability. The U.S. Supreme Court has not held that defendants have a right to a jury of peers of their own age. In 1985, a lower federal court reversed one of its earlier decisions and held that a young defendant did not have a right to a new trial because young adults from ages 18 to 34 had been underrepresented on the jury. The court held that a "mere statistical disparity in the chosen age group" is not sufficient to establish a violation of the Sixth Amendment right to a jury of one's peers. The defendant must show that the underrepresented group is defined and limited by factors or characteristics that can be defined easily; that the group may be distinguished by a common thread of similarity in attitude, ideas, or experience; and that they have a community of interest. The U.S. Supreme Court refused to hear the case, thus permitting the lower court's decision to stand.[17]

Disability is another issue that must be considered in jury selection. With the emphasis on the rights of persons with disabilities, exemplified by the passage of and the numerous cases being brought under the Americans with Disabilities Act (ADA), consideration must be given to extending the right to serve on juries to those whose physical or mental challenges might have precluded such service in the past.

Finally, those who serve on juries must conduct themselves properly both in and outside the courtroom. In a Houston, Texas, case a juror, age 19, was sentenced to six days in jail and fined $300 for oversleeping and appearing late for jury duty, thus delaying a trial.[18]

8-1d Other Constitutional Issues at Trial

Some constitutional rights of defendants discussed in earlier chapters in connection with the police or with pretrial procedures are applicable during the trial of a criminal case as well. Some of those rights take on their fullest meaning during the trial. For example, defendants must be notified of the charges against them. That notice must occur during the early pretrial stages, but formal charges must be read to the defendant at the trial. A confession obtained or evidence secured in violation of a defendant's rights should not be introduced during the trial because of the exclusionary rule.

Defendants have the right to compel witnesses to testify on their behalf and the right to confront and to cross-examine witnesses who testify against them. These rights and others have been interpreted to mean that defendants have a right to be present at their trials. That right, however, is subject to the defendant's good behavior, as illustrated by the classic case of *Illinois* v. *Allen*, which involved a defendant who appealed his conviction for armed robbery on the grounds that he had been improperly excluded from his trial.

At the beginning of the trial, Allen insisted on being his own lawyer, rejecting the services of his court-appointed counsel. Defendants have the right to refuse counsel, but generally attorneys will be appointed and available for defendants who choose to exercise that right. In the *Allen* case, when the defendant Allen began questioning prospective jurors, the judge interrupted him and asked him to confine his questions to the matters relating to their qualifications. Allen responded in an abusive and disrespectful manner. The judge asked appointed counsel to proceed with the examination of prospective jurors. Allen continued to talk, "proclaiming that the appointed attorney was not going to act as his lawyer. He terminated his remarks by saying, 'When I go out for lunchtime, you're [the judge] going to be a corpse here.'"

Allen took a file from his court-appointed attorney, tore it, and threw it on the floor. The judge warned Allen that he would remove him from the trial if he continued in this manner, but the warning had no effect on Allen's conduct. Allen was removed from the courtroom, and the examination of the potential jurors continued in his absence. Later Allen was returned to the court but was removed again after another outburst. During the presentation of the state's case, Allen was occasionally taken to the courtroom for identification, but he used vile and abusive language in responding to a question from the judge. After assuring the court he would behave, Allen was permitted to be in the courtroom while his attorney presented the case for the defense.

Justice Hugo Black delivered the opinion for the U.S. Supreme Court, which upheld the right of the trial judge to exclude Allen from his own trial. Justice Black pointed out that the trial judge had three constitutionally permissible options in this case. He could have cited Allen for **contempt of court,** excluded him from the trial, or bound and gagged him and left him in the courtroom. Each option was discussed, with the Court noting the possible prejudicial effect that binding and gagging the defendant might have had on the jury.

> Not only is it possible that the sight of shackles and gags might have a significant effect on the jury's feelings about the defendant, but the use of this technique is itself something of an affront to the very dignity and decorum of judicial proceedings that the judge is seeking to uphold.[19]

The U.S. Supreme Court noted that another problem with gagging is that this procedure prevents the defendant from meaningful contact with his attorney. For that reason, the Court refused to hold that the state must use this method in lieu of excluding the defendant from the trial. Further, the Court emphasized the importance of maintaining decorum in the courtroom and concluded that

> [i]f our courts are to remain what the Founders intended, the citadels of justice, their proceedings cannot and must not be infected with the sort of scurrilous, abusive language and conduct paraded before the Illinois trial judge in this case.[20]

In a more recent case, which occurred in 1997 in Alpine, Texas, two members of the Republic of Texas separatist group were ejected eight times because of their attempts to disrupt a trial. Richard McLaren and Robert Otto interrupted the judge frequently while he was instructing the potential jurors. Judge Kenneth DeHart permitted the defendants to return to the courtroom because he wanted them to participate in their trial. The defendants were convicted, but those convictions were reversed on appeal. McLaren, however, is serving 12½ years for a federal fraud conviction. In December 2001, both McLaren and Otto, along with four other members of the Republic of Texas separatist group, were sentenced after their convictions on federal charges stemming from a 1997 standoff with law enforcement officers. McLaren was sentenced to 10 years, whereas Otto received a 5-year sentence.[21]

▶ **Contempt of court**   An act (usually committed in violation of a court order or rule) considered as embarrassing, humiliating, or undermining the power of the court; may be civil or criminal.

Spotlight 8-2   **Stages in the Trial and Appeal of a U.S. Criminal Case**

1. Opening of the court session
2. Jury selection
3. Opening statement by the prosecutor
4. Opening statement by the defense attorney
5. Presentation of evidence by the prosecutor
6. Cross-examination by the defense
7. Redirect examination by the prosecutor
8. Cross-examination by the defense
9. Presentation of the defense's case by the defense attorney
10. Cross-examination by the prosecutor

11. Redirect by the defense
12. Cross-examination by the prosecutor
13. Rebuttal proof by the prosecutor
14. Closing statement by the prosecutor
15. Closing statement by the defense
16. Rebuttal statement by the prosecutor
17. Submittal of the case to the jury
18. The verdict
19. Postverdict motions
20. Sentencing
21. Appeals and writs

8-2   The Trial Process

In this section the stages of a criminal trial are discussed in the order in which they generally occur. Spotlight 8-2 lists those stages, and the discussion follows the order in that list. These stages are not always distinct, however, and some of the procedures may occur at various stages. For example, motions might be made throughout the trial; an obvious motion is one to dismiss or to declare a mistrial, which is made by defense counsel after the prosecutor or a prosecution witness has said something improper. A defense motion for change of venue (change of place of trial) might be made before and during the trial as increased media attention to the trial leads the defense to argue that it is impossible for the defendant to have a fair trial in that area.

8-2a   Opening of the Court Session

When it is time for the trial court session to begin, the bailiff arrives and calls the court to order with such words as "Hear ye, hear ye, the court of the Honorable Judge Decider is in session—all rise." At that point everyone in the courtroom should rise. The judge, usually dressed in a robe, enters the courtroom and sits, after which everyone else may sit. The judge announces the case, "The State of California versus Susan Jones, Case No. 45629-16." The judge asks whether the prosecution is ready; if so, the judge asks whether the defense is ready. If both are ready, the case begins with jury selection, assuming that the court has no additional business regarding the case, such as pretrial motions, that needs to be heard prior to the beginning of the trial.

After the jury has been selected and sworn, the judge reads the indictment or information and informs the court that the defendant has entered a plea of not guilty (or not guilty by reason of insanity, if that is permitted), and the trial begins with opening statements. Variances may occur in these procedures; for example, the jury may be selected and sent home (or sequestered) while attorneys argue various motions before the judge.

8-2b   Jury Selection

Jurisdictions differ in their procedures for selecting persons to form the pool from which jurors will be selected. Those selected are notified by means of a **summons,** a formal document issued by the court to notify a person that his or her presence is required in court for a particular reason at a specified time and date. The potential juror, after arriving at the designated place, may sit all day and not be picked for a jury. If that happens, he or she may be instructed to return for jury selection the following day. This procedure may go on for days, but many judges try to avoid this inconvenience to potential jurors.

▶ **Summons** A formal document issued by the court to notify a person that his or her presence is required in court for a particular reason at a specified time and date.

Usually the members of the jury pool are seated in the courtroom before the judge enters for jury selection. After the formal opening of the court session, the judge instructs the jury pool about procedures. The minute clerk begins by selecting names from a jury wheel, drawing names out of a fish bowl, or using some other similar procedure. As each name is drawn, the minute clerk reads and spells the name. The first selected person sits in the first seat in the jury box and so on until the jury box is filled or contains the number the judge wishes to process at one time.

Questioning of the potential jurors follows, a process called *voir dire,* which means "to tell the truth." The defense attorney and the prosecuting attorney *voir dire* the jury pool; that is, they question each potential juror and decide whether or not they would approve the selection of that person. Judges may question potential jurors, too. In the federal system judges may refuse to permit attorneys to question prospective jurors. Normally in the federal system jury selection takes only a few hours; in some states the process may take weeks or even months.

After they are questioned, potential jurors may be excused from jury duty in two ways. First, if they are excused for *cause,* they are presumed to be biased in the case. Bias may be presumed on the basis of the potential juror's answers to the questionnaire or to questions in court, association with or knowledge of the defendant or some other person involved in the trial, personal financial interest in the case, or a background that might prejudice them. For example, a person whose spouse has been murdered might be presumed to be prejudiced against a defendant on trial for murder. Attorneys are entitled to an unlimited number of challenges for cause. The judge may also exclude potential jurors for cause.

The second way a potential juror may be excused is by *peremptory challenge,* which means that the attorneys may excuse without cause. No reason need be given; that is the purpose of the challenge. But the peremptory challenge may not be used for extralegal reasons, such as to exclude minorities from the jury, as noted in this chapter's earlier discussion (see again Section 8-1c). States vary in the number of peremptory challenges permitted.

Some attorneys retain consultants to assist them in the questioning and selection of jurors. Through empirical studies, social scientists have provided information on characteristics that are related to opinions and therefore may influence the decision of a juror. In a particular case a retained jury consultant may conduct a survey to determine factors that might influence a juror in that town on that case.

8-2c Opening Statements

After the jury is selected, attorneys may make opening statements. The prosecutor makes the first opening statement. This is the prosecution's chance to outline what he or she intends to prove during the trial. The opening statement is very important; it should be planned carefully and delivered convincingly.

The opening statement should be brief but long enough to present an adequate statement of the facts the prosecution expects to prove. It should be interesting but not overly dramatic. The prosecutor must be certain not to overstep his or her boundaries and raise the ire of the judge, the defense, and the jury. Inflammatory and prejudicial statements are not permitted.

The defense is entitled to follow the prosecution with an opening statement, and many defense attorneys do so. The same principles apply to the defense as to the prosecution. The opening statement should raise the jury's interest to listen further but should not be too long or too dramatic. A defense attorney has the option of waiving the opening statement until the prosecution has presented its evidence. Some do so in order to hear that evidence before revealing the defense. Prosecutors, knowing that this might occur, may make comments in their opening statements that would lead the jury to expect the defense to make a statement or to be suspicious if the defense does not do so.

Like the prosecution, the defense attorney should not include information that is misleading in the opening statement. For example, a defense attorney in the Scott Peterson case said in his opening statement that the defense would show that Peterson could not be guilty. That was more than the attorney, Mark Geragos could deliver, and he was criticized

> **▶ *Voir dire*** To speak the truth; the process of questioning prospective jurors to determine their qualifications and desirability for serving on a jury.

by legal analysts for that assertion. Although that may not have been a major influence on the jury, Peterson was convicted of first-degree murder in the death of his pregnant wife and second-degree murder in the death of their unborn son. The jury recommended the death sentence, and the judge imposed that sentence.

8-2d Presentation of the Evidence

Before looking at the types of evidence that may be presented by the prosecution and the defense, it is necessary to understand some general rules of evidence and to look at the categories of evidence that apply to both the prosecution and the defense. The rules of evidence in criminal cases are contained in statutory and case law. They are complex, and they differ from one jurisdiction to another; however, a few general rules are important to a basic understanding of the criminal trial.

Any evidence presented must be *relevant, competent,* and *material* to the case. The meaning of those words has been litigated often, and over time changes have been made concerning admissible evidence. For example, in rape cases, historically the defense was permitted to ask the complainant about her prior sexual experiences, to imply that the alleged rape was a voluntary sexual act, not one of force. If she had had sexual relationships with other men, particularly if it could be inferred that she had been promiscuous, a rape conviction was unlikely. Today many jurisdictions have changed that rule. Some permit such questions only if the evidence is relevant to motive or conduct during the alleged crime. Other jurisdictions do not permit any questions about the victim's sexual experiences other than with the defendant and may limit that evidence to the case on trial. This change in what is defined as material evidence may not only affect the outcome of the case but also may make it much more likely that victims will report rapes and agree to testify at trial.

Attempts by the prosecution or the defense to introduce evidence or to ask questions thought by the opposing side to be incompetent, irrelevant, or immaterial may be countered by an objection by opposing counsel. If the objection is sustained, the evidence is not admitted. If the objection involves a question posed to the witness, the judge tells the witness not to answer the question. If the question has been answered already, the judge instructs the jury to disregard the answer, unless the information is so prejudicial that the judge declares a **mistrial,** which means the case cannot continue with that jury. A new jury must be selected or the charges dropped.

An important evidence rule is that of *discovery,* which refers to the process during which one side obtains the information that will be presented in court by the other side. The purpose of discovery is to prevent surprise in the trial and to enable each side to prepare adequately for its cross-examination of the evidence introduced by the other side. If discovery procedures are violated, the judge may impose fines or more severe sanctions, such as excluding the evidence in question, or even citing the attorney for contempt.

Several types of evidence may be presented. **Demonstrative evidence** is real to the senses, in contrast to evidence presented by the testimony of other people. Examples are the weapon used in the crime, blood samples, hair samples, and clothing. The integrity of demonstrative evidence may be, and often is, challenged.

Some evidence may be competent, relevant, and material to the case but be excluded because it has been secured in violation of the defendant's rights or because it is considered to be too prejudicial or inflammatory. Deciding which evidence to admit and which to exclude is the responsibility of the judge. He or she may be overruled on appeal, but many of the decisions made at the trial (or pretrial) stages stand, and often they are crucial to the outcome of the case.

A second type of evidence that may be introduced at trial is that of witnesses, which is referred to as *testimonial evidence.* Witnesses may be called by the prosecution or by the defense, and they are sworn in before they are permitted to testify. If they do not tell the truth, they may be prosecuted for perjury. There are several types of witnesses.

The testimony of a *victim-witness* is a preferred type of testimonial evidence. In many cases, prosecutors drop charges if victims will not agree to testify against the accused. *Eyewitnesses* are prime candidates for being called to testify in criminal cases, although

> **Mistrial** A trial that cannot stand, that is invalid. Judges may call a mistrial for such reasons as an error on the part of the prosecution or the defense, the illness or death of any of the parties participating in the legal proceedings, or the jury's inability to reach a verdict.

> **Demonstrative evidence** Real evidence; the kind of evidence that is apparent to the senses, in contrast to evidence presented by the testimony of other people.

some psychologists question the use of eyewitnesses, finding evidence that some jurors place too much weight on their testimonies.

Expert witnesses may be called by the defense or the prosecution. Expert witnesses testify regarding subjects on which they have expertise beyond that of the average person. For example, ballistics experts may be called to testify about the specifics of when and where a gun was fired and what kind of gun was used. Medical experts might testify to the cause of death in a murder case. Psychiatrists might testify concerning the mental or emotional state of the defendant. Before expert evidence may be admitted, the judge must rule that the science about which the expert will testify is advanced sufficiently to qualify. The second issue regarding expert testimony is whether a particular person is qualified to testify on the subject in question. The attorney who introduces the expert offers evidence to qualify that person. Typically experts are asked where they received their education and training, how much experience they have, and whether they have testified previously in the type of case before the court. Opposing counsel may challenge the expert's credentials, but in most cases they are accepted, although after the expert finishes testifying opposing counsel will try to discredit the content of the testimony during cross-examination. Both the prosecution and the defense might present experts from the same field. If they disagree, it is the jury's responsibility to determine credibility. A particular expert may be allowed to testify to some but not all issues about which the attorney wishes to question him or her.

Generally witnesses must testify to facts, not opinion, although in some instances opinions are allowed. But witnesses are not permitted to testify to the ultimate question of fact in a criminal case: the guilt or innocence of the defendant. One way for counsel to get around the requirement of factual, not opinion, testimony is to ask hypothetical questions concerning facts similar to those in the case on trial. The expert witness may answer these hypothetical questions.

In most instances experts and other witnesses are permitted to testify only to what they know, not to what they have heard from others, which constitutes **hearsay evidence.** Hearsay evidence is not admissible because there is no opportunity to cross-examine the source of the information. However, there are a number of exceptions to the hearsay evidence rule, such as a *dying declaration*. Since it might be presumed that one who is dying has no reason to lie, courts may permit the individual to testify (either in a deposition or at trial) to information that otherwise would be considered hearsay.

One further distinction important to the presentation of evidence is the difference between direct and circumstantial evidence. For example, a witness who testifies that he or she saw the alleged weapon being used by the defendant is providing **direct evidence.** Much evidence, however, is not direct; rather, it is *inferred* from a fact or series of facts and is called **circumstantial evidence.** In the Oklahoma City federal bombing trial, for example, the prosecution was not able to present a witness who could testify that he or she saw Terry Nichols at the federal building in Oklahoma City when it was bombed. The evidence linking Nichols with that crime was inferred from other testimony, and that testimony did not involve inferences that he was there but, rather, that he had some involvement in the planning of the crime. The lack of direct evidence may account for the jury's decision to convict Nichols of manslaughter rather than murder. Subsequently, Nichols was tried in a state court in Oklahoma and convicted of multiple murders, but he was spared the death penalty.

After the prosecution presents its witnesses, in a process called **direct examination,** those witnesses may be questioned by the defense attorney in **cross-examination.** The defense may reserve the right to cross-examine a witness later in the trial. After the defense cross-examines a prosecution witness, the prosecutor may follow with additional questions, in a process called *redirect examination*. If that occurs, the defense may cross-examine the witness again. The same process occurs in reverse after the defense has presented its witnesses.

8-2e The Prosecution's Case

The prosecution is the first to present evidence in a criminal case. Its case may include the presentation of demonstrative evidence as well as the testimony of the alleged victim, other witnesses, and experts. Usually police officers involved in the arrest or the investigation of

▶ **Hearsay evidence**
Secondhand evidence of which the witness does not have personal knowledge but merely repeats something the witness says he or she heard another person say. Hearsay evidence must be excluded from trial unless it meets one of the exceptions to the hearsay rule.

▶ **Direct evidence** Evidence offered by an eyewitness who testifies to what he or she saw, heard, tasted, smelled, or touched.

▶ **Circumstantial evidence** Evidence that may be inferred from a fact or a series of facts. *See also* **direct evidence.**

▶ **Direct examination** The examination of a witness, which is conducted by the attorney who called the witness to testify.

▶ **Cross-examination** The questioning of a court witness by adversary counsel after one attorney concludes the direct examination.

the case are called to testify. The prosecutor's presentation of evidence may consume days, weeks, even months in some trials and may involve very complicated evidence.

After the defense has rested its case, the prosecutor has the option of presenting additional proof to rebut the case presented by the defense. Not all prosecutors choose to exercise this option to present what is called *rebuttal evidence*. When the option is exercised, the prosecution may call or recall police officers or others to testify regarding facts that have been in dispute among witnesses at the trial.

8-2f   The Defense Attorney's Case

After the prosecution has presented its case and all cross-examinations and redirect examinations have occurred, the prosecution rests and the defense presents its case. At this point some special issues arise.

First, the defendant has a right not to testify (see Appendix A, Fifth Amendment). The reason is that even innocent persons might appear guilty if they take the stand. If the defendant does not testify, neither the prosecution nor the judge may make unfavorable comments about that fact.

Some defendants choose to testify. In that case they are sworn in, and they may be prosecuted for perjury if they testify falsely. They may be cross-examined by the prosecutor. Rules vary, but generally the rules applied to other witnesses also apply to the defendant. In most jurisdictions this means that the cross-examination may encompass only those subjects covered on direct or redirect examination. Where that is the case, the defense attorney has the ability to limit the subject matter on which the prosecution may ask questions to the subjects included in direct examination. Some jurisdictions, however, permit the prosecution to go beyond those subjects once the defendant takes the stand.

The defense may call *character witnesses*, who testify about the defendant's character; however, if that occurs, the prosecution may call witnesses to testify to the defendant's bad character. The prosecution may not, however, begin this line of evidence. Character witnesses, like all other witnesses, may be subjected to stringent cross-examination. This is difficult for many people, and therefore it is important that attorneys who plan to call character or other kinds of witnesses spend time with those witnesses, preparing them for trial.

Another important element of the defendant's case is the presentation of defenses. Commission of a criminal act, even with the required criminal intent, is not sufficient for a guilty verdict if the defense proves a legally acceptable reason that the law should not be applied to this defendant. Many defenses might be raised. Infancy, intoxication, duress, involuntary action, entrapment, public duty, legal impossibility, self-defense or defense of others, action under authority of law (for example, a justifiable killing by a police officer), and insanity are some examples. Jurisdictions differ in which of these defenses are acceptable and under what conditions. Differences exist in the type of proof required for the defense to be successful.

8-2g   Closing Statements

After all of the evidence has been presented in a case, attorneys may offer closing statements. The closing statement is given first by the prosecution, then by the defense; this may be followed with a rebuttal by the prosecutor. In the closing statement, as in the entire trial, the prosecutor must be careful not to go too far. If he or she does so, the judge must determine whether the statements are so prejudicial or erroneous that they might have undue influence on the jury's determination of guilt. If so, they are considered **prejudicial errors,** and the judge orders a mistrial. If not, they are considered harmless errors. Prejudicial errors and harmless errors may be committed by the defense or the prosecution and may refer to actions or comments made at various stages in the criminal process.

The defense offers a closing statement after that of the prosecutor, unless the defense chooses to waive this step. The defense should be careful not to go beyond the evidence or be too emotional, but as a practical matter rarely are defense attorneys' closing statements the subject of appeal. This is because the prosecution may not appeal an acquittal; if the

> **Prejudicial errors** Errors made during legal proceedings that affect the rights of parties substantially and thus may result in the reversal of a case.

defendant is convicted and the defense appeals, that appeal will be concerned only with alleged errors made by the prosecution or rulings made by the judge.

8-2h   Submittal of the Case to the Jury

After all of the preceding steps have been completed, most cases are submitted to a jury. The judge may not direct the jury to return a guilty verdict. However, in many jurisdictions trial judges, on their own or by granting a motion from the defense, may order a **directed verdict,** a direction to the jury to return a verdict of not guilty.

> **Directed verdict**   Upon a finding of insufficient evidence to convict a defendant, the judge may direct the jury to return a verdict of not guilty. The judge may not direct a guilty verdict.

Why would a trial judge have that power? If the evidence is so weak that it is unreasonable to conclude beyond a reasonable doubt that the defendant is guilty, it would be a travesty of justice to send the case to the jury, let the jury return a guilty verdict, and then make the defendant wait for an appeal to get justice.

Before the case is given to the jury for deliberation, the judge has the responsibility of charging the jury, which means instructing jurors on matters of law relating to the case they must decide. In many jurisdictions, patterned jury instructions are given for the most commonly raised issues. The judge accepts suggested instructions from the prosecution and the defense and usually schedules a conference with them on the proposed instructions. The judge determines the final instructions (which may be subject to appeal) and presents them orally to the jury. The charge of the judge is very important, for it can be influential, perhaps determinative, in the jury's decision.

The jury charge should be as clear and as simple as possible without distorting the meaning of the law. The law as applied to many cases is complicated and difficult to understand, especially for people who are not legally trained, yet it is the jury's responsibility to apply that law to the case it has heard. It is the duty of the trial judge to explain the law in terms that the jury can understand. If the judge's charge is too complicated or is an inaccurate interpretation of the law in the case, the defense may appeal. In some instances the case is reversed and requires a new trial.

The judge's charge must explain to the jury the law that applies to the case, and it must clarify what the jury may do. For example, if the defendant has been charged with first-degree murder but the law permits the jury to return a verdict of guilty of second-degree murder, that must be explained, along with the elements that must be proved for conviction on each of those charges. The judge should explain the meaning of evidence and distinguish among the types of evidence. If conflict exists in the testimonial evidence, the jurors need to understand that they are the final determiner regarding the credibility of the testimony. This is true particularly when expert opinions conflict. Jurors may expect conflict between the testimony of a victim and that of a defendant but be very confused when two physicians give contradictory statements. Experts do differ; the jury is to decide whom to believe. On the other hand, jurors may ignore the testimony of any or all experts.

The judge may instruct the jury to disregard certain evidence that has been admitted but that for some reason should not be considered. In the federal as well as in some state systems, the judge is permitted to summarize and comment on the evidence when the charge is given to the jury. This is an immense responsibility, for the obligation of the judge to be a neutral party continues throughout the trial unless the right to a jury trial is waived and the judge is to determine guilt or innocence.

The judge might cover many areas of law in the instructions. The details of each charge depend on the nature of the case being tried. Two issues deserve further attention in this section: the presumption of innocence and the burden and standard of proof.

> **Presumption of innocence**   A cornerstone of the adversary system; it provides that a defendant is innocent unless and until the prosecution proves guilt beyond a reasonable doubt.

In U.S. criminal justice systems, the defendant is presumed innocent. The **presumption of innocence** is an important principle. It means that the prosecution has the responsibility of proving every element required for conviction and that the defendant does not have to prove innocence. The defendant can do nothing and still be acquitted if the government does not prove its case.

Most judges instruct the jury regarding the presumption of innocence, although the U.S. Supreme Court has held that it is not constitutionally required that an instruction be given. According to the Supreme Court, all circumstances must be examined to determine whether the defendant had a fair trial without an instruction on the presumption. If so, the case will not be reversed for failure to give the instruction.

The presumption of innocence is essential in protecting those who are falsely accused. Innocent people are convicted in some cases, and these convictions may be devastating to their personal and professional lives. The criminal justice system is impaired when the rights of innocent persons are violated, particularly when a violation leads to a conviction (or, in some cases, execution).

The standard of proof in a criminal case is **beyond a reasonable doubt.** That burden is a heavy one; it means that, when jurors look at all the evidence, they are convinced, satisfied to a moral certainty, that guilt has been established by the facts. Some judges refuse to define *beyond a reasonable doubt* on the assumption that not much more can be said. We all understand those words, and any attempt to define them further might be confusing or misleading.

After the charge is read to the jury, the bailiff takes the jurors to the jury room to deliberate. These deliberations must be conducted in secret. It is the bailiff's responsibility to ensure that no one talks to the jurors; nor are the jurors permitted to seek advice. If they need further instruction they may send the bailiff to ask the judge, who may or may not give that instruction, depending on the nature of the request.

If the jurors are sequestered, they are escorted by the bailiff (or another court person, such as a deputy sheriff) not only in and out of the courtroom but also to all meals and to the hotel rooms where they are staying. Access to television and newspapers is not permitted unless special arrangements are made to avoid any possibility that jurors are exposed to media accounts of the trial. For example, jurors might be offered newspapers only after the articles about the trial have been removed.

Normally when the jurors deliberate they have access to the demonstrative evidence that has been introduced during the trial. If they have been permitted to take notes during the trial, they may have their notes for the deliberation. Generally it is left to the discretion of the trial judge whether jurors may take notes.

In some trials jurors deliberate for hours and do not reach verdicts. They report to the judge, who may tell them to go back and try again. The number of times a judge may send them back and how long they must deliberate is a matter of jurisdictional rules and judicial discretion, but the judge may not require jurors to deliberate for an unreasonable period of time. The definition of *reasonable* depends on the complexity of the trial. If it cannot reach a verdict, the jury is deadlocked, also called a *hung jury,* and the judge should declare a mistrial.

Mistrials may also be declared under other circumstances, such as the serious illness or death of the judge or one of the attorneys or jurors. Mistrials may be declared during the trial as a result of a prejudicial error made by one of the parties involved in the trial. Other reasons include prejudicial media publicity that comes to the attention of the jury and efforts of someone to bribe some or all of the jurors.

If the jury is not deadlocked and returns a verdict, the verdict may be not guilty. In that case the judge may order a verdict of acquittal, and the case is ended. The judge may not reverse a not guilty verdict. The judge may, but rarely does, reverse a guilty verdict. This may happen if the judge believes the evidence was not sufficient to support the guilty verdict. In addition, as noted in Chapter 6 (Spotlight 6-2), the judge may find the defendant guilty of a lesser charge than the one on which the jury based its verdict. In the case discussed in Spotlight 6-2, involving defendant Louise Woodward, the jury was instructed only on murder charges and found the defendant guilty of second-degree murder, but the judge reduced that conviction to manslaughter.

After the verdict and before sentencing, the attorneys may file postverdict motions. If the jury returns a guilty verdict, the defense may make a motion for a judgment of acquittal. That motion may be made before the case goes to the jury and probably is more appropriately done at that time. The motion is based on the argument that the evidence is not sufficient to support a guilty verdict. The court may be more likely to grant that motion before the jury has returned a verdict, particularly in a close case.

▶ **Beyond a reasonable doubt**
The standard for evidence required for a conviction in an adult criminal court or a juvenile court; a lack of uncertainty; the facts presented to the judge or jury are sufficient to lead a reasonable person to conclude without question that the defendant committed the act for which he or she is charged.

The more common motion made by the defense after a guilty verdict is a motion for a new trial. This motion may be made on several specific grounds or on general grounds; that is, a new trial is in the interest of justice. Court rules or statutes may enumerate the specific grounds on which this motion may be based.

8-3   Sentencing

After a guilty verdict, the court imposes a sentence, which may or may not involve a jury recommendation to the judge. In some jurisdictions the jury determines the sentence. In others the jury is permitted to make a sentencing recommendation, but the judge does not have to follow it, although there are exceptions in capital cases.

Frequently the sentencing process takes place at a later hearing to allow time for presentence reports. The court may hold an extensive sentencing hearing, or the judge may impose a sentence without a hearing, depending on the rules of the jurisdiction and, in some cases, the preferences of the judge. Sentencing is an important stage, and in recent years it has come under intense scrutiny by the public and the media, as well as by the courts.

8-3a   The Concept and Process of Sentencing

▶ **Sentence** The punishment imposed by the court on a convicted offender.

A **sentence** is a term of punishment imposed by a court on a convicted offender. Sentencing is one of the most controversial topics in criminal justice systems. It can be one of the simplest or one of the most complex processes. Sentencing involves numerous people, ranging from the legislators who formulate sentencing laws to the probation officers who compile the presentence reports used by judges in making sentence decisions.

An understanding of sentencing is complicated because it differs significantly from state to state, from court to court within a state, from county to county, and even from time to time within any of these jurisdictions. Sentencing policies in the federal system differ from those in the states. Finally, attitudes toward what is and is not appropriate in sentencing differ as well.

Sentencing Strategies

▶ **Indeterminate sentence**
A sentence to confinement without a definite term. Parole boards or professionals determine when the offender should be released.

Four main strategies are used for sentencing: indeterminate, presumptive, mandatory, and determinate sentences. Most states use a combination of these. An **indeterminate sentence** involves legislative specifications of sentence ranges that permit judges to exercise discretion in determining actual sentences. In its purest form, the indeterminate sentence would be from one day to life, but usually it involves legislative specification of a maximum and minimum term for each offense. For example, if the legislative sentence for armed robbery is not more than 25 or less than 10 years, judges have discretion to set the sentence at any point in between.

▶ **Presumptive sentence**
The normal sentence is specified by statute for each offense; judges are permitted to deviate from that sentence but usually may do so only under specified circumstances or must give reasons for the deviation.

Another sentencing strategy is the **presumptive sentence.** In presumptive sentencing the normal sentence is specified for each offense, but judges are permitted to deviate from that norm. Some jurisdictions require that any deviation from a presumptive sentence be accompanied by written reasons for the deviation. Furthermore, the law may specify which conditions and circumstances may be considered for deviating from the presumptive sentence.

▶ **Mandatory sentence** A sentence having a length imposed by the legislature, with no discretion given to the trial judge. If the defendant is convicted, the specified sentence must be imposed.

A **mandatory sentence** is one that must be imposed upon conviction. Mandatory sentences are specified by legislatures (or by Congress) and usually involve a prison term. The mandatory approach leaves the judge no discretion in sentencing. For example, if the provision is for a specific prison term, the judge may not suspend the sentence or impose a different term as an alternative to prison.

In recent years a popular approach in many jurisdictions, including the federal, has been the statutory requirement of imposing mandatory minimum sentences. Generally these sentences are very long; some examples are discussed later in this chapter, but at this point it is important to note that U.S. Supreme Court Associate Justice Anthony M. Kennedy, in speaking before the annual meeting of the American Bar Association (ABA) in

August 2003, called for that organization to review the nation's use of long mandatory sentences. Justice Kennedy noted that the United States

- Has the highest rates of incarceration in the world
- Spends approximately $40 billion a year incarcerating inmates
- Has an African American inmate population that constitutes approximately 40 percent of all of the inmates in the country[22]

The ABA assumed Justice Kennedy's challenge to revisit the federal sentencing guidelines, which, according to Kennedy, should be revised downward. The ABA appointed the Justice Kennedy Commission, which was chaired by Stephen A. Saltzburg, a law professor at George Washington University Law School. Justice Kennedy said that in many cases mandatory minimum sentences "are unwise and unjust." He compared the cost of incarceration to the cost of education, with these poignant words:

> When it costs so much more to incarcerate a prisoner than to educate a child, we should take special care to ensure that we are not incarcerating too many persons for too long. . . . It requires one with more expertise in the area than I possess to offer a complete analysis, but it does seem justified to say this: Our resources are misspent, our punishments too severe, our sentences too long.[23]

In August 2004, the ABA adopted some of the recommendations of the Kennedy Commission, "including repealing mandatory sentencing laws, and employing 'guided discretion' sentencing systems 'to avoid unwarranted and inequitable disparities in sentencing among like offenses and offenders, but permit courts to consider unique characteristics of offenses and offenders that may warrant an increase or decrease in a sentence.'" The ABA also adopted resolutions that would require law enforcement agencies to implement policies to eradicate ethnic and racial profiling; establish standards permitting inmates to request reductions of their sentences when exceptional circumstances occur; implement policies to ensure safe correctional facilities; and design programs to assist inmates with the problems of returning to society after incarceration.[24]

Another type of sentencing strategy is the **determinate sentence,** which requires a specific sentence for a particular crime, although the trial judge may have the option of suspending that sentence or imposing probation (or some other sanction, such as work service) rather than a jail or prison term. However, once the judicial sentence is imposed, the parole board does not have the discretion to reduce the sentence by offering early parole. The determinate sentencing scheme may involve a provision for mandatory parole after a specified portion of the determinate sentence has been served. It may include a provision for sentence reduction based on good time credits earned by the inmate.

Determinate sentences may include a provision for raising or lowering the sentence if there are **mitigating circumstances** or **aggravating circumstances.** For example, the determinate sentence for rape might be 15 years; however, if a weapon is used to threaten the victim, there may be a provision for increasing the penalty. Likewise, if there are circumstances that reduce the moral culpability of the offender, the sentence might be reduced. An example is extreme passion in a homicide, as when the accused finds his or her spouse in bed with another and, in a fit of anger, kills that person.

In any of the sentencing strategies, the power to determine sentence length may be altered by other factors. Power may be given to the governor to commute a sentence of life to a specified term of years or to commute a death sentence to a life sentence. The governor may also have the power to **pardon** an offender. In the case of a federal crime, the pardoning power resides in the president of the United States.

During his administration, President Bill Clinton granted numerous pardons. In 1999, he issued a pardon to an 80-year-old former sailor who was convicted during World War II. Freddie Meeks, one of the few survivors among the 50 African American sailors who were convicted of mutiny, said that, despite his failing health, he always believed he would live long enough to receive a pardon. After an explosion on 17 July 1944, resulting in the deaths of 320 men in California, Meeks and others refused to reload ammunition onto the ships, arguing that white officers were ordering African American sailors to engage in menial acts while ignoring the risks to their lives.[25]

Determinate sentence A sentence for a specific crime and determined by the legislature; the parole board, correctional officials, or a judge cannot make changes in the sentence length. In some jurisdictions the trial judge may have the power to suspend the sentence or to impose probation rather than the legislatively specified prison term.

Mitigating circumstances Circumstances that do not justify or excuse a crime but that, because of justice and fairness, make the crime less reprehensible; they may be used to reduce a crime to a lesser offense, such as to reduce murder to manslaughter. Mitigating circumstances must be considered before the death penalty can be imposed. *See also* **aggravating circumstances.**

Aggravating circumstances Circumstances that are above and beyond those required for the crime but that make the crime more serious; may be used in reference to many crimes, but the concept is critical particularly in capital punishment cases, where it is required.

Pardon An act by a state governor or the president of the United States (in federal cases) that exempts a convicted offender from punishment or, in the case of those already serving terms, further punishment and removes the legal consequences of the conviction. Pardons may also be granted after a person is released from prison. They may be absolute or conditional; individual or granted to a group, or class, of offenders; and may be full or partial, in which case the pardon remits only part of the punishment or removes some of the legal disabilities resulting from the conviction.

In 1998, President Clinton issued a posthumous pardon to the first African American graduate of West Point. Henry O. Flipper, who was born a slave in 1856 and graduated from West Point in 1877, was court-martialed in 1881 on charges of embezzling $2,500 in commissary money during his tour of duty in Texas. Although Flipper was acquitted of that charge, he was convicted of lying to investigators and of engaging in conduct unbecoming an officer. Flipper was dismissed from the army in 1882. Subsequently the judge advocate general of the army concluded that the charges against Flipper, which were brought by his commanding officer, were dubious charges that had resulted from racism. In 1976, the U.S. Army exonerated Flipper and changed his discharge to honorable. Flipper's remains were reburied with full honors in his birthplace in Thomasville, Georgia. When he granted the pardon, President Clinton said, "I welcome you all to an event that is 117 years overdue. . . . With great pleasure and humility, I now offer a full pardon." Today a section of the West Point library honors Flipper, and an annual award in his name is given to the outstanding cadet.[26]

President Clinton drew severe criticism, however, for the pardons he issued during the final days of his administration. Those pardons included a man under investigation by the Justice Department, his former partner in the Whitewater land deal, and a rich fugitive, whose wife gave the Clintons expensive gifts during their last year in office. The Clintons stated that they would pay for those gifts, but that gesture did not remove the controversy. Clinton issued approximately 140 pardons just before he left office, and some of those pardons were targeted for investigation.

One of the pardons issued by President Clinton was to William A. Borders Jr., who had been convicted of bribery. Borders was automatically disbarred as a result of that conviction. In 2003, he sought a hearing before the U.S. Supreme Court on the issue of whether the pardon, which eliminated his conviction, also removed the disbarment—that is, any prejudice resulting from that conviction. The Supreme Court refused to hear the case, thus leaving the lower court's decision. The District of Columbia Court of Appeals had ruled that, although a pardon removed the conviction and the law provided that disbarment was mandatory upon conviction of a crime of moral turpitude, the court that admitted the individual to the bar retained the power to reinstate after disbarment. Borders was convicted of soliciting bribes from two defendants to influence a federal district judge, Alcee L. Hastings, who was charged but not convicted in the scheme. Hastings was impeached by the U.S. House of Representatives, convicted by the U.S. Senate, and removed from his judicial position. Subsequently Hastings ran for and was elected to the U.S. House of Representatives, representing the state of Florida.[27]

Two final cases illustrate state pardons. In 2000, Elaine Bartlett was granted a pardon in New York after serving 16 years of a 20 years-to-life sentence under the state's strict drug possession laws, which among other provisions required that a defendant spend at least 15 years in prison.

In August 2003, Texas Governor Rick Perry pardoned 31 African Americans and 4 whites who were convicted after they were arrested in a drug sting in 1999 in Tulia, a small (population 5,000), predominantly African American Texas town, after the key witness against them, Tom Coleman, a white undercover narcotics agent, was indicted on three charges of perjury. Ed Bradley of CBS's *60 Minutes,* described the case as "one of the worst miscarriages of justice in recent memory" and noted that the defendants were sentenced to a total of 750 years. Coleman was convicted of aggravated perjury and sentenced to 10 years probation. He said he will appeal on the grounds that some of the special prosecutors had conflicts of interest in the case.[28]

The Sentencing Hearing

For less serious offenses, particularly when the case is not tried before a jury, the judge may pronounce sentence immediately upon finding the defendant guilty or upon accepting a guilty plea. Sentencing may be immediate when the judge has no option but to assess the statutory penalty. Sentencing may be set for a future date but may not involve any special investigations, with the judge taking recommendations from the defense and the prosecution. However, the trend is toward having a separate sentencing hearing. After the trial verdict the judge sets a formal date for sentencing, leaving sufficient time to consider appropriate presentence investigations. It is common in capital cases to have a separate hearing on the issue of whether the defendant will be sentenced to death, life, or a term of years.

The **presentence investigation (PSI)** may include information based on interviews with the defendant, family, friends, employers, or others who might have information pertinent to a sentencing decision. Medical, psychiatric, or other reports from experts may be included. Information on prior offenses, work records, school records, associates, pastime activities, attitudes, willingness to cooperate, and problems with alcohol or other drugs might be included as well.

If the PSI is conducted thoroughly, it is a time-consuming job. In some jurisdictions the reports are prepared by the Department of Corrections (DOC). Most of these departments have diagnostic facilities and may be better equipped to conduct the investigations than probation officers, who conduct the PSI in many jurisdictions.

The Sentencing Decision

Judges decide most sentences (unless the legislature has removed all judicial discretion), but in some cases (usually in serious offenses, such as first-degree murder) juries have sentencing power. The judge is not required to follow the jury's recommendation in all jurisdictions, although there are some restrictions placed on judges by U.S. Supreme Court decisions. Many of those decisions relate to sentencing in capital cases; they are complex and extensive and beyond the scope of this text. This discussion is limited to the general procedures that are followed during the sentencing process, with the mention of a case the U.S. Supreme Court decided during its 2003–2004 and 2004–2005 terms.

In October 2003, the U.S. Supreme Court agreed to hear the case of *Blakely* v. *Washington*, which raised the issue of whether the Supreme Court's decision in *Ring* v. *Arizona* applies to noncapital cases. In *Ring* the Supreme Court held that the aggravating circumstances used to make a defendant eligible for a capital sentence must be decided by a jury, not by a judge. Likewise, mitigating circumstances must be decided by a jury.[29]

In *Blakely* the U.S. Supreme Court faced the question of whether *Ring* applies to noncapital sentences for which state legislation requires the consideration of aggravating and mitigating circumstances. *Blakely* also raised issues concerning sentencing guidelines. The case came from Washington, which provided by statute that, for a variety of reasons, a trial judge may increase a sentence up to the statutory maximum. Blakely was sentenced to 90 months in prison after his conviction for kidnapping his wife. Kidnapping in Washington is a felony and could result in a sentence of up to 120 months. According to the sentencing guidelines of the state, given the circumstances of Blakely's crime, he should have received a 53-month sentence, but the judge increased that to 90 months after finding evidence of domestic violence and deliberate cruelty. The judge made those findings after a special sentencing hearing, during which the standard of proof was *a preponderance of the evidence* rather than that of the trial phase, *beyond a reasonable doubt*. Blakely appealed, arguing that the latter standard should apply and that a jury should make the decision. The Washington appellate court rejected those arguments. The U.S. Supreme Court reversed, stating that it was adhering to the 2000 controversial precedent case of *United States* v. *Apprendi*, in which the Supreme Court had ruled that any fact (other than a prior conviction) that could be used to enhance a sentence must be submitted to the jury and found to be true beyond a reasonable doubt.[30]

In 2004, the U.S. Supreme Court agreed to hear two cases that involved issues left unresolved by *Blakely*: (1) whether if a trial judge alone conducts fact finding at the sentencing hearing that violates the defendant's Sixth Amendment rights and (2) whether the federal sentencing guidelines were still viable.

United States v. *Booker* involved a defendant who was convicted of possessing and distributing crack cocaine. The amount of cocaine found on Booker when he was arrested (92.5 grams), combined with his 23 prior convictions, would, under the federal sentencing guidelines, result in a sentence of slightly less than 22 years. Because at the time of his arrest, however, Booker told police that in the previous few months he had sold 20 ounces

> **Presentence investigation (PSI)** An investigation of the background and characteristics of the defendant; it may include information that would not be admissible at the trial; it is presented to the judge to be used in determining sentence.

of cocaine, at the sentencing hearing, the trial judge "added" that amount to the 92.5 grams. The judge also "added" an obstruction of justice conviction based on his own determination that Booker had committed perjury at the trial. The result of these add-ons was a 30-year sentence, which was reversed by the court of appeals.[31]

The second case, *United States* v. *Fanfan,* involved Duncan Fanfan, who was convicted of conspiracy to distribute at least 500 grams of powdered cocaine. At the sentencing hearing the prosecution offered evidence that Fanfan also dealt in crack cocaine, which carried a longer sentence. Initially the federal sentencing judge sentenced Fanfan to 16 years in prison; however, based on *Blakely,* decided four days previously, the judge gave the defendant only a 6½-year sentence. That sentence was based on the amount of drugs involved in the jury decision. In agreeing to review the case, the U.S. Supreme Court bypassed the First Circuit Court of Appeals in Boston and accepted the case directly from the trial decision.[32]

In January 2005, the U.S. Supreme Court handed down its decisions in both *Booker* and *Fanfan,* with a 5-to-4 vote in each case. Justice John Paul Stevens, writing for the majority in one opinion, emphasized that the right to a trial by jury guaranteed by the Sixth Amendment (see Appendix A) is violated when a sentence is based on facts determined by the judge but not the jury. The second opinion, written by Justice Stephen G. Breyer, reduces the federal sentencing guidelines to an advisory role. According to Breyer, "The district courts, while not bound to apply the guidelines, must consult those guidelines and take them into account when sentencing." But Breyer noted that Congress could act to change the federal sentencing guidelines, when he said, "The ball now lies in Congress' court. The national legislature is equipped to devise and install, long-term, the sentencing system compatible with the Constitution, that Congress judges best for the federal system of justice." It can be presumed that this ruling, at least for now, leaves federal sentencing decisions up to trial judges, which could and probably will, result in widely varying sentences, a situation the federal guidelines were designed to avoid. Meanwhile, we can expect many defendants who were sentenced under the federal guidelines, to appeal those sentences. Even Justice Breyer said, "Ours is not the last word."

In December 2003, the U.S. Supreme Court agreed to hear a case in which the Ninth Circuit Court of Appeals held that *Ring* should be applied retroactively. If that decision had remained, the persons on death row in the states under the Ninth Circuit's jurisdiction (in December 2003, that included 124 inmates in Arizona, 16 in Idaho, and 6 in Montana) would have been entitled at least to a new sentencing hearing (although some had still not otherwise exhausted all of their appeals). In *Summerlin* v. *Stewart,* decided in 2004, the U.S. Supreme Court reversed the lower federal court and held that *Ring* does not apply retroactively to cases that were already final on direct review before *Ring* was decided.[33]

One final recent sentencing decision is important to this discussion. In *Shepard* v. *United States,* decided in March 2005, the U.S. Supreme Court reexamined the role of judges in sentencing. Recall that in *Apprendi,* discussed above, the Court had ruled that any fact that is used to enhance a sentence, other than a prior conviction, must be determined by a jury. The *Shepard* case involved a defendant who had previously entered guilty pleas to four burglaries, but his plea agreement did not contain the necessary details of those crimes. The federal statute under which Shepard entered a guilty plea to being a felon in possession of a firearm, the Armed Career Criminal Act (ACCA), permits enhanced penalties for offenders who are convicted of specified prior violent felonies. This provision includes burglaries but only if they are committed within a building or an enclosed space, such as a house. The burglary of a car or a boat does not meet the requirement for an enhanced penalty. Since Shepard's plea agreement did not note the required details of his burglary, and the district court ruled that the prosecutor did not present other evidence showing that Shepard's prior burglaries counted, the judge imposed a three-year sentence. The appellate court ruled that the trial judge should have looked at police reports to obtain the needed information, and, in effect, ordered the lower court to impose the 15-year mandatory, minimum sentence.

The U.S. Supreme Court reversed the decision of the appellate court, ruling by a 5-to-3 vote (Chief Justice William H. Rehnquist did not participate in the decision) that *Apprendi* and other recent cases limit trial judges to official court documents when they consider the nature of prior offenses for purposes of enhancing a sentence; thus, it was inappropriate to go beyond Shepard's plea agreement to determine whether his prior burglaries met the requirements for an enhanced sentence under the ACCA.[34]

In jurisdictions in which the jury has sentencing power, the judge instructs the jury concerning the law and its application to sentencing. Many factors might be considered in the sentencing decision. Those factors may be designated by statute. Some states have formalized and restricted the factors that may be considered. Many require that evidence of aggravating or mitigating circumstances be presented. Some jurisdictions use sentencing formulas, which indicate the weight to be given to specific factors, such as the nature of the crime.

If the defendant has been convicted of more than one offense, usually the judge has the authority to determine whether the sentences are to be imposed concurrently or consecutively. With a **concurrent sentence,** the defendant satisfies the terms of all sentences at the same time. For example, if the defendant is sentenced to 20 years for each of three counts of armed robbery, the total number of years served will be 20 if the sentences are concurrent. With a **consecutive sentence,** the defendant will have to serve 60 years (unless the term is reduced by parole or good time or is commuted or pardoned). Most multiple sentences are imposed concurrently.

After the sentence is determined, the judge reads the sentence to the defendant, and the sentence is recorded in court records. If the sentence involves incarceration, generally the defendant is taken into custody immediately (or returned to custody if he or she had not been released before trial). The judge may allow the defendant some time to prepare for incarceration, but that rarely occurs and generally applies only in the cases of government officials or other people who might, in the eyes of the judge, need time to get their affairs in order and who would not be a danger to society or flee the jurisdiction.

One final issue concerning the sentencing decision should be noted. In some jurisdictions crime victims are permitted to express their concerns and opinions on issues such as sentencing. The role of victims in sentencing was limited by the U.S. Supreme Court in a 1987 decision, *Booth* v. *Maryland,* in which the Court held that the defendant's constitutional rights are violated when Victim Impact Statements (VIS) contain information such as the severe emotional impact of the crime on the family, the personal characteristics of the victim, and the family members' opinions and characterizations of the crime and the offender. When the issue arose in the sentencing phase of a capital case, the Court emphasized its concern that, in such serious cases, decisions should be based on reason, not on emotion. Thus, the jury should not hear this type of information, which "can serve no other purpose than to inflame the jury and divert it from deciding the case on the relevant evidence concerning the crime and the defendant."[35]

In 1991, the U.S. Supreme Court reversed itself on the ruling in *Booth* and another case. In *Payne* v. *Tennessee* the Court ruled that a VIS may be used at capital sentencing hearings. "A state may legitimately conclude that evidence about the victim and about the impact of the murder on the victim's family is relevant to the jury's decision as to whether or not the death penalty should be imposed."[36] In 1995, the Washington Supreme Court upheld that state's provision for admitting victim impact evidence during the sentencing phase of a capital trial. The U.S. Supreme Court refused to hear an appeal, thus permitting the lower court decision to stand.[37]

8-3b   Types of Sentences

In some jurisdictions judges have numerous sentencing options. In addition to incarcerating defendants for short jail terms or for longer prison terms, judges may place offenders on probation or impose fines. Judges may use a combination of these possibilities along with others, such as work assignments. Sentencing options differ from jurisdiction to jurisdiction and vary by crime, but it is possible to examine the *types* of sentences. They are listed and defined in Spotlight 8-3 and are discussed briefly in this section.

A **fine** is a punishment in which the offender is ordered to pay a sum of money to the state in lieu of or in addition to other forms of punishment. Fines are used in combination

▶ **Concurrent sentence**   A sentence for more than one offense served at the same time. For example, if an offender receives a three-year prison term for robbery and a five-year prison term for assault, these sentences to be served concurrently, the total prison sentence is five years.

▶ **Consecutive sentence**   A term of imprisonment for more than one offense that must be served one following the other. If an offender receives a three-year term for robbery and a five-year term for assault, the consecutive sentence adds up to eight years.

▶ **Fine**   The payment of a sum of money to a court by the convicted defendant in addition to or instead of other punishment(s).

Spotlight 8-3   **Types of Sentences**

Death penalty—In most States, for the most serious crimes such as murder, the courts may sentence an offender to death by lethal injection, electrocution, exposure to lethal gas, hanging, or other method specified by State law.

Incarceration—The confinement of a convicted criminal in a Federal or State prison or a local jail to serve a court-imposed sentence. Confinement is usually in a jail, administered locally, or a prison, operated by the State or Federal Government. In many States offenders sentenced to 1 year or less are held in a jail; those sentenced to longer terms are committed to a State prison.

Probation—The sentencing of an offender to community supervision by a probation agency, often as a result of suspending a sentence to confinement. Such supervision normally entails specific rules of conduct while in the community. If the rules are violated a sentence to confinement may be imposed. Probation is the most widely used correctional disposition in the United States.

Split sentences, shock probation, and intermittent confinement— A penalty that explicitly requires the convicted person to serve a brief period of confinement in a local, State, or Federal facility (the "shock") followed by a period of probation. This penalty attempts to combine the use of community supervision with a short incarceration experience. Some sentences are periodic rather than continuous; for example, an offender may be required to spend a certain number of weekends in jail.

Restitution and victim compensation—The offender is required to provide financial repayment or, in some jurisdictions, services in lieu of monetary restitution, for the losses incurred by the victim.

Community service—The offender is required to perform a specified amount of public service work, such as collecting trash in parks or other public facilities.

Fines—An economic penalty that requires the offender to pay a specified sum of money within limits set by law. Fines are often imposed in addition to probation or as alternatives in incarceration.

Source: Bureau of Justice Statistics, *Report to the Nation on Crime and Justice: The Data*, 2d ed. (Washington, D.C.: U.S. Department of Justice, 1988), p. 96.

▶ **Restitution**   Punishment that requires an offender to repay the victim with services or money. This punishment may be imposed instead of or in addition to other punishment or fines and may be a requirement of parole.

▶ **Community work service** Punishment assigning the offender to community service or work projects. Sometimes it is combined with restitution or probation.

with probation and other alternatives to confinement. Historically fines were used primarily in cases involving traffic violations or other nonviolent offenses. Recently, with the increasing interest in victim compensation, including compensation for violent and property crimes, some jurisdictions have begun to assess fines against offenders convicted of violent crimes. Fines are used in conjunction with incarceration as well, with the latter being extended beyond the original sentence if the fine is not paid.

Another type of sentence that is growing in use is **restitution,** which requires offenders to reimburse victims financially or with services. The primary rationale for restitution is victim compensation; retribution is another. It is also argued that the state should assist crime victims, and restitution provides one source of revenue at the expense of the offender. And there is some evidence, especially among juveniles, that there is a greater chance of reducing the number of repeat offenders if defendants participate in some form of restitution, either financial or work service.

Restitution may be combined with work assignments. The work assignments may be designed to benefit only the victim or a larger group, as in the case of **community work service** assignments. Some administrative questions are left open by the statutes providing for restitution or community work service. Some are ambiguous about the kind of work that may be assigned. Others require work programs or restitution of a nature that aids the victim but also fosters rehabilitation of the offender. Usually community work service orders impose strict rules on the offender and, in many cases, are combined with probation, which is the most frequently used sanction for criminal activity.

Probation is used nearly three times as often as incarceration. It is a sentence in which the defendant is released into the community for a specified period, theoretically under supervision. It has been argued that probation is not a sentence, but it is in the sense that it may be imposed only by the judiciary, which may set terms and conditions for the sentence. These are discussed in more detail, along with other aspects of probation, in Chapter 11. It is important to understand at this point, however, that probation may be imposed in lieu of or in combination with a fine, restitution, or community service. It may be imposed in conjunction with a brief period of incarceration or with electronic monitoring, also discussed in Chapter 11.

Another type of sentencing, **corporal punishment,** is not a legal sentence in the United States at this time. The last statute to be repealed was the Delaware whipping statute in 1973. In the past three decades, however, some scholars have argued for a return to corporal punishment, considering it a less expensive and more humane punishment than incarceration.

Another type of sentence that was used extensively in the past is **capital punishment.** Over the years capital punishment has been in and out of favor, with abolition movements beginning in the 1700s, gaining momentum in the late 1800s, and leading to actual abolition of the death penalty in many states during the twentieth century, only to have it reinstated in most. We have already looked at some of the constitutional issues surrounding capital punishment. Other issues, along with a brief history of recent developments in U.S. capital punishment, are contained in Spotlight 8-4.

The final major type of punishment is confinement, or **incarceration.** Offenders may be incarcerated in a jail (generally used for those awaiting trial or sentenced to short terms, usually less than a year) or in a prison (used for offenders who have been convicted of serious crimes and sentenced to death or to long terms of confinement) or may be confined in a community treatment center. These facilities, along with the issues surrounding confinement and incarceration, are discussed in Chapters 10 and 11.

8-3c   Current Sentencing Issues

There are many issues in sentencing. This section considers four: sentence disparity, three strikes and you're out, truth in sentencing, and treatment and sentencing.

Sentence Disparity

Although there is great concern about alleged **sentence disparity,** its meaning is not clear. Some use the term to refer to any differences that they think are unfair or inappropriate. Thus, the differences between legislatively determined sentences in two jurisdictions might be viewed as disparate. Others limit the definition of the term to the differences in sentences imposed by judges in similar cases. Some include any differences; others look to the circumstances surrounding the crime before determining whether sentences are disparate.

Sentence disparity may stem from legislative, judicial, or administrative decisions. Sentence length may vary from jurisdiction to jurisdiction because legislatures establish different terms for the same crime. Legislatures may differ with regard to whether a defendant with multiple sentences serves them concurrently or consecutively. Legislative sentences may be disparate if within a system there are sentences that are considered unfair. Sentence disparity may also result from decisions made by others. For example, prosecutors may influence a sentence. In the plea bargaining process, the prosecutor may offer a deal that involves a lesser penalty for one offense if the offender pleads guilty to another or to several other offenses.

Juries also have considerable discretion, even when they are not empowered to determine sentences. If they think that the judge will be too harsh or if they perceive that the legislative sentence is unfair, jurors may refuse to convict. In that case juries have the ultimate power to decide sentences. Although parole has been abolished in some states, where it does exist parole authorities have great latitude in deciding actual time served. Even when the legislature specifies by statute the percentage of a term that must be served before an offender is eligible for parole, the parole board has the power to determine when, if ever, that person will be released before the end of the actual sentence (parole is discussed in Chapter 11).

Most of the allegations of sentence disparity have involved the variables of race and gender. Earlier studies examining race and gender in sentencing did not agree on whether discrimination existed and, if it did, to what extent and why. Modern scholars do not agree either, and the debate continues. A few studies are illustrative.

Some criminologists argue that criminal justice systems are racist in sentencing. Michael J. Lynch and W. Byron Groves, in their explanation of radical criminology (an approach to the study of crime and criminals that suggests a connection between economic

---

▶ **Corporal punishment**
Physical punishment, such as beatings or whippings.

▶ **Capital punishment**
Punishment by death for those convicted of capital crimes.

▶ **Incarceration**   Imprisonment in a jail, a prison, or another type of penal institution.

▶ **Sentence disparity**
Inequalities and differences that result when people found guilty of the same crime receive sentences varying in length and type, without reasonable justification for those differences.

Spotlight 8-4   **Capital Punishment in the United States: A Brief History**

In 1972 in *Furman v. Georgia,* the U.S. Supreme Court held that, although capital punishment is not per se unconstitutional, it is unconstitutional when in its application it involves discrimination caused by arbitrary and capricious administration of the sentence. *Furman* invalidated most capital punishment statutes in existence at the time, but the Supreme Court left the door open for new legislation providing for capital punishment if it is applied without violating defendants' constitutional rights.[1]

By 1976, 36 states had responded with new capital punishment statutes, although some of those have been challenged in the courts. In 1977, the constitutional issues were satisfied in the case of the Utah statute, and Gary Gilmore became the first person executed since 1967. In May 1979, after a long and complicated legal battle, John Spenkelink, convicted of murdering a man with a hatchet, was the first involuntary inmate to die of capital punishment in the United States since 1967 (Gilmore refused to appeal his sentence and asked that it be carried out). Spenkelink was executed in Old Sparky, Florida's electric chair.

The movement toward capital punishment was highlighted in 1995, when New York revived the death penalty after 18 years, making New York the 38th state with capital punishment. Governor George E. Pataki signed the bill with two pens owned by slain police officers. Former New York Governor Mario Cuomo had vetoed death penalty legislation 12 times. In June 2004, the state's highest court ruled that the legislation was unconstitutional as constructed, and by November 2004 legislators were predicting that, with the changing political climate, there was little chance the statute would be revised.[2]

In 1999, the U.S. Supreme Court agreed to decide whether electrocution as the only method of capital punishment in Florida constituted cruel and unusual punishment. In January 2000, how-ever, the Florida legislature enacted a new statute, which provides that inmates under a death sentence may choose between electrocution and lethal injection. The Supreme Court dismissed the Florida appeal because the issue, which came from a death row inmate who would be able to choose lethal injection, was moot.[3]

Another recent issue that has been given considerable attention in the media as well as in the courts is the possibility that innocent people may be convicted of capital murder and executed. After evidence (primarily DNA) showed that a death row inmate in Illinois was innocent, in early 2000 Governor George H. Ryan announced that he would impose a moratorium on the death penalty in Illinois until the completion of an inquiry on why so many innocent people had been given the death sentence. This action gave significant impetus to the current movement toward a moratorium on executions, although some states (for example, Texas and Florida) continued with them. Before Illinois Governor Ryan left office in January 2003 he pardoned four death row inmates and commuted to life the rest of the death row sentences. His successor, Rod Blagojevich, continued the execution moratorium. In the fall 2003, the Illinois legislature overrode the governor's veto on a new capital punishment bill designed to decrease the chances of sending an innocent person to death row. The governor indicated that he would keep the moratorium on capital punishment in place until it could be determined whether the new statute accomplishes its purpose.[4] In 2004, the Illinois Supreme Court upheld the commutations made by Governor Ryan.[5]

In June 2001, the U.S. Supreme Court reversed the death sentence of Johnny Paul Penry, a Texas death row inmate, who came within three hours of execution on 16 November 2000. The case was decided on narrow procedural grounds involving jury instructions and did not reach the issue of whether the

---

reality and social phenomena, such as racism), referred to numerous studies that support this position.

These studies show that minorities, particularly blacks, are discriminated against in the sentencing process. Blacks receive longer sentences than whites for the same crime, and blacks who victimize whites receive longer sentences than blacks who victimize blacks. Recent research . . . on rape indicates that this bias remains in force today.[38]

In a 1994 publication, law professor Michael Tonry reported his analysis of jail and prison data and concluded that racial disparities in sentencing had "steadily gotten worse since 1980." Tonry attributed this to politically motivated decisions by Republican administrations to increase penalties for drug violations, when they knew that such increases would impact minorities negatively but would not result in a significant reduction of the crime rate. Tonry gave several reasons for his conclusions. He charged that drug arrests are easier to make in inner-city minority areas than in areas dominated by the middle and upper classes. Increased penalties have been aimed primarily at the illegal use of crack cocaine, used by minorities more frequently than powder cocaine, "a pharmacologically indistinguishable drug used primarily by middle-class Whites."[39]

In one case, the differences between African Americans and whites in drug sentences were raised by African American defendants, who claimed that they were denied equal protection because of the higher sentences (approximately 100-to-1) for the illegal distribution or possession of crack, as compared with powder cocaine. In 1996 in *United States* v. *Armstrong,* the U.S. Supreme Court held that the African American defendants had not

mentally ill may be executed.[6] But in 2002 the U.S. Supreme Court held that it is unconstitutional to execute a mentally retarded (but not necessarily mentally ill) person. *Atkins* v. *Virginia* involved a man who was sentenced to death for a murder he committed when he was 18. Daryl R. Atkins has an IQ of 59. The U.S. Supreme Court left it to the states to determine when a person is mentally retarded and did not provide much guidance for making that determination. In March 2003, Texas executed James Colburn, who had been diagnosed as paranoid schizophrenic since he was 14. Colburn had made approximately 15 suicide attempts, claiming that voices in his head told him to take his own life. But there was also evidence that Colburn knew what was happening to him, understood the process, and even apologized to the victim's family before he was executed.[7]

In its annual report on capital punishment, issued in 2004 and reporting 2003 data, the Bureau of Justice Statistics (BJS) noted the following:

- In 2003, 65 inmates were executed, 6 fewer than in 2002....
- Of persons executed in 2003
  – 42 were white
  – 20 were black
  – 3 were Hispanic (all white)
  – 1 was American Indian
- Of those executed in 2003
  – 65 were men
- Lethal injection accounted for 64 of the executions; 1 was carried out by electrocution....
- The number of prisoners under sentence of death at yearend 2003 decreased for the third consecutive year....

37 States and the Federal prison system held 3,374 prisoners under sentence of death, 188 fewer than at yearend 2002.
- At yearend, the youngest inmate under sentence of death was 19; the oldest was 88.[8]

According to the Death Penalty Information Center, as of 17 March 2005, 956 persons had been executed since 1976, with 12 of those executions occurring in 2005. Of the 956 inmates, 58 percent were white; 81 percent of the victims were white. Since 1973, 119 inmates have been released from death row based on new evidence of their innocence.[9]

Chapter 7 discusses the issue of lawyer competence, especially as it relates to the trial of capital cases. Chapter 12 discusses the issue of whether juveniles should be executed.

1. Furman v. Georgia, 408 U.S. 238 (1972).
2. "Lawmakers See Little Chance to Fix Flaws in New York's Death Penalty Statute This Year," *New York Times* (18 November 2004), p. 25. The case is People v. Lavalle, 783 N.Y.S.2d 485 (2004).
3. "New York Revives Death Penalty after Eighteen Years," *New York Times* (8 March 1995), p. 1. See New York Penal Code, Section 60.06 (2005).
4. "At Last, Death Penalty Reform," *Chicago Tribune* (20 November 2003), p. 30.
5. People *ex rel*. Madigan v. Synder, 804 N.E. 2d 546 (Ill 2004).
6. Penry v. Johnson, 532 U.S. 782 (2001).
7. Atkins v. Virginia, 536 U.S. 304 (2002); "A Mentally Ill Killer Is Executed in Texas," *New York Times* (27 March 2003), p. 12.
8. Bureau of Justice Statistics, *Capital Punishment Statistics* (Washington, D.C.: U.S. Department of Justice, 2004), p. 1; on the Internet at www.ojp.usdoj.gov/bjs/cp.htm, retrieved 22 December 2004.
9. "Facts about the Death Penalty," Death Penalty Information Center, 5 February 2004, on the Internet at www.deathpenaltyinfo.org, retrieved 22 December 2004.

shown racial discrimination. According to the Court, the fact that 88.3 percent of all federal prosecutions for crack cocaine violations were against African Americans did not in itself prove racial discrimination.[40] The U.S. Sentencing Commission has proposed to change the ratio, but thus far Congress has not agreed to do so.

It has also been alleged that sentence disparity is related to the offender's gender. Some researchers say that women are treated differentially at every stage in U.S. criminal justice systems and that this treatment is sexist; that is, women are discriminated against because of their gender.

Others say the system is more lenient toward women than toward men at every level and that, in particular, women receive lighter sentences than men for the same offenses. That, too, must be analyzed in terms of the legal factors courts may consider in sentencing, such as prior convictions and the seriousness of the current offense. It is argued that, when these factors are analyzed, there is little or no evidence of gender bias in sentencing.[41]

In one study, Darrell J. Steffensmeier reviewed the empirical evidence concerning the differential sentencing of women and concluded that, although preferential treatment exists, it is of small magnitude. He argued that the "changing sex role definitions and the contemporary women's movement have had little impact on sentencing outcomes of either male or female defendants" and that the differentials by gender have been diminished.[42]

In a much later study, Steffensmeier and his colleagues analyzed gender and imprisonment decisions during a two-year period in Pennsylvania. They found support for earlier research, concluding that in general the women received more lenient sentences than the men. However, unlike some of their predecessors, these scholars concluded that the differences were due to "the type or seriousness of the crime committed and the defendant's prior record, not the defendant's gender (or, for that matter, age, race, or other background/contextual variables)."[43]

Judicial sentences are another potential source of disparity. Most allegations of sentence disparity are aimed at judges, and many of the recent changes in sentencing laws have been aimed at controlling or removing judicial discretion in sentencing. Various solutions to sentence disparity have been proposed, but most of the reform efforts have centered on two approaches: either controlling judicial discretion or removing it from the sentencing process. This is done primarily through the imposition of sentencing guidelines, or requirements. Sentencing guidelines are seen as a way to control discretion without abolishing it, while correcting the extreme disparity that can result from individualized sentencing.

Basically guidelines work as follows. A judge has an offender to sentence. Without guidelines the judge may consider the offender's background, the nature of the offense, and other variables. When guidelines are available, presumably the relevance of these and other variables has been researched. Thus, the judge has a benchmark of an appropriate penalty in such circumstances. However, the judge may decide that it is reasonable in a given case to deviate from the guidelines; in that situation, reasons should be given.

Sentencing guidelines may be based on an empirical analysis of what *has* been done in the jurisdiction, not a philosophy of what *ought* to be done. Sentencing guidelines may be based what it is thought *should* be done. This may occur in a variety of ways. The guidelines may be recommended by a committee and accepted and thus mandated by the legislature, or they may be adopted by judges to apply to their jurisdictions.

Sentencing guidelines have, however, been challenged in many cases, at both the federal and state levels. In 2003, U.S. Department of Justice (DOJ) officials announced that they would begin monitoring federal judges who sentenced below federal guidelines. This move was understood by some to mean that the DOJ would be making a list of judges who exercise more discretion than the justice department thinks wise. Specifically, federal prosecutors were directed to notify the DOJ when federal judges sentence below the guidelines; decisions would then be made concerning whether those sentences should be appealed. Attorney General John Ashcroft issued a policy statement in a memo to federal prosecutors on 28 July 2003, which included these words:

> The public in general and crime victims in particular rightly expect that the penalties established by law for specific crimes will be sought and imposed by those who serve in the criminal justice system.[44]

The federal judiciary reacted sternly to this memo and to a law enacted 30 April 2003 as a part of the Protect (Prosecutorial Remedies and Other Tools to End the Exploitation of Children Today) Act of 2003. Among other provisions, the Protect Act limits the cases in which a federal judge may issue a lighter sentence than the federal sentencing guidelines, gives Congress (without the permission of the sentencing judge) access to certain documents from the case, and requires the reporting of lighter sentences. The act also requires that, when a federal court of appeals reviews a sentencing decision of a federal district court, it must do so *de novo*, which means anew, as if the hearing had not been held before. Some federal judges have protested the new law and called for its repeal, with some retiring rather than enforce the law. In September 2003, the Judicial Conference of the United States, which is headed by U.S. Supreme Court Justice William H. Rehnquist and includes the 27 federal judges who make policy for the federal judiciary, called for a repeal of the law.[45]

In January 2004, Chief Justice Rehnquist focused his annual state of the judiciary on the Protect Act. The chief justice stated that the law "could appear to be an unwarranted and ill-considered effort to intimidate individual judges in the performance of their judicial duties." The chief justice continued by declaring, "It seems that the traditional interchange between the Congress and the judiciary broke down" when the law was passed without any formal input from the judiciary. The chair of the House Judiciary Committee, Representative F. James Sensenbrenner Jr., said there was no breakdown in communication. Congress knew the judiciary would oppose the bill, but it was necessary because federal judges were using "downward departures" (that is, lighter sentences) in applying the federal sentencing guidelines.[46] But, as noted earlier in this chapter, significant changes have been made in the impact of the federal sentencing guidelines as a result of the *Booker* and *Fanfan* cases decided by the U.S. Supreme Court in January 2005.

The proposal to reduce or remove judicial sentencing discretion was manifested primarily in the adoption of determinate sentencing, which began in the 1970s. One of the most rigid of the new determinate sentencing statutes was that of California, the state that pioneered the indeterminate sentence and that used it most extensively. The California statute removed the rehabilitation philosophy and substituted punishment as the reason for incarceration. It specified that sentences were not to be disparate and that individuals charged with similar offenses should receive similar sentences. The judge may decide on the basis of aggravating or mitigating circumstances to raise or lower the presumed sentence, but written reasons must be given for deviating from it.

The California statute abolishes the parole board, with its discretion to determine release, but it provides that all releasees be placed under parole *supervision* for one year upon release. Good time credits for good behavior in prison are available to reduce sentence length. The law permits sentencing judges to add up to three years to a sentence imposed on a defendant whose crime results in great bodily injury to the victim.[47] On the other hand, California has moved somewhat toward a treatment philosophy, as noted in Chapter 11.

Three Strikes and You're Out

The emphasis on reducing sentence disparity has been manifested most clearly in the national focus on the habitual offender, summarized in the 1994 political slogan **three strikes and you're out.** The phrase figured prominently at the state as well as the national level, after Polly Klaas, a 12-year-old who was kidnapped from her home in 1993 while her parents and her friends—who were attending her slumber party—were sleeping. Polly was sexually assaulted and murdered. Richard Allen Davis, who had two prior kidnap convictions, was convicted and sentenced to death for the crimes against Polly. California led in the enactment of three strikes legislation and was quickly followed by most states and the federal government. But California's legislation is one of the toughest. It provides for a mandatory sentence for all persons convicted of a third felony, and that third strike may be any felony. The first two felonies, however, must be serious or violent ones. California also provides harsher penalties for two strikes.

The alleged lack of justice in the California statute has been evidenced in many sentences, but one in particular should be noted. A defendant received a sentence of 25 years-to-life after his conviction for stealing a $20 bottle of vitamins, his third strike. The U.S. Supreme Court refused to review the case, but a written opinion signed by associate justices John Paul Stevens, David Souter, and Ruth Bader Ginsberg raised issues concerning the legality of such a long sentence and urged inmates with similar sentences to challenge their sentences.[48]

In 2003, the U.S. Supreme Court decided two three strikes cases and upheld the legislation in question. These cases are critical ones in sentencing, and excerpts from one of them is included here. The following excerpt, from *Ewing* v. *California,* states the facts of the case as well as the history and rationale for three strikes legislation. Note the U.S. Supreme Court's discussion of the discretion that still remains within the sentencing structure of this strict law, as the Court explains what is meant by a *wobbler.*[49]

▶ **Three strikes and you're out**
Legislation enacted in most states and in the federal government in recent years designed to impose long sentences on persons who commit three or more serious crimes.

Ewing v. *California*

In this case we decide whether the Eighth Amendment prohibits the State of California from sentencing a repeat felon to a prison term of 25 years to life under the State's "Three Strikes and You're Out" law.

California's three strikes law reflects a shift in the State's sentencing policies toward incapacitating and deterring repeat offenders who threaten the public safety. The law was designed "to ensure longer prison sentences and greater punishment for those who commit a felony and have been previously convicted of serious and/or violent felony offenses." . . .

Under California law, certain offenses may be classified as either felonies or misdemeanors. These crimes are known as "Wobblers." Some crimes that would otherwise be misdemeanors become "wobblers" because of the defendant's prior record. Both types of "wobblers" are triggering offenses under the three strikes law only when they are treated as felonies....

In California, prosecutors may exercise their discretion to charge a "wobbler" as either a felony or a misdemeanor. Likewise, California trial courts have discretion to reduce a "wobbler" charged as a felony to a misdemeanor either before preliminary examination or at sentencing to avoid imposing a three strikes sentence. In exercising this discretion, the court may consider "those factors that direct similar sentencing decisions," such as "the nature and circumstances of the offense, the defendant's appreciation of and attitude toward the offense, ... [and] the general objectives of sentencing."

California trial courts can also vacate allegations of prior "serious" or "violent" felony convictions....

[The U.S. Supreme Court then stated the facts of this case.]

On parole from a 9-year term, petitioner Gary Ewing walked into the pro shop.... He walked out with three golf clubs, priced at $399 a piece, concealed in his pants leg. A shop employee, whose suspicions were aroused when he observed Ewing limp out of the pro shop, telephoned the police. The police apprehended Ewing in the parking lot.

Ewing is no stranger to the criminal justice system. In 1984, at the age of 22, he pleaded guilty to theft. The court sentenced him to six months in jail, three years' probation, and a $300 fine. In 1988, he was convicted of felony grand theft auto and sentenced to one year in jail and three years' probation. After Ewing completed probation, however, the sentencing court reduced the crime to a misdemeanor, permitted Ewing to withdraw his guilty plea, and dismissed the case. In 1990, he was convicted of petty theft with a prior and sentenced to 60 days in the county jail and three years' probation. In 1992 Ewing was convicted of battery and sentenced to 30 days in the county jail and two years' summary probation. One month later, he was convicted of theft and sentenced to 10 days in the county jail and 12 months' probation. In January 1993, Ewing was convicted of burglary and sentenced to 60 days in the county jail and one year's summary probation. In July 1993, he was convicted of appropriating lost property and sentenced to 10 days in the county jail and two years' summary probation. In September 1993, he was convicted of unlawfully possessing a firearm and trespassing and sentenced to 30 days in the county jail and one year's probation.

In October and November 1993, Ewing committed three burglaries and one robbery at a Long Beach, California, apartment complex over a 5-week period. He awakened one of his victims, asleep on her living room sofa, as he tried to disconnect her video cassette recorder from the television in that room. When she screamed, Ewing ran out the front door. On another occasion, Ewing accosted a victim in the mailroom of the apartment complex. Ewing claimed to have a gun and ordered the victim to hand over his wallet. When the victim resisted, Ewing produced a knife and forced the victim back to the apartment itself. While Ewing rifled through the bedroom, the victim fled the apartment screaming for help. Ewing absconded with the victim's money and credit cards.

On December 9, 1993, Ewing was arrested on the premises of the apartment complex for trespassing and lying to a police officer. The knife used in the robbery and a glass cocaine pipe were later found in the back seat of the patrol car used to transport Ewing to the police station. A jury convicted Ewing of first-degree robbery and three counts of residential burglary. Sentenced to nine years and eight months in prison, Ewing was paroled in 1999.

Only 10 months later, Ewing stole the golf clubs at issue in this case. He was charged with, and ultimately convicted of, one count of felony grand theft of personal property in excess of $400. As required by the three strikes law, the prosecutor formally alleged, and the trial court later found, that Ewing had been convicted previously of four serious or violent felonies for the three burglaries and the robbery in the Long Beach apartment complex.

At the sentencing hearing, Ewing asked the court to reduce the conviction for grand theft, a "wobbler" under California law, to a misdemeanor so as to avoid a three strikes sentence. Ewing also asked the trial court to exercise its discretion to dismiss the allegations of some or all of his prior serious or violent felony convictions, again for purposes of avoiding a three strikes sentence. Before sentencing Ewing, the trial court took note of his entire criminal history, including the fact that he was on parole when he committed his latest offense. The court also heard arguments from defense counsel and a plea from Ewing himself.

In the end, the trial judge determined that the grand theft should remain a felony. The court also ruled that the four prior strikes for the three burglaries and the robbery in Long Beach should stand. As a newly convicted felon with two or more "serious" or "violent" felony convictions in his past, Ewing was sentenced under the three strikes law to 25 years to life....

[The U.S. Supreme Court then began its lengthy analysis of the legal issues in the case, reviewing the relevant case law concerning the proportionality of sentences before continuing with the following statement of the history and rationale of three strikes legislation.]

For many years, most States have had laws providing for enhanced sentencing of repeat offenders ... [but between 1993 and 1995 the current three strikes legislation approach began]. These laws responded to widespread public concerns about crime by targeting the class of offenders who pose the greatest threat to public safety: career criminals.... Throughout the States, legislatures enacting three strikes laws made a deliberate policy choice that individuals who have repeatedly engaged in serious or violent criminal behavior, and whose conduct has not been deterred by more conventional approaches to punishment, must be isolated from society in order to protect the public safety....

Our traditional deference to legislative policy choices finds a corollary in the principle that the Constitution "does not mandate adoption of any one penological theory." A sentence can have a variety of justifications, such as incapacitation, deterrence, retribution, or rehabilitation. Some or all of these justifications may play a role in a State's sentencing scheme. Selecting the sentencing rationales is generally a policy choice to be made by state legislatures, not federal courts.

When the California Legislature enacted the three strikes laws, it made a judgment that protecting the public safety requires incapacitating criminals who have already been convicted of at least one serious or violent crime. Nothing in the Eighth Amendment prohibits California from making that choice....

California's justification is no pretext. Recidivism is a serious public safety concern in California and throughout the Nation. According to a recent report, approximately 67 percent of former inmates released from state prisons were charged with at least one "serious" new crime within three years of their release. In particular, released property offenders like Ewing had higher recidivism rates than those released after committing violent, drug, or public-order offenses. Approximately 73 percent of the property offenders released in 1994 were arrested again within three years, compared to approximately 61 percent of the violent offenders, 62 percent of the public-order offenders, and 66 percent of the drug offenders....

[The U.S. Supreme Court then cited other studies of recidivism before discussing deterrence theory.]

The State's interest in deterring crime also lends some support to the three strikes law. We have long viewed both incapacitation and deterrence as rationales for recidivism statutes....

[The U.S. Supreme Court emphasized that after the passage of three strikes legislation there was a dramatic decrease in the number of parolees who committed additional crimes and, further, that many of those paroled in California left the state. The Court discussed some of the criticisms of the legislation and noted that those should be directed at the legislature, which is free to enact such legislation as long as it has a reasonable basis for doing so.]

Against this backdrop, we consider Ewing's claim that his three strikes sentence of 25 years to life is unconstitutional. . . . [The U.S. Supreme Court pointed out that it was not only the current crime of shoplifting golf clubs—although that is a serious crime—but also Ewing's entire history that was at issue. The Court concluded as follows.]

Ewing's sentence is justified by the State's public-safety interest in incapacitating and deterring recidivist felons, and amply supported by his own long, serious criminal record. Ewing has been convicted of numerous misdemeanor and felony offenses, served nine separate terms of incarceration, and committed most of his crimes while on probation or parole. His prior "strikes" were serious felonies including robbery and three residential burglaries. To be sure, Ewing's sentence is a long one. But it reflects a rational legislative judgment, entitled to deference, that offenders who have committed serious or violent felonies and who continue to commit felonies must be incapacitated. The State of California "was entitled to place upon [Ewing] the onus of one who is simply unable to bring his conduct within the social norms prescribed by the criminal law of the State." Ewing's is not "the rare case in which a threshold comparison of the crime committed and the sentence imposed leads to an inference of gross disproportionality."

We hold that Ewing's sentence of 25 years to life in prison, imposed for the offense of felony grand theft under the three strikes law, is not grossly disproportionate and therefore does not violate the Eighth Amendment's prohibition on cruel and unusual punishments.

Truth in Sentencing

> **Truth in sentencing** The concept requiring that actual time served by offenders is closer to the time allocated for the sentence. Many jurisdictions are establishing 85 percent as their goal, meaning that offenders may not be released for any reason until they have served 85 percent of their sentences.

Another current trend in sentencing is illustrated by California's statutory provision for **truth in sentencing,** which requires that anyone in California convicted of a violent or serious crime serve at least 80 percent of the imposed sentence. This provision applies to all crimes and is designed to negate the previous policy, by which inmates could earn good time credits and reduce their sentences by 50 percent.[50]

Truth in sentencing laws require that inmates serve a specified percentage of their sentences before they are released from prison. Most states have such laws, which are encouraged by federal government grants. The Violent Offender Incarceration and Truth-in-Sentencing Incentive Grants Act of 1995 offers states some grants for prison construction and operation but provides that those states require violent offenders to serve 85 percent of their sentences.[51] Some states require that murderers (or other specified types of offenders) must serve all of their time before they are released. For example, an Illinois law provides that "a prisoner who is serving a term of imprisonment for first degree murder shall receive no good conduct credit and shall serve the entire sentence imposed by the court." The statute then specifies that inmates serving sentences for certain crimes (such as aggravated kidnapping and attempted first-degree murder) may receive only 4.5 days of good conduct (toward early release) per month. Those serving time for crimes that are not enumerated may receive one day of good conduct credit for each day they serve.[52]

As expected, truth in sentencing and three strikes statutes have increased the number of persons incarcerated. In a publication released in January 1999, the Bureau of Justice Statistics (BJS) reported that the average time served by violent criminals in state prisons rose from 43 months in 1993 to 49 months in 1997, representing serving 54 percent rather than only 47 percent of their sentences. During the same period the number of state inmates eligible for release fell, leaving most state prisons with more inmates in 1997 than in 1993. In fact, the number of persons incarcerated in state prisons between 1990 and 1997 rose by 60 percent, although there was only a 17 percent increase in the number of persons sent to prison during those years.[53]

Treatment and Sentencing

The final sentencing issue to which we give attention is a relatively new one. After years of "locking them up and throwing away the key," some jurisdictions are beginning to review that approach and back away. The recent changes have come about because of the increased costs of incarceration at a time when government budgets have been cut significantly. There has also been some concern that the punitive approach, at least in some cases, is less effective than a treatment approach.

In 2001, a major newspaper ran the headline "States Ease Laws on Time in Prison." According to the *New York Times,* a 20-year trend toward tough sentencing laws was being "quietly rolled back" in some states. Mandatory minimum sentences were being reduced by statute. States, which were spending a total of $30 billion a year to operate prisons, some of which had been built at significant expense in recent years to house the inmates resulting from the get-tough approach, were reconsidering their approaches to punishment. One lawmaker in Louisiana, where prison populations increased by 50 percent as a result of the get-tough approach, referred to the punitive system as one that "was bankrupting the state and was not reducing crime."[54]

By 2003, with most states facing severe budget cuts, many state legislatures had begun changing sentencing policies in order to reduce the number of inmates on the states payrolls. According to one professional organization, "with the third straight year of budget shortfalls looming and most of the easy cuts already enacted, services once considered untouchable were falling prey to legislators desperate for additional savings."[55] More attention is given in Chapter 11 to the issue of treatment rather than punishment.

8-4 Appeals and Writs

Spotlight 8-5 explains the appeals process, along with what might happen to a case after appeal. A successful appeal does not necessarily mean that the case is over and the defendant is released from the criminal justice system. Generally a successful appeal means that the case is retried, and in most cases the defendant is convicted again. A successful appeal on a sentence—for example, the death penalty—may result in another death sentence. The difference is that, in the retrial (or resentencing), the state must not commit the errors made in the previous trial. As Spotlight 8-5 notes, on appeal a defendant may be successful on some issues but not on others.

In addition to appeals, defendants may petition for a **writ,** which is an order from the court. It gives permission to do whatever was requested or orders someone to do something specific. A common writ filed by offenders is a writ of *habeas corpus,* which means "you have the body." Originally a writ of *habeas corpus* was an order from the court to someone, such as a sheriff or a jailer, to have the person in court at a specified time and to state the legal theory under which the person was being held. Today it is more extensive, and its use is governed by statutes, which differ from jurisdiction to jurisdiction. Often it is used by inmates who are questioning the legality of their confinement. It does not question the issue of guilt or innocence but asserts that some due process rights of offenders are being violated or have been violated.

Under some circumstances sentences may be appealed. Occasionally a sentence is reversed, and the case is sent back for resentencing. In practice this rarely occurs. Appellate courts have given judges wide discretion in sentencing. As long as the sentence is within the statutory provisions and the sentencing judge has not abused his or her discretion or shown undue prejudice, it is difficult for defendants to challenge a judicial sentence successfully. In rare cases, courts may declare a legislatively determined sentence to be in violation of the defendant's rights.

> **Writ** An order from the court. *See also* **writ of certiorari** and **habeas corpus.**

> **Habeas corpus** Technically a written court order requiring that the accused be taken to court to determine the legality of custody and confinement; also refers to writs filed by inmates regarding the alleged illegality of their confinement.

Spotlight 8-5   The Appeals Process

An appeal occurs when the defendant in a criminal case (or either party in a civil case) requests that a court with appellate jurisdiction rule on a decision that has been made by a trial court or administrative agency.

Appellate courts receive two basic categories of cases: appeals and writs. Appeals, by far the most time-consuming and important, occur when a litigant's case receives a full-scale review after losing at the trial level (or, in several States, after losing in certain administrative proceedings).

The appeal begins when the party losing the case in the trial court, the "appellant," files a notice of appeal, usually a month or two after the trial court decision. Then within a few months the appellant files the trial court record in the appellate court. The record, often bulky, consists of the papers filed in the trial court along with the transcript of the trial testimony. Next the appellant and the opposing party, the "appellee," file briefs that argue for their respective positions. The briefs are usually followed by short oral presentations to the judges. Finally, the judges decide the case and issue a written opinion. An increasing number of courts, but still a minority, decide some appeals without written opinions.

State supreme court decisions are usually issued by the full court; intermediate court decisions are generally issued by three-judge panels. The whole decision process takes roughly a year, although it ranges from six months in some courts to several years in courts with large backlogs.

In making its final disposition of the case, an appellate court may

- "Affirm," or uphold the lower court ruling.
- "Modify" the lower court ruling by changing it in part, but not totally reversing it.
- "Reverse," or set aside, the lower court ruling and not require any further court action.
- "Reverse and remand" the case by overturning the lower court ruling but requiring further proceedings at the lower court that may range from conducting a new trial to entering a proper judgment.
- "Remand" all or part of the case by sending it back to the lower court without overturning the lower courts ruling but with instructions for further proceedings that may range from conducting a new trial to entering a proper judgment.

Thus, the termination of an appellate court case may or may not be the end of the case from the perspective of the parties involved in the case. They may be required to go back to the lower court for further proceedings. If federal law is involved, a party can petition for review in the U.S. Supreme Court. In criminal cases, defendants can file further petitions in a federal court or state court.

Source: Bureau of Justice Statistics, *Trends: The Growth of Appeals* (Washington, D.C.: U.S. Department of Justice, 1986), p. 3.

One final word on appeals and writs relates to the inability of some defendants to file them. A federal commission has requested that prosecutors as well as defense attorneys and other criminal justice system personnel assist inmates who need help in filing appeals for new trials, especially when DNA testing might reveal that they could not have committed the crimes for which they have been convicted. Attorney General Janet Reno directed the National Institute of Justice to establish the commission in 1998, and it issued a report the following year. Reno acted after she was presented with documentation of 28 cases in which DNA evidence had exonerated inmates. Other cases have subsequently been identified. According to Reno, the justice systems are not perfect, and those who are "charged with the administration of justice have a responsibility to seek its continued improvement."[56]

Chapter Wrap-Up

This chapter focused on the criminal trial, sentencing, and appeal. The procedures and issues surrounding these aspects of U.S. criminal justice systems are extensive and complicated and are governed by numerous statutes and court decisions. It is not possible to state "the law" in many of these areas because often the judges of state courts and lower federal courts differ in their analyses of how statutes and constitutions apply to the facts before them.

Even when the U.S. Supreme Court agrees to hear and decide some of the controversies, often we do not know how these decisions will be applied in similar cases. Some of the Court's decisions are close, with many of those decided by a 5-to-4 vote. Thus, a change of one member of the Court may alter the direction of what has been called the revolution in criminal procedure of the past several decades.

It is possible, however, to state generally what happens in the trial of a criminal case and how the constitutional guarantees apply to any or all of the stages of a trial. This chapter began with a brief overview of those constitutional rights and gave closer attention to the rights that are more specific to the trial and appellate stages. The right to a speedy trial, the right to a public trial by an impartial jury, and the right to the confrontation and cross-examination of witnesses, along with defendants' right to remain silent and not be forced to testify against themselves, are crucial to understanding the implementation of the various stages of the trial. Although states have considerable freedom in establishing the procedures by which they will conduct criminal trials, they may not violate federal (or state) constitutional provisions.

In that sense, every stage of the trial must be understood and analyzed in light of the federal constitutional rights to which all criminal defendants are entitled. The right to a public trial by an impartial jury precludes selection of the jury in secret. It prohibits implicit or explicit exclusion of people because of their race, gender, religion, or ethnic origin. However, understanding the right to a jury of one's peers may seem elusive, for most juries are not representative of young adults, and courts have held that lack of representation to be permissible in most cases.

The importance of constitutional rights that apply to the trial is underscored by the fact that, when those rights are violated, with only a few exceptions, the demonstrative or testimonial evidence secured as a result of those violations should be excluded from the trial. In some cases it is not possible to prove guilt beyond a reasonable doubt without this tainted evidence; thus, the case must be dismissed.

This use of the exclusionary rule has led to considerable controversy concerning U.S. criminal justice systems. Its implications are extensive. Police may become discouraged and refuse to arrest in certain situations, thinking the case will not result in a conviction. Society may become critical of a system that appears to let the guilty go free. Potential criminals may decide to commit crimes, thinking they will not be convicted even if arrested. But those protections are to ensure that, when people are convicted of crimes, their convictions occur only after proper procedures have been followed and constitutional safeguards have been observed.

In this chapter each stage of the criminal trial was explained and discussed, beginning with the opening of the court session, in which charges against the defendant are read, through jury selection, the presentation of evidence, the final arguments, and the verdict. In all of these stages the defense, the prosecution, and the judge are primary figures in assuring that proper procedures are followed. But following proper procedures does not end the matter. It is important to consider and reconsider the issues involved in U.S. criminal justice systems.

Some of those important issues were raised in this chapter. The right of the public to know and of the media to tell may conflict with the right of the defendant to be tried fairly and impartially. Which right should give way? The right of the defendant to a trial by jury creates enormous expenses and consumes considerable time of all participants in the criminal trial. At what point, if ever, should that right give way to cost?

The criminal trial has an enormous effect on the rest of the criminal justice system. Long criminal trials increase the backlog in civil and criminal courts and result in a greater likelihood that defendants are denied their right to a speedy trial and that society must spend more money to keep the system operating. Mistrials increase the amount of time and money devoted to trials. Failure to convict in numerous cases might lead the public to question the effectiveness of the system. Conviction of the innocent undermines the entire system, but acquittal of those whom most believe guilty has led to rioting. Repeated appeals lead many to question whether there is any finality in the law.

Throughout this discussion of the procedures and issues of the trial, however, it should be remembered that the vast majority of defendants do not go to trial. Therefore, it is important not to let the issues of the trial overshadow the need to give attention to the pretrial stages of criminal justice systems. In addition, it is important to understand and analyze what happens after defendants plead guilty or are found guilty at trial. Sentencing is a critical stage of the system and was the focus of the next major section of the chapter.

The sentencing process, ranging from the sentencing hearing to the formal stage of imposing the sentence on the convicted defendant, involves numerous issues and problems. The major ones were discussed in this chapter, beginning with an overview of the various sentencing strategies. The sentencing hearing was noted, along with some of the processes and issues involved in the decision-making process of sentencing.

The various types of sentences, ranging from probation to the most severe, capital punishment, were noted, followed by a discussion of the current issues and trends in sentencing. The concern with alleged sentence disparity led to a return to determinate sentences, many of which are longer than previously. The current concepts of truth in sentencing and three strikes and you're out embody this return to longer and more determinate sentences. More recently, however, some jurisdictions have turned to treatment rather than punishment in an attempt to balance budgets and reduce crime.

The final section of the chapter focused on appeals and writs, both means by which individuals may challenge the legality of their incarceration, their sentences, or even their convictions.

This chapter concluded our study of what happens in adult criminal court systems. As we have seen, most people accused of crimes do not go through the entire system. But for the small percentage who do, and for a society that needs and deserves protection from property as well as from violent offenders, confinement and incarceration have become the solutions. Whether they are adequate solutions is the underlying issue in the next section of the text, which includes three chapters.

Key Terms

aggravating circumstances (p. 225)	*demonstrative evidence (p. 219)*	*jury (p. 212)*
beyond a reasonable doubt (p. 223)	*determinate sentence (p. 225)*	*mandatory sentence (p. 224)*
capital punishment (p. 231)	*directed verdict (p. 222)*	*mistrial (p. 219)*
circumstantial evidence (p. 220)	*direct evidence (p. 220)*	*mitigating circumstances (p. 225)*
community work service (p. 230)	*direct examination (p. 220)*	*pardon (p. 225)*
concurrent sentence (p. 229)	*fine (p. 229)*	*peremptory challenge (p. 213)*
consecutive sentence (p. 229)	*habeas corpus (p. 239)*	*petit jury (p. 212)*
contempt of court (p. 216)	*hearsay evidence (p. 220)*	*prejudicial errors (p. 221)*
corporal punishment (p. 231)	*incarceration (p. 231)*	*presentence investigation (PSI) (p. 227)*
cross-examination (p. 220)	*indeterminate sentence (p. 224)*	*presumption of innocence (p. 222)*

presumptive sentence (p. 224)
restitution (p. 230)
sentence (p. 224)
sentence disparity (p. 231)

summons (p. 217)
three strikes and you're out (p. 235)
trial (p. 210)

truth in sentencing (p. 238)
voir dire (p. 218)
writ (p. 239)

Apply It

1. Explain the importance of constitutional rights in a criminal trial.
2. What is the purpose of the Speedy Trial Act of 1974? What kinds of delays does it permit?
3. Why is the right to a public trial important to defendants? What are the legal problems and issues with public trials as far as the media are concerned?
4. Why is the jury system considered important in the United States? Should it be abolished? Why or why not? Do you think a fair and impartial jury can be selected in high-publicity trials?
5. What are the requirements for jury size and the selection of names for the jury pool? What is meant by *an impartial jury? A jury of peers?*
6. What is the role of the judge in controlling the conduct of defendants at trial?
7. Should people who are chosen for the jury pool be permitted to be excused from jury duty at their own request, or should all persons called be required to serve? Which, if any, requests should be honored? Which reasons should not be considered?
8. What is the significance of *Batson* v. *Kentucky*? Does the case apply to gender?
9. How do opening statements differ from closing statements? Are both required for the prosecution and the defense?
10. Define demonstrative evidence. How does it differ from witness testimony as evidence?
11. What is the *hearsay rule*?
12. What is the difference between direct and circumstantial evidence?

13. What is meant by *direct examination, cross examination,* and *redirect*?
14. Contrast the prosecution's case with that of the defense.
15. Describe the role of the judge in presenting the case to the jury.
16. Describe and evaluate the role of the jury in a criminal trial.
17. Discuss the importance of sentencing and explain sentencing strategies.
18. Is a sentencing hearing necessary? Is it required? What occurs in a sentencing hearing? What is the value of a presentence investigation? Should the presentence investigation be available to the prosecution and the defense, as well as the judge? Why or why not?
19. What are the legal issues concerning the role of victims in the sentencing process? What is your opinion regarding the role they should be permitted to play?
20. Should capital punishment be abolished? Why or why not?
21. What is meant by *sentence disparity*? Discuss the issues of gender and racial discrimination in sentencing.
22. What problems have arisen with federal sentencing guidelines?
23. What is the difference between *determinate* and *indeterminate sentences*?
24. What do you think will be the effect of three strikes and you're out legislation? Evaluate the U.S. Supreme Court's recent decision on this concept. What is the effect of truth in sentencing?
25. Should we treat rather than punish? Discuss.
26. Explain the meaning of *appeals* and *writs*.

Endnotes

1. "U.S. Suits Multiply, but Fewer Ever Get to Trial, Study Says," *New York Times* (14 December 2003), p. 1.
2. Klopfer v. North Carolina, 386 U.S. 213 (1967).
3. U.S. Code, Title 18, Sections 3161–3174 (2005).
4. N.Y. Civil Rights Law, Section 12 (2005).
5. Tex. Code Crim. Proc., Art. 32A.01 (2004).
6. Tex. Code Crim. Proc. Art. 32A.02, Section 1 (2004).
7. Sheppard v. Maxwell, 384 U.S. 333, 356 (1966), quoting 135 N.E.2d 340, 342 (1956).
8. Globe Newspaper Co. v. Superior Court, 457 U.S. 596 (1982).
9. United States v. McVeigh, 955 F.Supp. 1281 (1997), *cert. denied sub nom.,* 522 U.S. 1142 (1998).
10. Duncan v. Louisiana, 391 U.S. 145, 149 (1968).
11. "New York State Ends the Mandatory Sequestration of Jurors," *New York Times* (31 May 2001), p. 20; N.Y. Penal Code, Section 310.10 (2005)
12. Taylor v. Louisiana, 419 U.S. 522, 523 (1975), footnotes and citations omitted.
13. Swain v. Alabama, 380 U.S. 202 (1965).
14. Batson v. Kentucky, 476 U.S. 79 (1986).

15. Miller-El v. Cockrell, 537 U.S. 322 (2003), *on remand,* Miller-El v. Johnson, 330 F.3d 690 (5th Cir. 2003), *subsequent appeal,* Miller-El v. Dretke, 361 F.3d 849 (5th Cir. 2004), *rev'd., remanded,* 125 S.Ct. 2317 (2005).
16. J.E.B. v. Alabama *ex rel.* T.B., 511 U.S. 127 (1994).
17. Barber v. Ponte, 772 F.2d 982 (1st Cir. 1985), *cert. denied,* 475 U.S. 1050 (1986).
18. "Juror Who Overslept Gets Jail for Delaying Court," *Orlando Sentinel* (4 January 1998), p. 22.
19. Illinois v. Allen, 397 U.S. 337 (1970).
20. Illinois v. Allen, 397 U.S. 337 (1970).
21. "Separatists Kicked Out of Court as Trial Opens," *Miami Herald* (28 October 1997), p. 4; "Separatists' Leader Acquitted in Texas," *New York Times* (28 August 1999), p. 9; "Separatists Sentenced in Firearms Case," *Dallas Morning News* (8 December 2001), p. 37.
22. "ABA Creates Kennedy Commission on Sentencing and Prison Policies," *Criminal Justice Newsletter* (3 November 2003), p. 6.
23. Ibid.
24. "ABA Passes Resolutions Dealing with Sentencing Guidelines," *Wisconsin Law Journal* (18 August 2004).

25. "Sailor from Mutiny in '44 Wins a Presidential Pardon," *New York Times* (24 December 1999), p. 12.

26. "First Black from West Point Gains Pardon," *New York Times* (20 February 1999), p. 7.

27. "Court Refuses Case on a Presidential Pardon," *New York Times* (24 September 2003); the case is Borders v. D.C. Office of Bar Counsel, 797 A.2d 716 (D.C. App. 2002), *cert. denied,* 540 U.S. 966 (2003).

28. "Texas Governor Pardons 35 Arrested in Tainted Sting," *New York Times* (23 August 2003), p. 7; "Tulia, Texas: Narcotics Officer Accused of Targeting the Black Community of Tulia, Texas, in a Drug Sting," *Show: 60 Minutes* (7:00 P.M. ET) – CBS (28 September 2003); "Inadmissible," *Texas Lawyer* 20, no. 47 (24 January 2005), p. 3.

29. Ring v. Arizona, 534 U.S. 1103 (2002).

30. State v. Blakely, 47 P.3d 149 (Wash.App. 2002), *rev'd, remanded,* Blakely v. Washington, 124 S.Ct. 2531 (2004); United States v. Apprendi, 530 U.S. 466 (2000).

31. United States v. Booker, 375 F.3d 508 (7th Cir. 2004), *aff'd, remanded,* 125 S.Ct.738 (2005).

32. United States v. Fanfan, 2004 U.S. Dist. LEXIS 18593 (D.Me., 2004), *petition granted, motion granted,* 2004 U.S. LEXIS 4789 (U.S. 2004); *and mot. granted, mot. denied,* 125 S.Ct. 26 (2004), *and subsequent appeal, remanded,* 125 S.Ct. 738 (2005).

33. "Judges' Rulings In Giving Death Are Overturned," *New York Times* (3 September 2003), p. 1; Summerlin v. Stewart, 341 F.3d 1082 (9th Cir. 2003), *rev'd, remanded,* 124 S.Ct. 2519 (2004).

34. Shepard v. United States, 125 S.Ct. 1254 (2005).

35. Booth v. Maryland, 482 U.S. 496 (1987), *overruled in part,* Payne v. Tennessee, 501 U.S. 808 (1991).

36. Payne v. Tennessee, 501 U.S. 808 (1991). The other case that was overruled is South Carolina v. Gathers, 490 U.S. 805 (1989).

37. State v. Gentry, 888 P.2d 1105 (Wash. 1995), *cert. denied,* 516 U.S. 843 (1995).

38. Michael J. Lynch and W. Byron Groves, *A Primer in Radical Criminology,* 2d ed. (New York: Harper and Heston, 1989), pp. 106–107, citations omitted.

39. Michael Tonry, "Racial Politics, Racial Disparities, and the War on Crime," *Crime & Delinquency* 40 (October 1994): 475, 483–488.

40. United States v. Armstrong, 517 U.S. 456 (1996).

41. For an analysis of gender and sentencing, see Marian R. Williams, "Gender and Sentencing: An Analysis of Indicators," *Criminal Justice Policy Review* 10, no. 4 (1999): 471–490.

42. Darrell J. Steffensmeier, "Assessing the Impact of the Women's Movement on Sex-Based Differences in the Handling of Adult Criminal Defendants," *Crime & Delinquency* 26 (July 1980): 344–357.

43. Darrell J. Steffensmeier et al., "Gender and Imprisonment Decisions," *Criminology* 31 (August 1993): 411–446; quotation is on p. 435.

44. "Justice Dept. to Monitor Judges for Sentences Shorter Than Guidelines Suggest," *New York Times* (8 August 2003), p. 12.

45. "In Angry Outbursts, New York's U.S. Judges Protest New Sentencing Procedures," *New York Times* (8 December 2003), p. 25; "Judges Seek Repeal of Law on Sentencing," *New York Times* (24 September 2003), p. 17. The Protect Act is codified as Public Law 108–21 (2005).

46. "Chief Justice Attacks a Law As Infringing on Judges," *New York Times* (1 January 2004), p. 10.

47. Cal. Penal Code, Section 1170 *et seq.* (2005).

48. Riggs v. California, 525 U.S. 1114 (1999).

49. Ewing v. California, 538 U.S. 11 (2003), footnotes and case citations omitted. The statute in question is Cal. Penal Code, Section 667(b) (2005). See also Lockyer v. Andrade, 538 U.S. 63 (2003).

50. Cal. Penal Code, Title 16, Section 667 (2005).

51. Violent Offender Incarceration and Truth in Sentencing Incentive Grants, U.S. Code, Title 42, Section 13701 *et seq.* (2005).

52. Ill. Crim. Stat., Chapter 730, Section 5/3-6-3 (2004).

53. Bureau of Justice Statistics, *Truth in Sentencing in State Prisons* (Washington, D.C.: U.S. Department of Justice, 1999), p. 1.

54. "States Ease Laws on Time in Prison," *New York Times* (2 September 2001), p. 1.

55. "Budget Deficits Forcing Changes in Sentencing, Lawmakers Say," *Criminal Justice Newsletter* (1 October 2003), p. 8, referring to the report *Dollars and Sentences: Legislators' Views on Prisons, Punishment, and Budget Crisis,* available from the Vera Institute of Justice, 233 Broadway, 12th Floor, New York, NY 10279, (212) 334-1300. On the Internet: www.vera.org.

56. *Postconviction DNA Testing: Recommendations for Handling Requests,* 1999, available from the National Criminal Justice Reference Services, Box 6000, Rockville, MD 20849-6000, (800)851-3420. On the Internet: www.ncjrs.org.

Confinement and Corrections

After the processes of convicting and sentencing, society is faced with the issue of what to do with offenders. Historically convicted offenders were treated informally by means of various psychological and physical punishments. Physical, or corporal, punishments became severe, however, and for humanitarian and other reasons reformers decided corporal punishment should be replaced with confinement.

Confinement facilities—formerly used primarily for detaining the accused temporarily while they awaited trial or the convicted while they awaited corporal or other forms of punishment—were viewed as places for punishment and reformation. Although many reformers saw confinement facilities as a replacement for corporal punishment, others saw them as an environment in which offenders would be reformed through work; would have time for reflection; and, in some cases, would be subjected to corporal punishment.

The history of the emergence of prisons and jails as places of punishment is a fascinating study, but it is laced with controversy, idealism, and unfulfilled promises. Part 4 traces that development from its beginning through modern times. Chapter 9 focuses on the history and structure of confinement, pointing out the differences between state and federal systems, the different levels of security that characterize confinement, and the emergence of prisons as places for punishment. The nature of private corrections is discussed, along with the problems of prison and jail overcrowding. This chapter provides the background needed for an analysis of some of the issues surrounding modern correctional practices.

Chapter 10 examines the administration and inmate life of modern prisons, looking particularly at the ways in which the internal structure of the prison may be used to control inmates. That control is not always successful, however, as illustrated by the discussions on prison violence and the lawsuits filed as a result of alleged violations of inmates' constitutional rights. Part 4 closes with a chapter on community corrections, probation and parole.

The History and Structure of Confinement

9

In the past, when the confinement of offenders was necessary, it was not for long periods. Lengthy confinements would have been impractical in a less populated world, where formal police protection did not exist and conditions were so unstable that populations moved from one place to another in search of food and shelter. Under those conditions, usually the punishment of persons who violated society's norms was carried out by quick methods, such as corporal punishment, or, in extreme cases, capital punishment. Generally confinement was for very short periods while defendants awaited corporal punishment or trial.

Places of confinement for suspects or convicted defendants should reflect the purposes for which they are intended. If confinement is for holding a person until trial or corporal punishment, little attention need be paid to that confinement facility except to keep it secure. The architecture, conditions, and administration should reflect the security goal. If humanitarian concerns are not important, the conditions of confinement are relatively unimportant. Likewise, if the reason for confinement is to remove offenders from society and punish them for their criminal acts, then programming, treatment personnel, and prison conditions are unimportant. Prison is a place of custody and punishment; being there is the punishment. The rationale is that offenders are getting what they deserve as a result of their criminal acts.

If the purpose of confinement is to rehabilitate offenders, more attention should be given to the total confinement program. The location of confinement facilities is important; facilities should be close enough to inmates' homes to enable family members to visit. Confinement conditions are important because they are related to inmates' rehabilitation. Treatment programs, educational and work opportunities, fairness in discipline, and many other activities behind prison walls are relevant. Administration and management must reflect a treatment-rehabilitation orientation and, at the same time, maintain security within the institution.

This chapter looks at the historical development of the incarceration of persons in prisons and jails for the purposes of detention and punishment. Throughout the discussion, the purposes of confinement—retribution, incapacitation, deterrence, and rehabilitation—should be kept in mind (see again the discussion on these philosophies in Chapter 1, Spotlight 1-2). The focus on one or more of these purposes is not necessarily chronological in the history of prisons, but the purpose is tied to the type of prison that emerges.

LEARNING
OBJECTIVES

After reading this chapter, you should be able to do the following:

- **Explain the reasons for the emergence of institutions for confining offenders**
- **Explain the significance of the Walnut Street Jail**
- **Distinguish the Pennsylvania system from the Auburn system and evaluate the contributions of each**
- **Recall the contributions of Europeans to the emergence and development of prisons**
- **Explain the relevance of the Elmira Reformatory**
- **Summarize the development of modern U.S. prison systems**
- **Distinguish among jails, prisons, and community corrections**
- **List and describe the purposes of prison security levels**
- **Analyze the differences between prisons for men and women**
- **Describe state and federal prison systems and evaluate the differences between them**
- **Discuss the implications of the growth in jail and prison populations, with particular attention to the negative effects of overcrowding**
- **Discuss the distinguishing features of jails and analyze the role of the federal government in local jails**
- **Explain boot camps and evaluate these programs**
- **Analyze the role of privatization in correctional facilities**

9-1   The Emergence of Prisons for Punishment

The use of secure facilities for *confinement* is an ancient practice. Persons were confined awaiting trial or sentencing. But the use of secure facilities, such as prisons or jails, for *punishment* is a relatively recent practice.

The transition from corporal punishment to prison as punishment took place in the eighteenth century. In 1704, Pope Clement XI erected the papal prison of San Michele in Rome. In 1773, the prison in Ghent, Belgium, was established by Hippolyte Vilain XIII. In 1776, England was faced with a rising crime rate, the elimination of the need for galley slaves, and decreasing opportunities for the **transportation** of criminals to its colonies. England legalized the use of hulks, usually broken-down war vessels. By 1828, at least 4,000 **offenders** were being confined in English prison hulks. The ships were unsanitary, poorly ventilated, and vermin-infested. Contagious diseases killed many inmates, and punishments were brutal. There was little work for inmates, and idleness was demoralizing. Moral degeneration set in because of the "promiscuous association of prisoners of all ages and degrees of criminality."[1] This system of penal confinement in England lasted until the middle of the nineteenth century.

The spirit of **humanitarianism** that arose during the Enlightenment was among the reasons for the substitution of imprisonment for transportation and corporal and capital punishment. People began to realize the horrors inherent in the treatment of incarcerated offenders. The French prison built in Paris in the fourteenth century, the Bastille, became a symbol of such treatment, as well as of tyrannical prison administration. French philosophers, shocked by what they called *judicial murders,* sought changes in criminal justice systems.[2]

Another important philosophical development in France during the French Revolution was the emphasis on rationalism. This approach was important in the history of prisons because of its influence on social and political philosophy. The philosophers believed that social progress and the greatest happiness for the greatest number would only occur through revolutionary social reform, which could be brought about only by applying reason.

▶ **Transportation**   Historically the practice of punishing criminals by exiling them to another country, usually far away.

▶ **Offenders**   Persons who have committed a criminal offense.

▶ **Humanitarianism**   In penal philosophy, the doctrine advocating the removal of harsh, severe, and painful conditions in penal institutions.

It was logical that these reform ideas would flourish in the United States because many French people lived here during the French Revolution and many influential Americans had been to France. Because the Constitutional Convention was influenced significantly by the political philosophy of French philosophers, it is not unreasonable to assume that its members were aware of French social philosophy.

There are other important reasons for the rise of the prison system in America. The increasing emphasis on personal liberty meant that the deprivation of liberty could be seen as punishment. In addition, after the Industrial Revolution there was an increasing need for labor, which could be supplied by inmates. It has been argued, too, that prisons were developed by those in power for the purpose of suppressing persons who were not in power.

Although these general conditions are important in explaining the rise of prisons, attention must also be given to one individual who was highly influential in the process: John Howard (1726–1790), known as the great European prison reformer. Howard, an Englishman, was credited with the beginning of the **penitentiary** system. Howard traveled throughout Europe and brought to the world's attention the sordid conditions under which inmates were confined. Howard's classic work, *State of Prisons*, published in 1777, was extremely influential in prison reform in Europe and in the United States. Among his other ideas, Howard suggested that inmates should be housed individually in sanitary facilities and provided clean clothing. Women and children should be segregated. Jailers should be trained and well paid.[3]

> **Penitentiary** Historically an institution intended to isolate convicted offenders from one another and from society, giving them time to reflect on their bad acts and become penitent; later, synonymous with prison.

9-1a The Emergence of American Penitentiaries

The history of correctional institutions can be traced back to Roman, French, and English systems. An early English gaol (jail) is featured in Spotlight 9-1. The unique contribution of America was the substitution of imprisonment for corporal punishment, an innovation of the Quakers of West Jersey and Pennsylvania in the eighteenth century. They combined the prison and the **workhouse** to achieve a system of confinement at hard labor.

In 1787, Pennsylvania enacted a statute reducing the number of capital crimes, substituting imprisonment for many felonies, and abolishing most corporal punishments. A 1794 statute abolished capital punishment except for first-degree murder and substituted fines and imprisonment for corporal punishment in the case of all other crimes. The Pennsylvania criminal code reform set the stage for similar developments in other states. The main feature of early Pennsylvania reform was the Walnut Street Jail.

> **Workhouse** An English institution used to confine offenders who were forced to work at unpleasant tasks; offenders were punished physically as well. The term is used in some places today to refer to institutions that emphasize reformation or rehabilitation through work.

The Walnut Street Jail

In 1787 in Pennsylvania, Benjamin Rush, Benjamin Franklin, and others met to discuss punishment. Rush proposed a new system for the treatment of offenders. This system included classification, individualized treatment, and prison labor to provide jobs for inmates and to make prisons self-supporting. A 1790 statute codified the principle of solitary confinement and established the Walnut Street Jail, in which individual cells were provided for serious felons. Other inmates were separated by gender and by whether they had been sentenced after being convicted of a crime or were being detained awaiting a trial or punishment. This law was the beginning of the modern prison system in the United States, and the Walnut Street Jail is often cited as the first U.S. prison.

Some scholars have argued that the Walnut Street Jail was not the first American prison. Alexis M. Durham III has written extensively about the development of early prisons. According to Durham, the honor goes to Connecticut's Newgate Prison, the "first true colonial prison for the long-term punishment of serious offenders."[4] That prison was used for the incarceration and punishment of offenders who committed the following crimes: robbery, burglary, forgery, counterfeiting, and horse thievery. Unlike the Walnut Street Jail, Newgate was much more like the English houses of corrections and other early penal facilities, with an emphasis on punishment rather than rehabilitation.[5]

Offenders in the Walnut Street Jail worked an 8- to 10-hour day and received religious instruction. They labored in their cells and were paid for their efforts. Guards were not permitted to use weapons, and corporal punishment was forbidden. Inmates were allowed to

| *Spotlight 9-1* | **The First London Gaol** |

Built shortly after the Norman Conquest in 1066, the Fleet Prison was the first London facility constructed solely for the purpose of holding prisoners. It was called the Gaol of London until 1188, when that name was taken over by the Newgate Prison and the original gaol became known as the Fleet Prison. The early gaol was built of stone and surrounded by a moat, typical of many structures in those days, serving the dual purpose of keeping the inmates in and outsiders out.

The primary purpose of this first London jail was the detention of suspects awaiting trial, after which they were punished elsewhere. One exception was debtors, who were held until their debts were paid. On occasion, jail inmates were permitted to leave the institution for limited periods, although generally a fee was charged for this privilege. Early physical conditions in the Fleet Prison were better than those in most English institutions, which is "not saying much since the state of the early English prisons was generally quite deplorable." Over time conditions deteriorated and "soon the Fleet had the reputation of being one of the worst in all the country."

The Fleet was burned in 1666, soon rebuilt, destroyed over 100 years later, rebuilt again, and closed in 1842. "The Fleet Prison was demolished some four years later, thus ending the career of one of the oldest English institutions, the original Gaol of London."

Source: Paraphrased from J. M. Moynahan, "The Original Gaol of London," *American Jails* 1 (Winter 1988): 88.

---

talk only in the common rooms at night before retiring. With some variations, this plan was followed in other states. By 1800, problems with the system had become obvious. Crowded facilities made work within individual cells impossible; there was not enough productive work for the large number of inmates, and vice flourished. Ultimately the Walnut Street Jail failed as a result of politics, finances, lack of personnel, and crowding, but not before it had gained recognition throughout the world.

The Walnut Street Jail and other early prisons faced serious problems. Despite the thick walls and high security, **inmates** escaped. To combat that problem, some **wardens** required inmates to wear uniforms; in some prisons the color of the uniform reflected whether the convict was a first-, second-, or third-time offender. Discipline was a major issue; some wardens reinstituted corporal punishment, whereas others used solitary confinement.

> **Inmates** Convicted persons whose freedom has been replaced by confinement in a jail, prison, mental ward, or similar institution.

Funding was another challenge in these early prisons, and facilities were needed for exercise. To alleviate these problems, work programs (such as gardening) were begun, but they were not effective. Inmates were neither reliable nor efficient, and administrators were not skilled in managing prison labor. The result was that most prisons operated at a loss. In 1820, the viability of the entire prison system was in doubt, and its most dedicated supporters conceded a nearly total failure. Institutionalization had failed to pay its own way and had encouraged and educated the criminal to a life in crime.[6]

> **Wardens** Historically, the chief administrative officers in corrections facilities.

In response to these problems, two types of prison systems developed: the Pennsylvania, or separate, system, based on solitary confinement; and the New York, or Auburn, system, known as the **silent system.** These two systems were the subject of intense debate. Tourists flocked to see the prisons; foreign nations sent delegates to examine the two systems. By the 1830s, the two American penitentiary systems were famous around the world.

> **Silent system** In penitentiaries, the historical practice of not allowing offenders to speak with one another.

The Pennsylvania System

With the demise of the Walnut Street Jail, solitary confinement at hard labor appeared to be a failure. Consideration was given to a return to corporal punishment. But in 1817 the Philadelphia Society for the Alleviation of the Miseries of Prisons began a reform movement, which led to a law providing for the establishment of the separate system of confining inmates in solitary cells without labor.

The first separate system prison was opened in Pittsburgh in 1826 and subsequently was known as the Western Penitentiary. Due to the problems resulting from inmate idleness in this prison, the law was changed to permit work in solitary confinement before the establishment of the Eastern Penitentiary in Philadelphia. The design of its building became the basic architectural model for the Pennsylvania system.

The Eastern Penitentiary—or Cherry Hill, as it was called because of its location in a cherry orchard—was established in 1829. It was the first large-scale attempt at implementing the philosophy of solitary confinement at all times, with work provided for inmates in their cells. The law that authorized construction of this prison specified that, although the commissioners could make some alterations and improvements in the plan used for the Western Penitentiary, the principle of solitary confinement must be incorporated.

John Haviland, the architect of Cherry Hill, was faced with the problem of creating a design that would permit solitary confinement but would not injure inmates' health or permit their escape. His solution was seven wings, each connected to a central hub by covered passageways. Each inmate had a single inside cell with an outside exercise yard. Inmates were blindfolded when taken to the prison and were not permitted to see other inmates. They were not assembled even for religious worship. The chaplain spoke from the rotunda, with inmates remaining in their cells.

Before Cherry Hill was completed, it became the focus of discussion among prison reformers around the world. Although it was the architectural model for most of the new prisons in Europe, South America, and later Asia, the design was not popular in the United States. Despite that fact, Haviland's contributions to prison architecture in American should not be minimized, as one criminologist stated:

> Compared with the penitentiaries of their day, Haviland's prisons were overwhelmingly superior, both technically and stylistically. . . . Haviland's great service to penology would seem to be in establishing high standards of construction, standards which were to have an influence on almost all of the prison construction of the nineteenth century.[7]

Haviland should also be remembered for the fact that his prison architecture embodied a treatment philosophy.

The Auburn System

The prison system that became the architectural model for the United States was the Auburn System. In 1796, New York enacted a statute that provided for the building of two prisons. Newgate in New York City was first occupied in 1797. That prison soon became so crowded that, to make room for new inmates, as many inmates had to be released as were admitted.

The second prison, Auburn, was similar to Newgate, with workshop groups during the day and several inmates to a cell at night. Discipline was a problem, however, so a new system, which became known as the Auburn system, developed. The Auburn system featured congregate work during the day, with an enforced silent system. Inmates were housed in individual cells at night. The architecture created a fortresslike appearance, with a series of tiers set in a hollow frame, a much more economical system than that of Cherry Hill.

The silent system was strictly enforced at Auburn. The inmates ate face to back. They stood with arms folded and eyes down, so that they could not communicate with their hands. They walked in lockstep with a downward gaze. Strict regulation of letters and visits with outsiders and few or no newspapers isolated them further. Inmates were brought together for religious services, but each sat in a boothlike pew, which prevented their seeing anyone other than the speaker.

Discipline was strictly enforced at Auburn. The warden, Captain Elam Lynds, thought that the spirit of a person must be broken before reformation could occur. He was credited with the Auburn punishment philosophy. It is said that he changed discipline rules without legislative authority, instituted the silent system, fed inmates in their cells, and required lockstep in marching. A committee from the legislature visited the prison, approved of the way it was being run, and persuaded the legislature to legalize the new system.

In 1821, a system of **classification** was instituted. It placed dangerous offenders in solitary confinement, which led to mental illness, inmates' pleadings for work, and sometimes even death. A commission established to study prisons recommended abolishing solitary confinement and putting all inmates to work.

▶ **Classification** The assignment of new inmates to the housing, security status, and treatment programs that best fit their individual needs.

Comparison of the Pennsylvania and Auburn Systems

Architecture is important in distinguishing the Pennsylvania system from the Auburn system. The latter emphasized the congregate but silent system; the former, solitary confinement. Both emphasized the importance of a disciplined routine and isolation from bad influences. Both reflected the belief that, because the inmate was not inherently bad but, rather, the product of defective social organization, he or she could be reformed under proper circumstances. Scholars, practitioners, and politicians debated the advantages and disadvantages of these two systems, but few questioned the premise on which both rested: incarceration is the best way to handle criminals.[8]

The architecture of the two systems resulted in cost differentials. The Auburn system was more economical to build, although the Pennsylvania system was less expensive to administer. It was argued that the Auburn system was more conducive to productive inmate labor and less likely to cause mental illness. The silent system continued into the twentieth century, not for the original purpose of preventing cross-infection, but because it was easier to run an institution if the inmates were not allowed to speak to each other.

Both the Pennsylvania and the Auburn systems sound harsh today, but they must be viewed in historical perspective, as noted by one authority:

> The most that can be said for this period of American prison history is that, despite all its stupidities and cruelties, it was better than a return to the barbarities of capital and corporal punishment for crime. In the face of public indignation at the chaos existing in early American prisons in 1820, it maintained the penitentiary system.[9]

The Pennsylvania and Auburn systems were also important in that both were based on treatment philosophies, with architecture designed to accommodate those philosophies.

9-1b   The Emergence of the Reformatory Model

The disagreement over the Pennsylvania and Auburn systems led to an emphasis on reformation, along with a prison system characterized by indeterminate sentences, parole, work training, and education. Before looking at the emergence of that system in the United States, it is important to look briefly at the European developments that influenced U.S. prison systems.

We look to the works of Captain Alexander Maconochie, an Englishman, and Sir Walter Crofton, an Irishman, for the beginnings of a reformatory movement. Maconochie began the movement in 1840, when he was placed in charge of the British penal colony on Norfolk Island, off the coast of Australia. Norfolk Island was used by England for the worst offenders, who had been transported from England to mainland Australia, where they committed further crimes. Previously England had transported its offenders to the American colonies. After the American Revolution, that was no longer an option, so many offenders were sent to Australia.

Maconochie was critical of the use of transportation. The conditions of transportation were dreadful. Offenders were chained together and in some cases had only standing room on the ships. Fevers and diseases were rampant; food was meager; sanitary conditions were unbelievable; and homosexual rape and other forms of violence were common.

Upon his arrival at Norfolk, Maconochie began to implement his reformation philosophy. He emphasized that he was not lenient and that society had a right to punish those who broke its laws, but

> we have no right to cast them away altogether. Even their physical suffering should be in moderation, and the moral pain framed so as, if possible, to reform, and not necessarily to pervert them. The iron should enter both soul and body, but not so utterly to sear and harden them.[10]

Maconochie's reform program was characterized by his advocacy of the indeterminate sentence and his belief that inmates should work, improve their conduct, and learn frugality of living before they were released. While in prison, they should work for everything they received. Their work earned them the required number of "marks." When they were qualified by discipline to do so, they should work in small groups of about six or seven, with all of the offenders answerable for the behavior of the entire group, as well as of each member. Before they were released, while still required to earn their daily tally of marks, offenders should be given a proprietary interest in their labor. They should be subjected to less rigorous discipline in order to be prepared to live in society without the supervision of prison officials.

Maconochie never was given the authority that he thought he would have when he went to Norfolk. His ideas were controversial and not greatly appreciated by the British authorities, but he made many changes in the penal colony, and it was a more humane place when he left.

Maconochie described his accomplishments as follows: "I found a turbulent, brutal hell, and left it a peaceful well-ordered community." Evidence proved him right. But the controversy over his methods and philosophies led to his recall in 1844:

> He was replaced by Major Childs, an incompetent who sought to carry out instructions to restore the previous evil methods in place of Maconochie's reforms. This led, on 1 July 1846, to a revolt by some of the convicts, and four of the penal staff were murdered.[11]

Sir Walter Crofton, a disciple of Maconochie, applied Maconochie's reform ideas to the Irish prisons, where he served as chairman of the board of directors. The Irish system was recognized for its emphasis on the following:

1. A reward system—all advantages, including release, were based on rewards for good behavior
2. Individual influence of the prison administrators on the inmates—prison populations were to be kept small (300 in ordinary prisons, 100 in intermediate prisons) to permit this influence
3. Gradual release from restrictions—restrictions were gradually removed until during the last stage, the intermediate prison, one-half of the restrictions were removed
4. A parole system involving strict supervision after release and revocation for infractions of the rules[12]

American reformers visited the Irish prison system in the 1860s and returned with great enthusiasm for their reformation philosophy. On 12 October 1870, a meeting led by penologist Enoch C. Wines was held in Cincinnati, Ohio, to settle the dispute between the Pennsylvania and Auburn systems. This meeting led to the organization of the American Correctional Association, then called the *National Prison Association*. The group drafted 37 principles calling for indeterminate sentences, cultivation of inmates' self-respect, inmate classification, and advancement of the philosophy of reformation rather than punishment.

The Elmira Reformatory, established in 1876, emerged from this meeting. It became the model for a **reformatory,** which was designed for young offenders. The architecture was similar to that of the Auburn system, but greater emphasis was placed on educational and vocational training. Indeterminate sentences with maximum terms, opportunities for parole, and the classification of inmates according to conduct and achievement were the greatest advances of this new institution.

Elmira was established at the same time that other reforms, such as the juvenile court, probation, parole, and indeterminate sentences, were emerging. It was predicted that Elmira would dominate U.S. prison systems.[13]

The significant contribution of the Elmira reformatory system was its emphasis on rehabilitation through education, which led to greater prison discipline, indeterminate sentences, and parole. The system declined eventually, mainly as a result of the lack of trained personnel to conduct the educational programs and to carry on the classification system adequately. Some scholars argue that the Elmira system was never intended to be a real reform but, rather, was developed for the purpose of controlling the lower classes, women, and minorities. The system promised benevolent reform but delivered only repression.[14]

An increase in the prison population in the late 1800s resulted in severe overcrowding. Eventually, new prisons were built, including Attica (New York) in 1931, and Stateville (Illinois) in 1925. Most of these followed the Auburn architectural plan and were characterized by increasing costs per inmate, Sunday services, a chaplain on duty most of the time, and insufficient educational and vocational training programs. The training programs were

▶ Reformatory An early corrections facility, which was less physically secure and which emphasized changing or reforming the offender; usually used to refer to an institution.

based on the needs of institutions, not the interests or needs of inmates. Insufficient funds were available to hire and retain adequate personnel.

Those institutions provided work for some inmates, and the prison products were sold on the open market. This industrial period of prison history irritated those in private industries, who complained that competition from prisons was unfair because of the low wages. In 1929, the Hawes-Cooper Act was passed, followed in 1935 by the Ashurst-Summers Act to restrict the sale of prison goods:

> These [federal statutes] in turn were followed by state laws designed to do the same. With the passage of these laws, the Industrial Prison was eliminated. In 1935 for the great majority of prisoners the penitentiary system had again reverted to its original status: punishment and custody.[15]

9-2 Modern Prisons: An Overview

When they emerged, United States prisons were viewed as a substitute for corporal punishment, but corporal punishment continued. Supposedly prisons emerged as places in which inmates could be reformed.[16] However, the early reform approach was abandoned eventually in favor of a custody philosophy. According to David Rothman, this occurred for several reasons. The change was not inherent in prison designs. Some disappointment was inevitable because of the great expectations the founders had for the success of the prison movement. Change also came about as a result of the resources drained from prisons during the Civil War. Additionally, the rehabilitation goal promoted but also disguised the shift from reformation to custody. Too often, prison administrators assumed that incarceration was reformation, and no one recognized that reformation programs were lacking. The administrators relaxed their reformative efforts, and abuses of power arose within the prisons.

The nature of inmates' offenses was also related to the change from a reformation to a custodial emphasis. The silent, segregated systems were not designed for hardened offenders serving long-term or life sentences. The founders who envisaged reformation of the offender had not contemplated what to do with the hardened adult offender or the juvenile already committed to a life of crime. When the situation arose, **custody** seemed the best answer. The public accepted that approach because of the need for safety and security.[17]

The custodial institution seemed the best way to handle changes in the composition of inmate populations. As cities became larger and their populations became more heterogeneous, including an influx of immigrants as well as distinct social classes, traditional methods of social control became ineffective. When those persons entered prison, an emphasis on custody seemed appropriate.

By the late 1800s, it had become clear that reformation was no longer a major punishment goal. Later studies reported corruption between correctional officers and inmates, cruel punishment of inmates, overcrowded prisons with financial problems, and severe criticism of both the Pennsylvania and Auburn systems. As hardened offenders were held for long periods of time, prisons turned into holding operations, where wardens were content if they could prevent riots and escapes.

Some reformers began to express dissatisfaction with incarceration per se, criticizing long sentences as counterproductive and large expenditures on prisons as foolish and unnecessary. Probation and parole were advocated but slow to be adopted. Most reformers and the public seemed content to incarcerate for the sake of security.

Why did the public stand for the decline of the original prison philosophy? David Rothman suggests that part of the explanation is that usually it is easier to capture public interest "with predictions of success than with the descriptions of corruption." Some may have believed that incarceration was synonymous with rehabilitation. But, says Rothman, the reasons went deeper. Many persons saw the prison as performing an important social function, for they noted that the majority of inmates were from the lower social class and many were immigrants. Few upper-class or upper-middle-class persons were incarcerated.[18]

In recent years reformation and rehabilitation have been dealt a severe blow by researchers who claim that empirical evidence shows that rehabilitation has failed. Some evidence of the rehabilitative ideal remains, but no longer is it the dominant reason for

▶ **Custody** Legal control over a person or property; physical responsibility for a person or thing.

punishment. It has been replaced by an emphasis on deterrence and retribution. In those jurisdictions in which reformation or rehabilitation is emphasized, the focus is usually on diversion from prison rather than on prison programs designed to reform.

Many aspects of modern U.S. prisons are examined in this chapter and in Chapter 10, which demonstrates that modern prisons are characterized by disruption, violence, monotonous daily routine, lack of work opportunities, and unconstitutional living conditions. Some jails and prisons are under federal court orders to improve inmates' living conditions and to reduce inmate populations or be closed. We may question whether these modern prisons are an improvement over the earlier ones. Some may say the question is not relevant; offenders should be punished, just what the system is doing.

9-3   Confinement Institutions

Offenders are confined in various types of institutions. These institutions are classified most commonly as jails, prisons, and community-based correction facilities.

Although the terms **jail** and **prison** are used interchangeably and the two types of institutions have many common characteristics, they can be distinguished by their purposes. Jails and detention centers are used for the confinement of persons awaiting trial. They are also used for the short-term detention of persons in need of care when no other facilities are available immediately. For example, a public drunk might be detained until sober or until arrangements are made for admittance to a treatment facility. Occasionally jails are used to detain witnesses to a crime if it is thought that otherwise they might not be available for trial. Finally, jails are used for the incarceration of convicted offenders who are sentenced to short terms, usually less than one year. Prisons are used primarily for the incarceration of offenders sentenced for lengthy terms (usually over one year) and for more serious offenses, such as felonies.

A third type of facility that is used for confinement is a **community-based correction facility,** which houses offenders but permits them to leave during part of the day to work, attend school, or engage in treatment programs. Offenders may also be confined in special-purpose facilities, such as treatment centers for abusers of alcohol or other drugs, for sex offenders, or for the mentally ill.

9-3a   Prison Security Levels

Prison security levels may be divided into three main categories: maximum, medium, and minimum custody. The federal government and most states have all three types. Characteristics of the levels differ from one jurisdiction to another.

Many of the maximum-security prisons currently in use were built before 1925, and most inmates were housed in maximum-security prisons, although for many of them that security level was excessive. Unfortunately, this also occurs in some jurisdictions today. Maintenance of these old maximum-security facilities is difficult and costly; many of the complaints about prison conditions are related to the problems of maintaining these old facilities. An example is that of San Quentin.

San Quentin, located in San Quentin Village, California (close to Oakland and San Francisco), was built in the 1850s on land purchased for $10,000. San Quentin is the third oldest prison in the United States, following the New York prisons at Auburn and Sing Sing. In 1934, its death row was constructed to handle 68 inmates, but today the number of condemned persons is often over 600. Most of these inmates live in two overcrowded buildings that were originally built to house regular inmates. In 1984, a federal court ruled that the San Quentin facility was unfit because of needed repairs. Approximately $35 million was spent on renovation and, for the first time, inmates had hot running water in their cells. A study completed in 2001 recommended closing San Quentin because of the cost of repairs needed to make the facility more secure as well as more accommodating to its inmates. It appears, however, that this plan will not be implemented. California's governor, Gray Davis (who was recalled in the fall of 2003 and Arnold Schwarzenegger was then elected), had proposed building a new death row facility at San Quentin. This unit would have cost approximately $220 million, and the need to get approval for that expenditure came at a

---

Jail   A local, regional, or federal facility used to confine persons awaiting trial, as well as those serving short sentences.

Prison   A federal or state penal facility for detaining adult offenders (although juvenile offenders are also incarcerated in adult facilities on occasion) sentenced to a year or longer after conviction of crimes.

Community-based correction facility   A facility in which the punishment emphasizes assimilation into the community. Instead of imprisonment, the offender may be put on probation or placed in programs such as work release, foster homes, halfway houses, parole, and furlough.

time (in 2003) when the state faced a multibillion-dollar shortfall in its budget, resulting in cuts in many state programs and institutions.[19]

The issue of what to do with San Quentin rose again in late 2004, with the *New York Times* featuring the prison on its front page. With a color photo of the prison in the background, the paper related that California's death row had grown sufficiently that the state was preparing to spend $220 million to build a new one next door. The article noted, however, that the prison is on an expensive piece of property with a spectacular view. Opponents were increasing their attempts to block the expansion, based on the value of the real estate and the views, urging that the new death row be built elsewhere. But by April 2005, the environmental impact statements, along with the legal analysis of the issue of moving death row, were complete. The conclusion was that San Quentin is the only place to build the new death row facility because that state's law requires that all male death row inmates be confined at San Quentin and that all executions occur at San Quentin. "The California Department of Corrections has no authority to change this law." Construction was to begin in the fall of 2005 on the planned $220 million facility. California has the largest death row population in the United States but does not conduct many executions.[20]

Maximum-, medium-, and minimum-security prisons differ in the emphasis on treatment and related programs and in the freedom permitted inmates. In maximum-security prisons, inmates are detained in their cells for longer periods of time and are given less freedom of movement within the cell blocks than are those in the other security levels.

Another type of prison is the *open prison*. Open prisons make use of the natural environment for security. An example is Alcatraz Island, located in San Francisco Bay. Called "the Rock" because the island is mainly rock, Alcatraz has been used for numerous purposes, including a military prison and a maximum-security federal prison. Officially it became a federal prison on 1 January 1934, and its purpose was to incarcerate the most dangerous federal offenders. A former U.S. attorney general described Alcatraz as a prison that would make no pretense at rehabilitation. Rather, it was a place for "the ultimate punishment society could inflict upon men short of killing them; the point of no return for multiple losers." Alcatraz was described by one writer as "the great garbage can of San Francisco Bay, into which every federal prison dumped its most rotten apples."[21]

Alcatraz incarcerated some of the most notorious federal offenders, men such as George "Machine Gun" Kelly, a college-educated man from a prosperous family, convicted of bootlegging, and Robert F. Stroud, a young pimp who killed a customer after he had attacked one of Stroud's prostitutes. Stroud became known as the "Birdman of Alcatraz" because of his knowledge of bird diseases. Men such as Kelly and Stroud were sent to Alcatraz because it was considered the most secure U.S. prison at the time. It was assumed that no one could survive in the icy waters and current long enough to swim to San Francisco. There are no records of successful escapes, although on 11 June 1962 three inmates escaped, and their bodies were never found.

The cost of keeping an offender at Alcatraz was three times as high as it was at any other federal prison, and costly capital improvements were needed. On 21 March 1963, the facility was closed as a federal penitentiary. Inmates were transferred to other federal prisons. After a period of occupation by Native Americans between 1969 and 1971, Alcatraz became a tourist attraction and currently is the most frequently visited one in the San Francisco area. In recent years Alcatraz has been renovated, and in 1991 a museum filled with "Alcatrivia" was opened on the island. By the summer 2003 tourists were able to buy a piece of one of the concrete buildings, as the administrators decided it would be less expensive to sell the concrete than to have it hauled off the premises. And a British travel agency was offering couples a package, including a wedding at Alcatraz. Numerous books have been written about the prison and the island, some by former inmates and others by prison staff or their families.[22]

Alcatraz illustrated some of the problems with open prisons. They may be more secure, but they are costly and inconvenient. Land is scarce, and finding appropriate places for prison colonies is difficult. It is unlikely, therefore, that the open prison system will be used extensively in the future. The federal penitentiary on McNeil Island off the coast of Washington State remains in use, although it is now part of the Washington state prison system.

In recent years special prisons for high security needs have been built. These secure facilities are referred to as *maxi-maxi prisons* or *supermaximum-security* prisons. By 1998, according to the National Institute of Corrections (NIC), more than 30 states had one of these high-security prisons, although the definitions of them varied. The author of a federal correctional report urged a conservative approach toward classifying inmates for supermax prisons and implored states not to use them to confine mentally ill inmates, those who need protective custody from other inmates, or those who are merely a nuisance. Supermax prisons are expensive to build and to operate, but they are popular with politicians. It is argued that the presence of these institutions—and thus the threat of being incarcerated in them—serves as a deterrent to inmates who might otherwise become disruptive within less secure facilities.[23]

A federal maxi-maxi or supermax prison was opened in 1994 in Colorado. It is a state-of-the-art prison designed and built specifically for predator inmates—those who have demonstrated that they cannot live in other prisons without causing trouble for inmates as well as staff and administration. The facility, located at the foot of the Rockies, was built for 400 inmates. The inmates live in a "super-controlled environment that enforces a hard-edged solitude to contain the risk of social mixing and violence. Even the cell windows deny them all views of the outside except the sky above."[24] A British newspaper described this prison as looking "more like a chemical weapons installation than anything else" because of the obvious security measures, including 14-foot-high razor wire bundles and a "triangular ring of mirrored-glass towers guarding the new tomb-like highest security prison," which "can be seen from six miles across the prairie wastelands of Colorado's Rockies."[25] More information on this secure federal prison is contained in Spotlight 9-2.

Spotlight 9-2　Supermax Prisons: A Look at the Federal System

The federal supermax prison in Florence, Colorado, is the most secure in the federal system, having surpassed Marion, Illinois, which held that position for many years. One of its newest occupants is Eric Rudolph, who in April 2005, pleaded guilty to multiple terrorist acts in the 1990s, including the 1996 bombings at Atlanta's Olympic games. Another inmate at the Colorado Supermax prison is Richard Reid, the shoe bomber terrorist who attempted to blow up a flight from Paris, France, to Miami, Florida. The Colorado supermax prison also houses other terrorists, such as Theodore "Ted" Kaczynski, the Unabomber (who used the mail to kill 3 people and injure 22 over a period of 17 years, serving 4 life sentences plus 30 years); Ramzi Abmed Yousef (convicted of masterminding the 1993 bombing of the World Trade Center, which killed 6 and injured more than 1,000 people, serving a life sentence); and Khalfan Khamis Mohamed, also serving life, who, along with 3 others, was convicted of bombing the U.S. embassies in Kenya and Tanzania in 1998, killing 224 people. Timothy McVeigh, who bombed the federal building in Oklahoma City in 1995, was incarcerated in this prison before he was flown to the federal death row facility at Terre Haute, Indiana, where he was executed. McVeigh's accomplice, Terry Nichols, was also housed in Florence until he was transferred to Oklahoma to stand trial for state murder charges. Nichols was convicted of 168 murders and sentenced to life in prison without parole.

The inmates at the Florence prison spend most of their days and nights in their cells in isolation. As one behavioral therapist said, Florence is the only U.S. prison "specifically designed to keep every occupant in near-total solitary confinement. . . . The worst behaved men could serve an entire sentence—decades—in isolation." The isolation is brutal but, said the therapist, so are the inmates. "This is it. The end of the line."[1] Some of the inmates are under court orders that severely restrict their communications with the outside world—for example, Yousef is not permitted to communicate by mail, telephone, or visits without court permission. Inmates are constantly monitored by surveillance cameras. The prison was opened in 1994; it cost $150 million to build, and it costs approximately $100 a day for each inmate. No one has ever escaped from the institution.[2]

The model of a supermax prison emerged in the 1970s and 1980s after numerous correctional officials were murdered by inmates. Various security measures were taken, including locking down an entire prison population. Soon the idea of building special facilities for the "worst of the worst" emerged, with the philosophy of almost total lockdown for these inmates.

Supporters claim that the supermax prisons have resulted in fewer deaths of inmates and staff; critics warn that locking inmates down in almost total isolation for years may have serious repercussions. Further, there is evidence that in some states the guidelines for supermax eligibility are ignored, resulting in the incarceration of some inmates who do not need or deserve such intense security and isolation. As one news article concluded, "[T]he available numbers suggest that casual overuse of these facilities is common. For in tough-on-crime America, imposing grim conditions on prisoners is all too often seen as a good in itself, regardless of the long-term costs."[3]

The treatment of mentally ill inmates within these supermax prisons is noted in Chapter 10. Noted also in Chapter 10 are allegations of sex between female correctional officers and male inmates in the Colorado supermax prison.

1. "Monsters Doomed to Rot in a Hellish Dungeon," *New York Post* (19 October 2001), p. 6.
2. Ibid.
3. Sasha Abramsky, "Return of the Madhouse: Supermax Prisons Are Becoming the High-Tech Equivalent of the Nineteenth-Century Snake Pit," *The American Prospect* (11 February 2002), p. 26.

9-3b Women's Prisons

Until the late nineteenth century, women, men, and children occupied the same dungeons, almshouses, and jails. The institutions were plagued with physical and sexual abuses. Prison reform led to segregated areas for women within the existing institutions. There were few female inmates, and that fact was used to justify not providing separate facilities. Some women's sections did not have a female matron. Vocational training and educational programs were not considered important.

In 1873, the first separate prison for women, the Indiana Women's Prison, was opened. Its emphases were rehabilitation, obedience, and religious education. Other institutions followed: in 1877 in Framingham, Massachusetts; a reformatory for women in 1891 in New York; the Westfield Farm (New York) in 1901; and in 1913 an institution in Clinton, New Jersey.

In contrast to institutions for adult men, most institutions for women are more aesthetic and less secure. Most female inmates are not considered high security risks and are not as violent as male inmates. There are some exceptions, but on the whole the institutions are built and maintained to reflect the assumption that the occupants are not great risks to themselves or to others. Usually female inmates are permitted greater privacy than incarcerated men.

Historically female inmates have had fewer educational, vocational, and treatment programs than their counterparts in all-male penal institutions. The movement toward inmates' rights in the 1970s led to a recognition of these discrepancies. However, in a provocative article on the need for research on women's issues, one scholar emphasized that we already know that male and female inmates differ in terms of their backgrounds and their needs. More attention must be given to the classification of female inmates, which affects the types of institutions in which they will be incarcerated, along with the treatment programs they will receive.[26]

There are some signs of improvement. In a 2000 study, the National Institute of Corrections (NIC) surveyed all state correctional departments to determine which had systems for identifying and accommodating the differences in the risks and needs of male and female inmates. The special needs of female inmates are discussed in more detail in Chapter 10, but here the overall issue of classification is important. The NIC study found that only four states (Idaho, New York, Massachusetts, and Ohio) had separate custody classification systems for women and that "only eight states used a system [of classification] that identify needs in a gender-responsible manner." Most classification models were developed for male inmates or for both genders but not specifically for women. The study found that female inmates respond more positively when classification is geared toward the variables that are most important to women upon release: "children, relationships, abuse, early trauma, mental illness and job skill."[27]

Some of those issues are being faced by the Federal Bureau of Prisons (BOP). The BOP director testified in May 2003 before a congressional committee, stating that "female offenders have different social, psychological, educational, family, and health care needs." As a result of recognizing these factors, the BOP "continues to design and implement special programs for female offenders. Several facilities operate intensive programs that focus on helping women who have histories of chronic sexual, emotional, or physical abuse by addressing their victimization and enabling positive change."[28]

Construction of women's prisons has also become a high-priority item in some state budgets, despite budget cutbacks. In February 2003, a correctional journal published information concerning state budgets and proposed prisons, especially for women. It was stated that more facilities for women is a need that has been generated by the increase in nonviolent, drug-related crimes committed by women countrywide. For example, in North Dakota the number of female inmates rose from 55 in 2001 to 125 by early 2003.[29]

But recently some states have closed women's prisons, and others have closed prisons that incarcerated both men and women. To illustrate, the South Carolina State Park Correctional Center, which housed female inmates at the time of its closure (the institution previously housed male inmates), was closed in 2002.[30]

9-4 State and Federal Prisons

Most U.S. prisons are state institutions, but the federal government has a large prison system as well. This section examines both of these systems.

9-4a   The Federal System

The chapter's earlier discussion of the emergence of U.S. prisons referred to state-supported prisons. The federal government, which did not have prisons until the 1900s, contracted with states to incarcerate federal inmates. One of the first acts of Congress was to pass a statute encouraging states to permit the incarceration of federal inmates, at the federal government's expense, in state prisons. Most federal inmates with less than a year to serve or those awaiting trial were kept in local jails.[31]

In 1870, Congress established the Department of Justice (DOJ), which had a general agent in charge of the federal inmates in local jails and state prisons. Later that position was called the *superintendent of prisons.* The superintendent was in charge of the care and custody of federal inmates and reported to an assistant attorney general in the DOJ.

Overcrowding in state prisons after the Civil War made some state officials reluctant to house federal offenders; other states accepted only federal offenders from within their borders. Transporting federal offenders to other states was expensive. In 1891, Congress authorized the purchase of land for three federal prisons.

The first federal prison was taken over from the War Department at Fort Leavenworth, Kansas. The facility had been used to house military offenders. It was found to be inadequate for the federal prison system, and Congress authorized the building of a prison on the Fort Leavenworth military reservation. Federal offenders housed at Fort Leavenworth built the prison. On 1 February 1906, inmates were moved to the new prison, and Fort Leavenworth was returned to the War Department. Final work on Leavenworth was not completed until 1928. Leavenworth remains in use as a prison, but serious physical problems exist with the facilities.[32]

Leavenworth was followed by the construction of federal prisons—all for men—in Atlanta, Georgia, and McNeil Island, Washington (which, as noted earlier, is now a state prison). These prisons followed the architecture and philosophy of the Auburn system.

Prison overcrowding, poor conditions, and inconsistent administration of prisons, which were run primarily by local wardens, led to the need for more organization in the Federal system. On 14 May 1930, President Herbert Hoover signed the law that created the federal Bureau of Prisons (BOP). Today that bureau is a complex system, headed by a director, Harley G. Lappin (who took office in 2003, becoming the seventh director since the bureau was established, and replacing Kathleen Hawk Sawyer, who retired). Lappin, who was the warden at the federal prison in Terre Haute, Indiana, when Timothy McVeigh was executed in June 2001, reports to the U.S. DOJ. The BOP has a prison industries division as well as a research arm, the National Institute of Corrections (NIC). The regional offices of the BOP facilitate the supervision and administration of all federal correctional institutions, inmates, and staff. The bureau has an extensive legal department as well as divisions overseeing programming, medical services, and administration.

On 14 May 2003, Lappin testified before the House Judiciary's subcommittee on crime, terrorism, and homeland security. Among other information supplied by Lappin was the following:

- The BOP continues to meet its mission to "protect society by confining offenders in facilities that are safe, humane, cost-efficient, and appropriately secure, and that provide work and other self-improvement opportunities to assist offenders in becoming law-abiding citizens."

- Earlier in 2003, the BOP added to its strategic plan the goal "to enhance our efforts regarding the prevention, disruption, and response to terrorist activities."

- Since 1980, the number of facilities has increased from 41 to 103 and the number of federal inmates has increased from 25,000 to 169,000 (approximately 144,000 of them living in federal institutions, the rest in private facilities or those managed by state and local governments).

- Since 1980, the BOP budget has increased from $330 million to over $4.4 billion.

- The bureau's primary mission is to incarcerate federal inmates, but it also houses some pretrial detainees and unsentenced convicted offenders under the jurisdiction of the U.S. Marshals Service (USMS). It also houses approximately 2,600 detainees of the Bureau of Immigration and Customs Enforcement, now located within the Department of Homeland Security.

- The BOP has four levels of security for its prisons, along with detention centers and medical facilities.
- New technology and changes in staff training (and drug testing) have been implemented to improve the safety and security of federal prisons.

In 2005, in testifying before the House Appropriations Committee, Lappin acknowledged that Congress had appropriated funds in 2005 to open 10 new prison facilities; that the number of inmates had increased to 182,000 and was expected to reach 200,000 in 2006, 208,000 in 2007, and 220,000 in 2009. The BOP was requesting over $5 billion for its 2006 budget, with $170 million of that allocated for buildings and facilities.[33]

Despite the claims of the new director concerning the operation of the BOP, a study released shortly before Lappin took office, and conducted by the DOJ's Office of the Inspector General, noted that illegal drugs were present in nearly all of the institutions within the BOP and that 50 inmates had died of drug overdoses since 1997. Further, the highest rates of positive results found during drug testing of federal inmates were at the most secure institutions. The inspector general stated that many of the drugs had been smuggled into the prisons by employees. The report concluded that the "BOP's failure to implement new [drug] interdiction activities, such as those that we recommended and which have been frequently adopted on the state level, results in significant gaps in the BOP's drug interdiction strategy." Simply stated, the BOP "has failed to take adequate measures to prevent drug smuggling by its staff." The report made suggestions for improvement, such as searching employees when they enter and limiting the type and number of items employees may bring to work. BOP officials argued that the drugs are brought in by visitors and noted that they have taken significant steps to control this method of smuggling. The solicitor's report was that the officials need to do more.[34]

In comparison with state prisons, federal prisons are more costly. Officials of the federal system say the cost differential is justified by the federal system's increased educational, vocational, and recreational facilities and lower inmate-staff ratio, a difference that results in easier control of inmates and a reduction in long-term operating costs.[35] Professions 9-1 contains the mission statement of the Federal Bureau of Prisons, along with a list of career opportunities in that system.

As of the end of December 2002, the federal prison system became the largest prison system in the United States, with 164,043 inmates, compared with 161,412 in California and 146,476 in Texas. And, according to a corrections journal, "As quickly as state prison systems are working to diminish their inmate populations by honing sentencing laws, instituting construction bans on new facilities, and reviewing alternatives to incarceration, the federal government has continued to build and plan for new facilities and stiffen policies that result in increased prison populations." The article suggested that these trends could be expected to continue through about 2007.[36]

9-4b State Systems

All states have correctional systems; most are centralized and headed by a director, who reports to the governor. The director is responsible for overseeing all correctional facilities. Most states have all levels of security for male offenders, in addition to separate institutions for juveniles and women and treatment centers in the communities. Not all levels of security are available for women because of the smaller number of female inmates.

States may contract with other states for the incarceration of some inmates. After a riot, it is not uncommon for inmates to be transferred to another state until the riot-damaged facilities are remodeled, repaired, or replaced. Such transfers may be made to remove the riot's leaders. States may also contract with other states to house inmates whose lives are in danger in their own states. Such arrangements might be made between a state and the federal system as well. State prison systems differ considerably from each other in size and

Professions 9-1

Federal Bureau of Prisons

Mission Statement

The Federal Bureau of Prisons protects society by confining offenders in the controlled environments of prisons and community-based facilities that are safe, humane, cost-efficient, and appropriately secure, and that provide work and other self-improvement opportunities to assist offenders in becoming law-abiding citizens.[1]

Career Opportunities: Job Descriptions[2]

General Schedule (GS) Careers

Accountant

Accounting Technician

Attorney and Summer Law Intern

Chaplain

Contract Specialist

Correction Officer

Correctional Treatment Specialist

Drug Treatment Specialist

Employee Services Assistant

Employee Services Specialist

Information Technology Specialist

Legal Instruments Examiner

Recreation Specialist

Safety Specialist

Secretary

Teacher

Training Instructor

Wage System (WS) Careers

Air Conditioning Equipment Mechanic (HVAC)

Automotive Mechanic

Carpentry

Electrician

Fabric Worker

Food Service

Maintenance Mechanic

Painting

Plumbing

Sheet Metal Mechanic

Upholstering

Utility Systems Repairing-Operating

Health Care Careers (GS)

Clinical Psychologist and Predoctoral Psychology

Internships

Dental Hygienist

Dental Officer

Health System Administrator

Medical Officer

Medical Records Technician

Registered Nurse

Nurse Practitioner

Pharmacist

Physical Therapist

Physician's Assistant

1. Federal Bureau of Prisons, www.bop.gov/ (retrieved 25 April 2005).
2. Federal Bureau of Prisons, www.bop.gov/jobs/descriptions.jsp (retrieved 25 April 2005).

complexity, as well as in prison conditions, administrative problems, and the cost of maintaining inmates. Most incarcerated persons are in local jails, rather than in state or federal prisons.

9-5 Local Systems: The Jail

Jails are "local (usually county) institutions used to confine individuals awaiting trial or other legal disposition, adults serving short sentences, or some combination of both."[37] Jails may be the most important facilities in criminal justice systems because they affect more people than do any other criminal justice facilities. The "jail is [not only] a major intake center . . . for the entire criminal justice system, but also a place of first or last resort for a host of disguised health, welfare, and social problem cases."[38] Other functions of local jails are included in Spotlight 9-3.

Jails may be traced far back into history, when they made their debut "in the form of murky dungeons, abysmal pits, unscaleable precipices, strong poles or trees, and suspended cages in which hapless prisoners were kept."[39] The primary purpose of those jails, also

Spotlight 9-3   **The Function of Jails**

- Receive individuals pending arraignment and hold them awaiting trial, conviction, or sentencing
- Readmit probation, parole, and bailbond violators and absconders
- Temporarily detain juveniles pending transfer to juvenile authorities
- Hold mentally ill persons pending their movement to appropriate health facilities
- Hold individuals for the military, for protective custody, for contempt, and for the courts as witnesses
- Release convicted inmates to the community upon completion of sentence

- Transfer inmates to Federal, State, or other authorities
- House inmates for Federal, State, or other authorities because of crowding of their facilities
- Sometimes operate community-based programs as alternatives to incarceration
- Hold inmates sentenced to short terms (generally under 1 year)

Source: Paige M. Harrison and Jennifer C. Karberg, Bureau of Justice Statistics Bulletin, *Prison and Jail Inmates at Midyear 2003* (Washington, D.C.: U.S. Department of Justice, May 2004), p. 7.

called *gaols* (see again Spotlight 9-1), was to detain people awaiting trial, transportation, the death penalty, or corporal punishment. The old jails were not escape-proof, and frequently the person in charge received additional fees for shackling inmates. Inmates were not separated according to classification; physical conditions were terrible; food was inadequate; and no treatment or rehabilitation programs existed.

These early detention centers were followed in the fifteenth and sixteenth centuries in Europe by facilities characterized by work and punishment, called workhouses, or houses of correction. After the breakup of the feudal system, all of western Europe experienced a significant increase in pauperism and public begging. To combat this problem, a workhouse called the Bridewell was established in London in 1557. The dominant philosophy at the Bridewell was a belief that, if people had to work at hard and unpleasant tasks, they would abandon their wantonness and begging. The sordid conditions of jails and workhouses in Europe were brought to the attention of the world by John Howard, the prison reformer mentioned earlier. After his tour of European institutions, Howard said in 1773 that more inmates died of jail fever than of execution.[40]

The first jails in the American colonies were places of confinement used primarily to hold suspects awaiting trial, persons who could not pay their debts, and convicted offenders waiting to be taken to prison. Jails were rarely used for punishment. Most of the offenses for which people may be sentenced to jail or prison today were handled in other ways then: by corporal punishment, capital punishment, fines, or publicly humiliating activities, such as sitting in the stock or pillory, where people could jeer at the offenders. In the stocks, the victim's ankles were chained to holes in a wooden frame. The pillory was a device of varying shapes and sizes, to which the offender was secured in several ways, one of which was to be nailed to boards. The pillory was driven through town, so that people could throw rotten eggs or vegetables at the offenders.

In the 1600s, to replace such severe punishments, Pennsylvania Quakers suggested what they considered to be a more humane form of treatment, the use of jails as punishment. U.S. jails came to be used not only for the detention of those awaiting trial but also as confinement for those serving short-term sentences.

The horrible conditions of American jails continued over the years. In 1923, Joseph Fishman, a federal prison inspector, investigator, and consultant, wrote a book, *Crucible of Crime*, in which he described U.S. jails. He based his descriptions and evaluations on visits to 1,500 jails. He said that some of the convicted would ask for a year in prison in preference to six months in jail because of the inhumane jail conditions.

According to Fishman, most jails were characterized by a lack of space; inadequate amenities, such as meals, bathing facilities, and hospitals; and no separate facilities for juveniles. Although Fishman said jail conditions were terrible nationwide, the facilities were worse in the South. Fishman's conclusion might be summarized by his definition of a U.S. jail as

> an unbelievably filthy institution. . . . Usually swarming with bedbugs, roaches, lice, and other vermin; has an odor of disinfectant and filth which is appalling; supports in complete idleness thousands of able-bodied men and women, and generally affords ample time and opportunity to assure inmates a complete course in every kind of viciousness and crime. A melting pot in which the worst elements of the raw material in the criminal world are brought forth, blended and turned out in absolute perfection.[41]

Today the typical U.S. jail is small, at least 30 years old, and in need of renovation. It is located in a small town, usually the county seat of a predominantly rural county. These small, rural jails constitute the majority of jails but house a minority of the total U.S. jail population. Some are used infrequently, and many are not crowded, in contrast to jails in urban areas. The typical jail is financed and administered locally.

Some states have assumed partial control of their jails and have established statewide minimum standards. Professional organizations have been involved with jail standards, too. In the 1980s, the American Correctional Association sponsored the Commission on Accreditation for Corrections. That commission develops jail standards and certifies jails that meet those standards, but supervision or evaluation by states or professional organizations may not be sufficient to raise jail standards to an acceptable level. Federal courts have become involved, and their actions are discussed in Chapter 10 in conjunction with court orders concerning jail and prison conditions.

The influence of the federal government on jails is seen in other areas, such as federal technical assistance, financial assistance, and the imposing of standards. In addition, the federal government has provided states and local governments with assistance to build new correctional facilities and to remodel existing ones.

9-6   Shock Incarceration: The Boot Camp Approach

A recent approach to incarceration is the use of military-style boot camps, which have been utilized for the shock incarceration of some offenders, usually young ones with their first prison term for drug offenses. Although there was some initial criticism of boot camps, the concept spread quickly in the 1990s. For example, in 1991 a private association that had been critical of the correctional system in New York praised the boot camp program and called for its expansion. According to the Correctional Association of New York, "In contrast to many other prisons, shock camps are safe, drug-free, and well-run institutions."[42]

Not everyone agreed. Some scholars noted that the boot camp model is conducive to abuses of power, as well as to aggressive behavior by both inmates and staff. Further, as criminologists found, "Research does not provide indications that there will be beneficial effects."[43] A 1994 National Institute of Justice (NIJ) study of boot camps concluded that "the boot camp experience in itself does not successfully reduce recidivism." But graduates of boot camps were more likely than those released from prison to state that the experience had been a positive one. It is important, however, to control for the supervision factor, for there is evidence that close supervision within the community after release from boot camp is important to the success of the shock incarceration experience.[44]

A 1995 research article reporting on the NIJ data from eight state boot camp programs noted the variation in the programs and the difficulty of measuring all the variables that might influence results. The authors suggested that programs should be evaluated on a state-by-state basis and concluded that "those who complete boot camp do not inevitably perform either better or worse than their comparison group counterparts."[45]

Other scholars have reported that their initial research showed overall positive results from boot camps.[46] In 1996, the New York program, which combined shock incarceration and boot camp training, was hailed by a state agency as a "rehabilitation model." According to the Correctional Association of New York, "with its intensive stress on both discipline and therapy, shock provides in six months a far better chance of rehabilitation than a sentence of one and one-half to three years in an ordinary prison."[47]

Some jurisdictions have found, however, that boot camps work only until youths leave. Researchers who evaluated boot camp programs for the NIJ reported in 1996 that "what appeared to be a promising prognosis at the conclusion of boot camp disintegrated during aftercare."[48]

A study published in 2003 by Abt Associates, a research firm, questioned the effectiveness of boot camps in reducing recidivism. The scholar who conducted the study pointed out that boot camps have had difficulty meeting their goals of reducing prison populations, prison costs, and recidivism. There have been some positives, however, such as a reduction in impulsive behavior, anxiety, and depression and an improvement in the social attitudes of boot camp participants. In the study, reading and math skills, along with self-esteem, improved among some. The study suggested that the time spent in boot camps (90 to 120 days in most) may be too low to make marked reductions in recidivism.[49]

Other jurisdictions have experienced sufficient problems with boot camps that the programs have been eliminated. For example, an investigation into the Maryland program revealed widespread abuse of juveniles by correctional officers. Fourteen officers were suspended during both criminal and civil investigations; five top justice officials (including Gilberto de Jesus, juvenile justice secretary) were fired; and all boot camp programs were closed. The governor declared that the "trust of the people of Maryland has been violated" by the officers' actions. Boot camps have also been questioned in other jurisdictions. Georgia began phasing out its experimental programs after a study by the U.S. Department of Justice reported that boot camps are harmful and ineffective. Some deaths have been reported in boot camps in other states, leading to the reevaluation of those programs as well.[50]

In 2001, Tony Haynes, age 14, died in a privately owned and operated Arizona boot camp, the Buffalo Soldier's Camp. In February 2002, the director of the camp, Charles F. Long II, age 56, was arrested on second-degree murder and child abuse charges. It was alleged that Haynes was forced to stand for 5 hours in 116-degree heat and that he was dehydrated; he was then taken to a motel and put in a bathtub to cool off. Several staffers were also charged in the boy's death. Troy A. Hutty, 29, a former corporal at the camp who was charged with manslaughter, pleaded guilty to negligent homicide and was promised probation as he agreed to testify against Long.[51]

Long's trial began in October 2004. Just before the trial recessed for the Thanksgiving holidays, Long's wife, Carmelina, was called to testify. She blurted out that the alleged victim's mother, upon hearing that her son died, had said, "I can't believe he did it." According to Carmelina, who worked with her husband, the mother "said he [her son] had been trying to kill himself for three years and he finally did it." Prosecutors objected to the comment, but the judge overruled that objection and downgraded some of the child abuse counts against Long to lesser felonies.[52] In January 2005 Long was convicted of reckless manslaughter and sentenced to six years in prison.

The following section considers some of the effects of jail and prison overcrowding and the efforts to combat them. The legal issues surrounding overcrowding are discussed in Chapter 10.

9-7   Prison and Jail Overcrowding

During the last two decades of the twentieth century, federal and state prisons experienced dramatic population growth, as well as continued expansion, even as crime rates were going down. Figure 9-1 diagrams the growth of the incarceration rate between 1980 and 2003, showing that the rate more than tripled. This increased incarceration rate was due in part to the three strikes and truth in sentencing policies, discussed in Chapter 8, as well as to stricter laws and enforcement.

Spotlight 9-4 contains information about jail and prison populations at mid-year 2004. In 2002, for the first time in history, U.S. prisons and jails held more than 2 million people, and that figure reached 2,131,180 by mid-year 2004. In 2004, state and federal prisons incarcerated 1,410,404 inmates; local municipal and county jails held or supervised 784,538 inmates, with 9 percent of those under supervision outside of the jails, such as in community correction facilities. In 12 states, led by Alabama, prison populations

Figure 9-1
Incarceration Rate, 1980–2003
Source: Bureau of Justice Statistics,
Correctional Populations in the United States,
1997 and *Prisoners in 2002,* (Washington,
D.C.: U.S. Department of Justice, July 2003),
p. 1; *Prisoners in 2003* (November 2004), p. 3.

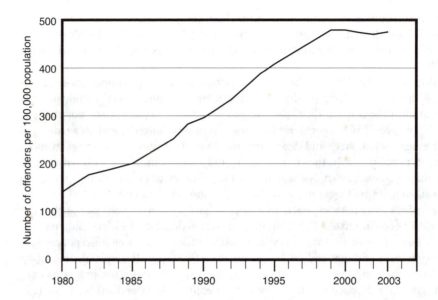

decreased. The total number of women under the jurisdiction of state and federal prison authorities increased by 2.9 percent, compared with a 2.0 percent increase for men.[53]

These increases in inmate populations have come as a surprise to some jurisdictions. In California, for example, the forecast in 2004 for prison populations in 2005 was that decreases would result in prison closings. To the contrary, the number of inmates in that state's prisons increased by 165,000, described by one paper as "a record number that jammed prisons to twice their intended capacity." The increase "punched a $207-million hole in the $6.25-billion corrections budget." In 2005, California was not closing prisons but opening a new one and reopening a facility that was privately managed. Corrections officials were warning that the overcrowding in California's prisons is "a recipe for unrest, as well as health and fire safety problems."[54]

A *New York Times* editorial, in commenting on the crime data through mid-2003, concluded as follows:

> The increase comes at a time when crime is falling and state and local governments are struggling to close budget deficits. The price of imprisoning so many Americans is too high, in scarce tax dollars and in wasted lives. Congress and state legislatures should find ways to reduce the number of people behind bars. . . . The nation's incarceration rate is among the world's highest, 5 to 10 times as high as in many other industrialized nations. . . .
>
> Congress and state legislatures should build more discretion into sentencing and look for ways to release prisoners who are no longer a threat to society. Locking the door and throwing away the key may make for good campaign sound bites, but it is a costly and inhumane crime policy.[55]

9-7a   The Effects of Overcrowding

Social scientists and federal judges have noted the negative impact of jail and prison overcrowding on inmates. In an earlier Texas prison case, the court opinion concluded that "inmates are routinely subjected to brutality, extortion, and rape. . . .The overcrowding . . . exercises a malignant effect on all aspects of inmate life." The court noted that inmates were in the presence of other persons almost constantly, sleeping only with the knowledge that they might be attacked by cellmates. "There is little respite from these conditions, for . . . inmates have wholly inadequate opportunities to escape the overcrowding in their living quarters."[56]

In 1995, it was reported that the Cook County (Chicago) Jail was so overcrowded that one out of every seven inmates was sleeping on the floor. The facility holds primarily accused persons awaiting trial, and thus it was not designed to provide educational or other rehabilitative facilities and programs. "The chronic tedium breeds violence, gang warfare,

Spotlight 9-4 Highlights of Jail and Prison Populations, Mid-Year 2004

In the year ending June 30, 2004
- The number of inmates in custody in local jails rose by 22,689; in State prison by 15,375; and in Federal prison by 10,095.
- The smaller State prison systems had the greatest percentage increase: Minnesota (up 13.2%) and Montana (up 10.5%).

At midyear 2004
- A total of 2,477 State prisoners were under age 18. Local jails held a total of 7,083 persons under age 18.
- State and Federal correctional authorities held 91,789 noncitizens, up from 90,566 (1.4%) at midyear 2003.
- In both jails and prisons, there were 123 female inmates per 100,000 women in the United States, compared to 1,348 male inmates per 100,000 men.
- An estimated 12.6% of black males, 3.6% of Hispanic males, and 1.7% of white males in their twenties were in prison or jail.
- Local jails were operating 6% below their rated capacity. In contrast, at yearend 2003 State prisons were estimated to be at capacity to 16% above capacity, and Federal prisons were 39% above their rated capacity.

- Privately operated prison facilities held 98,791 inmates (up 3.4% since yearend 2003). The Federal system reported the largest increase among inmates in private prisons (up 2,641).

Number of Jail Inmates up to 3.3% in 12 Months Ending June 30, 2004

Year	Number of Inmates in Jail Custody	Incarceration Rate*	Percent of Capacity Occupied
2004	713,990	243	94%
2003	691,301	238	94
2002	665,475	231	93
2001	631,240	222	90
2000	621,149	220	92
1995	507,044	193	93
1990	405,320	163	104

*Number of inmates per 100,000 residents

Source: Paige M. Harrison and Allen J. Beck, Bureau of Justice Statistics, *Prison and Jail Inmates at Midyear 2003* (Washington, D.C.: U.S. Department of Justice, May 2005), p. 1.

and drug trafficking," according to jail officials. A new facility was under construction, but officials said it would not solve the overcrowding problems, as more and more persons are arrested and tried. "We will never be able to build our way out of the problem," said one official at the John Howard Association, which serves as a watchdog on prisons.[57]

The harmful effects of prison overcrowding have led to numerous lawsuits, some of which are discussed in Chapter 10. In 2002, 15 Alabama female inmates filed a lawsuit alleging that the "outrageously overcrowded and dangerous conditions" in which women were serving time were causing physical assaults by inmates who were slashing each other with razors. In spring 2003, a district court admonished state prison officials for their failure to submit an acceptable plan for alleviating the unconstitutional conditions under which Alabama's female inmates were confined in the Julia Tutwiler Prison for Women and two other institutions. The court stated that a lack of money was not an acceptable reason for failure to submit the plan. On 2 December 2002, the court had ordered prison officials to submit a plan to correct the unconstitutional conditions; in spring 2003, the court decided, after hearing oral arguments, that the submitted plan was not sufficient. The court ordered state officials to devise a new plan to solve the unconstitutional conditions under which Alabama female inmates were being held.[58]

During several months in 2004, both parties to this suit negotiated and reached settlements, which were accepted by the court. The terms range from safety and security to medical issues and are quite extensive. Numerous inmates participated in giving their comments when they had the opportunity to do so, and the judge, in accepting the settlement agreements, commended them and the other parties to the litigation, noting that, as recently as December 2002, this court had described the conditions at Tutwiler as "essentially a time bomb ready to explode facility-wide at any unexpected moment." When he accepted the agreements in the summer 2004, the judge noted the improvements in conditions at the prison, attributed those to the work of the warden, and emphasized that the "court has full confidence that, in accordance with the provisions of the settlement agreements, [the warden] will build on her notable success." To ensure that occurs, the court appointed a special master, which is an expert, often an attorney or a prison official, who oversees the implementation of the court orders.[59]

A review published in 2003 by the Justice Policy Institute (JPI), which conducts research and promotes alternatives to incarceration, reported that 10 states (representing one-third of the U.S. population) had seen reductions in their prison populations, but most states were facing budget cuts that severely affected corrections. Some were reducing their prison populations solely for budgetary reasons. Michigan's outgoing governor signed legislation repealing mandatory minimum sentences for drug offenders. Kentucky's governor granted early release to 567 nonviolent offenders for a reported savings of $5 million. That state saved over $20 million by postponing construction on three proposed prison projects, cutting correctional staff positions, and reducing spending on private correctional facilities. According to Kentucky's governor, "Kentucky and most other states simply don't have the revenue it takes to house increasing prisoners." JPI cited other states with proposals to reduce the number of inmates, along with three public opinion polls showing that the public supported policies that deemphasize incarceration. For example, one poll revealed that two-thirds of its respondents favored treatment rather than incarceration for nonviolent drug offenders.[60]

9-7b Prison and Jail Expansion

Some jurisdictions have responded to overcrowding by building new facilities, an extremely costly measure. Others have remodeled existing facilities, resulting in a corrections business that is one of the fastest-growing industries in the United States.

Construction costs are not the only expenses to be considered. Operational costs of jails and prisons are high, and they continue to increase, outstripping the ability of many jurisdictions to cover them. Construction time is a factor as well. Because many jurisdictions are under federal court orders to reduce their prison and jail populations, they need available space quickly. As a result, some have sought faster construction plans and methods.

Hasty planning and construction have created unanticipated difficulties. A national survey of correctional officials revealed that security problems, designs conducive to inmate suicides, and increased vulnerability to lawsuits regarding confinement conditions had resulted from the design of some new facilities and renovations. In addition, faulty architecture has "resulted in multi-million-dollar cost overruns."[61]

By the spring 2003, with most states having overspent their budgets, prison budgets were being cut. Some were cut by early release. Between March and June 2003, Utah freed about 400 convicted felons because of overcrowding; Kentucky released 567 nonviolent inmates. According to a corrections professional journal, the average cost of incarceration was $20,000 to $25,000 per inmate, and state corrections departments were "facing the worst fiscal crises of a half-century or more." The article continued, "But after states and counties have trimmed their corrections departments as much as they dare, released as many prisoners as allowed, unscrewed light bulbs, turned down heaters and scrimped on supplies, they are finding the money still won't stretch."[62]

Some prison budget cuts may lead to lawsuits. For example, in the summer 2003 Virginia prisons began serving only two meals a day on weekends, calling one brunch. Texas prison inmates found their calories reduced from 2,700 to 2,500 per day. But the Nevada governor opposed food cuts in prisons, noting that the state was paying less to feed its inmates than its wild horses. Thirty-four states had overspent their general budgets, and 27 others had deficits to close before 1 July 2003. In many states budget cutting began with corrections.[63]

9-7c Private Correctional Facilities

One solution to prison problems has been to hire private firms to build and operate prisons or to provide special services, such as medical care or food. Privatization of correctional facilities, thought by many to be a modern movement, was actually used in the 1800s, in many cases for the same reasons as today, such as prison overcrowding. The recent emphasis on privatization can be attributed to "the failure of reform and rehabilitation, penal crowding, and concern with institutional costs."[64]

The latest trend is different from previous privatization of prisons in several ways. For a long time, correctional facilities, particularly jails and juvenile and adult community-based correction facilities, relied on outside agencies to provide certain goods and services. Studies showed this practice to be more cost-effective than each institution's providing every service and product that it needed. Medical service contracts were mentioned most frequently as more cost-effective than in-house services.[65]

The involvement of the private sector in corrections exists in three main areas: (1) prison work programs, (2) the financing of construction, and (3) the management of facilities. A state or the federal government might contract for one, two, or all of these.

Many states and the federal government use some private contractors for the management and operation of correctional institutions. In April 2003, Corrections Corporation of America (CCA) celebrated its twentieth anniversary of providing private services to government correctional facilities. CCA is the sixth largest correctional system in the United States, behind the federal system and the state systems in California, Texas, New York, and Florida. CCA controls more than 50 percent of the private correctional sector.[66]

In January 2005, a corrections journal reported that the three largest private prison companies look "like solid investments." Due to state and federal budget cuts, increasing prison populations, and resulting prison overcrowding, states and the federal government were turning to private corporations to solve the problems of the "chronic scarcity" of jail and prison beds. Over one-half of state facilities were over capacity, along with 33 percent of federal institutions.[67]

Several advantages to the use of private correctional facilities have been cited. For example, a study released in April 2003 and conducted by two Vanderbilt University professors concluded that states with private prisons had more success in keeping public spending for corrections under control than did states that did not have private prisons. Even states that had small levels of private prison use saved significant amounts in their correctional budgets.[68] Although we do not know whether private prisons can exist successfully with traditional government programs, some believe there are definite advantages. The private sector can concentrate on special offenders. This includes women, juveniles, illegal aliens, and inmates who are at risk in the general prison population, such as child molesters, former law enforcement officials, and prison informants.

The private sector may also provide an invaluable service simply by showing jail and prison officials that efficient and flexible management is possible in corrections, too. In most government facilities, competitive business principles, the creative use of staff, the adaptation of existing buildings and programs to meet changing needs, and experimentation with new ideas all seem to lag behind the private sector. Private involvement in corrections may encourage correctional administrators to modernize management styles, staff relations, and inmate care.[69]

The involvement of the private sector in corrections, however, raises many questions. First is the issue of whether private companies can deliver what they promise, such as "high-tech prisons that offer a full-range of rehabilitative programs, including college courses and job training, . . . pristine facilities that are efficiently managed without crowding problems" and at a lower cost than current facilities. These types of promises are made by companies such as Wackenhut Corrections Corporation and Corrections Corporation of America.[70]

There are also allegations that privatization of correctional facilities may be dangerous. Specifically, it is argued that private security firms cut security short to save money. One labor economist stated that "the daily pressures that these [private] companies face to satisfy Wall Street [cause] them to pay employees low wages, and to under-staff facilities, under-train employees and hire unqualified staff." The labor economist concluded that, if the government thinks airport security is so critical that it requires government rather than private regulation, it does not make sense to contract out the security of our prisons. A noted criminal justice policy analyst also believes that government prisons are better managed than private ones and that "inmate assaults on other inmates and guards, drug use and escapes occur at higher rates in private prisons."[71]

There are specific examples of violence within private prisons. In 1999, a New Mexico prison, the Guadalupe County Correctional Facility in Santa Rosa, was scrutinized after a correctional officer was killed at the institution, operated by Wackenhut Corrections Corporation. Public Safety Secretary Darren P. White accused Wackenhut employees of delaying the reporting of the riot to the state police and state correctional officials. The Guadalupe riot was the latest of four in recent months at private facilities in New Mexico. In addition to the officer's death, four inmates were killed and several other inmates and correctional officers were injured in those riots. The chief executive officer of Wackenhut alleged that it was the state's negligence in classifying inmates, not his company's response to the riot, that caused the deaths and injuries. The state transferred 109 inmates from New Mexico to a super-maximum-security prison in Virginia.[72]

There are other issues concerning private prisons. Politically it is argued that corrections is a government function, which should never be delegated. To do so increases problems, leading to lobbying for programs that might not be in the best interests of the public or corrections. The profit motive reduces the incentive to decrease the number of incarcerated people. The profit incentive encourages larger and larger private prisons. To make a profit, those facilities must be occupied. When the incentive for full prisons is combined with the public's call for longer and harsher sentences, the result may be more inmates serving more time.

Another issue concerns what happens if an inmate in a private correctional facility sues. Still other concerns are as follows:

- Will the government be held legally liable along with the private business?
- Should the government be involved in internal discipline or staff training?
- Will the short-term relief offered by private prisons turn into long-term, costly government obligations?
- Will public employees accept the presence of private staff?
- Will corrections administrators allow the transfer of inmate control to private business?
- Will the public lose its voice in determining the location of private prisons?[73]

Chapter Wrap-Up

This chapter set the stage for the next two chapters, which discuss life in prison and community corrections. It is important to understand the history of jails and prisons in order to evaluate what is happening today. The chapter began with the European background of incarceration, emphasizing the reform efforts of John Howard. Howard was influential in America, but the Quakers led the movement toward incarceration, intended as a milder sanction to replace the death penalty and the inhuman methods of corporal punishment that prevailed in U.S. criminal justice systems.

Two systems that emerged in the United States—the Pennsylvania system, with its emphasis on solitary confinement, and the Auburn system, with its emphasis on the silent system—competed for recognition in the United States and in Europe. The influence of the systems is seen today; many of our maximum-security prisons, built in the late 1800s and early 1900s, reflect an architecture typical of the Auburn system.

In Europe many prisons built on the architectural model of the Pennsylvania system remain in use. The Elmira Reformatory did not survive long as a place of reformation, but it set the stage for the movement toward rehabilitation and established the reformatory model that became characteristic of institutions for juveniles.

It is impossible to talk about a prison system in the United States, because states have their own unique systems; the jail systems of local communities differ widely; and the federal government has a separate system. The federal system has traditionally been considered the most efficient and effective, but it is also the fastest growing. State prisons have been the sites of most of the riots and overcrowded conditions that are discussed in subsequent chapters. But many local jails also face problems of overcrowding and inadequate facilities, leading to the establishment of jail standards by the federal government, the American Correctional Association, and some states. Overcrowding has also led to inmate lawsuits, some resulting in federal court orders to reduce prison and jail populations or make changes in prison conditions.

The use of military-style boot camps, once popular in recent years, has had numerous problems, including inmate deaths. In some jurisdictions boot camps have been abolished. The concept has some support remaining, however, for it gives the appearance of punishment as well as some semblance of preparing inmates to live more productive lives.

Many of the problems of incarceration are related to overcrowding. There are two basic ways to solve this problem. First, we can build more facilities. The costs, however, are overwhelming. Perhaps even more important, if we build them, we fill them, and the problem of a lack of prison space remains. The second solution is to reduce prison populations. This has been done in some states by enacting statutes that permit governors to declare an emergency when prison populations reach 95 percent (or some other figure) of legal capacity. Problems occur, however, when the releasees commit new crimes.

The cost of building new facilities to handle the overcrowding of jails and prisons, coming at a time when many government budgets are being cut, has led to the involvement of the private sector in the financing and management of jails and prisons. This is a controversial innovation, as the chapter's discussion demonstrates.

Inadequate conditions, overcrowding, and management problems in jails and prisons increase the problems of living behind the walls, as we will see in Chapter 10.

Key Terms

classification (p. 250)
community-based correction facility (p. 254)
custody (p. 253)
humanitarianism (p. 247)
inmates (p. 249)

jail (p. 254)
offenders (p. 247)
penitentiary (p. 248)
prison (p. 254)
reformatory (p. 252)

silent system (p. 249)
transportation (p. 247)
wardens (p. 249)
workhouse (p. 248)

Apply It

1. Explain why prisons emerged in Europe, and relate your discussion to the contributions of John Howard.
2. What characterized the emergence of prisons in the United States, and how did the Walnut Street Jail contribute to this development?
3. Compare and contrast the Pennsylvania and the Auburn systems.
4. What is a reformatory? Why were they developed? Explain the importance of European reformers to this development and compare that with the emergence of the Elmira Reformatory.
5. How do jails differ from prisons? From community-based correction facilities?
6. What is the difference between prisons centered on a philosophy of custody and those that focus on rehabilitation?

7. Distinguish among the levels of prison security. What is meant by a *supermax* or a *maxi-maxi* prison? Evaluate.
8. Explore the general and unique features of prisons for women and compare them with the features of those for men.
9. Distinguish between the state and federal prison systems and analyze population growth in each.
10. How does the present-day purpose of jails compare with its historical purpose? What are the problems of administering jails? What role, if any, should the federal government play in the administration of local jails?
11. What are boot camps? How effective are they?
12. What are the effects of prison and jail overcrowding?
13. What is the place of the private sector in jails and prisons?

Endnotes

1. Harry Elmer Barnes, *The Story of Punishment* (Boston: Stratford, 1930), pp. 117, 122. The introductory material on the history of prisons is based on this source unless otherwise noted.
2. Stephen Schaefer, *Theories in Criminology* (New York: Random House, 1969), pp. 104–105.
3. John Howard, *State of Prisons,* 2d ed. (Warrington, England: Patterson Smith, 1792).
4. Alexis M. Durham III, "Social Control and Imprisonment during the American Revolution: Newgate of Connecticut," *Justice Quarterly* 7 (June 1990): 293.
5. Alexis M. Durham III, "Newgate of Connecticut: Origins and Early Days of an Early American Prison," *Justice Quarterly* 6 (March 1989): 89–116.
6. David J. Rothman, *The Discovery of the Asylum: Social Order and Disorder in the New Republic* (Boston: Little, Brown, 1971), pp. 92–93.
7. Norman B. Johnston, "John Haviland," in *Pioneers in Criminology,* ed. Herman Mannheim (Montclair, N.J.: Patterson Smith, 1960), p. 122.
8. Rothman, *The Discovery of the Asylum,* p. 83.
9. Howard Gill, "State Prisons in America 1787–1937," in *Penology,* ed. George C. Killinger and Paul F. Cromwell (St. Paul, Minn.: West, 1973), p. 41.
10. Quoted in John Vincent Barry, "Alexander Maconochie," in *Pioneers in Criminology,* 2d enlarged ed., ed. Hermann Mannheim (Montclair, N.J.: Patterson Smith, 1972), p. 90.

11. Ibid., pp. 91, 95–97. For a recent account of Maconochie's contributions, see Norval Morris, *Maconochie's Gentlemen: The Story of Norfolk Island and the Roots of Modern Prison Reform* (New York: Oxford University Press, 2002).
12. Barry, "Alexander Maconochie," pp. 99–100.
13. Orlando G. Lewis, *The Development of American Prisons and Prison Customs* (1922; reprint, Montclair, N.J.: Patterson Smith, 1967), p. 7.
14. See Alexander W. Pisciotta, *Benevolent Repression* (New York: New York University Press, 1994).
15. Gill, "State Prisons in America," p. 53.
16. See Michael Foucault, *Discipline and Punish: The Birth of the Prison,* trans. Alan Sheridan (New York: Pantheon, 1977).
17. Rothman, *The Discovery of the Asylum,* pp. 238–239.
18. Ibid., pp. 243–253.
19. "Fabled Prison's Uncertain Fate," *New York Post* (12 August 2001), p. 26; "San Quentin Village Fights to Save Neighborhood Prison," *Corrections Professional* 6, no. 21 (27 July 2001); "New Life for Death Row in Marin," *San Francisco Chronicle* (26 April 2002), p. 1; "California's Death Row Opened for Governor," *Corrections Professional* 8, no. 11 (3 March 2003).
20. "San Quentin Debate: Death Row vs. Bay Views," *New York Times* (18 December 2004), p. 1.
21. Francis J. Clauss, *Alcatraz: Island of Many Mistakes* (Menlo Park, Calif.: Briarcliff, 1981), p. 35. The brief history of Alcatraz comes from this source.

22. See, for example, Jolene Babyak, *Eyewitness on Alcatraz: Life on THE ROCK as Told by the Guards, Families & Prisoners* (Berkeley, Calif.: Ariel Vamp Press, 1988, revised 1996); Darwin E. Coon (former inmate), *Alcatraz: The True End of the Line* (Sacramento, Calif.: New Desmas Press, 2002); Pierre Odier, *Alcatraz: The Rock: A History of Alcatraz: The Fort/the Prison* (Eagle Rock, Calif.: L'Image Odier, 1982).

23. National Institute of Corrections, *Supermax Prisons: Overview and General Considerations,* summarized in "Supermax Prisons Established in Most States, Study Finds," *Criminal Justice Newsletter* 29 (15 December 1999): 4–5. For a scholarly discussion of high-custody prisons, see Michael D. Reisig, "Rates of Disorder in Higher-Custody State Prisons: A Comparative Analysis of Managerial Practices," *Crime & Delinquency* 44 (April 1998): 205–228.

24. "A Futuristic Prison Awaits the Hard-Core 400," *New York Times* (17 October 1994), p. 1.

25. "There Are Jails . . . ," *The Daily Telegraph* (10 August 1996), p. 22.

26. Kathryn Ann Farr, "Classification for Female Inmates: Moving Forward," *Crime & Delinquency* 46 (January 2000): 3–17.

27. "Classification Systems Adapted for Women Offenders," *Corrections Professional* 8, no. 4 (18 October 2002).

28. Capitol Hill Hearing Testimony of Harley G. Lappin, director, Federal Bureau of Prisons, before the House Judiciary Committee on Crime, Terrorism, and Homeland Security (14 May 2003).

29. "States Propose Unprecedented Number of Women's Prisons," *Corrections Professional* (3 February 2003).

30. "Female Prison Closes in S.C.," *Corrections Professional* 7, no. 14 (5 April 2002).

31. This history of the federal prison system comes from a publication by Gregory L. Hershberger, The Development of the Federal Prison System (Washington, D.C.: U.S. Department of Justice/Federal Prison System, 1979).

32. "Inmates Say Military Prison Is Near Collapse," *New York Times* (17 August 1997), p. 19.

33. Harley G. Lappin, Testimony before the House Subcommittee on Crime, Terrorism, and Homeland Security (14 May 2003); Lappin, Testimony before the House Appropriations Committee (17 March 2005).

34. *The Federal Bureau of Prisons' Drug Interdiction Activities, Report Number 1-2003-002,* available on the Internet at www.usdoj.gov/org.

35. "Study: U.S. Prisons Cost More Than States," *Miami Herald* (1 November 1991), p. 9. The study was conducted by the General Accounting Office.

36. "BOP Emerges as Largest Prison System in United States," *Corrections Professional* 8, no. 8 (20 January 2003).

37. Advisory Commission on Intergovernmental Relations, *Jails: Intergovernmental Dimensions of a Local Problem: A Commission Report* (Washington, D.C.: U.S. Government Printing Office, May 1984), p. 2.

38. Hans Mattick, "The Contemporary Jails of the United States: An Unknown and Neglected Area of Justice," in *Handbook of Criminology,* ed. Daniel Glaser (Skokie, Ill.: Rand McNally, 1974), p. 781.

39. Edith Elisabeth Flynn, "Jails and Criminal Justice," in *Prisoners in America,* ed. Lloyd E. Ohlin (Englewood Cliffs, N.J.: Prentice Hall, 1973), p. 49.

40. Jerome Hall, *Theft, Law and Society* (Boston: Little, Brown, 1935), p. 108.

41. Joseph F. Fishman, *Crucible of Crime: The Shocking Story of the American Jail* (New York: Cosmopolis Press, 1923), pp. 13–14.

42. "New York Correctional Group Praises Boot Camp Programs," *Criminal Justice Newsletter* 22 (1 April 1991): 4.

43. Merry Morash and Lila Rucker, "A Critical Look at the Idea of Boot Camp as a Correctional Reform," *Crime & Delinquency* 36 (April 1990): 204.

44. National Institute of Justice Update, *Researchers Evaluate Eight Shock Incarceration Programs* (Washington, D.C.: U.S. Department of Justice, October 1994), p. 2.

45. Doris Layton Mackenzie et al., "Boot Camp Prisons and Recidivism in Eight States," *Criminology* 33 (August 1995): 327–358; quotation is on p. 327.

46. See, for example, Doris Layton MacKenzie and James W. Shaw, "Inmate Adjustment and Change during Shock Incarceration: The Impact of Correctional Boot Camp Programs," *Justice Quarterly* 5 (March 1990): 125–147.

47. Quoted in "New York's Shock Incarceration Called a Rehabilitation Model," *Criminal Justice Newsletter* 27 (15 April 1996): 1.

48. "Boot Camps Seem to Work—Until Youths Leave, Study Finds," *Criminal Justice Newsletter* 27 (3 June 1996): 3.

49. "Boot Camps Found Ineffective in Reducing Offender Recidivism," *Criminal Justice Newsletter* (1 October 2003), p. 1, summarizing the report by Dale G. Parent, *Correctional Boot Camps: Lessons from a Decade of Research* (NCJ-197018), available from the National Criminal Justice Reference Service, Box 6000, Rockville, MD 20849-6000. On the Internet: www.ncjrs.org/pdffiles1/nij197018.pdf (retrieved 26 June 2005).

50. "Maryland Is Latest of States to Rethink Youth 'Boot Camps,'" *New York Times* (19 December 1999), p. 1.

51. "Ex-Camp Worker Pleads Guilty," *Arizona Republic* (21 February 2002), p. 1B.

52. "Wife of Man Accused in Camp Death Shocks Courtroom," *Arizona Republic* (19 November 2004), p. 6B.

53. Paige M. Harrison and Allen J. Beck, Bureau of Justice Statistics, *Prison and Jail Inmates at Midyear 2004* (Washington, D.C.: U.S. Department of Justice, April 2005), pp. 1, 5.

54. "Crowding at Prisons Has State in a Jam," *Los Angeles Times* (13 March 2005), p. 1A.

55. "The Growing Inmate Population," *New York Times* (1 August 2003), editorial, p. 22.

56. Ruiz v. Estelle, 503 F.Supp. 1265, 1281–1282 (S.D. Texas, 1980), *aff'd. in part, vacated in part, modified, in part, appeal dismissed in part,* 679 F.2d 1115 (5th Cir. 1983), *cert. denied,* 460 U.S. 1042 (1982). Other proceedings occurred, resulting in the most recent ones, *later proceeding sub nom.,* 981 F.2d 1256 (5th Cir. 1992), *dismissed without opinion,* 114 F.3d 1180 (5th Cir. 1997).

57. "Overcrowding Keeps the Fuse Lit at Jail: New Cells Won't Solve Problem, Experts Say," *Chicago Tribune* (7 February 1995), p. 1.

58. Laube v. Campbell, 255 F.Supp. 2d 1301 (M.D. Ala. 2003), *settlement, judgment entered,* 333 F.Supp. 2d 1234 (M.D. Ala. 2004).

59. Laube v. Campbell, 333 F.Supp. 2d 1234 (M.D. Ala. 2004). The 2002 statement is from Laube v. Haley, 234 F.Supp. 2d 1227 (M.D. Ala. 2002).

60. "Detroit Jails May Be Forced to Release Inmates," *Corrections Professional* 8, no. 14 (11 April 2003).

61. "Surveyed Officials Cite Errors in Design of Prisons and Jails," *Criminal Justice Newsletter* 21 (1 May 1990): 2, referring to a report by Juvenile and Criminal Justice International, Inc.: *Design, Equipment, Construction and Other Blunders in Detention and Correctional Facilities: Who Is to Blame?*

62. "States Fight Back as Prison Population Growth Strains Budgets," *Corrections Professional* 8, no. 18 (6 June 2003).

63. "Meals Hit the Chopping Block," *Corrections Professional* 8, number 18 (6 June 2003).

64. Alexis M. Durham III, "Origins of Interest in the Privatization of Punishment: The Nineteenth and Twentieth Century American Experience," *Criminology* 27 (February 1989): 109.

65. See Camille G. Camp and George M. Camp, *Private Sector Involvement in Prison Services and Operations,* Criminal Justice Institute for the National Institute of Corrections (Washington, D.C.: U.S. Government Printing Office, February 1984), cited in *Corrections and the Private Sector,* Joan Mullen, National Institute of Justice (Washington, D.C.: U.S. Government Printing Office, March 1985), p. 2.

66. "CCA Marks 20th Anniversary," *Corrections Professional* 8, no. 15 (25 April 2003).

67. "Private Prison Stocks Poised to Break Out," *Corrections Professional* 10, no. 9 (21 January 2005).

68. "Details of the Study," *Corrections Professional* 8, no. 16 (9 May 2003).

69. See Anthony P. Travisono, "Is 'for-Profit' a Wolf at the Door?" *Corrections Today* 47 (July 1985): 4.

70. "Prisons Turn Profit for Private Firms: Lawmakers Seek OK to Buy Services," *St. Louis Post-Dispatch* (30 March 1995), p. 1, Illinois Section.

71. "Experts Argue against Prison Privatization," *Federal Human Resources Week* 9, no. 3 (29 April 2002).

72. "New Mexico Prison Officer Death Prompts Review of Privatization," *Criminal Justice Newsletter* (15 April 1999), p. 3.

73. Joan Mullen, National Institute of Justice, *Corrections and the Private Sector* (Washington, D.C.: U.S. Government Printing Office, March 1985), pp. 2–8.

Life in Prison

From the point of view of inmates, imprisonment is a series of status degradation ceremonies that serve two functions: to destroy their identities and to assign them new identities of a lower order.[1] The way offenders are treated when they enter prison exemplifies society's rejection; they are stripped of most of their personal belongings, given a number, searched, examined, inspected, weighed, and documented. To the inmates, these acts represent deprivation of their personal identities. The actions may be conducted in a degrading way that emphasizes their diminished status. They face the correctional officers, who have contacts and families in the outside world but who are there to ensure that the inmates conform to institutional rules.

Gresham M. Sykes referred to the psychological and social problems that result from the worst punishment, deprivation of liberty, as the "pains of imprisonment." In his classic study of male inmates in a maximum-security prison, Sykes discussed the moral rejection by the community, which is a constant threat to the inmate's self-concept; the deprivation of goods and services in a society that emphasizes material possessions; the deprivation of heterosexual relationships and the resulting threat to his masculinity; and the deprivation of security in a population in which the inmate faces threats to his safety and sometimes to his health and life.[2]

In their attempts to adjust to the pains of imprisonment, inmates devise ways of manipulating the prison environment. Sometimes this manipulation creates serious control problems for the correctional officers, staff, and administrators charged with the ultimate responsibility of maintaining safety and order within the prison and keeping inmates from escaping. This is not an easy task, and the problems are becoming more serious. But at the same time federal courts have interpreted various constitutional amendments as providing standards for the treatment of inmates, along with reasonable accommodations while they are incarcerated.

This chapter examines life in prison for inmates, as well as for the prison administrators and correctional officers charged with the responsibility of maintaining prisons. We begin with an overview of life in prison before looking at some of the major issues connected with incarceration. The traditional approach to inmates' rights is contrasted with the modern approach as we analyze substantive and procedural issues raised by the U.S. Constitution and the modern cases interpreting that document.

The roles of the primary persons charged with administering prisons, administrators and correctional officers, are explored historically and in light of recent developments. Their respective

LEARNING
OBJECTIVES

After reading this chapter, you should be able to do the following:

- **Relate the historical to the more recent position of federal courts on the issue of inmates' rights**
- **State the general criteria the U.S. Supreme Court uses to determine whether inmates' rights, such as to be free of cruel and unusual punishment, have been violated**
- **Trace the evolution of prison management styles and compare them with today's needs**
- **Explain the functions of correctional officers, exploring ways in which they controlled inmates historically and how that has changed recently**
- **Analyze correctional officer recruitment and training**
- **Discuss gender and racial issues concerning correctional administrators**
- **Identify some of the issues faced by new inmates and give a brief overview of inmate prison life**
- **Explain the inmate subculture, discuss its origin, and explore how it affects the adjustment of male and female inmates**
- **Analyze the social control role of the inmate system**
- **Discuss the influence of prison gangs in men's prisons**
- **Analyze the needs of female inmates and of those requiring special care and programs and discuss how those needs are or are not met**
- **Discuss the nature and analyze the impact of the Prison Rape Elimination Act of 2003**
- **Contrast same-gender sexual behavior of female and male inmates**
- **Discuss the impact of AIDS in a prison setting**
- **Comment on the problems of physically challenged, elderly, or mentally ill inmates and discuss the latest developments in these areas**
- **Discuss briefly the nature and availability of prison programs**
- **Analyze the impact of prison violence**

roles are scrutinized, along with issues such as recruitment, training, and the importance of diversity.

The next major section of the chapter is devoted to an explanation of what it is like to live in prison. It focuses on how inmates adapt to prison life. A general discussion of inmate subcultures is followed by a look at the inmate social system as a method of social control. The special needs of female inmates, such as the ways in which they provide for their children and their unique health needs, are noted. Inmate sexual behavior is also examined, with a comparison of male and female inmates. Among other critical issues associated with prison life are the subjects of AIDS (and ways to deal with those who are infected) and the growing concerns with inmates who are physically challenged, elderly, or mentally ill.

Prison programs, such as education, work, and recreation, are highlighted before the chapter closes with a discussion of prison violence, a growing concern in many institutions.

10-1   The Incarceration of Offenders

After offenders have been sentenced, official papers are prepared to turn them over to the custody of the state's department of corrections (or the Federal Bureau of Prisons in the federal system). They may be transported to prison immediately or retained in jail for a short period. In some states they are sent to a diagnostic center for a physical examination, psychological testing, and orientation. Assignment to a particular institution is made after a thorough evaluation of the test results. In other states the decision regarding placement is made according to the seriousness of the offense, the age and gender of the offender, and whether the offender has a prior record (and, if so, the extent and nature of that record). In the case of women there may be no choice; the state may have only one institution, which must accommodate all security levels, unless the state contracts with another state or the federal system.

If the state has a central diagnostic unit, offenders must be transported from that unit to their individual assignments for incarceration. Upon arrival at the assigned institution, usually offenders are isolated from the general population for several days, a week, or even longer. During that period they are told the rules or given a rule book to read. Physical exams are given. In most institutions they are strip searched for drugs and weapons. They may be required to take a bath with a disinfectant soap and shampoo. Urine samples are collected to determine whether they are on drugs, and laxatives may be given to determine whether they are smuggling drugs.

The inmates' clothing may be taken and special prison clothing issued. In lower-security institutions, especially in some women's prisons, inmates are permitted to wear their own clothing, although there may be restrictions on the type of clothing. The rules differ from state to state and even within states, depending on the institution's security level and other factors. When inmates are not allowed to keep personal clothing, they may be required to pay to have the clothing shipped home or may find upon release that it has been donated to a charity. When the inmate is released, many prisons issue only one new set of clothing.

During the orientation period, inmates are required to complete numerous forms concerning their background, medical history, and individuals who might be visiting. They may be asked whether they fear any persons in the prison; it is necessary to place some inmates in protective custody for protection from the rest of the population. Other inmates and correctional officials may test the inmate during the orientation period; most inmates advise that it is wise to be respectful to the officers and to be careful about making friends among other inmates. Generally inmates are not permitted to have visitors during this orientation period. Phone calls are prohibited or limited. Thus, it is a lonely, frustrating, and stressful time. Inmates may be interviewed for job assignments or educational programs in an effort to determine placement within the institution.

Inmates are permitted to buy a few personal items from the **commissary,** but times for purchases and frequency of purchases are limited. Money may not be kept by inmates in most institutions; it is placed in a trust fund, against which they may draw for purchases. Money that may be received from outside is limited. Any or all of the rules in effect during the orientation period may also apply to the inmate's life in the general population.

> ▶ **Commissary** The prison store as well as incidental items sold to inmates. Also an inmate's account, which is debited when an item is purchased.

Eventually inmates are relocated in the facility to which they are assigned and normal prison life begins. Before looking at the details of adaptation to prison life, it is important to discuss the legal implications of incarceration.

10-2   The Legal Implications of Incarceration

The recognition of inmates' legal rights has had a short history. The earlier judicial position on inmates' rights was expressed in an 1872 case, in which a federal court declared bluntly that, by committing a crime, the convicted felon forfeits his or her liberty and "all his personal rights except those which the law in its humanity accords to him. He is for the time being the slave of the state."[3]

From 1872 until the 1960s, for the most part the federal courts observed a **hands-off doctrine** toward inmates and prisons, reasoning that prison administration is a part of the executive, not the judicial, branch of government. In 1974, however, the U.S. Supreme Court held that, although an incarcerated person loses some rights because of institutional needs, "a prisoner is not wholly stripped of constitutional protections when he is imprisoned for crime. There is no iron curtain drawn between the Constitution and the prisons of this country."[4]

> ▶ **Hands-off doctrine** A policy used by courts to justify nonintervention in the daily administration of corrections agencies.

Even before the 1974 decision, however, lower federal courts had begun looking into inmates' claims that they were being denied basic constitutional rights. By the 1980s, numerous lawsuits had been filed by inmates, and federal courts had scrutinized prison conditions, particularly regarding overcrowding. Entire prison systems had been placed under federal court orders to reduce populations and to make other changes in prison conditions. By the 1990s, extensive problems of jail and prison overcrowding had resulted in an explosion of federal lawsuits concerning incarceration conditions. Recently, however, many jurisdictions have been taking steps to remove their prison systems from federal court oversight. They are doing this under a federal law enacted for this purpose.[5]

What was responsible for the increasing recognition of inmates' rights in federal courts? Among other issues, the **civil rights** activism of the 1960s included the treatment of inmates, and during that period federal courts began to look at what was happening inside prisons. Many of the earlier cases involved allegations of physical brutality as well as questionable living conditions. For example, a federal district court heard evidence on the prison conditions in Arkansas, concluded that inmates were living under degrading and disgusting conditions, and found the prison system unconstitutional. The need for judicial intervention into the administration of prisons was stated emphatically by the federal court: "If Arkansas is going to operate a Penitentiary System, it is going to have to be a system that is countenanced by the Constitution of the United States."[6]

Since the 1970s, federal courts have heard many cases on prison conditions. Federal intervention has been extended to jails as well. Some prison officials have been ordered to close facilities until conditions are corrected; others have been ordered to change specific conditions. Some officials who have defied these orders have been held in contempt of court. Judges continue to defer to prison authorities concerning day-to-day prison operations, but they intervene when federal constitutional rights are violated. It is important to look at those rights more closely, considering the differences between rights and privileges. It is also important to consider how actions are brought by inmates who seek legal remedies to alleged conditions.

Historically prison officials spoke of the difference between *rights* and *privileges*. Rights require constitutional protection; privileges are there by the grace of prison officials and may be withdrawn at their discretion. In 1971, the U.S. Supreme Court rejected the position that "constitutional rights turn upon whether a governmental benefit is characterized as a 'right' or a 'privilege.'"[7]

It is clear, however, that a hierarchy of rights is recognized. Some rights are considered more important than others and therefore require more extensive due process before they may be infringed upon. For example, an inmate's right to be released from illegal confinement is more important than the right to canteen privileges. Some of the other rights high in the hierarchy are the right to protection against willful injury, access to courts, freedom of religious belief, freedom of communication, and freedom from cruel and unusual punishment. If an inmate succeeds in a lawsuit against prison officials, he or she may be entitled to civil damages, as noted in Spotlight 10-1.

The recognition of inmates' rights and of the hierarchy of rights does not mean that the government (or prison officials acting as government agents) may not restrict those rights. Rights may be restricted if prison officials can show that the restriction is necessary for security or for other recognized penological purposes, such as discipline and order.

Another important issue concerns the tests used for determining whether an inmate's constitutional rights have been violated. One right is illustrative—the Eighth Amendment's ban on cruel and unusual punishment (see Appendix A). Generally the U.S. Supreme Court's tests are stated broadly and thus open to interpretation. In 1976, in examining allegations of cruel and unusual punishment with regard to prison conditions, the Court held that an inmate may bring a successful action against prison officials who deny him or her adequate medical care for a serious medical problem only if it can be shown that the officials acted with *deliberate indifference* to the inmate's needs. In *Estelle* v. *Gamble* the Court stated that allegations of "inadvertent failure to provide adequate medical care" or of a "negligent . . . diagnos[is]" do not establish the requisite state of mind for a violation of the cruel and unusual punishment clause.[8]

▶ **Civil rights** Sometimes called civil liberties; all the natural rights guaranteed by the U.S. Constitution (or by individual state constitutions), such as free speech and the right to religious beliefs and practices; also the body of law concerning natural rights.

Spotlight 10-1   Enforcing Inmate Rights through Civil Cases

In September 1971, the bloodiest prison uprising in U.S. history took place in New York State's Attica prison (approximately 30 miles from Buffalo). Inmates were angry about their living conditions and the food they were served. They asked for better educational programs, higher pay for prison work, and more minority guards. The inmates took control of the prison for four days, after which guards armed with pistols and shotguns ascended the prison's roofs and towers and fired 2,000 rounds of ammunition. When the riot ended, 29 inmates and 10 hostages were dead; many more were wounded. Inmates who survived claimed that correctional officers had tortured and brutalized them. Finally, in February 2000, some of those victims had an opportunity to tell a judge what had happened to them. The inmates testified regarding the issue of whether the $8 million the state had offered to settle the remaining claims was a reasonable and fair provision.[1] The money was distributed in December 2000.

This was not the first civil suit in the Attica case. In 1989, a New York court awarded a total of $1.3 million in seven lawsuits brought by inmates or their estates for damages caused in the Attica prison riots and their aftermath. These awards were granted to inmates who did not take part in the riots but were subjected to excessive force by authorities attempting to regain control of the prison. Police efforts (the governor had sent in 500 national guards) during that uprising were described by a state investigating committee as constituting the "bloodiest encounter between Americans since the Civil War." Individual damage awards ranged from $35,000 to $473,000.[2]

In 1997, a federal judge awarded a former Attica inmate $4 million for damages sustained when he was beaten and tortured by correctional officers during the 1971 Attica riot. The suit, first filed in 1974, alleged that Frank Smith was "forced to walk over broken glass, beaten with batons, locked in his cell for four days, . . . [and] made to lie on a picnic table [naked] for hours with a football under his chin." During that time officers "struck his testicles with batons" and burned his body with cigarettes while threatening to kill him or castrate him if he allowed the ball to roll away. Mr. Smith commented after the verdict: "The jury has sent a message that people everywhere need to be treated like humans, not animals." The principal attorney for Mr. Smith, Elizabeth Fink, had spent her entire career representing inmates who were incarcerated at Attica at the time of the uprising.[3] In observance of the 30th anniversary of the Attica riot, Court TV produced a documentary, "Ghosts of Attica," which featured Elizabeth Fink and her paralegal, former inmate Frank Smith. Also in September 2001, Fink alleged that the conditions that had precipitated the Attica riot still existed in many U.S. prisons.[4]

In a 2003 case a Texas jury awarded $4 million to a former inmate who alleged that a correctional officer at the prison camp in which she was incarcerated had slammed her up against a wall in a supply room (where she had been summoned for a drug test) and raped her. The jury took only 30 minutes to reach its verdict. The victim kept the clothing she was wearing at the time of the attack, and the semen stains provided incriminating evidence when she turned them over to authorities after she was released from the camp. She testified that as she was being raped the officer, Michael Miller, asked, "Do you think you're the first? This happens all the time." Miller was being investigated for criminal charges.[5]

Allegations of brutality, even sexual abuse, are not limited to charges by female inmates against male officers. In January 2003, a male inmate of a Las Vegas correctional center filed a lawsuit asking $3 million in damages and alleging that he was forced to become a sex slave by a female officer. Ryan Layman claimed that between November 2000 and January 2001 he was forced to submit to sexual relations with correctional officer Jennifer Burkley on numerous occasions. Burkley and another officer pleaded guilty to having sex with an inmate, a misdemeanor. Both were accused of performing oral sex on jailed teens. They were each sentenced to two years' probation. When she was sentenced, Burkley said, "It was wrong. . . . It should never have happened."[6]

1. "Ex-Inmates Hurt at Attica Tell the Judge Their Tales," *New York Times* (15 February 2000), p. 27.
2. "Court Awards $l.3 Million to Inmates Injured at Attica," *New York Times* (26 October 1989), p. 14.
3. "Ex-Attica Inmate Wins $4 Million in Suit over Reprisals after 1971 Uprising," *New York Times* (6 June 1997), p. 20.
4. UPI news release (7 September 2001).
5. "Rape Victim Wins Suit against CO," *Corrections Professional* 8, no. 19 (20 June 2003).
6. "Lawsuits Increasingly Allege Sexual Assault by Female Correctional Officers," *Corrections Professional* 8, no. 14 (11 April 2003).

In subsequent years the U.S. Supreme Court has construed the cruel and unusual punishment issue further. In 1991 in *Wilson* v. *Seiter*, the Court held that, "if the pain inflicted is not formally meted out *as punishment* by the statute or the sentencing judge, some mental element must be attributed to the inflicting officer before it can qualify." The Court interpreted the Constitution to require that, when inmates question prison conditions, they must show a negative state of mind of officials in order to win their cases. Specifically they must prove that prison officials harbor *deliberate indifference*. Dissenters noted correctly that in many cases this standard will be difficult if not impossible to prove.[9]

In 1994, the U.S. Supreme Court applied a subjective rather than an objective standard to determine whether prison officials had the required state of mind to constitute deliberate indifference. *Farmer* v. *Brennan* involved an inmate who was biologically male but had some characteristics of a woman. He alleged that he was raped by another inmate after he was incarcerated in an all-male prison. He argued that placing a transsexual in an all-male population constituted deliberate indifference to his safety. Officials should have known of the risks involved. The Supreme Court rejected that objective standard, stating that prison officials may be held liable for unsafe prison conditions only if they "know that inmates face a substantial risk of serious harm and disregard that risk by failing to take reasonable measures to abate it."[10]

In 1992 in *Hudson* v. *McMillian,* the U.S. Supreme Court held that inmates may bring actions for cruel and unusual punishment against prison officials who engage in physical force that results in injuries, even if those injuries are not significant. Justice Sandra Day O'Connor wrote the majority opinion, in which she stated, "When prison officials maliciously and sadistically use force to cause harm, contemporary standards of decency always are violated."[11]

Although there has been improvement in the conditions at some prisons, others remain subject to court order. For example, in March 2003 a federal district court judge admonished Alabama correctional authorities for their failure to submit an acceptable plan, as ordered earlier by the court, to alleviate unconstitutional prison conditions at three state prisons that house women. The court stated that a lack of funds was not an acceptable reason for failure to submit the plan. Further, the court refused to accept the recommendation of correctional officials that the court prohibit the transfer of additional female inmates from county jails to the Julia Tutwiler Prison for Women. The resolution of this lawsuit through court-accepted settlements was discussed in Chapter 9.[12]

10-3 Prison Administration

State prison systems have a director, who reports to the governor or a corrections board. In the federal system the director of the U.S. Bureau of Prisons (BOP), who reports to the U.S. attorney general's office in the Department of Justice (DOJ), also serves as commissioner of the Federal Prison Industries (FPI). In spring 2003, Harley G. Lappin became the director of the BOP, replacing retiring Kathleen Hawk Sawyer, who is featured in Professions 10-1 as an example of a woman who rose to a position of power within the correctional field. Serving as the chief prison administrator in a state or in the federal system is a high-pressure job, and turnover is high.

10-3a Wardens or Superintendents

Prison directors hire and fire wardens or superintendents of the institutions within their respective jurisdictions and manage the correctional agency's central staff. Preparing and managing a budget is one of the director's most important functions. Directors must justify to the legislature the need for additional funds for operating the prisons, a difficult problem today, with so many jurisdictions facing budget cuts while prison populations increase. Despite the importance of the director's position, the day-to-day administration of adult prisons is the responsibility of the warden or superintendent of each institution.

In early prisons, wardens had great power. Although some exercised control as a result of strong personalities, most controlled their institutions with the authority that came from their positions. The strict chain of command from the warden down to the inmates was emphasized by the military atmosphere of most institutions: the wearing of uniforms, the use of job titles, lockstep marching, and total deference to the warden and his staff. Strict discipline, and in some cases corporal punishment, were part of that traditional, authoritarian management style.

The earlier prison wardens exercised authoritarian management styles in their interactions with the staff, too. They had total authority to hire and fire the staff, and they required undivided loyalty, which in staff selection was a more important factor than competence. The warden controlled the institution's resources as well. Most wardens lived on the grounds of the institutions, and the warden's household budget was included in that of the prison. The authoritarian style dominated prison management until the middle of the twentieth century.[13]

Professions 10-1

Women in Corrections

During an internship at the Federal Correctional Institution in Morgantown, West Virginia, Kathleen M. Hawk decided on a career in corrections. Until the spring 2003, when she retired, Kathleen Hawk Sawyer, who holds a bachelor's degree in psychology and master's and doctoral degrees in counseling and rehabilitation, was the director of the Federal Bureau of Prisons. Prior to assuming the highest position in the bureau, Sawyer had served as its assistant director. She had also been a staff psychologist, the chief of psychology services, an associate warden, and a warden. In her earlier years she served in training administration in the federal system. While she served as assistant director, she made the following statement:

> I feel strongly that as women we should take full positive advantage of the marvelous career opportunities available to us today and pursue them not as our given right, but rather as occasions to demonstrate our talents and abilities so that many more doors will be open for generations of women after us.[1]

Kathleen Hawk Sawyer's elevation to the highest position in the Federal Bureau of Prisons demonstrates that women are assuming administrative positions in the criminal justice field.

Women have made contributions to corrections as well as to other criminal justice functions. "Beginning in the mid-1800s, they chaired, as well as served on, governing boards and citizen committees overseeing correctional agencies." They served as volunteers and later as correctional officers, assistant and associate wardens, and more recently as wardens.[2] Today they serve as correctional officers in men's as well as women's prisons, and they have been appointed to some of the higher administrative positions as well, as Hawk's appointment illustrated.

1. Karen Carlo Ruhren, "Kathleen M. Hawk: Profile: BOP Programming Administrator Sees Opportunities for Women," *Corrections Today* 54 (August 1992): 132.
2. Ibid.

During the 1970s, significant changes took place in many American prisons. First, there were demographic changes. Harsh drug laws led to the incarceration of more young people (some from the middle class) with drug problems. The percentage of the prison population that was poor, minority, and urban increased. Attempts to suppress gang activity resulted in the incarceration of greater numbers of gang members, many of whom maintained close ties to their colleagues outside prison. Increased politicalization within prisons occurred as the younger, more radical prison population viewed incarceration as a political process. They looked with disdain on the traditional rewards the officers might offer in exchange for their cooperation.

A second factor that precipitated change during the 1970s was the warden's decreased power. Many inmates and correctional officers were unwilling to accept the authoritarian governance style, and their rejection of that style has been supported by federal court orders. Court decisions that require changes in prison physical conditions as well as provisions for due process in some correctional proceedings have reduced the traditional power of prison administrators and correctional officers.

There are numerous obstacles to significant changes in prison management. First, the values of each social group within the prison may clash. Second, the conflict between the goals of custody and rehabilitation remains. Third, there are insufficient facts on which to base decisions. Part of this results from limited research, a lack of evaluation of treatment programs, and insufficient knowledge of the applicability of new management techniques to prison settings. With a lack of knowledge of treatment and management, the prison administrator tends to fall back on rule books and manuals, which are likely to produce a more rigid and authoritarian type of organization.

Finally, prisons continue to be faced with serious financial problems, which have reduced expenditures for management training programs and have resulted in difficulties in recruiting trained persons at competitive salaries. Decreased funding has also reduced the degree to which prison managers can provide the resources that are needed for other programs within the institution, as well as sufficient staff and officers.

Some signs of progress are evident in the area of corrections management. First, more institutions are implementing research techniques to measure the success of programs and evaluation strategies for personnel. Therefore, an increasing amount of information is available to correctional managers. Second, professional organizations are developing standards for criminal justice administration, including correctional administration. These standards reflect a general concern with effective management. More important, the standards being developed by correctional managers in the field may be more responsive to problems and more acceptable to administrators.

The third, and the most important, reform in prison administration is the increased attention to professionalism. More attention has been given to attracting highly educated people to the correctional field. Management has sought to improve correctional training and to introduce new management techniques. An issue arises, however, when professionalism is viewed as the *solution* to organizational problems, which may result in a better image of the organization without sufficient attention to underlying problems.

Some research suggests, for example, that more highly educated correctional officers do not have more positive and humane attitudes toward inmates than do less educated officers. Furthermore, the more highly educated officer may be more frustrated in the job. Thus, the appearance of professionalism may be only that, unless adequate prior and on-the-job training programs are implemented to prepare correctional officers for the difficulties they will face. Important organizational changes must be made, too.

10-3b Correctional Officers

The goals of the correctional institution and the management style of the warden or superintendent are very important in determining the success or failure of an institution. However, the individuals with the most extensive contact and perhaps the greatest effect on inmates are the **correctional officers,** or **guards.**

> **Correctional officer (guard)** A corrections employee with supervisory power over a suspect or convicted offender in custody.

Correctional officers in maximum-security prisons spend almost all of their workdays behind bars in close contact with inmates. It is impossible to generalize the working conditions or the reactions of correctional officers, but often the job is monotonous and boring. Salaries are low; fringe benefits are limited; the risk is tremendous. Stress is high, recruiting is difficult, and the turnover among officers is high in most institutions.

Attempts are being made, however, to assist officers in adjusting to the stress caused by violence and other problems within prisons. Stress management is becoming an important element of officer training. The American Correctional Association (ACA) provides numerous publications to assist officers in dealing with the daily problems they face. The ACA provides correspondence courses; criminal justice institutes provide continuing education programs. Some prison systems are giving correctional officers a taste of life as an inmate by sending them to prison to be treated as inmates for a short period of time, but these programs are expensive and not used widely.

The initial formal training of correctional officers is critical, too. Usually training is conducted at a central place within the prison system, and the nature of the training varies from one system to another. Of necessity, it covers institutional security; however, in addition, officers must learn how to protect themselves from inmates who attack them physically and how to react when inmates curse at, spit at, or urinate on them. Recruits are taught the rules and regulations that govern inmate behavior in prisons, and they must learn the rules and constitutional provisions that govern the behavior of correctional officers in relation to inmates.

> **Social system**
> The interrelationship of roles, acts, and statuses of people who make up the social structure; a social group or set of interacting persons or groups considered a unitary whole because it reflects the common values, social norms, and objectives of the individuals whom it comprises, even though the group is considered distinct from those individuals.

The fact is, however, that the primary function of correctional officers is to maintain internal security and discipline. In the past, when corporal punishment was allowed, officers controlled inmates by physical force and, if necessary, brutality. Although courts have held that excessive force is not permitted constitutionally, there is recent evidence that some correctional officers have brutalized inmates, as noted in Spotlight 10-2.

Another method correctional officers have used to control inmates is to manipulate the inmates' **social system.** Correctional officers permit selected inmates to have positions of authority and control over other inmates. In recent years, however, federal courts have prohibited the practice of elevating certain inmates to positions of power over other inmates. In some cases, the changes resulting in the removal of inmate power over other

Spotlight 10-2   Correctional Officers and Allegations of Brutality

In February 2000, eight Florida correctional officers were indicted in the beating death of inmate Frank Valdes in the summer 1999. An autopsy of Valdes revealed that all of his ribs were broken; the upper part of his body contained boot marks; and his testicles were swollen. The officers were part of the so-called *cell extraction team* that had removed Valdes from his cell prior to his death. Valdes, age 36, was on death row for killing a correctional officer in 1987. He had been in the prison system since he was 17 years old.[1] Three officers were tried and acquitted. Florida's attorney general decided not to prosecute the other five officers accused in the death, stating that he had no reason to believe he could get a conviction after losing the case against the officers he tried. In January 2003, the warden who was in charge of the prison when Valdes was killed was named by Florida Governor Jeb Bush as the head of the state's department of corrections.[2]

In January 2000, two correctional officers at the Nassau County Jail in Uniondale, New York, pleaded guilty to beating an unarmed inmate who was serving a 90-day sentence for violating traffic ordinances. The officers admitted that the inmate, Thomas Pizzuto, age 38, had done nothing to provoke them, although the former heroin addict was noisy and demanding methadone. The officers, Edward Velazquez and Patrick Regnier, faced a maximum sentence of 30 years-to-life in prison for murder, but, after two appeals, received sentences of approximately 11 years. Joseph Bergen, also a correctional officer at the jail, was sentenced to 5 years and 10 months for altering paperwork in an attempt to cover up the crime. In 2003 Pizzuto's widow and son settled their civil lawsuit for $7.75 million.[3]

Seven county jail correctional officers in Charleston, West Virginia, were fired in 1990 after investigators concluded that, without any provocation, they had beaten a handcuffed inmate who had been arrested for public intoxication and resisting arrest. At the time of the beating, the suspect was so drunk that he could not even give his name to authorities.[4]

In the fall 1992, 14 former employees of the women's prison in Georgia at Hardwick were indicted on charges of sexually abusing female inmates. It was labeled the worst case of such abuse in prison history, with alleged offenders charged with trading sex for coerced abortions, prostitution rings, rape, and sodomy. The accused included men and women. One of the accused was a former deputy warden. The indictments stemmed from a 1984 lawsuit against the institution's officials. The recently appointed female warden, Mary Esposito, said the charges reflected the change in attitudes toward women's rights in prison.[5]

In March 1993, after a state prison employee was killed at the Hardwick prison, ABC News reported that the killing occurred to prevent the victim from testifying in the case of alleged sexual abuse. By that time, almost 200 female inmates at the Georgia Women's Correctional Institution and two from other Georgia prisons had accused officers and other staff and former staff of sexual and other forms of abuse.[6] By July 1994, Cornelius Stanley, a former deputy warden accused of sexual molestation in the Georgia case, had been rehired, and all charges against him had been dismissed. Stanley was rehired as a lieutenant at the same salary he had held formerly at the rank of captain. Stanley received more than $58,000 in back pay plus another $50,000 from the state. It was the second time Stanley had been rehired after a firing involving alleged misconduct. He may not, however, work at a prison that houses female inmates. Of the 15 men and women indicted in the Georgia prison sex case, charges against three were dropped because the statute of limitations had expired. Two entered guilty pleas and received probationary sentences. One officer was acquitted.[7]

In 1999 and 2000, a total of 51 prison correctional officers and staff members were fired for improper behavior toward inmates in South Carolina. The investigation was begun after reports that one or two correctional officers had had sex with inmate Susan Smith, who is serving a life sentence for driving her two little boys into a lake and leaving them to drown while she escaped. By January 2003, 20 former prison employees had entered guilty pleas or had been convicted of drug, sex, or other misconduct offenses within South Carolina prisons and 29 more cases were pending. Houston Cagle, who had had sex with Smith, was sentenced to 10 years in prison but the sentence was suspended upon service of 90 days.[8]

In November 2002, seven guards at the federal supermax prison in Florence, Colorado, were indicted for alleged abuse of inmates. Those allegations were described as follows:

> According to court documents, those guards were a renegade group called "The Cowboys" who roamed the maximum-security penitentiary in 1995 and 1996 administering punishment ranging from smashing inmates' heads into walls to mixing human waste into prisoners' food.[9]

In June 2003, three of the former officers were convicted of beating handcuffed or shackled inmates; four were acquitted.[10]

1. "Guards Indicted in Slaying," *St. Petersburg Times* (3 February 2000), p. 1.
2. "Bush's Choice of Prison Boss Sparks Debate," *Orlando Sentinel* (7 January 2003), p. 5B.
3. "Two Guards Plead Guilty and Describe Fatal Beatings of a Prisoner," *New York Times* (13 January 2000), p. 26; "7.75M Deal in Jail Killing," *Daily News* (New York) (1 April 2003), p. 21. The federal case is United States v. Regnier and Velazquez, 2002 U.S. App. LEXIS 17749 (2d. Cir. 2002).
4. "Guards Fired over Beating of Prisoner," *Tallahassee Democrat* (31 May 1990), p. 1B.
5. "Fourteen Are Charged with Sex Abuse in Women's Jail," *New York Times* (14 November 1992), p. 1.
6. "ABC: Prison Worker's Death May Be Part of Sex Scandal," *Orlando Sentinel* (16 March 1993), p. 6.
7. "Prison Guard Accused of Abusing Female Inmates Is Rehired," *Atlanta Journal and Constitution* (12 July 1994), p. 1.
8. "Prison Vice Probe Over," *Greenville News* (20 January 2003), p. 1.
9. "Guards Accused of Sex at Prison: Women Indicted on Federal Counts," *Denver Post* (12 July 2002), p. 1B.
10. "US Prison Guards Guilty of Brutality," *Morning Star* (26 June 2003), p. 2.

inmates have occurred quickly without the addition of more correctional officers to fill the power void. In other cases, inmates have gained control of institutions for temporary periods, leading to devastating riots.

In some institutions correctional officers' use of inmates to help control other inmates has led to corruption, including officers' acceptance of bribes from inmates. Some officers have taken contraband into prisons. Contraband is any forbidden material, such as alcohol, other drugs, and weapons.

More recently some institutions have permitted correctional officers to use force—such as mace, pepper spray, or stun devices—in an attempt to cut down on prison violence. For example, a *stun belt* is a device attached to a person's waist. From a distance as far as 300 feet, the device can be activated to send an eight-second, 50,000-volt electric stun. Some judges permit the use of the device for the purpose of keeping defendants in order; others do not approve its use. The director of Virginia's prison systems, Ron Angelone, who left his position in 2002, claimed that the number of assaults per 1,000 inmates decreased from 7.98 in the mid-1990s to 4.3 in 1999 as the result of his policy of equipping correctional officers with stun guns.[14]

One suggestion for improving the control correctional officers have over inmates is increased professionalism and training of officers. In many jurisdictions a high school diploma is sufficient for the entry-level officer, although it would be difficult today for someone without college experience to advance to an administrative position. Good physical health is also required, for the duties of a correctional officer may involve strenuous physical work, particularly during a riot or another prison disturbance. Mental and emotional health are important, too, although many jurisdictions provide inadequate testing and training in these areas.

Finally, the recruitment of correctional officers poses problems. The administrator in charge of the New York City jails blamed the violence at the Rikers Island facility in the early 1990s on inadequate hiring practices of correctional officers.[15] Recruiting correctional officers did not improve significantly in the following decade, as highlighted by a 2001 front-page article in the *New York Times* entitled "Desperate for Prison Guards, Some States Even Rob Cradles." The article focused on Kansas, where the minimum age for correctional officers had recently been dropped from 21 to 19, but it also covered other jurisdictions. It quoted one prison authority as stating that, if recruiters were honest, they would advertise using such words as "Come to work with us. Have feces thrown at you. Be verbally abused every day."[16]

A more enthusiastic article on recruiting correctional officers was published in 2004 and referred to the efforts at a new prison in Forrest City, Arkansas. The facility provided approximately 300 new jobs, including teachers, drug treatment personnel, and medical personnel, as well as correctional officers. The ad read "Get your foot in the door as a correctional officer, and after that, opportunities abound." But the starting salary for that position ($34,000 annually) and the lowest for any of the new positions ($22,193 annually) concerned the state's correctional department head, who feared the salaries would not be competitive.[17]

A focus on South Carolina corrections revealed a doubling of workers quitting their jobs between 1997 and 2003. During 2002, nearly one-fourth of the state's correctional employees, 1,300 persons, left. Of that number, 331 were fired. A former prison administrator and current professor, Joann Morton, emphasized that with such high turnover the state was losing its investment in time and money. Further, Morton noted, about one-third of correctional officers nationally leave their jobs each year.[18]

A look at the correctional situation in New York in 2003 is illustrative of some of the problems we continue to face. In 2002, the rate of inmate assaults against correctional officers in New York fell to a 23-year low. The prison population was at its lowest since 1993, yet correctional officers were taking more worker's compensation leave time; the amount had increased significantly. In New York correctional officers receive full pay for the first six months of worker's comp leave. Many of the reasons given for requesting a leave were minor injuries that were not related to assaults by inmates. Authorities did not agree on the reasons officers were requesting compensation leaves, but the cost in 2002 alone was

$23 million. In addition, when officers are on leave, others must work overtime to cover the shifts. The cost of overtime pay in 2002 in New York was $82.4 million. Officers complain that the state allows only six months of compensation leave and that it overlooks valid reasons for leaves, such as the stress and strain of correctional work. For example, one correctional officer was denied stress leave after an inmate threw feces and urine at him 13 times.[19]

Despite problems of high turnover, corruption and brutality, difficulties in recruiting, and stress, some correctional officers see themselves as correctional agents (not just as officers primarily responsible for maintaining security and order), with a belief that the system can have positive effects on inmates.

10-3c Female and Minority Officers

It is important that women and minorities have opportunities to participate fully in all professions, and they are vital in corrections, which has a high representation of minorities and an increasing number of women. Despite the small number of female inmates in corrections overall, women have unique problems in the correctional setting, and those problems might best be understood by female officers. In addition, female officers allege that, to gain parity with male officers, they must be able to work in prisons that incarcerate male inmates.

Several court cases have established the right of women to work in correctional institutions for men and have affected their hiring and promotion, but these changes have occurred only within the past decade or so. In 1997, for example, in order to settle a lawsuit, Arkansas hired 400 more female correctional officers to work in the state's prisons for men.[20] In 1995, a federal court held that the U.S. Constitution does not prohibit the viewing of a male inmate by a female correctional officer. Thus, women may work in men's prisons even when those jobs involve monitoring nude male inmates. The court stated,

> How odd it would be to find in the eighth amendment a right not to be seen by the other sex. Physicians and nurses of one sex routinely examine the other. In exotic places such as California people regularly sit in saunas and hot tubs with unclothed strangers. . . . Women reporters routinely enter locker rooms after games. How could an imposition that male athletes tolerate be deemed cruel and unusual punishment?[21]

In 2003, a federal judge in Boston, Massachusetts, awarded damages to two female correctional officers who alleged that male officers in their work environment, the jail and house of correction operated by the Franklin County Sheriff's Office, had created a hostile working environment. The plaintiffs also alleged that they were retaliated against after they made complaints about the sexually harassing situation. The judge awarded each of the two plaintiffs $150,000 in compensatory damages and $20,000 in punitive damages; one was awarded $10,000 and the other $5,000 for the reimbursement of medical fees associated with their damages. They were also entitled to compensation for their respective attorney fees.[22]

In spite of potential problems and some negative attitudes in their work environments, female correctional officers seem able to establish and maintain personal authority in a prison setting; they are not manipulated by inmates any more often than male officers. One study reported that "the authority of women correctional officers is as legitimate as that of their male colleagues."[23]

Many women find the position of correctional officer to be rewarding and challenging. And there is evidence that female officers contribute to a reduction of violence in prisons. A Minnesota corrections consulting firm that secured data from one maximum-security prison in each of the contiguous 48 states, the District of Columbia, and the federal prison system, reported that, "over the course of a year, 12.3 percent of the male officers were assaulted by inmates, compared to 3.4 percent of female officers." The differences did not appear to be caused by female officers being too lenient with male inmates. The president of the firm concluded that "other facilities should consider employing more female officers. . . . It appears that if a greater percentage of women were employed, an overall reduction in assaults on officers might result."[24]

10-4 Daily Prison Life

Life in prison is monotonous and routine. In maximum-security prisons, inmates are regulated for most of each day, beginning with the time for rising in the morning. Meal schedules may be unusual; for example, in some prisons inmates eat breakfast at 3 or 4 A.M. and then go back to bed for naps before beginning the regular workday. This is done because of the long time period required to feed a large population in a secure facility. Dinner may be served as early as 3 P.M. Some inmates are fed in their cells. During lockdown, when there has been internal trouble among inmates and particularly after riots, inmates may be confined to their cells most of the day, with all meals served in there.

Most prisons do not have sufficient jobs for all inmates to work an eight-hour day, so many inmates must find ways to fill their time. The security needs of the institution determine how free they are to do so, but in some prisons inmates are permitted to move about rather freely within certain areas of the prison and to mingle with other inmates.

Recreational facilities may be available in the prison's common areas. Ping-Pong and basketball are examples. Some prisons have gyms; others have weight rooms or a provision for outdoor recreation, such as baseball or basketball, but hours of use are limited. Some books are available for inmates to take to their cells or rooms. In large prisons, particularly maximum-security institutions, inmates are limited to a specified number of showers per week—three, for example; they are marched to and from and are supervised during their showers. Privacy is nonexistent in most prisons. During the hours of the regular workweek, inmates may be assigned to jobs or be permitted to attend educational or vocational classes. Others may have no organized activities.

After dinner inmates may be permitted to socialize with other inmates in common areas. The institution may provide activities, such as movies, Alcoholics Anonymous meetings, drug abuse seminars, or other therapeutic programs. Many institutions make television available; some permit inmates to have a television and radio in their cells, provided the equipment is purchased from the commissary to avoid the problem of contraband being brought into the institution by this means. However, as prisons have become crowded and more expensive in a society that has become more punitive, some prison officials have eliminated television and other amenities for inmates.

Part of the inmate's day may be spent writing letters to friends and family, although there may be limits on the number of letters that may be sent and received. Gifts are limited or excluded. Inmates may spend time taking care of their personal or prison-issued clothing and working at institutional assignments.

In minimum-security institutions some inmates may be permitted to leave the institution from time to time for various purposes. For the most part, however, inmates are confined day and night for the duration of their sentences. During confinement, particularly in maximum-security prisons for men, inmates may be subjected to violence by other inmates; some are raped. Prison life is bleak for most inmates.

10-4a Adaptation to Prison

How do inmates adapt to the prison environment? In earlier prisons they were not allowed to interact with other inmates. With the end of the segregated and silent systems came the opportunity for inmates to interact. One result of this interaction has been the opportunity for inmates to form a prison subculture, or community. The new inmate encounters this subculture through the process of socialization, or **prisonization.**

In 1940, Donald Clemmer reported his study of the male prison community of Illinois's maximum-security prison at Menard. Many of the more recent studies of prisons have been conducted as tests of Clemmer's theories, the most important of which was his concept of prisonization. Clemmer defined prisonization as "the taking on, in greater or lesser degree, of the folkways, mores, customs, and general culture of the penitentiary." The process begins as the newcomer learns his or her status as an inmate. The most important aspects of prisonization are "the influences which breed or deepen criminality and antisociality and make the inmate characteristic of the ideology in the prison community."[25]

> ▶ **Prisonization** The process of an inmate's becoming accustomed to the subculture of prison life.

The degree to which prisonization is effective in a given inmate depends on several factors: (1) the inmate's susceptibility and personality; (2) the inmate's relationships outside the prison; (3) the inmate's membership in a primary group in prison; (4) the inmate's placement in the prison, such as which cell and cellmate; and (5) the degree to which the inmate accepts the dogmas and codes of the prison culture. Clemmer contended that the most important of these factors is the primary group in prison.

Clemmer saw prisonization as the process by which new inmates become familiar with and internalize prison **norms** and values. He argued that, once inmates become prisonized, they are, for the most part, immune to the influences of conventional value systems.

Other scholars have tested Clemmer's conclusions. Stanton Wheeler found strong support for Clemmer's position on prisonization in his study at the Washington State Reformatory. Wheeler found that the degree to which inmates became involved in prisonization varied by the length of time the inmate was in prison. Inmates were more receptive to the larger, institutional values during the first and the last six months of incarceration, but during their middle period of incarceration they were more receptive to the values of the inmate subculture.[26]

In comparing the prisonization of male and female inmates, researchers have questioned the Wheeler hypothesis. Geoffrey P. Alpert and others have found that, although time spent in prison is related significantly to prisonization among female inmates, this is not the case among male inmates. In their study of inmates in the Washington State prison system, these researchers found that other variables were predictive of prisonization, too. Among the women, attitudes toward race and the police were significant. Among the men, age was a significant variable, as were attitudes toward law and the judicial system.[27]

The Inmate Subculture: Models for Analysis

In earlier studies, scholars analyzed the emergence and development of the inmate subculture and created two models for explaining the phenomenon: deprivation and importation. In the **deprivation model,** the inmate's pattern of behavior is an adaptation to the deprivations of his or her environment. The inmate social system is functional for inmates; it enables them to minimize the pains of imprisonment through cooperation. For example, inmate cooperation in the exchange of favors not only removes the opportunity for some to exploit others but also enables inmates to accept material deprivation more easily. Their social system redefines the meaning of material possessions. Inmates come to believe that material possessions, so highly valued on the outside, result from connections instead of hard work and skill, which enables them to insulate their self-concepts from failures in work and skill.

In addition, those goods and services that are available may be distributed and shared if the inmates have a cooperative social system. Because of the pains of imprisonment and the degradation of inmates, which result in a threat to their self-esteem, inmates repudiate the norms of the staff, administration, and society and join forces with each other, developing a social system that enables them to preserve their self-esteem. By rejecting their rejecters, they avoid having to reject themselves.[28]

The more traditional approach to an understanding of the inmate subculture, according to John Irwin and Donald R. Cressey, is that inmates take patterns of behavior with them to prison. This constitutes the **importation model.** Irwin and Cressey argued that social scientists have overemphasized inside influences as explanations for the prison inmate culture. In reality the prison subculture is a combination of several types of subcultures imported by inmates from past experiences and used within prison to adjust to the deprivations of prison life.[29]

Research on the deprivation and importation models was conducted by Charles W. Thomas at a maximum-security prison for men. Thomas's research was designed to show the importance of both importation and deprivation variables. When an inmate arrives at prison, both the formal organization and the inmate society compete for his allegiance; these two represent conflicting processes of socialization. Thomas calls the efforts of the

▶ **Norms** The rules or standards of appropriate behavior shared by members of a social group.

▶ **Deprivation model** A model of prisonization based on the belief that the prison subculture stems from the way inmates adapt to the severe psychological and physical losses imposed by imprisonment.

▶ **Importation model** A model based on the assumption that the inmate subculture arises not only from internal prison experiences but also from the external patterns of behavior the inmates take into prison.

formal organization *resocialization* and those of the inmate society *prisonization.* The success of one requires the failure of the other. The prison is not a closed system.

In explaining the inmate culture, one must examine all of the following factors: preprison experiences, both criminal and noncriminal; expectations of prison staff and fellow inmates; the quality of the inmate's contacts with persons or groups outside the walls; postprison expectations; and the immediate problems of adjustment that the inmate faces. Thomas found that, the greater the degree of similarity between preprison activities and prison subculture values and attitudes, "the greater the receptivity to the influences of prisonization." Thomas also found that inmates from the lower social class are more likely to become highly prisonized, as compared with those from the upper social class; those who have the highest degree of contact with the outside world have the lowest degree of prisonization; and those having a higher degree of prisonization are among inmates who have the bleakest postprison expectations.[30]

Other researchers have concurred with one or the other of the models. In his study of race relations in a maximum-security prison for men, Leo Carroll found support for the importation model, although he concluded that it needed refinement. Carroll criticized the deprivation model as diverting attention from important factors within prison, such as racial violence.[31] Support for both the importation and the deprivation models has been found in studies of prisons in other countries.[32]

Studies of jail inmates are important in determining whether the inmate subculture is imported into the institution or results from adaptations to the institutional setting. Findings from these studies support both the importation and the deprivation theories.[33]

The Inmate System as a Social Control Agency

The inmate social system may create problems for correctional officers and other prison personnel, for inmates upon release, and for society. The inmate social system serves as a social control agency within the prison, wielding a powerful influence over inmates because it is the only reference group available. It is powerful because inmates need status. In addition, they may be more susceptible than usual to peer-group pressure and more prone to look to the peer group than to authority figures for social support. This form of social control is functional to the prison when it maintains order within the institution. To understand it, we must look more carefully at the problems of control faced by penal institutions.

Within the prison, two powerful groups seek to control one another: the correctional officers, whose primary responsibilities are custody and security, and the inmates, who are interested in escaping as much as possible from the pains of imprisonment. Richard A. Cloward studied the power struggle between these two groups. Cloward noted that in most institutions inmates reject the legitimacy of those who seek to control them. A serious social control problem may result. In many ways the job of the custodian in prison is an impossible one. He or she is expected to maintain control and security within the institution but may not use the traditional method of doing this—force. The new, more liberal philosophy of recognizing due process and other inmates' rights has increased problems of social control for correctional officers.[34]

Under the authoritarian regime of prison administration and management, inmate cooperation was necessary to maintain peace within institutions. The few officers could not have kept a disorganized body of inmates under control. Inmates ran the institutions, and the officers cooperated. For example, correctional officers permitted the leaders to take the supplies they needed. When a "surprise" search was conducted, they told the inmate leaders in advance. Those inmates spread the word as a form of patronage. The officers were aiding certain inmates in maintaining their positions of prestige within the inmate system; in return, inmate leaders maintained order. The system was a fairly stable one, with little disorder.

Federal court orders to abolish inmate power positions changed the traditional system of inmate-officer interaction and altered the role of the inmate social system in social control. The results are illustrated by the Texas prison system, which has been plagued with administrative attempts to maintain order. After a disturbance in 1985, during which 8 inmates were killed in 8 days, Texas prison officials announced that they were declaring war on the prison system. They locked down 17,000 inmates in 13 prisons. Sociologists studying the Texas prison system had reported earlier that the elevation of inmates to positions of power had kept racial tension in check, and little violence existed.[35] Inmates were removed from those positions as the result of a federal court order. The consequence was a power vacuum, which was then filled by gangs, beginning with one in 1983 (the Texas Syndicate, 56 members) and increasing to 8 gangs with a total of 1,400 members less than 2 years later. Violence increased, with gang warfare occurring between the Texas Syndicate and the Mexican Mafia, 2 of the largest prison gangs. In his analysis of the organizational structure of these 2 gangs, one scholar described them as similar. Among other characteristics, each follows a code of rules, called the *constitution*. The penalty for violating any of these rules is death.[36]

Gangs may be very influential in prison social control, with activities ranging from sex to murder. Effective control of gang influence demands knowledge of the gang members and their activities. Such knowledge is compiled and disseminated by computers. Gangs are difficult to control, and one administrator has emphasized that prisons do not create the gangs, "and they will not be eliminated no matter how successful our programs." The public needs to keep in mind that prisons are small societies, "temporary places of custody and control for individuals that society has chosen to reject from its membership."[37]

The collection of data on gang crime and the analysis of gang activities and memberships have increased in recent years. Some of these studies include prison settings; others do not. Some of the research focuses on gangs and drugs. One general review of research on gangs led its author to conclude that violent youth gang problems have increased and that gang members are committing more violent offenses. "However, it is unclear whether the growth in urban violence should be attributed largely to gangs, law-violating youth groups, or nongang youths." A number of gangs are appearing in smaller cities, but "family migration, not gang unit relocation, and local genesis appear to be the main explanatory factors." In short, there are a lot of unanswered questions about gang activity.[38]

Despite the unanswered questions, it is clear that prison life has been affected by gangs. Gang formation has been cited by inmates as one of the reasons for the increased turmoil within prisons. The presence of gangs, along with administrative policies concerning them, adds to the increasingly unpredictable world in which inmates live. Youth gangs are discussed in greater detail in Chapter 12.

Female Inmates and Special Needs

Characteristics of the female offender may help explain the nature of her adaptation to prison life and the differences between her methods of adapting and those of the typical male offender. Women constituted 6.9 percent of state and federal prison inmates in 2003, and their numbers have increased more rapidly than those of male inmates in recent years, as noted in Spotlight 10-3, and as chapter 9 noted, that differential continued through midyear 2004. Women are more likely than men to be serving time for drug offenses and to have used crack cocaine. More than three-fourths of female inmates are mothers, with two-thirds having children under the age of 18. In comparison with male inmates, women are more likely to be married and unemployed at the time of their incarceration.

In her 1974 classic study of the Federal Reformatory for Women, Rose Giallombardo considered the issue of whether the female inmate subculture is an adaptation to the pains of imprisonment or is imported from outside experiences. Giallombardo concluded that the prison inmate culture, or social system, cannot be explained solely as a response to prison deprivations, although they may precipitate its development. She illustrated her point primarily by looking at gender roles within correctional institutions for women and girls. Those gender roles reflected the roles women play in society. Her point was that attitudes and values, as well as roles and statuses, are imported into the prison system. Prison deprivations provide the structure in which these roles are performed.[39]

The evidence seems to suggest that, although roles within the inmate systems of men and women differ, they reflect the differences in the attitudes, values, and roles that have distinguished men and women traditionally. For example, in his study of a men's prison, Sykes suggested that loss of security is the greatest problem the male inmate faces. For the

Spotlight 10-3 The Growth of the Population of Female Inmates

The number of female prisoners increased 3.6%—higher than that of men, 2.0%—during 2003

During 2003 the number of women under the jurisdiction of State or Federal prison authorities increased by 3.6% (table 1). The number of men in prison rose 2.0%. At yearend 2003, 101,179 women and 1,368,866 men were in prison. Since 1995 the annual rate of growth of the female inmate population averaged 5.0%, higher than the 3.3% increase in male inmate population. By yearend 2003 women accounted for 6.9% of all prisoners, up from 6.1% in 1995 and 5.7% in 1990.

Relative to their number in the U.S. resident population, men were almost 15 times more likely than women to be incarcerated in a State or Federal prison. At yearend 2003 there were 62 sentenced female inmates per 100,000 women in the United States, compared to 915 sentenced male inmates per 100,000 men.

Since 1995 the total number of male prisoners has grown 29%; the number of female prisoners, 48%. At yearend 2003, 1 in every 1,613 women and 1 in every 109 men were incarcerated in a State or Federal prison.

Over a third of female prisoners held in the 3 largest jurisdictions

Texas (13,487), the Federal system (11,635), and California (10,656) held more than a third of all female inmates ... Mississippi (134 sentenced female inmates per 100,000 female residents), Oklahoma (127), and Louisiana (104) had the highest female incarceration rates. States with the lowest female incarceration rates were concentrated in the Northeast—Rhode Island (10 sentenced female prisoners per 100,000 female residents), Massachusetts (12), and Maine and New Hampshire (both with 18).

Twelve States had an average annual increase of more than 10% between 1995 and 2003, led by North Dakota (18.5%),

Montana (17.9%), and Maine (16.7%). During this period the State female prison population increased an average of 4.9% per year; the Federal female prison population increased 5.8% per year.

Table 1. Prisoners under the jurisdiction of State or Federal correctional authorities, by gender, yearend 1995, 2002, and 2003

	Men	Women
All inmates		
2003	1,368,866	101,179
2002	1,342,513	97,631
1995	1,057,406	68,468
Percent change,		
2002–2003	2.0%	3.6%
Average annual		
1995–2003	3.3%	5.0%
Sentenced to more than 1 year		
2003	1,316,495	92,785
2002	1,291,450	89,066
Percent change,		
2002–2003	1.9%	4.2%
Incarceration rate*		
2003	915	62
1995	789	47

*The number of prisoners with sentences of more than 1 year per 100,000 residents on December 31.

Source: Paige M. Harrison and Allen J. Beck, Bureau of Justice Statistics, *Prisoners in 2003* (Washington, D.C.: U.S. Department of Justice, November 2004), pp. 4–5.

---

female inmate it appears that the loss of liberty and autonomy is the major deprivation. Women miss the freedom to come and go and resent the restrictions on communications with family and friends. In the institutions everything is planned for them. Furthermore, female inmates may be frustrated because they have no control over events that occur in the outside world: their children may be neglected; a loved one may become sick or die; and husbands or boyfriends may be unfaithful.

For some female inmates prison life is a deprivation of the goods and services to which they are accustomed. As soon as they enter the institution they are stripped of most of their worldly possessions, a "kind of symbolic death." They must endure supervised baths and body examinations for drugs and contraband. They may have to give up their personal clothing and wear prison uniforms, although in some institutions female inmates are permitted to wear their own clothes. Generally personal items, such as jewelry, pictures, cosmetics, and other beauty products, are banned or limited.[40]

Although some male inmates have children, the issue of child care is usually a more critical factor with female inmates. Not only do most have children, but they were living with those children when they were incarcerated. Care for their children is a primary concern of many inmate mothers, and separation from them is one of the greatest pains of their incarceration.

An inmate mother must face her inability to care for her children along with the loss of self-esteem that may come with incarceration. She must cope with the readjustment she and her children face when she is released from prison. She must deal with the lack of visitation opportunities for children and the difficulty of telling her children what is happening. Some may face lawsuits over the legal custody of their children. All of these factors affect the ways in which incarcerated mothers adapt to prison life.

A recent study underscores the harm children suffer when one or both parents are incarcerated. Young children may suffer separation anxiety, which appears to be magnified when it is the mother who is incarcerated. The reason may be that, when women are incarcerated, their children usually live with grandparents (53 percent of the cases) or other relatives, or even in foster homes (almost 10 percent), rather than with their fathers. But when men are incarcerated, the children of 90 percent of them live with their mothers. Women are incarcerated in institutions that are, on the average, 160 miles from their homes; men, only 100 miles. Most incarcerated parents do not have any visits from their children while they are in prison.[41]

Some jurisdictions have developed programs to encourage interaction between incarcerated parents and their children. For example, in 2000 Florida began its program Reading Family Ties: Face-to-Face. This program permits women at the Lowell and Hernando Correctional Institutions to have live video visits with their children each week. The children go to a special center, where they may interact with their mothers for one hour, while the incarcerated mothers are in a room with a video camera, a computer, and a speaker phone. Officials claimed that the program had improved the conduct of the mothers and of the children.[42]

Also in 2002, the Tennessee Prison for Woman opened a child visitation unit, which was dedicated to the memory of a former warden, Penny A. Bernhardt, who was instrumental in the success of the program. The new unit, which contains 16 beds, permits children from three months to six years of age to spend the weekends with their parents in relative privacy. Activities oriented toward child development are provided, and an outdoor recreational area is planned.[43]

Some states—for example, Ohio, Nebraska, New York, and Washington—have made provisions for inmates who give birth to keep their babies with them while they are incarcerated. Although historically mothers were permitted to keep their children in prison, the practice was abandoned in most jurisdictions in the 1970s and 1980s because of legal liability issues.[44]

Some provisions have also been made for incarcerated fathers to interact with their children. The first program was developed in the early 1990s in Ft. Worth, Texas, at the all-male federal correctional facility. According to one psychologist, "The one concern I hear the most often from inmates is not about legal battles, but concerns about their families. . . . Family communication and support is extremely important to the inmate."[45]

In addition to the need to address the issue of parenting for both male and female inmates is the issue of sexual abuse. Female inmates are more frequently the victims of sexual abuse, and that situation necessitates special treatment. See again Spotlight 10-2, which highlights some examples of the sexual abuse of female inmates.

A recent case of sexual abuse of inmates occurred in Texas, when, in June 2003, Dr. Carlos Baez was charged with three counts of sexual abuse of a ward. Dr. Baez, a gynecologist at the Federal Bureau of Prisons facility in Fort Worth, Texas, was accused of having engaged in sexual intercourse with three inmates who were under his custodial, supervisory, and disciplinary authority. In October, Dr. Baez pleaded guilty to two counts of sexual abuse of a ward and was given the maximum possible sentence under federal guidelines: 14 months in a federal prison. Dr. Baez was given until 1 December 2004 to report to prison; he relinquished his medical license.[46]

Female inmates are not the only targets of sexual activity in prisons. In summer 2002, two female former correctional officers at the supermax federal prison in Florence, Colorado (for a discussion of that prison, see again Chapter 9), Kellee S. Kissinger, 34, and

Christine Achenbach, 42, were accused of having had oral sex or sexual intercourse with inmates. Achenbach, who held the fourth highest position at the prison, that of executive assistant to the warden, was convicted in December 2002. In May 2003, she was sentenced to five years' probation and four months' home detention and was fined $3,000. The sentencing judge, commenting that she had no option but to require the defendant to register as a sex offender (for a discussion of this requirement, see Chapter 11), stated, "Even though I personally would not want to see this kind of conviction treated as a sex-offender conviction, I must apply the law as it is written, not as I wish it were written." Of the inmates, the judge said, "I don't think they felt victimized at all. . . . They probably enjoyed it." Kissinger, who accepted a plea bargain that Achenbach refused, was sentenced to four years' probation and a $2,400 fine. She was given the option of serving 100 hours of community service in lieu of the fine.[47]

Sexual abuse may cause low self-esteem and depression, especially when that abuse is by force, as is often the case when correctional officers have sex with female inmates. Some techniques used to combat these conditions are meditation, breathing techniques, vocal expression, movement classes to improve physical strength, and counseling.

Female inmates also have special medical needs. The issue of whether special medical care for women should be available in prisons, along with legal issues surrounding the differences in programs that are available to male as compared with female inmates, has led to numerous court cases. In a 1996 case, *Women Prisoners of the District of Columbia Department of Corrections* v. *District of Columbia,* a federal court of appeals held that the district court had gone too far in its orders for the plaintiffs in a class action suit. The court noted that, if all prisons were required to provide *identical* programs for men and women, prison administrators might not provide programs at all, especially with current budget problems in most prisons. The court held that physical restraints used on women during the third trimester of pregnancy, sexual harassment by correctional officers, a lack of adequate fire safety provisions, and the quality of the general living conditions at the institution in question constituted cruel and unusual punishment and thus must be changed. However, with regard to programs and work opportunities, the court emphasized that there is no constitutional right to these programs; some are available only for women, some for men. This is not unconstitutional, especially given the differences in the sizes of the institutions involved. A specific program provided for men but not for women does not in and of itself violate equal protection. But on remand, numerous orders were made concerning the medical and other treatment of female inmates.[48]

In 1995 in the California correctional system, female inmates filed a suit concerning special health care and other needs. Subsequently the parties entered into a stipulated agreement that the California Department of Corrections would provide or exceed the minimum Eighth Amendment requirements for health care for inmates. The women had originally alleged inadequate health care, including delays and disruptions in receiving medications, inadequate sick call, triage (determining priorities for help in an emergency), emergency care, nurses, urgent care, chronic case, care for AIDS/HIV, and many other areas.[49] Prior to the final settlement in 2000, the attorneys for the inmates, referring to their allegations that the state had not complied with all of the earlier agreements, did recognize some success but warned as follows:

> [These plaintiffs] have endured too much suffering and taken too many risks by coming forward for us to consider that this case is over. . . . We hope that the Department of Corrections will implement the settlement in good faith, but in case they do not, we are prepared to return to the court to protect the women's constitutional rights. . . .
>
> The women who brought this suit aren't asking for "Cadillac care" and they aren't out for money or fame. . . . They've stuck their necks out and stood up to the state for one simple reason—to hold the state of California responsible for meeting their basic medical needs.[50]

A professor who studied the conditions encountered by female inmates by interviewing them and correctional officers in two Texas prisons concluded that the system has not kept up with the changing female populations; in short, the special needs of female inmates have been neglected. According to Denise Huggins of the University of Arkansas, the prison system "delivers secondhand services and offers inadequate or inappropriate training, treatment and educational programs." Huggins continued, claiming that the "daily lives of female inmates is mind-numbing time punctuated by inadequate educational programs and humiliating treatment."[51] As humiliating treatment, Huggins cited strip searches, conducted as frequently as five times daily. Job training programs often train women for work in primarily male-dominated fields (such as plumbing or auto repair), in which they are not likely to get jobs. The few educational programs may be reserved for younger inmates or for those with five years or less to serve and thus may not be available to most inmates. Huggins concluded, "It is clear that we need to take a good look at the way we treat female inmates and come up with solutions that are more appropriate and more realistic for their needs."[52]

Sexual Behavior

Inmates face sexual harassment and abuse from other inmates, and this occurs more frequently among male than among female inmates. The issue of same-gender sex, and especially rape, has been a topic of research in male prisons for years.

Isolation from the opposite gender implies abstinence from the satisfaction of heterosexual relationships at a time when the sex drive is strong. Some inmates turn to same-gender behavior, not by preference but because they need an outlet for sexual expression. Early studies reported that between 30 and 40 percent of male inmates had some same-gender experiences while in prison. These estimates were discussed at a conference on prison homosexuality in the early 1970s. Peter C. Buffum wrote a synthesis of the five working papers presented at that conference. Buffum contended that the belief that we can eliminate same-gender sex in prisons by establishing other outlets for sexual drives is a myth.[53] Others have not agreed, however, and the subject deserves further attention.

Same-gender sexual behavior among male inmates seldom involves a close relationship. In some cases a man who is vulnerable to sexual attacks enters into a sexual relationship with another man who agrees to protect him from abuse by other inmates. Earlier studies found that sexual acts between male inmates seemed to be a response to their sexual needs coupled with their socialization. Men are taught to be aggressive, and playing the male role (the wolf) in a sexual act with another man might enable the inmate to retain this self-concept. Further, male inmates may see a prison sexual relationship as little more than a search for a casual, mechanical act of physical release.[54]

Same-gender sexual behavior among men and the forms it takes in prison should be viewed in light of the importation and deprivation models discussed earlier. Prison presents the inmate with a problem of sexual deprivation, but "the meaning, amount, and character of these adjustments will be strongly dependent on the meaning that these same behaviors had for the inmate before he or she was incarcerated."[55]

Some researchers have found prostitution to be the most frequent type of same-gender sexual behavior among male inmates. Usually the behavior is not the result of violence; however, when violence occurs, it often has racial implications.[56] It is a power play, which can be compared to the rape of a woman by a man. It represents the need to dominate, to control, to conquer.

Daniel Lockwood, who reported on his study of male inmates in New York prisons, interviewed men designated as targets of sexual propositions or sexual abuse, as well as those who were identified as sexual aggressors. He found that many verbal threats of sexual aggression did not result in actual aggression.[57]

Most inmate same-gender rape victims do not report the acts, primarily because of the fear of reprisal by other inmates. Some fear for their lives if they cooperate with officials in trying to solve violent acts. These fears may not be unreasonable.

Other inmates have filed lawsuits after being victimized by same-gender rape. The standard used by courts in analyzing these claims is whether officials were *deliberately indifferent* to the needs of inmates and the situations in which they were placed. This standard was illustrated by a 1991 case, in which a heterosexual jail detainee alleged that he had been raped by a gay male with whom he was assigned a cell. An appellate court held that the inmate had stated a sufficient claim that his due process rights were violated when he showed that prison officials engaged in a custom or policy of placing aggressive gay males in the general population while isolating passive ones. This action permitted aggressive gays to prey on other inmates, especially in an overcrowded facility. Defendants in the case argued unsuccessfully that inmates should have to prove that prison officials showed a *reckless indifference* to their welfare or that officials acted with *callous disregard*.

The appellate court rejected those standards and held that the same standard required for cases involving a lack of medical treatment should be used: that of deliberate indifference. According to the court, this standard is an appropriate balance between the responsibility of jail officials to manage the facility and maintain security and the right of pretrial detainees to personal security. Although the case involved pretrial detainees (who had not been convicted and thus should not be punished), it is reasonable to expect the same standard to be applied in prisons, which house convicted persons who are eligible for punishment.[58]

In a more recent case, heard by the U.S. Supreme Court and sent back to the lower court for reconsideration, an inmate who considered herself a woman, but whom prison officials classified as a man, sued for rape by a male inmate in a men's prison. Dee Farmer alleged that on April Fool's Day in 1989 she was raped in her cell in a high-security federal prison in Terre Haute, Indiana, where she was incarcerated for credit card fraud. Subsequently Farmer was transferred to a low- and medium-security prison in North Carolina. Farmer claimed that federal officials purposely put her at risk. Her suit for $200,000 and placement in a facility that housed both genders was dismissed by a federal court in Wisconsin and by a federal appeals court. Farmer, who has a penis, had enhanced her female appearance through silicone breast implants and hormone injections.

In deciding Farmer's case, the U.S. Supreme Court focused on the meaning of *deliberate indifference,* defining the term for the first time. The concept is similar to criminal negligence and calls for subjective rather than objective knowledge. "The officials must both be aware of facts from which the inference could be drawn that a substantial risk of serious harm exists, and [they] must also draw the inference." The case was sent back to determine more facts.[59]

In contrast to the sexual behavior of gay male inmates, same-gender sexual behavior among female inmates may develop out of mutual interest to alleviate the depersonalization of the prison and to gain status.[60] For a female inmate, a lesbian relationship may take the place of the primary group relationship for some male inmates. Talk of loyalty, sharing, trust, and friendship among female inmates may refer to the same-gender relationship, not to primary groups per se. Lesbian relationships represent an attempt to simulate the family found outside the prison and are not primarily for sexual gratification. One study reports that same-gender relationships are the most important relationships among female inmates.[61]

For female inmates, pseudofamilies may compensate for the lack of the close family environment on the outside. These relationships permit the exercise of dominant and submissive roles, which the women learned outside of prison. Within these pseudofamilies is an opportunity for sexual behavior, but the primary reason for forming family relationships appears not to be for that purpose.[62]

Another characteristic of the sexual behavior of female inmates distinguishes their behavior from that of male inmates' sexual involvement. Whereas in most cases male sexual behavior, especially rape, is manifested in actual physical sexual contact (oral or anal sex), for female inmates sexual relationships may involve only a strong emotional relationship, with some bodily contact that would be acceptable outside prison (for example, embracing upon seeing one another). On the other hand, some women may hold hands or fondle breasts, whereas others engage in more serious forms of sexual contact, such as oral-genital contact and bodily contact that attempts to simulate heterosexual intercourse.[63]

Another issue regarding sexual behavior in women's prisons is that of relationships (including rape) with correctional officers. Allegations of sexual abuse by male correctional officers against female inmates have been substantiated in several recent studies; some are noted in Spotlight 10-1. One is a study of the correctional facilities in the District of Columbia, along with the three largest systems: California, Texas, and the federal system, which house more than one-third of all female inmates in the United States. The study conducted by the General Accounting Office (GAO) revealed that the three largest correctional systems had 506 allegations of sexual misconduct from 1995 to 1998. Of those allegations, 18 percent were substantiated. During the same period, women in the District of Columbia made 111 allegations of sexual misconduct, of which 11 percent were substantiated. It was concluded that the actual number of incidents is not known because "many female inmates may be reluctant or unwilling to report staff sexual misconduct, and jurisdictions lack systematic data collection and analysis of reported allegations." Sexual misconduct includes "consensual" sexual activities due to the inherently coercive nature of the prison environment. Most of the reported incidents involved "verbal harassment, improper visual surveillance, improper touching, and/or consensual sex," with allegations of rape and related forms of sexual violence noted only rarely.[64]

More recent studies, however, have shown that more than half of the sexual assaults committed against female inmates are perpetrated by other female inmates, not male staffers. Two researchers from the University of South Dakota studied sexual abuse in three midwestern medium- and maximum-security prisons that house women. The researchers included sexual activity by coercion as well as by force. They found greater coercion (about double) in the larger prison, which was more racially diverse and housed women who had committed the more serious crimes. In that institution approximately 25 percent of the interviewed women said they had been sexually coerced while in prison, over 33 percent of them by one assailant and 40 percent by two or three persons together. Less than one-third of these victims reported the attacks to prison officials. The two researchers concluded as follows:

> Overall the female situation is not as violent and serious as what happens typically in a male prison. . . . There are some women's prisons that are so well-managed that this problem is kept to a very low level. That's good. But we need to recognize that women in prison are sexually coercing other women. It's not just male corrections officers.[65]

One solution to sexual assaults on female inmates has been offered by Alanco Technologies, which developed a belt alarm system. The component, called PSD-II, a belt equipped with a transmitter, could be worn by all prison staff. When that belt is removed the system will record the event and can be used to verify where the staffer was at a particular time and how long the person was in that area.[66]

Another attempt to reduce or eradicate sexual assaults against both female and male inmates is to pass a law. In July 2003, the U.S. Senate unanimously passed Senate Bill 1435, the Prison Rape Elimination Act of 2003. Lara Stemple, the executive director of Stop Prisoner Rape (SPR), a national organization devoted to stopping prison rape, which Stemple refers to as "dehumanizing and sometimes deadly. . . . Victims have been left beaten and bloodied, they have suffered long-term psychological harm, they have been impregnated against their will, and they have contracted HIV. It's time to take this important step to address the problem." According to SPR, one in five inmates has been sexually abused; among female inmates the number is one in four. Stemple emphasizes that many of the abuse incidents are not reported by frightened inmates; when reported, they may be ignored by the administration. She concluded, "We hope federal legislation will not only create incentives for states to take this problem seriously, but also give facilities the tools and information they need to prevent it."[67]

The U.S. House of Representatives also passed the Prison Rape Elimination bill, and it was signed by President George W. Bush in 2003. This new law pertains not only to sexual assaults but also to other prison issues, such as AIDS, mental illness, general violence, and psychological problems. Portions of the law are included in Spotlight 10-4.

| *Spotlight 10-4* | **Prison Rape Elimination Act of 2003** |

[I]n 2003, the U.S. Congress passed and President George W. Bush signed the Prison Rape Elimination Act, which is designed to reduce the extensive problems resulting from prison rape. This Spotlight relates some of the major findings as well as the provisions of the new law, the purpose of which is to] provide for the analysis of the incidence and effects of prison rape in Federal, State, and local institutions and to provide information, resources, recommendations, and funding to protect individuals from prison rape.[1]

Section 15601. Findings

Congress makes the following findings: ...

(2) Insufficient research has been conducted and insufficient data reported on the extent of prison rape.... [The estimates are that over 1 million inmates have been assaulted during the past 20 years.]

(3) Inmates with mental illnesses are at increased risk of sexual victimization. America's jails and prisons house more mentally ill individuals than all of the Nation's psychiatric hospitals combined. As many as 16 percent of inmates in State prisons and jails and 7 percent of Federal inmates, suffer from mental illness.

(4) Young first-time offenders are at increased risk of sexual victimization. Juveniles are 5 times more likely to be sexually assaulted in adult rather than juvenile facilities—often within the first 48 hours of incarceration.

(5) Most prison staff are not adequately trained or prepared to prevent, report, or treat inmate sexual assaults.

(6) Prison rape often goes unreported, and inmate victims often receive inadequate treatment for the severe physical and psychological effects of sexual assault—if they receive treatment at all.

(7) HIV and AIDS are major public health problems within America's correctional facilities.... Prison rape undermines the public health by contributing to the spread of these diseases, and often giving a potential death sentence to its victims.

(8) Prison rape endangers the public safety by making brutalized inmates more likely to commit crimes when they are released....

(9) The frequently interracial character of prison sexual assaults significantly exacerbates interracial tensions....

(10) Prison rape increases the level of homicides and other violence against inmates and staff, and the risk of insurrections and riots.

(11) Victims of prison rape suffer severe physical and psychological effects that hinder their ability to integrate into the community and maintain stable employment upon their release from prison. They are thus more likely to become homeless and/or require government assistance....

(13) The high incidence of sexual assault within prisons involves actual and potential violations of the United States Constitution....

(14) The high incidence of prison rape undermines the effectiveness and efficiency of United States Government expenditures through grant programs such as those dealing with health care; mental health care; disease prevention; crime prevention; investigation, and prosecution; prison construction, maintenance, and operation; race relations; poverty; unemployment and homelessness. The effectiveness and efficiency of these federally funded grant programs are compromised by the failure of State officials to adopt policies and procedures that reduce the incidence of prison rape.

Section 15602. Purposes

The purposes of this Act are to—

(1) establish a zero-tolerance standard for the incidence of prison rape in prisons in the United States;

(2) make the prevention of prison rape a top priority in each prison system;

(3) develop and implement national standards for the detention, prevention, reduction, and punishment of prison rape;

(4) increase the available data and information on the incidence of prison rape, consequently improving the management and administration of correctional facilities;

(5) standardize the definitions used for collecting data on the incidence of prison rape;

(6) increase the accountability of prison officials who fail to detect, prevent, reduce, and punish prison rape;

(7) protect the Eighth Amendment rights of Federal, State, and local prisoners;

(8) increase the efficiency and effectiveness of Federal expenditures through grant programs such as those dealing with health care; mental health care; disease prevention; crime prevention, investigation, and prosecution; prison construction, maintenance, and operation; race relations; poverty; unemployment; and homelessness; and

(9) reduce the costs that prison rape imposes on interstate commerce.

[The statute provides for the collection of data on prison rape, the reporting of such data, the establishment of a Review Panel on Prison Rape within the U.S. Department of Justice, and many other provisions.]

1. Prison Rape Elimination Act of 2003 is codified at U.S. Code, Title 42, Sections 15601 *et seq.* (2005). The appropriate section numbers for each section quoted are noted in the Spotlight.

10-4b AIDS and Other Medical Issues

We have already seen that female inmates have special medical needs. But medical issues are important for both male and female inmates. The first major issue is that of AIDS.

Acquired immune deficiency syndrome (AIDS) has become a household word in the United States, as educational efforts to alert people to the deadly and rapidly spreading disease have had some success. Thousands of people have died of AIDS, and there is no known cure. There is evidence that AIDS is spread primarily through sexual contacts and intravenous drug use.

HIV and AIDS are major concerns in correctional facilities, as well as in other areas of criminal justice systems. The number of cases of AIDS among prison inmates has dropped recently, and the number of AIDS-related deaths in prison dropped more than 80 percent between 1995 and 2000, but the number of confirmed cases of AIDS has remained significantly higher in prison than in the general population (four times higher in 2000).[68] As Spotlight 10-4 notes, AIDS is one focus of the Prison Rape Elimination Act of 2003.

The most common disease among inmates is hepatitis C, with approximately 29 percent of inmates in a recent study in Maryland testing positive (compared with about 2 percent of the general population). The analysis reported that approximately 65 percent of the prison inmates with HIV were also infected with hepatitis C. A study conducted by the American Civil Liberties Union in Virginia reported that 39 percent of inmates were infected with hepatitis C.[69] In addition to the problem of spreading the disease within the prison is that of infecting others upon release. In 2003, the Centers for Disease Control and Prevention (CDC) held a conference of prison medical personnel to discuss the public health issues associated with released inmates infected with contagious diseases. The CDC expressed concern that inmates were not being treated for contagious diseases, while the American Civil Liberties Union and 24 other organizations concerned with issues of health within prisons called for Congress to investigate the state of medical care within U.S. prisons and jails.[70]

The most extensive study of prison health issues was conducted by the National Commission on Correctional Health Care, a nonprofit group that focuses on prison health. The study was funded by the U.S. Department of Justice and the CDC. The research, which focused on a three-year period during the mid-1990s, was presented to Congress in May 2002. Some of the findings were as follows:

- An estimated 34,800 to 46,000 inmates as of 1997 were infected with HIV, with an estimated 9,000 with full-blown AIDS.

- An estimated 98,500 to 145,500 HIV-positive inmates were released from prisons and jails during that time.

- As much as one-fifth of the nationwide jail and prison population of 2 million could be infected with hepatitis C.

- There were an estimated 1,400 cases of tuberculosis in jails and prisons across the country as of 1997, and as many as 12,000 inmates carrying the disease were released that same year.[71]

Many states do not have adequate medical facilities or staff to handle contagious diseases. In the case of HIV inmates, two states—Mississippi and Alabama—isolate the inmates from the general population, which means those inmates are unable to participate in most prison programs. Prison officials argue that it would be too expensive to establish programs just for isolated inmates and that to be forced to do so would go beyond the reasonable accommodations required by federal legislation for inmates with disabilities. Under the Americans with Disabilities Act (ADA) of 1990, individuals who pose a "direct threat to the health and safety of others" may be excluded from prison programs. The ADA defines direct threat as "a significant risk to the health or safety of others that cannot be eliminated by reasonable accommodation" or through the modification of existing programs. Alabama inmates filed a lawsuit against the prison system in 1985 under the federal Rehabilitation Act, which is similar to the ADA. In April 1999, the Eleventh Circuit Court of Appeals upheld the prison policy because of the risk of death for those infected with HIV and because of security problems in prisons. In January 2000, the U.S. Supreme Court refused (without comment) to accept the case for review, thus allowing the lower appellate court ruling to stand.[72]

Other lawsuits have been more successful for inmates or their estates. For example, Washington State settled a wrongful death suit for $1 million after the death of Phillip Montgomery, age 32, who died a few hours after he was turned away from a prison health clinic. Montgomery had contracted hepatitis C. Class action lawsuits concerning the lack of diagnosis and treatment for hepatitis C within prisons have been filed in several states.[73]

One final point concerning AIDS in prisons is the issue of contact visits between inmates and their families. In 1987, New York's highest court upheld the decision of prison officials to prohibit **conjugal visits** between an inmate infected with AIDS and his wife. The court held that this refusal was not an unreasonable interference with the rights of the inmate or of his spouse.[74] This is not an issue in most institutions, as they do not permit conjugal visits for any inmates.

By 2005, however, there was some encouraging news in a few jurisdictions concerning both the treatment of AIDS and attempts to prevent the spread of hepatitis C within prisons. To cite only a few examples, in December 2004, Michigan's governor signed legislation that provides $1.2 million for a new hepatitis C testing program. In Mary 2005 a corrections publication noted that approximately one-third of all U.S. residents with hepatitis C and 15 percent of residents with AIDS are in prison but that few prisons provide adequate means of preventing the spread of these diseases. Specifically, the article noted that 95 percent of prisons ban the distribution or possession of condoms. However, in June 2005, the California Assembly voted to permit the distribution of condoms in the state's prisons. According to one assemblyman, California's prisons are "HIV infection factories and we are paying tens of millions of dollars a year for not making condoms available." The condoms will be provided by health and nonprofit agencies.[75]

> ▶ **Conjugal visits** Visits that permit inmates to engage in sexual and other social contacts with their spouses in an unsupervised, private setting.

10-4c Inmates Who Are Physically Challenged, Elderly, or Mentally Ill

Another characteristic of changing prison life is the increase in the number of inmates who are physically challenged, elderly, or mentally ill. The incarceration of persons with disabilities has taken place for years, but recently some courts have held that the Americans with Disabilities Act (ADA) and its predecessor, the 1973 federal Rehabilitation Act, apply to inmates in some circumstances. The Ninth Circuit Court of Appeals has held that, in its administration of programs, prison officials may not discriminate against inmates with disabilities who are "otherwise qualified" (a requirement of the statute).[76] It has been held, however, that the statutes do not apply to inmate employment.[77]

The aging of the prison population also presents new challenges. In the United States the inmate population age 55 or older grew 85 percent between 1995 and 2003, from 32,600 in 1995 to 60,300 in 2003, representing the largest increase of any age grouping during that period. That age group, combined with ages 40 to 44, accounted for 46 percent of the total growth in U.S. prison populations between 1995 and 2003. Even with the 85 percent increase, inmates ages 55 or older constituted only 4.3 percent of the prison population in 2003.[78] Despite that, older inmates have significantly different needs, such as food and medical care, than other inmates. In states with a large retired population, such as Florida and Arizona, the increase in older inmates may present acute financing problems.

The special needs of mentally challenged inmates should also be addressed. In its 2001 special report on mental illness (based on data through June 2000), the Bureau of Justice Statistics (BJS) reported that approximately 191,000 inmates in state prisons (16 percent of the total inmates) were identified as mentally ill and that approximately one-fifth of those were not receiving therapy or counseling. Mentally ill male inmates received less treatment (1 in 10, or 10 percent), compared with mentally ill female inmates (1 in 4, or 25 percent). Further, 30 percent of state prison facilities did not screen inmates for mental illness. Approximately two-thirds of the mentally ill inmates who were receiving therapy or medications were in units that did not specialize in mental illness. Three states—Wyoming, North Dakota, and Rhode Island—had no psychiatric facilities for mentally ill inmates. The lead researcher described the study as a modest survey that did not delve into the types of mental illness. Nevertheless, he concluded, "The numbers support that mental illness is a significant problem for state prisons. How inmates are diagnosed and how easily they can receive treatment is a subject worthy of attention."[79]

Another study, published in 2001 and conducted by the U.S. Public Health Service, focused on the mental health problems of minorities and noted several significant problems they had in getting adequate treatment both outside and inside prisons. Their difficulties outside prison may make minorities more likely to be drawn into the criminal justice system through inappropriate behavior. In general, we do not know how to react to people who act out problems because of a lack of medication or treatment—other than to lock them up. They are arrested rather than diverted to medical care. In analyzing these issues, one commentator noted that Texas was paying approximately $22,000 a year to incarcerate each inmate and that some mentally ill offenders could be treated less expensively in group homes or other diversion facilities. He concluded that there is a "clear correlation with mental illness, the state's minority populations, poverty and prisons."[80]

Concerned persons and organizations have called for investigations into the way mentally ill inmates are treated. Many are kept in isolation at least 24 hours a day in tiny rooms with little ventilation or light, conditions that, according to mental health experts, may lead to deterioration, depression, and even suicide. After judges found that a disproportionate number of mentally ill inmates were being housed in isolation in the prisons in Wisconsin and Ohio in 2002, those states agreed to be monitored. The American Civil Liberties Union (ACLU) filed suit in 2002 after eight mentally ill inmates died in Colorado's El Paso County Jail.[81]

There are some encouraging signs. In 2002, a plan submitted by Texas prison officials concerning the care of mentally ill inmates in solitary confinement (called *administrative segregation* in Texas) received a guarded endorsement by attorneys who have been involved in the general prison lawsuit that has gone on in that state since 1972.[82]

Minnesota prison systems stand out in the mental health field. For example, the Linda Berglin Mental Health Center at the Minnesota Correctional Facility–Red Wing, is one of the newest correctional health facilities. It was supported by an $800,000 grant from the state in 2000. The center provides treatment for seriously mentally ill inmates.[83]

In New York City, officials agreed in principle to a settlement that would end a three-year lawsuit and provide inmates with help—such as transition medications, assistance in finding housing, transportation from incarceration to their homes, and help in getting Medicaid and welfare benefits—after they are released from jail. A lawyer representing the inmates called the plan one that requires sweeping changes and is, as far as he knows, the only lawsuit of its kind in the country. Another lawyer involved in the case said, "New York City has developed a program unique in the country in its content and scope which we believe will provide significant assistance to mentally ill inmates with the hope that these inmates will be able to successfully reintegrate into the community."[84]

In 2003, a federal appeals court upheld the decision of a U.S. district judge in Portland, Oregon, who ruled that the state violated the rights of mentally ill persons by keeping them in county jails for weeks or months before they were sent to the state hospital, where they could receive psychiatric care. According to the Ninth Circuit Court of Appeals, mentally ill persons who are awaiting trial have a higher rate of suicide and "are often locked in their cells for 22 to 23 hours a day, which further exacerbates their mental illness." Only the state hospital is charged with their psychiatric care; thus, if they are held in jail and not transferred to that facility, they will not get the psychiatric care they need to become competent to stand trial.[85]

A mental health program in New York has gained recognition. The Albany County Correctional Facility was the scene of the tragic death of a mentally ill inmate in 1995. After that incident the superintendent and the president and chief executive officer of the Mental Health Association in New York met to discuss what they could do to prevent another such occurrence. With the assistance of grants, they began a program to divert mentally ill offenders from prisons. In their efforts, the officials engaged housing officials, support groups, mental health experts, legislators, and corrections officials and formed the Options Committee to develop diversion plans. Between January and June 2003, the committee diverted 11 inmates, with plans to have 25 by September and 75 by 2004. The diversion program saves money, as mental health inmates are usually incarcerated 30 percent longer than other inmates and cost approximately 30 percent more to incarcerate. The Options

Committee needs additional funding, and that comes at a time when city, county, and state budgets are being cut (it received some funding from United Way), but if the program can get adequate funding, it is thought that it can divert 50 percent of the mentally ill persons from jails.[86]

Despite these efforts, the treatment of mentally ill offenders remains a problem, as noted by the congressional findings in the Prison Rape Elimination Act of 2003, discussed in Spotlight 10-4. And in 2003 a major study by Human Rights Watch concluded that, although significant progress has been made in the treatment of mentally ill offenders in prisons, much remains to be done. The 215-page report concluded that prisons were "never intended as facilities for the mentally ill, yet that is one of their primary roles today." Other conclusions are as follows:

- On any given day, 70,000 inmates are psychotic.

- Between 200,000 and 300,000 inmates are mentally ill.

- Correctional officers who are not trained to recognize mental illness often punish these offenders for their illnesses (for example, citing an offender for "creating a disturbance" when the inmate is screaming because he or she "hears voices").

- Mentally ill offenders who do not receive proper treatment are "afflicted with delusions and hallucinations, debilitating fears, and extreme and uncontrollable mood swings. . . . They huddle silently in their cells, mumble incoherently, or yell incessantly. They refuse to obey orders and lash out without apparent provocation. They beat their heads against cell walls, smear themselves with feces, self-mutilate, and commit suicide."

- Untrained correctional officers may escalate the problems when they use excessive force to discipline mentally ill offenders. "Several mentally ill prisoners have died from asphyxiation after struggling with guards who used improper methods to control them."[87]

One encouraging development is the diversion of some mentally ill offenders from criminal justice systems to treatment programs by processing their cases through mental health courts, which are discussed in Chapter 11. At this point, however, it is relevant to note that, in the fall 2004, Congress enacted the Mentally Ill Offender Treatment and Crime Reduction Act of 2003, which is to divert mentally ill persons to special courts for treatment. The bill provides up to $100 million a year in grants for states and localities. According to Senator Mike DeWine, who introduced the bill, "Unfortunately, the reality of our criminal justice system is that jails and prisons do not provide a therapeutic environment for the mentally ill, and are unlikely to do so any time soon. Indeed the mentally ill inmate often is preyed upon by other inmates or becomes even sicker in jail. Once released from jail or prison, many mentally ill people end up on the streets. With limited personal resources and little or no ability to handle their illnesses alone, they often commit further offenses resulting in their rearrest and reincarceration. This 'revolving door' is costly and disruptive for all involved." Portions of this legislation are contained in Spotlight 10-5.[88]

Finally, brief attention should be given to the 2003 U.S. Supreme Court decision holding that it is permissible to medicate defendants so they will be competent to stand trial. That decision, *Sell* v. *United States,* which was decided by a 6-to-3 vote, did not, however, answer the question of whether it is constitutional to forcibly medicate mentally ill death row inmates so that they are legally competent for execution. In *Sell* the justices stated that it should be a rare case in which involuntary medication is used. It is appropriate "only if the treatment is medically appropriate, is substantially unlikely to have side effects that may undermine the fairness of the trial, and, taking account of less intrusive alternatives, is necessary significantly to further important governmental trial-related interests." The defendant in this case, Charles Sell, had a long history of mental illness. He was charged with numerous crimes, including mail fraud, Medicaid fraud, and attempted murder. Since 1999, Sell, a former dentist, had been held in the U.S. Medical Center for Federal Prisoners in Missouri. He had refused antipsychotic medications. The Eighth Circuit Court of Appeals found that Sell was not dangerous and held that he could be medicated against his

Spotlight 10-5　Mentally Ill Offender Treatment and Crime Reduction Act of 2003

[The Mentally Ill Offender Treatment and Crime Reduction Act of 2003 became law in the fall 2004 and is designed to improve the correctional systems' work with mentally ill inmates. Some of its provisions are reprinted here.[1]]

(1) According to the Bureau of Justice Statistics, over 16 percent of adults incarcerated in United States jails and prisons have a mental illness.

(2) According to the Office of Juvenile Justice and Delinquency Prevention, approximately 20 percent of youth in the juvenile justice system have serious mental health problems, and a significant number have co-occurring mental health and substance abuse disorders.

(3) According to the National Alliance for the Mentally Ill, up to 40 percent of adults who suffer from a serious mental illness will come into contact with the American criminal justice system at some point in their lives.

(4) According to the Office of Juvenile Justice and Delinquency Prevention, over 150,000 juveniles who come into contact with the juvenile justice system each year meet the diagnostic criteria for at least 1 mental or emotional disorder.

(5) A significant proportion of adults with a serious mental illness who are involved with the criminal justice system are homeless or at imminent risk of homelessness; and many of these individuals are arrested and jailed for minor, nonviolent offenses.

(6) The majority of individuals with a mental illness or emotional disorder who are involved in the criminal or juvenile justice systems are responsive to medical and psychological interventions that integrate treatment, rehabilitation, and support services.

(7) Collaborative programs between mental health, substance abuse, and criminal or juvenile justice systems that ensure the provision of services for those with mental illness or co-occurring mental illness and substance abuse disorders can reduce the number of such individuals in

adult and juvenile corrections facilities, while providing improved public safety.

Section 3. Purpose.

The purpose of this Act is to increase public safety by facilitating collaboration among the criminal justice, juvenile justice, mental health treatment, and substance abuse systems. Such collaboration is needed to—

(1) reduce rearrests among adult and juvenile offenders with mental illness, or co-occurring mental illness and substance abuse disorders;

(2) provide courts, including existing and new mental health courts, with appropriate mental health and substance abuse treatment options;

(3) maximize the use of alternatives to prosecution through diversion in appropriate cases involving non-violent offenders with mental illness;

(4) promote adequate training for criminal justice system personnel about mental illness and substance abuse disorders and the appropriate responses to people with such illnesses;

(5) promote adequate training for mental health treatment personnel about criminal offenders with mental illness and the appropriate response to such offenders in the criminal justice system;

(6) promote communication between criminal justice or juvenile justice personnel, mental health and co-occurring mental illness and substance abuse disorders treatment personnel, nonviolent offenders with mental illness or co-occurring mental illness and substance abuse disorders, and support services such as housing, job placement, community, and faith-based organizations; and

(7) promote communication, collaboration, and intergovernmental partnerships among municipal, county, and State elected officials with respect to mentally ill offenders.

1. The Mentally Ill Offender Treatment and Crime Reduction Act of 2003 is codified as Public Law 108-414 (2005).

will in order to make him competent to stand trial. The U.S. Supreme Court upheld that decision.[89]

10-4d　Prison Programs

The special needs of female inmates—as well as of inmates who are HIV-positive or who have already contracted AIDS, of elderly inmates, and of those who are physically or mentally challenged—should not be ignored. But neither should the mental, social, and physical needs of the inmates who do not fall into these categories. Our discussion in this section delves into the programs that might be implemented for the well-being of all inmates. In particular, education, work, and recreation are examined.

Despite the importance of education, insufficient attention is given to educational opportunities in correctional institutions. It is estimated that as many as 50 to 75 percent of American adult inmates are illiterate. Over 50 percent have not completed high school, and there is evidence that, whatever grades they have completed, inmates' skills are lower than those of noninmates who have completed the same grades. If these inmates are to return to society as law-abiding individuals, they must have skills, many of which are gained primarily through formal education. Most prisons provide some educational opportunities; some have college courses. Jails lag far behind prisons in this, as well as in many other areas.

Despite the evidence of the beneficial effects of education, those who argue that prisons should be for punishment and that state or federal government money should not be used for educating inmates, may be winning in some jurisdictions. For example, the 1994 revision of the federal criminal code eliminated grants that were being used to provide college courses in prisons. Further, courts have not ruled that inmates have a *right* to any educational opportunities they may choose, and some courts have held that inmates do not have a right to a free college education.[90]

With the severe local and state budget cuts that are becoming all too familiar, some jurisdictions have chosen to eliminate prison education and other programs. For example, in 2003 Maryland was facing a freezing of its prison education budget. That budget had been increased from $12.6 million to $14.2 million the previous year but then frozen. In 2003, the state had 10,000 inmates who needed to take state-mandated GED (high school equivalency) classes but for whom there was no room in the programs. Corrections officials predicted that by the end of 2004 approximately 60 percent of the state's inmates would be without a high school diploma and thus need the GED classes. The correctional program coordinator at the Maryland State Department of Education said, "We can guarantee at least a 20 percent drop in recidivism from educational participation, but we need more staff and more resources."[91]

In 2003, the Kentucky legislature cut that state's education program budget for correctional facilities from over $5 million to less than $3 million. Originally the entire budget was cut, but part was restored after the department of corrections officials emphasized that without any education programs the rates of recidivism would increase when inmates were released and that they might commit more infractions while incarcerated. The previous year, 410 inmates had received GEDs and 629 had earned diplomas or certificates in technical courses, all of which better prepared the inmates for getting jobs upon release from incarceration. The education programs in Kentucky prisons ended 1 April 2003. In addition to the loss to inmates, 99 full-time and 10 part-time teachers were out of work.[92]

Budget cuts continued in 2004. In March, 40 inmates graduated from high school at California's Lancaster facility, but prison officials emphasized that the program was in danger of being cut. As a result of budget cuts, this institution's prison vocation education department lost 33 of its 46 programs.[93] In the fall 2004, it was announced that the Flint, Michigan, school district had cut its ties with a program designed to help jail inmates and drug offenders earn their GEDs after the state cut over one-half of the $1 million to $1.5 million a year it had provided for these efforts. According to school officials, "It's a real sad thing. It's a program we held on to as long as we could, but we had to do what we had to do."[94]

Another area of important focus in prison programming is work. A noted criminologist has said that "the most difficult prison to administer is the one in which prisoners languish in idleness. Absence of work leads to moral and physical degradation and corrupts institutional order."[95] Work has been an important part of U.S. prisons historically, and some of the early prison industries were profitable economically. State laws prohibiting the sale of prison-made goods to the general public, along with federal laws prohibiting shipping prison-made goods across state lines into states with these statutes, changed the nature of prison labor. Prisons were confined primarily to making goods for state (or federal) use.

In recent years additional attempts have been made to introduce meaningful vocational opportunities into prisons, along with "just plain work" to keep inmates busy and provide needed services for state and federal institutions. The federal Bureau of Prisons (BOP) led the way, announcing in 1994 the need to expand its Federal Prison Industries (FPI). All federal inmates are required to work, but the increase in the inmate population is outstripping available jobs. Further, most of the inmates work in jobs that maintain the institution and thus may not prepare them for the marketable skills they need when they are released from prison. Federal prisons are limited to producing goods for federal institutions in order to avoid competition, but some have suggested a change in that policy.[96]

In 2003, the U.S. House of Representatives voted 350 to 65 to limit the FPI by placing new restrictions on the contracts of the agencies. It was argued that the federal government was taking away jobs from U.S. citizens and giving them to federal inmates, who are already being housed and fed at the expense of U.S. taxpayers. A similar bill was referred to the Senate Committee on Government Affairs but did not pass. In June 2005, the bill, now entitled the Federal Prison Industries Competition in Contracting Act of 2005, was reintroduced into the House of Representatives.[97]

Inmates may be but do not have to be paid for their work. A 1990 federal court ruling held that "compelling an inmate to work without pay is not unconstitutional."[98] Inmates' wages are very low (some as low as 25 cents an hour), although it has been suggested that inmates should be paid the minimum wage but required to pay for room and board.

In 1995, the BOP finalized its regulations on requiring inmates to pay for the cost of incarceration. The regulations apply to all inmates convicted after 1 January 1995.[99] Legal issues have been raised concerning requiring inmates to pay the costs of their incarceration, and courts are not uniform in their reactions to these issues.

A final area of focus on programming is recreational. It is in this area that many budget cuts have been made in recent years. In particular, institutions have cut cable television and phone use by inmates. According to a Department of Justice (DOJ) investigation, some federal inmates had abused phone privileges by conducting illegal drug sales and in some cases by ordering the murders of witnesses. The report concluded that the federal BOP needed to "squarely address what appears to be widespread inmate abuse of prison telephones and take immediate and meaningful actions to correct the problem."[100] The DOJ has prosecuted more than 100 cases of phone abuse in federal prisons in recent years.[101]

One final issue regarding phone use in prisons should not go unnoticed. Numerous prison systems have permitted phone companies to charge artificially high rates for long-distance collect calls made by inmates from prisons and jails. A *New York Times* editorial on the subject concluded, "It is wrong to penalize and profit from the families of inmates, and unconscionable that New York should lead the pack."[102]

10-4e Prison Violence

Prison officials are warning that one of the results of reducing or eliminating prison programs may be increased violence, manifested in the murders of other inmates or prison officials; escapes; or riots that may result in serious property damage, injuries, or deaths. For example, on 13 December 2000, seven dangerous inmates escaped from a Texas maximum-security prison. They were not captured until January, when four of the seven were arrested in Colorado, where a fifth inmate killed himself after officers arrived. The other two were captured later. The inmates were charged with, among other crimes, killing a law enforcement officer. Four were convicted and sentenced to death. In June 2003, the fifth inmate, Randy Halprin, 25, was convicted and sentenced to death. In November 2003, Patrick Murphy Jr. was also convicted and sentenced to death.

Prison violence also involves injuries to and the deaths of other inmates, as illustrated by the killing of defrocked priest John J. Geoghan in August 2003 in a Massachusetts state prison. Geoghan, who had been accused of molesting children for decades, admitted to engaging in sexual acts with three boys. The inmate accused of Geoghan's murder allegedly wrote a letter received by a newspaper; the author of the letter stated that he had been sexually abused when he was a child; he apologized to Geoghan's sister for murdering her brother. The letter was signed "Regretfully but sincerely, Joseph L. Druce." Subsequently Druce entered a plea of not guilty to beating and strangling Geoghan. In December 2003, the director of the Massachusetts Department of Corrections, Michael Maloney, began a medical leave after defending his administration and assuring the pubilc that Massachusetts prisons are safe and secure. The state's governor, Mitt Romney, appointed an independent commission to investigate whether that is the case.[103]

Other types of prison violence involve riots. Although few in number, prison riots are serious in their injuries to humans—injuries that in some cases result in death—and in their destruction of property.

Spotlight 10-6 Selected Disturbances or Riots in American Prisons, 1985–2003

Calico Rock, Arkansas: June 2003

Twelve inmates were injured and sent to the infirmary and 16 more were transferred to the isolation unit of the medium-security prison of the North Central Unit of the Arkansas Prison System. The fighting broke out in three cell blocks after one inmate was sent to isolation for refusing to leave the shower during a fire drill. Other inmates, especially the cousin of the isolated prisoner, began protesting with comments such as "We are not going to take this." No prison personnel were injured, and the unit's emergency response team brought the fighting under control quickly. Prison officials, who refused to characterize the incident as a riot, stated that such events seldom occur at that prison.

Lamesa, Texas: April 2000

One inmate was killed and 31 were injured, some critically, in a minimum- to medium-security prison after approximately 300 African American and Hispanic inmates became involved in a riot, which lasted only a few hours before prison officials brought the institution under control by using pepper spray. The riot began after two inmates started fighting in the dining hall.

Crescent City, California: February 2000

One inmate was killed and 8 were injured, 1 critically, after approximately 200 African American and Hispanic inmates began fighting with handmade weapons. The incident occurred on the day that a federal grand jury indicted 2 former correctional officers for violating the civil rights of inmates by the use of brutality, which resulted in the death of 1 victim. This prison at Pellican Bay, located on the West Coast about 20 miles south of the California/Oregon border, houses the state's most violent inmates. It was designed for 2,280 inmates but contained 3,400 at the time of the 2000 riot. In a 1997 riot at the institution, 6 inmates were killed.[1]

Lucasville, Ohio—Southern Ohio Correctional Facility: April 1993

In March 1995, Jason Robb, an inmate accused of helping lead a 1993 riot, which resulted in the deaths of 9 inmates and 1 correctional officer, was convicted of killing the officer and 1 inmate. Robb was convicted of 6 of 7 charges against him, including aggravated murder and kidnapping. The riot began on Easter Sunday, when a fight broke out as inmates returned from the recreation yard to their cell blocks. It lasted 11 days. Inmates surrendered after they agreed with prison officials on 21 issues, including numerous improvements in prison conditions. Officials agreed that inmates would not be subjected to retaliations by correctional officers, although it was made clear that those who committed crimes, such as murder, would be subject to prosecution, but it was not until 10 years later, in May 2003, that the last of 4 inmates charged in the death of officer Robert Vallendingham was convicted. For the second time, a jury found James Were, 46, guilty of kidnapping and two counts of aggravated murder, one for plotting the death of the officer and the second for killing him during the kidnapping. Were's first conviction was overturned by the Ohio Supreme Court. The prosecution was seeking the death penalty, but Were's mental condition was at issue. He was given a second death sentence, but the state supreme court ordered a new trial. In December 2004, the state supreme court upheld the conviction and death sentence of George Skatzes, who was considered a leader in the riot.[2]

Two of the most destructive and highly publicized U.S. prison riots occurred in 1971 in Attica, New York, and in 1980 in Santa Fe, New Mexico. The Attica riot is summarized in a 1985 opinion of a federal judge whose court heard allegations of violations of constitutional rights in that facility. The judge noted that 43 persons (32 inmates and 11 correctional employees) were killed during the riot. Prior to the riot, the prison was overcrowded, with 2,200 inmates in a facility built for 1,700. Although 54 percent of the inmates were African American and 9 percent were Puerto Rican, all officers were white. The institution had no meaningful programs for inmates. As noted in Spotlight 10-1, the civil suits regarding this riot continued for years.[104]

On 2 February 1980, a riot as devastating as the Attica riot occurred at the state prison in Santa Fe, New Mexico. Estimates of damage ranged from $20 million to repair to $80 million to replace the prison. At least 90 persons required hospitalization, and 33 inmates were killed. Characteristic of the violence was the torture and incredible brutality of inmates toward inmates, which led national guardsmen to regurgitate on the scene and firefighters who had fought in Vietnam to proclaim that they had not seen such atrocities as those that were committed during this riot.[105]

Although no major riots have occurred in U.S. prisons in recent years, there have been many in other countries. For example, in June 2003, Manaus, a city in northern Brazil, South America, was the scene of a prison riot that lasted 12 hours and resulted in 13 deaths. Some of the more recent U.S. prison riots or disturbances are featured in Spotlight 10-6. In early 2004, two inmates held two correctional officers hostage for two weeks in an Arizona

Maryland and New York Prisons: May 1991

Fourteen correctional officers and 44 inmates were injured when Maryland inmates rioted in the Correctional Institution at Hagerstown on 25 May 1991. Of the 1,600 inmates at the institution, approximately 1,000 were involved in the riot, "which officials described as the most serious disturbance at the prison in decades." Inmates caused over $1 million of damage before the riot was quelled. The prison was approximately 60 percent overcrowded at the time of the riot.[3]

On 28 May 1991, a disturbance began at the Southport Correctional Facility at Pine City, New York. This facility is a maxi-maxi prison designed to house the state's most serious and dangerous offenders. Three correctional officers, taken hostage by approximately 50 inmates, were held for 26 hours before being released. Although there were no deaths in this riot, several officers were stabbed or beaten. Inmates were protesting the institution's lock-down policy, which kept them in their cells 23 hours a day, with only 1 hour out for supervised exercise; poor living conditions and food; and some of the restrictions on visitation.[4]

Moundsville, West Virginia—West Virginia Penitentiary: January 1986

Inmates wielding homemade weapons took correctional officers hostage and seized control of the prison; 3 inmates were killed; 16 hostages were taken; and the prison was held by inmates for 43 hours. Officers taken hostage were forced to watch inmates brutalize, torture, and then kill inmates thought to be snitches. The body of 1 inmate, a convicted murderer and child molester, was dragged up and down a cell block as other inmates spat on him. The riot was triggered by inmate anger over restrictions on contact visits with family and friends and the cancellation of a Christmas open house.

Officials in the state blamed each other for the problems. The current governor and the former governor "traded charges of accusing each other of cowardice and misguided policies." The current governor said the killed inmates were accused of being informants for the administration and that the informant policy was started by the previous governor, who retorted that during the three-day crisis the current governor was not available. On 16 January 1986, inmates began a work strike to protest continued restrictions of their activities since the riot. In February, 25 inmates who had been placed in isolation since the New Year's Day riot broke out of their cells. Correctional officers persuaded 23 of the inmates to surrender and then captured the other 2. Sixty-eight inmates were in isolation as a result of the riot.

The West Virginia Penitentiary had been placed under court order in 1983 after the court found unconstitutional conditions, including maggot-infested food and raw sewage in living areas. The prison at that time was overcrowded, and officials were ordered to reduce the population.

1. "Inmate Dies and 8 Are Hurt in California Prison Riot," *New York Times* (24 February 2000), p. 21.
2. "Lucasville Inmate's Conviction Upheld," *Columbus Dispatch* (9 December 2004), p. 8C. The case is State v. Skatzes, 2004 Ohio LEXIS 2859 (Sup.Ct. Ohio, 2004).
3. "Maryland and New York Prisons Suffer Serious Disturbances," *Criminal Justice Newsletter,* 22 (3 June 1991): p. 5.
4. Ibid.

prison. Steven Coy, 39, was charged with sexual assault against the female hostage. Coy and the second inmate, Ricky Wassenaar, were charged with kidnapping and assault, and Wassenaar was also charged with attempted murder. In these incidents we see brutality, physical injury, death, and destruction of property. We see inmates protesting prison conditions and demonstrating their anger at prison officials who have not changed those conditions. Coy pleaded guilty so he could be sent to a prison near his family in Maine; he received seven life sentences. Wassenaar asked for a trial, which was in process in April 2005. He represented himself, although the court appointed an advisor to assist.

One final form of violence is less obvious but very important, and that is inmate self-inflicted violence. This violence may not be reported in jails and prisons for a variety of reasons, but, when such violence leads to suicide, the acts become known and may trigger investigations by public officials and lawsuits by survivors. Suicides are more common in jails than in prisons, and little is known about the reasons for inmate death by suicide. The issue gained national attention in 1993, when U.S. Attorney General Janet Reno ordered a federal investigation of the 46 hanging deaths that had occurred in Mississippi jails since 1987. Some argued that these deaths of young African Americans were lynchings, not suicides. After an eight-month investigation, federal officials ordered the state to correct "gross deficiencies" in Mississippi jails or face closure of the facilities. In 1995, after almost two years of additional investigation, the FBI reported that it had found no evidence of misconduct on the part of jail officials. Not all agreed with that finding, however, with some alleging that the FBI had not talked to all of the witnesses.[106]

According to an American Bar Association publication, approximately one-third of all jail suicides occur in the South, which is characterized by more lax jail standards, compared with other jails throughout the nation. For example, during the Mississippi suicides under investigation between 1993 and 1995, one-fourth of all of the jails in that state were under federal court order for failure to comply with national safety standards. Three southern states—Georgia, Mississippi, and Alabama—did not conduct jail inspections and had no state standards for jail conditions. An expert on jail suicides stated, "Jail officials in the South pay extremely low wages, hire unqualified jailers and offer no training in suicide recognition and prevention." A Mississippi medical examiner, who ruled that the deaths he investigated were all suicides, concluded that the suicide issue in that state was "much more of a public health issue . . . than it is a criminal justice issue. . . . There's nobody watching the inmates." But an independent pathologist from Chicago, who examined the autopsy of one of the dead inmates, concluded that the inmate did not commit suicide but was murdered. The pathologist stated that it was "almost impossible to hang oneself" in the position in which that inmate was found, but the official federal investigation ruled that all of the inmate deaths under investigation were suicides.[107]

The reasons for self-inflicted violence and suicide in jails and prisons are varied. Such violence and suicides have been linked to overcrowded institutions, mental illness, the extended use of solitary confinement, and the psychological consequences of being a victim in jail or prison. Some inmates who are threatened with rape or other violence become depressed and desperate about their physical safety, because their only options are fight and flight. If they submit to violence, they are branded as weak and forced to face further violent attacks from aggressive inmates. If they seek help from the prison administration, they are branded as snitches or rats. Furthermore, the inmate social system rewards violence against weaker inmates.

In June 2003, the superintendent of a Virginia jail requested a federal investigation into the fact that three inmates had hanged themselves within the previous eight months. A fourth inmate who died was a suicide victim, according to the jail officials' investigation; however, according to the medical examiner, the cause of death was asphyxiation.[108]

What can be done to prevent jail and prison suicides? In the Shelby County Correction Center (Memphis, Tennessee), which had three suicides between 1990 and 1999, increased security was added. Jail officials estimated that as a result they thwarted about one suicide a week for that period. The chief jailer said that his staff had increased its monitoring of potentially suicidal inmates. An article citing these figures quoted a nationally recognized mental health expert, Dr. Fuller Torrey, as stating that jail suicides are high because, after closing many of the mental health facilities in the 1960s and 1970s, jails became the "dumping ground for the mentally ill. . . . I think there is no question there is a relationship in jail suicides and the large number of mentally ill people we are putting in jail now." Dr. Torrey continued,

> We should not be surprised to see that because most jails are not set up to take care of people who are mentally ill. So we are basically asking them to do a job that they are not trained or set up to do. These people belong in a psychiatric ward. They don't belong in jail.[109]

According to Shelby County Jail officials, approximately 20 to 35 percent of their inmates have a history of mental illness, and the percentage has been increasing over the years. The jail has also been plagued with other problems. Three times prior to 1999, federal courts had cited the Shelby County Jail officials as engaging in unconstitutional practices and held that the facility was infested with gangs. As a result the jail had not been accredited since 1990 and its officials were under a court order to use a classification system in deciding housing assignments and to increase their monitoring of inmates.[110]

Other approaches to the prevention of jail suicides have been taken. A jail that opened in South Bend, Indiana, in 2001 placed a psychiatrist on duty in an attempt to prevent suicides after two suicides occurred in the county jail. And after two jail inmates committed suicide within a six-month period in 2002, a new cell block was opened in early 2003 at the Madison County Jail (Missouri). The facility houses male inmates who may be suicide risks because of depression or mental illness. The sheriff commented, "We want to see the inmates who walk into this jail walk out, and not be carried out."[111]

The belief that jail suicides can be prevented, at least in many cases, is implicit in the lawsuits for wrongful death won by the families of deceased inmates who committed suicide. In April 2003, a New Mexico mother whose daughter committed suicide in jail, won a settlement consisting of attorney fees plus a $5,500 annuity for each of her daughter's three children. The children will receive the money when they reach age 25. The lawsuit alleged that the jail officials were negligent in their failure to provide adequate medical and psychiatric care. And a Maine family filed both state and federal lawsuits for the wrongful death of their loved one, a man who committed suicide in the Maine State Prison mental health unit. The family of Adam J. Dupuis alleged that prison officials were deliberately indifferent to Dupuis's medical needs and that corrections officials were playing cards when Dupuis hanged himself in his cell. Dupuis, who was in a mental health unit and had been diagnosed as bipolar, was on medication for severe anxiety and depression. The treatment was successful but had been changed. On the day in question, Dupuis placed a sign in his window to block the corrections officers' view of him and was not seen for 45 minutes, during which time he committed suicide. He had made an unsuccessful suicide attempt a week prior.[112]

Chapter Wrap-Up

In 1984, the U.S. Supreme Court said that the continuing guarantee of substantial rights to prison inmates "is testimony to a belief that the way a society treats those who have transgressed against it is evidence of the essential character of that society."[113] This chapter explored life in prison historically and currently. It began with a brief look at the events that might accompany an inmate's arrival at prison and proceeded to an overview of the legal issues that govern incarceration today.

The U.S. Supreme Court has made it clear that some rights are forfeited by inmates and that security needs may justify the restriction of rights normally recognized in prison. This chapter surveyed the historical and current approaches to inmates' legal rights, beginning with a look at the traditional hands-off doctrine, in which federal courts refused to become involved in daily prison administration and maintenance. As a result of the recognized abuse of inmates and the civil rights movement, which brought the nation's attention to the problems not only of minorities in society but also of the conditions under which inmates lived, courts began to abandon the hands-off policy. Courts continue to defer to prison officials, but they no longer tolerate violations of basic rights. The concept of cruel and unusual punishment, along with ways of determining what that means, was discussed as an example.

The chapter focused next on prison administration and its relationship to security goals. In the earlier days, authoritarian prison wardens or superintendents and correctional officers maintained security by keeping inmates separate; by not permitting them to talk to each other; or by using fear and force, often involving corporal punishment. Those methods are not permitted today; new management techniques are necessary.

Corrections officers are crucial to prison management. They have primary responsibility for maintaining internal discipline, order, and security. Their jobs are difficult and at times boring, but the position is challenging and rewarding to many who have chosen the profession of corrections officer. The chapter emphasized the importance of selecting and training officers carefully and of including women and minorities within their ranks. It also noted examples of brutality by prison correctional officers.

When we think of life behind bars, however, we think mainly of inmates serving time within those facilities. This chapter noted how inmates adjust to prison life through the prisonization process. The resulting subculture was discussed in view of its origin: whether inmates develop the subculture as a method of adapting to the deprivations of prison or whether they acquire the values of the subculture and then import them into prisons.

The male inmate subculture is characterized by social roles that assist inmates in maintaining some self-esteem and positive self-concepts. Some accomplish these goals at the expense of other inmates: social control through economics, through racial and gang violence, and through homosexual attacks. Prison gangs play a critical role in these interactions.

Female inmates develop patterns of adaptation to prison life, too, but normally their adaptations are less violent than those of male inmates. Their social roles mirror the roles they have played in society. Women face many of the same deprivations as male inmates, but they face the additional problems of adjusting to daily life without their children. Mothers behind bars have become a subject of research only recently, and even today few provisions are made for female inmates to interact with their children. Women also have special medical needs, and institutions are attempting to accommodate those needs, although some are doing so only under court orders or the threat of such orders. Sexual harassment of female inmates is a serious problem, although it is not limited to them; harassment of males was also noted. Particular attention was given to the Prison Rape Elimination Act of 2003 and its implications.

The sexual behavior of male and female inmates was contrasted and discussed in the context of a relatively recent issue of prison life: AIDS. The complications are increasing, too, as officials must determine how to cope with AIDS without violating inmates' constitutional rights. The chapter also discussed the existence and implications of contagious diseases, such as hepatitis C and tuberculosis, in prisons.

Attention was also given to the special needs of inmates who are physically challenged, elderly, or mentally ill.

Adaptations to prison are made more difficult by the lack of activities, including education, work, and recreational programs and facilities. Recent attention to the need for such programs, along with budget cuts that have reduced prison programs, was discussed in the chapter.

The final section looked at the impact of prison violence, with particular attention given to major prison riots. The Attica riot of 1971 and subsequent studies of the riot illustrate the devastation of riots in terms of personal injury, death, and property damage, as well as the slowness with which meaningful changes are made. The

New Mexico and West Virginia riots illustrate the torture and brutality of which inmates are capable. The more recent riots remind us that serious prison disturbances still occur.

Another type of violence in prison is self-inflicted violence, apparently the only way some inmates find to adjust. In some cases, suicide results.

This chapter's discussion of the problems of controlling inmates within prison looked at the issues historically and in terms of recent events. But eventually most inmates are released from prison. The meaning that has for them and for society is the topic of Chapter 11.

Key Terms

civil rights (p. 276)
commissary (p. 275)
conjugal visits (p. 296)
correctional officer (guard) (p. 280)

deprivation model (p. 285)
hands-off doctrine (p. 275)
importation model (p. 285)

norms (p. 285)
prisonization (p. 284)
social system (p. 280)

Apply It

1. What is the *hands-off doctrine*, and to what extent (and why) has it been abandoned?
2. What is meant by a *hierarchy of rights*?
3. What were the characteristics of the authoritarian warden? What do you think should be the characteristics of the ideal warden or prison superintendent?
4. What events have occurred within prisons during the past three decades and forced changes in prison administration?
5. How did early correctional officers control inmates? If permitted, would those techniques be effective today?
6. Discuss recruitment and training issues with regard to correctional officers. Note the issues regarding gender and race.
7. Describe some of the daily aspects of inmate prison life.
8. Define prisonization and subculture, and explain the development and importance of each in a prison setting. Would the importance be different in prisons for female inmates, as compared with male inmates?
9. Distinguish between the importation and deprivation models, and explain the social control role of inmate social systems.
10. What is the significance of prison gangs? What could be done to lessen their influence?
11. What provisions do you think should be made for incarcerated women who have children at home or for women who give birth during incarceration? What provisions

should be made for incarcerated fathers to visit with their children? Do female inmates have special problems other than child care, and, if so, how should they be handled? Should inmate fathers have the same access to visitation arrangements that inmate mothers have?
12. Analyze sexual relations between correctional officers and inmates.
13. Explain the Prison Rape Elimination Act of 2003, and discuss what you think its impact will be on prison life.
14. Distinguish the sexual behavior in prison of gay males from that of lesbians.
15. What has been the impact of AIDS on prisons? How should the problems be handled? What about the spread of other contagious diseases, such as tuberculosis and hepatitis C?
16. Discuss the situations faced by prison officials as a result of an aging inmate population. What are the special needs of inmates who are disabled? Mentally ill?
17. If most inmates are relatively poorly educated, why do we not make a greater effort to provide education classes in prisons?
18. Should inmates be required to work within the prisons? If there is a lack of jobs, how should that problem be solved?
19. What policies would you recommend to prison administrators if they were to ask you how to prevent prison riots? What policies might prevent jail or prison suicides?

Endnotes

1. See Harold Garfinkel, "Conditions of Successful Degradation Ceremonies," *American Journal of Sociology* 61 (March 1956): 420–424.
2. Gresham M. Sykes, *The Society of Captives* (Princeton, N.J.: Princeton University Press, 1958), pp. 63–83.
3. Ruffin v. Commonwealth, 62 Va. 790, 796 (1872).
4. Wolff v. McDonnell, 418 U.S. 539 (1974).
5. See "States and Cities Removing Prisons from Courts' Grip," *New York Times* (30 January 2000), p. 1.
6. Holt v. Sarver, 309 F.Supp. 362 (E.D.Ark. 1970). This case has a long history of remands and reversals leading to the U.S. Supreme Court case Hutto v. Finney, 437 U.S. 678 (1978).
7. Graham v. Richardson, 313 F.Supp. 34 (D.Ariz 1970), *aff'd.,* 403 U.S. 365, 375 (1971).
8. Estelle v. Gamble, 429 U.S. 97, 106 (1976).
9. Wilson v. Seiter, 501 U.S. 294 (1991).
10. Farmer v. Brennan, 511 U.S. 895 (1994).
11. Hudson v. McMillian, 503 U.S. 1 (1992).
12. Laube v. Campbell, 255 F.Supp. 2d 1301 (M.D.Ala. 2003), *settlement, judgment entered,* 333 F.Supp. 2d 1234 (M.D. Ala. 2004).
13. Norman Holt, "Prison Management in the Next Decade," *Prison Journal* 57 (Autumn/Winter 1977): 17–19. Unless otherwise noted, this discussion of prison management comes from this source.
14. "Virginia Prison Chief to Step Down," *Corrections Professional* 7, no. 17 (24 May 2002).

15. "Correction Chief Faults Hiring Methods at Rikers," *New York Times* (25 August 1990), p. 11.

16. "Desperate for Prison Guards, Some States Even Rob Cradles," *New York Times* (21 April 2001), p. 1.

17. "Federal Prison Hunting Recruits: Forest City Lockup to Provide 300 Jobs, Not All as Guards," *Arkansas Democrat-Gazette* (8 July 2004).

18. "Prison Worker Turnover Doubles," Greenville News (10 March 2003), p. 1B.

19. "Although Prisons Are Safer, Officers' Use of Leave Soars," *New York Times* (28 November 2003), p. 10.

20. "Female Guards at Men's Prisons," *Orlando Sentinel* (20 June 1997), p. 10.

21. Johnson v. Phelan, 69 F.3d 144 (7th Cir. 1995), *cert. denied,* 519 U.S. 1006 (1996).

22. Brissette v. Franklin County Sheriff's Office, 235 F.Supp. 2d 63 (D. Mass. 2003).

23. Rita J. Simon and Judith D. Simon, "Female COs: Legitimate Authority," *Corrections* 50 (August 1988): 132.

24. "Female Correctional Officers Said to Reduce Prison Violence," *Criminal Justice Newsletter* 27 (1 April 1996): 2.

25. This discussion of Clemmer's concept of prisonization comes from his book, *The Prison Community* (New York: Holt, Rinehart and Winston, 1958), pp. 298–301.

26. Stanton Wheeler, "Socialization in Correctional Communities," *American Sociological Review* 26 (October 1961): 697–712.

27. Geoffrey P. Alpert et al., "A Comparative Look at Prisonization: Sex and Prison Culture," *Quarterly Journal of Corrections* 1 (Summer 1977): 29–34.

28. See Sykes, *Society of Captives;* and Gresham M. Sykes and Sheldon L. Messinger, "The Inmate Social System," in *Theoretical Studies in Social Organization of the Prison,* ed. Richard A. Cloward et al. (New York: Social Science Research Council, 1960).

29. See John Irwin and Donald R. Cressey, "Thieves, Convicts and the Inmate Culture," *Social Problems* 10 (Fall 1962): 142–155.

30. Charles W. Thomas, "Prisonization or Resocialization: A Study of External Factors Associated with the Impact of Imprisonment," *Journal of Research in Crime and Delinquency* 10 (January 1975): 13–21.

31. Leo Carroll, "Race and Three Forms of Prisoner Power Confrontation, Censoriousness, and the Corruption of Authority," in *Contemporary Corrections: Social Control and Conflict,* ed. C. Ronald Huff (Beverly Hills, Calif.: Sage, 1977), pp. 40–41, 50–51.

32. Ronald L. Akers et al., "Prisonization in Five Countries: Type of Prison and Inmate Characteristics," *Criminology* 14 (February 1977): 538.

33. See James Garofalo and Richard D. Clark, "The Inmate Subculture in Jails," *Criminal Justice and Behavior* 12 (December 1985): 431.

34. Richard A. Cloward, "Social Control in the Prison," in *Theoretical Studies,* ed. Cloward et al.

35. James W. Marquart and Ben M. Crouch, "Coopting the Kept: Using Inmates for Social Control in a Southern Prison," *Justice Quarterly* 1, no. 4 (1984): 491–509.

36. Robert S. Fong, "The Organizational Structure of Prison Gangs," *Federal Probation* 54 (March 1990): 36–43.

37. Michael P. Lane, "Inmate Gangs," *Corrections Today* 51 (July 1989): 98–102.

38. James C. Howell, "Recent Gang Research: Program and Policy Implications," *Crime & Delinquency* 40 (October 1994): 494–515; quotation is on p. 509.

39. Rose Giallombardo, *The Social World of Imprisoned Girls: A Comparative Study of Institutions for Juvenile Delinquents* (New York: John Wiley, 1974).

40. David A. Ward and Gene G. Kassebaum, "Women in Prison," in *Correctional Institutions,* ed. Robert M. Carter et al. (Philadelphia: J. B. Lippincott, 1972), p. 215.

41. Justice Policy Center, *Families Left Behind: The Hidden Costs of Incarceration and Reentry,* a 12-page report, available on the Internet at http://urban.org/url.clm?ID=310882. The report is summarized in "Incarceration of Parents Causes Enormous Problems, Report Says," *Criminal Justice Newsletter* (17 November 2003), p. 5.

42. "DOC Program Strengthens Family Ties," *Corrections Professional* 8, no. 4 (18 October 2002).

43. "Child Visitation Unit Added to Female Prison," *Corrections Professional* 7, no. 15 (19 April 2002).

44. "Mothering behind Bars," *State Legislatures* 28, no. 10 (1 December 2002): 11.

45. "Prison Systems Slowly Implementing Parent Training Programs for Males," *Correctional Educational Bulletin* 6, no. 3 (26 November 2002).

46. "Prison Doctor Charged with Sex Abuse," *Corrections Professional* 8, no. 18 (6 June 2003); "Prison Doctor Sentenced in Sex-with-Inmate Case," *Houston Chronicle* (24 October 2003), p. 30.

47. "Official Gets Probation for Inmate Sex," *Denver Post* (16 May 2003), p. 4B.

48. Women Prisoners of the District of Columbia Department of Corrections v. District of Columbia, 899 F.Supp. 659 (D.D.C. 1995), *vacated, in part, remanded,* 93 F.3d 910 (D.C.Cir. 1996), *cert. denied,* 520 U.S. 1196 (1997), *on remand,* 968 F.Supp. 744 (D.D.C. 1997).

49. The case is Shumate v. Wilson, filed in the U.S. District Court, Eastern District of California, in 1995; "Plaintiff Class," *AIDS Policy and Law* 18, no. 12 (20 June 2003).

50. "Lawyers to Get $1.2M in Prison Settlement," *The Recorder* (American Lawyer Media, L.P.) (14 August 1997), p. 1.

51. "Services for Women Inadequate," *Correctional Educational Bulletin* 6, no. 4 (24 December 2002).

52. "Study: Programs Could Help Humiliated, Bored Female Inmates: Researchers Say More Education Is Needed," *Corrections Professional* 8, no. 8 (20 January 2003).

53. Peter C. Buffum, *Homosexuality in Prisons* (U.S. Department of Justice et al., Washington, D.C.: U.S. Government Printing Office, 1972), p. 13.

54. Sykes, *Society of Captives,* p. 97.

55. Buffum, *Homosexuality in Prisons,* p. 9.

56. Leo Carroll, *Hacks, Blacks, and Cons: Race Relations in a Maximum Security Prison* (Lexington, Mass.: D.C. Heath, 1974), p. 194.

57. Daniel Lockwood, *Prison Sexual Violence* (New York: Elsevier Science, 1980), p. 21.

58. Redman v. San Diego County, California, 942 F.2d 1435 (9th Cir. 1991), *cert. denied,* 502 U.S. 1074 (1992).

59. Farmer v. Brennan, 511 U.S. 825 (1994).

60. Ward and Kassebaum, "Women in Prison," pp. 217–219.

61. Rose Giallombardo, *Society of Women: A Study of a Woman's Prison* (New York: John Wiley, 1966).

62. John Gagnon and William Simon, "The Social Meaning of Prison Homosexuality," *Federal Probation* 32 (March 1968): 27–28.

63. David Ward and Gene Kassebaum, "Sexual Tensions in a Women's Prison," in *Crime and Justice: The Criminal in Confinement,* ed. Leon Radzinowicz and Marvin E. Wolfgang (New York: Basic Books, 1971), pp. 146–155.

64. "Study Describes Extent of Staff-on-Inmate Sex Misconduct," *Criminal Justice Newsletter* 30 (2 March 1999): 5–6. The full report, *Women in Prison: Sexual Misconduct by Correctional Staff,* is available without charge from the General Accounting Office, Box 37050, Washington, DC 20013 (202) 512-6000. Fax: (202) 512-6061. On the Internet: www.gao.gov.

65. "Inmates Commit Most Sexual Assaults in Women's Prisons," *Corrections Professional* 8, no. 8 (20 January 2003).

66. "Belt Alarm Could Curb Sexual Abuse in Women's Prisons," *Corrections Professional* 8, no. 14 (11 April 2003).

67. "U.S. Senate Passes Legislation to Curb Prisoner Rape; House to Vote Wednesday," *Business Wire* (22 July 2003).

68. Bureau of Justice Statistics Bulletin, *HIV in Prisons, 2000* (Washington, D.C.: U.S. Department of Justice, October 2002), pp. 1–5.

69. "Maryland Prison System Has High HIV Rate," *Corrections Professional* 8, no. 17 (23 May 2003).

70. "Infections in Newly Released Inmates Are Rising Concern," *New York Times* (28 January 2003), p. 14.

71. "When Prison Cells Breed Disease," *Legal Times* (9 December 2002), p. 1.

72. Davis v. Hopper, 171 F.3d 1289 (11th Cir. 1999), *cert. denied,* 528 U.S. 1114 (2000).

73. "When Prison Cells Breed Disease," p. 1.

74. Doe v. Coughlin, 523 N.Y.S.2d 782 (N.Y.Ct.App. 1987), *cert. denied,* 488 U.S. 879 (1988).

75. "Michigan Prisons Test Inmates for Hepatitis C," *Corrections Professional* 10, no. 7 (17 December 2004), no page number; "Doctors Encourage Inmate Condom Access," *Corrections Professional* 10, no. 16 (13 May 2005), no page number; "California Chamber Approves Measure to Give Inmates Condoms: Cost of AIDS Care weighs Heavy on Decision," *Corrections Professional* 10, no. 18 (24 June 2005), no page number.

76. Bonner v. Lewis, 857 F.2d 559 (9th Cir. 1988), *cert. denied,* 498 U.S. 1074 (1991). The ADA is the Americans with Disabilities Act of 1990, Public Law 101-336, U.S. Code, Title 42, Section 12101 *et seq.* (2005).

77. Paige M. Harrison and Allen J. Beck, Bureau of Justice Statistics, *Prisoners in 2003* (Washington, DC: U.S. Department of Justice, November 2004), p. 8.

78. Paige M. Harrison and Allen J. Beck, Bureau of Justice Statistics, *Prisoners in 2003* (Washington, DC: U.S. Department of Justice, November 2004), p. 8.

79. "Federal Government Report Says Mentally Ill Convicts Sometimes Go Untreated," *Corrections Professional* 6, no. 22 (10 August 2001). The original report is Bureau of Justice Statistics, *Mental Health Treatment in State Prisons* (Washington, D.C.: U.S. Department of Justice, 2001), on the Internet at www.ojp.usdoj.gov/bjs/abstract/mhtsp00.htm.

80. James C. Harrington, "Criminal Justice System Fails Those with Mental Disabilities," *Texas Lawyer* 17, no. 31 (8 October 2001): 47.

81. "Courts Review Solitary Confinement for Mentally Ill Inmates: Several States Are under Fire from Civil Rights Groups," *Corrections Professional* 8, no. 5 (8 November 2002).

82. "Inmates' Lawyers Support Care for Mentally Ill," *Corrections Professional* 7, no. 10 (12 February 2002).

83. "Minnesota DOC," *Corrections Professional* 7, no. 21 (9 August 2002).

84. Tom Perrotta, "City Settles Class Action, Agrees to Provide Health Care to Released Mentally Ill Inmates," *New York Law Journal* 229 (9 January 2003): 1. The case is Brad H. v. City of New York, 185 Misc. 2d 420 (Sup.Ct. 2000), *aff'd., mot. denied, mot. granted,* 716 N.Y.S.2d 852 (1st Dep't. 2000).

85. "Court Orders Swifter Review of Mentally Ill Defendants," *Metropolitan News Enterprise* (Los Angeles, California) (7 March 2003), p. 3. The case is Oregon Advocacy Ctr. v. Mink, 322 F.3d 1101 (9th Cir. 2003).

86. "Funding the Program," *Corrections Professional* 8, no. 19 (20 June 2003).

87. *Ill-Equipped: U.S. Prisons and Offenders with Mental Illness,* summarized in "Report Cites Limited Progress in Prison Mental Health Programs," *Criminal Justice Newsletter* (3 November 2003), p. 2. The report is available from Human Rights Watch, 350 Fifth Avenue, 34th Floor, New York, NY 10118. (212) 290-4700. On the Internet: www.hrw.org.

88. "Bill Would Fund Treatment of Mentally Ill Criminal Offenders," *Criminal Justice Newsletter* (16 June 2003), p. 2; quotation is on p. 3. The bill is the Mentally Ill Offender Treatment and Crime Reduction Act of 2003, Public Law 108-414 (2005).

89. Sell v. United States, 539 U.S. 166 (2003).

90. See Hernandez v. Johnston, 833 F.2d 1316 (9th Cir. 1987).

91. "Maryland Prison Budget Cuts Freeze Number of Teachers, Salaries," *Correctional Educational Bulletin* 6, no. 7 (19 March 2003).

92. "Kentucky Budget Cuts Most Prison Vocational, Educational Programs," *Correctional Educational Bulletin* 6, no. 8 (15 April 2003).

93. "40 Inmates Graduate High School at California's Lancaster Facility," *Correctional Educational Bulletin* 7, no. 7 (22 March 2004).

94. "Michigan School District Drops Correctional Program," *Correctional Educational Bulletin* 8, no. 2 (1 November 2004).

95. Elmer H. Johnson, *Crime, Correction, and Society,* rev. ed. (Homewood, Ill: Dorsey, 1968), p. 559.

96. "Bureau of Prisons Cites Need to Expand Prison Industries," *Criminal Justice Newsletter* 25 (16 May 1994): 4.

97. Federal Prison Industries Competition in Contracting Act of 2005, HR 2965 (2005).

98. Murray v. Mississippi Department of Corrections, 911 F.2d 1167 (5th Cir. 1990), *cert. denied,* 498 U.S. 1050 (1991).

99. The statute providing for such fees is Public Law 102-395, Section 111, enacted in 1992.

100. "Bureau of Prisons Criticized for Inmate Abuse of Phones," *Criminal Justice Newsletter,* 30 (1 April 1999): 3.

101. "Justice Dept. Wants to Curb Federal Inmates' Phone Use," *New York Times* (15 August 1999), p. 14.

102. "When Johnny Calls Home, from Prison," *New York Times* (6 December 1999), p. 28.

103. "Embattled Prisons Chief Takes Leave," *Chicago Tribune* (3 December 2003), p. 20.

104. Abdul Wali v. Coughlin, 754 F.2d 1015 (2d Cir. 1985).

105. Cited in Joseph W. Rogers, "Postscripts to a Prison Riot" (paper presented at the Annual Meeting of the Academy of Criminal Justice Sciences, Louisville, Ky., 25 March 1982).

106. See, for example, "After Mississippi Hangings, Feds Order Jails to Shape Up," *Atlanta Journal and Constitution* (31 December 1993), p. 1; "Around the South: Mississippi Jail Deaths Probe Ends; FBI Finds No Evidence of Civil Rights Violated," *Atlanta Journal and Constitution* (26 January 1995), p. 3.

107. Mark Curriden, "Suicide or Lynching? Human Rights Commissions Holds Hearings on Jail Hangings," *American Bar Association Journal* 79, no. 14 (June 1993).

108. "Va. Jail Requests Federal Review after 3 Hangings," *Washington Post* (10 June 2003), p. 4B.

109. "Jail Suicides Beg Question: How Could This Happen? Vulnerable Include Mentally Ill Inmates," *Commercial Appeal* (Memphis, TN) (21 November 1999), p. 1.

110. Ibid.

111. "Jail Changes to Target Inmate Suicide," *South Bend Tribune* (Indiana) (22 May 2003), p. 4D; "Jail Adds Unit for Suicidal Inmates," *St. Louis Post-Dispatch* (25 February 2003), p. 1B.

112. "Inmate Suicide Lawsuit Settled," *Albuquerque Journal* (New Mexico) (21 April 2003), p. 8B; "Family to Sue State over Prison Inmate's Suicide," *Portland Press Herald* (5 December 2002), p. 1B.

113. Hudson v. Palmer, 468 U.S. 517, 523, 525 (1984).

Community Corrections, Probation, and Parole

11

Supervision of offenders within the community is a frequent alternative to imprisonment, although the conditions placed on offenders may be severe. This chapter focuses on community treatment of offenders, probation, and parole. It begins with an overview of community-based corrections, noting the historical development and discussing problems offenders face when they enter these programs. It focuses on diversion programs, such as drug courts, and the general treatment approach characteristic of some jurisdictions today. It examines how problems might be minimized through programs that prepare inmates for their release from prison back into the community.

Probation, the most frequently imposed sentence, and parole, until recently a major form of release from prison, are discussed in their historical contexts and with their modern changes. Both have been the focus of considerable attention in recent years. Crimes committed by probationers and parolees frequently receive widespread publicity, leading to public pressure to reduce the use of probation and parole. In some cases these pressures have been successful.

Like other changes in criminal justice systems, however, changes in the use of probation and parole must be viewed in terms of their effects on the rest of the system. A significant reduction in the use of one or both of them places severe strain on correctional systems, increasing prison overcrowding and all of its consequences. In addition, it may result in the incarceration of offenders who do not need such severe restraints. But crimes committed by probationers and parolees reduce the safety and security of society. It is not possible to predict with great accuracy who will harm society while on probation or parole.

The chapter considers some of the major federal constitutional issues that govern community corrections, probation, and parole. Finally, it focuses on Megan's laws, which evolved in an effort to protect the community from released sexual predators.

OBJECTIVES

After reading this chapter, you should be able to do the following:

- **Explain the meaning of the term** *community corrections* **and state the advantages of using this approach**
- **Discuss the development and impact of drug courts and other diversionary programs**
- **Comment on mental health issues regarding community corrections**
- **Assess the contributions of California to the modern treatment approach toward minor, nonviolent drug offenders**
- **Explain furlough, work release, and prerelease programs**
- **Distinguish probation from parole and analyze recent data on each**
- **Explain felony probation and analyze recent approaches to its use**
- **Analyze the use of electronic monitoring and house arrest**
- **Discuss the legal limitations on probation and parole conditions**
- **Recognize the advantages and disadvantages of intensive probation supervision**
- **Analyze the process of searching and seizing parolees**
- **Identify three organizational models of parole systems**
- **Explain the parole process, with particular attention to due process**
- **Explain the legal controls on parole and probation revocation**
- **Analyze the future of probation and parole**
- **List and discuss the major constitutional issues relating to community corrections, probation, and parole, noting in particular the impact of the Americans with Disabilities Act (ADA)**
- **Discuss the issues surrounding probation or parole revocation**
- **Assess the impact of Megan's Laws and analyze the constitutional issues raised by these statutes**

11-1   Supervision of Offenders in the Community

Discussions in earlier chapters described some methods used in the past to permit the accused or the convicted offender to remain in the community. Family members, friends, and attorneys served as sureties to guarantee the presence of the accused at trial. Later, sureties were replaced by a variety of methods of posting bond. Early reformers, such as John Augustus, were successful in their efforts to have convicted persons placed on probation in the community. In the late 1880s in New York City, halfway houses were used to permit inmates a gradual readjustment to the community.

11-1a   Overview

The major impetus for the modern movement toward supervision of the offender within the community grew out of the Federal Prisoner's Rehabilitation Act of 1965 and the President's Commission on Law Enforcement and the Administration of Justice. The latter stated in its 1967 report that the new direction in corrections recognized that crime and delinquency are community as well as individual failures. The commission saw the task of corrections as one of reintegrating offenders into the community, restoring family ties, assisting offenders to get an education or employment, and securing for them a place in the normal functioning of society. That required changes in the community and in offenders. The commission described the traditional methods of institutionalizing offenders as fundamentally deficient. It concluded that **reintegration** is likely to be more successful if society works with offenders in the community rather than confining them in prisons.[1]

▶ **Reintegration** A punishment philosophy emphasizing the return of the offender to the community, so that employment, family ties, and education can be restored.

In 1973, the National Advisory Commission on Criminal Justice Standards and Goals called for an increased emphasis on probation. The commission concluded, "The most hopeful move toward effective corrections is to continue to strengthen the trend away from confining people in institutions and toward supervising them in the community."[2]

Reintegration of the offender into the community is not a one-way process, however. The community must take an active role in the process of treating offenders. It might not be sufficient to try to reintegrate the offender into the community; the community may need to change along with the offender. For example, if resources for reintegration are not available, they must be provided.

Some punishments that do not involve incarceration do not fall within the definition of community-based corrections. Fines and restitution are alternatives to incarceration, but they are not community-based corrections. The important factor in community-based corrections is the relationship between those involved in the program, both clients and staff, and the community. Community-based programs involve an element of supervision aimed at assisting offenders to reintegrate into the community. In some programs supervision may not be adequate, but it is the effort to supervise and improve that distinguishes community-based programs from fines and restitution, both of which can be combined with community-based corrections.

Community-based corrections should be distinguished from *diversion,* a process of directing the offender away from the adult criminal (or juvenile) systems and into other programs. Diversion usually occurs instead of, not in addition to, court processing. Diversion has been used primarily in the processing of juveniles, but it can be used for adult offenders as well. The alcoholic or drug addict who is apprehended for petty theft might be counseled to enter a substance abuse treatment program in the community and told that successful completion of that program will result in the dropping of criminal charges. That program could be a community-based treatment program. Because of the importance of the recently enacted approach of diverting offenders convicted of minor drug offenses, attention is given to that subject in this chapter.

Supervised programs may be offered within prisons to prepare offenders for release. They may also be offered outside of prisons, with inmates reporting back to their prisons on a part-time basis before their release. Or the programs may be provided for convicted offenders who are placed on probation or released on parole.

Community-based programs and supervision may be provided in residential facilities, such as community treatment centers, group homes, foster homes, and halfway houses. Foster homes and group homes may be used for juveniles who do not need specialized treatment programs but who have experienced difficulties living in their own homes. They may house juveniles who need specialized programs, which may be provided in nonresidential community treatment centers, schools, or other institutions.

Halfway houses can be viewed as places for offenders nearing the end of their terms to live during a period of gradual reentry into society. The offender lives in a supervised environment but may leave that facility during the day to work or to participate in vocational, treatment, or educational programs.

Residential facilities can be used for more than halfway programs. Some are viewed as long-term housing for offenders, usually juveniles, who need intensive treatment and supervision. They may be designed for offenders with particular needs. For example, some are limited to first offenders; others are limited to repeat offenders who do not function effectively without intensive supervision. Residential facilities may include community treatment centers that provide housing and supervision for persons who have not been to prison, such as those who are on probation and need more supervision than may be provided in a nonresidential environment.

Some community treatment facilities are nonresidential. Offenders live in their own homes or with relatives or friends but go to treatment centers for individual or group therapy and for participation in seminars and other programs designed to assist them with adjustment problems. However, before offenders are placed in community corrections following time in prison, attention should be given to the problems they will face after release, which is done later in this chapter. But first, attention is given to a recent focus in community treatment: diverting nonviolent drug offenders from incarceration.

11-1b   Diversion of Nonviolent Drug Offenders

Prison overcrowding and the expenses it entails, dissatisfaction with severe sentencing, and humane concern have led in some states to recently enacted statutes providing for the diversion from incarceration of minor, nonviolent drug offenders. This is accomplished primarily in two ways: by processing those offenders through special drug courts or by making statutory provisions for the treatment rather than the incarceration of offenders processed through the adult criminal courts.

Drug Courts

Spotlight 6-3 noted that approximately one-third of all persons investigated by U.S. attorneys are suspected of having committed drug offenses, and approximately 29 percent of all federal arrests are for drug offenses. In recent years drug arrests and convictions have increased significantly, and imposed sentences as well as time required to serve have increased. In the federal system alone, between the enactment of the Sentencing Reform Act of 1984 and 1999, the proportion of drug offenders who were sentenced to prison increased from 79 to 92 percent. Drug prosecutions in federal courts increased from 21 percent of the total cases in 1982 to 36 percent in 1999. In 1988, a federal drug offender could expect to spend 39.3 months in prison; in 1999, he or she could expect to spend 61.8 months in prison. In 1999, most federal prison inmates were incarcerated for drug offenses—57 percent, compared with 11 percent for violent crimes, 7 percent for property offenses, 8 percent for an immigration offense, and 9 percent for other offenses.[3] And according to a 2003 publication of the Bureau of Justice Statistics, "Drug prosecutions have comprised an increasing proportion of the federal criminal caseload—from 21 percent of defendants in cases terminating in U.S. district court during 1982 to 37 percent during 2001."[4]

This increase in drug prosecutions has led to an attempt to process some of the offenders through special drug courts. Drug courts may focus on particular types of offenses or problems, such as those that occur in families when parents are accused of drug violations and their children are removed from the families for their own protection. Reintegrating those children back into the family is important.[5] Drug courts may also focus on types of offenders, for example, first- or second-time minor offenders, or they may focus on types of drug offenses.

Drug courts began in Miami, Florida, in 1989 and have spread to all states. According to a December 2003 speech by a Massachusetts judge, Peter Anderson, in 2000 all of the chief justices and court administrators in the 50 states signed a statement supporting drug courts. Judge Anderson explained drug courts as follows:

> The typical drug court combines substance-abuse treatment in the community, strict case management with direct judicial involvement, regular drug testing, and graduated incentives and sanctions based on performance in treatment. The ultimate reward is avoidance of a jail sentence or the expunging of criminal charges. The ultimate sanction is imprisonment.[6]

Judge Anderson maintains that mandatory treatment within drug courts is more effective than voluntary treatment or imprisonment "if the goal is to keep addicts from relapsing into drug habits and crime." He claims that the war on drugs is not only expensive but also ineffective in reducing both drug addiction and crime; further, the sentences for drug offenders are too harsh. Also, decriminalization, which offers treatment with little threat of punishment, "diverts scarce resources from those who can most benefit: addicted offenders. Drug courts deal with the shortcomings of both approaches, favoring treatment over jail but constructing a system that allows treatment to stick."[7]

Judge Anderson contends that in his 13 years on the bench he has learned the following:

- "Substance abuse is a significant factor in the majority of criminal cases that enter the judicial system each year. . . .
- Almost all substance abusers and addicts need treatment to become clean and sober. The vast majority of them will not do it on their own.

- The longer someone remains in treatment, the more successful he or she generally is in maintaining sobriety and law-abiding behavior. . . .
- Coerced treatment works. Most addicts and substance abusers will not enter treatment or stay very long if treatment is voluntary. . . .
- Treatment that is not only coerced but coordinated has an even higher success rate. . . .
- Success in treatment should be rewarded. Treatment is hard work. Most addicts have zero self-esteem and no track record of accomplishment in life. Rewarding offenders is a strange concept to most judges and court officials, but it is essential in substance-abuse cases."[8]

New York's chief judge Judith Kaye agreed. Referring to what she called a "startling fact" that almost one-half of New York's inmates were serving sentences for drug-related offenses, Kaye emphasized that drug offenses cannot be ignored by courts. Because of the serious impact of drug offenses on the state's courts, New York instituted drug courts less than a decade ago, and, said Judge Kaye, "Their effectiveness in halting the destructive cycle of addiction and criminality is indisputable." To support her conclusions, the judge referred to a study by the U.S. Department of Justice (DOJ) and the Center for Court Innovation. That report, one of the most comprehensive about state drug courts, was published in 2003. It concluded that the New York drug courts reduced recidivism by almost 32 percent. Over 18,000 offenders had participated in the state's drug courts, resulting in an estimated savings to the state of over $254 million in incarceration costs alone.[9]

A variation of the drug court is the family drug court in Kentucky. This court is designed to help mothers who are addicted to drugs, and as a result have lost custody of their children, to "come clean" and recover the custody of their children. By the end of 2003, the program, which had been in existence about two years, had 5 mothers (out of 25 enrolled) who had succeeded in getting their children returned to them. A recent publication, citing a successful mother who had just regained custody of her children, said of the woman, "She's a great mother. She may have made mistakes but that's why they put erasers on pencils, because everyone makes mistakes."[10]

The federal government has been supportive of drug courts. In May 2002, the government announced through the Substance Abuse and Mental Health Services Administration (SAMHSA) that it was appropriating an additional $10 million for drug courts. And when the U.S. drug czar, John P. Walters, testified before a congressional committee in February 2003, he announced that the White House would be supporting more funding for drug courts. Finally, in his proposed budget for 2006, President George W. Bush increased drug court funding from $30 million to $70 million, although he recommended no funding for the Safe and Drug-Free Schools and Communities State Grants program, for which $441 million was appropriated for the 2005 fiscal year.[11]

Statutory Provisions for Treatment

A second approach to the treatment rather than punishment of selected categories of drug offenders was led by California. That state's statute is reproduced in Spotlight 11-1. California led the way in this most recent emphasis on the treatment rather than the punishment of minor, first- or second-time drug offenders. Under the California system, once a drug offender completes the treatment program successfully, that person's conviction is removed from the records. The California statute does not apply to those who *sell* drugs, however. Some states (for example, Ohio, Nevada, and Arizona) have been unsuccessful in their recent attempts to pass legislation similar to that of California, but efforts to do so continue in several states.

There is concern, however, that with state budget cuts drug courts and other treatment programs for drug offenders will be reduced or even cut. For example, in September 2003 it was announced that the Alameda (California) Probation Department was pulling staff out of many of its diversion programs, including drug courts. Judges claimed that these

Spotlight 11-1	**Treatment of Minor Drug Offenders: The California Approach**

One of the boldest treatment approaches for substance abuse is that of California, which provides treatment rather than punishment for minor first and second offenders. The California statute is as follows:[1]

> (a) Notwithstanding any other provision of law, and except as provided in subdivision (b), any person convicted of a nonviolent drug possession offense shall receive probation. As a condition of probation the court shall require participation in and completion of an appropriate drug treatment program. The court may also impose, as a condition of probation, participation in vocational training, family counseling, literacy training and/or community service. A court may not impose incarceration as an additional condition of probation. Aside from the limitations imposed in this subdivision, the trial court is not otherwise limited in the type of probation conditions it may impose. Probation shall be imposed by suspending the imposition of sentence.
>
> In addition to any fine assessed under other provisions of law, the trial judge may require any person convicted of a nonviolent drug possession offense who is reasonably able to do so to contribute to the cost of his or her own placement in a drug treatment program. [The statute then specifies the types of offenders who are excluded from this statute.]

1. Possession of Controlled Substances; Probation; Exceptions, California Penal Code, Section 1210.1 (2005).

cuts would "cripple the superior court's 11-year-old drug court—the first such program in the state and the second in the nation."[12]

11-1c   Diversion of Mentally Challenged Persons

In Chapter 10 we noted that many offenders are mentally challenged. Spotlight 10-5 reproduced portions of the Mentally Ill Offender Treatment and Crime Reduction Act of 2003, which went into effect in late 2004. That act emphasizes that the majority of mentally challenged persons who come into contact with criminal justice agencies can benefit from treatment. One suggestion for diverting these offenders is to process them through mental health courts rather than juvenile courts or adult criminal courts.

Mental health courts were started in Broward County, Florida, in 1997; other states have followed. The Center for Court Innovation (the research and development arm of the New York State court system) studied the mental health courts in Florida, California, Washington, and other states. These courts were established specifically for handling mentally ill offenders. They are similar to drug courts in that they are geared toward the treatment rather than punishment of offenders. The courts are optional; treatment is not available unless the offender is willing to participate. The targets for these courts—which have their own special judges and some support staff, such as clinical persons—are seriously mentally ill and facing nonviolent misdemeanor charges. According to the Center for Court Innovation report, these special courts aim "to move beyond standard case processing to address the underlying problems that bring people to court. . . . In the process, they seek to shift the focus of the courtroom from weighing past facts to changing the future behavior of defendants."[13]

In 2000, Congress enacted a provision for federal mental health courts. The bill, passed unanimously by the Senate and by a voice vote in the House, provides for federal grants for up to 100 programs to establish special mental health courts, which target offenders who are charged with nonviolent offenses or misdemeanors. The statute provides for training law enforcement and judicial personnel to identify persons who should qualify for the special programs. There is a provision for "voluntary outpatient or inpatient mental health treatment, in the least restrictive manner appropriate, as determined by the court, that carries with it the possibility of dismissal of charges or reduced sentencing upon successful completion of treatment." It also provides for the centralized management of all charges against a defendant. Finally, the statute provides for "continuing supervision of treatment plan compliance for a term not to exceed the maximum allowable sentence or probation for the charged or relevant offense and, to the extent practicable, continuity of psychiatric care at the end of the supervised period."[14]

For offenders who are incarcerated, however, assistance is needed for their transition back into society.

11-2   Problems of Offenders Upon Release

Each year approximately 400,000 persons are released from prisons back into the community. Many of them will be apprehended again, some rather quickly. All will face problems; some problems will be individualized; others will be difficulties that most if not all releasees face. For example, releasees need street and work clothing. Although most prisons provide clothing or permit inmates to receive it from home, usually this is insufficient. The prison may allow only one set, and the inmate may not have family or friends who provide additional clothing. Even a prearranged job may not be much help, for the inmate will not get a paycheck for a week or longer.

Many prison systems give inmates a small amount of money upon release. The amount varies from state to state but may be as low as $50. With these funds, inmates must pay for additional clothing and room and board; and in many cases repay debts incurred before incarceration and restitution. They may also have families to support.

Employment is another problem faced by the released offender. Institutions may or may not provide offenders assistance in seeking employment. Inmates also face social adjustments upon release. The day of release may be characterized by a sense of optimism, the belief that life will be different and more pleasant. Release from prison has been called a positive life change, but people experience uncertainty, loneliness, depression, and disorganization as well.

For many ex-offenders, release from prison means frustration and anxiety over how to act and what to say in social situations and on the job. Feelings of helplessness, insecurity, fear, indecision, and depression may result in physical problems, such as loss of appetite, chronic exhaustion, sleeping problems, or sexual difficulties. Fear of the unknown may be particularly acute for inmates who have not been able to maintain close ties with their families during incarceration.

Relationships with family members may create problems for ex-offenders. Spouses and children suffer as a result of the offender's incarceration; anger and hostility may greet the offender who returns home. Years of absence, with few opportunities for family members to visit their loved ones in prison, may create interpersonal problems that are beyond repair. Financial hardships caused by the offender's absence may compound the interpersonal tensions.

Financial, economic, social, and other difficulties that inmates encounter on release from prison may be eased if adequate services are provided for ex-offenders by the community, but preparation for release is also important.

11-2a   Furlough and Work Release Programs

A **furlough** involves permitting the inmate to leave the institution once or occasionally for a specified purpose other than work or study. The offender may be given a furlough to visit a sick relative, to attend a family funeral, or to look for a job. The leave is temporary and is granted for a short period of time. It may involve supervision.

In **work release** programs, inmates are released from incarceration to work or to attend school. They may participate in work study, take courses at an educational institution, or work at jobs in the community. Work release is referred to by other names as well: day parole, outmate program, day work, daylight parole, free labor, intermittent jailing, and work furlough.

The first work release law, the Huber Law, became law in Wisconsin in 1913. The next statute, in North Carolina, was not enacted until 1957. The first furlough program was introduced by legislation in Mississippi in 1918. A few states passed laws providing for

▶ **Furlough**   An authorized, temporary leave from a prison or other penal facility in order to attend a funeral, visit the family, attempt to secure employment, or engage in any other approved activity.

▶ **Work release**   The release of an inmate to attend school or to work outside the institution but requiring that person to return to the institution at specified times.

work release or furloughs before 1965, but most of the programs in existence today were established by state laws after the passage of the 1965 federal law, the Prisoner Rehabilitation Act.

State legislation varies regarding who decides which inmates are placed on work release and whether inmates may retain any or all of the money they earn. Most legislation permits states to contract with other political subdivisions for housing of inmates who cannot find work near the institution. Some provide halfway houses or work release centers, and some use county jails. Generally inmates may not work in areas where there is a surplus of labor. They must be paid the same as others doing the same jobs. If a union is involved, it must be consulted, and the releasee may not work during a labor dispute.

Furlough and work release programs are important for several reasons. Work release programs enable offenders to engage in positive contacts with the community, assuming, of course, that work placement is satisfactory. They permit offenders to provide some support for themselves and their families. This can eliminate the self-concept of failure that may be the result of the loss of the supporter role, which is so important in American society. Through work release the offender may obtain more satisfying jobs than the prison could provide.

Work release and furlough programs provide a transition for the incarcerated inmate from a closely supervised way of life in prison to a more independent life within society. These programs give the community a transition period to accept offenders back into society. These programs have permitted some states to close one or more correctional facilities, thus decreasing the cost to taxpayers.

Problems with work release involve the process of selecting the participants; finding sufficient jobs for them; gaining community acceptance; and ensuring that inmates do not commit crimes while they are on release. There is no guarantee, of course, that offenders placed on furlough or work release will not commit crimes: in fact, the possibility that they will do so has led to community action to eliminate these methods of early release in some jurisdictions. However, many U.S. correctional systems have retained work release and educational release programs. In some of these programs inmates are required to pay room and board, to help support their families, to pay fines and costs, or to contribute to victims' compensation funds.

11-2b Prerelease Programs

Before release, all inmates should have an opportunity to participate in prerelease programs. It is unreasonable to expect that the difficulties faced by releasees will be solved by inmates without any assistance from counselors and other professionals.

Prerelease centers are another solution for preparing inmates who have serious adjustment problems but who are being released because they have completed their terms. In a residential environment that provides more supervision than offenders would have under probation or parole but less than they experience in prison, releasees may be able to make the adjustment to freedom gradually enough to succeed upon final release. In these cases, for a specified period before their release, inmates are transferred to prerelease facilities to finish their terms. The housing facility alone, however, is not sufficient for most inmates. Ideally those facilities would provide the full range of services needed to prepare inmates for release, including meaningful work opportunities.

The preparation of inmates for release is not sufficient to ensure that they will make adequate adjustments when they leave prison. Inmate families also need to be prepared for the adjustments that they must make when their loved ones are released from prison; thus, counseling should be provided for families.

11-3 Probation and Parole: An Overview

Probation and parole have been the most frequently used alternatives to prison and probably the most controversial. Probation is a sentence that does not involve confinement but may involve conditions imposed by the court, usually under supervision.

TABLE 11-1

Persons under Adult Correctional Supervision in the United States: 1995–2003

Year		Total Estimated Correctional Populationª	Community Supervision		Incarceration	
			Probation	Parole	Jail	Prison
1995		5,342,900	3,077,861	679,421	507,044	1,078,542
2000		6,445,100	3,826,209	723,898	621,149	1,316,333
2001		6,581,700	3,931,731	732,333	631,240	1,330,007
2002	June 30		—	—	665,475	1,355,494
	December 31	6,759,100	4,024,067	750,934	—	1,367,856
2003	June 30		—	—	691,301	1,387,269
	December 31	6,889,800	4,073,987	774,588	—	—
Percent change, 2002–03		1.9%	1.2%	3.1%	3.9%	2.3%
Average annual Percent change, 1995–2003ᵇ		2.9%	2.9%	1.7%	4.0%	3.4%

Note: Counts of probationers, parolees, and prisoners are for December 31, unless specified elsewhere. All jail counts are for June 30. Jail and prison counts include inmates held in private facilities. Totals in 2000 through 2003 exclude probationers held in jail or prison.
— Not available.
ªBecause some offenders may have multiple statuses, totals were rounded to the nearest 100.
ᵇPercent change based on comparable reporting agencies, excluding 193,607 probationers in agencies added since 1995.

Source: Lauren E. Glaze and Seri Palla, Bureau of Justice Statistics, *Probation and Parole in the United States 2003* (Washington, D.C.: U.S. Department of Justice, July 2004), p. 1.

The term **probation** is used to refer to the status of a person placed on probation, to the subsystem of the criminal justice system that handles this disposition of offenders, and to a process that involves the activities of the probation system: preparing reports, supervising probationers, and providing or obtaining services for probationers.

Parole is the release of persons from correctional facilities after they have served part of their sentences. It is distinguished from *unconditional release,* which occurs when the full sentence (or the full sentence minus time reduced for good time credits) has been served.

Probation and parole permit convicted persons to live in the community, with conditions imposed on their behavior and, in some cases, under supervision. Both are based on the philosophy that the rehabilitation of some individuals might be hindered by imprisonment (or further imprisonment) and could be aided by supervised freedom. The processes differ in that parole is granted after a portion of the prison term has been served, whereas probation is granted in lieu of incarceration. Probation is granted by the judge. Usually parole is granted by a **parole board** appointed or elected specifically for that purpose.

In recent years probation and parole have come under severe attack, and attempts have been made to reduce the number of people who are permitted to participate. However, the programs have not been cut back as severely as some had hoped, primarily because of overcrowded prisons and jails. Problems arise; security of the community and supervision cost are the two biggest.

Despite these problems, probation and parole are important elements of criminal justice systems, with probation the most widely used sentence overall. Table 11-1 reports the numbers of adult correctional populations in 1995, 2000, 2001, 2002, and 2003, showing the differences in the numbers confined in jail or prison, compared with those on probation or parole. Spotlight 11-2 highlights information on probation and parole from the latest Bureau of Justice Statistics (BJS) data.

Probation A type of sentence that places the convicted offender under the supervision of a probation officer within the community instead of in prison. Also, the part of the criminal justice system that is in charge of all aspects of probation.

Parole The status of an offender who is released before the completion of a prison sentence; usually the parolee must be supervised in the community by a parole officer.

Parole board A panel at the state or federal level that decides whether an inmate is released on parole from a correctional institution before the expiration of his or her sentence.

Spotlight 11-2   Probation and Parole in the United States: Highlights, 2003

Probation

- The adult probation population grew 1.2% in 2003, an increase of 49,920 probationers, less than half the average annual growth of 2.9% since 1995.
- 49% of all probationers had been convicted of a felony, 49% of a misdemeanor, and 2% of other infractions. Twenty-five percent were on probation for a drug law violation, and 17% for driving while intoxicated.
- Four States had an increase of 10% or more in their probation population in 2003: Kentucky (up 17%), Mississippi (up 15%), and Nebraska and New Hampshire (each up 12%). The adult probation population decreased in 19 States, led by Minnesota with the only double-digit decrease (down 10%).
- Washington State had the highest rate of probationers per 100,000 residents, 3,767; New Hampshire had the lowest, 426.

Parole

- Overall, the Nation's parole population grew by 23,654 in 2003, or 3.1%, almost double the average annual growth of 1.7% since 1995.
- Mandatory releases from prison as a result of a sentencing statute or good-time provision comprised 51% of those entering parole in 2003; in 1995 they were 45%.
- A total of 17 States had double-digit increases in their parole population in 2003. Five States had a parole population increase of 20% or more: North Dakota (up 53%), Alabama (up 31%), Kentucky (up 27%), New Hampshire (up 25%), and New Mexico (up 23%).
- 12 States had a decrease in their parole population. Hawaii (down 11%) was the only State with a decrease of more than 10%.

Source: Lauren E. Glaze and Seri Palla, Bureau of Justice Statistics, *Probation and Parole in the United States 2003* (Washington, D.C.: U.S. Department of Justice, July 2004), p. 1.

11-4   Probation

In the United States probation is traced to John Augustus, a prosperous Boston shoemaker. He asked that offenders be given their freedom within the community under his supervision, and Massachusetts responded with a statute in 1878. By 1900, six states had probation statutes; by 1915, 33 states had statutes providing for adult probation; and by 1957, all states had probation statutes. In 1925, a statute authorizing probation in federal courts was enacted.[15]

11-4a   Types of Probation

Probation is administered in several ways. In some cases it is reserved for only minor offenses; supervision may or may not be imposed. But there are several other types of probation: felony probation, house arrest, and shock probation combined with periodic sentencing.

> **Recidivists** Those who commit crimes repeatedly.

The use of probation for offenders convicted of *serious* offenses is referred to as *felony probation.* Studies by the Rand Corporation disclosed that many felony probationers commit additional crimes while they are on probation. Thus, they are **recidivists.** In 1985, the Rand Corporation published the results of its study of 16,000 felons on probation. Over a 40-month period, the research team tracked 1,671 felons; a total of 2,608 criminal charges had been filed against them. Of the felony probationers, 65 percent were arrested, 51 percent were convicted, and 34 percent were returned to jail or prison. Most of the offenses committed by the probationers were serious. The director of the Rand research warned that this information should not be used to abolish probation. Rather, it should be used to assess the problems that were created by increasing the use of probation rapidly without adequate increases in funds and staff. As the lead investigator noted, "No single human can adequately evaluate, report on, and supervise 300 criminals at a given time."[16]

The Rand Corporation study concluded that probation in its current form is not successful, but the researchers emphasized that sending felons to overcrowded prisons would not solve the problem, either. They suggested alternatives:

> The answer may be intensive surveillance programs that include intense monitoring and supervision, real constraints on movement and action, requirement of employment, mechanisms to immediately punish infractions, and added requirements of community service, education, counseling, and therapy.[17]

Studies in other states have suggested that some felony probation programs are more successful than those evaluated by Rand. After reviewing the Rand research and studies of more successful programs, such as those in Kentucky and Missouri, one scholar used data from New Jersey to examine the effectiveness of felony probation programs. He recommended that more attention be given to such problems of probationers as drug abuse and employment and that the studies of felony probation be scrutinized more carefully:

> The major conclusion is that probation is an acceptable sentencing alternative for some felony offenders in some states but that recidivism rates can be alarmingly high for particular categories of offenders.[18]

Probation may be combined with **house arrest** (or home detention or confinement), a relatively recent development in the United States, dating back only a couple of decades. Offenders who are confined by house arrest are placed under specific restrictions. They may live at home or in another designated facility, but they may leave only under specified conditions.

In some jurisdictions house arrest is accompanied by *electronic monitoring*, in which monitors are attached to the offender, usually to the ankle or the wrist. The devices are monitored by probation officers or other personnel who can determine whether the probationer leaves home (or another area of confinement, such as the place of employment) during restricted hours.

Although electronic monitoring is not new to criminal justice systems, the technology has become increasingly sophisticated. An expert on electronic monitoring and tracking emphasizes that global positioning systems (GPS) have been used effectively in tracking terrorists as well as offenders. "The U.S. military invented GPS during the Cold War to mobilize troops and missiles. These electronic products are so resourceful that they're also being implemented here at home for other 'enemies of the state': convicted criminals." Here is how the system works:

> Subjects under GPS tracing and monitoring wear a removable tracking unit (PTU) and a non-removable wireless ankle cuff. The ankle cuff is the size of a large wristwatch. The cuff communicates with the PTU to ensure that both items are always within a close and specific proximity of each other. If communication with the cuff is lost, the PTU assumes that the user has abandoned it and a violation is recorded. The PTU acquires its location from the Department of Defense's GPS satellites, and records this time and location into an Internet-based database system.
>
> This information is communicated back to probation, parole, bonding, and court officials using a Web browser; authorities are able to look at a detailed map to determine where the person has been. If a violation is detected, that is, if a person was in a forbidden area, authorities can take action.[19]

The use of government satellites gives local and state law enforcement officials extensive coverage. For example, child abductions often result in the child's being taken to another state; this could be tracked with GPS. As of spring 2003, 27 states had begun to use some form of global tracking, and it was predicted that the number would increase quickly.[20]

The following are some examples of the use of electronic monitoring. Katrina Leung, an accused double agent for China (in January 2005, the charges were dropped, and the prosecution planned an appeal) was released on $2 million bail, provided she wore a device that monitored her at all times. She was fitted with a device that was hooked to a global positioning satellite system, which uses U.S. Defense Department satellites. The device is about the size of a car stereo. A spokesperson for the company that manufactures these devices described their security as second only to keeping inmates behind bars. In June 2003, about 1,000 persons in Los Angeles were wearing the device, for which they each paid approximately $40 a month. During 2002, Los Angeles County saved $18 million by using electronic monitoring over the detention of persons sentenced to 60 days or less. The offenders are required to pay for the monitoring services, however, and that raises a legal issue for those who cannot afford to pay. Further, approximately 2 offenders per month attempt to elude the system; most are back in jail within 2 days.[21]

▶ **House arrest** A form of confinement, usually on probation, in which the offender is permitted to live at home (or some other approved place) but is restricted in his or her movements to and from the area. A curfew may be imposed, and the offender may be subject to unannounced visits from a probation officer. In some cases electronic devices are used to monitor the probationer's location.

In Wausau, Wisconsin, electronic monitoring used to keep minor offenders out of jail saves the county $12,000 a month per offender, while permitting offenders to remain in their jobs and with their families.[22]

Some empirical research is available on the use of electronically monitored home confinement. An early study concluded that the operation of electronic equipment is successful; most local criminal justice personnel accept the program; no serious legal problems appeared to develop when the plan was used as an alternative to detention. A significant savings resulted when the cost of electronic monitoring was compared with that of detention.[23]

A more recent study of electronic monitoring, which compared types of supervision provided for those monitored, along with probationers and inmates, concluded that electronic monitoring "added little value to more traditional forms of community control." Although rates were high for program completion, the rates of recidivism were not reduced significantly by the use of electronic monitoring.[24]

In another analysis of electronic monitoring programs, researchers emphasized that there are significant differences in the behavior of program administrators as well as participants of each program. Thus, any evaluations must take into account these differences, such as the ability of administrators to detect and apprehend violators. The types of participants involved and the nature of the programs are other issues that must be considered.[25]

A critical factor in the success of electronic monitoring is that the programs be adequately staffed. As a Connecticut probation officer noted, "One of the critical issues we face in releasing individuals into the community so abruptly, is that funding has been cut for a reasonable number of trained probation and parole officers to effectively work with offenders." She continued by stating, "My ability to work successfully with offenders is compromised when large number [sic] of offenders are suddenly released into the community and I am forced to be held accountable to monitor probationers using the same policies, standards and guidelines as when I have an ideal caseload." However, in 2002 and 2003 most states faced the worst budget crises they had encountered since World War II. As a result, the executive director of the American Probation and Parole Association concluded as follows: "My concern is that at a time when probation and parole agencies could be more effectively utilized as a successful alternative to incarceration, they are being set-up for failure by being overburdened."[26] That comment also applies to the use of electronic monitoring with probation, parole, or diversion.

Electronic monitoring is used extensively with abusers of alcohol and other drugs. As substance abuse violations have increased in number and have swelled court dockets and prison populations, many jurisdictions have turned from incarceration to alternative treatment programs combined with electronic monitoring. One problem with this approach, however, is that the dropout rate in substance abuse treatment programs is high, especially when those programs are voluntary and unsupervised. As noted earlier, there is some evidence that substance abuse treatment is more effective when it is mandatory and supervised.

Electronic monitoring may also be used with violent offenders, such as sexual predators. In Iowa, for example, authorities are using sophisticated systems to track sex offenders and other dangerous offenders placed on probation or released from prison on parole. The system notifies authorities when the offenders are near areas that they are forbidden to visit, such as any place in which children can be expected to play.[27] There is some empirical evidence that electronic monitoring is reasonably safe with sex offenders, although not with violent offenders in general.[28]

Most jurisdictions, however, limit their electronic monitoring offenders to those convicted of misdemeanors. For example, in spring 2003 Los Angeles County officials planned to release 2,600 inmates from the county jail. Some were to be on supervised work release; others were to be electronically monitored, with a panel, including a retired judge, deciding which inmates would go to each program. The sheriff expected to save $17 million as a result of these releases. In August 2003, the sheriff stated that, because of budget cuts and federal mandates to keep the population under certain levels, he had no choice but to free some inmates from custody or place them in other programs, such as work release or drug treatment.[29]

One of the primary reasons for using electronic monitoring is cost, but despite the cost savings, a significant problem with electronic monitoring is that it may be used without sufficient inquiry into the legal implications of this type of surveillance. Two lawsuits illustrate the civil implications of recidivism among offenders released with electronic monitoring. In both of these cases, plaintiffs alleged that the equipment was not maintained properly and that officials knew the bracelets broke down repeatedly. Some judges in the districts in which the cases occurred stopped ordering electronic monitoring, stating that they had lost faith in the system. In the first case, a Chicago jury awarded $3 million to the estate of a firefighter, a brother of Philadelphia 76ers all-star Maurice Cheeks. Cheeks was murdered by a gang, one of whom had succeeded in removing his electronic bracelet.[30]

The second case involved the murder of Holly Staker, an 11-year-old baby-sitter. The suit claimed that she was attacked by a convicted burglar, Juan Rivera, who had slipped off his electronic monitor. Rivera was convicted of stabbing the sitter 27 times and raping her as she died and the child looked on. He was sentenced to life in prison, but the conviction was overturned for technical reasons. He was convicted in a second trial and again sentenced to life in prison. However, in May 2005 the prosecution and the defense were preparing for hearings on the defense motion for a new trial. The defense claims that DNA evidence shows that the semen on Staker's body was not that of Rivera. The hearings were postponed to provide the state time to do its own DNA testing.[31]

But even if an offender does not violate the terms of his or her release as monitored electronically, problems may arise. In January 2001, authorities charged Keon Lipscomb with the rape and murder of his girlfriend's small child. Lipscomb was on electronic monitoring from Cook County (Chicago) Jail and was not in violation of his monitoring agreement. If he did kill the child, it was done while he was in a place to which he was confined. Lipscomb's trial was scheduled to begin 18 July 2005. In addition to the charges concerning the child, he faced numerous charges stemming from his violent behavior while in the Cook County Jail, although his trial was not expected to include those charges or the sexual assault of the child, just the murder charge. Lipscomb, only 23 and without a high school education, who has never held a job and who faces the death penalty, insisted on representing himself. The judge stated that he had no choice but to grant that request. Lipscomb was examined by a psychiatrist, who determined that the defendant does understand his rights and that he could be sentenced to death if convicted.[32]

Another problem with electronic monitoring is escape. In the early part of 2003, Andrew Luster, a great grandson of Max Factor, the cosmetics mogul, was on trial in San Diego for multiple rape counts. It was alleged that Luster had spiked the drinks of his dates and later raped the women. Luster, who was wearing an electronic bracelet, was permitted to be away from his home during the day. He fled in the morning, and the signal was not acknowledged until he missed his 8 P.M. curfew that night.[33] The trial was continued in his absence; he was convicted and sentenced in February 2003. In June 2003, he was captured in Mexico and returned to the United States to serve his prison sentence of 124 years.[34]

One final argument against electronic monitoring and house arrest is that the sentence is too lenient, but either or both may be accompanied by **intensive probation supervision (IPS)** (discussed in Section 11-4d, "Probation Supervision"), fines, or restitution. They may also be combined with brief jail or prison sentences, which constitute the third type of probation.

Some statutes permit sending offenders to prison for a short period of time and then placing them on probation. It is assumed that this procedure will shock the offender into appropriate behavior. This process is called *shock probation*, although technically that term is incorrect because probation is an *alternative* to incarceration. The purpose of shock probation is to expose offenders to the shock of prison before placing them on probation and to release them before they are influenced negatively by the prison experience.

Probation may also be combined with a jail term, a procedure called *periodic sentencing*. The offender may be confined to jail during the night but be permitted to go to work or school during the day. The jail term might be served on weekends only, with the offender free to move about in the community during the week, although under some probation terms. The weekend alternative has been used frequently for offenders who have been convicted of driving while intoxicated, particularly in jurisdictions in which jails are crowded and the offender has a steady job.

▶ **Intensive probation supervision (IPS)** With small caseloads, probation officers provide more careful supervision than they could provide with larger caseloads.

11-4b Probation Administration

In most jurisdictions probation administration is a court function, meaning that it is located in the judicial branch of government. The trial judge, who presides over probation hearings, may reject a probation recommendation made by the attorneys.

Despite the role of the trial judge in making probation decisions, it is possible for various courts within a particular jurisdiction to have probation departments, resulting in an overlap of services and other administrative problems. Other jurisdictions may have a statewide probation system with branches at the city and county levels. Probation departments may be found in the executive branch, too, reporting to the governor in the case of statewide systems. Probation departments differ in size and complexity and in the extent and quality of the services they provide for clients.

One division of the probation department provides services to courts. Usually the *presentence investigation (PSI)* is prepared by the probation department through interviewing clients and related parties, investigating and compiling materials relevant to each case, and developing recommendations for the sentencing body. In addition, the department provides the court with processing and reporting services for probation cases. This section keeps records of all persons on probation, the status of their probation, whether probation has been revoked, and other pertinent data.

Probation departments provide services for probation clients, too. Counseling, referral to other community sources, and supervision are the most common services provided by probation departments to their clients. Counseling alcoholics and their families is a service offered by some probation departments.

Usually probation departments are headed by a chief probation officer, who has functions typical of a chief executive officer of any organization. The primary responsibility for hiring, training, and firing probation officers and for managing all sections of the probation department is in the hands of this officer. The chief probation officer has public relations functions as well, working with community leaders, attorneys, police officers, and court personnel.

If the probation department is large enough, it may have an assistant chief probation officer, who reports to the chief probation officer and may be assigned such responsibilities as coordinating volunteer efforts and administering the department. A supervisor might be in charge of coordinating the efforts of those who prepare the PSI, assign cases, and handle other administrative functions.

Probation officers work directly with probationers. These officers should have training in the various aspects of probation work, including skills in interpersonal relationships. They provide counseling for probationers and engage in surveillance to determine whether their clients are violating probation conditions.

Probation officers do most of the investigative work in preparing the PSI and may be required to make a sentence recommendation to the judge before sentencing. This involvement in the sentencing decision and then in supervising the probationer may present problems. Probationers may resent the position the probation officer has in relation to the judge. Furthermore, it is questionable whether probation officers can be effective counselors while being responsible for surveillance.

Average beginning salaries for probation officers are not high enough to attract many well-qualified people, particularly if the goal is to attract people who have baccalaureate degrees, as the National Advisory Commission recommended. Efforts must be made to raise salaries and to improve working conditions for probation officers. Opportunities to work in the federal probation system are discussed in Professions 11-1.

A moving tribute to careers in probation was made by Sylvia Johnson, the chief probation officer for the Alameda County Probation Department in Oakland, California, when she said,

> I still have hope and love for my profession, probation. I owe a lifetime debt to the countless numbers of judges, referees, probation staff, foster parents, community-based organizations, and volunteers who have both supported me and taught me new ways of providing services. . . . Our society must not forget or abandon all children and families in need, and through public policy and a private sector call to action, we can and must improve their quality of life.[35]

Professions 11-1

Federal Probation Services

Most people in the United States who are under the supervision of criminal justice systems are on probation. Most probationers are supervised by probation officers. These officers perform a variety of functions and offer young people interesting and challenging career choices. This Professions box features the federal probation system, but many state systems are similar. Reference is made to several specialties within the federal probation system.

The Function of Federal Probation Officers[1]

Probation officers have two basic duties: presentence investigations and the supervision of offenders. Both require written and oral skills; a broad understanding of criminal justice systems; knowledge of federal probation and parole systems; knowledge of the federal prison system, federal sentencing guidelines, and federal case law; and an ability to work with diverse populations.

Presentence investigations require a probation officer to prepare for the court a document that includes information on the offense in question, the offender's history and personal characteristics, sentencing options, and the application of federal sentencing guidelines. Collecting and analyzing the data may require extensive time by the officer, who must make recommendations regarding the offender's potential risk, as well as the need for restitution, treatment, or other options. Probation officers prepare these reports by interviewing the offender and other persons, reading available documents, and analyzing other evidence. Probation officers also supervise inmates. Such supervision may involve extensive visits or be limited to phone calls, depending on the officer, the offender, the offense, and available resources.

The Function of Federal Pretrial Services Officers[2]

Federal pretrial services officers have two main functions: investigation and supervision. They investigate each offender in order to recommend to the court whether the individual should be released pending trial. If the offender is released, they provide supervision for some but not all offenders. The court may determine that some offenders do not pose a threat to themselves or to society and can be predicted to show up for trial; thus, they need no supervision.

Pretrial services officers also attend court sessions concerned with pretrial services and detention. They prepare release status reports for the courts. These reports summarize the offender's compliance with prerelease orders and make recommendations for release or detention if the offender is released after sentencing and pending an appeal. Supervision may include meeting with offenders to counsel them about the details of their release, the need to attend treatment programs for the abuse of alcohol or other drugs, other treatment programs, job opportunities, and so on.

To be eligible for the position, an applicant must have a bachelor's degree in an academic subject, such as sociology, criminology or criminal justice, psychology, or some other social science, although occasionally those with majors in other disciplines, such as business, are hired. Many individuals working as pretrial services officers have graduate degrees, and many of the federal officers have experience at the local or state level.

Substance Abuse Specialists[3]

Most probation officers must deal with offenders who have abused alcohol or other drugs, but the substance abuse specialist is a senior-level officer whose job is to oversee and manage a substance abuse program. This person is in charge of the budget for substance abuse, which includes the contracts for substance abuse treatment programs. He or she may provide in-service training for those who supervise offenders with drug problems; the individual may or may not have his or her own caseload.

1. Adapted from John P. Storm, "What United States Probation Officers Do," *Federal Probation* 61 (March 1997): 13–18.
2. Adapted from Thomas J. Wolf, "What United States Pretrial Services Officers Do," *Federal Probation* (March 1997): 19–24.
3. Adapted from Edward M. Read, "Challenging Addiction: The Substance Abuse Specialist," *Federal Probation* 61 (March 1997): 25–26.

One final point on the administration of probation systems is that some charge for their services. According to a 2003 report, in 2001 Texas adult probationers paid $237 million in court-ordered fines and probation fees and performed 8.5 million hours of unpaid community service, which otherwise would have cost the state approximately $45 million in pay to minimum-wage workers. These fees, fines, and work service accommodated approximately one-half of the probation supervision costs of the state.[36]

11-4c   Probation Conditions

The purpose of probation is to assist offenders in making social adjustments and in reintegrating into society as law-abiding citizens. Thus, the policy is to impose restrictions on offenders' freedom when they are released. Restrictions differ from jurisdiction to jurisdiction, but some are common to all.

It is customary to require probationers to report to an officer periodically at specified times and places; the officer may visit the client, too. Probationers may change residence only with the permission of the supervising officer. They must work (or attend school or some other approved activity); any changes must be reported. In some cases probationers are not allowed to make changes without the prior permission of the supervising officer or the court.

Most probationers are required to submit periodic reports of their activities and progress. They are not permitted to use nonprescription drugs and may be restricted (or prohibited) in the use of alcoholic beverages and forbidden to frequent bars or other questionable places. They may be required to submit to periodic drug testing if the facts of their cases suggest drug violations. Substance abuse is a serious problem among probationers. The first national survey of adults on probation, conducted in 1995, revealed that nearly 70 percent of adult probationers had engaged in drug use; 32 percent stated that they had been using illegal drugs in the month before the offense for which they were currently on probation. Fourteen percent of that 32 percent were under the influence of drugs when the current offense was committed.[37] Review Spotlight 11-2 (see again Section 11-3, "Probation and Parole: An Overview"), which notes that 25 percent of the probationers in 2003 were sentenced for violating a drug law and 17 percent were convicted of driving while intoxicated.

Among other restrictions, probationers are not permitted to own, possess, use, sell, or have deadly weapons or firearms under their control. Their personal associations are restricted. In some jurisdictions, probationers are not permitted to drive an automobile; in others, driving is permitted only with prior permission of the supervising officer. Normally probationers may not leave the county or state without permission, which is granted infrequently and only for extraordinary reasons. They are required to refrain from violating laws, and they must cooperate with their probation officers. In some cases courts impose curfews or restrictions on where probationers may live. Their civil rights may be affected as well. Usually they are not permitted to marry, engage in business, or sign contracts without permission.

Probation conditions must comply with certain court restrictions. Just as courts have been reluctant to interfere with daily prison administration, traditionally they have also taken a hands-off policy toward the imposition of probation conditions. In recent years, however, courts have rejected some restrictions as constituting improper restraints on probationers' rights.

Several cases illustrate constitutional issues with regard to probation conditions. A federal court in Illinois held that it was reasonable for a court to order a probationer to get a paying job rather than become a missionary. The probationer had been ordered to pay restitution and fines after conviction of a series of religious scams. A federal court in New York held that it is unconstitutional to require a convicted drunk driver to attend Alcoholics Anonymous (AA) meetings while on probation. The court noted the spiritual and religious nature of AA meetings and held that requiring one to attend them violated the probationer's First Amendment rights (see Appendix A). The case was affirmed on appeal, and the U.S. Supreme Court refused to review it.[38]

In a Wisconsin case the state supreme court held that the trial judge did not abuse discretion is his decision that, as a condition of probation, the father of nine children must agree not to father any more children unless he could prove that he could support them. The Wisconsin Supreme Court gave its reasons, along with the factual allegations, in the following brief excerpt. The state court twice denied a reconsideration, and the U.S. Supreme Court declined to hear the case.[39]

United States vs Myers

State v. Oakley

We conclude that in light of Oakley's ongoing victimization of his nine children and extraordinarily troubling record manifesting his disregard for the law, this anomalous condition—imposed on a convicted felon facing the far more restrictive and punitive sanction of prison—is not overly broad and is reasonably related to Oakley's rehabilitation. Simply put, because Oakley was convicted of intentionally refusing to pay child support—a felony in

Wisconsin—and could have been imprisoned for six years, which would have eliminated his right to procreate altogether during those six years, this probation condition, which infringes on his right to procreate during his term of probation, is not invalid under these facts. Accordingly, we hold that the circuit court did not erroneously exercise its discretion.

A recent example of a case in which the appellate court did not approve of a probation condition is that of *United States* v. *Sofsky*. This case involved a defendant who entered a guilty plea to receiving more than 1,000 still and moving pictures of child pornography over the Internet. One of his probation conditions was that he would not access the Internet without the permission of his probation officer. The appellate court stated its position regarding the probation condition as follows:

> We conclude that the [probation] condition exceeds even the broad discretion of the sentencing judge with respect to conditions of supervised release, and must be substantially modified. [In a separate action the court also rejected Sofsky's appeal of his conviction. The U.S. Supreme Court refused to review the decision.][40]

Other recent cases demonstrate varying probation conditions approved by courts. The key is whether the conditions are reasonably related to the offense for which the individual is on probation. For example, an order requiring that a probationer "make every attempt to avoid being in contact with children" was held reasonable in a case involving an offender who had been convicted of a sex crime against a 12-year-old. The court held that the condition fell within the statutory provision "as the court, in its discretion, deems reasonably necessary to insure that the defendant will lead a law-abiding life or to assist him to do so." It also met the provision that the court has discretion to require a defendant to "[s]atisfy any other conditions reasonably related to his [or her] rehabilitation."[41]

A probation order designed solely to embarrass or humiliate an offender may not be upheld. A California judge "whose penchant for innovative sentencing has made him a media darling"[42] ordered an offender to wear a T-shirt proclaiming, "I am on felony probation for theft." That condition was held to be a violation of the offender's right to privacy. The appellate court noted that the statute provides that a purpose of probation is rehabilitation, but the requirement in question was designed to expose the offender to public ridicule and humiliation. Further, the order would have made it impossible for the offender to fulfill another probation condition, which was to get a job. The court stated that the questionable probation order

[*People v. Griffith* handwritten annotation]

> could adversely affect [the probationer's] ability to carry on activities having no possible relationship to the offense for which he was convicted or to future criminality. . . . The condition was unreasonably overbroad and as such was invalid.[43]

Likewise, requiring that one convicted of aggravated battery erect a large sign on his property stating, "WARNING! A violent felon lives here: Enter at your own risk," was held to be unreasonable. The condition might hinder the offender's rehabilitation as well as cause psychological problems for him and for the innocent members of his family. The sign was viewed as a "drastic departure" from the state's sentencing provisions.[44] Warnings might be appropriate, however, in some cases, such as those involving sex offenders.

[*People v Hackler* handwritten annotation]

Finally, an issue arises concerning prohibiting a probationer from engaging in an activity such as drinking alcohol, which is legal for other adults. In 1997, a California court upheld abstention from alcohol as a probation condition. The court noted that, when a probationer is required to abstain from conduct that is otherwise legal, the requirement must be "reasonably related to the underlying crime or to future criminality." The court cited data linking alcohol use and crime, concluding, "It is well-documented that the use of alcohol lessens self-control and thus may create a situation where the user has reduced ability to stay away from drugs." The probationer in this case had been placed on probation for three years after a guilty plea to simple possession of methamphetamine and possession of the substance for sale.[45]

[*People v Meyer* handwritten annotation]

11-4d Probation Supervision

▶ Probation officer
A government official responsible for supervising persons on probation and for writing the presentence reports on offenders.

One of the primary functions of the **probation officer** is to supervise probationers. The type and degree of supervision vary. In some probation departments it is the probation officer's job to counsel probationers. In other departments a probation officer is expected to supervise only the activities of probationers, and that supervision may be limited. The model that is chosen depends on the availability of resources, the caseloads of probation officers, their professional training, probationers' needs, and many other factors. Essentially the officer's function is to assist the probationer in making important transitions—from law-abiding citizen to convicted offender; from free citizen to one under supervision; and, finally, back to free citizen.

Some probation officers may prefer to have close interpersonal relationships with the clients they are assisting. The literature contains numerous articles discussing ways in which probation officers can improve their supervisory relationships with their clients. Many articles discuss the expectation that probation officers will go beyond supervision and serve as treatment agents for their clients. Treatment of probationers may be multidimensional. Many probationers need to learn the social skills involved in successful interpersonal relationships. Most offenders have long histories of personal failures, and probation officers are crucial people in helping them increase confidence in themselves and acquire the social skills and habits necessary for successful interpersonal relationships.

When probation officers go beyond the supervision of their clients and begin a treatment process, some problems may occur. Many officers lack sufficient training in treatment techniques. Even if probation officers are trained, skilled, and licensed in treatment techniques, the very nature of the position may preclude successful treatment. Because of the legal nature of probation work, realistically probation officers cannot promise the confidentiality that an effective treatment relationship needs. In reality, probation officers have a conflict of interest. The officers not only represent the interests of the state in taking action against violations of probation agreements or of the law but also represent the interests of clients in treatment and supervision.

The National Institute of Corrections (NIC) has suggested that probation, parole, and community corrections staff need more training to cope with their dual roles of treatment *and* surveillance. In the past these workers were primarily social workers who focused on the rehabilitation of their clients. While performing that role only, the staff rarely had to be concerned with safety. Now, however, the supervisors may be in danger of physical harm as they check on their clients to determine whether they are violating the terms of their releases, even arresting them in some cases. In a recent study the NIC emphasized that social workers need training in how to protect themselves from physical harm by their clients. The report cited examples in which probation and parole officers were injured, some killed, while performing their jobs. Among other recommendations, the NIC listed appropriate training in the use of firearms under the circumstances in which these supervisory officers must perform. Officers should be trained to recognize and respond appropriately to the escalation of violence, or what the report called *continuum training*. In conclusion, the NIC stated as follows:

> Under stress, in a crisis, officers instinctively respond the way they have been trained. If trained only in verbal skills and then given a firearm, an officer will likely first try to control a situation verbally and then jump to the use of lethal force. In failing to provide defensive tactics training, the agency is failing to provide the officer with skills to deal with statistically the largest assailant population: offenders who use physical assault that requires a response of less-than-lethal force.[46]

Probation supervision has come under severe criticism, especially when persons on probation have committed additional crimes. In 1999, a panel of probation experts (including several from the American Parole and Probation Association), called the Reinventing Probation Council (RPC), suggested much stronger probation supervision, with such measures as no "free" violations—that is, any probation violation would carry sanctions. Probationers would not be told in advance that they might be subject to drug testing. Furthermore, probation supervisors should meet with probationers in the probationers' homes at all hours—not just regular probation office hours—a process the panel called *fortress probation*. The panel recommended lighter caseloads, noting the absurdity of expecting any meaningful supervision when an officer has a caseload of 500. The panel also noted that attitudes and policies of probation staff must be changed. For example, the policy of avoiding dangerous neighborhoods may increase the safety of officers, but it makes it essentially impossible to be a probation officer, as many probationers live in those areas. The RPC concluded as follows: "We believe probation is at once the most troubled and the most promising part of America's criminal justice system."[47]

The subject of probation supervision needs to be explored in more detail. In the past, researchers debated the effect of the officer's caseload size on the success or failure of probationers. That issue is not settled, and many factors are important in determining what type of caseload is most efficient. Today the focus of probation has shifted in many jurisdictions. No longer is rehabilitation the primary purpose of probation. The function of probation is to divert from prison persons who might not need that intensive security and supervision and, through that diversion process, reduce the populations that are swelling prisons. It is argued that many offenders can succeed on probation if they are under intensive probation supervision (IPS).

IPS programs began developing in the 1960s. Two researchers who studied earlier programs suggested that three conclusions could be drawn from those analyses:

1. Intensive supervision is difficult to achieve.
2. Close contact does not guarantee greater success.
3. Intensive supervision produces an interactive effect.

The third conclusion refers to the evidence that, although IPS appears to assist some offenders, "it is entirely reasonable that intensive supervision might interfere with the functionings of some clients who would otherwise be successful."[48]

In a comparison of IPS clients with regular probation clients, it was found that the former had more technical probation violations, but that probably was the result of the fact that they were watched more closely. The IPS probation clients, however, were not more likely to be rearrested or incarcerated. However, if IPS does not result in lower recidivism, why continue with the program, given its higher costs over minimal-supervision probation? Further research needs to be conducted, but one consideration is that probation conditions for IPS may be too severe.[49]

A research monograph that contains several articles on IPS, including a review of several specific programs and the research findings concerning those and other programs, concluded that more research is needed on the effectiveness of IPS. Although there is some evidence that increased supervision decreases recidivism among some offenders, "there is mounting evidence that increased supervision of low-risk offenders actually increases their rate of failure." The researchers stated that the "research issues are complex, but society can ill afford to let them go unanswered."[50]

11-5 Parole

Parole is an administrative decision to release an offender after he or she has served time on a sentence to a correctional facility. It may be distinguished from other methods of release from prison. Some inmates are released before serving their full sentences because they have accumulated credits given for good behavior during incarceration. The amount of prison time that may be reduced for good time credits is determined by prison policies or by legislation. Some offenders are not released from prison until they serve the full term imposed at sentencing, at which time they must be released.

Rehabilitation, justice, prison overcrowding: these are the three main reasons for parole in the United States. Ironically, the movement to abolish parole, a movement that paralleled the one toward determinate sentencing in the late 1970s and 1980s, was propelled by the cry for justice, disillusionment with rehabilitation, and the argument that the lack of justice in the parole decision process hindered rehabilitation. Parole was called the "never-knowing system" by many inmates who argued that it was granted for arbitrary and capricious reasons.

Parole has come under severe attack in the United States, primarily as a result of violent crimes committed by persons released on parole. For example, the killing of a police officer in New York City in 1998 led to proposals to abolish parole. Officer Anthony Mosomillo, age 36 and the father of two, was called a hero by New York City's mayor, who proclaimed Mosomillo "an exceptional police officer." Mosomillo was gunned down by a parolee whom he and his fellow officers were attempting to arrest for a parole violation. The offender, Jose Serrano, managed to get another officer's gun and shot Mosomillo four times in the neck and body. Before he died, Mosomillo killed Serrano.

Serrano was on parole after serving time for a drug conviction, but he was wanted for a parole violation when he was arrested in April 1998 on a minor drug offense. At that time he was released from custody after giving police an alias. He was ordered to return to court on 18 May. Serrano had been fingerprinted, but those prints were not available when he gave police the alias.

When Serrano failed to show up for his 18 May court date, a warrant was issued for his arrest. Mosomillo and his colleagues apprehended Serrano, who was hiding under a bed. Serrano's girlfriend, who was on probation until the year 2005 for her conviction for smuggling heroin, struggled with a female officer, whose gun was knocked away. Serrano then grabbed the gun and began shooting. Mosomillo was taken to a hospital, where he died—with his wife and children, one a toddler, by his side.

The killing of Officer Mosomillo by a parolee led to calls for the abolition of New York's parole system. In August 1998, the state enacted a statute that limits access to early release for first-time violent felons. The statute requires that these felons serve 85 percent of their maximum sentences before they are covered by mandatory release. Previously these offenders were released after they had completed two-thirds of their maximum sentences, unless they had been involved in disciplinary problems while in prison. The law is the result of lobbying by the parents of Jenna Grieshaber, who was killed in her Albany apartment in 1997, and it is called "Jenna's Law," although it was Mosomillo's death that gave impetus to the law's passing. Spotlight 11-3 contains another example of reaction to the crimes of a parolee.

Such crimes give rise to cries for parole abolition. After a decade of attempts, the federal criminal code was revised when President Ronald Reagan signed the Comprehensive Crime Control Act of 1984. That act abolished early release by parole in the federal system and, over a five-year period, phased out the U.S. Parole Commission. Under the statute, inmates in the federal system may receive only a maximum of 15 percent good time credit on their sentences. Under the former statute, they were eligible for parole after serving only half of their sentences.[51]

By January 1999, 15 states had abolished parole boards, although criminologists had warned that there was no significant evidence that abolishing parole reduces crime. Some of the states that had abolished parole boards later reinstituted them because of prison overcrowding, which resulted in a need to release some inmates before they had completed their sentences. Some politicians argued that parole boards are such failures that their abolition would have no effect on criminal justice systems, anyway. Others insisted that parole boards may actually result in some inmates serving longer terms than they would under some sentencing structures that allow for a reduction in sentences for good time and other reasons. For example, criminologist Joan Petersilia notes that Richard Allen Davis, who was convicted of killing Polly Klaas (whose case was discussed in Chapter 8), was rejected for parole six times before California abolished its parole board. But Davis had to be released after he had served a specified period of time; shortly thereafter, he killed Klaas. This crime led to the three strikes legislation in California and subsequently other states, as noted in Chapter 8.[52]

Despite the abolition of parole and its declining use in the 1980s and 1990s, in recent years some states have reevaluated the need for parole. In June 2003, the governor of New Mexico announced that he was opposed to building new prisons but that his state had one of the fastest-growing inmate populations in the country. Thus, early parole release, which was abolished in 1996 by the previous governor, was being considered as a viable solution to prison overcrowding. Some were skeptical, however, because of one of the state's most horrendous crimes, which had been committed by a person on parole.[53]

Spotlight 11-3   Paroled Murderer Convicted of Rape and Murder

In December 1969, Reginald McFadden and three other men were accused of killing a 60-year-old woman during a burglary. McFadden was convicted and sentenced to life without parole. In 1992, McFadden's sentence was commuted by a 4-to-1 vote of the Pennsylvania Board of Parole, but the board required that he spend 2 years in a halfway house program. Due to mistakes in paperwork and a long delay by the governor's office in signing the appropriate papers, McFadden did not enter a halfway house; nor did he receive any other type of supervised release.

By October 1994, McFadden was back in custody, charged with kidnapping, beating, and raping a 55-year-old woman. On 27 March 1995, he was indicted for the murder of Robert Silk, who was abducted from his home and killed. He was convicted of these crimes and sentenced to prison.

In 1997, McFadden sued the Department of Corrections for $1.05 million in damages, claiming that through "gross negligence" they had failed to rehabilitate him, thus causing the crimes he committed after his release. His case was dismissed, but later in the year it led to the passage of Senate legislation limiting frivolous lawsuits filed by inmates. Pennsylvania's attorney general, in praising the bill, noted that the state issued an average of 90 times a week, and many of those lawsuits are filed by inmates.[1]

After McFadden's rape conviction, the victim, Jeremy Brown, made a public statement. Brown described herself as the "only living victim" of the defendant. She promised to work to change the state's parole law. Brown spoke angrily about the trial in which McFadden served as his own attorney: "I think it is perfectly ludicrous that I was tortured by this man for five hours and then to have to sit there and answer his ridiculous questions.... I think it's crazy."[2]

When he was sentenced in 1996, McFadden told the judge he was proud that he was the symbol of "everything that is wrong with society" and that he would take the life of the judge "as quick as you can blink your eye.... Think about that." In a sentencing the previous year, McFadden told the judge not to give him any mercy. "If I was sitting where you are at, I wouldn't show you a bit of mercy."[3]

It is expected that McFadden will spend the rest of his life in prison.

1. "Pennsylvania Attorney General Fisher Applauds Legislation Limiting Frivolous Lawsuits," PR Newswire, State and Regional News (4 June 1997).
2. "Rape Victim Takes Spotlight and Aims It at Parole System," *New York Times* (25 August 1995), p. 1.
3. "Why We Need the Death Penalty," *The Record* (Bergen Record Corp. 15 April 1996), p. 16.

In recent years paroles have been denied to several well-known criminals. In 2000, Mark David Chapman, who had murdered John Lennon, was denied parole. In 2002, a follower of Charles Manson, Leslie Van Houten, was turned down for parole for the 14th time. Van Houten was involved in the Manson cult killings of Rosemary and Leno La Bianca in 1969. Van Houten and her lawyers claimed that she was under the spell of Manson when she engaged in those murders. She stated, "I believed that he was Jesus Christ.... I bought into it lock, stock and barrel." The prosecutor argued that Van Houten knew exactly what she was doing. But even if Van Houton's parole had been recommended by the state's parole board, she probably would have remained in prison. In California, parole recommendations must be approved by the governor. During his tenure, California Governor Gray Davis approved only 2 of the 148 cases recommended to him, and both of those involved women who claimed they had been physically abused by the men they killed. The battered woman defense was not permitted in California until 1992.[54]

Governor Davis (who was recalled as governor in the fall of 2003) frequently refused (as permitted by state law) to grant parole to offenders recommended for parole by the State Board of Prison Terms. Just three days after his election in 2003, Governor Arnold Schwarzenegger paroled a man who had been convicted of murder; in November 2003, he paroled a woman who had been convicted of killing her husband's lover. Rosario Munoz, whose parole was rejected twice by Governor Davis, was recommended by the board for parole because she was not considered at high risk of reoffending and she had raised money for her victim's daughter by selling portraits that she had painted.[55]

For those in California who oppose these and other paroles, a study can be cited in support of their positions. A state watchdog agency, the Little Hoover Commission, published its findings in 2003: the parole system in California was a "costly, colossal failure," resulting in the fact that 67 percent of the offenders incarcerated in the state each year are parolees who have violated one or more terms of their previous release. According to one California paper, "[T]his staggering return rate, double the national average, means that California is getting a miserable return on its $1.4 billion parole system."[56]

In 2004, it was reported that only 21 percent of California's parolees complete parole without being returned to prison, but it was also noted that many of those returned were the result of decisions of parole officers, not courts. A study of the parole system emphasized that many of today's parole officers have backgrounds as prison guards, unlike previous ones, who were usually trained as probation officers or social workers. The result is a tendency to "nail and jail" parolees, sending them back to prison, rather than referring them to community treatment programs. In 2004, the California Department of Corrections announced that it was instituting a graduated sanctions policy, using such programs as halfway houses, electronic monitoring, and restitution, rather than sending so many parolees back to prison. The state was facing a $200 million budget deficit in its prison system at the end of 2004. That compared with a $544 million deficit at the end of 2003.[57]

The release of particular offenders on parole has resulted in severe criticism. A parole in London, England, that shocked many was granted in 2001 to the two 18-year-olds who had kidnapped and killed James Bulger, a 2-year old, when the offenders were only 10 years old. Bulger's mother said she was devastated by the news and that the killers, Robert Thompson and Jon Venables, should have served at least 15 years. Thompson and Venables were given new identities (new birth certificates, social security cards, bank accounts, identification cards, and even invented pasts) before they were released. A judge had ruled that they were no longer threats to society and that they should be released before they reached the age of 19, which would qualify them for incarceration in a prison for young convicts.[58]

In the United States, a 2003 parole also brought intense reaction. Kathy Boudin, age 60, a 1960s radical who served 22 years in prison for participating in an armed car robbery that resulted in deaths, was paroled from the Bedford Hills Correctional Facility in New York. The radical groups the Black Liberation Army and the Weather Underground stole $1.6 million from a Brink's armored car at a mall in 1981. They said the money would be distributed to poor African Americans. Boudin, who is white, pleaded guilty to robbery and murder in 1984. She was a passenger in the rented van used for the getaway after the robbery, during which a security guard was killed. Two police officers were slain during the shootout with the robbers. Boudin's request for a parole was denied in May 2003 but granted in August. The state's governor, George E. Pataki, denounced the parole board's decision and declared that there would be changes in the parole system. The parole commissioners refused requests to reconsider their decision. While she was in prison, Boudin had helped organize programs for AIDS patients as well as inmates who had children; upon her release she had a job at Manhattan's St. Luke's Hospital, developing programs for HIV-positive women.[59]

11-5a The Organization of Parole Systems

The organization of parole is complex. One reason for this complexity is the variety of sentencing structures under which parole systems must operate. In jurisdictions where sentences are long with little time off for good behavior, parole may involve a long supervision period. In jurisdictions where sentences are short, parole may be unimportant as a form of release, and supervision is for shorter periods.

Despite the wide variety of parole programs, there are three organizational models: institutional, independent authority, and consolidated models. Under the *institutional model,* found mainly in the juvenile field, the decision to release is made by the correctional staff. The assumption is that those who work closely with the offender are in the best position to make a decision concerning his or her release. Arguments against this model are that institutions may make decisions in their own best interests, not in the best interests of the offender or the community. Decisions may be based on institutional overcrowding. Staff members may be less objective in the decisions because they are closely involved with the offender. Abuse of discretion may be a greater possibility under this model than in the independent authority model.

As a result of those problems, many parole boards for adult correctional facilities follow the *independent authority model,* in which the parole board is established as an agency independent of the institution. This model has been criticized severely. Frequently the parole board is composed of people who know little or nothing about corrections. The board is removed from the institution and may not understand what is taking place there. Decisions may be made for inappropriate reasons; as a result, parole boards may release those who should not be paroled and retain those who should be released.

A new model has emerged, a *consolidated model* of organization for parole boards, and there is a trend toward adopting it. This trend accompanies a move toward consolidating correctional facilities into one common administration, usually a department of corrections. Under the consolidated model, the parole-granting board is within the administration of the department of corrections but possesses independent powers.

It is important for parole board members to have an understanding of all correctional programs in the system. It is more likely that such understanding will occur under the consolidated model than under the other two models. However, the board should possess independence, so that it can act as a check on the rest of the system.

With the exception of the institutional model, most parole systems are located in the executive branch of government and are administered at the state level. Most systems have one parole board, whose members are appointed by the executive branch. In most states that board has final authority to decide who is granted parole (see again the discussion of the parole of Kathy Boudin). In other states the board makes recommendations to someone else who has the final decision-making authority. That person might be the governor, as noted earlier concerning the state of California.

Some parole board members serve full-time; others serve part-time. They may or may not have specific qualifications for the position. As political appointees, they may be appointed for reasons unrelated to expertise in the kind of decision making that is the board's function. The board may have the authority to revoke as well as to grant parole.

The parole system has a division responsible for parole services, which includes parole supervision. Parole services may be delegated to smaller divisions throughout the state. Generally the parole system provides some parole services at the institutions in which inmates are incarcerated. Often one person has the responsibility of interviewing all those eligible for parole and making written recommendations to the parole board.

Parole officers should have the same qualifications as probation officers. Increasingly professional organizations and commissions are recommending that parole and probation officers hold a bachelor's degree, and some recommend that additional education be required. In-service training is very important as well and should be continued throughout the officer's period of work and evaluated periodically.

Finally, in some states parole as such has been replaced with statutory provisions for early release when prison and jail populations reach a crisis stage. Even in those cases, however, parole supervision remains important.

11-5b The Parole Process

In jurisdictions with a parole release system, the parole process is very important, and adequate preparation should be made for the parole hearing. The inmate's ability to convey an improved self-image and to demonstrate an ability to work with others and stick with a job may influence the board's decision. Inmates who have maintained strong family ties may have an edge in the decision-making process. Inmates who have had successful experiences on work release, education release, or furlough may also have an advantage. And a good behavior record in the institution may be viewed favorably.

Inmates should be told what to expect regarding the timing of the decision and the kinds of questions to anticipate. Demeanor and behavior are important; some inmates are put through mock decision-making situations to prepare them for the parole board hearing. It is also important to prepare the inmate for the parole board's decision; a negative decision may have a disastrous effect on an inmate who has not been adequately prepared for that result.

Eligibility for Parole

The determination of eligibility for parole varies, but usually there are statutory specifications, such as requiring that inmates serve a certain percentage of their sentences before they are eligible for parole. Good time credits may reduce that period. Many jurisdictions require that inmates have job commitments before parole is granted; others grant parole on the condition that the inmate has a job by the time he or she is released on parole.

The Parole Hearing

The parole candidate may appear before the entire parole board or only a committee of the board. Larger boards may split into smaller groups to process paroles faster. Usually the parole hearing is held at the institution where the inmate is incarcerated. However, if only a few inmates at one institution are eligible, they might be transported by the state to a central location for the hearing.

Many parole systems allow inmates to participate in the hearings, although that participation might be very short. This gives inmates a greater sense of fairness in that they have an opportunity to express to the board members their perceptions of their chances for success.

Numerous factors may be considered in a parole decision. Those factors require information from the past, present, and future. They include statements made by the sentencing judge concerning the reasons for sentencing, as well as the inmate's plans for the future. They include disciplinary action, if any, that has occurred during the inmate's incarceration. Documentation on changes in attitude and ability are also important. The crime for which the inmate is serving time, along with any prior experience on parole or probation, is considered, as are family relationships, the ability to get along with others, and jobs.

Parole Board Discretion

Historically parole boards have had almost total discretionary power in determining parole. Parole was viewed as a privilege, not a right. Because parole was not a right, no reasons had to be given for denial. Elements of due process were not required at the time the decision was made. Courts reasoned that due process was not required at the determination of parole because parole granting was not an adversary proceeding. Parole granting was a complicated decision, and the parole board needed to be able to use evidence that would not be admissible in an adversary proceeding, such as a trial. The general lack of due process at the parole decision stage resulted in bitter complaints from inmates. Perhaps the late Justice Hugo Black of the U.S. Supreme Court best summarized the view of many inmates toward the parole board:

> In the course of my reading—by no means confined to law—I have reviewed many of the world's religions. The tenets of many faiths hold the deity to be a trinity. Seemingly, the parole boards by whatever names designated in the various states have in too many instances sought to enlarge this to include themselves as members.[60]

Due Process and the Parole Hearing

The Fourteenth Amendment (see Appendix A) prohibits the denial of life, liberty, or property without due process of law. Claims by inmates for due process at the parole decision are based on the argument that they have a liberty interest in parole. The U.S. Supreme Court has held that, although there is no constitutional right to parole, statutes may create a protected liberty interest. When that is the case, parole may not be denied if the conditions of those statutes are met.

How do we know whether a protected liberty interest has been created and therefore due process is required? According to the U.S. Supreme Court, if a state creates a parole system and provides that, if inmates meet certain conditions they are entitled to parole, a liberty interest has been created. Under those circumstances, the state has created a presumption that inmates who meet certain requirements will be granted parole. If the statute is general, however, giving broad discretion to the parole board, no liberty interest is created.

In *Greenholtz* v. *Nebraska* the U.S. Supreme Court examined the Nebraska statute, which provided for two hearings before a final parole decision. At the first hearing, an informal one, the inmate is interviewed and all relevant information in the files is considered. If the board decides the inmate is not ready for parole, parole is denied and the inmate is given reasons. If the board finds evidence that the inmate might be ready for parole, it notifies the inmate of a formal hearing, at which time the inmate may present evidence, call witnesses, and be represented by retained counsel.

In *Greenholtz* the Court found that a liberty interest was created by the Nebraska statute but that the procedures required by the statute met due process requirements. "The Nebraska procedure affords an opportunity to be heard and when parole is denied it informs the inmate in what respects he falls short of qualifying for parole; this affords the process that is due under these circumstances. The Constitution does not require more."[61]

In 1987, while analyzing the Montana parole statute, the U.S. Supreme Court reaffirmed its holding in *Greenholtz* that, although the existence of a parole system does not by itself give rise to an expectation of parole, states may create that expectation or presumption by the wording of their statutes. In *Board of Pardons* v. *Allen* the Supreme Court held that the Montana statute, like the Nebraska statute examined in *Greenholtz*, creates an expectation of parole, provided certain conditions are met. Thus, if those conditions are met, parole must be granted.[62]

In both of these cases, the U.S. Supreme Court emphasized that the language—the use of the word *shall* rather than *may*—creates the presumption that parole will be granted if certain specified conditions are met. Thus, the Supreme Court injected some procedural requirements into the parole-granting process in the states that use mandatory language in their parole statutes.

Control of Parole Decisions

Parole boards are criticized by inmates, and many scholars find some parole decisions to be arbitrary and capricious. Criticism of parole decisions has led to the suggestion that some restrictions be placed on this important decision-making process.

In the 1920s, sociologists developed scales to be used in situations such as predicting success in marriage. Some of those scales were adapted to the parole decision. Charts involved factors such as age, education, and prior criminal record to predict whether most inmates with certain characteristics would be successful if paroled. The application of prediction scales yielded conflicting results, although the various approaches are difficult to compare. The only general conclusion that might be drawn from statistical prediction studies is that it may be easier to predict nonviolent than violent crime.

Social scientists have used the clinical approach to prediction as well, looking at the specific characteristics of a particular inmate and trying to predict whether that person would be successful on parole. Generally this approach has led to an overprediction of dangerousness, which means that fewer inmates who are thought to be dangerous actually are.

Another method of control over parole is to require written reasons for denying parole. In the past most parole boards did not give reasons for denial, and courts did not require them to do so. Today some jurisdictions that have retained parole require that reasons be given for its denial. Although the result may be only a checklist given to the inmate, this information lets the inmate know what is required for a successful parole hearing in the future.

Parole guidelines are used as a method of control over parole decision making. Not only has the use of systemwide guidelines given inmates a feeling of greater fairness in the parole process, but also, in some states, guidelines have had the advantage of being used to reduce prison overcrowding. Critics of objective guidelines for parole decision making argue that they do not result in greater fairness and may actually increase prison overcrowding.

Parole Conditions

Parole conditions are an essential element of the release process. The U.S. Supreme Court has stated,

> The essence of parole is release from prison, before the completion of sentence, on the condition that the prisoner abide by certain rules during the balance of the sentence. . . .
> [T]he conditions of parole . . . prohibit, either absolutely or conditionally, behavior that is deemed dangerous to the restoration of the individual into normal society.[63]

Parole conditions vary from jurisdiction to jurisdiction and are similar to probation conditions. Many parole conditions have been challenged in court. They are valid, however, if they are reasonably related to the crimes in question, if they are not against public policy, and if it is reasonably possible for the parolee to comply with them.

11-5c   Parole Supervision

When inmates are released from prison on parole, they must report to a parole supervisor or **parole officer.** They are told the circumstances under which they are to report, how often, when and where to file reports, and what to expect regarding visits from parole officers.

Parole supervision has come under attack. The surveillance function of parole officers may be undermined by large caseloads; officers may not have time for anything more than brief contacts with their parolees. Because of this, some argue that home visits and monthly reports are costly and useless devices for the control of parolee behavior and that this function would be better performed by police. Changing the conditions of parole supervision is another suggested reform. Conditions that have only slight relevance to criminal behavior could be eliminated. This change would leave parole officers free to concentrate on the service aspect of supervision: helping with employment, housing, and other adjustments to the community.[64]

> ▶ **Parole officer** A government employee who supervises and counsels inmates paroled to the community.

11-6   Constitutional Issues

Some of the constitutional issues that govern probation and parole are the same as those that govern other aspects of criminal justice systems and have been discussed earlier in the text. Examples are due process, equal protection, and unusual punishment. Other constitutional issues are discussed here. We begin with search and seizure.

11-6a   Search and Seizure

In 1987 in *Griffin* v. *Wisconsin,* the U.S. Supreme Court held that probation officers who suspect their clients of probation violations may search their homes (without a warrant) for evidence of such. The Ninth Circuit held that the standard established by *Griffin* does not apply to law enforcement officers searching for evidence of a crime. But in 2001 in *United States* v. *Knights,* the U.S. Supreme Court held that the Fourth Amendment's protection against unreasonable searches and seizures (see Appendix A) is restricted in the case of probationers and that the warrantless search of a probationer's home by law enforcement officers in this case was constitutional. The facts and the reasoning are articulated in the following excerpt from the case.[65]

United States v. Knights

A California court sentenced respondent Mark James Knights to summary probation for a drug offense. The probation order included the following conditions; that Knights would "submit his ... person, property, place of residence, vehicle, personal effects, to search at anytime [sic], with or without a search warrant, warrant of arrest or reasonable cause by any probation officer or law enforcement officer." Knights signed the probation order, which stated immediately above his signature that "I HAVE RECEIVED A COPY, READ, AND UNDERSTAND THE ABOVE TERMS AND CONDITIONS OF PROBATION AND AGREE TO ABIDE BY SAME." In this case, we decide whether a search pursuant to this probation condition, and supported by reasonable suspicion, satisfies the Fourth Amendment.

Three days after Knights was placed on probation, a Pacific Gas & Electric (PG&E) power transformer and adjacent Pacific Bell telecommunications vault near the Napa County Airport were pried open and set on fire, causing an estimated $1.5 million in damage. Brass padlocks had been removed and a gasoline accelerant had been used to ignite the fire. This incident was the latest in more than 30 recent acts of vandalism against PG&E facilities in

Napa County. Suspicion for these acts had long focused on Knights and his friend, Steven Simoneau. The incidents began after PG&E had filed a theft-of-services complaint against Knights and discontinued his electrical service for failure to pay his bill. Detective Todd Hancock of the Napa County Sheriff's Department had noticed that the acts of vandalism coincided with Knight's court appearance dates concerning the theft of PG&E services. And just a week before the arson, a sheriff's deputy had stopped Knights and Simoneau near a PG&E gas line and observed pipes and gasoline in Simoneau's pickup truck.

After the PG&E arson, a sheriff's deputy drove by Knight's residence, where he saw Simoneau's truck parked in front. The deputy felt the hood of the truck. It was warm. Detective Hancock decided to set up surveillance of Knights's apartment. At about 3:10 the next morning, Simoneau exited the apartment carrying three cylindrical items. Detective Hancock believed the items were pipe bombs. Simoneau walked across the street to the bank of the Napa River, and Hancock heard three splashes. Simoneau returned without the cylinders and drove away in his truck. Detective Hancock entered the driveway and observed a number of suspicious objects in the truck: a Molotov cocktail and explosive materials, a gasoline can, and two brass padlocks that fit the description of those removed from the PG&E transformer vault.

After viewing the objects in Simoneau's truck, Detective Hancock decided to conduct a search of Knights's apartment. Detective Hancock was aware of the search condition in Knights's probation order and thus believed that a warrant was not necessary. The search revealed a detonation cord, ammunition, liquid chemicals, instruction manuals on chemistry and electrical circuitry, bolt cutters, telephone pole-climbing spurs, drug paraphernalia, and a brass padlock stamped "PG&E."

Knights was arrested, and a federal grand jury subsequently indicted him for conspiracy to commit arson, for possession of an unregistered destructive device, and being a felon in possession of ammunition. Knights moved to suppress the evidence obtained during the search of his apartment. The District Court held that Detective Hancock had "reasonable suspicion" to believe that Knights was involved with incendiary materials. The District Court nonetheless granted the motion to suppress on the ground that the search was for "investigatory" rather than "probationary" purposes. The Court of Appeals for the Ninth Circuit affirmed. The Court of Appeals relied on its earlier decisions holding that the search condition in Knights's probation order "must be seen as limited to probation searches, and must stop short of investigation searches."

The Supreme Court of California has rejected this distinction and upheld searches pursuant to the California probation condition "whether the purpose of the search is to monitor the probationer or to serve some other law enforcement purpose." We granted certiorari to assess the constitutionality of searches made pursuant to this common California probation condition.

Certainly nothing in the condition of probation suggests that it was confined to searches bearing upon probationary status and nothing more. The search condition provides that Knights will submit to a search "by any probation officer or law enforcement officer" and does not mention anything about purpose. The question then is whether the Fourth Amendment limits searches pursuant to this probation condition to those with a "probationary" purpose. . . .

[The Court refers to the reasoning of *Griffin,* interpreting that case as providing that a "special need" exists for the state to supervise probationers in such a way as to ensure that they honor the terms of their release.]

In Knights's view, apparently shared by the Court of Appeals, a warrantless search of a probationer satisfies the Fourth Amendment only if it is just like the search at issue in

Griffin—i.e., a "special needs" search conducted by a probation officer monitoring whether the probationer is complying with probation restrictions. [The U.S. Supreme Court stated its disagreement with this position.] . . .

The Government, advocating the approach of the Supreme Court of California, contends that the search satisfied the Fourth Amendment under the "consent" rationale of cases such as [case names and citations omitted]. In the Government's view, Knights's acceptance of the search condition was voluntary because he had the option of rejecting probation and going to prison instead, which the Government argues is analogous to the voluntary decision defendants often make to waive their right to a trial and accept a plea bargain. . . . [The Court stated that it need not decide the consent issue] because we conclude that the search of Knights was reasonable under our general Fourth Amendment approach of "examining the totality of the circumstances."

The touchstone of the Fourth Amendment is reasonableness, and the reasonableness of a search is determined "by assessing, on the one hand, the degree to which it intrudes upon an individual's privacy and, on the other, the degree to which it is needed for the promotion of legitimate governmental interests." . . .

The judge who sentenced Knights to probation determined that it was necessary to condition the probation on Knights's acceptance of the search provision. It was reasonable to conclude that the search condition would further the two primary goals of probation—rehabilitation and protecting society from future criminal violations. The probation order clearly expressed the search condition and Knights was unambiguously informed of it. The probation condition thus significantly diminished Knights's reasonable expectation of privacy. . . .

The State has a dual concern with a probationer. On the one hand is the hope that he will successfully complete probation and be reintegrated back into the community. On the other is the concern, quite justified, that he will be more likely to engage in criminal conduct than an ordinary member of the community. The view of the Court of Appeals in this case would require the State to shut its eyes to the latter concern and concentrate only on the former. But we hold that the Fourth Amendment does not put the State to such a choice. Its interest in apprehending violators of the criminal law, thereby protecting potential victims of criminal enterprise, may therefore justifiably focus on probationers in a way that it does not on the ordinary citizen.

We hold that the balance of these considerations requires no more than reasonable suspicion to conduct a search of this probationer's house. The degree of individualized suspicion required of a search is a determination of when there is a sufficiently high probability that criminal conduct is occurring to make the intrusion on the individual's privacy interest reasonable. Although the Fourth Amendment ordinarily requires the degree of probability embodied in the term "probable cause," a lesser degree satisfies the Constitution when the balance of governmental and private interests makes such a standard reasonable. . . .

The District Court found, and Knights concedes, that the search in this case was supported by reasonable suspicion. We therefore hold that the warrantless search of Knights, supported by reasonable suspicion and authorized by a condition of probation, was reasonable within the meaning of the Fourth Amendment. The judgment of the Court of Appeals is reversed, and the cause is remanded for further proceedings not inconsistent with this opinion.

The *Knights* case is included here not only to demonstrate the reduced privacy rights of probationers but to emphasize the U.S. Supreme Court's reasoning regarding balancing those rights against public safety. Some lawyers argue that this case has broad implications for the war on terrorism. As an attorney for the Criminal Justice Legal Foundation in

Sacramento, California, stated, "This decision is important because it recognizes that public safety, rather than the privacy rights of criminals, should be the government's chief concern when it comes to conditions of probation." And, according to a publication of the American Bar Association, "Although the case had nothing to do with the war on terrorism, some lawyers say the Sept. 11 attacks made it unlikely that any justice would champion the rights of a criminal who appeared intent on bombing a local utility."[66]

The Ninth Circuit was not to be deterred by the U.S. Supreme Court's reversal of its decision in *Knights*. In March 2003, the Ninth Circuit held unconstitutional the search of a parolee's home without a warrant and without reasonable suspicion. The case involved a parolee who had signed a "Fourth waiver," which gave permission for parole officers to search his home. The FBI agent who conducted the parole search admitted that he did not expect to find any evidence of criminal activity and nothing to connect the parolee to an unsolved robbery that had occurred two years previously. But he thought the pressure might entice the parolee to confess to that robbery. In less than two hours the parolee confessed. In the case of *United States* v. *Crawford*, a panel of the Ninth Circuit stated as follows:

> We hold that the search of Crawford's home without any reasonable suspicion, although pursuant to a parole condition authorizing such searches, violated the Fourth Amendment. Because Crawford's confession resulted from the suspicionless search of his residence, we reverse the district court's decision denying his motion to suppress and remand to allow him to withdraw his guilty plea.

The entire court of the Ninth Circuit agreed to hear this case and reached a different decision. The full court affirmed Crawford's conviction but remanded the case for resentencing. The U.S. Supreme Court declined to hear the case.[67]

11-6b   The Americans with Disabilities Act (ADA)

A second area of constitutional issues concerning probation and parole is that of the Americans with Disabilities Act (ADA). In 2002 in a California case, the Ninth Circuit Court of Appeals ruled that the ADA applies to parole decisions. The case of *Thompson* v. *Davis* involved two inmates incarcerated in Vacaville, California, and serving terms of 15 years-to-life for second-degree murder. The appellants argued that the Board of Prison Terms had not recommended them for parole because they were drug addicts. The federal court found that the appellants, who had received substance abuse treatment while in prison, had been drug-free for many years, one since 1984 and the other since 1990. Past drug addiction is considered a disability under the ADA. Both had been eligible for parole release since 1993. The Ninth Circuit ruled that the appellants met the conditions of the ADA and concluded, "Since a parole board may not deny African-Americans consideration for parole because of their race, and since Congress thinks that discriminating against a disabled person is like discriminating against an African-American, the parole board may not deny a disabled person parole because of his disability." The case was sent back to the district court to determine whether the paroles were denied because of the inmates' former drug addiction or for some other reason. The U.S. Supreme Court refused to review the case, thus permitting the Ninth Circuit decision to stand.[68]

11-6c   Probation and Parole Revocation

Historically **probation revocation** or **parole revocation** occurred without due process hearings. In probation cases in which the offender had been sentenced to prison but the judge suspended the sentence and placed the offender on probation, violation of probation conditions resulted in incarceration to serve the original sentence.

In 1967 in *Mempa* v. *Rhay*, the U.S. Supreme Court held that, when sentencing has been deferred and the offender placed on probation, the revocation of that probation and the determination of a sentence of incarceration require the presence of counsel. The Court reasoned that this situation, in which in reality the offender is being sentenced, invokes the requirement that, "at every stage of a criminal proceeding where substantial rights of a criminal accused may be affected," counsel is required. This case and others pertinent to

Probation revocation The process of declaring that a sentenced offender violated the terms of probation. If probation involved a suspended prison or jail sentence, the revocation may mean that the original sentence is invoked and the individual is sent to a prison or jail.

Parole revocation The process of returning a released offender to an institution for technical violations of parole conditions or for committing a new crime.

probation and parole revocation are summarized in Spotlight 11-4. Probation revocation that does not involve deciding a sentence, however, does not always require counsel, although there are some due process requirements.

Like probation, historically parole revocation was conducted with little concern for due process. Lack of due process was justified on the basis that parole was a privilege, not a right, or that it involved a contract. The inmate contracted to behave in exchange for freedom from incarceration. If that contract were broken, the inmate could be returned to prison. Others argued that parole is a status of continuing custody, during which the offender is subject to prison rules and regulations; thus, revocation requires no greater due process than that required for any action against the inmate while incarcerated.

In 1972 in *Morrissey* v. *Brewer,* the U.S. Supreme Court looked at parole revocation in the case of two offenders, Morrissey and Booher. Morrissey's parole was revoked for these allegations:

1. He had bought a car under an assumed name and operated it without permission.
2. He had given false statements to police concerning his address and insurance company after a minor accident.
3. He had obtained credit under an assumed name.
4. He had failed to report his place of residence to his parole officer.

Booher's parole was revoked because allegedly

1. He had violated the territorial restriction of his parole without consent.
2. He had obtained a driver's license under an assumed name.
3. He had operated a motor vehicle without permission.
4. He had violated the employment condition of his parole by failing to keep himself in gainful employment.[69]

No hearing was held before parole was revoked in these two cases. In its discussion of the cases, the U.S. Supreme Court made several findings. According to the Court, the purpose of parole is rehabilitation. Until parole rules are violated, an individual may remain on parole, and parole should not be revoked unless those rules are violated. Parole revocation does not require all the due process rights of a criminal trial, but some due process elements must be observed. Informal parole revocation hearings are proper, and the requirements of due process for parole revocation change with particular cases.

In *Morrissey* the U.S. Supreme Court enumerated the minimum requirements for revocation; they are reproduced in Spotlight 11-4. The Court also ruled that there should be two hearings before the final decision is made. The first is to determine whether there is probable cause to support a parole violation. At the second, more formal hearing, the final decision is made whether to revoke parole.

One year after *Morrissey* the U.S. Supreme Court extended these minimum due process requirements to probation revocation, but in *Gagnon* v. *Scarpelli* the Supreme Court also discussed whether counsel is required at probation and parole revocation; the Supreme Court had not decided that issue in *Morrissey.* In *Gagnon* the Court held that there might be some cases in which counsel is necessary in order for the offender to have a fair hearing, but counsel is not constitutionally required in all revocation cases.[70]

Two other cases of significance to revocation hearings are summarized in Spotlight 11-4. Taken together, *Bearden* v. *Georgia* and *Black* v. *Romano* demonstrate that there are some restrictions on probation revocation. In *Bearden* the U.S. Supreme Court held that it is improper to revoke the probation of an indigent who has not paid a fine and restitution unless there is a finding that the indigent has not made a sufficient effort to pay. Even then, the court must look at other alternatives before revoking probation and incarcerating the offender. But in *Romano,* when the offender's probation was revoked because he was charged with leaving the scene of an automobile accident (a felony), the U.S. Supreme Court held that due process does not require that, before incarcerating the offender on the original sentence, other sentencing alternatives be considered.[71]

Spotlight 11-4 — Due Process and Parole and Probation Revocation: The Supreme Court Responds

Mempa v. *Rhay,* 389 U.S. 128 (1967)

A probationer is entitled to be represented by appointed counsel at a combined revocation and sentencing hearing. This is because sentencing is a stage of the actual criminal proceeding, "where substantial rights of a criminal accused may be affected."

Morrissey v. *Brewer,* 408 U.S. 471 (1972)

Before parole can be revoked, the parolee is entitled to two hearings. The first is a preliminary hearing at the time of arrest and detention, and is for the purpose of determining whether there is probable cause to believe that parole has been violated. The second hearing is a more comprehensive hearing, which must occur before making a decision to revoke parole.

Minimum due process requirements at that second hearing are

1. Written notice of the alleged violations of parole
2. Disclosure to the parolee of the evidence of violation
3. Opportunity to be heard in person and to present evidence as well as witnesses
4. Right to confront and cross-examine adverse witnesses unless good cause can be shown for not allowing this confrontation
5. Right to judgment by a detached and neutral hearing body
6. Written statement of the reason for revoking parole, and of the evidence used in arriving at that decision

The Court did not decide whether retained or appointed counsel is required at a parole revocation hearing.

Gagnon v. *Scarpelli,* 411 U.S. 778 (1973)

The minimum due process requirements enumerated in *Morrissey* v. *Brewer* apply to revocation of probation. A probationer is entitled to the two hearings before revocation.

The Court considered the issue of whether counsel is required and held that there is no constitutional right to counsel at revocation hearings, and that the right to counsel should be determined on a case-by-case basis. The Court left the matter of counsel to the discretion of parole and probation authorities and indicated in part that an attorney should be present when required for fundamental fairness. An example is a situation in which the parolee or probationer is unable to communicate effectively.

Bearden v. *Georgia,* 461 U.S. 660 (1983)

The state may not revoke probation in the case of an indigent who has failed to pay a fine and restitution, unless there is a determination that the probationer has not made a bona fide effort to pay or that there were not adequate alternative forms of punishment. "Only if alternative measures are not adequate to meet the state's interests in punishment and deterrence may the court imprison a probationer who has made sufficient bona fide efforts to pay."

Black v. *Romano,* 471 U.S. 606 (1985)

The due process clause generally does not require a sentencing court to indicate that it considered alternatives to incarceration before revoking probation. This case did not involve the indigency issue regarding failure to pay a fine and restitution, as did the *Bearden* case.

It is clear from these decisions, read in conjunction with those involving the decision whether to grant parole, that the U.S. Supreme Court sees a significant difference between granting parole and revoking parole. The Court stated it this way:

> The Court has fashioned a constitutional distinction between the decision to revoke parole and the decision to grant or to deny parole. Arbitrary revocation is prohibited by *Morrissey* v. *Brewer* . . . whereas arbitrary denial is permitted by *Greenholtz* v. *Nebraska Panel Inmates*.[72]

The courts have continued to hear cases involving parole and probation revocation. In a 1998 decision a divided U.S. Supreme Court held that the exclusionary rule, which bars the use at trial of illegally seized evidence, would not bar the use of the same material at a parole revocation hearing. In *Pennsylvania Board of Probation and Parole* v. *Scott,* Justice Clarence Thomas, writing for the majority, emphasized, "The costs of allowing a parolee to avoid the consequences of his violation are compounded by the fact that parolees (particularly those who have already committed parole violations) are more likely to commit future criminal offenses than are average citizens." Thus, the U.S. Supreme Court held that a weapon found during a home search of a parolee, who was forbidden to have weapons, was admissible at his parole revocation hearing. The four dissenting justices argued unsuccessfully that, if the exclusionary rule is necessary to deter police from making unreasonable searches and seizures, it is also necessary to deter parole officers from doing so.[73]

In 1998, the California Supreme Court ruled that law enforcement officers may search the person or property of a parolee without reasonable suspicion and that any evidence of a crime may be used against the parolee at a subsequent trial for that crime. In *People* v. *Reyes* an anonymous phone called tipped Rudolph Reyes's parolee officer that Reyes (1) was using methamphetamine; (2) had lost his job because his employer suspected that he was stealing; (3) had made a false report to police that his home had been burglarized; and (4) had threatened his wife with a gun. The parole officer asked police to visit Reyes's home. When they did so, they saw Reyes exiting a shed on his property. Reyes did not appear to be under the influence of drugs; however, after the police conversed with the parole officer by phone, they conducted a search of the shed and found methamphetamine. After Reyes was charged with illegal possession, he moved to suppress the drugs because they had been seized illegally. The trial judge denied the motion, and Reyes was convicted. On appeal he argued that the drug evidence should have been suppressed because the police did not have reasonable suspicion to search his shed, as required by previous cases. The court of appeals agreed that the drug evidence should have been suppressed. The California Supreme Court reversed and held that reasonable suspicion is no longer required for a search and seizure of the property of a parolee. The court concluded, "Because of society's interest both in assuring the parolee corrects his behavior and in protecting its citizens against dangerous criminals, a search pursuant to a parole condition, without reasonable suspicion, does not intrude on a reasonable expectation of privacy, that is, an expectation that society is willing to recognize as legitimate." The court emphasized that its decision does not mean that all searches are reasonable. For example, a search could be unreasonable if it were "made too often, or at an unreasonable hour, or if unreasonably prolonged, or for other reasons establishing arbitrary or oppressive conduct by the searching officer." In addition, a search that is made at the "whim or caprice" of an officer or one that is motivated by "personal animosity toward the parolee" is not reasonable; such a search would constitute a "form of harassment." The U.S. Supreme Court refused to review the case.[74]

11-7 Megan's Laws

Another measure taken in some jurisdictions to avoid recidivism by offenders released from prison or parole is to require registration and notice. In 1994, New Jersey enacted a community notification statute, commonly called *Megan's Law,* after Megan Kanka, who was sexually assaulted and murdered earlier that year. Jessee K. Timmendequas, a neighbor with two sex offender convictions, was charged, convicted, and sentenced to death for her murder.[75]

Megan's parents turned the tragedy into a national effort to enact legislation requiring that, when sex offenders are released from prison, notification must be given to the law enforcement officers in the areas in which the offenders plan to live. New Jersey's statute was followed by statutes in most other states and the District of Columbia, as well as the federal system.[76] The statutes vary in their provisions, but many require that residents be notified of the presence of a sex offender in the neighborhood.

Megan's Laws may also require that schools, community organizations, and entire neighborhoods be notified when sex offenders move into the area. Notification includes the offender's name, address, description, picture, license plate number, and place of employment, depending on the assessment assigned to the offender by the prosecutor's office. That office is required to assess whether the released sex offender is at low, moderate, or high risk for subsequent sex crimes, a difficult task that is requiring much prosecutorial time.

There are problems with registration, however, and a lack of resources to check on registered sex offenders has resulted in offices "losing" them. For example, in early 2003 it was announced that California had lost track of more than 33,000 sex offenders, representing 44 percent of the 76,350 who had registered at least once. This information was reported by the Associated Press, which stated that it had made repeated requests over a nine-month period to get this information. The AP release noted that, although no one knows how many of those sex offenders had committed additional sex crimes, Department of Justice (DOJ) data show that over 52 percent of sex offenders in the nation are recidivists.[77] The

AP release prompted a child advocacy group, Parents for Megan's Law, to contact all 50 states by telephone and request information about their sex offender registrations. This group reported in February 2003 that, on the average, states were unable to account for 24 percent of their registered sex offenders. The executive director of this nonprofit agency said that states are enacting Megan's Laws but doing little to implement those laws.[78]

The California picture regarding the registration of sex offenders was even more bleak later in 2003, when a study conducted by the Bureau of State Audits reported that in California the Megan's Law data base contained "thousands of errors, inconsistencies, and out-of-date information" and that these mistakes placed the public at risk. On the one hand, the public could be misled in checking the database and finding no sex offenders in their neighborhoods, when they, in fact, do reside there. On the other hand, the public could become unreasonably alarmed by the erroneous reporting that 1,142 incarcerated sex offenders are in the community. In addition, the state violated the privacy of 42 juvenile sex offenders by including their names within the registry, thus making public the names of juvenile offenders. And although the failure of a sex offender to register is a crime, the state rarely knows who is avoiding the registry unless those offenders, most of whom move often, are arrested for other crimes.[79]

On 15 December 2004, California began posting the names of registered sex offenders on its website, Meganslaw.ca.gov. By evening of that day, the site was too busy to navigate; in only four days it had received 14 million visits. But the site has been criticized as inadequate. Approximately 22,000 names are omitted, and of the 63,000 included, there is insufficient information on many. And for the 63,000 registered sex offenders on whom data are available online, exact addresses can be retrieved for only the 33,500 who have been convicted of the most serious sex crimes. Further, it is not possible to search any of the names by physical characteristics or vehicle registration information.[80]

Problems with keeping track of sex offenders gained national attention in 2005, when John E. Couey, 46, a convicted sex offender, allegedly confessed to the kidnapping, rape, and murder of 9-year-old Jessica Lunsford. Jessica's body was found approximately 150 yards from the home she shared with her father and grandparents. Couey was reportedly staying with his half-sister in a home near that in which Jessica lived. Couey reportedly had failed to keep authorities informed of his living arrangements. After Jessica's death (and that of Sarah Lunde, 13, whose death in 2005 was also attributed to a released sex offender), Florida, along with other states, began efforts to strengthen their sex offender registration laws. In early May 2005, Florida's Governor Jeb Bush signed a bill, to become effective September 2005, that requires all released offenders who are convicted of sexually molesting children under age 12 to wear satellite monitoring devices for life. These devices will enable law enforcement officials to know whether the sex offenders go near schools or other places they are forbidden to visit. In addition to meeting registration requirements, released sex offenders will be required to check in twice a year with their local county jail; failure to do so could result in felony charges. The statute also increases the time sex offenders must serve in prison, with a 25-year minimum sentence for offenders who are convicted of lewd and lascivious acts against a child, representing approximately three times the average prison sentence previously served by Florida's sex offenders. Implementation of the statute will cost Florida $13 million during its first year.[81]

Important legal developments with regard to Megan's Laws have also occurred in courts, with some upholding state statutes but others declaring the statutes (or parts of them) unconstitutional. But the important point is that in 2003 the U.S. Supreme Court upheld sex offender registration laws in two states: Alaska and Connecticut. The Alaska case raised the issue of whether the law violated the *ex post facto* clause of the U.S. Constitution, whereas the Connecticut case raised the due process issue. The Alaska case was challenged by two men, each having served eight years for sexually molesting his own daughter. After the Alaska Megan's Law was enacted in 1994, the men (both of whom had been released from prison in 1990) were required to register as sex offenders. They argued on appeal that, since the law was not in effect when they committed their crimes, it could not be imposed on them. To do so would constitute additional punishment, which is prohibited by the *ex post facto* clause. The Connecticut statute was challenged by appellants who argued that the lack of a requirement to determine whether a released sex offender was dangerous before requiring registration violated due process. The U.S. Supreme Court rejected both challenges. By a 6-to-3 vote in *Smith* v. *Doe*, the Court held that the Alaska statute does not violate the *ex post facto* clause, which bars additional punishment. According to the majority, sex offender registration requirements do *not* constitute punishment. The *purpose* of required registration is to protect society, not to punish defendants.[82]

In *Connecticut Department of Public Safety* v. *Doe*, by a unanimous vote, the U.S. Supreme Court upheld the Connecticut statute, which, the Court stated, does not violate due process of law. No hearing on the issue of whether a sex offender is dangerous is necessary prior to requiring that offender to register. About one-half of the state Megan's Laws do not require a hearing.[83]

The legal challenges to Meagan's Laws are expected to continue, along with local and state efforts to publicize information on sex offenders. In addition to the legal challenges to sex offender registration laws, treatment-oriented persons have noted the burden the laws place on sex offenders who committed their crimes many years ago and have been rehabilitated. Since the laws generally apply to all sex offenders, they sweep within their coverage teenagers who have impregnated their underage lovers, whom they plan to marry; gay males or lesbians convicted of engaging in oral sex (as noted in Chapter 1, Spotlight 1-4)—such laws have been held unconstitutional by the U.S. Supreme Court; and so on. Critics of the sex registration statutes refer to them as the swift reaction to a high-profile case and a lack of attention to the details by which the statutes are implemented.[84]

Supporters argue that, by making the public more aware of the location of sexual predators in their neighborhoods, sex offender registration statutes will deter additional sexual offenses. The only other alternative, they argue, is to confine sex offenders for longer periods of time. They cite the Kansas Sexually Violent Predator Act, which was enacted in 1994 and upheld by the U.S. Supreme Court in 1997. This act permits the potentially indefinite confinement of "sexually violent predators." But the act reaches only those offenders who have "been convicted of or charged with a sexually violent offense" and who suffer from a "mental abnormality or personality disorder which makes the person likely to engage in . . . predatory acts of sexual violence."[85]

Chapter Wrap-Up

This chapter covered some critical areas of criminal justice. Despite the current public demand for stricter reactions to criminals, the crisis of overcrowded jails and prisons forces most jurisdictions to use some types of community corrections. And even though many jurisdictions have retreated from rehabilitation as a purpose for punishment and corrections, offenders are (and will continue to be) in the community, usually with limited or no supervision. The issue is not whether we wish to have community corrections; the issue is how much attention and funding we will provide to make sure the use of community corrections does not impair the goal of security.

In recent years there has been somewhat of a return to a rehabilitation philosophy, especially in the processing of substance abuse offenders. The chapter covered the use of drug courts as well as statutory provisions for the treatment, rather than punishment, of first- or second-time drug offenders, as illustrated by the California approach.

This chapter began, however, with an overview of community-based corrections: it considered the history of this approach to corrections, along with the cost. Financing is a problem, particularly with the cutbacks in federal and state budgets; however, the costs of corrections in the community are far lower than the costs of incarceration, and that is true even when intensive supervision is provided for offenders residing in the community. The problems that offenders face when they live in the community were discussed in this chapter, along with the need for services in assisting them to cope with these adjustments. In particular, attention was given to furlough, work release, and prerelease programs.

Probation and parole were discussed in greater depth in this chapter than were other community corrections because they are the methods used most frequently. Probation is the sentence imposed most often and is used today for serious as well as minor offenders. The prognosis for success is not great, although it is thought that with intensive probation supervision the probability for success improves. Special attention was given in the chapter to felony probation, house arrest, and shock probation, as well as to electronic monitoring.

Brief attention was given to the administration of probation systems before focusing on probation conditions. Courts uphold most restrictions on the daily lives of probationers, provided the imposed conditions are reasonably related to the offenses in question and do not interfere with constitutional rights. The chapter's final section on probation gave attention to the supervision of probationers and, in particular, the process of search and seizure.

Parole has been the most frequently used method of release from prison, but its use for early release has been restricted in recent years. The various methods of organizing parole systems were discussed in the chapter, along with the parole process, including eligibility for parole and the parole hearing. The due process requirements for the parole decision-making hearings were also discussed. Attempts to decrease the perceived arbitrariness of parole decisions have involved the use of parole guidelines. Due process in the revocation of probation and parole has helped remove the arbitrariness and unfairness of those important processes.

The movement away from rehabilitation has resulted in problems for community corrections. Perhaps the most bitter criticisms have been hurled at parole, resulting in action in many states to abolish or at least curtail its use. Despite the call for parole abolition, it has become obvious that some form of discretion in the release of offenders must be retained, especially if sentences are long.

No one can say which is the real problem: the failure of parole per se or the abuse of discretion by parole-granting authorities. In 1975, Maurice H. Sigler, chairman of the U.S. Board of Parole, argued that parole "has now become the scapegoat of all of corrections' ills." He suggested that the system deserves the same objective, dispassionate analysis that its critics demand of parole decisions:

To those who say "let's abolish parole," I say that as long as we use imprisonment in this country we will have to have someone, somewhere, with the authority to release people from imprisonment. Call it parole—call it what you will. It's one of those jobs that has to be done.[86]

The abolition of parole may result only in the shifting of discretion to another area, such as prosecution. Prosecutors may refuse to prosecute; juries may refuse to convict in cases involving long, mandatory sentences with no chance of parole. Efforts to control discretion within the parole system may be a more reasonable approach than the total abolition of the system.

The final section of the chapter analyzed Megan's Laws, now enacted in most states and in the federal system and upheld by the U.S. Supreme Court. The discussion detailed the types of notification that are required and looked at the constitutional issues raised by these statutes, which were passed after the 1994 rape and murder of Megan Kanka, age seven, of New Jersey. We can expect continued controversy over these sex offender registration laws as courts balance society's rights with those of ex-offenders.

Key Terms

furlough (p. 317)
house arrest (p. 321)
intensive probation supervision (IPS) (p. 323)
parole (p. 319)
parole board (p. 319)

parole officer (p. 336)
parole revocation (p. 339)
probation (p. 319)
probation officer (p. 328)

probation revocation (p. 339)
recidivists (p. 320)
reintegration (p. 312)
work release (p. 317)

Apply It

1. Define *community-based corrections* and give reasons that some argue that it is to be preferred over incarceration of offenders.
2. Evaluate the role of drug courts and other diversionary treatments of substance abusers.
3. Do we need mental health courts? Why or why not?
4. What problems do offenders face when they return to the community from incarceration? What is being done to assist them in coping with those problems? Evaluate furlough, work release, and prerelease programs.
5. What is the difference between probation and parole? Which is used more frequently and why? What are the trends in the use of probation and parole?
6. What are the arguments for and against the use of house arrest?

7. What is electronic monitoring? Should its use be increased?
8. Discuss and evaluate shock probation.
9. What typical restrictions or conditions are placed on probationers? What should be the guidelines, legally or practically, for such restrictions?
10. What is meant by *intensive probation supervision?* How does it compare in effectiveness with traditional methods of supervision?
11. Describe and analyze recent trends in parole systems.
12. What effect do due process requirements have on parole granting? On parole revocation?
13. Explain and discuss the implications of Megan's Laws. Comment on the constitutionality of these laws.

Endnotes

1. President's Commission on Law Enforcement and Administration of Justice, *The Challenge of Crime in a Free Society* (Washington, D.C.: U.S. Government Printing Office, 1967), p. 121.
2. National Advisory Commission on Criminal Justice Standards and Goals, *A National Strategy to Reduce Crime* (Washington, D.C.: U.S. Government Printing Office, 1973), p. 121.
3. Bureau of Justice Statistics, *Federal Criminal Case Processing* (Washington, D.C.: U.S. Department of Justice, February 2001), p. 1.
4. Bureau of Justice Statistics, *Federal Criminal Case Processing, with Trends 1982–2001* (Washington, D.C.: U.S. Department of Justice, January 2003), p. 14.

5. See "Innovative Drug Court Program Offers Early Intervention, Reunites Families," *Alcoholism & Drug Abuse Weekly* 14, no. 27 (15 July 2002): 1.
6. "Treatment with Teeth: A Judge Explains Why Drug Courts That Mandate and Supervise Treatment Are an Effective Middle Ground to Help Addicts Stay Clean and Reduce Crime," *The American Prospect* (December 2003), p. 45.
7. Ibid.
8. Ibid.
9. "Drug Courts Reduce Recidivism by 32 Percent," *The Daily Record of Rochester* (Rochester, New York) (14 November 2003).
10. "Drug Court Is All about Family," *The Courier-Journal* (Louisville, KY) (24 December 2003), p. 1B.

11. The testimony of Walters can be found in the *Federal News Service* (27 February 2003). The enactment statute for drug courts can be found in Sections 50001-50002 of the Violent Crime Control and Law Enforcement Act of 1994, Public Law 103–322 (13 September 1994). The information on Bush's proposed budget came from "President's Fiscal 2006 Budget Would Eliminate School-Based Prevention Program," *Alcoholism & Drug Abuse Weekly,* 17, no. 7 (14 February 2005): 1042–1394.

12. "Alameda Probation Department Drops Drug Court, Diversion Cases: Budget-Cutting Move Upsets Judges, Surprises County Supervisors," *The Recorder,* 9, no. 4-2003 (4 September 2003).

13. "Mental Health Courts Offer Detention Alternatives," *Legal Intelligencer* 231, no. 12 (19 July 2004): 4.

14. "Congress Approves Grants for Mental Health Courts," *Criminal Justice Newsletter* 31, no 2 (18 January 2000): 4. The statute is codified at U.S. Code, Title 41, Section 379611 (2005).

15. See Sanford Bates, "The Establishment and Early Years of the Federal Probation System," *Federal Probation* 51 (June 1987): 4–9.

16. Joan Petersilia, "Rand's Research: A Closer Look," *Corrections Today* 47 (June 1985): 37.

17. *Criminal Justice Research at Rand* (Santa Monica, Calif.: Rand Corp., January 1985), p. 11.

18. John T. Whitehead, "The Effectiveness of Felony Probation: Results from an Eastern State," *Justice Quarterly* 8 (December 1991): 525–543.

19. "GPS Tracking Is the Wave of the Future for Law Enforcement Authorities," *Journal of Counterterrorism & Homeland Security International* 9, no. 1 (Winter 2003).

20. Ibid.

21. "Long Arm of the Law Has Them By the Anklet," *Los Angeles Times* (27 June 2003), Part 2, p. 2.

22. Parolee Ditches Monitor, Escapes," *Wausau Daily Herald* (14 July 2003), p. 1.

23. Daniel Ford and Annesley K. Schmidt, "Electronically Monitored Home Confinement," *National Institute of Justice Report* (Washington, D.C.: U.S. Department of Justice, November 1985), p. 2.

24. James Bonta et al., "Can Electronic Monitoring Make a Difference? An Evaluation of Three Canadian Programs," *Crime & Delinquency* 46 (January 2000): 61–75; quotation is on p. 61.

25. Terry L. Baumer, "A Comparative Analysis of Three Electronically Monitored Home Detention Programs," *Justice Quarterly* 10 (March 1993): 121–142.

26. "Community-Based Supervision Dilemma: Corrections Programs Targeted for Cuts as Prison Populations Rise," *State Government News* 46, no. 5 (1 May 2003): 15.

27. "Officials Hail Novel Tracking System," *Corrections Professional* 8, no. 4 (18 October 2002).

28. See the study by Mary A. Finn and Suzanne Muirhead-Steves, "The Effectiveness of Electronic Monitoring with Violent Male Parolees," *Justice Quarterly* 19, no. 2 (June 2002): 293–312.

29. "L.A. Inmates to Be Released," *Corrections Professional* 8, no. 14 (11 April 2003); "Prisoners Being Freed before Serving Full Sentence," *Long Beach Press-Telegram* (12 August 2003).

30. "Electronic Bracelets Flawed, Suits Claim," *American Bar Association Journal* 81 (April 1995): 30.

31. Ibid; Attorneys Seek New Trial in Murder Case," *Chicago Daily Herald* (14 May 2005), p. 3.

32. "Home Monitoring Doesn't Stop Crime in Homes," *Chicago Daily Herald* (5 February 2001), p. 1, "Man Who Faces Death Will Represent Himself," *Chicago Daily Herald* (3 May 2005), p. 3.

33. "Long Arm of the Law Has Them by the Anklet."

34. United States v. Luster, 2000 U.S. App. LEXIS 15987 (8th Cir. 2000).

35. Sylvia J. Johnson, "Probation: My Profession, My Lifetime Employment, My Passion," *Crime & Delinquency* 44 (January 1998): 117–120; quotation is on p. 120.

36. "Probationer Fees Cover Half of Supervision Costs in Texas," *Criminal Justice Newsletter* (2 January 2003), p. 7.

37. Bureau of Justice Statistics, *Substance Abuse and Treatment of Adults on Probation, 1995* (Washington, D.C.: U.S. Department of Justice, March 1998), p. 1.

38. United States v. Myers, 864 F.Supp. 794 (N.D.Ill. 1994); Warner v. Orange County Department of Probation, 870 F.Supp. 69 (S.D.N.Y. 1994), *aff'd.,* 115 F.3d 1068 (2d Cir. 1996), *cert. denied,* 528 U.S. 1003 (1999).

39. State v. Oakley, 629 N.W.2d 200 (Wis. 2001), *recons. denied, clarified,* 635 N.W.2d 760 (Wis. 2001), *cert. denied,* Oakley v. Wisconsin, 537 U.S. 813 (2002).

40. United States v. Sofsky, 287 F.3d 122 (2d Cir. 2002), *supplemental opinion,* 2002 U.S. App. LEXIS 5296 (2d Cir. 2002), *cert. denied,* Sofsky v. United States, 537 U.S. 1167 (2003).

41. People v. Griffith, 657 N.Y.S.2d 823 (App.Div.3d Dept. 1997).

42. Stephanie B. Goldberg, "No Baby, No Jail: Creative Sentencing Has Gone Overboard, a California Court Rules," *American Bar Association Journal* 78 (October 1992): 90.

43. People v. Hackler, 13 Cal.App.4th 1049 (5th Dist. 1993).

44. People v. Meyer, 680 N.E.2d 315 (Ill. 1997).

45. People (California) v. Beal, 70 Cal.Rptr.2d 80 (Cal.App.4th Dist. 1997), *review denied,* 1998 Cal. LEXIS 2172 (Cal. 1998).

46. National Institute of Corrections, *New Approaches to Staff Safety,* www.nicic.org., summarized in "New Enforcement Duties Require Safety Training, Report Says," *Criminal Justice Newsletter* (1 May 2003), p. 7; quotation is on p. 8.

47. *"Broken Windows" Probation: The Next Step in Fighting Crime,* available from the Manhattan Institute, 52 Vanderbilt Avenue, New York, NY 10017 (202) 599-7000. On the Internet: www.manhattan-institute.org. The publication is summarized in "Leading Officials Issue Plan for 'Reinventing' Probation," *Criminal Justice Newsletter* 30 (1 April 1999): 1–2.

48. Todd R. Clear and Patricia L. Hardyman, "The New Intensive Supervision Movement," *Crime & Delinquency* 36 (January 1990): 42–44. The entire journal is devoted to issues on IPS.

49. Quoted in *Criminal Justice Newsletter* 24 (1 July 1993): 1.

50. James M. Byrne et al., "The Effectiveness of the New Intensive Supervision Programs," *Research in Corrections* 2 (September 1989): 42.

51. The Sentencing Reform Act was passed as part of the Comprehensive Crime Control Act of 1984, Public Law 98-473, 98 Stat. 1837, 1976 (1984), and is codified with its subsequent amendments in U.S. Code, Title 18, Sections 3551 *et seq.* (2005) and U.S. Code, Title 28, Sections 991–998 (2005).

52. "Eliminating Parole Boards Isn't a Cure-All, Experts Say," *New York Times* (10 January 1999), p. 11.

53. "State Might Revive Early-Parole Plan," *Santa Fe New Mexican* (8 June 2003), p. 1. New Mexico's Probation and Parole Act is codified at N. Mex. Stat. 31-21-3 *et seq.* (2004).

54. "Parole Denied to a Follower of Manson," *New York Times* (29 June 2002), p. 8.

55. "Schwarzenegger Paroles Killer," *New York Times* (28 November 2003), p. 23.

56. "Revolving Door: Parole System Is Expensive Failure," *San Diego Union-Tribune* (24 November 2003), p. 6B.

57. "Must Reduce Inmate Numbers," *San Gabriel Valley Tribune* (13 May 2004); "California's Prison Deficit Soars Past $200 Million," *Scripps Howard News Service* (16 December 2004).

58. "Killers of British 2-Year-Old Win Parole," *New York Times* (23 June 2001), p. 5.

59. "Decision to Grant Parole to Ex-Radical Will Stand," *New York Times* (23 August 2003), p. 12; "Parole for '60s Radical Meets with Protest," *Corrections Professional* 9, no. 3 (14 October 2003).

60. Quoted in Jessica Mitford, *Kind and Usual Punishment: The Prison Business* (New York: Alfred A. Knopf, 1973), p. 216.

61. Greenholtz v. Nebraska, 442 U.S. 1 (1979).

62. Board of Pardons v. Allen, 482 U.S. 369 (1987).

63. Morrissey v. Brewer, 408 U.S. 471, 478 (1972).

64. Andrew von Hirsch and Kathleen J. Hanrahan, *Abolish Parole?* (Washington, D.C.: U.S. Government Printing Office, 1978), p. 21.

65. United States v. Knights, 534 U.S. 112 (2001), footnotes and case citations omitted. Griffin v. Wisconsin may be found at 483 U.S. 868 (1987).

66. David G. Savage, "Searches at Stake: New Limits on Probationers' Privacy Rights May Have Post–Sept. 11 Implications," *American Bar Association Journal* 88 (February 2002): 30.

67. United States v. Crawford, 323 F.3d 700 (9th Cir. 2003), *and vacated, reh'g., en banc, granted*, 2003 U.S. App. LEXIS 18402 (9th Cir. 2003), *and different results reached on reh'g., remanded*, 372 F.3d 1048 (9th Cir. 2004), *cert. denied*, 125 S.Ct. 863 (2005).

68. Thompson v. Davis, 295 F.3d 890 (9th Cir. 2002), *cert. denied*, 538 U.S. 921 (2003).

69. Morrissey v. Brewer, 408 U.S. 471 (1972).

70. Gagnon v. Scarpelli, 411 U.S. 778 (1973).

71. Black v. Romano, 471 U.S. 606 (1985); Bearden v. Georgia, 461 U.S. 660 (1983).

72. Jago v. Van Curen, 454 U.S. 14 (1981).

73. Pennsylvania Board of Probation and Parole v. Scott, 524 U.S. 357 (1998).

74. People v. Reyes, 968 P.2d 445 (Cal. 1998), *cert. denied*, 526 U.S. 1092 (1999).

75. The statute is codified in N.J.Stat., Section 2C:7-1 *et seq.* (2004).

76. The federal statute is part of the Violent Crime Control and Law Enforcement Act of 1994, Public Law 103-323 (13 September 1994), Section 20417.

77. "Nearly Half of Calif. Sex Offenders Not Tracked," *St. Petersburg Times* (8 January 2003), p. 5.

78. "States Losing Track of Sex Offenders, Survey Says," *Tallahassee Democrat* (7 February 2003), p. 1.

79. *California Law Enforcement and Correctional Agencies: With Increased Efforts, They Could Improve the Accuracy and Completeness of Public Information on Sex Offenders*, on the Internet at www.bsa.ca.gov/bsa/index.html.

80. "Sex-Offender List Draws Quick Criticism," *New York Times* (26 December 2004), p. 27.

81. "After 2 Cases in Florida, Crackdown on Molesters," *New York Times* (1 May 2005), p. 18. The Florida sex offender registration statute is codified at Fl. Stat. 943.0435 (2005).

82. Smith v. Doe, 538 U.S. 84 (2003).

83. Connecticut Department of Public Safety v. Doe, 538 U.S. 1 (2003).

84. "Registry Laws Tar Sex-Crime Convicts with Broad Brush," *New York Times* (1 July 1997), p. 11.

85. Kan. Stat. Ann., Section 59-29a01 *et seq.* (2004). The case is Kansas v. Hendricks, 521 U.S. 346 (1997).

86. Maurice H. Sigler, "Abolish Parole?" *Federal Probation* 39 (June 1975): 48.

Juvenile Justice:
A Special Case

Juvenile court systems have emerged as separate systems for processing juveniles who engage in criminal and delinquent activities or who are dependent or neglected. Historically these special courts and systems were viewed as being concerned with the welfare of children who did not need the procedural safeguards characteristic of adult criminal court systems.

In recent years that orientation has changed. Some but not all procedural safeguards recognized in adult criminal courts have been extended to juvenile court systems, leaving the two systems far less distinguishable than was originally the case. Whether these are positive or negative changes is debatable, but clearly the increased attention given to the involvement of juveniles in violent crimes has resulted in efforts to change juvenile justice systems or process violent juveniles in adult criminal court systems.

Chapter 12 discusses the early development and the recent changes that have been made in juvenile court systems, along with the development and changes that have occurred in juvenile correctional systems.

Juvenile Justice Systems

12

Criminal responsibility in adversary systems is based on the premise that the accused has the ability to understand and control his or her behavior. Most people are presumed to have this ability, but among the exceptions have been persons of tender years. Separate systems for them emerged in the late 1800s in the United States. In recent years these systems have gone through significant changes, leading criminologist Alida V. Merlo to state in her 2000 presidential address before the members of the Academy of Criminal Justice Sciences (ACJS) the following:

> We are at a unique point in our history, a crossroads. First, there is a paradox: on the one hand, official crime statistics demonstrate that juvenile violent crime is decreasing. On the other, punitiveness toward juvenile offenders continues to increase. . . .
>
> Second . . . evidence suggests that public attitudes are softening. Support for early intervention efforts may even be growing.[1]

This chapter looks at some of the changes discussed by Merlo in her presidential address. It begins with a brief historical overview of the background of U.S. juvenile justice systems. The origin of juvenile courts is discussed, along with the dispute over the purposes of juvenile justice systems. Data on delinquency are analyzed, with particular emphasis on violent crimes by and against juveniles, as well as the impact of youth gangs. The chapter examines how U.S. Supreme Court decisions have changed traditional juvenile justice systems before looking more closely at how those systems operate today. The constitutionality of juvenile curfews is noted, along with a look at race and gender issues relating to juveniles.

Juvenile court organization and procedures are examined, followed by an analysis of juveniles in adult criminal courts, including the role of attorneys. Megan's Laws, discussed in Chapter 11 with reference to adults, are analyzed here as they apply to juveniles. The chapter gives attention to juveniles in corrections as well as to the issue of capital punishment. The final section contains a brief assessment of adult criminal and juvenile justice systems.

LEARNING
OBJECTIVES

After reading this chapter, you should be able to do the following:

- **List and explain the basic procedural and philosophical differences between juvenile and criminal courts historically and currently**
- **Discuss current data on delinquency, especially data on violent crimes**
- **Analyze the impact of youth gangs on our society**
- **List and explain the major U.S. Supreme Court cases regarding juveniles' constitutional rights and assess the impact of the right to counsel**
- **Enumerate and explain the purpose and practice of juvenile curfews and discuss the legal issues involved**
- **Explore the racial and gender issues of juvenile justice systems**
- **Discuss the general procedures of juvenile courts**
- **Analyze the role of attorneys in juvenile courts**
- **Explain the processing of juvenile offenders in adult criminal courts and relate your discussion to persistently violent juvenile offenders**
- **Discuss the application of Megan's Laws to juveniles**
- **Assess the importance of drug courts to juvenile justice systems and compare them with those in adult criminal court systems**
- **Summarize recent changes in juvenile corrections**
- **Evaluate the 2005 U.S. Supreme Court decision concerning capital punishment and juveniles**
- **Assess the future of juvenile court systems**

12-1 Juvenile Justice Systems: An Overview

Special justice systems for children rest on the belief that a **juvenile delinquent** should be treated separately from and differently than adults. Juveniles need special handling and processing when they engage in delinquent or criminal acts. They are considered amenable to treatment, to change, and to rehabilitation.

Although the first discussion of **juvenile** problems of which we have record dates back 4,000 years to the Code of Hammurabi, the treatment of children in the United States can be traced to the philosophy of the English, who in the eleventh and twelfth centuries developed the practice of treating children differently than adults. A child under the age of 7 was considered incapable of forming the intent required for criminal prosecutions. A child between the ages of 7 and 14 years was presumed to be incapable of forming the intent, but that presumption could be refuted. A child over 14 was treated as an adult.

During this earlier period of English history, when the death penalty was provided for many crimes, children were not exempted, although few children were executed. Later in England the *chancery,* or equity courts, were established for the purpose of avoiding the harshness of the strict technicalities of the English common law. Equity courts were to decide cases on the principles of justice and fairness. These courts were called *chancery courts* because they were under the jurisdiction of the king's chancellor. Equity courts had jurisdiction over many types of cases, including those involving children.

The English king could exercise the power of a parent over children and others, a concept called ***parens patriae,*** literally meaning the "parent of the country." In time this concept became so important that England enacted statutes permitting the legal rights of parents and other family members to be terminated in the cases of persons who needed the legal guardianship of the king.

Parens patriae was interpreted in England to mean that the sovereign had the responsibility to oversee any children in the kingdom who might be neglected or abused. The

---

Juvenile delinquent A person under legal age (the maximum age varies among the states from 16 to 21, but 18 is the most common) whom a juvenile court has determined to be incorrigible or in violation of a criminal statute.

Juvenile A young person under age for certain privileges, such as voting or drinking alcoholic beverages. If accused of a criminal or juvenile offense, usually a juvenile is not tried by an adult criminal court but is processed in the juvenile court.

Parens patriae Literally, "parent of the country"; the doctrine from English common law that was the basis for allowing the state to take over guardianship of a child. In the United States the doctrine forms the basis for juvenile court jurisdiction. The doctrine presumes that the state acts in the best interests of the child.

▶ **Status offense** A class of crime that does not consist of proscribed action or inaction but, rather, of the personal condition or characteristic of the accused—for example, being a vagrant. In juvenile law, a variety of acts that would not be considered criminal if committed by an adult—for example, being insubordinate or truant or running away from home.

▶ **Juvenile court** The court having jurisdiction over juveniles who are accused of delinquent acts or offenses or criminal acts or who are in need of supervision because they are being neglected or mistreated by their parents or guardians.

▶ **Detention centers** Facilities for the temporary confinement of juveniles in custody who are awaiting court disposition.

▶ **Petition** A formal document for filing an action in juvenile court, in contrast to a grand jury indictment or prosecutor's presentment in the adult criminal court.

▶ **Detention** *See* **pretrial detention.**

▶ **Adjudication** The process of decision making by a court; normally used to refer to juvenile proceedings. The term is also used to refer to rule enforcement by administrative agencies.

▶ **Disposition** The final decision of a court in a criminal proceeding to accept a guilty plea, to find the defendant guilty or not guilty, or to terminate the proceedings against the defendant.

court exercised this duty only when it was thought necessary for the welfare of the child, and that rarely occurred. The protection of society and the punishment of parents were not considered to be sufficient reasons to invoke the responsibility. In the English system and in the system as adopted during the early period of American history, the *parens patriae* doctrine applied only to children who were in need of supervision or help because of the actions of their parents or guardians, not to children who were delinquent. These children had various names, such as *children in need of supervision (CINS)*, *persons in need of supervision (PINS)*, and *dependent* or *neglected children.* The extension of juvenile court jurisdiction over delinquent children was an innovation adopted in Illinois in 1899.[2]

In the United States, juvenile court jurisdiction was extended to children considered incorrigible because they would not obey their parents or other adults. Even if they were not violating the law, these juveniles could be accused of committing a **status offense.** The trend in recent years has been to remove status offenses from juvenile court jurisdiction; however, where jurisdiction remains, generally the status offender is included within the definition of juvenile delinquent. Some states have a minimum age for juvenile court jurisdiction, but as a practical matter most courts do not decide cases involving very young children.

Prior to the emergence of the **juvenile court,** children in the United States were treated as adults. Capital punishment was permitted but seldom used; however, many children were deprived of adequate food, were incarcerated with adults, or were subjected to corporal punishment. Some institutions were established to separate incarcerated juveniles from adults. The New York House of Refuge, established in 1824, was the first and served as a model. These early institutions eliminated some of the evils of imprisoning children with adult criminals, although some scholars have questioned whether they provided much improvement in the treatment of juveniles.[3]

By the mid-1800s in the United States, probation for juveniles had been established and separate **detention centers** had been built. The 1800s saw the evolution of progressive ideas in the care and treatment of dependent and neglected children. Protective societies, such as the Society for the Prevention of Cruelty to Children (developed in New York in 1875), paved the way for the first juvenile court, established in 1899 in Illinois. Other states followed quickly.

Spotlight 12-1 lists some of the historical differences between U.S. adult criminal courts and juvenile courts. The juvenile court, with its emphasis on individualized treatment, was visualized as a social agency or clinic rather than a court of law, a vision that has encountered much criticism in recent years. The court was to be a social institution designed to protect and rehabilitate the child rather than to determine the child's guilt or innocence. Juvenile courts were to be treatment—not punishment—oriented. The purpose of juvenile courts was to prevent children from becoming criminals by catching them in the budding stages and giving them the protection and love that a parent would be expected to provide.

The vocabulary of juvenile and criminal courts differed, too. Children would not be arrested but, rather, summoned or apprehended; they would not be indicted, but a **petition** would be filed on their behalf. If **detention** were necessary, the children would be placed in special facilities separate from adults, not in jails. They would not have a public trial but a private hearing, in which juries and prosecuting attorneys would rarely, if ever, be used. In most cases they would not have an attorney.

The juvenile hearing would be informal, for the ordinary trappings of the courtroom would be out of place. Judges would not act as impartial observers, as was their function in criminal courts. Rather, they would act as wise parents, disciplining their children with love and tenderness and deciding informally what was best for those children. Juveniles would not be sentenced as the concept is used in adult criminal courts. Instead, after the hearing there would be an **adjudication.** A **disposition** would be made only after a careful study of the juvenile's background and potential, and the decision would be made in the best interests of the child.

The juvenile court hearing differed from that of the adult criminal court in procedure as well as in philosophy. Rules of evidence required in criminal courts were not applied to

| *Spotlight 12-1* | U.S. Adult Criminal and Juvenile Courts: Some Historically Important Contrasts |

Adult Criminal Court	**Juvenile Court**
Court of law	Social institution, agency, clinic
Constitutional rights	*Parens patriae* approach—supra constitutional rights
Purpose to punish, deter	Purpose to salvage, rehabilitate
Begins with arrest	Begins with apprehension, summons; process of intake
Indictment or presentment	Petition filed on behalf of child
Detained in jails or released on bail	Detained in detention centers or released to family or others
Public trial	Private hearing
Strict rules of evidence	Informal procedures
Right to trial by jury	No right to trial by jury
Right to counsel	No right to (or need for) counsel
Prosecuted by state	Allegations brought by state
Plea bargaining	No plea bargaining; state acting in child's best interests
Impartial judge	Judge acting as a wise parent
Pleads guilty, innocent, or *nolo contendere*	Admits or denies petition
Found guilty or innocent	Adjudicated
Sentenced	Disposition of the case
Probation	Probation
Incarcerated in jail or prison	Placed in reformatory, training school, foster home, etc.
Released on parole	Released to aftercare

juvenile courts. Adult criminal court procedural safeguards were set aside in the interest of treatment and the welfare of children. Because the state, in recognizing its duty as parent, was helping, not punishing, children, no constitutional rights were violated. The emphasis in juvenile court was not on what the child *did* but on who the child *was*. Juvenile courts were to be concerned with the children as individuals, and this enabled judges to save children from criminal careers through proper treatment. In contrast, the adult criminal court was concerned at trial with the narrow issue of the guilt or innocence of the accused.

Early advocates of juvenile courts believed that law and humanitarianism were not sufficient for the treatment of juveniles. They expected juvenile courts to rely heavily on the findings of the physical and social sciences. It was anticipated that these research findings would be applied scientifically in the adjudication and disposition of juveniles. The failure of the social sciences to develop sufficient research to implement this philosophy adequately, the failure of the legal profession to recognize and accept these findings that would be of assistance, and the abuse of discretion by correctional officials all contributed to the tensions that developed over the lack of procedural safeguards in juvenile courts.

The rehabilitative ideal of the founders of juvenile courts has not been realized. In actuality, many juveniles receive punishment, not treatment, and being processed through juvenile rather than adult criminal courts does not remove the stigma of *criminal*.

Not only may a juvenile suffer the worst of both the adult criminal and the juvenile court worlds, but some scholars take the position that this was the intent. Disputing the benevolent motives of the founders of the juvenile court system, some scholars have argued that juvenile courts diminish the civil liberties and privacy of juveniles and that the child-saving movement was promoted by the middle class to support its own interests.[4]

Others have contended that the development of juvenile courts represented neither a great social reform nor an attempt to diminish juveniles' civil liberties and to control them arbitrarily. Rather, it represented another example of the trend toward bureaucratization and an institutional compromise between social welfare and the law. The juvenile court "was primarily a shell of legal ritual within which states renewed and enacted their commitment to discretionary social control over children."[5]

Professions 12-1

Careers in Juvenile Justice

The increase in violent crimes by juveniles has led officials to pay greater attention to research into juvenile crime. Research provides numerous job opportunities for those who are trained in research methodology. The opportunities exist in all areas of criminal justice, but juvenile justice is one area that often appeals to young people. The desire to find out why crime happens and what to do—how to treat—may lead to intriguing days at the office.

Those who prefer the hands-on approach will also find numerous chances to become involved in juvenile justice. Jobs are available in juvenile detention and corrections facilities, juvenile probation and parole, school service, community treatment programs, court services, and many other areas. Students may be interested in teaching positions that focus on children with behavior problems as well as on those who have already committed juvenile or criminal offenses.

Another area of service to juveniles is in victimization, as larger numbers of children, some very young, become crime victims, often at the hands of other children or juveniles. The

government has developed an action plan to break the cycle of juvenile crime and victimization, with then—U.S. attorney General Janet Reno concluding:

> More and more of our Nation's children are killing and dying. The only way we can break the cycle of violence is through a truly national effort implemented one community at a time. Everyone has a role—businesses, schools, universities, and especially parents. Every community and every citizen can find practical steps in the Action Plan to do something now about youth violence.[1]

The implementation of the government's plan provides various career and job opportunities for those interested in focusing their work on juveniles.

1. Attorney General Janet Reno, quoted in Sarah Ingersoll, "The National Juvenile Justice Action Plan: A Comprehensive Response to a Critical Challenge," *Juvenile Justice: Kids and Guns: From Playgrounds to Battlegrounds* (Washington, D.C.: U.S. Department of Justice, Office of Juvenile Justice and Delinquency Prevention, September 1997), p. 11.

Changes have occurred in the juvenile court philosophy and procedures. However, before discussing those, it is appropriate to take a brief look at delinquency data, an area of research that provides interesting job opportunities, as noted in Professions 12-1.

12-2   Juvenile Delinquency Data

▶ **Delinquency**   *See* **juvenile delinquent.**

It is impossible to get accurate data on the amount of **delinquency,** since jurisdictions differ in their definitions of the term. Theoretically *delinquency* does not refer to children processed through juvenile courts because they are in need of supervision, because they are dependent or neglected, or because they are abused. Nevertheless, some jurisdictions include in delinquency data all categories of juveniles over which juvenile courts have jurisdiction.

Methods of collecting delinquency data vary, too, and in most cases juvenile records are considered confidential; some states require that the records be destroyed or sealed. How, then, do we know about juvenile offenses? Chapter 2 discussed the use of self-report studies, in which respondents are asked to state the types of offenses they have committed and how often they have committed them. From carefully selected samples of the population, predictions can be made on the overall extent of delinquency.

Official arrest rates recorded by age brackets and published by the FBI are another source of data. The official data reveal that, in 2003, persons under age 18 accounted for 15.5 percent of all arrests for violent crimes and 28.9 percent of all arrests for property crimes. Figure 12-1 graphs the percentage of total arrests in 2003 of persons under 18 for all serious offenses and several other crimes. The figure demonstrates that, according to official data, juveniles under the age of 18 do *not* commit most of the violent crimes. If the age is extended from 18 to 25, however, the picture is different. In 2003, those under 25 constituted 44.3 percent of all arrests for violent crimes and 57.4 percent of all arrests for property offenses.[6]

Some states have become more sensitive toward juveniles. For example, 62 percent of California voters endorsed Proposition 21, which became effective 8 March 2000. Proposition 21 provides that a teen age 14 or over who is accused of committing one of a list of crimes (such as murder, rape, or lewd and lascivious acts on a child under 14) "shall be prosecuted under the general law in a court of criminal jurisdiction."[7] Other juveniles

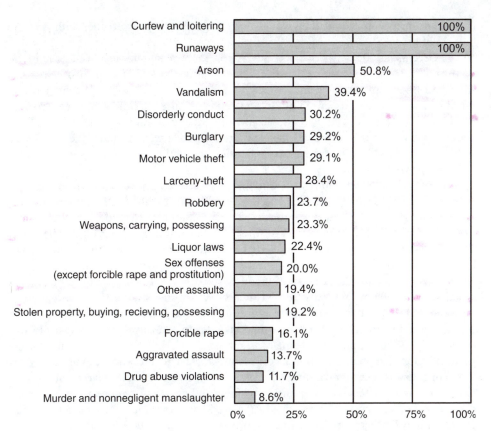

Figure 12-1
Percentage of Total Arrests in 2003 Involving Youths Under 18 Years of Age
Source: Federal Bureau of Investigation, *Uniform Crime Reports, 2003* (Washington, D.C.: U.S. Government Printing Office, 2004), p. 286.

are under the jurisdiction of the juvenile court. The statute contains language stating that serious crimes by juveniles had increased and were expected to continue doing so. According to the findings and declarations of the statute, although overall crime had declined, "juvenile crime had become a larger and more ominous threat."[8] Other states have also become more punitive toward violent juveniles, and the issue of juvenile violence deserves closer attention.

12-2a Violence by and against Juveniles

It is the violence by juveniles, often with juvenile victims, that raises great concern, along with the types of violent crimes that are being committed. Perhaps the most publicized and shocking was the violence at Columbine High School in Littleton, Colorado. On 20 April 1999, two students, Eric Harris and Dylan Klebold, went on a shooting spree, which resulted in the deaths of 12 students and a teacher and injuries to two dozen others. In December of that year tapes made by Harris and Klebold were released, revealing their anger and their plans to kill up to 250 people. The "tapes are a macabre documentary of the meticulous planning for the attack, which the two youths called retaliation for years of taunting that they said friends and relatives had inflicted on them because of an unwillingness to dress and act as others wanted." Their anger had built to the point that they could no longer cope.[9]

In December 1999, a Florida youth, Michael Ian Campbell of Cape Coral, age 18, was arrested for sending a threat over the Internet, suggesting that he needed to finish the plans begun by Harris and Klebold. As a result of the threat, Columbine High School was closed 2 days early for Christmas vacation. After a guilty plea, Campbell served 16 weeks in a federal prison in Florida.

In the spring 2000, a six-year-old boy allegedly pulled a gun from his pants and shot a six-year-old girl in front of their teacher and other students. Kayla Rolland was struck in the neck by a bullet from a .32-caliber gun and died within the hour.[10] The boy and his brother were placed in a foster home (subsequently their mother released her rights to them), and prosecutors said they would not charge the alleged offender with a crime because of his age.

In December 2003, an 11-year-old boy, Aaron Kean, was sentenced to 18 years in the custody of the New Jersey juvenile justice system after he admitted that he had kidnapped Amir Beeks, a 3-year-old boy, from a library, beat the child with a baseball bat, and left him for dead in a creek behind Aaron's house, apparently because the child kept bothering him about his scooter. Kean, who was also accused of sexually assaulting Beeks, is one of the youngest persons in the custody of the New Jersey juvenile system. Under the New Jersey system, the boy will be under the control of authorities (either in custody or under supervision on parole) until he is 35.[11]

Sixteen-year-old Antonio Nunez, who was 14 when he kidnapped a businessman and shot at police in California, was sentenced to life without parole and four additional life terms plus 121 years in prison for the crimes of attempting to murder a police officer, assault, evading a police officer, street terrorism, and committing crimes for the benefit of a street gang. Nunez is one of the youngest persons in California history to be sentenced to life in prison without parole.[12]

In addition to murder, youths are committing sex crimes, usually against other youths or children. In 1997 in Texas City, Texas, two boys, ages 10 and 14, were held in the rape of a 4-year-old girl. The boys were caught assaulting the little girl, whom they allegedly lured into a school bus by telling her they would take her to a carnival. The 14-year-old was found guilty of kidnapping and sexually assaulting the victim. The victim would not say what had happened on the bus, but she did identify the defendant, who faced up to 40 years in prison. He was sent to a **training school** for juveniles, but after 48 referrals of disciplinary behavior and 70 incidents of misbehavior (including masturbating in view of female correctional officers and admitting that he fantasized about raping them), the judge transferred Andrew Feathers, age 16, to an adult prison in February 2000. Feathers could spend up to 17 more years in prison; had he remained in the juvenile facility, he would have been released no later than his 21st birthday. Feathers's young accomplice, who had planned the rape, was placed on probation.[13]

In 2003, four Mephan High School (New York) football players were charged with numerous crimes, including the sexual abuse of younger players at a preseason training camp in Pennsylvania. Two of the players were sentenced to juvenile facilities; the youngest, who was 15 at the time of the crimes, was sentenced to probation. The juvenile charges against those three players are sealed but will remain on their records and can be accessed by law enforcement officials. The fourth and oldest player, who was charged with three felonies, entered a guilty plea to the misdemeanor of reckless endangerment in exchange for a promise of probation. Apparently the prosecutors were agreeable to this plea because the testimony of the witness/victims was contradictory. The fourth player is eligible for a program entitled "accelerated rehabilitation." If he completes that program with no problems, his record will be expunged. In addition, he must complete 50 hours of community service and write a paper explaining the impact of his actions on himself, his family, the community, and the victims. Finally, he is required to write a letter of apology to his victims. Although his plea ended the court actions on the crimes, civil lawsuits remained to be resolved.[14]

Juvenile violence often occurs in gangs, a subject that has received increased research attention in recent years.

12-2b Youth Gangs

Gang membership is not limited to juveniles, but juvenile gangs are a major focus in today's efforts to combat crime, especially violent crime. Research on gangs and delinquency is not a new phenomenon, but the nature of gang activities has changed in recent years. Although violence might have been characteristic of some early gangs, it appears to be the focal point of today's gangs. Whereas the gangs that were the focus of early sociological research may have fought over turf, today's gangs go to war over drug trafficking, even killing their own members if they become informers.

> ▶ **Training school**   A secure corrections facility to which juveniles are confined by court order.

The violent nature of gangs was emphasized by the president of the California Gang Investigators Association when he testified before a U.S. Senate committee in 2003. Wesley D. McBride reported that the Los Angeles-based gangs had spread throughout the country and that the "most important weapon in the gang's arsenal is fear." McBride continued:

> Gangs are the master predators of the urban landscape. Their ability to instill fear into the people of a community knows no bounds. This fear percolates through the community [and becomes] part of the atmosphere. After a time, physical threats are not needed; the threat is unspoken but part of the community culture.[15]

There are many types of gangs. Experts warn that it is not easy to distinguish among, for example, youth gangs, street gangs, and organized crime enterprises. One U.S. Department of Justice (DOJ) study of youth gangs (those applicable to this chapter's focus) accepted criminologist W. B. Miller's definition of youth gang as follows:

> a self-formed association of peers, united by mutual interests, with identifiable leadership and internal organization, who act collectively or as individuals to achieve specific purposes, including the conduct of illegal activity and control of a particular territory, facility, or enterprise.[16]

The importance of research on youth gangs is emphasized by a study of juvenile violence and gangs that disclosed that most juvenile crime is committed by gang members. The study tracked 808 children for seven years and found that 85 percent of robberies by youths were committed by the 15 percent of the youths who had joined gangs. These gang members committed 54 percent of the felony thefts; 58 percent of the juvenile crimes; and 62 percent of drug sales committed by the sample youths. Data were obtained from self-report studies from those surveyed as well as from juvenile court records; both sources showed that most crimes committed by youths were by those who had joined gangs. Other conclusions were that, with the exception of drug involvement, youth crimes dropped when the teens left the gangs. The following factors were found to be associated with joining gangs: "poverty, unstable family living conditions, the availability of drugs and alcohol, parents who tolerate or commit violence, falling behind or failing in school, and 'hanging out' with delinquents."[17]

In 2003, the Office of Juvenile Justice and Delinquency Prevention (OJJDP) released its analysis of 2001 data, noting that juvenile gangs exist in U.S. cities and towns of all sizes and that these gangs are a substantial problem. In cities with a population of over 250,000, all responding law enforcement agencies reported gang problems. Gang activity was reported in 35 percent of suburban counties and 11 percent of rural counties, and of those jurisdictions that reported gang activity in the previous survey (based on 1996 data), 95 percent reported gang activity in 2001. The OJJDP concluded, "Based on survey results, it is estimated that nearly 3,000 jurisdictions across the United States experienced gang activity in 2001." In addition, most jurisdictions reported that gang members who returned to their areas after incarceration "noticeably contributed to an increase in violent crimes" in those areas.[18]

The impact of gangs is illustrated by a look at Los Angeles, where gang murders have played a significant role in that city's position as the murder capital of the United States. Although crime remained relatively unchanged throughout the country in 2002 and murders were down in New York City, this incidence of serious crime in Los Angeles increased from 581 in 2001 to 654 in 2002. The police chief in New York City during the decline in that city's murder rate was William J. Bratton, who subsequently became the Los Angeles police chief. Bratton admitted that in LA he would need a new approach to lowering the crime rate, especially the murder rate, because that city has large and highly organized gangs, which are thriving. In June 2003, Bratton admitted that he did not yet have the solution to the LA gang problem.[19]

In November 2003, LAPD Chief Bratton called for a program similar to the one he instituted in New York City. Bratton declared that it is not possible to "just arrest your way out of the situation." Hiring more police for the streets will not solve the problems created by the estimated 96,000 gang members in Los Angeles County (50,000 of whom are in the city of Los Angeles). In addition, said Bratton, it is necessary to provide after-school programs and jobs for youths in order to remove Los Angeles as the gang capital of the nation. Chief Bratton made significant changes in his administration and proclaimed that he was refocusing the department's crime-fighting efforts. The new focus is on gang members, ex-cons, and the rest of the 10 percent of the population responsible for 50 percent of the area's crimes. Bratton was described as wanting to "build on efforts that saw homicides drop 24 percent during his first year in office . . . and violent crimes decrease 5.4 percent." According to Bratton, "We have started some momentum that I don't want to lose."[20]

By early 2004, Los Angeles city officials had increased efforts to combat the city's 100,000 gang members, whom Chief Bratton refers to as *violent sociopaths*. In January 2004, the Los Angeles police, along with federal authorities, raided a large public housing project in the Watts section of Los Angeles, arresting 41 members of the Bounty Hunters gang. The men were charged with conspiracy to sell narcotics and to distribute cocaine.[21] In December 2003, when Chief Bratton met with 50 of his officers, he reported to them that, compared with the same time the previous year, murders in Los Angeles had dropped 22 percent. Bratton stated that he would continue to focus on gangs, which he referred to as a "domestic-terrorist problem."[22]

Although Los Angeles is the gang capital of the United States, the murder rate in Chicago has also been pushed up by gangs. The Chicago Police Department announced in June 2003 that it would begin a policy of assessing crime trends daily, followed by deployment of a special unit to gang-infested areas in an attempt to prevent gang-related violence before it occurs. The police said the recent surge in violence was caused primarily by gang wars over drug turf. With regard to prevention, one Chicago police official said, "You can't be thinking weeks or months ahead when they are thinking hours and days ahead. . . . You must be able to assess daily trends and activity by the hour." Officials estimated that approximately one-half of Chicago's homicides in 2002 were the result of gang murders.[23]

In an earlier effort to curb gangs in Chicago, that city enacted an antiloitering ordinance that permitted police to disburse people gathered in a public place "with no apparent lawful purpose." In 2000, the U.S. Supreme Court decided the case of *City of Chicago* v. *Morales*, in which the Court held that the Chicago ordinance was unconstitutional because it was vague and gave police too much discretion to arrest people who might not be engaging in any illegal acts.[24] In February 2000, the city tried again, with an ordinance designed to inconvenience gangs by disbursing them so frequently that they could not keep a hold on a community or an area within one. Three Hispanic men, who were among the first to be arrested under the new ordinance, challenged its constitutionality. On 19 March 2002, a Chicago judge ruled that the ordinance is constitutional. According to Cook County (Illinois) Circuit Judge Mark Ballard, the U.S. Supreme Court's opinion in *Morales* drew a road map for an acceptable plan and "the Chicago framers of the revised ordinance knew how to read the map."[25]

Officials in other cities have also taken measures to intervene in gang activities and to prosecute the extreme cases, but district attorneys report that their efforts are being met with serious problems. They complain about the leniency of the juvenile justice system and the intimidation of victims and witnesses by gang members. Prosecutors complain that many gang members "pass through the system without serving any sentence." Prosecution efforts are hindered further by the changing roles of the persons involved. "In gang crime, today's victim may become tomorrow's perpetrator seeking revenge."[26]

Some law enforcement authorities have concluded that prevention is more effective than prosecution. A city near Los Angeles is an example. Officials in Paramount, California, began in the early 1980s to recognize their gang problems. According to a recent report published by researchers at the University of Southern California (USC), a prevention program called Gang Resistance Is Paramount (GRIP) has been successful in reducing gang activities and membership. GRIP focuses on educating students in the second, fifth, and ninth grades about gangs, gang violence, vandalism, peer pressure, drug abuse, and other negatives, as well as the positives of self-esteem, family, and many other topics. GRIP attempts to get to children before they are recruited by gangs. The USC researchers reported, "There has been a significant decrease in the activity of major gangs, gang members, and the ratio of gang members to residents in Paramount since 1982."[27]

Gangs and gang activities are not limited to male members. Earlier sociological researchers reported that female juveniles participated in gangs, too, and that they did so for some of the same reasons as their male counterparts: to find a sense of belonging that they had not found elsewhere. One researcher found that female gang members did not view themselves as criminals, even when they engaged in behavior that violated the law. They rationalized their behavior by saying that it was necessary in their society or by denying responsibility for what they did. Generally female gang members were aggressive against other women but not against men.[28]

A 1999 report by the Chicago Crime Commission, based on a two-year study of female teen gangs, concluded the following:

> They are stepping to the forefront, selling their own drugs, making their own decisions, and avenging their own wrongs. Females are willing to participate in the full range of violent criminal activity at the same rate and the same level—and sometimes more—as their male counterparts.[29]

12-3   The Constitutional Rights of Juveniles

The U.S. Supreme Court has held that the U.S. Constitution extends some but not all of the rights of adult defendants to juveniles. In most situations juveniles have a right to counsel (and to have counsel appointed if they cannot afford private defense counsel), the right not to be tried twice for the same offense, and the right to have the allegations against them proved by the same standard—beyond a reasonable doubt—that is used in a criminal trial. They do not have a federally recognized constitutional right to a trial by jury, although some state statutes provide for one.

The U.S. Supreme Court has not decided the issue of whether juveniles have the right to a public trial, but it has held that the press may not be punished criminally for publishing the name of a juvenile delinquent when it obtains the name by lawful means.[30] Some states have statutes permitting the press to attend juvenile hearings. Others leave the decision to the discretion of the judge or prohibit the press entirely. The issue of whether juveniles have a federal constitutional right to a speedy trial has not been decided, but many states have provided by statute for limitations on the period of time the state may take to process a juvenile case. Two recent cases illustrate.

In 1999, the Pennsylvania Superior Court held that the Sixth Amendment (see Appendix A) right to a speedy trial applies to juvenile delinquency proceedings. *Commonwealth* v. *Dallenbach* involved a juvenile who was accused of harassing and threatening a Spanish family. Dallenbach's hearing was not set until 5 months after the petition was filed, but shortly before the scheduled hearing the state requested and obtained a continuance. The hearing was scheduled for 13 months later. The court noted that, although the U.S. Supreme Court had not ruled on this precise issue, it had ruled that juveniles are entitled to fundamental fairness. With that in mind, the Pennsylvania court said,

> To ensure successful rehabilitation, the reformation program (including punishment) must commence within a reasonable time of the child's delinquent act so that the child can comprehend the consequences of his act and the need for reform. As a result, the concept of "fundamental fairness" in juvenile proceedings would seem to require that at least some time limit be placed on the length of time between the delinquent act and the case disposition, including any associated punishment.[31]

Also in 1999, the New York Court of Appeals ruled that, under that state's constitution, juveniles have the right to a speedy trial. In addition to the problems that delays may create for adults, juveniles may have a less acute memory and thus be even more disadvantaged in recalling the facts of the alleged incident. Furthermore, the court stated that delay hinders rehabilitation, which is still an important part of juvenile justice.[32]

12-3a U.S. Supreme Court Cases

Recognition of juveniles' constitutional rights has occurred in a limited number of cases decided by the U.S. Supreme Court, beginning with *Kent* v. *United States,* decided in 1966. Technically this case does not apply to juvenile courts in other jurisdictions because it involved the interpretation of a District of Columbia statute. The case is important, however, because it signaled the beginning of the movement to infuse juvenile court proceedings with some due process elements.[33]

Morris A. Kent Jr., a 16-year-old, was arrested and charged with rape, six counts of housebreaking, and robbery. In accordance with a Washington, D.C., statute, the juvenile court waived its jurisdiction over Kent, who was transferred to the adult criminal court for further proceedings. Kent requested a hearing on the issue of whether he should be transferred, and his attorney requested the social service file used by the court in the transfer decision. Both requests were denied.

Although the D.C. statute required a full investigation prior to the waiver of a juvenile from the jurisdiction of the juvenile court to that of the adult criminal court, the juvenile court judge did not state any findings of facts; nor did he give reasons for his decision to transfer Kent to the criminal court, which might lead one to think a full investigation did not occur.

Kent was indicted by a grand jury and tried in a criminal court. A jury found him not guilty by reason of insanity on the rape charge and guilty on the other charges. He was sentenced to serve from 5 to 15 years on each count, for a total of 30 to 90 years in prison. Kent appealed his case. The first appellate court affirmed; the U.S. Supreme Court reversed. The U.S. Supreme Court agreed that juvenile courts need great latitude; it affirmed the doctrine of *parens patriae* but concluded that this doctrine does not constitute "an invitation to procedural arbitrariness." The Court suggested that the "original laudable purpose of juvenile courts" had been eroded and that there "may be grounds for concern that the child receives the worst of both worlds; that he gets neither the protection accorded to adults nor the solicitous care and regenerative treatment postulated for children."[34]

The first juvenile case from a state court to be heard by the U.S. Supreme Court was *In re Gault.* On 8 June 1964, 15-year-old Gerald Gault and a friend were taken into custody in Arizona after a Mrs. Cook complained that two boys had been making lewd phone calls to her. Gault's parents were not notified that their son was in police custody. When they returned home from work that evening and found that Gerald was not there, they sent his brother to look for him and were told that he was in police custody.

Gault's parents were not shown the petition that was filed the next day. At the first hearing, attended by Gerald and his mother, Mrs. Cook did not testify; no written record was made of the proceedings. At the second hearing, Mrs. Gault asked for Mrs. Cook, but the judge said that Mrs. Cook's presence was not necessary. The judge's decision was to commit Gerald to the state industrial school until his majority (age 21 in Arizona). When the judge was asked on what basis he adjudicated Gerald delinquent, he said he was not sure of the exact section of the code. The section of the Arizona Criminal Code that escaped his memory defined as a misdemeanant a person who "in the presence or hearing of any woman or child . . . uses vulgar, abusive, or obscene language." For this offense a 15-year-old boy was committed to a state institution until his majority. The maximum legal penalty for an adult was a fine of $5 to $50 or imprisonment for a maximum of two months. In contrast to an accused juvenile, an adult charged with this crime would be afforded due process at the trial.

The case was appealed to the U.S. Supreme Court, which reversed. Justice Abe Fortas delivered the opinion for the majority. Counsel had raised six basic rights: notice of the charges, right to counsel, right to confrontation and cross-examination, privilege against self-incrimination, right to a transcript, and right to appellate review. The Supreme Court ruled on the first four of these issues. The Court limited the extension of procedural safeguards in juvenile courts to those proceedings that might result in the commitment of juveniles to an institution in which their freedom would be curtailed. Justice Fortas excluded from the Supreme Court's decision the preadjudication and the postadjudication, or dispositional, stages. Justice Fortas reviewed the humanitarian philosophy of juvenile courts, but he said that the reality of juvenile courts is an unfulfilled dream. Courts that had been designed to act in the best interests of the child had become courts in which arbitrary and unfair procedures frequently occurred.[35]

The U.S. Supreme Court explained the importance of due process and of the procedural rules that protect it, especially the right to counsel. The Supreme Court compared procedure in law to the scientific method in science. The Court noted that Gault had been "committed to an institution where he may be restrained of liberty for years." Calling the institution an industrial school made no difference. The fact was that the juvenile's world became "a building with whitewashed walls, regimented routine and institutional hours . . . peopled by guards, custodians, state employees, and 'delinquents' confined with him for anything from waywardness to rape and homicide." In light of the seriousness of this confinement, it would be "extraordinary if our Constitution did not require the procedural regularity and the exercise of care implied in the phrase 'due process.' Under our Constitution, the condition of being a boy does not justify a kangaroo court."[36]

Despite the ruling by the U.S. Supreme Court in the *Gault* case that juveniles have a right to counsel, a study published by the American Bar Association (ABA) in 2003 concluded that "the spirit and promise" of the case "had been largely unfulfilled." Among other findings the report stated the following:

- Many juveniles waive their right to counsel because no one has sufficiently explained the importance of that right to them.

- Most courts in the study did not even keep track of the number of juveniles who waive their right to counsel.

- Many juvenile court officials continue to believe that the juvenile proceedings should be adversarial.

- Those juveniles who are represented by counsel are often represented by less than ideal counsel, characterized by a lack of preparation and advocacy. "At least 90 percent of detained youth did not even know their public defender's name."

- Most public defenders who represent juveniles spend very little time with their clients.

This ABA study of the Maryland system concluded that "the majority of youth in detention are incarcerated without effective representation" and that youths are routinely detained in secure facilities for the purpose of punishment. The ABA recommended that juveniles not be permitted to waive their right to counsel until they have spoken with counsel; that defense counsel who represent juveniles receive increased training and greater resources; that juvenile court actions have oversight and monitoring to avoid disparate treatment of minorities, youths with educational needs, and those who are mentally ill; and that the "misuse and abuse of secure detention" be put to an end.[37]

The U.S. Supreme Court has considered other constitutional rights for juveniles. In 1970 in *In re Winship*, the Supreme Court faced the issue of whether juvenile court proceedings require the same standard of proof as that of adult criminal courts or whether a lesser standard can be used. The Court applied the criminal court standard, concluding that "the observance of the standard of proof beyond a reasonable doubt will not compel the States to abandon or displace any of the substantive benefits of the juvenile process."[38]

In 1971 in *McKeiver* v. *Pennsylvania*, the U.S. Supreme Court refused to extend the right to a trial by jury to juvenile court proceedings. The Supreme Court emphasized that the underlying reason for its decisions in *Gault* and *Winship* was the principle of fundamental fairness. When the issue is one of fact finding, elements of due process must be present. But a jury is not a "necessary component of accurate fact-finding." The Supreme Court concluded that, unlike adult criminal courts, juvenile courts should not become full adversary systems. The Court left open the possibility for state courts to experiment, *inviting* them to try trial by jury in juvenile proceedings but refusing to require them to do so.[39]

In 1975 in *Breed* v. *Jones*, the U.S. Supreme Court held that the constitutional provision that defendants may not be tried twice for the same offense applies to juveniles. Breed,

17, was apprehended for committing acts while armed with a deadly weapon. He was adjudicated in the juvenile court, which found the allegations to be true. At the hearing to determine disposition, the court indicated that it intended to find Breed "not . . . amenable to the care, treatment and training program available through the facilities of the juvenile court," as required by the statute. Breed was transferred to criminal court, where he was tried and found guilty of robbery in the first degree. Breed argued on appeal that the transfer after a hearing and decision on the facts in juvenile court subjected him to two trials on the same offense. The U.S. Supreme Court agreed.[40]

In 1984 in *Schall* v. *Martin*, the U.S. Supreme Court upheld the New York statute that permitted preventive detention of juveniles. The Supreme Court held that preventive detention fulfills the legitimate state interest of protecting society and juveniles by detaining those who might be dangerous to society or to themselves. The Court reiterated its belief in the doctrines of fundamental fairness and *parens patriae*, stating that it was trying to strike a balance between the juvenile's right to freedom pending trial and society's right to be protected. The juveniles in this case were apprehended for serious crimes. According to the U.S. Supreme Court, the period of preventive detention was brief and followed proper procedural safeguards. Three justices disagreed with the Supreme Court's decision.[41]

In 1994, the California Supreme Court interpreted *Schall* v. *Martin* as not requiring that juveniles be granted a probable cause hearing within 48 hours after arrest, as is required for adults. The California court recognized significant differences in the detention of juveniles as compared with adults, noting that in many cases it is in the juvenile's best interest that detention occur. The court cited specific sections in the California statute that provide adequate safeguards for detained juveniles. For example, a juvenile may not be detained for more than 24 hours without written review and approval. The U.S. Supreme Court refused to hear the case, thus leaving the California decision intact.[42]

In 1992 in *United States* v. *R.L.C.*, the U.S. Supreme Court held that juveniles may not be punished more harshly in sentencing than they would have been had they been charged and convicted of the same crime as an adult.[43] And in 2004, the U.S. Supreme Court decided a case concerning the issue of whether juveniles must be given the *Miranda* warning before the police question them at the police station. In the case of *Yarborough* v. *Alvarado*, the Los Angeles police questioned a 17-year-old suspect at the police headquarters without giving him the *Miranda* warning. The police argued that the warning was not necessary because the suspect was free to leave. The Ninth Circuit Court of Appeals had ruled in the suspect's favor, holding that a person his age would not feel free to leave the police station. The U.S. Supreme Court reversed, holding that, under the facts of the case, when the police questioned the appellant, he was not in police custody for purposes of the *Miranda* warning; he was free to leave. Alvarado was suspected of being involved with a group of teens who were at a mall the night of the killing in question. About a month after the shooting, the officer in charge of the investigation left word at Alvarado's house and called his mother at work, stating that the officer would like to talk with Alvarado. The parents took Alvarado to the sheriff's office and waited in the lobby while the officers interviewed him for about two hours; the *Miranda* warning was not given.[44] This case is to be distinguished from the issue of whether juveniles have a constitutional right to the *Miranda* warning, a subject that is discussed later in this chapter. The issue in this case was whether the juvenile had come within the *Miranda* warning embrace—that is, whether at the time he was free to go and thus the *Miranda* warning was not required.

12-3b   Juvenile Curfews

Constitutional issues have arisen in recent years with the imposition of curfews in an attempt to reduce crime by keeping juveniles who are not accompanied by an adult off the streets after specified hours. One example of this trend, which is being adopted by more and more cities, is the Dallas, Texas, ordinance. This ordinance provides that youths under 17 must be off the streets from 11 P.M. to 6 A.M. During those hours juveniles may not be in public places or establishments. The exceptions are youths who are running errands for their parents or other adults; returning from school, civic, or religious functions; passing time on sidewalks in front of their homes; or exercising First Amendment rights (see Appendix A). Violations may result in a fine not to exceed $500 for each offense.

In 1993, the U.S. Court of Appeals for the Fifth Circuit upheld the Dallas ordinance, emphasizing that the ordinance was narrowly tailored to further the city's compelling interest in reducing and preventing juvenile crime and victimization. The U.S. Supreme Court refused to hear the case, thus allowing the decision of the Fifth Circuit to stand.[45]

The U.S. Supreme Court took a similar position in 1999, when it refused to review a challenge to a Charlottesville, Virginia, midnight weekday curfew for teens. Parents had challenged the curfew as an infringement on their parental discretion and their children's freedom, claiming that the ordinance puts their children under "house arrest." The ordinance covers teens under 17 and provides that, from midnight to 5 A.M. on weekdays and 1 to 5 A.M. on Saturdays and Sundays, they may not be on the streets. Some exceptions are permitted, such as a teen who is running an errand for a parent and is carrying a note from a parent.[46]

Some curfews are more restrictive. In New Orleans, for example, the juvenile weekday curfew is 8 P.M. during the school year and 9 P.M. during summer vacations. Some curfews extend beyond the streets; for example, the Mall of America in Minneapolis is included in the teen curfew of that city.[47] And some curfews have been held unconstitutional. In 1997, for example, a federal appellate court in California held that the San Diego ordinance, which made it illegal for minors to "loiter, idle, wander, stroll or play" after 10 P.M. was unconstitutional.[48]

What distinguishes these cases? Why are some curfew ordinances constitutional but others are not? Portions of the decision involving the Charlottesville, Virginia, ordinance are included here to clarify. The opinion is lengthy and involves numerous constitutional issues. Only a few are included here.[49]

Schleifer v. City of Charlottesville

This appeal involves a challenge to the constitutionality of a juvenile nocturnal curfew ordinance enacted by the City of Charlottesville. The district court held that the ordinance did not violate the constitutional rights of minors, their parents, or other affected parties and declined to enjoin its enforcement. We agree that the ordinance is constitutional and affirm the judgment of the district court.

On December 16, 1996, the Charlottesville City Council, after several months of study and deliberation, amended Section 17-7 of the City Code to enact a new juvenile nocturnal curfew ordinance. The City Council designed the curfew ordinance to:

(i) promote the general welfare and protect the general public through the reduction of juvenile violence and crime within the City;

(ii) promote the safety and well-being of the City's youngest citizens, persons under the age of seventeen (17), whose inexperience renders them particularly vulnerable to becoming participants in unlawful activities, particularly unlawful drug activities, and to being victimized by older perpetrators of crime; and

(iii) foster and strengthen parental responsibility for children.

Effective March 1, 1997, the ordinance generally prohibits minors, defined as unemancipated persons under seventeen, from remaining in any public place, motor vehicle, or establishment within city limits during curfew hours. The curfew takes effect at 12:01 A.M. on Monday through Friday, at 1:00 A.M. on Saturday and Sunday, and lifts at 5:00 A.M. each morning.

The ordinance does not restrict minors' activities that fall under one of its eight enumerated exceptions. Minors may participate in any activity during curfew hours if they are accompanied by a parent; they may run errands at a parent's direction provided that they possess a signed note. The ordinance allows minors to undertake employment, or attend supervised activities sponsored by school, civic, religious, or other public organizations. The ordinance exempts minors who are engaged in interstate travel, are on the sidewalk abutting their parents' residence, or are involved in an emergency. Finally, the ordinance does not affect minors who are "exercising First Amendment rights protected by the United States Constitution, such as the free exercise of religion, freedom of speech and the right of assembly."

The ordinance sets forth a scheme of warnings and penalties for minors who violate it. For a first violation, a minor receives a verbal warning, followed by a written warning to the minor and the minor's parents. For subsequent violations, the minor is charged with a Class 4 misdemeanor. The ordinance also makes it unlawful for certain other individuals, including parents, knowingly to encourage a minor to violate the ordinance....

Plaintiffs are five minors under age seventeen who are subject to the ordinance, one eighteen-year-old, and two parents of minor children. The minors allege that, with their parents' permission, they occasionally wish to engage in lawful activities which the curfew will not permit. These activities include attending late movies; getting a 'bite to eat'; playing in a band; socializing with older siblings; and attending concerts in Richmond, which would bring them back through Charlottesville during curfew hours. The eighteen-year-old plaintiff alleges that he has been deprived of opportunities to associate with his younger friends by the ordinance. The parent plaintiffs allege that the ordinance interferes with their decisions on which activities, at what times, are appropriate for their children....

[The court discussed the constitutional tests that should be used to determine this case and contrasted the San Diego curfew ordinance, which was held unconstitutional.]

The San Diego curfew applied to all minors under the age of eighteen, began at 10:00 P.M., and extended until 'daylight immediately following.' It contained four exceptions: (1) when a minor is accompanied by a parent or other qualified adult; (2) when a minor is on an emergency errand for his parent; (3) when a minor is returning from a school-sponsored activity; and (4) when a minor is engaged in employment.

By contrast, Charlottesville's curfew applies only to minors less than seventeen years of age, does not begin until midnight on weekdays and 1:00 A.M. on weekends, lifts at 5:00 A.M. each morning, and contains no fewer than eight detailed exceptions.... [Those are listed; see the same list earlier in the opinion.]

The Charlottesville ordinance carefully mirrors the Dallas curfew ordinance.... Like the Charlottesville ordinance, the Dallas curfew covered fewer hours than San Diego's and affected minors under the age of seventeen, not eighteen.... [The court listed the exceptions in the Dallas curfew ordinance, which are similar to those in the Charlottesville one, and concluded that the Charlottesville curfew,] with its narrow scope and comprehensive list of exceptions, represents the least restrictive means to advance Charlottesville's compelling interests....

[The court notes the stated purposes of the Charlottesville curfew ordinance and the arguments regarding whether those purposes were being met and concludes as follows:]

The Charlottesville curfew serves not only to head off crimes before they occur, but also to protect a particularly vulnerable population from being lured into participating in such activity. Contrary to the dissent's protestation, we do not hold that every such curfew ordinance would pass constitutional muster. The means adopted by a municipality must bear a substantial relationship to significant governmental interests; the restrictiveness of those means remains the subject of judicial review. As the district court noted, however, the curfew law in Charlottesville is 'among the most modest and lenient of the myriad curfew laws implemented nationwide.' Charlottesville's curfew, compared to those in other cities, is indeed a mild regulation: it covers a limited age group during only a few hours of the night. Its various exceptions enable minors to participate in necessary or worthwhile activities during this time. We hold that Charlottesville's juvenile curfew ordinance comfortably satisfies constitutional standards.

Accordingly, we affirm the judgment of the district court. We do so in the belief that communities possess constitutional latitude in devising solutions to the persistent problem of juvenile crime.

Recall that the U.S. Supreme Court refused to hear this case; thus the decision stands. The opinion gives some of the reasons the Charlottesville and Dallas ordinances are constitutional, whereas that of San Diego was not. In 2003, the Washington Supreme Court held that the juvenile curfew in Sumner, Washington, was unconstitutional. That ordinance was challenged by a father who permitted his son, age 14, to go to a convenience store during curfew hours. The Sumner curfew prohibited teens under 18 from "remaining" in public places or businesses between the hours of 11 P.M. and 5 A.M. Sunday through Thursday and later on Fridays, Saturdays, or holidays. The police could cite parents who permitted their children to violate the curfew. The court held that the word *remaining* was unconstitutionally vague. The court pondered, for example, whether stopping to tie a shoe while walking, or stopping for gasoline on the way home from a football game, would constitute *remaining*. According to the court, "[A]n ordinance which affords a police officer broad discretion to determine if a juvenile is in violation when tying his or her shoe or pumping gas does not withstand a vagueness challenge." The ordinance did not offer standards for distinguishing unpermitted behavior from permitted behavior.[50] After that decision, Sumner city council members decided to wait a year and assess the juvenile crime data in the area before deciding whether to draft another curfew.[51]

An issue separate from the constitutionality of juvenile curfews is whether we *should* have them. One study of the effects of juvenile curfews led the researchers to conclude that the preventive effect of such ordinances "appeared to be small."[52]

12-3c   Race and Gender Issues

Both race and gender are important factors to consider in analyzing juvenile justice systems. A study published in 1994 disclosed that, even after controlling for the influence of social factors and the seriousness of the offense in question, "African American and Latino youth were more likely to be detained at each decision point in the juvenile justice system."[53] Another study of African American youths had similar findings with regard to differential treatment but found that the differences varied among jurisdictions. This suggests the need for a more careful analysis of factors other than race that might be involved in producing the differences.[54]

In 2000, a study sponsored by the National Council on Crime and Delinquency (NCCD) reported that, at every stage of criminal justice systems, African American youths are overrepresented. Although they constitute only 15 percent of all youths under age 18, of those juvenile cases coming to the attention of the police, African American youths, as compared with whites, represent the following:

- Twenty-six percent of all juvenile arrests
- Thirty-one percent of those referred to juvenile courts (rather than processed informally outside the system)
- Forty-four percent of the youths who are detained pending adjudication
- Thirty-two percent of those who are adjudicated delinquent
- Forty-six percent of those who are transferred to adult criminal courts
- Forty percent of the youths who are sent to residential juvenile facilities
- Fifty-eight percent of the youths who are sent to adult jails or prisons[55]

The NCCD report found that Latino youths are also overrepresented in the system, although it is difficult to assess the extent, since some Latinos are classified as white. But the data did indicate that, when Latino and white youths are charged with the same offenses, Latinos are three times more likely than whites to be incarcerated (African Americans are six times more likely). The NCCD referred to the juvenile justice system as having a "double standard of justice"—one for whites and one for minorities—and concluded that "kids of color are much more likely to spend their formative years behind bars." Officials warned that there is a danger in concluding that these differences are *caused* by racist police, prosecutors, and juvenile court officials. Rather, the evidence *suggests* that justice systems for juveniles are not racially neutral. Despite the warnings, the report concluded, "Throughout the system, minority youth—especially African American youth—receive different and harsher treatment. This is true even when white youth and minority youth are charged with similar offenses. This report documents a juvenile justice system that is 'separate but unequal.'"[56]

A 2002 report comparing the treatment of white and Latino youths in criminal justice systems also concluded that Latinos are "significantly over-represented in the U.S. justice system and receive harsher treatment than white youth, even when charged with the same types of offenses." When youths are charged with drug offenses, Latinos are 13 times more likely than whites to be incarcerated.[57]

In contrast, a 2003 publication by two criminologists, supported by a grant from the Office of Juvenile Justice and Delinquency Prevention, concluded that police decisions to take juveniles into custody are not based on race. According to this report, the data

> offer no evidence to support the hypothesis that police are more likely to arrest nonwhite juvenile offenders than white juvenile offenders, once other incident attributes are taken into consideration. . . . The data do indicate, however, an indirect bias effect in the arrest of nonwhite juveniles in that they are more likely to be arrested when the victim is white than when the victim is nonwhite.[58]

Earlier in the chapter, we noted that there is evidence that juveniles do not have adequate legal assistance. The same study, by the American Bar Association (ABA), reported that the situation may be worse for minorities:

> [T]oo many children, particularly of color, fall victim to conveyer-belt justice—with kids rushed through a system riddled with institutional flaws, without regard for their individual cases or needs.
>
> Collectively, the reports paint a disturbing picture [according to the ABA president, with the overall result being] a massive misdirection of resources that fails children and undermines public safety.[59]

There are some signs of successful efforts to reduce apparent racial disparity among juveniles in our justice systems. In 2002, a study of the detention of juveniles in the Oregon county that contains Portland concluded as follows: "Maltnomah County has shown the country that you can reduce racial disparities in juvenile justice, make more modest use of detention, and still uphold public safety." The study was conducted by the Justice Policy Institute (JPI), a criminal justice research group based in Washington, D.C. The successful efforts included hiring more minority personnel, seeking additional alternatives to detention, and establishing written criteria for selecting those youths who should be detained.[60]

Another factor crucial to an analysis of differential reactions within juvenile justice systems is that of gender. The 1974 Juvenile Justice and Delinquency Prevention Act (JJDPA) encouraged states to find means other than incarceration for juveniles who had committed nonserious offenses (status offenders, most of whom were girls) and for juveniles who were dependent or neglected but who had not committed any offenses. The statute called for an end to incarcerating juveniles with adults.[61]

Often race and gender are combined, as juvenile justice systems discriminate against minority females. In a 2001 publication, *Justice by Gender: The Lack of Appropriate Prevention, Diversion, and Treatment Alternatives for Girls in the Justice System*, the author, an expert on juvenile delinquency, noted the various ways in which she believed the data provided evidence of discrimination against youthful female offenders. These were more likely to be apprehended for minor or status offense violations, such as running away from home, behaviors associated with mental health problems, disorderly conduct, and violation of probation or court orders. In recent years the apprehension and incarceration rates for female teens have increased significantly, whereas overall juvenile crime has decreased. Female youths now account for approximately one-fourth of all juvenile arrests and, while incarcerated, young females are more likely than young males to be sexually abused. The author advocated that "the vast majority of female juvenile offenders should be diverted from formal court proceedings and placed in individually tailored programs." She emphasized that these programs should be sensitive to racial and ethnic differences as well as to the educational, health, and family problems that contributed to the misbehavior of female youths.[62]

12-4   Juvenile Court Organization and Procedures

Juvenile courts differ somewhat from jurisdiction to jurisdiction, but our discussion in this section involves the organization and procedures that are found in most U.S. juvenile court systems. Figure 12-2 diagrams a typical organizational model and should be used as a reference for this discussion.

12-4a   Court Procedures

Juveniles may be referred to a juvenile justice system in various ways. Although most juvenile offenders are referred by law enforcement agencies, some referrals come from parents, relatives, schools, probation officers, other courts, and miscellaneous other sources. Juveniles may be counseled and released to their parents. Some are diverted to social services or other programs. In juvenile systems historically **diversion** was used to remove the juveniles from *official* juvenile or criminal proceedings before a hearing. If a decision is made

▶ **Diversion** The removal of the offender from the criminal proceeding before or after guilt is determined and disposition through other procedures, such as work release, drug treatment, or community service.

Figure 12-2
The Stages of Delinquent Case Processing in the Juvenile Justice System
Note: This chart gives a simplified view of caseflow through the juvenile justice system. Procedures vary among jurisdictions.
Source: Melissa Sickmund, Bureau of Justice Statistics, *Juveniles in Court* (Washington, D.C.: U.S. Office of Juvenile Justice and Delinquency Prevention, U.S. Department of Justice, June, 2003), p. 3.

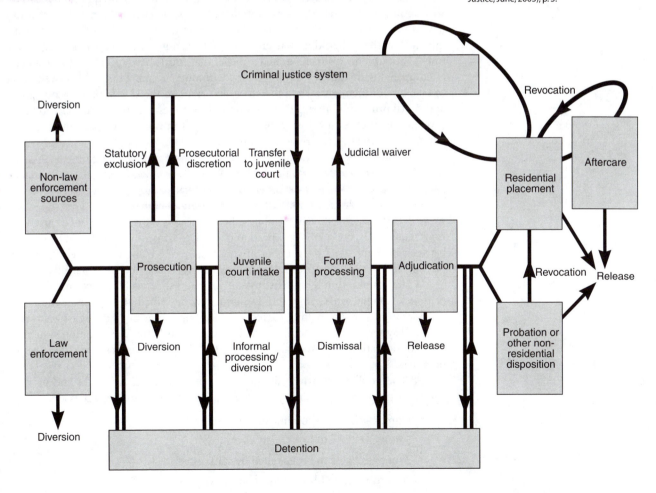

not to divert the juvenile to some other agency or to his or her parents, other dispositions must be made.

In some cases, after a referral has been made and the police have observed delinquent behavior, or an offense has been reported and juveniles are suspected, the police may begin surveillance and investigation. There is no way of knowing how many cases are handled by the police without any formal action being taken, but most juveniles are not taken into custody upon apprehension by police. Police are not the only people who may take children into custody. Officials in child protective services, probation officers, family services, and youth services may do so in many jurisdictions.

Historically there were few guidelines for taking juveniles into custody. In the *Gault* case the U.S. Supreme Court excluded prejudicial activities (such as police apprehension) that occur prior to a court appearance from the due process requirements of that case. Some lower courts have held that taking a juvenile into custody is not an arrest and, therefore, the due process requirements that must be observed in the arrest of an adult are not applicable. But most courts appear to consider the process an arrest, which should be accompanied by due process requirements.[63]

If a juvenile is taken into custody, the issues of search and seizure may arise. Most state courts have interpreted *Gault's* fundamental fairness test to mean that the constitutional prohibition against unreasonable searches and seizures applies to juvenile proceedings. Some states have incorporated exclusionary rules into their statutes; thus, evidence seized illegally in juvenile cases may not be admitted as evidence against the offenders.

Whether or not a search is conducted, there may be a decision to detain the juvenile. Most often, juveniles are taken into custody without a summons or a warrant. Police must then decide what to do with the juveniles in their custody. Most are released to their parents. When that is not possible or reasonable, most jurisdictions require that juveniles be placed in juvenile detention centers. As noted earlier in this chapter, in *Schall* v. *Martin* the U.S. Supreme Court upheld preventive detention for juveniles. After noting that juveniles have a substantial interest in liberty, the Supreme Court said, "But that interest must be qualified by the recognition that juveniles, unlike adults, are always in some form of custody." The Supreme Court reiterated its belief that courts have special powers over children, as compared with adults. "[C]hildren, by definition, are not assumed to have the capacity to take care of themselves" and therefore, according to the U.S. Supreme Court, they need additional protection. Preventive detention of juveniles may be appropriate to protect the juveniles themselves, not just to protect society, as in the case of preventive detention of adults, which the U.S. Supreme Court upheld in 1987.[64]

The power to detain juveniles does not mean the power to detain them in jails rather than in juvenile detention facilities. The Juvenile Justice and Delinquency Prevention Act, passed by Congress in 1974 and amended in subsequent years, provides that funds be made available for juvenile justice and delinquency projects and programs to those states that comply with the statute's mandates. Among other provisions is the phasing out of juvenile detention in *adult* jails, but a 1999 publication of the Department of Justice (DOJ) reported that between 1994 and 1997 the number of youths under 18 being held in jails increased by 35 percent, and in 1997 they constituted approximately 2 percent of the total jail population.[65]

A 2001 publication by the Institute of Crime, Justice, and Corrections, along with the National Council on Crime and Delinquency, described the "phenomenon of youth offender incarceration in adult correctional facilities" as a "burgeoning issue in many correctional systems" and recommended changes such as better classification systems to take into consideration the "special needs or the maturation issues presented by youthful offenders."[66]

A 2002 publication, which focused on Latino youths in adult jails and prisons, concluded, "Compared to youth in juvenile facilities, youth in adult facilities are:

- 8 times as likely to commit suicide.
- 5 times as likely to be sexually assaulted.
- 2 times as likely to be assaulted by staff.
- 50 percent more likely to be attacked with a weapon."[67]

Placing juveniles in adult prisons is a serious and controversial measure. According to the DOJ, juveniles accounted for almost 2 percent of all new court commitments to adult prisons in 1996. Over three-fourths of these juveniles were minorities. Most were 17; most were males.[68] In its data analysis published in June 2004, the DOJ stated that, according to the Bureau of Justice Statistics's (BJS) latest Annual Survey of Jails, on 30 June 2000, 7,600 inmates under the age of 18 were being held in adult jails, accounting for 1.2 percent of the total U.S. jail population on that date. Most of these juveniles had already been convicted or were awaiting trials in adult criminal courts.[69] In November 2004, the BJS published data on inmates in U.S. correctional facilities in 2003, noting that "fewer than 0.2 percent of all sentenced prisoners were under age 18 at yearend 2003." The total number of inmates who were under 18 at that time was approximately 2,800, compared with 4,800 at yearend 1995.[70] As noted in Spotlight 9-4 in Chapter 9, at midyear 2004, state prisons held 2,477 persons under age 18, while local jails confined 7,083 persons under that age.

Some courts have upheld committing juveniles to adult prisons. In 1997, the Washington Supreme Court upheld that state's provision that juveniles deemed to constitute a "continuing and serious threat to the safety of others at the institution" may be transferred administratively from a juvenile facility to an adult prison. The juvenile who appealed the case argued that, since his juvenile court hearing did not provide him with all of the procedural protections of an adult court, he was denied his constitutional rights. The court responded that changing the location of detention did not alter the system: the youth offender remained under the juvenile system and retained the benefits of that system.[71]

The issue of incarcerating juveniles in adult prisons was raised in the case of *Ratliff* v. *Cohn*, decided by the Indiana Supreme Court in 1998. Donna Ratliff was 14 when she set fire to her home, killing her mother and 16-year-old sister. Ratliff claimed that she had been beaten repeatedly by her mother and sexually molested by another older sister and an uncle. Ratliff was charged in an adult criminal court and entered guilty pleas to arson and two counts of reckless homicide. Although the trial court recommended that Ratliff be placed in an alternative facility, the Indiana Department of Corrections sent her to the Indiana Adult Women's Prison, where she was confined in a special-needs unit away from the general population. On appeal Ratliff raised several issues, most of which were denied. The state supreme court held that the state constitution and laws did not require that all juveniles be incarcerated in facilities designed especially for them but only that such facilities must exist. The court upheld the decision to incarcerate Ratliff in the women's prison and rejected most of her claims concerning her incarceration there. But the court did state that Ratliff had a due process claim with regard to her allegation that she was "subjected to hostility and threats by adult inmates . . . and fears for her safety" and that "she has been sexually propositioned and harassed by older inmates." The court expressed no view with regard to the accuracy of these claims but sent the case back to the trial court for consideration. Subsequently Ratliff was transferred to a private juvenile facility. In 1999, she was removed to a dorm for youthful offenders at the Indiana Women's Prison.[72]

Another issue with regard to juvenile detention or incarceration is that of bail. Some states have granted juveniles the right to release on bail; others have denied that right; still others have decided that it is not an issue because of the provision of special facilities for juvenile detention.

Another issue in juvenile court systems is whether juveniles should be interrogated by police. Originally it was assumed that it would be therapeutic for children to confess; thus, juveniles had few procedural protections concerning police interrogation. Today the rule is that juvenile confessions may be used against them in court, provided those confessions are made voluntarily.

Certain procedures conducted by police may not be applicable in juvenile cases. Most statutes covering juvenile proceedings attempt to protect juveniles from some of the harshness of adult criminal courts and therefore prohibit publication of the pictures of suspects and the taking of fingerprints. The use of lineups and showups, however, has been left to the courts, most of which have held that the standards applicable to adults must also be applied in juvenile proceedings.

If a decision is made to detain a juvenile, that individual is taken to intake screening, which is designed to remove the juveniles who should be diverted if that decision was not made earlier. A decision might be made at this stage to refer the juvenile to another agency or to his or her parents to await a hearing. A third alternative is to detain (or continue to detain) the juvenile before the hearing.

The **intake decision** is made by an intake officer, who may also be a probation officer. Theoretically these officers conduct an investigation before making the intake decision; however, with heavy caseloads, this may not be done thoroughly, if at all. Some states have placed statutory requirements on the intake officer regarding referrals out of the system or dismissals. For example, in some jurisdictions the intake officer may not dismiss a case without the prosecutor's written permission. In others the case may not be dismissed or diverted if the complaining witness insists that formal action proceed beyond this stage.

If the juvenile is detained with the intent that a petition will be filed to bring formal procedures, usually a hearing is held to determine whether there is reason to continue with the case. This is true whether the juvenile is being held as a dependent and neglected child or for alleged delinquency. The hearing must be held within a reasonable period after detention begins, but it does not involve all of the specific procedural safeguards.

After the preliminary inquiry or hearing, the juvenile may be released from detention, or the case may be dismissed. If the case is not dismissed, it may proceed only with the filing of a petition, the formal document for initiating a case in the juvenile system. This petition is in contrast to a grand jury indictment or a prosecutor's presentment in adult criminal courts.

The *Gault* case requires that juveniles and their parents be given adequate notice of the charges and of the proceedings to follow. Most states require that the adjudicatory hearing be held within a specified period after the petition is filed. If this does not occur, in some jurisdictions the case must be dismissed.

Juveniles may admit or deny guilt; most admit that they committed the acts of which they are accused. This plea must be a knowing and voluntary one, and juveniles have the right to counsel if they are involved in proceedings that could lead to confinement in an institution.

Since the *Kent* case, some jurisdictions have enacted statutes to permit juveniles some discovery procedures. *Discovery* involves the right to find out the evidence and witnesses the opposing side plans to use in the case. This information is necessary for the juvenile and his or her attorney to know how best to proceed with the case, and it might affect the juvenile's decision to admit or deny the allegations.

12-4b   The Role of Attorneys

In traditional juvenile court systems, there was no place for attorneys. The proceedings were not considered adversarial; all parties were thought to be acting in the child's best interests, and no need was seen for attorneys.

Prosecutors were not needed because the decision to proceed was made by intake officers. In reality, however, whether the individual is called an intake officer or a prosecutor, a person permitted to decide who will or will not be processed in the juvenile court system has considerable power. The question is not whether prosecutors have power but how much power they have. Some jurisdictions restrict prosecutorial power to dismiss the case after the petition is filed, but even in those cases prosecutors retain considerable discretion over determining whether to proceed with cases referred by the police or others.

The defense attorney's primary function in a juvenile case is to ensure that the juvenile's constitutional rights are protected during all of the proceedings. The attorney should be familiar with all the facts of the case and be prepared to present a defense at the hearing. The lack of formality in the hearing does not mean that the defense is any less important in a juvenile than in a criminal court hearing.

An important issue in juvenile court cases is whether the *Miranda* case applies to juveniles. In 1971, when the U.S. Supreme Court decided *McKeiver*, the Court stated in a footnote that, although it had not ruled that *Miranda* applies to juveniles, it was assuming that the *Miranda* principles were applicable to the proceedings in *McKeiver*, despite the Court's holding that juveniles are not entitled to all procedures applicable to criminal trials. Most

> ▶ **Intake decision**
> In prosecution, the first review of a case by an official in the prosecutor's office. Weak cases may be weeded out at this stage; in juvenile courts the reception of a juvenile against whom complaints have been made. The decision to dismiss or proceed with a case is made at this stage.

courts ruling on the question have held that *Miranda* applies to juvenile cases.[73] The issues arise over whether juveniles may waive their *Miranda* rights. Some courts have refused to accept a juvenile waiver without parental guidance. Others have held that children may not waive complicated legal rights, and thus it is permissible for police to question children in custody, provided they do so in a fair manner. Recall that, earlier in the chapter, in our discussion of the quality of legal assistance provided for juveniles, we noted a recommendation by the American Bar Association that courts not recognize a juvenile's waiver of the right to counsel unless that juvenile had the assistance of counsel in making the waiver decision.

The interaction between those who serve as prosecutors and those who serve as defense attorneys is as important in juvenile as in adult criminal court systems. The relationship between prosecutors and defense attorneys in juvenile systems is similar to the relationship they share in adult criminal court systems. They may serve as checks on the potential abuse of power, or they may cooperate to the point of violating juveniles' rights. They may serve diligently and competently, with the best interests of juveniles as their goals. But in some cases those who take that perspective find their goals thwarted by a system that has inadequate resources and insufficient personnel.

Another interaction that occurs between prosecutors and defense attorneys in criminal court proceedings is also applicable to juvenile proceedings. Plea bargaining does occur, and some have argued that in many cases this process is in the best interests of the child and of society.

The juvenile hearing is less formal than that of the adult criminal court, but the same general procedures occur. The prosecutor presents the evidence against the juvenile; the defense has an opportunity to cross-examine the witnesses; and some rules of evidence apply. Hearsay evidence may be presented in a juvenile hearing, in contrast to an adult criminal court trial. Evidence is presented to a judge and not to a jury, unless the jurisdiction provides for a trial by jury and the juvenile has not waived that right.

At the end of the presentation of evidence, there is an adjudication of whether the juvenile did what he or she has been accused of doing. Technically the terms *guilty* and *not guilty* are not used in juvenile proceedings, although the obvious purpose is to determine whether the alleged acts were committed. To support a finding of responsibility, the evidence must be sufficient to convince the judge beyond a reasonable doubt.

In traditional language, juveniles are not sentenced; dispositions are made. Dispositions tend to be indeterminate, although the court loses jurisdiction over the child when he or she reaches the age of majority. Several types of dispositions are available. Figure 12-2 illustrates that the court may take one of three routes. Nominal dispositions, such as warnings and reprimands, may be made. Conditional dispositions in juvenile courts are similar to those in adult criminal courts: restitution, fine, community service, suspended disposition, or community supervision (probation). A final method of disposition is to place juveniles in secure or nonsecure facilities.

What procedures must be followed at the disposition hearing? In *Gault,* the U.S. Supreme Court stated that it was not answering the question of which federal constitutional due process rights apply to the pre- or postadjudicatory hearing stages of the juvenile process. Therefore, the required procedures are established by state statutes or by state court decisions, and they vary from state to state. Because most juvenile cases do not involve a dispute over the facts, the disposition hearing becomes the most significant part of the process, and the right to counsel is important. Normally, disposition of a juvenile case involves a separate hearing from that of adjudication, and it is preceded by an investigative report, or social report, on which the decision may be based.

The social report is crucial to the philosophy that juveniles are to be treated individually and that it is possible to rehabilitate them. The social report should include any information that might have a bearing on assessing the needs of the particular child. The types of evidence that may be admitted at the dispositional stage are much broader than those permitted at the adjudicatory hearing.

After the disposition, the juvenile may have grounds for an appeal. In *Gault* the U.S. Supreme Court refused to rule that there is a constitutional right to appeal from a juvenile court decision, but since *Gault* all jurisdictions have made some statutory provisions for appeals.

12-5 Juveniles in Adult Criminal Courts

Concern with what appears to be an increasing number of juveniles involved in violent crimes has resulted in a push for more stringent treatment of these offenders. As Spotlight 12-2 reports, most states provide that in certain cases juveniles may be tried in adult criminal courts. This may be permitted because both the adult criminal courts and the juvenile courts have jurisdiction; the offenses are excluded from the jurisdiction of juvenile courts, or there is a *waiver* from the juvenile to the adult criminal court. This last procedure, also called *transfer* or **certification,** means that the juvenile court waives jurisdiction; the case is transferred from the juvenile court to the adult criminal court; or the juvenile court certifies that the juvenile should be tried as an adult. When certification occurs, the juvenile goes through the same procedures as those required in adult criminal courts and has the same constitutional rights as others who are tried in those courts.

Certification to an adult criminal court is important because it may result in more severe consequences to the juvenile, although this is not always the case. The certification process that must be followed differs from state to state. In some states the prosecutor makes the decision; in others the decision is made by the juvenile court judge.

The procedural requirements for waiver were articulated by the U.S. Supreme Court in the *Kent* case. As noted earlier, although the *Kent* case applied only to a statute at issue in Washington, D.C., most courts have interpreted the case as stating the minimum due process requirements for transfer from a juvenile court to an adult criminal court. The juvenile is entitled to a hearing on the issue of transfer, and the right to counsel attaches to that hearing. Upon request, the defense counsel must be given access to the social record that the court has compiled on the juvenile. If jurisdiction is waived from the juvenile court to the adult criminal court, the juvenile must be given a statement of the reasons for the waiver.

Some statutes give adult criminal courts jurisdiction over juveniles who commit specified serious crimes, such as murder, but permit the adult criminal court to transfer the case to a juvenile court. New York is an example. Under the New York statute, children age 13 or older who are charged with second-degree murder and children 14 or older who are charged with any one of a number of serious crimes (including burglary, sodomy in the first degree, aggravated sexual abuse, manslaughter in the first degree, murder, rape, and robbery) are under the *exclusive* original jurisdiction of adult criminal courts. But those courts may transfer the cases to juvenile courts by a process known as *reverse certification*.[74]

The Colorado Court of Appeals has held that, when a juvenile is transferred to an adult criminal court, due process does not require that the evidence supporting transfer be clear and convincing. Under the Colorado statute, a juvenile who is 14 or older and is accused of an act that would be a felony if committed by an adult may be transferred to an adult criminal court at the request of the prosecutor, provided the juvenile court conducts an investigation. The purpose of that investigation is to determine whether there is probable cause to believe that the juvenile committed the act and, if so, whether it is in the interests of society and of the accused juvenile that the case be transferred. The Colorado appellate court noted that the decision of whether or not to transfer is more analogous to a sentencing hearing than to a trial to determine guilt. The court emphasized that there is no constitutional right to be tried as a juvenile and that the risk to society of not trying the juvenile as an adult may outweigh any reasons for leaving the case in the juvenile court.[75]

The transfer of juveniles to adult criminal courts has been severely criticized by some juvenile court judges. According to the National Council of Juvenile and Family Court Judges, the "assumption is that . . . [adult] criminal courts will be tougher and can serve as a more effective deterrent for juvenile crime. . . . This assumption is not borne out by the facts."[76]

Two scholars who tested the results of Idaho's statutory automatic waiver to adult criminal courts of juveniles who are accused of violent crimes found that the process did

> **Certification** The process used to remove juveniles from the jurisdiction of the juvenile court to that of the adult criminal court; also called *transfer* or *waiver*.

Spotlight 12-2 Juveniles in Adult Criminal Courts

Many States Have Changed the Boundaries of Juvenile Court Jurisdiction

Traditionally discretionary judicial waiver was the transfer mechanism on which most states relied. Beginning in the 1970s and continuing through the present, however, state legislatures have increasingly moved juvenile offenders into criminal court based on age and/or offense seriousness, without the case-specific consideration offered by the discretionary juvenile court judicial waiver process.

State transfer provisions changed extensively in the 1990s. From 1992 through 1997, all but six states enacted or expanded transfer provisions. An increasing number of state legislatures have enacted mandatory waiver or exclusion statutes. Less common, then and now, are concurrent jurisdiction provisions.

In Most States, Juveniles Convicted in Criminal Court Cannot Be Tried in Juvenile Court for Subsequent Offenses

In thirty-one states, juveniles who have been tried as adults must be prosecuted in criminal court for any subsequent offenses. Nearly all of these "once an adult/always an adult" provisions require that the youth must have been convicted of the offenses that triggered the initial criminal prosecution.

Judicial Waiver Is the Most Common Transfer Provision

In all states except Nebraska, New Mexico, and New York, juvenile court judges may waive jurisdiction over certain cases and transfer them to criminal court. Such action is usually in response to a request by the prosecutor; in several states, however, juveniles or their parents may request judicial waiver. In most states, statutes limit waiver by age and offense.

Waiver provisions vary in terms of the degree of decision-making flexibility allowed. Under some waiver provisions the decision is entirely *discretionary*. Under the others there is a rebuttable *presumption* in favor of waiver. Under others waiver is *mandatory* once the juvenile court judge determines that certain statutory criteria have been met. Mandatory waiver provisions are distinguished from statutory exclusion provisions in that the case originates in juvenile rather than criminal court.

Statutes Establish Waiver Criteria Other Than Age and Offense

In some states, waiver provisions target youth charged with offenses involving firearms or other weapons. Most state statutes also limit judicial waiver to juveniles who are "no longer amenable to treatment." The specific factors that determine lack of amenability vary but typically include the juvenile's offense history and previous dispositional outcomes. Such amenability criteria are generally not included in statutory exclusion or concurrent jurisdiction provisions.

Many statutes instruct juvenile courts to consider other factors when making waiver decisions, such as the availability of dispositional alternatives for treating the juvenile, the time available for sanctions, public safety, and the best interests of the child. The waiver process must also adhere to certain constitutional principles of fairness.

Source: Howard N. Snyder and Melissa Sickmund, *Juvenile Offenders and Victims: 1999 National Report* (Washington, D.C.: Office of Juvenile Justice and Delinquency Prevention, U.S. Department of Justice, September 1999), p. 103.

not result in a reduction of violent juvenile crime. The authors concluded that their results were similar to those of a study of New York's automatic waiver statute: "there does not appear to be a deterrent effect of legislative waiver on rates of juvenile violent crimes." The researchers noted that the finding is interesting particularly in light of the vast differences between the two states: one a highly urbanized state with high crime rates, the other a much more rural state with low crime rates.[77]

In his dissertation at the University of Maryland, David L. Myers reported that juveniles processed through adult criminal courts, in comparison with those in juvenile courts, were more likely to be released prior to trial but that their recidivism rates were higher. If they went to trial they were more likely than juveniles in the juvenile court system to be convicted and incarcerated, and their sentences were longer. Myers concluded, "This suggests that the price of any short-term public safety achieved through prosecuting juveniles as adults might be an increase in long-term criminal offenses. . . . Although the transferred offenders received harsher punishment than did their counterparts retained in juvenile courts, public safety did not appear to be enhanced." Dr. Larry Sherman, chairman of the University of Maryland's Department of Criminology and Criminal Justice, where Myers was a student when he conducted this study, described this result as an unintended result of the "get-tough" laws: "It shows the bankruptcy of the legislative process where such crucial decisions are made in the absence of scientific evidence. . . . If the Food and Drug Administration had been asked to approve this policy, they would have rejected it for lack of evidence that the policy was safe and effective."[78]

According to data released in 1998 by the U.S. Bureau of Justice Statistics (BJS), of the juveniles in the 75 largest U.S. counties who were transferred to adult criminal courts, two-thirds had been charged with violent offenses. Those who were convicted were sentenced to an average 10-year term. Most juveniles who are transferred to adult criminal courts are convicted, and, if convicted, they are more likely than those in juvenile courts to be incarcerated. This is true even for the crime of murder. For example, 100 percent of juveniles convicted of murder in adult criminal courts during the BJS study were sentenced to prison, compared with only 77 percent of juveniles adjudicated of murder in juvenile court proceedings. The remaining 23 percent were given probation or other forms of sentences.[79]

Florida leads the nation in the number of juveniles tried as adults, with about 7,000 per year. Florida houses approximately 10 percent of the juveniles who are incarcerated in U.S. prisons.[80] Two recent cases—those of Lionel Tate and Nathaniel Brazill—caught the nation's attention. Tate's case was discussed in Chapter 7 in the context of plea bargaining.

Brazill, like Tate, was 14 when he was tried in a Florida adult criminal court, but unlike Tate, who was convicted of first-degree murder, Brazill was convicted of second-degree murder and thus escaped the mandatory sentence of life without parole specified by Florida law for first-degree murder convictions. Brazill, who was 13 when he shot and killed his favorite teacher, faced a possible 25 years-to-life sentence. He received 28 years. In May 2003, Brazill's conviction and sentence were upheld by a Florida court of appeals. Brazill's prosecutor, Marc Shiner, described the defendant as a killer whose "demeanor sends chills up my spine." But he also said that it was very difficult for him to prosecute a young man who was not much older than his own son. "There was something wrong with the picture. It just didn't fit. It didn't fit that you had a schoolteacher killed by a kid, either." Shiner subsequently became a defense attorney, and one of his first clients was a 16-year-old girl accused of killing her newborn son.[81]

Not all juveniles who commit serious crimes are tried in adult criminal courts, and not all who are tried in those courts receive such harsh punishment as Tate and Brazill. (Recall from the earlier discussion that Tate's conviction was reversed on appeal; rather than retry him, the prosecution offered him the same plea deal as previously, and Tate took it, resulting in his release. But Tate was arrested in Spring 2005 for allegedly engaging in the armed robbery of a pizza delivery person, although the juvenile who named Tate subsequently recanted. If Tate was involved in the armed robbery, he could be returned to prison for life). For example, the youngest child ever tried for murder in an adult court was convicted and sentenced to only 7 years in a maximum-security juvenile facility. Nathaniel Abraham, age 13 at sentencing and 11 when he murdered Ronnie Greene Jr., age 18, could have been sentenced to life in prison. Abraham was tried under a 3-year-old Michigan statute that permitted trying juveniles of any age in adult courts. The judge criticized the law as "fundamentally flawed" and assailed the criminal justice system for failing young people, such as Abraham, stating, "The Legislature has responded to juvenile criminal activity not by helping to prevent and rehabilitate, but rather by treating juveniles more like adults. . . . The real solution is to prevent an adult criminal population ever coming into existence."[82]

Successful constitutional challenges have been made to some automatic waivers from juvenile to criminal courts. For example, the Delaware provision that a juvenile who turns 18 before trial should be transferred to an adult criminal court automatically if one or more enumerated crimes were charged, was held to violate the state and federal constitutions because it removed from the judiciary the authority to make the transfer decision. In essence, the decision was made by the prosecutor, who had the power to effect a transfer by bringing charges of an enumerated offense.[83]

There are a number of reasons for and against certification or waiver. One of the strongest arguments in favor of waiver is that it sends a message to juveniles and thus serves as a deterrent. It serves as notice to society that we are getting tough on juvenile crime. But some experts argue that the get-tough approach is not working, giving only the *appearance* of toughness and deterrence. If the system is too severe, police may not arrest; prosecutors may not prosecute or will charge lesser offenses; juries may not convict. In addition, there is evidence that many juveniles who are tried in adult courts are not legally competent. A study published in 2003 by the MacArthur Foundation and conducted by a nine-member team led by a physician at the University of Massachusetts Medical School, concluded that juveniles who are tried in adult criminal courts are far more likely than adult defendants to have serious impairment of their competency. They are less likely to understand that it may be to their advantage not to talk freely to the police during interrogation. The report concluded that "states should consider implementing policies and practices designed to ensure that young defendants' rights to a fair trial are protected." That might mean requiring competency evaluations before a juvenile is transferred to an adult court.[84]

12-6 Megan's Laws and Juveniles

Recall Chapter 11's discussion of Megan's Laws. In some jurisdictions Megan's Laws extend to juvenile sex offenders, who may be required to register for life. In 2003, the Illinois Supreme Court upheld the sentencing of a 12-year-old who is required to register as a sex offender for the remainder of his life. In a 5-to-1 decision the court rejected the argument that lifetime registration conflicts with the rehabilitative purposes of juvenile systems. The defendant in *People* v. *J.W.* pleaded guilty to two counts of aggravated sexual assault on two 7-year-old boys (in exchange for the state's dropping other charges). The acts included oral and anal sex, as well as bestiality (in this case, sex with a dog). The defendant was placed on probation for 5 years and required to register as a sex offender for life. He appealed the registration requirement but the appellate court held that, because of the nature of his sex acts, he is a sexual predator under Illinois law and thus required to register as a sex offender for the rest of his life. In 1999, the Illinois legislature amended the juvenile statutes to include not only rehabilitation of juveniles but also protection of the public as goals; thus, said the judge, the sentence is rational in light of that purpose. Another term of the defendant's probation was that he could not live in or even return to the village in which the incidents took place. The defendant's parents said that they would move; until that occurred, the boy was to live with his aunt. He was eventually placed in a treatment center.[85]

Not all applications of Megan's Laws to juveniles have been upheld. In 1999, the Alabama Court of Criminal Appeals held that Alabama's Megan's Law was unconstitutional as applied to juveniles. The statute was applied to juveniles by a 1998 amendment, which required that juveniles who are adjudicated on the basis of certain enumerated acts must declare their intention to reside in a specific location before they can be released from custody. The juvenile's offense history, fingerprints, and photograph are provided to law enforcement officials in the designated area. In larger cities this information is distributed on fliers, which are sent to residences within a specified distance of schools, day care centers, and other places that care for children, and all schools within 3 miles of the offender's declared residence. The court ruled that the statute's provision that an adult may return to a home that has a minor but a juvenile may not do so (although an exception may be made for a juvenile offender who is the parent of the minor in the designated home) violates the juvenile's right to equal protection. Further, the court ruled that the statute violated the *ex post facto* rights of all juveniles who had committed their acts before the statute was amended to include them.[86]

12-7 Juvenile Drug Courts

Previous discussions in this text have encompassed drug courts, which are designed primarily for treatment rather than punishment. Because of that emphasis, drug courts are particularly applicable to juveniles. A comprehensive study by the National Drug Court Institute (NDCI) and the National Council of Juvenile and Family Court Judges (NCJFCJ) published in 2003 emphasized, however, that drug courts for juveniles should not mirror those for adults. The NDCI and the NCJFCJ created a council to develop a plan for drug courts for juveniles.

One main difference between juvenile and adult drug courts is that the former deal primarily with individuals who are usually not yet addicted to alcohol or other drugs. Thus, it is important for the drug courts to assess the level of juvenile involvement in drugs, ranging

Spotlight 12-3   Substance Abuse and Juveniles: A Report

[In 2004, the National Center on Substance Abuse at Columbia University (CASA) published a groundbreaking report on substance abuse among juveniles, based on a 5-year study. Some of the findings were as follows:]

- At least 30 percent of adults in prison for felony crimes were incarcerated as juveniles.
- Ninety-two percent of arrested juveniles who tested positive for drugs, tested positive for marijuana; 14.4 percent, for cocaine.
- Up to three-quarters of incarcerated 10- to 17-year-olds have a diagnosable mental health disorder.
- As many as eight out of 10 incarcerated juveniles suffer from learning disabilities.
- Compared to juveniles who have not been arrested, those who have been arrested once in the past year are: more than twice as likely to have used alcohol; more than 3.5 times likelier to have used marijuana; more than three times likelier to have used prescription drugs for non-medical purposes; more than seven times likelier to have used Ecstasy; more than nine times likelier to have used cocaine and more than 20 times likelier to have used heroin....
- The arrest rate for black juveniles is more than 1.5 times the rate for white juveniles.

[As a result of its findings, CASA] is calling for a complete overhaul of the juvenile justice system [including some of the following recommendations:]

- Creating a model juvenile justice code to set practice standards and accountability for states in handling juvenile offenders.
- Training all juvenile justice system staff, including juvenile judges, law enforcement and other court personnel, how to recognize and deal with substance-involved offenders.
- Extending to juveniles diversion programs such as juvenile drug courts and comprehensive home-based services.
- Making available treatment, healthcare, education and job training programs to children in juvenile justice systems.
- Expanding grant programs through the U.S. Office of Juvenile Justice and Delinquency Prevention and conditioning such grants on providing appropriate services to juvenile offenders....
- Ensuring that each child receives a comprehensive assessment to determine needs....

Source: Selections from the report by the National Center on Substance Abuse at Columbia University (CASA), as published in "Report Indicts Juvenile Justice System for Lack of Treatment: CASA Calls for Overhaul of State Systems," *Alcoholism & Drug Abuse Weekly* 16, no. 40 (18 October 2004), p. 1.

from abuse to dependency, and in some cases to addiction. But substance abuse is a serious problem among juveniles, as Spotlight 12-3 notes.

A second contrast between juveniles and adults who might benefit from drug courts is that most juveniles are living with their families, so the courts must focus on the entire family, not just the individual in trouble. The NDCI and NCJFCJ report emphasized the need to focus on positive rather than negative aspects of the juvenile's family. Juvenile drug courts must focus on "the idea that youth and their families—even though they have problems—have innate resources that can positively change their lives." Further, the court should treat juveniles and their families as "experts on their own case. As youth and families become more aware of their strengths, they begin to feel more capable. This in itself is a powerful intervention tool."

A third difference is that most juveniles are in school—or at least are required by law to be there. Thus, school systems should be involved in the drug court treatment plans. Fourth, juvenile drug courts must comply with the privacy and confidentiality requirements of juvenile court systems—which are not part of adult criminal court systems. Finally, although drug testing is important in both juvenile and adult drug courts, it should be utilized frequently with juveniles, but the youth's behavior should be watched carefully, as another measure of drug involvement.[87]

12-8   Juveniles in Corrections

The placement of juveniles in closed institutions is a relatively new practice. In the 1700s and early 1800s, it was thought that the family, the church, and other social institutions should handle juvenile delinquents. Jail was the only form of incarceration, and it was used primarily for detention pending trial. From 1790 to 1830, the traditional forms of social control began to break down as mobility and town sizes increased. Belief in sin as the cause of delinquency was replaced by a belief in community disorganization. A method was needed whereby juveniles could be put back into orderly lives. It was decided that the institution—

the house of refuge, the well-ordered asylum patterned after the family structure—was the answer.

The institutional model was used for juveniles, adult criminals, elderly persons, the mentally ill, orphans, unwed mothers, and vagrants. It was thought that by institutionalizing these persons their lives could become ordered as they were removed from the corruption of society. Life in the total institution was characterized by routine, head counts, and bells signaling the beginning and end of activities.[88]

By the 1850s, many people were admitting that custody was all the institutions offered. Problems such as overcrowding, lack of adequate staff, and heterogeneous populations led to the realization that institutionalization was not accomplishing its goal. The next concept for juveniles was the training school, typically built around a cottage system. It was thought that cottage parents would create a homelike atmosphere. Hard work, especially farmwork, was emphasized.

In recent years overcrowding, shortage of staff, and a lack of resources, along with due process violations, have characterized juvenile corrections. The first nationwide investigation of juvenile institutions, published in 1993, disclosed that 75 percent of juveniles were housed in institutions that violated at least one standard relating to living space. Forty-seven percent lived in overcrowded institutions, up from 36 percent in 1987. Overcrowding was described as a "pervasive and serious problem across the nation."[89]

The study, mandated by Congress in 1988, found that only 27 percent of juvenile facilities met security standards. Only 25 percent of juveniles were in facilities that met standards for controlling suicidal behavior, and 11,000 youths committed more than 17,000 suicidal acts in a year, although only 10 were completed in 1990. The study disclosed that between 1987 and 1991 the proportion of confined juveniles who were minorities increased from 53 percent to 63 percent, with Hispanics increasing from 13 percent to 17 percent and African Americans from 37 percent to 44 percent.[90] The results of this congressionally mandated study led then–U.S. Attorney General Janet Reno to declare, "This study puts an exclamation point on the obvious conclusion that America must take better care of its children before they get into trouble and not abandon them once they are in trouble."[91]

In 1999, the results of the first Census of Juveniles in Residential Placement (CJRP) was published. This census provides the most detailed information available on juveniles in corrections. According to the CJRP, on 29 October 1997, 106,000 juveniles were being held in juvenile residential placement facilities. Most (95 percent) had been committed by juvenile courts, with the remaining 5 percent there on orders from adult criminal courts. Twenty-six percent of the juveniles were being detained awaiting adjudication, disposition, or placement. Twenty-five percent of all juveniles in residential facilities had been charged with violent offenses, and 7 of 10 of those were minorities. Custody rates for African American juveniles were substantially higher than rates for other groups. Female juveniles represented only a small proportion of the juveniles in residential facilities (1 in 17), and they tended to be younger than male juveniles.[92]

Later studies of juvenile facilities also reported findings of overcrowded facilities. In a 2002 publication, the Office of Juvenile Justice and Delinquency Prevention (OJJDP) stated that approximately 40 percent of the juvenile facilities in its study were overcrowded. The OJJDP concluded that, although its census could not "establish a causal relationship, these crowded facilities were more likely than other facilities to report that they had transported youth to an emergency room in the last month because of injuries resulting from a conflict with another resident or individual."[93]

12-8a Types of Institutions for Juveniles

Despite the movement toward diverting juveniles from closed institutions, today most juveniles who are under the care and custody of the state are confined in public institutions or in traditional training schools. Detention centers and shelters are used to confine those who have been referred to juvenile courts and are awaiting disposition by those courts. These facilities are used for detaining juveniles who cannot be confined in their own homes. A child who is to be placed in a correctional institution may be held temporarily in a reception or diagnostic center, pending a decision concerning which institution would be the best placement for the child. Our primary concern in this section is with the facilities in which the juveniles are placed for their more lengthy confinement, and those are of three basic types: training schools, boot camps, and group homes

Generally the training school, which houses most confined juveniles, is the largest of the facilities. It was the first type of facility that was widely accepted for the confinement of juveniles, and it is the most secure. Some jurisdictions operate other types of facilities that are less secure, such as ranches, forestry camps, and farms. Most of these facilities are located in rural areas and permit greater contact with the community than the training school provides.

Boot camps, discussed in greater detail in chapter 9, are also used to incarcerate juveniles. In the boot camp atmosphere the offender must participate in a strongly regimented daily routine of physical exercise, work, and discipline, which resembles military training. Many of the programs include rehabilitative measures, such as drug treatment and educational programs, but this method of incarcerating offenders has its critics, and some programs have been abolished.

The least physically secure facilities are *group homes.* Unlike *foster homes,* which are community-based facilities in which juveniles live with families, many group homes are small institutions. Most are operated by a staff, not a family. The cost per juvenile resident is twice as high for staff-operated group homes as for foster care. Group homes have been criticized as a poor substitute for foster care homes because they remove the positive influence of the family atmosphere.[94]

The staff of many juvenile institutions attempt to make the facilities as homelike as possible. A campuslike environment or cottage setting, with a small number of juveniles housed in each building along with cottage or house parents, is typical. Despite these efforts, the architecture of many juvenile facilities reflects the premise that all who are confined there must face the same type of security as those few who need the more secure environment. Security is very important, but the facilities should not preclude opportunities for rehabilitation.

Institutions for detaining juveniles have come under criticism. After complaints about how incarcerated juveniles were being treated in Georgia, the Civil Rights Division of the U.S. Department of Justice (DOJ) began investigating some of the institutions that house juveniles. In February 1998, researchers reported that their investigation had "identified a pattern of egregious conditions violating the federal rights of youths in the Georgia juvenile facilities we toured." Among other violations, the DOJ report cited the failure to provide adequate health care for mentally disturbed juveniles, abusive disciplinary practices, overcrowding in some sections, inadequate educational and rehabilitative services and programs, and, in some facilities, a lack of adequate medical care. The DOJ described some of the conditions as abusive, egregious, and grossly substandard. The DOJ and Georgia state correctional officials reached an agreement under which the latter agreed to spend millions of dollars to institute significant changes in the housing and treatment of juveniles in the state's correctional facilities.[95] Extensive improvements were made in Georgia's juvenile justice system during the next three-to-four years.[96]

During an investigation of the juvenile institution in Jena, Louisiana, the DOJ found that inmates were physically abused and deprived of food and clothing while the institution was under the control of Wackenhut Corrections Corporation (WCC), the largest private prison company. In 2002, WCC abandoned its contract with Louisiana after the DOJ sued WCC and the state, alleging that conditions at Jena were "dangerous and life-threatening, and in need of emergency action to protect inmates." The state assumed temporary control of the institution, and changes were being made. In January 2003, the state and the DOJ reached an agreement that replaced the one noted earlier and acknowledged that Louisiana was primarily in compliance with the DOJ reforms. Under the new agreement the youthful offenders will have increased access to courts, forms for filing administrative procedure complaints, greater protection from harm and investigations of reported excessive force against them, more mental health treatment, and other treatment programs.[97]

One other state's juvenile correctional facilities have received significant attention in recent years. In 2003, the DOJ cited abuses in the Mississippi correctional system, charging the system with violating the constitutional rights of juveniles and failing to provide general and special education services at two institutions: the Oakley Training School (which confines serious male offenders) and the Columbia Training School in Clarion (which confines both female and male juveniles). Among the findings were the following:

- The schools violated the juveniles' First Amendment rights by forcing them to engage in religious activities.
- The juveniles were subjected to unsafe living conditions and received inadequate treatment and care.
- Disciplinary practices included pole-shackling, the improper use and overuse of restraints and isolation, pepper spray, and staff assaults on juveniles.[98]

The report documented the following specific abuse cases:

- A 13-year-old boy under suicide watch at Columbia was hog-tied face down, with his hands and feet shackled together.
- Suicidal girls at Columbia were forced to undress and then were placed naked in a dark room for three days to a week, with only a hole in the floor as a bathroom.
- A girl at Columbia was sprayed with pepper spray for yelling at an employee during an exercise drill.
- Several girls at Columbia were forced to eat their own vomit if they threw up during exercise.

The U.S. representative who filed a complaint about the schools, Bennie Thompson, recommended that the state employees of these two schools be prosecuted. "Those Draconian policies have been outlawed by every court in the land, and the fact these are juveniles . . . makes it even more egregious."[99]

After a year-long investigation, in December 2003 the DOJ filed a lawsuit, in which it challenged the conditions under which young offenders were being held in Mississippi, referring to the situation as constituting "unconscionable abuse." According to DOJ officials, the lawsuit is a necessity because they were unable to negotiate acceptable terms for improvement with Mississippi officials. The assistant attorney general for civil rights stated, "We do not lightly seek to place state facilities under consent degrees, but believe that one is necessary in this case." The official stated his conclusion that the only way to "effect lasting and systemic change" is to have the federal judiciary involved. The allegations include physical abuse and humiliation and some of the abuses cited earlier in this discussion. The lawsuit includes two juvenile facilities, the Oakley Training School (for boys) in Raymond, Mississippi, and the Columbia Training School in Columbia (for both boys and girls). Most of the youths in those facilities are there for nonviolent offenses. The response of the Mississippi attorney general was, "We should be spending our time and our money protecting our children instead of wasting it on unnecessary litigation and legal fees."[100]

In April 2005, the Mississippi governor signed into law a bill that is designed to improve conditions at the Columbia and Oakley training schools, and in May 2005 the DOJ and Mississippi settled the lawsuit that DOJ had filed against the state for civil rights violations at the juvenile institutions. Under the terms of the settlement, the state will continue to oversee daily operations, but a monitor was retained to ensure compliance with, among other provisions, the agreement to improve "protection from harm, suicide prevention, medical care, mental health care, rehabilitative treatment, and education." The national news release announcing this agreement quoted DOJ officials as stating that investigations were pending in California, Hawaii, Indiana, Maryland, Ohio, Oklahoma, and Virginia.[101]

Finally, attention should be given to the increasing need for facilities to house female juveniles. A look at Florida illustrates the problem and, perhaps, the solution. In the decade ending in 2002, the number of girls apprehended for delinquent or criminal behavior in Florida increased by 67 percent, compared with a 25 percent increase for boys. In 2002, girls constituted one out of every four juvenile offenders in Florida. The changes made in Florida to accommodate this increase in female juvenile offenders were described by a

Texas legal publication as "the most progressive and the most punitive programs in the nation for female juvenile offenders." In April 2002, Florida opened a maximum-security facility for young female felons, such as those convicted of carjackings, manslaughter, murder, aggravated battery, and other serious violent crimes. Only a few other such facilities exist in the nation. The institution, the Florida Institute for Girls, has been praised but also criticized as being too harsh for the treatment of young female offenders. Florida spends about $45,815 a year to incarcerate each delinquent girl; by comparison, Texas spends about $35,000 a year.[102]

In July 2003, after two more violent altercations between inmates and staff, the director of the Florida Institute for Girls lost her job. Earlier that summer, the state attorney general announced that he was ordering a grand jury investigation into alleged sexual abuse of the inmates at the prison. According to experts, even consensual sex between female inmates and correctional officers is devastating (as well as inappropriate and illegal). Most of the girls have been sexually abused by others, even family and friends, and they learn that the way to deal with problems is through sexual abuse. As one clinician said, "It perpetuates that that's how you deal with people, you deal with them sexually."[103]

12-8b   Treatment and Juvenile Corrections

Originally special facilities were established to isolate juveniles from the harmful effects of society and from incarcerated adults. Later, with the development of juvenile courts, the treatment philosophy prevailed. During the past century, however, various commissions have pointed out the failure of juvenile corrections to provide adequate services and programs to enable the successful implementation of a treatment philosophy. In more recent years courts have entered the picture, requiring some elements of due process in the adjudication of juveniles, changes in the disciplinary handling of institutionalized juveniles, and changes in the degree and kinds of services provided in those institutions.

The assignment of juveniles to special facilities for the purpose of treatment after they have been through proceedings that do not involve all elements of due process raises the critical issue of whether juveniles have a constitutional right to treatment. Recall that the original reason for not infusing the juvenile court with due process requirements was that, unlike adult offenders, juveniles were not being punished. They were being treated; juvenile court judges acted in the best interests of the children. Thus, juveniles did not need due process requirements to protect them from governmental action.

The U.S. Supreme Court has discredited the practice of using the philosophy of rehabilitation to deny juveniles their basic constitutional rights, and it has acknowledged that rehabilitation has failed. However, the Supreme Court has also articulated its support for the retention of at least part of the *parens patriae* philosophy in juvenile proceedings while applying some but not all due process requirements. This has had a somewhat confusing result.

Scholars and many courts have taken the position that, under the doctrine of *parens patriae*, juveniles have given up some of their constitutional rights in order to be processed through a system that is based on treatment rather than punishment. Therefore, the state must provide that treatment or relinquish custody of the child. A juvenile's right to treatment is based on cases involving the legal rights of the confined mentally ill.

The U.S. Supreme Court has not decided a case on the constitutional right to treatment for juveniles, although in *O'Conner* v. *Donaldson*, a case involving confinement of the mentally ill, the opinion of the Court implied that the justices might not hold that juveniles have a constitutional right to treatment.[104]

Some courts, however, have ruled that specific constitutional rights of adults must be extended to incarcerated juveniles. For example, the Sixth Circuit Court of Appeals has held that the right to counsel applies to incarcerated juveniles when they raise claims involving other constitutional rights, as well as for civil rights actions that relate to their incarceration. If the juveniles cannot afford counsel, the state must provide it for them in these cases. The issue arose in a class action suit in Tennessee and involved incarcerated youths who claimed that they were being denied access to courts.[105]

There is little question, however, that some forms of treatment should be provided for juveniles. Like adults, juveniles are entitled to reasonable medical care, and some medical problems might be even more critical for them than for adults. For example, the U.S. Centers for Disease Control and Prevention (CDC) state that juveniles are particularly at high risk of contracting viral hepatitis. Incarcerated juveniles are more likely than their nonincarcerated counterparts to practice unsafe sex and to use injection drugs, both of which are highly associated with the spread of hepatitis. Since most juveniles are released from incarceration and from 50 to 75 percent of them will at some time be incarcerated in an adult facility, they have maximum opportunities to spread the disease to others.[106]

Juvenile offenders also have a higher rate of mental and emotional problems than their nonincarcerated counterparts, yet most do not receive adequate treatment (if at all) while they are confined. A representative of the U.S. Department of Education has alleged that the juvenile justice system "has largely become a warehouse for children suffering from mental illness. . . . Somewhere between 50 and 75 percent of incarcerated young offenders are estimated to have a diagnosable mental health disorder, yet the U.S. juvenile justice system is unprepared to adequately identify or treat them."[107]

12-8c   Juveniles in the Community

Juveniles may be released from institutions and placed on parole, usually called **aftercare.** Historically juveniles have had no right to early release, but most do not remain in confinement for long periods of time. Usually they are released to aftercare, but if they violate the terms of that release they may be returned to confinement. Many of the rules that the U.S. Supreme Court has applied to adult parole and probation revocation have been applied to juveniles.

The type of aftercare of juveniles is important. Aftercare should begin with a prerelease program while the juvenile is in confinement. There are two kinds of prerelease programs in juvenile institutions. In the first type, juveniles may be given furloughs or weekend passes to visit their families, a practice that permits gradual reentry into society. In the second type, juveniles may be moved to cottages within the institution, where they live for a period of time with other inmates who are almost ready to be released, and where special programs are provided to prepare them for that release. The length of the aftercare period depends on the needs of each juvenile.[108]

Another procedure for keeping the juvenile in the community is probation. Recall that probation is the most frequently used sanction for adults; the same is true for juveniles. And the same issues are raised. As with adults, the key issue with juveniles is whether serious offenders may be placed in the community without causing unreasonable harm to others. There is some evidence that intensive probation supervision (IPS) of serious juvenile offenders is an effective alternative to incarceration but that the cost-effectiveness of IPS is difficult to achieve without the widespread use of diversion.[109]

Another type of community care of juveniles is called *respite care.* These programs, which exist in various jurisdictions throughout the country, are designed for runaways and their families. Under respite care the children are given a break from their families and vice versa. A report on these programs states that some families actually lock their children out, practically begging the county or the state to take charge of children they have found to be incorrigible. Many of these children are not a threat to society, but they need a place to stay while problems with their families can be worked out. Respite care gives juvenile court judges an option other than the potentially detrimental detention centers and jails. These programs provide a cooling-off period followed by counseling for all involved parties. The goal is to reunite the child with his or her family as quickly as possible.[110]

Finally, several juvenile justice systems have developed aftercare programs that focus on the juvenile as soon as he or she is sentenced and continue through incarceration and the return of the juvenile to the community. The Intensive Aftercare Programs (IAP) are sponsored by grants from the DOJ's Office of Juvenile Justice and Delinquency Prevention (OJJDP). The model programs are in Denver, Colorado; Las Vegas, Nevada; and Norfolk, Virginia. The central component of the IAP is an "overarching case management system,"

▶ **Aftercare**   The continued supervision of juveniles after they are released from a correctional facility; similar to the term *parole* in adult criminal court systems.

which begins with risk-assessment and classification programs designed to target the juveniles who are most likely to commit additional delinquent or criminal acts. The programs are individualized to the participants, considering problems they face within their families and schools, drug abuse, and other issues. Random urinalysis and electronic monitoring of juveniles after their release from institutions are important in the maintenance of close supervision and control. Other features are a graduated set of sanctions for those who need to be punished and a reward system for those who show progress in their treatment plans. The goal of the current research on these model programs is to determine "whether a well-conceived and strongly implemented IPA model will have the desired effect of reducing recidivism and recommitments among high-risk parolees."[111]

12-8d   The Effect of Institutionalization on Juveniles

The National Advisory Commission on Criminal Justice Standards and Goals advocated that, where possible, juvenile delinquents should be diverted from institutionalization. The commission concluded as follows:

> The failure of major juvenile and youth institutions to reduce crime is incontestable. Recidivism rates, imprecise as they may be, are notoriously high. The younger the person when entering an institution, the longer he is institutionalized, and the farther he progresses into the criminal justice system, the greater his chance of failure.[112]

The advisory commission emphasized that these institutions are places of punishment, and they do not have a significant effect on deterrence. They remove juveniles from society temporarily. In that sense society is protected, but the changes in the offender during that incarceration are negative, not positive. The institutions are isolated geographically, which hinders delivery of services from outside the institution, decreases visits from families and friends, reduces opportunities for home furloughs, and limits the availability of staff. Many of these institutions have outlasted their functions. Because of their architecture, the institutions are inflexible at a time when flexibility is needed. They were built to house too many people for maximum treatment success. The large numbers have resulted in an excessive emphasis on security and control. The advisory commission maintained that these institutions are dehumanizing and that they create an unhealthy dependence.

The traditional juvenile correctional institution must change. It should not continue to warehouse failures and release them back into society without improvement. It must share a major responsibility for the successful reintegration of those juveniles into society; however, as institutions change their goals the public must be involved in the planning, goals, and programs, as well as in the efforts toward reintegration into the community. Most important, the public must fully accept these institutional and community programs for juveniles. The advisory commission concluded its discussion of juvenile corrections by saying, "It is no surprise that institutions have not been successful in reducing crime. The mystery is that they have not contributed even more to increasing crime."[113]

12-8e   Deinstitutionalization

Dissatisfaction with closed institutions has led to several movements. One is diversion. Another is community corrections. A third movement, related to diversion and community corrections, is deinstitutionalization. This movement began with an emphasis on probation, foster homes, and community treatment centers for juveniles. The establishment of the California Youth Authority in the early 1960s and the closing of Massachusetts's juvenile institutions in 1970 and 1971 gave impetus to the movement.

What caused this movement toward deinstitutionalization for juveniles? Some say it started in the early 1960s, when the government began granting money to localities to improve conditions in the processing and treatment of delinquency. Others say it emerged when social scientists began to assume the role of clinicians and became involved in policy decision making at local and federal levels. Still others point to the interest of lawyers in the 1960s and 1970s in reforming juvenile courts.

Some scholars take the position that the movement came primarily from a desire to save the costs of constructing new facilities and repairing existing ones. Whatever the reasons, it is clear that this movement is unlike most others in the field. It involves a major change: abandoning the large institution and replacing it with a different concept of corrections. The era of the large institution may be over, with some jurisdictions abolishing them. An example is that of Massachusetts.

In 1969, Jerome G. Miller took charge of the Department of Youth Services in Massachusetts. At first he attempted to reform the system; however, "after fifteen months of bureaucratic blockades, open warfare with state legislators, and sabotage by entrenched employees, Miller abandoned reform and elected revolution."[114] Between 1969 and 1973, Miller closed the state's juvenile institutions, placing juveniles in community-based facilities.

The Massachusetts experiment with deinstitutionalization was evaluated by a team of social scientists from Harvard University. In the early stages of evaluation the researchers guardedly concluded that the experiment was a success. In 1977, the tentative conclusions were questioned. The recidivism rates of the youths had not increased or decreased; therefore, it might be concluded that deinstitutionalization, though no better, was no worse than institutionalization and was certainly more humane. However, the evaluators reported a crisis in the reaction of the public, the courts, and the police.[115]

Empirical studies of the Massachusetts system conducted in the 1980s to determine the success of deinstitutionalization were contradictory, but in 1998 a researcher who looked at the Massachusetts situation concluded,

> Twenty-five years later, the fight remains a good one, and the cause remains just. Our strategies did not go far enough, but they went farther than anyone thought. Their failure was largely not a failure of will but rather a failure of our own political naivete, the general community's faith in its own compassion, and everyone's readiness to assume responsibility for our young people. Let us hope we have learned these lessons well.[116]

In evaluating deinstitutionalization, we must raise the issue of whether the negative effects of institutionalization, at least to some extent, will crop up in community treatment centers or other forms of handling juveniles as well. In responding to the argument that large juvenile institutions should be abolished because they are schools for crime, one researcher points out that in many cases those large institutions are confining juveniles who previously were in the smaller institutions. Thus, the smaller institutions must take responsibility for part of the failure of the correctional system to rehabilitate juveniles. Furthermore, replacing the large institutions with smaller facilities "may not really change the amount of teaching and learning that takes place among offenders."[117] If juveniles who already have a strong orientation toward crime are confined together, they may continue to infect and teach each other.

12-9 Juveniles and Capital Punishment

According to the Death Penalty Information Center, as of December 2004 there were 72 persons (all men) on death row in 12 states for murders they committed when they were ages 16 (19 percent of the 72) or 17 (81 percent), out of a death row population of 3,471 (as of 1 October 2004). Texas had the largest number, with 40 percent of the total of juveniles who were on death row. Two-thirds of the men who were juveniles when they committed the murders for which they were on death row were persons of color; over two-thirds of their victims were white; over one-half of the victims were female; 81 percent were adults.[118]

The 1986 execution of James Terry Roach, then 25 but executed for a crime he committed when he was 16, raised the issue of whether capital punishment should be imposed on juveniles. In an earlier case, Monty Lee Eddings, who was 15 when he murdered an Oklahoma highway patrol officer who had stopped him for a traffic violation, was successful in the appeal of his death sentence to the U.S. Supreme Court. Eddings's attorney argued that capital punishment for a crime committed while the offender was a juvenile constitutes cruel and unusual punishment. The Supreme Court did not decide that issue but sent the case back for resentencing on the grounds that at the sentencing hearing the lower court did not consider mitigating circumstances. The trial court considered the mitigating circumstances and resentenced Eddings to death. Before his case reached the U.S.

Spotlight 12-4   Capital Punishment for Crimes Committed as a Juvenile

During its 2004–2005 term, the U.S. Supreme Court heard the case of Christopher Simmons, 27, who was 17 when he committed murder. In 1993, Simmons solicited friends to assist him in committing a robbery, tying up the victim, and throwing her off a bridge. He boasted that they would get away with the crime because they were juveniles. One of his friends (age 15 and thus not eligible for the death penalty) agreed. The two broke into the home of Shirley Crook to commit burglary. Crook was home and recognized Simmons from an automobile accident in which both had been involved. Crook, age 46 and scantily clad, was bound and gagged, and her arms were taped behind her back. She was driven around in a minivan and, when she tried to escape, was beaten before being pushed off a railroad trestle, still conscious. Her dead body was later found in the river by fishermen.

Simmons was convicted of murder and sentenced to death. The Missouri Supreme Court initially upheld the conviction and the sentence but subsequently held that imposing the death penalty on a person who was 17 when the murder was committed constitutes cruel and unusual punishment. The court imposed a life sentence. The state of Missouri asked the U.S. Supreme Court to reverse. Eight states and numerous individuals—including former U.S. President Jimmy Carter and Soviet President Mikhail S. Gorbachev, along with organizations such as the American Bar Association and the American Medical Association (arguing that the brains of 16- and 17-year-olds are not fully developed in the areas that regulate decision making) and over 30 religious organizations—filed briefs with the U.S. Supreme Court, asking the Court to declare that executing a person for a murder committed as a juvenile is unconstitutional.[1]

The U.S. Supreme Court decided *Roper* v. *Simmons* in March 2005, holding that the execution of a person for a crime committed at age 17, constitutes cruel and unusual punishment. Portions of the opinion follow:[2]

> The State sought the death penalty. As aggravating factors, the State submitted that the murder was committed for the

purpose of receiving money; was committed for the pursrpose of avoiding, interfering with, or preventing lawful arrest of the defendant; and involved depravity of mind and was outrageously and wantonly vile, horrible, and inhuman. The State called Shirley Crook's husband, daughter, and two sisters, who presented moving evidence of the devastation her death had brought to their lives.

> In mitigation Simmons' attorneys first called an officer of the Missouri juvenile justice system, who testified that Simmons had no prior convictions and that no previous charges had been filed against him. Simmons' mother, father, two younger half brothers, a neighbor, and a friend took the stand to tell the jurors of the close relationships they had formed with Simmons and to plead for mercy on his behalf. Simmons' mother, in particular, testified to the responsibility Simmons demonstrated in taking care of his two younger half brothers and of his grandmother and to his capacity to show love for them.

> During closing arguments, both the prosecutor and defense counsel addressed Simmons' age, which the trial judge had instructed the jurors they could consider as a mitigating factor. Defense counsel reminded the jurors that juveniles of Simmons' age cannot drink, serve on juries, or even see certain movies, because "the legislatures have wisely decided that individuals of a certain age aren't responsible enough."

> Defense counsel argued that Simmons' age should make "a huge difference to [the jurors] in deciding just exactly what sort of punishment to make …"

> The jury recommended the death penalty after finding the State had proved each of the three aggravating factors submitted to it. Accepting the jury's recommendation, the trial judge imposed the death penalty….

> The prohibition against "cruel and unusual punishments," like other expansive language in the Constitution, must be interpreted according to its text, by considering history, tradition, and precedent, and with due regard for its purpose and function in the constitutional design. To implement this framework we have established the propriety and affirmed the necessity of referring to "the evolving standards of decency that mark the progress of a maturing society" to

Supreme Court a second time, however, Oklahoma's Court of Criminal Appeals changed the sentence from death to life imprisonment.[119]

In 1985, the U.S. Supreme Court upheld the death sentence of a defendant who was 18 at the time he committed his atrocious capital crime.[120] But in 1988 the Supreme Court decided *Thompson* v. *Oklahoma*, in which it reversed the capital sentence of William Wayne Thompson, who was 15 when he committed the crime for which he was given the death penalty. In *Thompson* a majority of the Supreme Court justices agreed that the execution of an individual who was 15 at the time he committed a capital crime is cruel and unusual punishment, even though the crime was heinous. In deciding the issue the Supreme Court used the standards established in *Trop* v. *Dulles*, decided in 1958. The standards are "the evolving standards of decency that mark the progress of a maturing society."[121]

The U.S. Supreme Court's decision in *Thompson* banned capital punishment for youths who are under 16 when they commit a capital offense; however, it did not answer the question of whether capital punishment is cruel and unusual when imposed on youths between the ages of 16 and 18 at the time the capital murder is committed. The Supreme

determine which punishments are so disproportionate as to be cruel and unusual. . . .

[The Supreme Court reviewed its precedent cases involving capital punishment of juveniles, along with those involving executing the mentally challenged. The Court then distinguished between the maturity levels of adults and juveniles and continued]

Three general differences between juveniles under 18 and adults demonstrate that juvenile offenders cannot with reliability be classified among the worst offenders. First, as any parent knows and the scientific and sociological studies respondent and his *amici* (friends of the court briefs) cite tend to confirm, "[a] lack of maturity and an underdeveloped sense of responsibility are found in youth more often than in adults and are more understandable among the young. These qualities often result in impetuous and ill-considered actions and decisions." . . .

It has been noted that "adolescents are overrepresented statistically in virtually every category of reckless behavior." In recognition of the comparative immaturity and irresponsibility of juveniles, almost every state prohibits those under 18 years of age from voting, serving on juries, or marrying without parental consent.

The second area of difference is that juveniles are more vulnerable or susceptible to negative influences and outside pressures, including peer pressure. This is explained in part by the prevailing circumstance that juveniles have less control, or less experience with control, over their own environment.

The third broad difference is that the character of a juvenile is not as well formed as that of an adult. The personality traits of juveniles are more transitory, less fixed.

These differences render suspect any conclusion that a juvenile falls among the worst offenders. The susceptibility of juveniles to immature and irresponsible behavior means "their irresponsible conduct is not as morally reprehensible as that of an adult." Their own vulnerability and comparative lack of control over their immediate surroundings mean juveniles have a greater claim than adults to be forgiven for failing to escape negative influences in their whole environment. The

reality that juveniles still struggle to define their identity means it is less supportable to conclude that even a heinous crime committed by a juvenile is evidence of irretrievably depraved character. From a moral standpoint, it would be misguided to equate the failings of a minor with those of an adult, for a greater possibility exists that a minor's character deficiencies will be reformed. . . .

Our determination that the death penalty is disproportionate punishment for offenders under 18 finds confirmation in the stark reality that the United States is the only country in the world that continues to give official sanction to the juvenile death penalty. . . .

Over time, from one generation to the next, the Constitution has come to earn the high respect and even . . . the veneration of the American people. The document sets forth, and rests upon, innovative principles original to the American experience, such as federalism; a proven balance in political mechanisms through separation of powers; specific guarantee for the accused in criminal cases; and broad provisions to secure individual freedom and preserve human dignity. These doctrines and guarantees are central to the American experience and remain essential to our present-day self-definition and national identity. Not the least of the reasons we honor the Constitution, then, is because we know it to be our own. It does not lessen our fidelity to the Constitution or our pride in its origins to acknowledge that the express affirmation of certain fundamental rights by other nations and peoples simply underscores the centrality of those same rights within our own heritage of freedom.

The Eighth and Fourteenth Amendments forbid imposition of the death penalty on offenders who were under the age of 18 when their crimes were committed. The judgment of the Missouri Supreme Court setting aside the sentence of death imposed upon Christopher Simmons is affirmed.

It is so ordered.

1. "Dozens of Nations Weigh in on Death Penalty Case," *New York Times* (20 July 2004), p. 1.
2. Roper v. Simmons, 125 S. Ct. 1183 (2005).

Court makes this very clear in its opinion, noting that it has been asked to declare capital punishment unconstitutional for all youths under 18:

> Our task today, however, is to decide the case before us; we do so by concluding that the Eighth and Fourteenth Amendments prohibit the execution of a person who was under sixteen years of age at the time of his or her offense.[122]

In 1989, the U.S. Supreme Court decided the cases of two other death row inmates who had committed murders while they were juveniles. One was approximately 17 years and 4 months old when he raped and sodomized a 20-year-old woman repeatedly, before he killed her with a bullet in the front and another in the back of her head. The second juvenile was approximately 16 years and 6 months of age when he killed a 26-year-old mother of two by multiple stab wounds in her chest. The U.S. Supreme Court held that capital punishment for these youths did not constitute cruel and unusual punishment.[123]

In June 2002, the U.S. Supreme Court held that a national consensus had emerged that executing mentally retarded persons constitutes cruel and unusual punishment. Some legal scholars thought the reasoning might be extended to executing persons who committed murders when they were 16 or 17 years old. The U.S. Supreme Court declined to make that extension, however, as demonstrated by its refusal in October 2002 to review the case of Kevin Stanford, who had been on Kentucky's death row since 1982 for raping and murdering a 20-year-old gas station attendant when Stanford was 17. Stanford argued that there is an emerging consensus that juveniles under 18 should not be executed. When the U.S. Supreme Court refused to review Stanford's case, the dissenting justices issued an opinion, stating, "The practice of executing such offenders is a relic of the past and is inconsistent with evolving standards of decency in a civilized society. We should put an end to this shameful practice." The dissent noted that, since its 1989 decision, five states had banned the execution of juveniles under 18.[124]

In August 2002, when the U.S. Supreme Court declined to stay the execution of Toronto M. Patterson, who was 17 when he committed murder, three justices urged their colleagues to reconsider their decision regarding the execution of offenders who were 16 or 17 when they committed capital murder. Patterson was executed.[125]

In January 2003, the U.S. Supreme Court rejected the appeal of Scott A. Hain, 32, an Oklahoma death row inmate who committed murder when he was 17. Hain was executed in April 2003.[126] In October 2003, the U.S. Supreme Court refused to review the case of Nanon McKewn Williams, a Texas inmate who was on death row for a murder he committed when he was 17. Williams's attorney said that, had the case been reviewed, he had planned to argue by analogy to the Supreme Court's 2002 decision that capital punishment is unconstitutional in the case of the mentally retarded.[127]

There was hope, however, that the sentencing of Lee Malvo would result in a closer look at executing juveniles. Malvo was convicted of committing murder when he was 17; he was involved in the 2002 sniper shootings in the Washington, D.C., area. Malvo was sentenced to life, and some experts argued that the jury's sparing of the life of a person who had committed such atrocious acts could create support for the abolition of the death penalty for crimes committed by juveniles.[128]

In January 2004, the U.S. Supreme Court accepted for review a case involving the constitutionality of executing offenders who were 16 or 17 when they committed a capital murder. In October 2004, the Court heard the case of Christopher Simmons, 27, who killed at age 17. The state of Missouri had overturned his death sentence in summer 2003. Despite the Court's decision to hear the case of *Roper* v. *Simmons,* Texas scheduled (between March and June 2004) the executions of four persons who were juveniles when they committed capital murder.[129] Subsequently the state agreed to stay those executions pending the U.S. Supreme Court's decision, which was handed down in March 2005. The *Simmons* case is discussed in Spotlight 12-4, which also reproduces portions of this important case.

12-10   Juvenile and Criminal Justice Systems: An Assessment

Gina Grant appeared to be a perfect candidate for Harvard University, which granted her early admission for the fall class of 1995. Grant, an orphan, had top grades in a highly rated high school, an IQ of 150, excellent references, and a high score on entrance exams. She was co-captain of the tennis team and tutored underprivileged kids. However, after a published article about her and other orphans, an anonymous source sent Harvard information about her previous life in South Carolina. When she was 14, Grant had entered a plea of no contest to manslaughter in the death of her mother, whose skull was smashed by at least 13 blows from a candlestick. Harvard revoked her early admission letter after notification of this incident.

The case of Gina Grant is an excellent one to note in closing this text's study of criminal and juvenile justice systems, for it raises many of the issues those systems face today. Although she had been accused of a violent crime, Grant was processed through the juvenile justice system. She was given only a short term of incarceration and placed on probation. Her records were sealed, and she was given a chance at rehabilitation. Many argued that she was successful; she had served her time; she deserved a chance for a new life; that is the purpose of the juvenile system. Others argued that the case illustrated that juveniles are becoming more violent and that juvenile justice systems are soft on crime. They stated that Grant should have been processed through the criminal justice system and sentenced to a long term and that Harvard officials acted appropriately in revoking their admissions offer.

Grant's case and others like it focus on many of the issues facing justice systems today. Should we continue to preserve juvenile justice systems, or should all serious crimes be processed through criminal justice systems? If we retain juvenile systems, how closely should they mirror criminal systems in structure and procedure? Most important, will crime rates be affected by changing the current systems?

We began the chapter with a reference to the 2000 presidential address at the annual meeting of the Academy of Criminal Justice Sciences. President Alida V. Merlo focused her address on juvenile justice, which she described as being at a crossroads between the get-tough, punitive legislative approaches despite the recent reductions in juvenile violence and the apparent softening of public attitudes toward juveniles. In her summary, Merlo stated the following:

> We can either continue to move toward more punitive juvenile justice policies, greater intolerance for adolescents, growing racism, more costly and more inhumane policies, and an ever-widening gulf between poor children and the rest of us, or we can blaze a new path. As teachers, scholars, researchers, students, and practitioners, we have the opportunity to infuse the system with a new kind of thinking—thinking that is informed by research, by the evaluation of programs, and by an understanding of the complex societal conditions that cannot be eliminated without substantial long-term investments.[130]

Chapter Wrap-Up

Historically, juvenile justice systems held the highest hopes for success in rehabilitation, reformation, and reintegration, but they contained some of the greatest deprivations of constitutional rights. In the name of "the best interests of the child," the state took away liberty without due process of law. Under the guise of treatment and rehabilitation, not punishment, juvenile court systems swept into their clutches many who otherwise would not have been processed by court systems.

There is a need to treat juveniles differently than adults; there is a need to segregate them from adults in confinement; there is a need to offer them opportunities for improvement, so that they can succeed in a competitive world. Those needs may not be met by violating their rights.

After an overview of juvenile justice systems, this chapter looked at the current data on juveniles as offenders and as victims. In particular, it considered violent acts by and against juveniles before looking closely at the impact of youth gangs on our society. Efforts to combat gang crimes were noted, with a special look at Los Angeles.

The constitutional rights of juveniles were considered in some detail, with the chapter focusing first on the critical U.S. Supreme Court cases and looking in particular at the right to counsel (noting that it is often not effective counsel). Juvenile curfews were explored, followed by legal issues concerning race and gender.

The chapter then turned to an analysis of the juvenile court, beginning with a look at court procedures. The discussion showed that, although not all procedural requirements of criminal courts have been applied to juveniles, many due process rights have been extended to them in juvenile courts. No longer is it sufficient to say that juveniles are not arrested; they are apprehended. They are not found guilty; they are adjudicated. They are not sentenced, but dispositions are made of their cases. The change in wording does not compensate for a lack of due process. In many respects present-day criminal and juvenile courts are similar, but states have some room to experiment in their juvenile systems. For example, trial by jury is not required by the U.S. Constitution but has been extended by statute to juvenile courts in some states.

Violent crimes by juveniles appear to be committed by a few, but those violent few commit a large percentage of the total crimes committed by juveniles. Concern with this violence and with recidivism has led some states to pass statutes giving adult criminal courts jurisdiction over juveniles who commit serious crimes. In other states, after a proper hearing, juvenile courts may waive jurisdiction over juveniles who have committed serious crimes.

All reforms have problems, and one problem with the get-tough laws concerning juveniles has been the unwillingness of courts and juries to convict if they know there will be an automatic penalty that they consider too severe. Thus, in some cases the get-tough policy results in less, not more, protection for the community. It is important to evaluate changes carefully for that reason. Insufficient attention has been given to evaluating legislative changes in juvenile systems.

Two major areas discussed earlier in the text with regard to adult criminal courts were also explored in this chapter as they relate to juveniles. The application of Megan's Laws and the use of drug courts were noted.

The next major focus of the chapter was on juveniles in corrections. Juveniles have received differential treatment in corrections, too, although it is not at all clear that those differences are positive. Indefinite detention of juveniles under the guise that they are being treated when they are being detained without treatment has been held by courts to be inappropriate. Unfortunately, disillusionment with treatment and rehabilitation in many jurisdictions has resulted in a decreased emphasis on treatment, even in the case of juveniles. At the other extreme has been the position that institutionalization is bad for juveniles and therefore should be abandoned, with juveniles being cared for in community treatment facilities.

The execution of juveniles is one of the most controversial areas in juvenile court systems. The chapter noted the recent changes in the legal aspects of executing juveniles, including excerpts from the U.S. Supreme Court's 2005 decision, *Roper* v. *Simmons.*

In conclusion, some scholars are questioning the wisdom and efficiency of retaining juvenile court systems if most of the procedures of adult criminal court systems become a part of juvenile court systems. Others note the unfairness of a system that is moving toward criminal court sentences without all of the elements of due process provided in those courts. One law professor stated the issue as follows:

> As juvenile courts' sentencing practices resemble increasingly those of their criminal counterparts, does any reason remain to maintain a separate court whose sole distinguishing characteristic is its persisting procedural deficiencies?[131]

Another scholar commented that juvenile court systems are old enough that we should consider whether it is time for them to die; however, after considering carefully the pros and cons of abolishing juvenile courts, he decided that on balance we should keep them.[132]

It may be that the future of criminal justice is related to what we do with juvenile court systems. Certainly this is an area to follow closely as the U.S. Supreme Court ponders and decides whether to continue the march toward greater due process and equal protection or to retract from that path into a more conservative approach to the interpretation of the U.S. Constitution.

Key Terms

adjudication (p. 352)
aftercare (p. 381)
certification (p. 372)
delinquency (p. 354)
detention (p. 352)
detention centers (p. 352)

disposition (p. 352)
diversion (p. 367)
intake decision (p. 370)
juvenile (p. 351)
juvenile court (p. 352)

juvenile delinquent (p. 351)
parens patriae (p. 351)
petition (p. 352)
status offense (p. 352)
training school (p. 356)

Apply It

1. How were juveniles treated historically?
2. What events led to the emergence of juvenile courts in the United States?
3. What are the basic ways in which juvenile courts and adult criminal courts differ?
4. Analyze current data on juveniles as offenders and as victims.
5. Briefly describe what the Supreme Court held in each of the following cases: *Kent, Gault, Winship, McKeiver, Breed, Schall,* and *R.L.C.*
6. What are the legal issues involved in juvenile curfews? What are the practical implications of curfews?
7. What are the major gender and racial issues today regarding juvenile offenders?
8. What is the relationship of the police to juveniles?
9. Define and discuss intake proceedings in juvenile systems.
10. Describe the role of the prosecutor and of the defense attorney in juvenile proceedings.
11. Discuss the disposition of a juvenile case and the appeal process.
12. Why are some juveniles tried in adult criminal courts, and how is this accomplished?
13. Should Megan's Laws be applied to juveniles? Why or why not?
14. Should drug courts be extended to juvenile offenders? Why or why not?
15. Why did separate institutions for juveniles develop? Are they successful? Should they be continued? What is meant by *deinstitutionalization?*
16. Discuss some of the recent findings about juvenile institutions.
17. What is the current legal status of the capital punishment of inmates who committed their capital crimes when they were juveniles?

Endnotes

1. Alida V. Merlo, "Juvenile Justice at the Crossroads: Presidential Address to the Academy of Criminal Justice Sciences," *Justice Quarterly* 17, no. 4 (December 2000): 639–661; quotation is on pp. 640–641.
2. Orman Ketcham, "The Unfulfilled Promise of the American Juvenile Courts," in *Justice for the Child,* ed. Margaret Keeney Rosenheim (New York: Free Press, 1962), p. 24.
3. See Alexander W. Pisciotta, "*Parens Patriae,* Treatment and Reform: The Case of the Western House of Refuge, 1849–1907," *New England Journal of Criminal and Civil Confinement* 10 (Winter 1984): 65–86.
4. See Anthony Platt, *The Child Savers* (Chicago: University of Chicago Press, 1969).
5. John R. Sutton, "The Juvenile Court and Social Welfare: Dynamics of Progressive Reform," *Law and Society Review* 19, no. 1 (1985): 142.
6. Federal Bureau of Investigation, *Crime in the United States: Uniform Crime Reports 2003* (Washington, D.C.: U.S. Government Printing Office, 2004), p. 286.
7. Cal. Wel. & Inst. Code, Section 602 (2005).
8. Proposition 21, the Gang Violence and Juvenile Crime Prevention Act of 1998, Section 2(a) (2005).

9. "Student Killers' Tapes Filled with Rage," *New York Times* (14 December 1999), p. 19.

10. "Boy, 6, Accused in Classmate's Killing," *New York Times* (1 March 2000), p. 14.

11. "Boy, 11, Gets 18 Years in the Juvenile System for Murder of 3-Year-Old," *New York Times* (13 December 2003), p. 14.

12. "California Teenager Given Life Sentence," *New York Times* (15 June 2003), p. 19.

13. "Two Youths Held on Charge of Raping Four-Year-Old Girl," *Orlando Sentinel* (27 June 1997), p. 5; "Judge Orders Teen Rapist Sent to Adult Prison," *Houston Chronicle* (24 February 2000), p. 21.

14. "L.I. Athletes Said to Admit Responsibility in Abuse Case," *New York Times* (14 November 2003), p. 5B; "Mepham Assault Case: 4th Player Admits Guilt," *Newsday* (New York: Nassau and Suffolk Edition) (28 April 2004), p. 3; "Ruling on Mepham Player," *Newsday* (New York: Nassau and Suffolk Edition) (29 May 2004), p. 5.

15. Quoted in "California Law Enforcement Praises School Anti-Gang Program," *Criminal Justice Newsletter* (3 November 2003), p. 4; quotation is on p. 5.

16. W. B. Miller, *Crime by Youth Gangs and Groups in the United States* (Washington, D.C.: U.S. Department of Justice, Office of Justice Programs, Office of Juvenile Justice and Delinquency Prevention, 1992—revised from 1982), p. 21, quoted in James C. Howell, *Youth Gang Programs and Strategies* (Washington, D.C.: U.S. Department of Justice, Office of Justice Programs, Office of Juvenile Justice and Delinquency Prevention, August 2000), p. 1.

17. "Most Juvenile Crime Committed by Gang Members, Study Finds," *Criminal Justice Newsletter* 28 (2 January 1997): 5.

18. Office of Juvenile Justice and Delinquency Prevention, *Highlights of the 2001 National Youth Gang Survey* (Washington, D.C.: U.S. Department of Justice, 2003), p. 1.

19. "Bratton's Challenge," *New York Times* (22 June 2003), Section 4, p. 2.

20. "Cops Seek Allies: Public Called Key to Beating Gangs," *Daily News of Los Angeles* (14 November 2003), p. 1N; "Bratton Shuffles LAPD Brass: Department to Focus on Top 10 Percent," *Daily News of Los Angeles* (18 November 2003), p. 3N.

21. SHOW: "All Things Considered," National Public Radio, headline: "Los Angeles Police Department and FBI Officials Continue Their Crackdown on Gangs in South Central LA," (28 January 2004).

22. "The Gang Buster: Bratton Cut Crime in New York, and Now He's Doing It in L.A. His Secret: Giving Cops More Power," *Time Magazine* (19 January 2004), p. 56.

23. "Chicago Tries Rapid Responses to Curb Gangs," *Christian Science Monitor* (30 June 2003), p. 2.

24. City of Chicago v. Morales, 527 U.S. 41 (2000).

25. "Anti-Loiter Ordinance: Does It Have a Leg to Stand On?" *South Bend Tribune* (Indiana) (1 April 2002), p. 1C.

26. "Prosecutors Cite Difficulties in Prosecuting Gang Members," *Criminal Justice Newsletter* 26 (3 April 1995): 3, referring to *Prosecuting Gangs: A National Assessment* (Rockville, Md.: National Criminal Justice Reference Service).

27. "California Law Enforcement Praises School Anti-Gang Program," p. 5.

28. Anne Campbell, "Self Definitions by Rejection: The Case of Gang Girls," *Social Problems* 34 (December 1987): 451–466.

29. Terry Carter, "'Equality with a Vengeance': Violent Crimes and Gang Activity by Girls Skyrocket," *ABA Journal* 85 (November 1999): 22. See also Karen Heimer and Stacy DeCoster, "The Gendering of Violent Delinquency," *Criminology* 37 (May 1999): 277–318.

30. Smith v. Daily Mail Publishing Co. 443 U.S. 97 (1979).

31. Commonwealth v. Dallenbach, 729 A.2d 1218 (Pa. Super. 1999).

32. *In re* Benjamin L., 708 N.E.2d 156 (N.Y. App. 1999).

33. Kent v. United States, 383 U.S. 541 (1966).

34. Kent v. United States, 383 U.S. 541, 554–555 (1966).

35. *In re* Gault, 387 U.S. 1 (1967).

36. *In re* Gault, 387 U.S. 1, 19–21, 26–28 (1967).

37. American Bar Association, *Maryland: An Assessment of Access to Counsel and Quality of Representation in Delinquency*, an 81-page report available on the Internet at www.abanet.org. The report is summarized and the quotations in this chapter were taken from "ABA Finds Right to Lawyer Is 'an Unfilled Promise,'" *Criminal Justice Newsletter* (17 November 2003), p. 2.

38. *In re* Winship, 397 U.S. 358 (1970), quoting *In re* Gault.

39. McKeiver v. Pennsylvania, 403 U.S. 528 (1971). For a discussion of the issue in today's courts, see John Gibeaut, "A Jury Question: Jurors Should Judge Youths in Juvenile Court, Some Say," *American Bar Association* 85 (July 1999): 24–25.

40. Breed v. Jones, 421 U.S. 519 (1975).

41. Schall v. Martin, 467 U.S. 253 (1984).

42. Alfredo A. v. Superior Court, 849 P.2d 1330 (Cal. 1994), *subsequent opinion on reh'g.,* 865 P.2d 56 (Cal. 1994), *cert. denied,* 513 U.S. 822 (1994).

43. United States v. R.L.C., 503 U.S. 291 (1992).

44. Yarborough v. Alvarado, 541 U.S. 652 (2004).

45. Qutb v. Strauss, 11 F.3d 488 (5th Cir. 1993), *cert. denied,* 511 U.S. 1127 (1994).

46. Schleifer v. City of Charlottesville, 159 F.3d 843 (4th Cir. 1998), *cert. denied,* 562 U.S. 1018 (1999).

47. "Time after Time, Curfews Prove Useless," *Boston Herald* (21 July 2003), p. 23.

48. Nunez by Nunez v. City of San Diego, 114 F.3d 935 (9th Cir. 1997).

49. Schleifer v. City of Charlottesville, 159 F.3d 843 (4th Cir. 1998), *cert. denied,* 562 U.S. 1018 (1999), case names and citations omitted. The ordinance is codified at Charlottesville, Va., Code Section 17-7.

50. City of Sumner v. Walsh, 61 P.3d 1111 (Wash. 2003).

51. "Sumner Takes Year Off from Curfew Law," *The News Tribune* (Tacoma, Washington) (5 July 2003), p. 1B.

52. David McDowall et al., "The Impact of Youth Curfew Laws on Juvenile Crime Rates," *Crime & Delinquency* 46 (January 2000): 76–92; quotation is on p. 76.

53. Madeline Wordes et al., "Locking Up Youth: The Impact of Race on Detention Decisions," *Journal of Research in Crime and Delinquency* 31 (May 1994): 149.

54. Edmund F. McGarrell, "Trends in Racial Disproportionality in Juvenile Court Processing: 1985–1989," *Crime & Delinquency* 39 (January 1993): 19–48.

55. Cited in "Race Disparity Seen throughout Juvenile Justice System," *Criminal Justice Newsletter* 30, no. 20 (25 April 2000): 6–7.

56. Ibid.

57. "Donde Está la Justicia?" News release by Building Blocks for Youth, available on the Internet at www.buildingblocksforyouth.org/latino_rpt/pr_english.html (18 July 2002).

58. Carl E. Pope and Howard N. Snyder, *Race As a Factor in Juvenile Arrests*, Office of Juvenile Justice and Delinquency Prevention (Washington, D.C.: U.S. Department of Justice, April 2003), pp. 1, 6.

59. "ABA Finds Right to Lawyer Is 'an Unfulfilled Promise," quoting *Maryland: An Assessment of Access to Counsel*, pp. 2–3.

60. Justice Police Institute, *Reducing Disportionate Minority Confinement: The Multnomah County, Oregon Success Story and Its Implications*, on the Internet: www.cjcj.org, cited in "Success Claimed in Oregon in Reducing Minority Detention," *Criminal Justice Newsletter* 32, no. 2 (11 February 2002): 5–6.

61. Juvenile Justice and Delinquency Prevention Act, U.S. Code, Title 42, Section 5633 (2005).

62. Deborah L. Rhode, "Injustice by Gender," *National Law Journal* (18 June 2001), p. 21.

63. See Lanes v. State, 767 S.W.2d 789 (Tex.Crim.App. 1989), requiring probable cause to arrest a juvenile.

64. Schall v. Martin, 467 U.S. 253, 265 (1984). The adult preventive detention case is United States v. Salerno, 481 U.S. 739 (1987).

65. Howard N. Snyder and Melissa Sickmund, Office of Juvenile Justice and Delinquency Prevention, *Juvenile Offenders and Victims: 1999 National Report* (Washington, D.C.: U.S. Department of Justice, September 1999), p. 208. The statute is codified at U.S. Code, Title 18, Section 5031 *et seq.* (2005).

66. *Juveniles in Adult Prisons and Jails: A National Assessment*, cited in "Juveniles in Adult Prisons 'a Burgeoning Issue,' Study Finds," *Criminal Justice Newsletter* 31, no. 5 (10 January 2001): 6.

67. "Donde Está la Justicia?"

68. Snyder and Sickmund, *Juvenile Offenders and Victims*, p. 209.

69. Melissa Sickmund, Bureau of Justice Statistics, *Juveniles in Corrections* (Washington, D.C.: U.S. Department of Justice, June 2004), p. 18.

70. Paige M. Harrison and Allen J. Beck, Bureau of Justice Statistics, *Prisoners in 2003* (Washington, D.C.: U.S. Department of Justice, November 2004), p. 8.

71. Monroe v. Soliz, 939 P.2d 205 (Wash. 1997).

72. "Girls' Needs Addressed in Prison's Special Unit; Younger Convicts Have Their Own Dorm, Along with Special Classes and Training," *Indianapolis Star* (12 September 1999), p. 4B; Ratliff v. Cohn, 693 N.E.2d 530 (Ind. 1998).

73. See, for example, State v. Whatley, 320 So.2d 123 (La. 1975).

74. New York CLS Family Court Act, Section 301.2 (2005).

75. *In re* A.D.G., 895 P.2d 1067 (Colo.Ct.App. 1994), *cert. denied sub nom.*, 1995 Colo. App. LEXIS 423 (Colo. 5 June 1995).

76. "Judges' Group Criticizes Trend toward Waiver to Adult Court," *Criminal Justice Newsletter* 25 (1 March 1994): 1.

77. Eric L. Jensen and Linda K. Mitsger, "A Test of the Deterrent Effect of Legislative Waiver on Violent Juvenile Crime," *Crime & Delinquency* 40 (January 1994): 102.

78. "Adult Court Is Stricter, but Recidivism Higher, Study Finds," *Criminal Justice Newsletter* 30 (4 January 1999): 3–4.

79. "Criminal Courts Give 10-Year Terms to Violent Juveniles, Study Finds," *Criminal Justice Newsletter* 29 (17 August 1998): 4.

80. "Florida Leads Nation in Trying Kids as Adults," *Tallahassee Democrat* (31 August 1999), p. 1; "Juveniles in Adult Courts: Editorials", *The Ledger* (Lakeland, Fla.) (17 December 2003), p. 12.

81. "After Conviction of Boy, Prosecutor Switches Sides," *New York Times* (18 November 2002), p. 14; Brazill v. State, 845 So.2d 282 (Fla. Dist. Ct. App. 4th Dist. 2003).

82. "Boy Who Killed Gets 7 Years, Judge Says Law Too Harsh," *New York Times* (14 January 2000), p. 1.

83. Hughes v. State, 653 A.2d 241 (Del. 1994), *clarified, reh'g. denied*, 1995 Del. LEXIS 36 (Del. 30 January 1995).

84. *Juveniles' Competence to Stand Trial: A Comparison of Adolescents' and Adults' Capacities as Trial Defendants* (Philadelphia, Pa.: MacArthur Foundation Research Network on Adolescent Development and Juvenile Justice, 2003), as cited in "Many Juveniles Lack Competence for Adult Court, Study Finds," *Criminal Justice Newsletter* (18 March 2003), p. 5.

85. People v. J.W., 787 N.E.2d 747 (Ill. 2003), *cert. denied*, 540 U.S. 873 (2003).

86. State v. C. M., 746 So.2d 410 (Ala.Crim.App. 1999).

87. "Juvenile Drug Courts Must Differ from Adults, Task Force Says," *Criminal Justice Newsletter* (1 May 2003), p. 4, referring to *Juvenile Drug Courts: Strategies in Practice*, a 78-page report available on the Internet at www.ncjrs.org/txtfilesl/bja/197866.txt.

88. See David J. Rothman, *The Discovery of the Asylum* (South Salem, N.Y.: Criminal Justice Institute, 1988), pp. 50, 51.

89. "Crowding of Juvenile Facilities Is 'Pervasive,' Study Finds," *Criminal Justice Newsletter* 24 (15 April 1993): 4.

90. Dale G. Parent et al., *Conditions of Confinement: Juvenile Detention and Corrections Facilities. Research Summary* (Washington, D.C.: U.S. Department of Justice, February 1994), p. 1. This publication is a summary of the congressionally mandated study, and it was prepared by Abt Associations, Inc., under a grant from the Office of Juvenile Justice and Delinquency, Office of Justice Programs, U.S. Department of Justice.

91. "Crowding of Juvenile Facilities," p. 5.

92. Snyder and Sickmund, *Juvenile Offenders and Victims*, pp. 186–198.

93. Melissa Sickmund, Office of Juvenile Justice and Delinquency Prevention, *Juvenile Residential Facility Census, 2000: Selected Findings* (Washington, D.C.: U.S. Department of Justice, December 2002), p. 1.

94. Joseph R. Rowan and Charles J. Kehoe, "Let's Deinstitutionalize Group Homes," *Juvenile and Family Court Journal* 36 (Spring 1985): 1–4.

95. "Justice Dept. Cites Abuses in Georgia Juvenile Justice System," *Criminal Justice Newsletter* 29 (2 February 1999): 1–2; and "U.S. and Georgia in Deal to Improve Juvenile Prisons," *New York Times* (22 March 1998), p. 16.

96. "Georgia Juvenile Department Overhauls Corrections Education," *Corrections Professional* 8, no. 2 (6 September 2002).

97. "Louisiana Assumes Operation of Wackenhut Prison," *Corrections Professional* 7, no. 18 (14 June 2002); "Louisiana Pressured for Change," *Corrections Professional* 8, no. 19 (20 June 2003); "Louisiana and Justice Dept. Settle on Juvenile Facilities," *Criminal Justice Newsletter* (4 March 2003), p. 3.

98. "Abuse Cited at Mississippi Youth Correctional Education Centers," *Correctional Educational Bulletin* 6, no. 12 (19 August 2003). See also "Care of Juvenile Offenders in

Mississippi Is Faulted," *New York Times* (1 September 2003), p. 11.

99. Ibid.

100. "Justice Dept. Sues Mississippi over Alleged Abuse of Juveniles," *Criminal Justice Newsletter* (2 January 2004), p. 4.

101. "Mississippi Juvenille Facility Suit Settled," *UPI News Release* (4 May 2005).

102. "News," *Texas Lawyer* 17, no. 24 (2 September 2002): p. 21.

103. "Reports of Abuse at Girls' Prison Prompt Review," *Orlando Sentinel* (18 June 2003), p. 2B.

104. O'Conner v. Donaldson, 422 U.S. 563 (1975).

105. Shookoff v. Adams, 750 F.Supp. 288 (M.D.Tenn. 1990, *aff'd. sub nom.*, 969 F.2d 228 (6th Cir. 1992). The U.S. Supreme Court case on which the decision relies concerns the right of adult offenders to access to courts. See Bounds v. Smith, 430 U.S. 817 (1977).

106. "Imprisoned Youth at High Risk for Viral Hepatitis," *Hepatitis Weekly* (14 May 2001).

107. "Teachers Must Handle Mental Health Students with Care," *Correctional Educational Bulletin* 4, no. 11 (30 July 2001).

108. For additional information on the aftercare of juveniles, see David M. Altschuler et al., Office of Juvenile Justice and Delinquency Prevention *Reintegration, Supervised Release, and Intensive Aftercare*, (Washington, D.C.: U.S. Department of Justice, July 1999).

109. See, for example, Richard G. Wiebush, "Juvenile Intensive Supervision: The Impact on Felony Offenders Diverted from Institutional Placement," *Crime & Delinquency* 39 (January 1993): 68–89.

110. *Respite Care: A Promising Response to Status Offenders at Risk of Court-Ordered Placements* (New York: The Vera Institute of Justice, 2003), as cited in "'Respite Care' Helping Runaways and Other Status Offenders," *Criminal Justice Newsletter* (16 January 2003), p. 3.

111. "Researchers Conducting Review of Juvenile Aftercare Programs," *Criminal Justice Newsletter* (15 October 2003), pp. 6–7, referring to the OJJDP publication *Aftercare Services* (NCJ-201800), available from the Juvenile Justice Clearinghouse, Box 6000, Rockville, MD 20849-6000. (800) 638-08736. On the Internet: www.ojp.usdoj.gov/ojjdp.

112. The National Advisory Commission on Criminal Justice Standards and Goals, *Corrections* (Washington, D.C.: U.S. Government Printing Office, 1973), p. 350.

113. Ibid., pp. 350–352.

114. *Time* (30 August 1976), p. 63.

115. Alden D. Miller et al., "The Aftermath of Extreme Tactics in Juvenile Justice Reform: A Crisis Four Years Later," in *Corrections and Punishment,* ed. David F. Greenberg, Sage Criminal Justice System Annuals (Beverly Hills, Calif.: Sage, 1977), p. 245.

116. Yitzhak Bakal, "Reflections: A Quarter Century of Reform in Massachusetts Youth Corrections," *Crime & Delinquency* 44 (January 1998): p. 116.

117. Maynard L. Erickson, "Schools for Crime?" *Journal of Research in Crime and Delinquency* 15 (January 1978): 32–33.

118. "Overview of Those under Juvenile Death Sentences," Death Penalty Information Center, referring to Victor L. Streib, "The Juvenile Death Penalty Today," on the Internet at www.deathpenaltyinfo.org/article.php?did=2048scid=27#streibstats;.

119. Eddings v. Oklahoma, 455 U.S. 104 (1982).

120. Baldwin v. Alabama, 472 U.S. 372 (1985).

121. Thompson v. Oklahoma, 487 U.S. 815 (1988); Trop v. Dulles, 356 U.S. 86, 101 (1958) (plurality opinion).

122. Thompson v. Oklahoma, 487 U.S. 815 (1988).

123. Stanford v. Kentucky, 492 U.S. 361 (1989).

124. Stanford v. Parker, 2001 U.S. App. LEXIS 26419 (6th Cir. 2001), *cert. denied,* 537 U.S. 831 (2002).

125. "3 Justices Call for Reviewing Death Sentences for Juveniles," *New York Times* (30 August 2002), p. 1; Patterson v. Cockrell, 2002 U.S. App. LEXIS 6396 (5th Cir. 2002), *cert. denied,* 536 U.S. 967 (2002).

126. Hain v. Mullin, 852 P.2d 744 (Okla. Crim. App. 1993), *cert. denied,* 537 U.S. 1173 (2003).

127. "High Court Passes on Local Case: Activists Sought Ruling on Killers Younger Than 18," *Houston Chronicle* (21 October 2003), p. 17. The case is Williams v. Texas, 540 U.S. 969 (2003).

128. "Penalty for Young Sniper Could Spur Change in Law," *New York Times* (25 December 2003), p. 9.

129. "Despite Upcoming Supreme Court Argument, Texas Schedules Execution Dates for Four Juvenile Offenders," Death Penalty Information Center (13 February 2004), on the Internet at www.deathpenaltyinfo.org/article.php?did=878&scid=64. The case is Roper v. Simmons, 112 S.W. 3d 397 (Mo. 2003), *aff'd.,* 125 S.Ct. 1183 (2005).

130. Merlo, "Juvenile Justice at the Crossroads," p. 657.

131. Barry C. Feld, "The Punitive Juvenile Court and the Quality of Procedural Justice: Disfunctions between Rhetoric and Reality," *Crime & Delinquency* 36 (October 1989): 443.

132. Robert O. Dawson, "The Future of Juvenile Justice: Is It Time to Abolish the System?" *Journal of Criminal Law and Criminology* 81 (Spring 1990): 136–155.

Selected Amendments to the United States Constitution

Amendment I (1791)

Congress shall make no law respecting an establishment of religion, or prohibiting the free exercise thereof; or abridging the freedom of speech, or of the press; or the right of the people peaceably to assemble, and to petition the Government for a redress of grievances.

Amendment IV (1791)

The right of the people to be secure in their persons, houses, papers, and effects, against unreasonable searches and seizures, shall not be violated, and no Warrants shall issue, but upon probable cause, supported by Oath or affirmation, and particularly describing the place to be searched, and the persons or things to be seized.

Amendment V (1791)

No person shall be held to answer for a capital, or otherwise infamous crime, unless on a presentment or indictment of a Grand Jury, except in cases arising in the land or naval forces, or in the Militia, when in actual service in time of War or public danger; nor shall any person be subject for the same offence to be twice put in jeopardy of life or limb; nor shall be compelled in any criminal case to be a witness against himself, nor be deprived of life, liberty, or property, without due process of law; nor shall private property be taken for public use, without just compensation.

Amendment VI (1791)

In all criminal prosecutions, the accused shall enjoy the right to a speedy and public trial, by an impartial jury of the State and district wherein the crime shall have been committed, which district shall have been previously ascertained by law, and to be informed of the nature and cause of the accusation; to be confronted with the witnesses against him; to have compulsory process for obtaining witnesses in his favor, and to have the Assistance of Counsel for his defence.

Amendment VIII (1791)

Excessive bail shall not be required, nor excessive fines imposed, nor cruel and unusual punishments inflicted.

Amendment IX (1791)

The powers not delegated to the United States by the Constitution, nor prohibited by it to the Sates, are reserved to the States respectively, or to the people.

Amendment XIV (1868)

Section 1. All persons born or naturalized in the United States, and subject to the jurisdiction thereof, are citizens of the United States and of the State wherein they reside. No State shall make or enforce any law which shall abridge the privileges or immunities of citizens of the United States; nor shall any State deprive any person of life, liberty, or property, without due process of law; nor deny to any person within its jurisdiction the equal protection of the laws.

Section 5. The Congress shall have power to enforce, by appropriate legislation, the provisions of this article.

How to Read a Court Citation

Pugh v. Locke, 406 F.Supp. 318 (M.D.Ala. 1976), *aff'd., remanded*, Newman v. Alabama, 559 F.2d 283 (5th Cir. 1977), *and rev'd. in part sub nom.*, 438 U.S. 781 (1978), *later proceeding sub nom.*, 466 F.Supp. 628 (M.D.Ala. 1979), *later proceeding*, 683 F.2d 1312 (11th Cir. 1982), *cert. denied*, 460 U.S. 1083 (1983), later proceeding sub nom., 740 F.2d 1513 (11 Cir. 1984).

This case has a number of citations, and that is not common among all cases, but it is common among cases involving unconstitutional conditions in prisons and jails. This case illustrates many elements of case citations, some of which are omitted because of their length.

Original Citation

[Pugh v. Locke][1] [406][2] [F.Supp.][3] [318][4] [M.D.Ala.][5] [1976][6].

1. Name of case
2. Volume number of reporter in which case is published
3. Name of reporter; see "Abbreviations for Commonly Used Reporters for Court Cases."
4. Page in the reporter where the decision begins
5. Court deciding the case
6. Year decided

Additional Case History

[*aff'd., remanded*][7] [Newman v. Alabama][8] [559][9] [F.2d][10] [283][11] [(5th Cir. 1977)][12] [*and rev'd., in part*][13] [438][14] [U.S.][15] [781][16] [1978][17] [*later proceeding*] or [*later proceeding*][18] [*cert. denied*][19]

7. Affirmed and remanded (sent back for further proceedings). The appellate court told the lower court that it agreed with part of its decision but that some aspect of the decision needed to be reconsidered.
8. The name under which the case was affirmed and remanded. In some cases the name will be omitted, and the citation will carry the notation *sub nom.*, which means "by another name." Several times that occurs in this case, but they are omitted here.
9. Volume number of the reporter in which the case is published
10. Abbreviated name of the reporter (Federal Reporter, second series)
11. Page number on which the opinion begins
12. The court deciding the case and the date the decision was given
13. Additional history—appeal to U.S. Supreme Court, which reversed the lower court in part, under another name

14. Volume number of the reporter in which the U.S. Supreme Court decision is published
15. Abbreviated name of the reporter
16. Page number on which the U.S. Supreme Court decision begins
17. Year in which the U.S. Supreme Court decided the case
18. The case had a later proceeding under a different name before the Middle District of Alabama court (in 1979) and another before the Eleventh Circuit in 1982.
19. The U.S. Supreme Court refused to grant *certiorari;* thus, the case was not heard by that Court.

Abbreviations for Commonly Used Reporters for Court Cases

Decisions of the U.S. Supreme Court

S.Ct.: Supreme Court Reporter

U.S.: United States Reports

Decisions from Other Courts: A Selected List

A., A.2d: Atlantic Reporter, Atlantic Reporter Second Series

Cal.Rptr: California Reporter

F.2d: Federal Reporter Second Series

F.3d: Federal Reporter Third Series

F.Supp: Federal Supplement

N.Y.S.2d: New York Supplement Second Series

N.W., N.W.2d: North Western Reporter, North Western Reporter Second Series

N.E., N.E.2d: North Eastern Reporter, North Eastern Reporter Second Series

P., P.2d: Pacific Reporter, Pacific Reporter Second Series

S.E., S.E.2d: South Eastern Reporter, South Eastern Reporter Second Series

Definitions

Aff'd Affirmed; the appellate court agrees with the decision of the lower court.

Aff'd. per curium Affirmed by the court. The opinion is written by the court instead of by one of the judges; a decision affirmed but without a written opinion.

Aff'd. sub nom Affirmed under a different name; the case at the appellate level has a different name from that of the trial court level.

Cert. denied *Certiorari* denied; the U.S. Supreme Court refused to hear and decide the case. Some state supreme courts use this terminology; others use *review denied*.

Concurring opinion An opinion agreeing with the court's decision but offering different reasons.

Dismissed The court dismissing the case from legal proceedings, thus refusing to give further consideration to any of its issues.

Dissenting opinion An opinion disagreeing with the reasoning and the result of the majority opinion.

Later proceeding Any number of issues could be decided in a subsequent proceeding.

Reh'g. denied Rehearing denied; the court refused to rehear a case.

Remanded The appellate court sent the case back to the lower court for further action.

Rev'd. Reversed, overthrown, set aside, made void. The appellate court reversed the decision of the lower court.

Rev'd. and remanded Reversed and remanded; the appellate court reversed the decision and sent the case back for further action.

Vacated Abandoned, set aside, made void. The appellate court set aside the decision of the lower court.

GLOSSARY

A

AIDS (acquired immune deficiency syndrome) A deadly disease that attacks the immune system; it is communicated through exchange of body fluids, especially during sexual activity and blood transfusions, but it can also be transmitted in other ways.

Acquittal Legal verification of the innocence of a person in a criminal trial.

Adjudication The process of decision making by a court; normally used to refer to juvenile proceedings. The term is also used to refer to rule enforcement by administrative agencies.

Administrative law Rules and regulations made by agencies to which power has been delegated by a state legislature or by the U.S. Congress. Administrative agencies investigate and decide cases concerning potential violations of these rules.

Adversary system One of two primary systems for settling disputes in court. The accused is presumed to be innocent. A defense attorney and a prosecuting attorney attempt to convince a judge or a jury of their versions of the case. *See also* **inquisitory system.**

Aftercare The continued supervision of juveniles after they are released from a correctional facility; similar to the term *parole* in adult criminal court systems.

Aggravated assault Technically an assault is a threat to commit a battery, but often the term is used to refer to a battery. Aggravated assault involves a battery inflicted by use of a deadly weapon.

Aggravating circumstances Circumstances that are above and beyond those required for the crime but that make the crime more serious; may be used in reference to many crimes, but the concept is critical particularly in capital punishment cases, where it is required.

Appeal The stage in a judicial proceeding in which a higher court is asked to review a decision of a lower court.

Appellant The loser in a court case, who seeks a review of the decision by a higher appellate court.

Appellee The winning party in a lower court, who argues on appeal against reversing the lower court's decision.

Arraignment A hearing before a judge, during which the defendant is identified, hears the formal reading of the charges, is read his or her legal rights, and enters a plea to the charges.

Arrest The act of taking an individual into custody in order to make a criminal charge against that person.

Arson The willful and malicious burning of the structure of another with or without the intent to defraud. Burning of one's own property with the intent to defraud is included in some definitions. Many modern statutes carry a more severe penalty for the burning of a dwelling than of other real property.

Assigned counsel An attorney appointed by and paid for by the court to represent a defendant who does not have funds to retain a private attorney.

Attendant circumstances Facts surrounding a crime, which are considered to be a part of that crime and which must be proved along with the elements of the crime.

B

Baby Moses laws Provisions for protecting mothers (or fathers) who abandon their newborn children in ways that will protect those infants; these laws are becoming more common in the United States as well as in some other countries. Normally the laws permit new parents to leave the babies in safe places and avoid prosecution.

Bail Money or property posted by the defendant (or a surety) to guarantee that he or she will appear for trial, sentencing, or imprisonment. If the defendant does not appear, the court may require that the money or property be forfeited.

Beyond a reasonable doubt The standard for evidence required for a conviction in an adult criminal court or a juvenile court; a lack of uncertainty; the facts presented to the judge or jury are sufficient to lead a reasonable person to conclude without question that the defendant committed the act for which he or she is charged.

Bond A written document indicating that the defendant or his or her sureties assure the presence of that defendant at a criminal proceeding and that, if the defendant is not present, the court may require that the security posted for the bond be forfeited.

Booking The official recording of the name, photograph, and fingerprints of a suspect, along with the offense charged and the name of the officer who made the arrest.

Bow Street Runners The mid-eighteenth-century London system that gave the police powers of investigation and arrest to constables, who were given some training and paid a portion of the fines in successfully prosecuted cases.

Burglary The illegal or forcible entering of any enclosed structure in order to commit a crime, usually theft. Some jurisdictions require that the intent be to commit a felony rather than a less serious crime.

C

Capital punishment Punishment by death for those convicted of capital crimes.

Case law Legally binding court interpretations of written laws or rules made by the courts. *See also* **common law.**

Causation In criminal law, the requirement that the act must be the cause of the harmful consequence.

Certification The process used to remove juveniles from the jurisdiction of the juvenile court to that of the adult criminal court; also called *transfer* or *waiver.*

Circumstantial evidence   Evidence that may be inferred from a fact or a series of facts. *See also* **direct evidence.**

Civil law   Distinguished from criminal law as that law pertaining to private rights.

Civil rights   Sometimes called civil liberties; all the natural rights guaranteed by the U.S. Constitution (or by individual state constitutions), such as free speech and the right to religious beliefs and practices; also the body of law concerning natural rights.

Classification   The assignment of new inmates to the housing, security status, and treatment programs that best fit their individual needs.

Commissary   The prison store as well as incidental items sold to inmates. Also an inmate's account, which is debited when an item is purchased.

Common law   Broadly defined, the legal theory and law that originated in England and are common in the United States as well. More specifically, common law consists of the guidelines, customs, traditions, and judicial decisions that courts use in decision making. It is contrasted with constitutions and written laws.

Community-based correction facility   A facility in which the punishment emphasizes assimilation into the community. Instead of imprisonment, the offender may be put on probation or placed in programs such as work release, foster homes, halfway houses, parole, and furlough.

Community work service   Punishment assigning the offender to community service or work projects. Sometimes it is combined with restitution or probation.

Concurrent sentence   A sentence for more than one offense served at the same time. For example, if an offender receives a three-year prison term for robbery and a five-year prison term for assault, these sentences to be served concurrently, the total prison sentence is five years.

Concurring opinion   A judge's written opinion agreeing with the result in a case but disagreeing with the reasoning of the majority opinion.

Conjugal visits   Visits that permit inmates to engage in sexual and other social contacts with their spouses in an unsupervised, private setting.

Consecutive sentence   A term of imprisonment for more than one offense that must be served one following the other. If an offender receives a three-year term for robbery and a five-year term for assault, the consecutive sentence adds up to eight years.

Constable   An officer of a municipal corporation who has duties similar to those of a sheriff, such as preserving the public peace, executing papers from the court, and maintaining the custody of juries.

Contempt of court   An act (usually committed in violation of a court order or rule) considered as embarrassing, humiliating, or undermining the power of the court; may be civil or criminal.

Continuance   The adjournment of a trial or another legal proceeding until a later date.

Contraband   Any item (such as weapons, alcohol, or other drugs), possession of which is illegal or violates prison rules.

Corporal punishment   Physical punishment, such as beatings or whippings.

Correctional officer (guard)   A corrections employee with supervisory power over a suspect or convicted offender in custody.

Crime   An illegal act of omission or commission that is punishable by the criminal law.

Crime rate   The number of crimes per 100,000 population.

Crimes known to the police   All serious criminal offenses that have been reported to the police for which the police have sufficient evidence to believe the crimes were committed.

Criminal   A person found guilty of an act that violates the criminal law.

Criminal justice system   The entire system of criminal prevention, detection, apprehension, trial, and punishment.

Criminal law   Statutes defining acts so offensive that they threaten the well-being of the society and require that the accused be prosecuted by the government. Criminal laws prescribe punishments that may be imposed on offenders.

Cross-examination   The questioning of a court witness by adversary counsel after one attorney concludes the direct examination.

Cruel and unusual punishment   The punishments prohibited by the Eighth Amendment to the U.S. Constitution, as interpreted by the courts. Some examples are torture, prison conditions that "shock the conscience," excessively long sentences, and the death penalty for rape but not murder of an adult woman.

Curtilage   The enclosed ground and buildings immediately around a dwelling.

Custody   Legal control over a person or property; physical responsibility for a person or thing.

D

Date rape   Forced sexual acts that occur during a social occasion. The alleged victim may have agreed to some intimacy but not to the activities defined in that jurisdiction as constituting the elements of rape.

Deadly force   Force likely to cause serious bodily injury or death.

Defendant   The person charged with a crime and against whom a criminal proceeding has begun or is pending.

Defense attorney   The counsel for the defendant in a criminal proceeding, whose main function is to protect the legal rights of the accused.

Defenses   Responses by the defendant in a criminal or civil case. They may consist only of a denial of the factual allegations of the prosecution (in a criminal case) or of the plaintiff (in a civil case). If the defense offers new factual allegations in an effort to negate the charges, there is an affirmative defense.

Delinquency   *See* **juvenile delinquent.**

Demonstrative evidence   Real evidence; the kind of evidence that is apparent to the senses, in contrast to evidence presented by the testimony of other people.

De novo   Literally "anew" or "fresh." A trial *de novo* is a case that is tried again, as if no decision had been rendered previously. In some jurisdictions a first appeal from a lower court may be a trial *de novo*. The term may be used to refer to other proceedings, such as hearings.

Department of Homeland Security (DHS)   The cabinet-level department created after the 9/11/01 terrorist attacks; its creation constituted the most extensive federal government reorganization in 50 years; it combines 22 federal agencies and constitutes the third largest federal agency.

Deposition   Oral testimony taken from the opposing party or a witness for the opposing party. Depositions are taken out of court but under oath. They are recorded verbatim, usually by a court reporter. Attorneys for both sides are present. Depositions may be used when the deposed is not able to appear in court. They may also be used to impeach the testimony of a witness in court.

Deprivation model   A model of prisonization based on the belief that the prison subculture stems from the way inmates adapt to the severe psychological and physical losses imposed by imprisonment.

Detention   *See* **pretrial detention.**

Detention centers   Facilities for the temporary confinement of juveniles in custody who are awaiting court disposition.

Determinate sentence   A sentence for a specific crime and determined by the legislature; the parole board, correctional officials, or a judge cannot make changes in the sentence length. In some jurisdictions the trial judge may have the power to suspend the sentence or to impose probation rather than the legislatively specified prison term.

Deterrence   A punishment philosophy based on the assumption that the acts of potential offenders can be prevented. *Individual deterrence* refers to the prevention of additional criminal acts by the specific individual being punished; *general deterrence* refers to the presumed effect that punishing one offender will have on other potential offenders.

Dicta   The written portions of a judge's opinion that are not part of the actual ruling of the court and are not legally binding precedents for future court decisions.

Directed verdict   Upon a finding of insufficient evidence to convict a defendant, the judge may direct the jury to return a verdict of not guilty. The judge may not direct a guilty verdict.

Direct evidence   Evidence offered by an eyewitness who testifies to what he or she saw, heard, tasted, smelled, or touched.

Direct examination   The examination of a witness, which is conducted by the attorney who called the witness to testify.

Discovery   A legal motion requesting the disclosure of information held by the opposing counsel and intended for use in the forthcoming trial.

Discretion   In the criminal justice system, authority to make decisions based on one's own judgment rather than on specified rules. The result may be inconsistent handling of offenders, as well as positive actions tailored to individual circumstances.

Disposition   The final decision of a court in a criminal proceeding to accept a guilty plea, to find the defendant guilty or not guilty, or to terminate the proceedings against the defendant.

Diversion   The removal of the offender from the criminal proceeding before or after guilt is determined and disposition through other procedures, such as work release, drug treatment, or community service.

Domestic violence   The causing of serious physical harm or the threatening of such harm to a member of one's family or household, including spouses, ex-spouses, parents, children, persons otherwise related by blood, persons living in the household, or persons who lived there formerly. May include relationships of persons who do not live together but who have had intimate relationships, such as courtship.

Due process   The constitutional principle that a person should not be deprived of life, liberty, or property without reasonable and lawful procedures that must be made available in any criminal action, including postconviction procedures, such as prison disciplinary hearings or parole revocations.

E

Equal protection   All persons under like circumstances must receive essentially the same treatment in criminal justice systems; they may not be discriminated against because of race, gender, minority status, ethnicity, disability, or religion.

Exclusionary rule   Evidence secured as a result of illegal actions by law enforcement officers should be excluded from a trial.

Expert witness   A person with extensive training or education in a particular field, such as medicine, who testifies at depositions or at trials concerning a critical issue of that case, such as what caused the death of the deceased.

F

Felony   A serious offense, such as murder, armed robbery, or rape. Punishment ranges from execution to imprisonment in a state or federal institution but also includes probation, community work service, fines, and other less punitive sanctions, as well as a combination of these measures.

Fetal abuse   The abusing of a fetus, which may or may not lead to its death. In some jurisdictions any resulting injury may lead to legal culpability; in a few states, killing a fetus may result in murder charges.

Fine   The payment of a sum of money to a court by the convicted defendant in addition to or instead of other punishment(s).

Fleeing felon rule   The common law rule that permitted police to shoot at any fleeing felon. The rule has been modified to require circumstances involving (1) the threat of serious injury or death of an officer or others, (2) the prevention of an escape if the suspect threatens the officer with a gun, or (3) the officer's having probable cause to believe that the suspect has committed or has threatened to commit serious bodily harm.

Forcible rape   *See* **rape.**

Frankpledge system   In old English law, a system whereby the members of a tithing had corporate responsibility for the behavior of all members

over 14 years old. Ten tithings formed a hundred, and hundreds were later combined to form shires, similar to counties, over which a sheriff had jurisdiction.

Frisk   An action by a law enforcement officer or a correctional officer consisting of patting down or running one's hands quickly over a person's body to determine whether the suspect or inmate has a weapon or other contraband. This is in contrast to a body search, which is a more careful and thorough examination of the person.

Furlough   An authorized, temporary leave from a prison or other penal facility in order to attend a funeral, visit the family, attempt to secure employment, or engage in any other approved activity.

G

General deterrence   *See* **deterrence.**

Good faith exception   The provision that illegally obtained evidence will not be excluded from a subsequent trial if it can be shown that the police secured the evidence in good faith, meaning that they had a reasonable belief that they were acting in accordance with the law.

Grand jury   A group of citizens, convened by legal authority, who evaluate evidence to ascertain whether a crime has been committed and whether there is sufficient evidence against the accused to justify prosecution. If so, the grand jury may return an indictment. In some jurisdictions grand juries are empowered to conduct investigations into alleged criminal activities.

H

Habeas corpus   Technically a written court order requiring that the accused be taken to court to determine the legality of custody and confinement; also refers to writs filed by inmates regarding the alleged illegality of their confinement.

Hands-off doctrine   A policy used by courts to justify nonintervention in the daily administration of corrections agencies.

Harmless error   A minor or trivial error not deemed sufficient to harm the rights of the parties who assert the error. Cases are not reversed on the basis of harmless errors.

Hate crime   As defined in the federal criminal code, a crime "that manifests evidence of prejudice based on race, religion, disability, sexual orientation, or ethnicity, including where appropriate the crimes of murder, non-negligent manslaughter, forcible rape, aggravated assault, simple assault, intimidation, arson, and destruction, damage or vandalism of property."

Hearsay evidence   Secondhand evidence of which the witness does not have personal knowledge but merely repeats something the witness says he or she heard another person say. Hearsay evidence must be excluded from trial unless it meets one of the exceptions to the hearsay rule.

House arrest   A form of confinement, usually on probation, in which the offender is permitted to live at home (or some other approved place) but is restricted in his or her movements to and from the area. A curfew may be imposed, and the offender may be subject to unannounced visits from a probation officer. In some cases electronic devices are used to monitor the probationer's location.

Humanitarianism   In penal philosophy, the doctrine advocating the removal of harsh, severe, and painful conditions in penal institutions.

Hundred   In English law, a combination of 10 tithings as part of the frankpledge system. *See also* **tithing** and **frankpledge system.**

I

Identity theft   The stealing of an individual's social security number or other important information about his or her identity and using that information to commit crimes, such as removing funds from the victim's bank account.

Importation model   A model based on the assumption that the inmate subculture arises not only from internal prison experiences but also from the external patterns of behavior the inmates take into prison.

Incapacitation   A punishment theory usually implemented by imprisoning an offender to prevent the commission of any other crimes by that person. In some countries (and in earlier days in the United States), incapacitation involved mutilation, such as removing the hands of thieves and castrating sex offenders.

Incarceration   Imprisonment in a jail, a prison, or another type of penal institution.

Indeterminate sentence   A sentence to confinement without a definite term. Parole boards or professionals determine when the offender should be released.

Index offenses   The FBI's *Uniform Crime Reports* of the occurrences of the eight crimes considered most serious: murder and nonnegligent manslaughter, forcible rape, robbery, aggravated assault, burglary, larceny-theft, motor vehicle theft, and arson. In June 2004, the FBI discontinued publishing data according to index offenses because of the misrepresentation of crime in an area that can be caused by a very high (or low) volume or rate of crime of only one of these serious crimes in that area.

Indictment   The written accusation of a grand jury, formally stating that probable cause exists to believe that the suspect committed a specified felony.

Individual deterrence   *See* **deterrence.**

Inevitable discovery rule   Evidence secured illegally by police will not be excluded from the suspect's trial, provided it can be shown that the evidence would have been discovered anyway under legal means.

Informant   A person who gives information to law enforcement officials about a crime or planned criminal activity.

Information   A formal written document used to charge a person with a specific offense. Prosecutors issue informations, in contrast to indictments, which are issued by grand juries.

Initial appearance   The first appearance of the accused before a magistrate; if the accused is detained in jail immediately after arrest, he or she must be taken quickly to a magistrate for the initial appearance. At that point the magistrate decides whether there is probable cause to detain the suspect and, if so, tells the suspect of the charges and of his or her constitutional rights, including the right to an attorney.

Inmates   Convicted persons whose freedom has been replaced by confinement in a prison, jail, mental ward, or similar institution.

Inquisitory system   A system in which the defendant must prove his or her innocence, in contrast to the adversary system, which has a presumption of innocence, requiring the state (or federal prosecutors in federal cases) to prove the defendant's guilt.

Intake decision   In prosecution, the first review of a case by an official in the prosecutor's office. Weak cases may be weeded out at this stage; in juvenile courts the reception of a juvenile against whom complaints have been made. The decision to dismiss or proceed with a case is made at this stage.

Intensive probation supervision (IPS)   With small caseloads, probation officers provide more careful supervision than they could provide with larger caseloads.

INTERPOL   A world police organization that was established for the purpose of cooperation among nations involved in common policing problems.

Interrogatories   A set of questions given to a party thought to have pertinent information that may be used at a trial or other legal proceedings. The party completing the interrogatories must sign an oath that the statements are correct.

J

Jail   A local, regional, or federal facility used to confine persons awaiting trial, as well as those serving short sentences.

Judge   An elected or appointed officer of the court who presides over a court of law; the final and neutral arbiter of law who is responsible for all court activities.

Judicial review   The authority of an appellate court to check the decisions of lower courts as well as those within the executive and legislative branches of government within its jurisdiction to determine whether any of those acts are in violation of statutes or constitutions.

Jurisdiction   The lawful exercise of authority; the area within which authority may be exercised, such as the geographical area within which a particular police force has authority. Courts may have *original* jurisdiction to hear the case; if more than one court has authority to hear the same case, those courts have *concurrent* jurisdiction. *Appellate* jurisdiction is the power of a court to hear a particular case on appeal. *Exclusive* jurisdiction means that only one court may hear the case.

Jury   In a criminal case, a group of people who have been sworn in at court to listen to a trial and to decide whether the defendant is guilty or not guilty. In some jurisdictions, juries may determine or recommend sentences.

Just deserts   The belief that those who commit crimes should suffer for those crimes; also the amount or type of punishment a particular offender deserves to receive.

Juvenile   A young person under age for certain privileges, such as voting or drinking alcoholic beverages. If accused of a criminal or juvenile offense, usually a juvenile is not tried by an adult criminal court but is processed in the juvenile court.

Juvenile court   The court having jurisdiction over juveniles who are accused of delinquent acts or offenses or criminal acts or who are in need of supervision because they are being neglected or mistreated by their parents or guardians.

Juvenile delinquent   A person under legal age (the maximum age varies among the states from 16 to 21, but 18 is the most common) whom a juvenile court has determined to be incorrigible or in violation of a criminal statute.

L

Larceny-theft   The unlawful removal of someone else's property with the intention of keeping it permanently. Historically small thefts were categorized as *petit larceny* and large thefts as *grand larceny*. The latter was punished by the death penalty, a punishment no longer permitted for larceny in the United States. Some modern theft laws do not distinguish between the two types of larceny.

Law Enforcement Assistance Administration (LEAA)   The agency established by Congress in 1965. It provided funding for the development of police departments, police techniques, police education, and police training. It was abolished in 1982. Money for education was provided through the Law Enforcement Education Program (LEEP).

Law Enforcement Education Program (LEEP)   *See* **Law Enforcement Assistance Administration (LEAA).**

Lineup   A procedure in which a group of people are placed together in a line to allow the complainant or an eyewitness to point out the alleged offender.

M

Magistrate   A judge in the lower courts of the state or federal court system. Usually magistrates preside over arraignments, preliminary hearings, bail hearings, and minor offenses.

Mala in se   Actions that are intrinsically immoral, such as murder, forcible rape, and robbery.

Mala prohibita   Actions that are wrong because legislation prohibits them, although there may not be general agreement that they are wrong in themselves.

Mandatory sentence   A sentence having a length imposed by the legislature with no discretion given to the trial judge. If the defendant is convicted, the specified sentence must be imposed.

Manslaughter   The unlawful killing of a human being by a person who lacks malice. Manslaughter may be *involuntary* (or negligent), the result of recklessness while committing an unlawful act (such as driving while intoxicated), or *voluntary*, an intentional killing committed in the heat of passion.

Marshal   A sworn law enforcement officer who performs the civil duties of the courts, such as the delivery of papers to begin civil proceedings. In some jurisdictions marshals serve papers for the arrest of criminal suspects and escort inmates from jail to court or into the community when they are permitted to leave the jail or prison temporarily.

Mens rea   The criminal intent of the accused at the time the criminal act is committed.

Miranda **warning**   The rule stemming from *Miranda* v. *Arizona,* which stipulates that anyone in custody for an offense that might result in a jail or prison term must be warned of certain rights before any questioning by law enforcement officials occurs. These rights include the right to remain silent, to be told that anything said can and will be held against the suspect, the right to counsel (which will be appointed if the suspect cannot afford to retain private counsel), and the right to cease talking at any time. If the warning is not given or is given and violated, any information obtained from the suspect may be inadmissible as evidence at trial. The rights may be waived if done so willingly and knowingly by one who has the legal capacity to waive them.

Misdemeanor   A less serious offense, punishable by a fine, probation, or a short jail term, in contrast to a felony, a more serious crime.

Mistrial   A trial that cannot stand, that is invalid. Judges may call a mistrial for such reasons as an error on the part of the prosecution or the defense, the illness or death of any of the parties participating in the legal proceedings, or the jury's inability to reach a verdict.

Mitigating circumstances   Circumstances that do not justify or excuse a crime but that, because of justice and fairness, make the crime less reprehensible; they may be used to reduce a crime to a lesser offense, such as to reduce murder to manslaughter. Mitigating circumstances must be considered before the death penalty can be imposed. *See also* **aggravating circumstances.**

Molly Maguires   A powerful secret police organization in the 1870s in Pennsylvania.

Moot   The term used to describe a controversy that has ended or evolved to the stage at which a court decision on that case is no longer relevant or necessary; this is a limitation on the power of courts to decide a case.

Motion   A document submitted to the court, asking for an order or a rule.

Motor vehicle theft   The stealing of an automobile, in contrast to the stealing of an automobile part or larceny-theft from an automobile.

Murder   The unlawful killing of another person with either express or implied malice aforethought.

N

National Crime Victimization Survey (NCVS)   Crime data collected by the Bureau of Justice Statistics (BJS) and based on surveys of people to determine who has been victimized by crime.

National Incident-Based Reporting System (NIBRS)   A reporting system used by the FBI in collecting crime data. In this system, a crime is viewed along with all of its components, including the type of victim, type of weapon, location of the crime, alcohol/drug influence, type of criminal activity, relationship of victim to offender, and residence of victims and arrestees, as well as a description of the property and its value. This system includes 22 crimes, rather than the 8 that constitute the FBI's Part I Offenses of serious crimes.

Negligence   In law, an act that a reasonable person would not do, or would not fail to do under similar circumstances. Negligence does not require a criminal intent.

Nolo contendere   Literally, "I will not contest it." In a criminal case this plea has the legal effect of a guilty plea, but the plea cannot be used against the defendant in a civil action based on the same act. The plea might be used in a case involving a felony charge of driving while intoxicated. A guilty plea could be used as evidence of liability in a civil action of wrongful death filed by the family of the victim who died in the accident, whereas a *nolo* plea requires that the plaintiff in the civil action prove liability.

Norms   The rules or standards of appropriate behavior shared by members of a social group.

O

Offenders   Persons who have committed a criminal offense.

P

Pardon   An act by a state governor or the president of the United States (in federal cases) that exempts a convicted offender from punishment or, in the case of those already serving terms, further punishment and removes the legal consequences of the conviction. Pardons may also be granted after a person is released from prison. They may be absolute or conditional; individual or granted to a group, or class, of offenders; and may be full or partial, in which case the pardon remits only part of the punishment or removes some of the legal disabilities resulting from the conviction.

Parens patriae   Literally, "parent of the country"; the doctrine from English common law that was the basis for allowing the state to take over guardianship of a child. In the United States the doctrine forms the basis for juvenile court jurisdiction. The doctrine presumes that the state acts in the best interests of the child.

Parole   The status of an offender who is released before the completion of a prison sentence; usually the parolee must be supervised in the community by a parole officer.

Parole board   A panel at the state or federal level that decides whether an inmate is released on parole from a correctional institution before the expiration of his or her sentence.

Parole officer   A government employee who supervises and counsels inmates paroled to the community.

Parole revocation   The process of returning a released offender to an institution for technical violations of parole conditions or for committing a new crime.

Penitentiary   Historically an institution intended to isolate convicted offenders from one another and from society, giving them time to reflect on their bad acts and become penitent; later, synonymous with prison.

Peremptory challenge   A challenge that may be used by the prosecution or the defense to excuse a potential juror from the jury panel. No reason is required. Each attorney gets a specified number of peremptory challenges. Peremptory challenges are distinguished from *challenges for cause,* which are unlimited and based on a reason for disqualification, such as a conflict of interest in the case.

Petition   A formal document for filing an action in juvenile court, in contrast to a grand jury indictment or prosecutor's presentment in the adult criminal court.

Petit jury   *Petit* literally means "small, minor, or inconsiderate"; a trial jury in contrast to a grand jury. *See also* **jury.**

Plain view doctrine   The legal doctrine that permits a law enforcement officer who is legally searching a place for particular items to seize those that are in plain view but not listed on a search warrant.

Plea bargaining   The process of negotiation between the defense and the prosecution before or during the trial of a defendant. The process may involve reducing or dropping some charges or a recommendation for leniency in exchange for a plea of guilty on another charge or charges.

Police   A government official authorized to enforce the law and to maintain order, using physical, including deadly, force if necessary.

Posse   The rural police system in which the sheriff may call into action any number of citizens over a certain age if they are needed to assist in law enforcement.

Prejudicial errors   Errors made during legal proceedings that affect the rights of parties substantially and thus may result in the reversal of a case.

Preliminary hearing   An appearance before a lower-court judge to determine whether there is sufficient evidence to submit the case to the grand jury or to the trial court. Preliminary hearings may include the bail decision.

Presentence investigation (PSI)   An investigation of the background and characteristics of the defendant; it may include information that would not be admissible at the trial; it is presented to the judge to be used in determining sentence.

Presentment   A document issued by a grand jury that states that probable cause exists to believe that the suspect committed the crime. Presentments are issued without the participation of the prosecutor. *See also* **indictment.**

Presumption of innocence   A cornerstone of the adversary system; it provides that a defendant is innocent unless and until the prosecution proves guilt beyond a reasonable doubt.

Presumptive sentence   The normal sentence is specified by statute for each offense; judges are permitted to deviate from that sentence but usually may do so only under specified circumstances or must give reasons for the deviation.

Pretrial detention   The detention of a defendant in jail between arrest and trial, either because the judge has refused bail or the defendant cannot meet the requirements of bail. Generally the purpose is to assure the presence of the accused at trial. Also, *preventive detention* of defendants who are detained because they are thought to present a danger to themselves, to others, or to both if released pending trial.

Preventive detention   *See* **pretrial detention.**

Prison   A federal or state penal facility for detaining adult offenders (although juvenile offenders are also incarcerated in adult facilities on occasion) sentenced to a year or longer after conviction of crimes.

Prisonization   The process of an inmate's becoming accustomed to the subculture of prison life.

Private security forces   Persons employed by private agencies instead of governmental ones to provide security from criminal activity.

Proactive   In policing, preparing for, intervening in, or taking the initiative in finding criminals, rather than depending on the reports of others.

Probable cause   In search warrant cases a set of facts and circumstances that leads to the reasonable belief that the items sought are located in a particular place. In arrest cases the facts and circumstances lead to the reasonable belief that the suspect has committed a crime.

Probation   A type of sentence that places the convicted offender under the supervision of a probation officer within the community instead of in prison. Also, the part of the criminal justice system that is in charge of all aspects of probation.

Probation officer   A government official responsible for supervising persons on probation and for writing the presentence reports on offenders.

Probation revocation   The process of declaring that a sentenced offender violated the terms of probation. If probation involved a suspended prison or jail sentence, the revocation may mean that the original sentence is invoked and the individual is sent to a prison or jail.

Property crimes   Crimes aimed at the property of another person rather than at the person. Serious property crimes include larceny-theft, burglary, motor vehicle theft, and arson.

Pro se   Literally, "on behalf of self"; acting as one's own attorney.

Prosecuting attorney   A government official responsible for representing the state or federal government against an offender in criminal proceedings.

Prosecution   The process that occurs when the state (or federal government) begins the formal process in a criminal case. The action is taken by a **prosecuting attorney.**

Public defender   An attorney retained and paid by the government to represent indigent defendants in criminal proceedings.

R

Racial profiling   The reaction by law enforcement officers to potential suspects based solely on their race or ethnicity.

Rape   Historically, unlawful vaginal intercourse with a woman; it is called *forcible rape* if engaged in against the will of the woman by the use of threats or force; it is called *statutory rape* if the sexual intercourse was consensual between a man and a woman who was under the age of consent. More recently some rape statutes have been rewritten to include male victims, as well as penetration of any body opening by any instrument, including but not limited to the male sexual organ.

Reactive   In policing, depending on the reports of citizens to find criminal suspects, rather than working independently; it is important because police are not in a position to observe most criminal behavior.

Recidivists   Those who commit crimes repeatedly.

Recusal   The removal of oneself from a proceeding, such as by a judge who has a conflict of interest in a case.

Reformatory   An early corrections facility, which was less physically secure and which emphasized changing or reforming the offender; usually used to refer to an institution.

Rehabilitation   A punishment philosophy based on a belief that the offender can and will change to a law-abiding citizen through treatment programs and facilities. Rehabilitation may be most likely to occur in community-based programs rather than during incarceration in penal institutions. The "rehabilitative ideal" was embodied in probation, parole, the indeterminate sentence, and the juvenile court.

Reintegration   A punishment philosophy emphasizing the return of the offender to the community, so that employment, family ties, and education can be restored.

Restitution   Punishment that requires an offender to repay the victim with services or money. This punishment may be imposed instead of or in addition to other punishment or fines and may be a requirement of parole.

Retribution   *See* **just deserts.**

Reversible error   An error in a legal proceeding, such as a trial, that is considered sufficient to require the reversal of a conviction or a sentence.

Right to counsel   The right to be represented by an attorney at crucial stages in the criminal justice system. Indigent defendants have the right to counsel provided by the state.

Robbery   The use of force or fear to take personal property belonging to another against that person's will.

S

Sanction   A penalty or punishment that is imposed on a person in order to enforce the law.

Search and seizure   The examination of a person or a person's property and the taking of items that may be evidence of criminal activity; it generally requires a search warrant. Unreasonable searches and seizures are prohibited.

Search warrant   *See* **warrant.**

Self-report data (SRD)   The process of collecting crime data by asking people about their criminal activity, usually by use of anonymous questionnaires.

Sentence   The punishment imposed by the court on a convicted offender.

Sentence disparity   Inequalities and differences that result when people found guilty of the same crime receive sentences varying in length and type, without reasonable justification for those differences.

Sheriff   The chief law enforcement officer in a county, usually chosen by popular election.

Shires   *See* **frankpledge system.**

Showup   An identification procedure during a police investigation; it involves showing the alleged victim only one person rather than several, as in a lineup; it is permitted only in extraordinary circumstances.

Silent system   In penitentiaries, the historical practice of not allowing offenders to speak with one another.

Social system   The interrelationship of roles, acts, and statuses of people who make up the social structure; a social group or set of interacting persons or groups considered a unitary whole because it reflects the common values, social norms, and objectives of the individuals whom it comprises, even though the group is considered distinct from those individuals.

Stare decisis   Literally, "let the decision stand." The doctrine that courts will abide by or adhere to the rulings of previous court decisions when deciding cases having substantially the same facts.

Status offense   A class of crime that does not consist of proscribed action or inaction but, rather, of the personal condition or characteristic of the accused—for example, being a vagrant. In juvenile law, a variety of acts that would not be considered criminal if committed by an adult for example, being insubordinate or truant or running away from home.

Statutory law   Law that the legislature has originated and passed by a written enactment.

Subculture   A group of significant size whose behavior differs significantly from the behavior of the dominant groups of society.

Subpoena   A command issued by a court, ordering a person to appear in court (or another designated place) at a specified time and place for the purpose of giving testimony on a specified issue. Persons may be ordered to bring documents pertinent to the case; that order is called a subpoena *duces tecum.*

Summons   A formal document issued by the court to notify a person that his or her presence is required in court for a particular reason at a specified time and date.

T

Three strikes and you're out   Legislation enacted in most states and in the federal government in recent years designed to impose long sentences on persons who commit three or more serious crimes.

Tithing   In English history, a system of 10 families who had responsibility for the behavior of members over the age of 14. Tithings were also important in protecting the group from outsiders.

Training school   A secure corrections facility to which juveniles are confined by court order.

Transportation   Historically the practice of punishing criminals by exiling them to another country, usually far away.

Transportation Security Administration (TSA)   A federal agency created by the Aviation and Transportation Security Act (ATSA), enacted two months after the 9/11/01 terrorist attacks. The TSA was developed to take over the security screening functions for all commercial flights in the United States.

Trial   In criminal law, court proceedings during which a judge, a jury, or both listen to the evidence as presented by the defense and the prosecution and determine whether the defendant is guilty beyond a reasonable doubt.

True bill   The prosecutor's indictment returned with the approval of the grand jury. After hearing the prosecutor's evidence, the grand jury determines that the indictment is accurate; that is, it is a true bill.

Truth in sentencing   The concept requiring that actual time served by offenders is closer to the time allocated for the sentence. Many jurisdictions are establishing 85 percent as their goal, meaning that offenders may not be released for any reason until they have served 85 percent of their sentences.

U

Uniform Crime Reports (UCR)   Official crime data, collected and published by the Federal Bureau of Investigation (FBI) and based on "crimes known to the police"—crimes that are reported to or observed by the police and that the police have reason to believe were committed.

USA Patriot Act   The United and Strengthening America by Providing Appropriate Tools Required to Intercept and Obstruct Terrorism Act of 2001, enacted in fall 2001 in response to the 9/11/01 terrorist attacks. The act expands the powers of the federal government to deal with terrorism. Some of those powers involve the expansion of wiretaps on terrorist suspects' email, telephone conversations, and use of the Internet.

V

Venue   The location of a trial; a change of venue is the removal of a trial from the location where it would be held normally to another location, either to avoid public pressure or to obtain an impartial jury.

Victim compensation programs   Plans for assisting crime victims in making social, emotional, and economic adjustments.

Victimology   The discipline that studies the nature and causes of victimization, as well as programs for aiding victims and preventing victimization.

Victim precipitation   Concept that a criminal act may have been brought on by the alleged victim's actions.

Vigilantism   Literally, "watchman"; action by a person who is alert and on guard, cautious, suspicious, ready to take action to maintain and preserve peace; actions of citizens who take the law into their own hands in an effort to catch and punish criminals.

Violent crimes   Crimes defined by the FBI's *Uniform Crime Reports* as serious crimes against a person. They include murder and nonnegligent manslaughter, robbery, forcible rape, and aggravated assault.

Voir dire   To speak the truth; the process of questioning prospective jurors to determine their qualifications and desirability for serving on a jury.

W

Waiver   The giving up of one's rights, such as the right to counsel or to a jury trial. Waivers must be knowing and intelligent; that is, the defendant must understand what is being relinquished. Some rights may not be waived.

Wardens   Historically, the chief administrative officers in corrections facilities.

Warrant   A court-issued writ authorizing an officer to arrest a suspect or to search a person, personal property, or a place.

Watch system   A system charged with the duties of overseeing, patrolling, or guarding an area or a person. Watchmen were prominent in the early watch system of policing.

White-collar crime   The illegal actions of corporations or individuals, committed while pursuing their legitimate occupations. Examples are consumer fraud, bribery, and embezzlement.

Workhouse   An English institution used to confine offenders who were forced to work at unpleasant tasks; offenders were punished physically as well. The term is used in some places today to refer to institutions that emphasize reformation or rehabilitation through work.

Work release   The release of an inmate to attend school or to work outside the institution but requiring that person to return to the institution at specified times.

Writ   An order from the court. *See also* **writ of *certiorari*** and ***habeas corpus.***

Writ of *certiorari*   *Certiorari* literally means "to be informed of." A writ is an order from a court giving authority for an act to be done or ordering that it be done; a writ of *certiorari* is used by courts that have discretion to determine which cases they will hear. It is used most commonly today by the U.S. Supreme Court when cases are appealed to that Court from lower courts.

Case Index

Name Index

Subject Index